MAFIA
KINGFISH

Also by John H. Davis

The Bouviers: Portrait of an American Family

Venice

The Guggenheims: An American Epic

The Kennedys: Dynasty and Disaster

John H. Davis

MAFIA
KINGFISH

CARLOS MARCELLO
and the Assassination of
JOHN F. KENNEDY

John H. Davis

New York
Dec. 6, 1988

McGRAW-HILL PUBLISHING COMPANY

New York   St. Louis   San Francisco
Toronto   Hamburg   Mexico

1 2 3 4 5 6 7 8 9 DOC DOC 8 9 2 1 0 9 8

ISBN 0-07-015779-0

Library of Congress Cataloging-in-Publication Data

Davis, John H.
Mafia Kingfish : Carlos Marcello and the assassination of John F. Kennedy

Bibliography: p.
Includes index.
1. Marcello, Carlos.   2. Crime and criminals—United States—Biography.   3. Mafia—Louisiana—Case studies. 4. Kennedy, John F. (John Fitzgerald) 1917–1963—Assassination. I. Title.

| HV6452.L82M344 | 1988 | 364.1'092'4 [B] | 88-13209 |
| ISBN 0-07-015779-0 | | | |

Book design by Patrice Fodero

For
SAHODRA
with love

Contents

PART IV: WAR WITH THE KENNEDYS, 1961–1963

PART V: AFTERMATH: NOVEMBER 22, 1963– AUGUST 17, 1965

PART VI: A PRECARIOUS POWER, 1965–1977

Prologue

New Orleans, 1981

The United States v.
Carlos Marcello

HAUSER: Do you have any juice down there?

MARCELLO: Yeah, I've got 'em all where I want 'em.

...

HAUSER: You can get Jefferson Parish, too?

MARCELLO: Yeah, that's the main one. I'm understand?

HAUSER: You talkin' about Lee and Allen?

MARCELLO: Yeah, they my kind o' people.

...

HAUSER: You got juice out there too?

MARCELLO: I got connections, yeah. I know everybody from fucking Grand Isle all the way to Raceland, man.... All the way to Houma, you know....It take me two days if I stop at each one of 'em house to say hello, right. Yeah, it's really somethin' to see....I got two Italian boys. They state representatives, Guarisco

and Siracusa....I know all these people....Go there
and gotta get the right people. Say 'Here $5,000,
$10,000....It takes time to get where I am at. To
know all dese people—governors, business, the attorney general. They know me.

HAUSER: You're the boss.

DAVIDSON: You have the respect, Carlos.

The scene was a crowded New Orleans courtroom in July 1981.
Carlos Marcello, reputed boss of the Louisiana Mafia, was being tried
on federal charges of racketeering and bribery as a result of a successful yearlong FBI undercover investigation that led to the indictments of Marcello, Washington lobbyist I. Irving Davidson, New
Orleans attorney Vincent Marinello, and Louisiana state official
Charles E. Roemer II.

It was one of those airless, suffocating New Orleans summer days
of 95-degree heat and 99 percent humidity that the sputtering courthouse air conditioners were almost powerless to overcome. Among
those sweltering in the courtroom, in addition to the principals in
the drama and the ladies and the gentlemen of the press, was a con-
tingent of over twenty Marcellos, sitting en bloc in the center of the
courtroom's spectators section. Carlos's tall, dark-haired, sweet-faced
wife, Jacqueline, was flanked by two of her daughters, Louise and
Jackie, and a son, Joseph Carlos, known as "Little Joe." Behind them
sat four of Carlos's six brothers, Joseph, Vincent, Anthony, and
Sammy, with their wives and children. Several Marcellos were wearing yellow ribbons—symbolizing betrayal—pinned to their lapels in
recognition of the presence in court of the family's nemesis, the prosecution's star witness, thrice-convicted swindler and notorious con man
Joseph Hauser. Hauser had brilliantly coordinated the FBI's sting
operation against his former associate and thus was more responsible than anyone else for the trial that was unfolding.

The prosecution was playing one of the 1400 reels of taped conversations between Carlos Marcello, Hauser, two FBI undercover
agents, Mike Wacks and Larry Montague, and others, that had been
secretly recorded over the course of an entire year—February 1979
to February 1980. They represented a concerted drive on the part of
the federal government to nail Marcello once and for all, to finally
put behind bars the wily Mafia boss who had successfully defied every effort of the Justice Department to convict him of a major crime
during the past thirty-five years.

The tape being played, in competition with the relentless drone of the courthouse air conditioners, had been recorded on April 2, 1979, by Joe Hauser at a meeting with Carlos Marcello and Irving Davidson in Marcello's Town & Country Motel office. The intrepid Hauser had brought along his specially designed attaché case with a tape recorder hidden in a false bottom. With the attaché case resting on Marcello's desk, Hauser had asked Carlos if he had any influence with the New Orleans City Council and with the officials who governed his home turf, Jefferson Parish.

Things had not been going very well for Carlos Marcello since his New Orleans trial began in May 1981. The squat, bullnecked 71-year-old Mafia boss had had no idea his supposed friends Joe Hauser, Mike Wacks, and Larry Montague had been secretly recording their conversations with him in his office and in the farmhouse of his 6400-acre swampland property on the West Bank. Why, they had even had the nerve to bug him in his favorite New Orleans restaurant. In the end, the boys he had trusted so completely had made a goddamned fool out of him. Now he had to put up with all this public embarrassment.

The tapes played on....On one tape Marcello reminisced with attorney Vincent Marinello about his relationships with former Louisiana Governor John McKeithen and present Governor Edwin Edwards.

MARCELLO: Man, I know better than you, man, 'bout them politicians....They take your fucking money, man, they tell you good-bye, man....I put $2000 in McKeithen's pocket....I hate the motherfucker, take my money and don't do nuttin' for me....I went with him before, when he wasn't nuttin'....I had McKeithen for eight years. That sonofabitch got $168,000 my money, and then that sonofabitch too scared to talk to me. How do you like that shit?...[Then about Governor Edwards:] Edmund and me all right, but I can't see him every day....He's the strongest sonofabitchin' governor we ever had. He fuck with women and play dice, but won't drink. How do you like dat?

No, things had not been going too well for the boss of Louisiana lately. Barely two years before, just as the FBI's sting operation against him was getting under way, a congressional committee charged with

reinvestigating the assassination of President John F. Kennedy had
concluded that the President had probably been murdered as a result of a conspiracy involving organized crime and that the Mafia
leader most likely to have participated in a plan to assassinate the
President was Carlos Marcello. The Assassinations Committee's final
report had cast a pall of suspicion over the Mafia boss and his family,
and the resultant publicity now threatened to prejudice his trial.
Marcello's defense team vigorously protested every attempt by the
prosecuting attorneys, during the pretrial hearings, to introduce into
evidence three taped conversations between Marcello and the undercover agents about the Kennedy assassination and the Assassinations
Committee's investigation of the murder. Finally, presiding Judge
Morey L. Sear ruled that the tapes could not be played in court and
ruled, as well, that they be put under permanent court seal.

What was played in court was sometimes so embarrassing to the
semiliterate Mafia boss that to him almost anything would have been
preferable to having to hear the courtroom audience snickering over
some of his remarks.

When asked by a local politico if he would ever testify against a
certain Louisiana politician, Marcello replied in his unique southern
Louisiana Sicilian drawl:

> "I'm as far as me, I ain't gonna tell 'em nothin'. They can, they
> can come here forty times, but I ain't, you know, I'm gonna
> take, tell him, look. Carlos don't care if he got subpoenaed forty
> times. I got subpoenaed with the President, the Vice, the, the,
> the, the United States…district attorney. I mean, uh, the attor-
> ney general and all. Tell him, I just take the Fifth Amendment
> and that's it. They ain't gonna get a fuckin' thing from me."

As the tapes unwound, day after day, week after week, with Carlos
unknowingly incriminating himself over and over again, it became
clearer and clearer to most observers of the trial that Carlos Marcello's
long criminal career was rapidly drawing to a close. The government
finally had the goods on him, and his fifty-year career in crime would
soon be over.

It had been an astounding success story: Carlos Marcello's rise
from New Orleans street thug to undisputed boss of a vast criminal
empire, an "invisible government" that at its zenith brought in $2
billion annually from criminal operations in Louisiana, Mississippi,
and Texas.

Yes, it had been a remarkable career, Carlos's long climb from planner of petty street robberies—when he was only 19 the New Orleans papers described him as a "young Fagin"—to the suspected mastermind of the crime of the century.

The intervening years had seen a drive for wealth and power of Napoleonic intensity as Carlos successfully defied every level of government that opposed him, from the local sheriff's office of Jefferson Parish, to the New Orleans chief of police, to two select committees of the United States Senate, to the United States Department of Justice, and finally to the attorney general and President of the United States.

It had been a long, arduous, and frequently violent struggle, the rise to prominence in Louisiana of the Marcellos of Jefferson Parish. Few American families of wealth and power have had to contend with adversaries as mighty as those who tried to thwart their advance. And few indeed began their adventure in the New World from surroundings as lowly and unpromising as the swamps and mud flats of the Louisiana bayou country, where, in an old ramshackle abandoned plantation house, the Minacores of Ravanusa, Sicily, put down their first American roots.

PART I

From Sicily to Louisiana

1908–1934

1

Taking Root in the Bayou

In October 1910, the Italian steamship *Liguria* docked in New Orleans after a twenty-two-day voyage from Palermo. On it were 625 steerage passengers, mostly Sicilians, who were seeking a better life for themselves in the New World. Among the Sicilian passengers was a young recently married woman, Luigia Minacore, and her son Calogero, a baby of seven months. She had come to join her husband, Giuseppe, a farm laborer, also Sicilian, who had emigrated to New Orleans a year earlier. Because Louisiana's climate was similar to Sicily's, Sicilian immigrants preferred New Orleans to all other American cities.

Before the passengers were allowed to disembark, a police detective boarded the ship, along with the usual customs officials, to determine whether any of the immigrants might be members of the dreaded Mafia that had been plaguing New Orleans for the past thirty years. When questioned by the detective and an immigration officer, Luigia Minacore stated she was a housewife carrying $10 in her purse and was not an "anarchist." Soon she was cleared by the authorities and allowed to join her husband on the dock. It was the first time Giuseppe Minacore had seen his infant son.

After working for a while as a field hand on a sugar plantation, Giuseppe Minacore managed to add enough money to his savings

9

and his wife's dowry to buy a small farm in the bayou country on the West Bank of the Mississippi near Algiers, a community roughly opposite New Orleans. Giuseppe and his family moved into the old abandoned plantation house that stood on the property, virtually a ruin. The farm was surrounded by swampland, a huge morass of twisting bayous, shallow lakes studded with tall, gaunt cypresses draped in Spanish moss, and mud flats populated by bright green palmettos and white egrets. On their parcel of spongy land Giuseppe and Luigia raised turnips, beans, spinach, carrots, and tomatoes for sale in New Orleans' old French market.

Giuseppe was a short, muscular man with the squat, rugged build of the Sicilian peasant. He had been brought up on a farm in southern Sicily near Ravanusa, a village about 70 miles north of Agrigento, the coastal town famous for its ruins of ancient Greek temples. Luigia, a strong young woman with a talent for languages—she was to speak six—had also come from Ravanusa and had married Giuseppe there in 1908. Shortly after the wedding the couple had gone to Tunisia, then a French protectorate with a large Italian colony, to find work. For a year and a half they lived in Carthage on the outskirts of Tunis, until, in the fall of 1909, Giuseppe decided to travel to New Orleans in search of better prospects, leaving his four-months-pregnant wife temporarily behind. On February 6, 1910, Luigia gave birth to a boy, whom she named Calogero. She joined her husband in New Orleans eight months later.

While Giuseppe was working on the sugar plantation, his overseer, also named Minacore but not a relative, forced him to change his name so that people would not confuse the boss with his underling. The name the overseer chose was Marcello, not a typical Sicilian name but one generally found in northern Italy and especially in Venice, where Marcello had been one of the great names of the old aristocracy. Later Giuseppe and Luigia changed their first names to Joseph and Louise and gave the name Carlos to their young son, Calogero.

Joseph and Louise Marcello labored hard on their soggy West Bank land, and their small vegetable farm prospered, enabling them to raise a large family of seven sons and two daughters. Eventually Joseph and Louise became naturalized American citizens, and the children Louise bore on Louisiana soil automatically acquired U.S. citizenship. For some reason, the couple never bothered to have their Tunisian-born son, Carlos, naturalized.

From his earliest years Carlos helped his father on the farm, and when he was old enough to handle a horse and cart, it was he whom his father entrusted with carting the vegetables to market. The young boy would take the cart onto the Algiers ferry for the journey across the Mississippi to the thriving old French market along Decatur Street on the fringe of New Orleans' Vieux Carré.

Young Carlos grew up to be a sturdy, hardworking youth—very short, like his father, but endowed with a powerful physique. Bold, courageous, and tireless in sports and work, he left no question about who was the leader in the family. Carlos easily dominated his six brothers and two sisters in the run-down plantation house in which they grew up. They in turn gave him their complete loyalty.

It cannot be said that the Marcellos of the south coast of Algiers were already "Mafia" when they emigrated to Louisiana. Their native village was in the province of Agrigento, a region of southern Sicily where the Mafioso mentality was prevalent but where highly organized criminal brotherhoods were rare. More than likely it was in New Orleans that Joseph and Louise Marcello, already Mafioso in outlook by virtue of the tradition in which they had grown up, came under the influence of a structured Mafia organization for the first time. The vegetable and fruit markets of the city had long been controlled by the Mafia, and it was virtually inevitable that Joseph and Carlos Marcello would become involved with what was already a flourishing Mafia organization in New Orleans.

2

The Louisiana Mafia

"They set up their hideouts and places of rendezvous in swamps....In the pathless tangle of bayous and morasses south of New Orleans are retreats where criminals of the Sicilian Mafia can conceal themselves indefinitely without any chance of the police finding them." So went an 1882 article in New Orleans' *Times-Picayune* about the growing menace of the Mafia in Louisiana.

The Mafia, as a loosely knit band of Sicilian criminals, had existed in New Orleans since the late 1860s, when more Sicilians were emigrating to New Orleans than to any other American city. It did not become a force to be reckoned with until the mid-1880s, however, when it developed into the first fully organized crime family in the United States.

In late-nineteenth-century Louisiana, the Sicilian Mafia found an ideal social soil in which to grow. Like Sicily's situation in relation to the rest of Italy, Louisiana had always remained somewhat outside the mainstream of American life. It was a separate culture with its own peculiar traditions and customs and a code of ethics where political corruption had long been an accepted way of life. Like Sicily, Louisiana had known the domination and misrule of both the French and the Spanish, and it was against its will that it eventually was absorbed into the United States. Both Louisiana and Sicily were, for brief periods, under Napoleonic rule, and Napoleon's policies directly affected both their destinies. The French emperor sold Louisiana to the United States in 1803, and his assumption of power in Sicily two years later created the social turmoil out of which the criminal brotherhoods of the Mafia evolved.

Like the Sicilians, the Louisianans had always been suspicious, and disrespectful, of the law and the courts. Hence, the Mississippi delta was a natural paradise for those who chose to live outside the law. Since the early days of the French colony, long before the Sicilian Mafia arrived, "the pathless tangle of bayous and morasses" of southern Louisiana had been the base of operations for countless pirates who consistently defied the law and the authorities as they preyed at will on the stream of shipping coming to and going from New Orleans' burgeoning port.

The Mafia, as both a state of mind and a criminal organization, had been imported into Louisiana from western Sicily in the second half of the nineteenth century, where it had existed as a secret criminal brotherhood since the early 1800s and as a state of mind and way of life for centuries.

No one knows for certain what the origins of this unique social phenomenon were. Since the area of Sicily in which it developed—the region surrounding the island's capital, Palermo—had once been occupied by Arab tribes for over 200 years, and one of these tribes was called the Mafir, some historians, mindful of the Mafia's defiance of Judeo-Christian ethics, have theorized that it might have sprung up at least as an attitude during the so-called Saracen, or Moslem, domination in the early middle ages.

The word "Mafia," however, did not always connote criminality. It first appeared in the Italian language as a descriptive term of possibly Arabic origin, peculiar to western Sicily, meaning beauty or excellence, with overtones suggesting manly bearing and courage. Before it was used to describe a form of criminal enterprise, "Mafia" meant a type of behavior, a kind of power. To behave like a Mafioso one had to make oneself respected, had to be strong enough to avenge oneself for any insult to one's person, or any extension of it, such as one's family or community. Honor and respect, for a Mafioso, were attained through the use of violence, and the surest way to attain power and prestige was to take another man's life.

How and why did this type, the Mafioso, come into being and win power and social acceptance in western Sicily? It is believed that it was the result of a kind of social degeneracy brought by centuries of misrule and oppression.

No people in Europe had been subjected to such frequent, and brutalizing, foreign domination as the Sicilians, especially those living in the western regions around Palermo. After the collapse of the Roman Empire in the west in the late fifth century, Sicily was in turn conquered and ruled by the Byzantines, the Saracens (or north African Arabs), the Normans, the Hohenstaufens, the Angevin French, the Aragonese Spanish, the Empire of Spain, the Spanish Bourbons, who became an independent dynasty, the Austrian Empire, Napoleonic France, the Bourbons again, and, finally, the Piedmontese House of Savoy, who, with the assistance of the guerrilla leader Giuseppe Garibaldi, finally brought the island into reluctant union with the rest of Italy.

During these centuries of foreign oppression the Sicilian people formed a deep-seated antagonism to all legally constituted authority, and social institutions gradually evolved that enabled them to take the law into their own hands. Landowners established small private militias to defend their families, workers, and estates against marauding bandits and armed tax collectors from whatever foreign regime held sway in Palermo at the time. Some of these militias became more powerful than their masters, broke away from their control, formed *compagni d'armi,* and established rule over large areas of countryside. Powerful Mafiosi emerged in villages and towns and came to serve as a sort of proxy of the state. In time, to be against the ruling establishment became the accepted attitude, to resist it the accepted behavior.

This Mafioso outlook, then, existed long before the secret criminal organizations that sprang into being in Sicily in the early nineteenth century and became a near universal state of mind in Sicily and much of southern Italy that has persisted to this day. The state and its laws are the enemy. They must be opposed and subverted. Taking their place in a given community is the Mafioso, the boss, the man of respect, the man of honor. As a mediator of disputes, the Mafioso replaces the courts. As a defender of public safety, he and his soldiers will take up arms against all offenders and protect the community from foreign exploiters. As the ruler of an invisible government, the Mafioso will impose his own code on his followers and his own laws on his constituents and will expect to receive their homage and a percentage of the fruits of their labor in return.

It is generally believed that it was not until the conquest of southern Italy and Sicily by the forces of Napoleon in 1806, which saw the expulsion of the Bourbon King of Naples and the temporary dissolution of his power, that the secret criminal organizations known today as the Mafia came into being. Upon the temporary collapse of Bourbon power the old Kingdom of the Two Sicilies fell into chaos, its judicial system, never a model of probity and fairness, became hopelessly corrupt, and the police and the courts became a standing joke not only to the Sicilians but to all of Europe. As a consequence, powerful local Mafiosi took law and political authority into their own hands and formed loosely organized societies under an unwritten code of laws and ethics that slowly replaced legally constituted power in the towns and villages.

In time these societies, which existed in perpetual defiance of the established regime, developed into secret criminal organizations governed by a specific code of behavior that, it is thought, had been derived from certain secret societies that had long existed in Spain, which in turn had been influenced by terrorist traditions inherited from the Moslem domination. This code imposed secrecy and silence upon the brotherhoods and ordered their members never to seek redress of grievances before the courts and never to give evidence before a court. To talk about the brotherhood to the authorities was considered the ultimate *infamitá*. For the guilty party, it meant death without trial.

Power in this brotherhood was vested in men who displayed exceptional courage and personal magnetism and who never hesitated to kill an adversary, if such an act was necessary, to avenge a wrong and restore honor and respect.

The Mafia brotherhoods were bound together by ties of friendship and kinship and a common opposition to the forces of law and order imposed by the ruling government. Their code demanded they must always aid one another and band together to combat the common enemy. To maintain their honor and respect they could never allow the smallest slights and insults to go unavenged.

By the early 1860s the secret criminal societies of western Sicily had developed into a system of terrorism founded on secrecy, fraternity, and murder. When the unification of Italy in 1860 left a political vacuum, the Mafia brotherhoods of Sicily quickly seized power. By the end of the 1860s they virtually controlled the island, functioning as a kind of invisible government. The ultimate source of their power was a code of behavior in dramatic contrast to that which prevailed in the rest of Europe: an unflinching willingness to commit murder to achieve one's ends.

During the economic depression that descended on Sicily after the unification, thousands of poverty-stricken Sicilians fled the island

and emigrated to North Africa, northern Italy, and the United States. Of all American cities, the Sicilians had long preferred New Orleans. Between 1841 and 1855 some 3000 Sicilians had emigrated to Louisiana, and after 1860 their numbers multiplied rapidly. Of these, a sufficient number had been associated with the criminal brotherhoods in the old country to be able to form similar criminal societies in their adopted land.

The necessity to band together against the system into which they had immigrated had soon become evident to the poverty-stricken, illiterate Sicilian immigrants as they encountered social conditions in Louisiana that were not much different from those they had experienced on their native soil. In America they soon found themselves a despised minority at odds with a ruling establishment of largely French and English ancestry, bent on keeping them down, that was reminiscent of the Spanish, French, Bourbon, and Austrian tyrannies under which their ancestors had suffered for centuries.

By the early 1870s this fledgling American Mafia, the first to take root in the United States, had seized control of New Orleans' lucrative and prestigious French market and was in the process of subduing the wharves and docks to its will. From then on it was only a matter of time before it came to control all the produce markets of the city and most of the loading and unloading of freight in the port. As might be expected, this conquest had been accomplished through much violence. Between 1869 and 1889 the New Orleans police attributed over a hundred murders to the infamous Sicilian Mafia. The willingness to kill to achieve one's ends had become just as much the cornerstone of Mafia power in Louisiana as it had been in Sicily.

3

The Murder of the Chief

By 1885 the New Orleans Mafia numbered some 100 members, all Sicilians, and was ruled by the Matranga brothers, Charles and Tony, assisted by a council of twenty. Its principal activity was extortion, mostly of law-abiding Italians who had emigrated from the Italian mainland or areas of Sicily not dominated by the Mafia. Its modus operandi: A threatening letter demanding protection money would be delivered to, let us say, an Italian shop owner; if he didn't pay up within a specified period, he would be given a last warning; then, if he still didn't pay up, he would be murdered, usually with a sawed-off shotgun.

In time Tony Matranga's mob came into conflict with the wealthy Provenzano family, a politically influential clan not connected to the local Mafia organization that maintained a monopoly of the unloading of fruit ships from South and Central America.

In an effort to intimidate the Provenzanos so they would relinquish their control of the docks, the Matrangas murdered two Provenzano workers, warning the Provenzanos that there would be more killings if they didn't give in. The Provenzanos responded by ambushing Tony Matranga, who emerged only slightly wounded from the shooting.

Finally the Provenzanos sought protection from the New Orleans

17

police, specifically from the police chief, David Hennessey, and Hennessey quickly took up the cause of the Provenzanos against the Matrangas. The stage was set for one of the bloodiest episodes in the history of New Orleans and the only incident of a popular uprising against the Mafia in American history.

On the night of October 15, 1890, around 11:25 P.M., Chief Hennessey was walking home with two companions, from whom he separated about a block away from his house. Half a minute later the two men heard a burst of shotgun fire followed by three or four revolver shots. Rushing in the direction of Hennessey's home, they found the chief collapsed on the stoop of a neighbor's house. He was bleeding from four gunshot wounds.

"They've given it to me," Hennessey moaned to his friends, "but I give it back to them the best I knew how."

"Who did it? Who did it?" the two men cried.

"The dagos," Hennessey whispered as he passed out. He died in a hospital the following morning.

The murder of Police Chief Hennessey created a tremendous sensation in New Orleans. In response to pressure from all quarters the mayor appointed a committee of fifty to assist the authorities in gathering evidence. Finally twenty-one members of the Matranga gang were arrested, nineteen of whom were indicted, eleven as principals, eight as accessories to the crime.

Later, in March 1891, amid rumors of witnesses being threatened and jurors bribed, all defendants were acquitted in a verdict that utterly enraged the people of New Orleans.

But in the Sicilian colony the mood was just the opposite. The Sicilian fruit and vegetable vendors decorated their stands with bunting and flowers. Many New Orleans citizens reported to the police that they had heard Sicilians all over the city boasting: "The Mafia is on top now, and will run this town to suit itself." At a large shrimp-boat landing, a gang of Sicilians tore down an American flag, trampled on it, and then hoisted it upside down below the flag of Italy.

While these celebrations were going on, a group of prominent New Orleans citizens announced a mass rally for the following morning to protest the verdict. Some 2000 or more citizens showed up, and after an exhortation from their leader, it was decided that they would take justice in their own hands by storming the jail in which the Mafia defendants were being kept.

Using huge battering rams, the crowd was able to break through one of the doors to the old prison. The raging mob then poured in to hunt for the Mafiosi. In the meantime prison officials had freed the Sicilians from their cells so they could hide from the avengers. Before long, seven of them were caught hiding in the yard of the women's section and were immediately shot dead. Two more were found crammed in a doghouse, where the warden kept his bull terrier, and were shot through the entrance at almost point-blank range. Two others were dragged out of jail and hanged, one from a lamppost, the other from a tree. Justice done, the mob disbanded. Later it was discovered that several witnesses had been threatened and some jurors bribed during the trial that had acquitted the Mafia conspirators.

As it turned out, the lynching caused a diplomatic crisis between Italy and the United States. The Italian Navy, the fourth largest in the world at the time, was put on alert to set sail for New Orleans. Ambassadors were recalled. Finally President Harrison settled the matter by paying the Italian government $25,000 in reparations. Some of the money was then sent to the Italian consul in New Orleans to be distributed to the families of those who had been killed in the lynching. Most of this money was then confiscated by the Matrangas.

After the crisis died down, the New Orleans papers rejoiced that the local Mafia organization had been defeated and would never raise its ugly head again. They were wrong. After lying low for a couple of years the Matranga gang regrouped and began a series of kidnappings, one of which resulted in murder. Extortion in the markets and along the waterfront picked up again. By the time the Marcello family had established itself during the second decade of the century, the New Orleans Mafia was as strong as ever. Before long there would be more assaults on public officials, a practice that came to distinguish the New Orleans Mafia from all other Mafia families, which for the most part tended to confine their killings to offenders and rivals within their own organizations and competitors from other families.

It was the Matrangas' successor, the Sicilian-born Sam "Silver Dollar" Carolla, who continued the New Orleans tradition of assault on public officials during the prohibition era, a period of rapid growth for the Louisiana Mafia. Carolla, a bootlegger and narcotics smuggler, shot and killed the one official who had had the courage and integrity to stand in his way in a city whose law enforcement agencies were thoroughly corrupt: a federal narcotics agent by the name of Cecil Moore. But times had changed. Carolla was not subjected to a lynching. For murdering a public official, a judge reputed to have been in the Mafia's pocket gave Silver Dollar Sam a slap on the wrist: two years in federal prison.

The outrageously light sentence was a portent of things to come. In the years ahead light sentences and generous executive clemency became the norm in Louisiana as the Mafia, growing steadily in wealth and power, gradually took control of the political machinery of the entire state.

4

The Young Mastermind

The Marcello family prospered modestly in the vegetable business during the first two decades of their emigration to Louisiana. As soon as a child was strong enough, he or she would be pressed into service on the farm. Carlos, the oldest son, entrusted with carting produce to market, had to bargain with the wholesalers. The others busied themselves in the spongy fields of their father's West Bank domain.

Carlos came into daily contact with the young toughs who policed the vegetable market for boss Sam Carolla. It wasn't long before the strapping young farmhand began thinking of ways to make some money on his own. Dropping out of school at the age of 14, he began drifting into a life of crime. The robust, pugnacious young man soon demonstrated a gift for leadership, especially when it came to the planning of crimes.

When he turned 18, Carlos left home and rented a room in the French Quarter for $2 a week. Parts of the French Quarter in those days were well known as the breeding grounds of criminals. There young Carlos became a street punk, pulling off petty burglaries and planning larger ones.

The next year, 1929, Carlos made a spectacular debut as a criminal by pulling off a $7000 bank robbery with three teenage accomplices. The bank was in Algiers, not far from Joseph Marcello's West

21

Bank farm. After abandoning their getaway car, the four made their way through a swamp to Joseph Marcello's farmhouse. There Joseph agreed to hide the cash if they would give him $400 of it. The four youths handed over the $400, and Joseph buried the money in his backyard.

The incident troubled some of the other members of the Marcello family who evidently were not in on the planning of the robbery. One of Carlos's younger brothers, Peter, fearing his father could get into serious trouble by harboring the thieves and their loot, ran into town and told the story of the robbery to the Algiers police.

When the police came to the Marcello farmhouse, described in the papers two days later as a "rambling structure of antebellum days, badly in need of paint," they confiscated the $6600 plunder and forced Joseph Marcello to show them where he had buried his $400 payoff. Joseph was then charged as an accessory to the crime. The police also detained Carlos, Peter, and one of the accomplices for questioning, then released them. The accomplice told the police that Carlos had planned the crime. Though the New Orleans *Times-Picayune* displayed a photograph of young Carlos on page one, claiming he had planned the bank robbery, charges against him and the others were eventually dropped. The bank had been satisfied to get its money back.

Undaunted, Carlos began planning his next robberies. According to the testimony of one of his teenage hirelings, who was eventually arrested by the police, Carlos got him and a 13-year-old boy to rob a grocery store in Algiers at gunpoint to raise enough money to stage a holdup of the same Algiers bank that Carlos had successfully robbed a few months before. Carlos argued that the grocery store robbery would net them enough money to buy pistols and a sawed-off shotgun that would make the bank holdup "easy going."

To effect the grocery store robbery, Marcello rented a gun for $5 from a friend and stole a car for the getaway. He then gave the two boys, aged 16 and 13, detailed instructions on how to rob the store, handed them the gun, and drove them to the store. The robbery went off without a hitch, and the boys got away with $65. After abandoning the getaway car, Carlos paid off the friend who had lent him the gun and divided the remaining $60 with the two boys.

During the weeks that followed, Carlos invited his two young accomplices up to his French Quarter apartment several times, where he meticulously planned with them the holdup of the Algiers bank. But as the day planned for the bank holdup approached, the clerk of the grocery store Marcello's youthful gang had robbed a few weeks before spotted the two boys on a street in Algiers and had them arrested by the police. It was then that the 13-year-old spilled the whole story. On the basis of the young boy's account, Carlos was arrested a few weeks later and charged with assault and robbery for the grocery store holdup and grand larceny for the theft of the getaway car.

The New Orleans papers carried the story prominently, characterizing Carlos as a 19-year-old "criminal mastermind," a "Fagin" who recruited "baby bandits" to carry out his crimes. As it turned out, Carlos was the only one of the three to be convicted. He was sentenced to serve nine to twelve years in prison and entered the state penitentiary in Angola on May 28, 1930. He was only 20 years old.

During his confinement in Angola, Carlos was able to further exercise his talents as a manipulator of men.

At first he was assigned to the prison's license-plate factory, one of the toughest jobs in Angola. However, he soon befriended an inmate known to have influence with the prison administration and through him was able to land an easier job as the warden's yard boy.

While running errands and doing odd jobs for the warden, Carlos learned that the warden was carrying on an affair with his female cook. Now he had something on the warden. In a shrewd and daring maneuver, varieties of which he would practice all his life, Marcello used his knowledge of this liaison to blackmail the warden into granting him special favors. One of these favors was easy access to the kitchen. This meant access not only to the cook's dishes but also to the cook, with whom young Carlos entered into a clandestine affair.

Meanwhile Carlos's father was doing everything possible to spring his son from prison. Joseph Marcello had cultivated a relationship with a member of the state legislature from Algiers, supplying him with loads of fresh vegetables free. Now he turned to him with plans to do something to get his oldest son out of jail. Finally this individual approached a former state legislator and convicted gambler, Peter Hand, who had special influence with Governor O. K. Allen, puppet successor to the powerful Huey Long, and Hand agreed to intervene on behalf of Joseph Marcello's son. In the end, Governor Allen issued a pardon for Carlos, and the young convict was able to leave prison after serving only four years of his nine- to twelve-year sentence.

During his term in Angola, Carlos had plenty of time to ruminate on his mistakes. He had learned that accomplices, even members of one's own family, could not be trusted. It was therefore necessary in planning a job either to insulate oneself from one's ac- complices, so they do not know who you are, or to silence them after they get the job done. Although Carlos was destined to make one more big mistake during his criminal apprenticeship, this strategy would one day make him invincible.

PART II

Rise to Power

1934—1947

"I have found it always true, that men do seldom or never advance themselves from a small beginning, to any great height, but by fraud, or by force."

—*Machiavelli*

5

Back in Business: Carlos
Joins the Mob

After Carlos was released from prison, at age 24, it was back to the mud flats and "floating prairies" of the West Bank and the raucous produce markets of New Orleans. There he resumed working for his father, on a temporary basis, until he was able to make a living on his own.

Joseph Marcello had in the meantime added to his landholdings around Algiers and had begun to venture into shrimping. A flourishing business in Louisiana, as it had been in Joseph's native Sicily for decades, shrimping was almost wholly dominated by Sicilians affiliated with the Mafia, many of whom had been shrimpers in the old country.

Carlos found that his brothers and sisters had grown up considerably since he had gone off to serve his time at Angola. Pete was now a well-built, handsome young man of 22; Rose, 20, and Mary, 18, were already being exhibited by their parents to prospective husbands; Pascal and Vince, the more gentle and sensitive of the brothers, were now 16 and 13; Joe Jr., at 10, was already an exceptionally strong boy, short and stocky like Carlos; Anthony, perhaps the best-looking of the brothers, was 8; and Sammy, the baby of the family, was a small, rotund boy of 6. Even though Carlos had been away from the family for four years, he easily resumed his role as undisputed leader of the clan. It would not be long before he would be recruiting his brothers, one by one, into his ventures.

Working for his father again was, as everyone in the family knew it would be, just a stopgap solution for Carlos. A penniless, almost illiterate parolee whom nobody "on the outside" would employ, he was nevertheless ambitious to make his mark in the world. As soon as he had saved up enough money, Carlos made the first business investment of his life; with a down payment of $500 he bought a run-down "colored" bar in nearby Gretna which was frequented almost exclusively by black workers. Carlos named it The Brown Bomber after the heavyweight boxing champion, Joe Louis, and brought his brother Peter in to tend bar.

Gretna at the time was a down-at-the-heels community on the West Bank in Jefferson Parish, controlled in large part by the Mafia in close collaboration with the long-corrupted parish police. Its principal attractions were illegal gambling halls, whorehouses, fronts for the sale of marijuana and other drugs, and bars for the underaged. In return for a percentage of the profits from these amusements, the police let their mob-affiliated owners and managers alone.

Not long after Carlos took over The Brown Bomber, he began using the place as a front for selling marijuana, and probably other drugs, to young black workers whom he would lure into his place with free samples. Through payments to the local Mafia hood who supervised his block, Carlos was able to keep the police at bay.

On Saturday nights The Brown Bomber's black clientele played cards and dice into the early morning hours while Carlos and Peter plied them with beer, whiskey, and pot. If a customer got unruly, Carlos himself would throw him out. Though not tall, Carlos had the reputation of being a brutal fighter who could easily overpower most men. A survivor from this era remembers the diminutive Carlos lifting huge six-foot-six blacks up and throwing them out on the street.

"It was real colored," Marcello later reminisced of his clientele in his unique Sicilian-American southern Louisiana drawl. "We had nuttin' but colored people in dere, and man did dey drink."

The bar was prosperous, as most working-class bars were during the depression. Soon Carlos was able to branch out and open a retail liquor store in a lopsided old wooden building he rented in nearby Algiers, the community he had attempted to plunder before being sent off to Angola. "De wholesalers gave me de stuff," he later recalled. "I didn't have to buy nuttin'."

It was at about this time that Carlos, now 25, was unofficially inducted into the Louisiana Mafia, then run by Sam "Silver Dollar"

Carolla. Carlos had met one of Carolla's "capos," or underbosses, Frank Todaro, and Todaro had immediately taken a liking to this young tough who got things done. Before long, Carlos was taking care of various jobs for Todaro, who, among his many activities, was involved in the violent drug trade for Sam Carolla at the time.

Soon the Todaros and the Marcellos grew close. Carlos's sister Mary became best friends with Frank Todaro's daughter Jacqueline and invited her to be a bridesmaid at her wedding to the young man her parents had selected for her to marry, Samuel Loria. Carlos was best man at the wedding and, so the story goes, immediately fell for bridesmaid Jacqueline, a tall, slender brunette who towered over him. Four months later, on September 6, 1936, Carlos and Jackie were married. The young couple went to live in a cramped, dingy apartment over Carlos's retail liquor store in Algiers. Jackie then took over the management of the store while Carlos and his brother Pete looked after The Brown Bomber and their growing marijuana trade.

But Carlos now had other responsibilities. As a soldier and son-in-law of a Mafia capo, eager to rise in Sam Carolla's organization, he had to keep himself available for whatever assignments Frank Todaro saw fit to send his way. It would not be long before Todaro would begin to entrust him with some of his biggest jobs.

It should be emphasized at this point that the Louisiana Mafia Carlos Marcello joined in 1936 was unlike any other Mafia brotherhood in the United States. The New York, Chicago, and New England mobs had prospered enormously off the illegal liquor trade during prohibition and had developed into highly structured organizations with quasi-military hierarchies which came to be known collectively as La Cosa Nostra, or "our thing." The boss, or father, of a given "family" was commander in chief of a small army of extortionists, burglars, loan sharks, swindlers, smugglers, and murderers, run by his underbosses, the *capiregime* and *consiglieri*, beneath whom functioned the lieutenants and soldiers, or "button men." It was a tight ship, in competition with other tight ships. The boss of one family could be eliminated at any time by the boss of another. The capi and button men down the chain of command were strictly accountable to the boss and could not found businesses or pull off jobs on their own.

Not so in Louisiana. In Louisiana, where as we know the Mafia had put down roots long before there was such a thing in New York, Chicago, and New England, the brotherhood was much more loosely structured and the boss had much more independence and authority. More a spontaneous grouping of individuals of like mind and inclination, usually but not always tied by bonds of kinship, each with a degree of autonomy, the Louisiana Mafia resembled more the Mafia of western Sicily from which it sprang than did the northern and midwestern families of the United States. Without rival gangs to challenge his power, the boss of the Louisiana Mafia was free to do more or less as he pleased and did not have to defer to the *commissione,* the national ruling body of Mafia bosses that had been created in the early thirties to establish territories and mediate disputes between the major families. The boss of the Louisiana Mafia tolerated a good deal of independence and autonomy on the part of his subordinates. They could carry on their own individual enterprises with little interference from above. So loosely structured was the Louisiana Mafia that its members, almost all of whom had businesses of their own, could easily deny being associated with the organization, if indeed they even admitted such membership to themselves. "Who me? In the Mafia? I don't know nothin' about it. I never even heard of it" was their usual refrain.

It was not long after Carlos's marriage to Jackie Todaro that he and his brother Vincent set up a business of their own within the loose, protective embrace of Silver Dollar Sam's network. It was a jukebox and pinball machine distributing outfit they named the Jefferson Music Company. In addition to jukeboxes and pinball machines, Jefferson also distributed pool tables and various gambling paraphernalia. In time, Carlos would succeed in strong-arming all the bars and restaurants in Algiers and Gretna into getting rid of the jukeboxes and pinball machines they already had and installing his own.

It was at about the time Carlos was beginning his apprenticeship in the mob under Frank Todaro that a major event took place in the New York underworld that was eventually to provide him with the first big break of his life. Frank Costello, a major Mafia potentate in New York, who at a 1929 meeting in Atlantic City had succeeded in facing down the great Al Capone, began relocating his huge slot machine operation to Louisiana.

Costello, the son of poor Italian immigrants, had grown up in the slums of New York's Lower East Side and had run away from home at the age of 16 to become a street hoodlum. Joining one of New York's fledgling Mafia families as a button man, he threw himself into the illicit bootleg liquor trade during prohibition in the twenties. Quickly he climbed to the top of his Mafia family and made a fortune; by the early thirties the press had dubbed him "prime minister of the Mafia."

During his rise to wealth and power, during prohibition, Costello claimed he entered into a loose partnership with another bootlegger, Joseph P. Kennedy of Boston, who moved to New York in the late twenties after having been snubbed in his native Boston. Kennedy's father, P. J. Kennedy, a small-time politician, had been in the liquor business in Boston before prohibition as an owner of working-class bars and retail liquor stores, and his son Joe took the business underground after the sale of alcoholic beverages was banned in 1919. Costello once told author Peter Maas that he "helped Kennedy get rich," and another Mafia figure, "Doc" Stracher, told journalists in Israel that there had been a falling out between the two. Mafia boss Joseph Bonanno also attested to the Costello-Kennedy relationship in his 1983 autobiography, *A Man of Honor.* After prohibition was repealed, Costello and Kennedy went their separate ways. Each had acquired lucrative Scotch franchises and had set up distributorships in competition with one another in New York, as did Mafia operatives Lucky Luciano and Meyer Lansky. Costello's Alliance Distributors handled King's Ransom and House of Lords Scotch, and Kennedy's Somerset Liquors distributed Haig and Haig's and Dewar's Scotch and Gordon's Gin. By the mid-thirties the two were in deadly competition, and it is generally believed that the Kennedy family's intense animosity toward the Mafia, which would surface so spectacularly during President Kennedy's brief administration, stemmed in part from this violent rivalry.

But liquor was by no means Costello's only profitable business. By the early thirties the prime minister of the Mafia was making huge sums of money from his vast network of slot machines in the New York metropolitan area. So violent had been the competition with other mob distributors, so corruptive to the New York police had the whole process been, and so huge were Costello's largely untaxed profits that New York's reform mayor Fiorello LaGuardia finally ordered them out of the city.

It was then that Costello ran into Louisiana's flamboyant Senator Huey Long, known throughout the country as "the Kingfish," in a Long Island nightclub. The two hit upon the idea of relocating Costello's slot machines to Louisiana. Long, who as governor of Louisiana had ruled the state as a virtual dictator, wanted them in his bailiwick to help finance certain state programs dear to his constituents' hearts. He would facilitate their introduction into Louisiana in return for a commission of 10 percent of the take. The fact that gambling in Louisiana was illegal was hardly even taken into consideration. Huey Long knew that the police would be only too delighted to share in the expected slot machine bonanza.

Soon Costello was in New Orleans conferring with Sam Carolla and conducting a survey to find out how many locations could be counted on to accept his slot machines. The day was not far off when the Marcello brothers' jukebox distribution company, Jefferson Music, would be recommended to Costello by Carolla as an ideal vehicle for distributing his machines on the West Bank.

But before that day dawned, Carlos blundered into trouble with the law again, this time by misjudging a marijuana customer who turned out to be a federal undercover agent.

Carlos and four partners had been running what the head of the federal Narcotics Bureau in New Orleans was to describe later as "one of the major marijuana rings in the New Orleans area" out of The Brown Bomber in Gretna. Over the past three years Carlos's initially modest marijuana trade had developed into a lucrative wholesale operation supplying mostly retailers from the West Bank. In March 1938 an FBI undercover agent posing as a dealer bought 23 pounds of marijuana from Carlos in his Gretna saloon and arrested him on the spot.

At his trial, Carlos was sentenced to a year and a day in the Atlanta Federal Penitentiary and was fined $76,830. As it turned out, with Sam Carolla pulling political strings for Frank Todaro's boy, Carlos got away with serving only nine months of his sentence and was allowed to pay only $400 of his fine. The leniency was provided by Governor O.K. Allen, a stooge of Huey Long until Long's assassination in 1935.

After his brief term in Atlanta, Carlos, now 30 years old, returned to his West Bank haunts and, getting out of the bar and liquor business, joined forces again with his brother Vincent to make their Jefferson Music Company his principal business. Helped by the muscle provided by Frank Todaro and Sam Carolla's West Bank thugs, Carlos was responsible for seeing that every bar and restaurant in Jefferson Parish took his jukeboxes and pinball machines. Soon the stocky, bullnecked, already locally infamous young tough became a familiar sight around Algiers and Gretna driving truckloads of jukeboxes here and there, and stories began circulating about the treatment he meted out to bar owners who refused to take his machines.

6

The Slot Machine Coup:
Carlos Joins Frank Costello

Before Frank Costello could begin moving his thousand slot machines down to New Orleans, he had to strike a deal with local Mafia boss Sam Carolla. It was a delicate situation. Costello's patron, Kingfish Huey Long, who had granted him a virtual slot machine monopoly in Louisiana, controlled the political machinery of the state but was at odds with the New Orleans municipal administration controlled by Carolla.

Frank Costello was known in the mob as a diplomat and a statesman. It was not for nothing that the eastern press had dubbed him the prime minister of the Mafia. After days of negotiations with Silver Dollar Sam, Costello came up with a mutually satisfactory arrangement.

It was agreed that Costello would operate his illegal slot machines as a franchise in Louisiana under the protection of Huey Long and Sam Carolla. New York and Louisiana would share key positions in the enterprise from which they could keep a vigilant eye on each other. In exchange for allowing Costello to operate freely in the city of New Orleans, Carolla demanded political protection from Huey Long for his activities in the rest of Louisiana, a privilege he did not yet have, for his influence had been restricted to the southern part of the state. Upon Costello's urging, the Kingfish agreed.

33

Sam Carolla's slot machine deal with Costello brought the previously insular Louisiana Mafia into the mainstream of organized crime in America for the first time. The move turned out to be an important milestone for the first family of the Mafia. Before long Costello, Carolla, and mob financier and adviser Meyer Lansky agreed to establish a national underworld communications center in New Orleans, and later a national clearinghouse for underworld money laundering operations was founded in the Crescent City.

So powerful had Frank Costello become by the mid-forties that FBI Director J. Edgar Hoover saw fit to personally establish informal contact with him in order to effect a degree of understanding, as it were, between the prime minister of the Mafia and the prime minister of the nation's investigative agencies.

It was *Time* magazine that first revealed Hoover's meetings with Costello to the public. In a 1975 cover story on Hoover, *Time* asserted that some FBI agents the magazine had interviewed spoke of Hoover "sometimes traveling to Manhattan to meet one of the Mafia's top figures, Frank Costello. The two would meet in Central Park." Later, historian Arthur M. Schlesinger, Jr., stated in his biography of Robert F. Kennedy that William Hundley, chief of the Justice Department's organized crime section under Kennedy, had confirmed the fact that Hoover had met with Costello in New York. In a 1988 interview, Hundley said it was Costello himself who told him about his friendship with Hoover. Hundley believes Hoover and Costello saw each other throughout the 1950s, and perhaps even into the 1960s.

Later, during the Kennedy administration, J. Edgar Hoover would deny that organized crime existed and would adopt a strangely lenient attitude toward Frank Costello's protégé, Carlos Marcello.

And so Frank Costello began moving his thousand slots from New York to New Orleans, secure in the knowledge that he could operate his illegal machines in Louisiana with no problems from law enforcement authorities, or from the FBI.

To look out for New York's interests in his New Orleans operations, Costello chose an old friend and associate, professional gambler "Dandy Phil" Kastel. Kastel was to operate in tandem with Carolla's man, James "Diamond Jim" Moran, born James Broccato, a former bootlegger, ex-prizefighter, and ex-bodyguard of Huey Long who worked on the fringe of Carolla's organization and would later open what became a famous New Orleans restaurant. Diamond Jim knew New Orleans' French Quarter inside and out, so he took Dandy

Phil around to find the best locations for Costello's machines and make sure the owners would accept them.

Before long, Costello's thousand slot machines were in place, and they became instantly popular. The machines were known as "chiefs" because of the elaborate bronze head of an Indian chief mounted above the dial. Now valuable collectors' items, they were said to have netted Frank Costello $70,000 on an investment of $9500 during their first year of operation.

Costello then formed three successive companies to distribute his machines: the Bayou Novelty Co., the Pelican Novelty Co., and the Louisiana Mint Co. All turned out to be gold mines. By 1940 the machines had proved their profitability in New Orleans many times over, and Costello was ready to expand operations throughout the rest of the state, beginning with the West Bank.

For some time Dandy Phil Kastel had been impressed by the success of the Marcello brothers' Jefferson Music Company, which had first been pointed out to him by Sam Carolla. It seemed that wherever he went on the West Bank he found the Marcellos' jukeboxes and pinball machines purring away making money. What is more, he learned what a ruthlessly efficient collector Carlos Marcello was.

Although Dandy Phil probably didn't know it at the time, another excellent reason for putting Marcello in charge of the West Bank slot machine operation was Carlos's uncanny ability to avoid prosecution by the law. Since his pardon by Huey Long's stooge, Governor O. K. Allen, in 1935, Carlos had been charged with two more assaults and robberies, violation of the federal Internal Revenue laws, assault with intent to kill a New Orleans police officer, sale of narcotics, and armed assault of a New Orleans investigative reporter. None of these charges were ever prosecuted, and the records of several of the arrests mysteriously disappeared. Then there were all the murders in which Carlos was a suspect but for which he was never charged.

Dandy Phil and Carlos Marcello sat down and talked, and they came up with an agreement whereby Jefferson Music would install and manage 250 of Costello's slots and be allowed to pocket two-thirds of the gross, with the remaining third going to Costello's Louisiana Mint Co.

From all indications Carlos, now 30 and the father of a 3-year-old girl, plunged into the slot machine business with a vengeance. He paid calls on every bar, restaurant, gambling hall, and whorehouse in Algiers and Gretna and bullied them into taking Costello's machines at terms very favorable to himself and Costello. When all 250 machines were in place, he was tireless and exacting in collecting his share of the loot. Bar owners feared the appearance of the quick-tempered little man when he would come to collect his due, and they often allowed him to take more than his agreed-on percentage to avoid arousing his ire. It wasn't long before the machines became phenomenally profitable. Since they were technically illegal, payoffs had to be made to the local police, and Carlos made sure they were handsome.

It was during this heady time that Carlos formed what was to be a lasting relationship with the Gretna police chief, Beauregard Miller, Jr.

"I used to give Miller $50,000 in cash every few months," Carlos boasted many years later to an FBI undercover agent, unaware the agent was recording his remarks. "I used to stuff de cash in a suitcase and carry it over to his office," he went on, adding that he took care to be generous to everyone under his command also. "I used to give 'em all cash money," he told the undercover agent. "I'd go out in de mornin' with my pants pockets full and say 'hello, here's a twenty for ya, pal,' 'here's a hundred bucks,' 'here's a fifty.' I took care of everybody."

Carlos also took care of himself and his family in the bargain. After Costello's 250 West Bank slots began gushing, Carlos gave up his cramped little apartment above the liquor store in Algiers and bought a two-story wood frame house with a porch in Gretna near the town line with Algiers and moved his family into it. Jacqueline Marcello, who had given birth to a second daughter, was relieved of her daily chores at the liquor store. After an unsettled and somewhat stormy five years with Carlos she could now lead the life she had always wanted, that of a modest middle-class housewife and mother in a respectable neighborhood.

While Carlos and his brother Vincent were establishing their West Bank slot machine operation for Costello, Carlos was also working at various jobs for his immediate superior in Sam Carolla's organization, Frank Todaro. It was the early forties, the war was on, and New Orleans had become a major center of black-market activities in every scarce commodity. The New Orleans Mafia, already heavily into smuggling narcotics, was quick to get involved with black-market goods, and Carlos got some of Todaro's choicest assignments, one from which he could collect a sizable share of the take.

The war was on, but since Tunisian-born Carlos had never become a U.S. citizen, he, unlike his American-born brothers, Peter and Vincent, avoided the draft. Thus, while Peter and Vincent went off to fight in Europe, Carlos was left free in New Orleans to exploit the war to the benefit of himself and his boss, Silver Dollar Sam Carolla.

It was a violent world, the Mafia-controlled port of New Orleans during World War II, but Carlos did not shrink from it. Almost his entire working life now was making people pay up: making the bar and restaurant owners of the West Bank who carried Costello's machines pay up, making the buyers of contraband goods in the sheds and warehouses along the wharves of New Orleans pay up, making the more clandestine buyers in the bayous and swamps of the Mississippi delta pay up. To the satisfaction of Dandy Phil, Diamond Jim, Frank Costello, Silver Dollar Sam, and Frank Todaro, Carlos always brought back the bacon. He could be relied on. There were rumors of fierce battles, brutal assaults, and an occasional murder along the way, but these were to be expected. The police, who should have been concerned, were taken care of. The important thing was the money. Carlos could always be counted on to bring back the money.

By the end of the war, Carlos's efforts on behalf of his various bosses had begun to pay off. Through his powers of intimidation he had gained the reputation of being a man to be reckoned with, a man who consistently delivered, and was widely talked of in mob circles as the logical successor to Silver Dollar Sam, who had fallen into imminent danger of being deported to Sicily. So pleased was Frank Costello with his young West Bank deputy that when, in 1944, his syndicate decided to open a plush new Las Vegas–style gambling house in Jefferson Parish on the East Bank, Carlos was brought in as a 12.5 percent partner. Among the other partners, besides Costello, was the notorious Meyer Lansky. Carlos was up with the big boys now. The 35-year-old West Bank hoodlum had arrived.

7

Gambling and Murder: Carlos Enters the Big Time

The scene was a wood-paneled office in the plush new Beverly Country Club casino in Jefferson Parish. Mike Maroun, a Shreveport lawyer, was paying a call on his old friend, and now casino owner, Carlos Marcello, whom he had not seen since the days of The Brown Bomber.

On entering the richly furnished office, Maroun beheld a short, stocky man seated behind a large desk, fedora tilted back on his head, a cigar in his mouth, his feet propped up on the desk. It was his old friend Carlos now in entirely different surroundings. Marcello immediately stood up and embraced Maroun, flashing a big grin. Then he grabbed him by the arm and took him on a quick tour of the casino. Though Carlos had certainly not grown any taller, Maroun was impressed by his commanding presence, his erect bearing, and his air of authority. As they strode through the lavish gaming rooms, the croupiers and dealers appeared to pause when Carlos passed their tables, coming to attention like troops being reviewed by their commanding officer. Maroun noted the look of fear and admiration on their faces. Carlos had come a long way, he reflected, from the dingy bar of The Brown Bomber when a good night was a roomful of peaceful drunks who could pay their checks and didn't have to be thrown out onto the street.

Carlos Marcello's rapid rise from colored-bar owner and soldier in Sam Carolla's organization to casino owner and man of authority had come about as a result of a series of high-level meetings in New Orleans in the early forties between Frank Costello, Phil Kastel, and Meyer Lansky to discuss the expansion of Costello's operations in Louisiana and the possible establishment of centers of communications and money laundering operations to be used by the underworld, on a national scale, in New Orleans. So profitable had Costello's slot machine operation been—in all, several thousand of his nickel and dime chiefs had been installed throughout Louisiana—that he decided to open up three big Las Vegas–style gambling casinos in the state, the first of which was to be in Jefferson Parish. At one of the last meetings it had been decided to bring Costello's young West Bank deputy, Carlos Marcello, into the partnership. The final percentages of ownership were to be Costello, 20 percent; Lansky, 20 percent; Kastel, 27.5 percent; New Orleans "high roller" A. G. "Freddie" Rickerfor, 17.5 percent; and Carlos Marcello, 12.5 percent. The remaining 2.5 percent would be reserved for political payoffs.

It was also agreed that Frank Coppola, a New York associate of Costello, would represent New York's interests in the new gambling operations and Carlos Marcello would represent the interests of Louisiana. For Carlos it was a virtual anointing, the equivalent in the business world of being promoted to vice president of a major corporation.

Carlos's elevation was primarily due to Frank Costello's estimate of his abilities. After Carlos installed the first 250 of Costello's chiefs on the West Bank and they paid off so well, and so punctually, Costello gave him a green light to place as many in the area as the market would bear. Carlos had succeeded in installing hundreds more throughout Jefferson Parish.

This accomplishment was partly due to Carlos's assiduous cultivation of Jefferson Parish's chief of police, Beauregard Miller, and veteran sheriff, Frank Clancy, known to his constituents over his two decades in office as "King Clancy." Costello was well aware of this and knew he needed the blessing and cooperation of Miller and Clancy if his plans for a casino were to get off the ground. He also knew that no one was in a better position to arrange that cooperation than Carlos Marcello.

Costello knew also that Sheriff Clancy posed a real obstacle to the realization of his plans. Clancy had allowed Marcello to place hundreds of illegal gambling machines in his parish and had countenanced the operation of many small illegal gambling halls, run by local Jefferson Parish citizens, in return for a percentage of their profits, but he balked at the idea of a huge, Mafia-backed casino in his bailiwick. The casino would compete with the parish's private gambling halls, and Clancy was well aware that the added Mafia presence might undermine his own power and attract national attention that could conceivably expose his own corruption.

Though all but illiterate and, having dropped out of school at 14, largely uneducated, Carlos possessed a shrewdness as a negotiator and an instinctual knowledge of human motivation worthy of a seasoned politician twice his age. Meeting with the outgoing governor of Louisiana, Jimmie Davis, and Sheriff Clancy, Marcello engineered an adroit compromise. With Governor Davis acting as arbiter, Marcello got Clancy to agree to let the Mafia open up three gambling casinos in his parish on the *East* Bank of the Mississippi. These would not compete directly with the gambling halls owned by his Jefferson Parish constituents on the West Bank, which was then the most populous side of the river. In return for his concession, Clancy would be given a 2.5 percent share of the casino profits and the right to hire all nonadministrative personnel—which meant he could dispense around 500 jobs to the faithful.

The new casino, named the Beverly Country Club, was opened on December 4, 1945, and soon became an extraordinary success. Described by the New Orleans *States-Item* as "the most sumptuous of all Jefferson's palaces of chance," it was about as lavish and luxurious a casino as could be built at that time. As Costello's brother-in-law, Dudley Geigerman, told a New Orleans reporter: "It couldn't have been better. If it could have been better we would have had it." The public agreed. Before long, the Beverly Country Club became the most popular place of entertainment in the New Orleans area as thousands flocked to its restaurants, bars, and gaming tables. Soon a nightclub was opened in the place, and big-name entertainers like Jimmy Durante, Zsa Zsa Gabor, Joe E. Lewis, and Sophie Tucker were performing nightly shows.

Even the sudden emergence of a powerful opponent not long after the casino opened ended up contributing to the Beverly's popularity. In the fall of 1945, reform candidate DeLesseps Morrison was elected mayor of New Orleans on a promise of ridding the city of corruption. Once elected, he attacked the "Costello-Kastel-Lansky combine" and succeeded in having 600 of Costello's chiefs removed from the city. The result was an influx of New Orleans gamblers into Jefferson Parish, where they could play Costello's slot machines at will. Many of these became new customers of the Beverly Country Club, which boasted an entire room full of chiefs.

It was during this period that Costello and Kastel made Carlos Marcello manager of the casino's day-to-day operations and later, upon the unexpected deportation of Frank Coppola, put Carlos in charge of all Costello's gambling operations in Louisiana. Carlos then brought in brothers Peter and Anthony to help out and began running the place with an iron hand. Inevitably one of his major jobs became paying off the Jefferson Parish police. Soon parish police deputies were functioning as doormen, "house drivers," and "ushers" at the casino and were paying regular visits to the cashier to collect their shares of the "ice."

Legend has it that Carlos had a tailor sew a foot-long pocket into the left leg of one of his trousers, which he would stuff with cash as he made his rounds through the parish paying off the police one by one. That he made huge payoffs to Beauregard Miller and King Clancy was eventually confirmed by remarks he made to FBI undercover agents during a federal sting operation against him over thirty years later.

By the middle of 1947, a year and a half after the Beverly Country Club opened, Carlos Marcello was doing very well indeed. In addition to his work at the casino, he was active in half a dozen other ventures. He and his brother Vincent were expanding the activities of the Jefferson Music Co. to include services for racetrack gamblers, including shortwave radio broadcast. In partnership with fellow Mafioso Joseph Poretto, Carlos gained control of the Southern News and Publishing Co., the largest racing wire service in New Orleans, serving Louisiana's statewide gambling network. Reaping huge profits from the narcotics trade for Sam Carolla and from the frantic gambling at the Beverly casino, Carlos shrewdly invested his money in West Bank real estate. Cognizant of the fact that Silver Dollar Sam was under an order of deportation, he began maneuvering to take Carolla's place in the event the Immigration and Naturalization Service (INS) dispatched the boss to his native Sicily.

The time had come for Carlos to display to the world his newly attained wealth and power, and so, a little over a year after the Beverly Country Club opened its doors, he bought an eight-bedroom Italianate mansion on Barataria Boulevard in Marrero, Jefferson Parish, and moved his growing family—he now had a son and three daughters—into the place six months later. Now his children would grow up in surroundings worthy of some of the grand old families of New Orleans.

Worthy, too, of some of the grand old families of the Louisiana Mafia. Among Carlos's new neighbors was the head of the wealthy old Provenzano clan, the family that had asked Police Chief David Hennessey for protection from the Matrangas in 1890 and in so doing had precipitated the chief's murder. But Carlos's new home far surpassed the Provenzanos' estate in splendor. The yellowish-beige stone and stucco building, with a gently sloping red-tiled roof, boasted an elegant central portico of three large, graceful arches supported by marble Corinthian columns surmounted by a long upper-story terrace. The portico was flanked by two imposing wings with huge arched windows that looked out over a wide expanse of lawn scattered here and there with classical Greek and Roman statuary. It was a magnificent residence, grander than any other on the West Bank, that proudly and ostentatiously displayed money earned and power fought for. Its 37-year-old owner was now, in the parlance of his father's people in Sicily, a "man of respect." He had arrived. His investments were highly profitable, his political contacts firmly in place. He was a man whose counsel was taken seriously by the governor of his state and by some of the top Mafia bosses of the nation. He controlled the law enforcement authorities and political machinery of the territory in which he lived and worked, Jefferson Parish. He stood at the threshold of assuming absolute control of the underworld in Louisiana. That was what the palace on Barataria Boulevard was supposed to say to the world.

It had been an extraordinary adventure, Carlos Marcello's seventeen-year ascent from New Orleans street thug to wealthy gambling casino owner and heir apparent to the rule of the oldest Mafia family in the United States. But what most people did not know, or at best were but dimly aware of, was the extent of the violence and brutality that accompanied that ascent. Along the way, Carlos had been the prime suspect in several murders for which he was never charged and which were never solved. One which was related in an FBI report over a year after the fact was particularly gruesome.

Constantine Masotto was a New York hoodlum who had been condemned to death without trial by his Mafia family for robbing his sister. Fleeing to New Orleans, he went into hiding under an assumed name. The head of his New York family got in touch with Silver Dollar Sam and announced that there was a price on Masotto's head. Sam notified his men. The police were keeping track of Masotto's movements. Then, one day, he suddenly disappeared.

The Marcello family owned a rustic tavern at the edge of a swamp on the West Bank. It was a place where Carlos and his brothers ate spaghetti and drank beer and wine with their friends and other members of Sam Carolla's gang. According to an FBI report, a year after Masotto was found missing by the New Orleans police, his lime-encrusted skeleton was discovered in the swamp behind the Marcellos' tavern. Masotto, the report stated, had been tied to a chair in the tavern and had been beaten to death with rubber hoses by Carlos Marcello and an accomplice. The body was then thrown into a tub of lye, and after decomposition, the partially liquefied remains were poured into the swamp. Although Carlos had been questioned by the police in the killing, as he had been for several other murders over the years, he was never charged with the crime.

8

Meeting at the Black Diamond: Carlos Anointed

On May 5, 1947, some waiters at the Black Diamond nightclub in New Orleans, a "colored" establishment in a run-down section of town, noted an unusual number of expensive-looking cars pulling up to the rear entrance and dropping off groups of well-dressed white men who quickly headed for the back rooms of the club.

The waiters, and also some of the musicians who played at the Black Diamond, had observed similar arrivals of well-dressed whites to the all-black club in the past. The rumor was that the gatherings, always held in the back of the club, were secret meetings of the city's Mafia big shots, but nobody seemed to know for sure. Once a musician inadvertently burst into a back room, interrupting what seemed to be a heated business discussion around a large table, and was surprised by the hostility he ran into.

"Listen here," growled one of the men, leaping up from the table, "if you knew how tough this is in here, you'd get out fast."

The waiters and musicians were correct in their suspicions. The meetings were held to conduct certain urgent business of the Louisiana Mafia. Sam Carolla had chosen the obscure "colored" nightclub to put the feds off his scent. Among those who attended the May 5, 1947, Black Diamond conclave, according to a Senate Crime Committee report issued four years later, were Carolla underbosses Frank

Todaro, Joseph Capro, Tom Rizzuto, Frank Lombardino, and Nick Grifazzi; Sam Carolla's son, Anthony; Marcello business associates Joseph Poretto and Nofio Pecora; and Carlos, Peter, Vincent, Joseph, Anthony, Jake, and Nick Marcello, the latter two being cousins of the Marcello brothers. The purpose of the meeting was to choose a successor to Silver Dollar Sam, who had just been deported by the United States government to his native Sicily. Or, to be more precise, a de facto successor, since, technically speaking, a Mafia boss remains boss for life, even though he may be living in exile, far from his domain.

The Justice Department had been trying to deport Carolla since the 1930s, but, for one reason or another, had repeatedly encountered obstacles and delays, not the least of which stemmed from the high-level political alliances Carolla had built up over the years.

Sam Carolla's criminal career went back to the early twenties when he became French market supervisor for Charles Matranga, whom he succeeded as boss of the local Mafia in 1925. Plunging into the illegal liquor trade during prohibition, as well as the burgeoning narcotics traffic of the Mississippi delta, he was charged with many crimes, including attempted murder, during his first five years as boss, but was not nailed on any of them until 1932 when he was convicted of murdering, in a gangland-style ambush, a federal narcotics official. At his trial a New Orleans prosecutor called him "the worst kind of gangster," but the judge, as we know, sentenced him to only four years in the federal penitentiary in Atlanta. After serving only two, he received a full pardon from the same politician who had let young Carlos Marcello go free before his sentence was up, Huey Long's puppet in Baton Rouge, Governor O.K. Allen, and returned to New Orleans to resume his direction of the mob.

The swarthy, sleepy-eyed Carolla, a ruthless and adroit businessman who never became a U.S. citizen, made a huge fortune off smuggling liquor and drugs during the twenties and thirties. Using his illicit gains to buy political protection and leverage, he rose to a position of such power in New Orleans that he virtually controlled the municipal government through bribery and intimidation.

Eventually the Justice Department initiated deportation proceedings against Carolla, which were continually frustrated by legal maneuvering and political interference. They were then indefinitely delayed by World War II, when the U.S. government was compelled to enlist the cooperation of the Mafia to ensure the loyalty of the mob-controlled longshoreman's union, and of the towns of southern Sicily during the Allied invasion. After the war, the Immigration and Naturalization Service resumed its efforts to deport the Sicilian-born Carolla, and on May 30, 1947, the INS finally got their man. Silver Dollar Sam was escorted by immigration officials to Galveston and flown to Sicily on a military transport.

During the months leading up to Carolla's deportation, Carlos Marcello emerged as the most likely candidate to take his place as boss of the Louisiana underworld. Carlos had, in fact, been promoting himself for the job for some time, both within the organization and among the politicians and police of Jefferson and New Orleans parishes.

Since striking it rich in the narcotics trade, the slot machine business, and casino gambling, Carlos had assumed the air of a big shot, something that was both expected and appreciated in a Mafia boss in Louisiana. Very much the politician, Carlos had a way of flattering people simply by recognizing them and calling them by their first names. Generous with his money, he made loans to people who could do him favors without insisting on their signing promissory notes. So openly corruptive was he with the police that some of the officers he paid off were often boastful of having taken money from "Uncle Carlos." Once he was stopped by the New Orleans Police while speeding on Gentilly Boulevard, and one of the officers pulled a gun as he approached Marcello's car. Carlos told the officer he was speeding because he thought his pursuers were holdup men. Then he quickly delved into his pockets and, according to the officer, "pulled out a wad of green bills that would have choked a horse," thrusting them into the officer's pocket. As if that were not enough, Carlos paid a visit to the officer at his post on Gentilly Boulevard the next day and gave him a gold cigarette lighter in the shape of a pistol. "Ya like to wave ya gun so much, I thought I'd give ya this," he laughed. The incident soon took its place in the growing Marcello legend.

That legend included rumors upon rumors of Carlos's rapidly escalating wealth. Since becoming a part owner of the Beverly Country Club and assuming administrative command of the casino, he had bought a gambling hall called the Old Southport Club on the East Bank near the New Orleans–Jefferson Parish border. He quickly transformed it into a lavish Las Vegas–style casino, like the Beverly, renaming it the New Southport Club, and it became instantly popular and phenomenally profitable. He had also become part owner of scores of bars and restaurants all over southern Louisiana and along the Mississippi coast—from Westwego and Morgan City to Gulfport and Biloxi—in which his jukeboxes and slot machines were constantly churning out cash. Then there were all the bookies who paid Carlos good money for subscribing to his racing wire, The Southern News Co., serving Louisiana's statewide gambling network. Carlos's income had probably increased tenfold over the past three years and, in the process, so had his ability to pay off cops and politicians. By the time of Silver Dollar Sam's deportation, there was no one in Carolla's organization who could match the financial and political clout of Carlos Marcello.

Nor was there anyone who could match Carlos's personal magnetism, his capacity for leadership, his energy, or his ambition. And, most important of all, in terms of the code by which the Mafia lived, there was no one in the ranks of Carolla's organization who inspired as much fear as did Carlos Marcello, despite his comparative youth. Already, by 1947, after only a decade of service in the Louisiana mob, the name of Carlos Marcello struck fear in the hearts of politicians throughout the state. The stories of decomposed bodies found in Marcello's swamp had had their cumulative effect.

And so the powers in the Louisiana underworld gathered on the night of May 5, 1947, in a back room of the Black Diamond to choose a new leader. Among them, as we know, was one member of the Carolla family, the son of the recently deported boss, and no fewer than six Marcellos.

It has been rumored that some of Carolla's men tried to promote the candidacy of Anthony Carolla, but soon realized they lacked adequate support. (Anthony would brood on his rejection over the years and would one day take his grievance to a sit-down of major Mafia bosses, including Carlos Marcello, in New York.) When the names of other Carolla loyalists—friends of Anthony—were raised, the six Marcellos glowered and the names were quickly withdrawn. When the meeting broke up, a waiter thought he saw a short, stocky man leave the club first. But it wasn't until the next morning that people began to figure out what had probably happened. Carlos's neighbors on Barataria Boulevard had noticed an unusually large flow of traffic in front of Marcello's house and an unusually large number of cars parked outside. Soon word spread among Marcello's connections, and before long, King Clancy was observed walking toward Carlos's front door. Since Carlos's "election" had taken place amid the utmost secrecy, there was no one from the press to record Sheriff Clancy's act of obeisance.

Later, it was said, Frank Costello sent his blessing from New York, and Sam Carolla sent word from Palermo that he approved Carlos's selection as caretaker-boss until he, Silver Dollar Sam, returned from exile.

In assuming the mantle of boss of the Louisiana Mafia, Carlos Marcello, now 38, inherited the direction of an invisible government, grounded in an ancient code of secrecy, fraternity, and murder, that had been steadily expanding its activities and influence in Louisiana for the past seventy-five years. This invisible government was not a discernible, structured organization, but was rather a vast network of professional criminals, shady businessmen, corrupt law enforcement officials, politicians, and government bureaucrats that resembled more a club than a corporation.

What Carlos Marcello inherited, then, in concrete terms, was the loyalty and income-producing services of a narcotics smuggler in Gretna, a madam in Morgan City, a bookmaker in New Orleans, a crooked sheriff in Gulfport, a loan shark in Algiers, a corrupt police chief in Metairie, and a compliant bureaucrat in Baton Rouge.

What held this far-flung network of outlaws together and kept them obedient to the boss's commands was a combination of greed and fear. Greed for the riches that cooperation with the boss promised. Fear of swift and certain punishment for any infraction of his rules, or failure to obey his commands.

Because the discipline enforced by fear was so crucial to the invisible government's continued growth and influence, it was absolutely essential that its leader be a man willing to commit murder to achieve his goals. In the end, Carlos Marcello's elevation to boss of Louisiana's invisible government was not so much due to his newfound wealth and political power, but to his reputation as a brutal killer.

By extension it was also due to the reputation of the Mafia brotherhood he represented. The long chain of murders committed by the Sicilians in New Orleans over the years was part of Louisiana's collective memory. The Mafia murder of Police Chief David Hennessey was just as much a chapter of Louisiana lore as Napoleon's sellout to Thomas Jefferson or the piratical raids of Jean Laffite.

Carlos Marcello had learned what exploiting greed and fear could get him. As a tough, streetwise young criminal from a despised minority, he had found out early in life how cowardly, weak, pliant, and greedy Louisiana's legally constituted officials were, from the cop on the beat to the sheriff of Jefferson Parish to the governor of the state. Threaten them with murder, or the murder of a family member, or offer them a chance to earn quick, easy money by betraying the public trust, and he had them where he wanted them.

As for his clients, the people, Carlos was well aware of their weaknesses too. As a young man in his mid-twenties, he had learned to exploit poor blacks' weaknesses for alcohol and drugs. As he grew older, he discovered he could make money exploiting the weaknesses of ever-increasing numbers of ordinary men and women. They wanted gambling and he gave them gambling. They wanted sex and he gave them whores. They wanted drugs and he sold them drugs. They wanted money and he paid them bribes.

If Carlos Marcello had been an ordinary man of ordinary ambitions, he would have been content to run an essentially provincial underworld enterprise in Louisiana, after his elevation to power in 1947. But there was nothing ordinary about Carlos Marcello. No sooner did he take control of Carolla's network then he began extending its operations beyond Louisiana's borders. Among other ventures, he soon gained control of the Nola Printing Co., a gambling wire serving bookmakers in Louisiana, Texas, Oklahoma, Arkansas, Chicago, Alabama, Missouri, and Mississippi. Before long he would extend operations to California, Central America, the Caribbean, and beyond.

Along with this business expansion went a progressive defiance of the authorities. Within four years of his assumption of power in Louisiana, he would defy a committee of the United States Senate. Within a decade and a half, so great would become his power and arrogance that he would even dare to defy the President and attorney general of the United States.

PART III

Making Enemies
1948–1960

9

Willswood Tavern

On the West Bank of the Mississippi, in Jefferson Parish, roughly opposite New Orleans, stretches a long and desolate tract of marshland whose waterways connect to the south with Lake Cataouatche and Lake Salvador and ultimately to Barataria Bay and the Gulf of Mexico. In the early nineteenth century the notorious pirates Jean and Pierre Laffite operated out of a base in Barataria, raiding shipping bound for the port of New Orleans at will. A hundred and fifty years later, a twentieth-century pirate established his lair on 6400 acres of this morass and used it as a base to plunder an entire state.

The Marcello family, gradually expanding their landholdings northward from the south coast of Algiers, had, at first, acquired a 178-acre tract of this swampland and had converted a ramshackle shed on the property into a rustic bar and restaurant that came to be known as Willswood Tavern. It was a small, nondescript structure at the edge of the swamp that looked to passersby like an abandoned building. In reality, it was anything but abandoned. Not long after Carlos was anointed boss of the local Mafia, he made Willswood his headquarters, the nerve center of almost all his criminal operations.

Every Sunday morning the don would hold court at Willswood for the key players in the rackets he controlled in Louisiana and Mississippi. From Lake Charles they came, and from Houma, and

Gretna, and Plaquemines and New Orleans, and Morgan City, and Gulfport on the Mississippi coast: the madams of all the Marcello whorehouses and call-girl rings, the operators of all the Marcello gambling enterprises—the bookmakers and the slot machine operators— the fencers of stolen goods, the drug smugglers, the loan sharks, and the corrupt sheriffs, mayors, and state bureaucrats who made these illegal activities possible, all would descend on Willswood Sunday mornings to pay homage to Carlos and render unto him his cut of their take.

Carlos Marcello was around 38 at the time, a short, bullnecked, muscular man with big hands, a disproportionately large head, and an imperious air. He had already made a small fortune from illegal gambling and other rackets, and had acquired a reputation as a man who would stop at nothing to achieve his goals. Feared by his underlings, and by politicians and police throughout the state, he would sit at the long table at Willswood on Sunday mornings and review the battles of the week with the urgency and authority of a commanding general addressing his staff in the midst of a major military campaign.

After business, Carlos would provide his faithful with food and drink, and by two in the afternoon a boisterous party would be under way as the madams and gamblers and smugglers feasted on oysters, shrimp, crayfish, fettuccine, salad, and cheese and swilled down bottles of beer, Chianti, and *vino bianco*. Carlos, who had an enormous appetite, had imported ex-convict Provino Mosca, Al Capone's former chef, from Chicago. His tasty Italian cooking soon became legendary in the underworld and among the corrupt politicians and law enforcement officials of Louisiana and Mississippi, who considered it something of an honor to be invited to Carlos's table. So popular did Mosca's kitchen become that Carlos built Mosca and his family a small house on the property. When Carlos eventually transferred his headquarters elsewhere, Willswood Tavern became Mosca's restaurant, still one of the most popular Italian eateries on the West Bank.

When the feasting at Willswood was over and Marcello's minions were dismissed, Carlos and one of his lieutenants would count the take and then head home with the loot accompanied by a bodyguard. Those who came to Willswood on Sunday morning knew that if they didn't pay up, or seemed to be holding money back, they might eventually disappear in the swamp. The boss had a way of handling cheats: death without trial. After the party at Willswood was over, Carlos's bodyguards would detain the suspected offender, the boss would grill him, and if he was satisfied he was guilty, one of the guards would strangle him and dump his body in a huge tub of lye. The partially decomposed corpse would then be poured into the swamp where what was left of it would flow into a waterway and disappear with hardly a trace.

This was Mafia justice, swifter and surer than the authorities' justice. As long as the Mafia had leaders powerful enough to enforce this brand of justice, and as long as there were sheriffs and district attorneys and judges willing to go along with it, the authorities, the courts, the government, would be powerless against them. Carlos Marcello knew this instinctively. His vast swamp not only absorbed corpses, it swallowed laws, courts, constitutions.

10

Carlos Defies the Kefauver Committee

COMMITTEE COUNSEL: Mr. Marcello, are you a member of the Mafia?

MARCELLO: I refuse to answer the question on the ground it might intend to criminate me.

...

COUNSEL: Have you attended a meeting at the Willswood Tavern with Frank Costello?

MARCELLO: I refuse to answer the question on the ground that it may tend to incriminate me.

...

COUNSEL: Did you attend a meeting at the Black Diamond Night Club on May 5, 1947, with Vincent, Joseph, Anthony, Jake, and Nick Marcello?

MARCELLO: I refuse to answer the question....

...

COUNSEL: Are you engaged in an oil enterprise in Pickens Field
with Joseph Poretto?

MARCELLO: I refuse to answer....

...

COUNSEL: Do you now or have you ever had interest in Tregle's
Dreamland Barroom in Jefferson Parish?

MARCELLO: I refuse to answer....

Carlos Marcello had taken the witness stand in New Orleans' federal courthouse, accompanied by his attorney, G. Wray Gill, before a
huge crowd of reporters, photographers, and onlookers eager to get
a look at the reported "evil genius of organized crime in Louisiana."
Wearing dark glasses and a conservative navy-blue double-breasted
suit and scowling defiantly at the tall, lanky, somewhat awkward senator from Tennessee, Chairman Kefauver, Carlos was in the midst
of his virtuoso performance of pleading the Fifth Amendment, in
his southern Louisiana drawl, before a committee of the United States
Senate, 152 times. Only one question would he answer: "What laws
have you violated?" To which he replied: "Not being an attorney I
would not know." Marcello even refused to tell the committee where
he was born, how old he was, and whether he was married, on the
grounds his answers might tend to incriminate him.

The occasion was the appearance in New Orleans on January 25,
1951, of the Special Committee to Investigate Organized Crime in
Interstate Commerce of the U.S. Senate, chaired by Senator Estes
Kefauver, to hold hearings on illegal gambling in Louisiana. Carlos
Marcello was the principal witness.

The rapid expansion of Carlos Marcello's criminal empire went largely unchallenged during the 1940s. What few rival gangs there were
in New Orleans were too fearful of Marcello to try to get in his way.
And local and state law enforcement officials and politicians were too
greedy for his generous payoffs ever to take anything but a token
stand against him. In the Louisiana underworld Carlos reigned supreme. He felt he could get away with anything and usually did. Not
only did Carlos's whirlwind rise to power go unchallenged, it also went
largely unnoticed. Although the Marcello name was certainly well
known to the leaders of the nation's principal Mafia families and to

the heads of certain labor unions, not to mention to his own underground network of criminal agents and bought officials in Louisiana, Texas, and Mississippi, it was still not yet known to the general public in those three states, and had never received national publicity. As a result of these ideal circumstances, Carlos developed a sense of invulnerability and self-importance that added still another dimension to his already inflated pride. For sheer cockiness of manner and exuberance of ego, few Mafia bosses in America could match the panache of Carlos Marcello.

It came as a rude shock, then, when in 1950 the muckraking Washington columnist Drew Pearson, in a nationally syndicated article, described Carlos Marcello as "the crime czar of New Orleans," and a year later Senator Estes Kefauver of Tennessee publicly referred to him as "the evil genius of organized crime in Louisiana."

Senator Kefauver had formed his Special Committee to Investigate Organized Crime in Interstate Commerce in the face of almost overwhelming opposition. As many senators opposed its formation as not, and if it had not been for the tie-breaking vote of Vice President Alben Barkley, the committee would never have come into existence. Also opposing the committee at the time was Attorney General J. Howard McGrath, who asserted publicly that the Justice Department had no persuasive evidence that a "national crime syndicate" existed.

McGrath's attitude toward organized crime was typical of law enforcement agencies throughout the United States at the time. Almost no one, least of all the Department of Justice and its investigatory arm, the FBI, wanted to know that such a secretive, sinister menace as the Mafia existed on an organized national scale, and therefore it was almost universally decreed not to exist.

Estes Kefauver was an exception. He knew from his experiences as an attorney and a senator fighting corruption that organized crime existed, probably on a national scale, and he was determined to do something about it. Upon forming his committee, Kefauver stated he wanted answers to three key questions: Did a national, highly organized criminal network exist? If it did, what were its chief sources of power? And to what extent had organized crime purchased the cooperation of local governments?

The Kefauver Committee hearings in New Orleans in January 1951 were held in the federal courthouse under the full glare of national press coverage. Among those called to testify were Carlos Marcello, his brother Anthony, and their associate Joseph Poretto. Others included gamblers "Dandy Phil" Kastel and "Diamond Jim" Moran (alias James Broccato), and such allegedly corrupt public officials as Jefferson Parish Sheriff Frank Clancy and New Orleans Mayor De-Lesseps Morrison. From the questions the committee asked, it became clear that Kefauver's advance investigators had done a thorough job of gathering intelligence on the Marcello organization. Among other things, it became evident from the questioning of Marcello that Carlos was no mere parochial phenomenon, that he had recently been in touch with the survivors of the old Al Capone gang in Chicago, and leaders of the Mafia in Los Angeles, Florida, and Texas.

The committee's grilling of Marcello covered a wide range of his alleged criminal activities and exposed, by inference, many of his most tenaciously guarded secrets. He was asked if he had now, or ever had, interest in a bewilderingly long list of slot machine distributors, gambling casinos, racing wire services, and assorted bars, restaurants, and nightclubs throughout southern Louisiana and Mississippi. Among the organizations and places named were the Jefferson Music Co., the Beverly Country Club Casino, the New Southport Club, the Dixie Coin Co. of Gulfport, Mississippi, the Willswood Tavern, and Tregle's Dreamland Barroom.

Referring obviously to the secret conclave at which he had been made de facto boss of the Louisiana Mafia, Carlos was asked if he had attended a meeting at the Black Diamond Night Club on May 5, 1947, along with what amounted to a roll call of the most powerful underworld figures in Louisiana: Anthony Carolla, Nofio J. Pecora, Tom Rizzuto, Frank Lombardino, Vincent, Joseph, and Anthony Marcello, among others.

He was asked if he ever had a meeting with Frank Clancy, Beauregard Miller, and Phil Kastel. He was asked if he had recently made a person-to-person telephone call to Harry Brooks, a close associate of Los Angeles crime boss Mickey Cohen, while Brooks was in Texas. He was asked if he had recently made a person-to-person call to "Joe Savela [sic] [Joseph Civello], the Mafia boss of Dallas." He was asked if he had recently made a person-to-person call to "Sam Garras [sic] [Sam Yaras], the brother of Dave Garras [sic], the Chicago hoodlum." He was asked if he knew Santos Trafficante, Jr., of Tampa, owner of casinos in Havana and boss of the Florida Gulf Coast Mafia.

When Marcello was asked whether he had made a person-to-person telephone call to Vincent Valloni in Houston, Texas, the questioning turned to the subject of murder:

"Did you know Vincent Valloni?"

"Do you know that Vincent Valloni was murdered?"

"Do you know that Vincent Valloni was murdered subsequent to your telephone call?"

"Do you know that the murderer of Vincent Valloni said that he killed him on instructions from Peter Duca?"

"In a Mafia-type killing?"

By the time Marcello took the Fifth for the 152nd time, Chairman Kefauver was utterly exasperated. Stating that the committee's investigative reports identified Marcello as "one of the principal criminals in the United States today," Kefauver told the packed courtroom:

"The record is long, the connections are bad, the implications according to our report are most sinister, and we wanted to find out among other things what was the trouble with our naturalization and immigration laws that a man who is apparently having such a detrimental effect on law enforcement and to decency in the community, how can he continue to stay here."

Compared to the grilling of Carlos Marcello, the questioning of the other witnesses was a mere sideshow. Brother Anthony and underboss Joe Poretto took the Fifth to fewer and less spectacular questions. So did Sheriff Clancy and "Dandy Phil" Kastel. The only major witness who enlivened the proceedings was ex-boxer "Diamond Jim" Moran, alias Broccato, who had this curious exchange with Chairman Kefauver:

"What does one do with the handle of a slot machine?" Kefauver asked.

"Pull it…it's good exercise," replied Broccato.

Then, to the amusement of the courtroom audience, Broccato boasted that the mayor of New Orleans, DeLesseps Morrison, had once visited his hunting camp and played a slot machine in his lodge. He then invited Senator Kefauver to be his guest at the camp: "I'll be your personal cook," he said with a twinkle.

Estes Kefauver was not amused. Genuinely outraged by the pervasive corruption he had encountered in Louisiana, he persuaded the committee to cite Carlos Marcello for contempt of Congress, a charge for which Marcello was eventually convicted and sentenced to six months in prison. Kefauver also recommended to the attorney general that deportation proceedings be initiated against Marcello as soon as possible.

Joseph Marcello posted as bond for his oldest son 175 acres of land on the West Bank and the Willswood Tavern. Eventually an appeals court overturned Marcello's conviction, claiming that Marcello had been within his rights to plead the Fifth 152 times, sparing him prison. However, in 1953 the U.S. government issued its first deportation order against Marcello, initiating a case, and a struggle, that has lasted to this day.

11

The Town & Country Motel

During the week of the Kefauver hearings, the Marcellos had to endure seeing Carlos's name and face on the front page almost every day. They had to endure reading Senator Kefauver's characterizations of Carlos as "the evil genius of organized crime in Louisiana," the "number one hoodlum," and "one of the principal criminals in the United States today." They also had to endure references in the press to Anthony and Vincent as alleged accomplices in their brother's crimes and see revealed, for the first time in print, the existence of their secret swampland headquarters and several of the bars, restaurants, and nightclubs they had secretly controlled, such as the Forrest Club, the Billionaires Club, and Tregle's Dreamland Barroom. Everything was out in the open. The family had become notorious in Louisiana. Now people would stare at Jacqueline Marcello when she went to the supermarket and the Marcello children would have to answer back to the gibes and taunts of their peers at school.

It was not long after this that Joseph and Louise Marcello decided to make a pilgrimage to their native Sicily, which they hadn't seen since their departure forty-four years before. Arriving in Palermo by steamer in June 1952, the Marcellos journeyed to the village in southern Sicily in which they had been raised. Ravanusa is in the province of Agrigento, a dry, rocky, hilly region known for its sulphur mines, its most famous son, Luigi Pirandello, and the magnificent ancient Greek temples that rise up out of the flowered plains along its Mediterranean coast. It is a region of intense natural beauty, a land of enormous distances, of hilltop medieval villages reaching toward vast, open skies, of rocky slopes spotted with olive trees, sheep, and goats.

Whether Joseph and Louise Marcello appreciated the beauty of their corner of Sicily is anyone's guess. Most likely what impressed them most about it was the unchanging poverty. They were rich now in comparison to the relatives who had remained behind. They had accomplished what tens of thousands of Sicilian emigrants to America had dreamed of but did not always achieve: they had escaped the cycle of Sicilian poverty and had won a share of the riches of the New World.

Sicily, to people of the Marcellos' class, held little charm. For the Sicilian peasants it had always been a place of *malafortuna*. And, as it turned out for the Marcellos, it was still a place of *malafortuna*. For not long after Joseph and Louise arrived in Ravanusa, Joseph suddenly took ill and had to be driven to a hospital in Palermo, where he died on June 17.

Louise accompanied her husband's body home to Louisiana, where Joseph was laid to rest in Gretna's Catholic cemetery. In his later years Joseph had built up a thriving shrimping business in the delta and had made several lucrative real estate investments. Among the assets he left to his wife were 178 acres of land in Marrero on the West Bank and the Willswood Tavern.

As it turned out, the Willswood Tavern became one of the first casualties of the Kefauver investigation. Exposed now as Carlos Marcello's headquarters, it was soon relegated to a mere restaurant. Presided over by its new owner, the widow Louise, its kitchen remained under the direction of Al Capone's former chef, Provino Mosca, who by the time of Joseph's death had attracted a considerable following.

It did not take Carlos long to establish a new headquarters. In 1953, he bought the Town & Country Motel on Airline Highway, that ugly stretch of commercial sprawl—an endless procession of gas stations, parking lots, billboards, striptease joints, sleazy bars, cheap motels, and neon signs—stretching from Moisant International Airport to New Orleans.

The Town & Country was the first of Carlos Marcello's many motel acquisitions. Located in New Orleans Parish, near the Jefferson

Parish line, it consisted of a main one-story building and two adjoining structures: the Town & Country Restaurant and Lounge, and Carlos's office. By the middle of 1953 the restaurant and lounge had become a meeting place for professional gamblers, the key men in Marcello's criminal organization, and corrupt politicians from all over Louisiana. There was a small room reserved for Marcello's slot machines, B girls hustled drinks and solicited for prostitution in the bar, and in a back room there was a long table with chairs for Carlos's Sunday meetings.

In charge of the Town & Country Motel complex were two of Carlos Marcello's highest ranking associates, Nofio Pecora and Joseph Poretto, and one of Carlos's younger brothers, Anthony. Pecora was an ex-convict with a history in heroin traffic and prostitution. Poretto a stocky New Orleanian, who had worked in the racing wire services in Chicago since the days of Moe Annenberg, comanaged, with Carlos's brother Joe, and co-owned, with Carlos, the Nola News wire service, a horseracing wire network. The network, which included a private, exclusive telephone line extending throughout Jefferson Parish, provided race tips and results to bookies throughout Louisiana and Texas and was tied in with the Mafia-owned and operated national racing wire network. From the Town & Country Motel, Nofio Pecora and his wife, Frances, who doubled as Carlos's personal secretary, ran a call-girl ring covering Texas, Louisiana, Mississippi, and Alabama. Every payday Frances would take a bus load of her girls down to the U.S. Naval Air Station in Harrison County, Mississippi, and position them outside its gates. The girls would then hustle the airmen back to a motel in town rented twice a month by the Marcello organization. Between the girls and the room rentals the Marcellos were able to absorb a healthy share of the Navy payrolls.

In 1956, the year in which one of Carlos's daughters, Louise, was named Queen of the Krewe of Midas for the Mardi Gras carnival season, the local police discovered that Carlos's Town & Country Motel was being used as a place of assignation for a prostitution ring using teenage girls, some of whom, it was learned, played hookey from school on a regular basis to meet their dates at the motel.

As for Carlos himself, he established an office in a squat, unadorned modern one-story building of cheap brick and gray cinder block directly behind the motel. In his spacious, carpeted office Carlos made calls and received visitors from behind a huge uncluttered mahogany desk. His secretary, Frances Pecora, had her office at the end of a corridor leading from Marcello's office to the building's entrance. Opposite Mrs. Pecora was the office of Carlos's "messenger boy" lawyer, Phillip Smith, who was on constant call to attend to whatever legal problems might come up. Although this unpretentious suite of offices appeared at first glance almost as benign as the name of the motel of which it was a part, uninitiated visitors would be rudely reminded by a sign on the door leading out precisely whom they were dealing with:

THREE CAN KEEP
A SECRET
IF TWO ARE DEAD

From his Town & Country headquarters Carlos Marcello ran a vast, complex array of operations—some legal, others illegal—concentrated mostly in Louisiana, Mississippi, and Texas, but extending also to California, Mexico, and the Caribbean.

According to the director of the New Orleans Metropolitan Crime Commission, Aaron Kohn, Marcello developed his venture capital "through extensive gambling operations, including casinos, slot machines, pinball, football pools, dice, card games, roulette and bingo, also narcotics, prostitution, extortion clip-joint operations, marketing stolen goods, robberies, burglaries and thefts." This criminal enterprise, again according to Kohn, "required, and had, corrupt collusion of public officials at every level including police, sheriffs, justices of the peace, prosecutors, mayors, governors, judges, councilmen, licensing authorities, state legislators, and at least one member of Congress."

With the capital raised from his illegal operations Marcello was able to finance a sizable array of legitimate businesses, including motels, restaurants, taverns, banks, beer and liquor distributorships, shrimp-boat fleets, shipbuilding, finance companies, taxi and bus firms, sight-seeing lines, linen supply companies, gas stations, souvenir shops, phonograph record distributorships, electrical appliance stores, and a tomato canning company. This last activity provided Marcello with his stock alibi for not having anything to do with organized crime. Under questioning from law enforcement agencies, Marcello always stubbornly insisted he was merely a $1500-a-month "tomato salesman." Then he would produce a can of tomatoes from the Pelican Tomato Company, and display receipts from Pelican's single largest customer, the U.S. Navy Department.

By 1953 Carlos, at 42, had developed a commanding presence. People observed that he "sat tall" at his Town & Country desk and had a regal, intimidating bearing. Fearless and ruthless since his teens, Carlos was given to occasional fits of rage that were frightening to behold. During one tantrum at Willswood he is said to have fired a bullet into the head of a treacherous underling as if he were swatting a fly. Fearless and ruthless since his teens, he had the reputation of rarely hesitating to take enormous risks or shrink from eliminating someone who stood in the way of his ambitions.

A hard worker, Carlos often woke up at 4:00 A.M. to scan the real estate ads in the papers to spot a bargain before anyone else. Otherwise he rose around 6:00 and immediately began phoning friends and associates throughout Louisiana over his morning coffee, priming them for the business of the day. By 8:00 he would be shaved, dressed, breakfasted, and ready to be driven in his bronze Cadillac to his Town & Country office. After a ten-hour workday there, he would come home promptly every evening around 7:00 for dinner with his wife.

Since Carlos dropped out of school at age 14, his English never advanced beyond that of a semiliterate white New Orleans unskilled laborer. In Marcello's vocabulary, "that" is "dat," "nothing" is "nuttin'," an oyster is an "erster." Although he was destined to earn and control millions of dollars, he was barely able to count, add, and subtract, and had to rely on relatives and subordinates to perform the most elementary arithmetic calculations for him. Yet he had been gifted with immense physical and emotional energy, a keen native intelligence, and a relentless will to power. It was these qualities that enabled him to dominate and control the highly educated professionals in the courts of law and seats of government in Louisiana whose formal education did not prevent them from ending up in his pocket.

After his father's death in 1953 Carlos became very much the loyal and affectionate family man, devoted to his six brothers, two sisters, four children, ten grandchildren, and numerous nieces and nephews. The seven Marcello brothers were remarkably supportive of one another. Each had his own responsibility in the Marcello criminal organization, as detailed by Aaron Kohn in his 1961 congressional testimony.

The one-eyed Pete Marcello, 40, who had, as we know, been arrested with brother Carlos in 1929 as a suspect in a bank robbery, had served a brief term in prison for a narcotics violation in 1944. He now managed several "Venus-trap" striptease joints owned by Carlos in the French Quarter and business district. Brother Pasquale, or Pascal, 36, operated an illegal gambling house in Gretna, Jefferson Parish, well known for selling drinks to under-age customers. Vincent, known as Vinnie or Vince, considered to be the most "gentlemanly" of the brothers, at 31 managed the family slot machine, pinball, and jukebox business, the Jefferson Music Company, owned fifty-fifty by himself and Carlos. Joe Jr., 28, Carlos's most trusted brother, functioned as Carlos's right-hand man, his immediate underboss, and helped Joe Poretto run the Nola wire service and the Marcello bookie network. Anthony Marcello, known as Tony, 26, helped manage the Town & Country Motel and also helped collect from the hundreds of jukeboxes and slot machines that Jefferson Music leased to bars and restaurants in Jefferson Parish and New Orleans. And finally there was Salvadore, or Sammy, the youngest brother at 24 and the most personable and gregarious of the seven brothers, who helped Vincent in the management of Jefferson Music and acted as a sort of public relations man for Carlos when Carlos needed to put up a sunny, charming front.

They were a rough, ruthless, cocksure, prosperous, and much-feared bunch, the seven Marcello brothers of Jefferson Parish, Louisiana. And they routinely got away with everything. With the Jefferson Parish sheriff and the local town chiefs of police in their pockets, they could do as they pleased. Such was their infamy that no one in New Orleans or Jefferson Parish would dare stand up to them. By the mid-fifties, in their corner of Louisiana, the seven Marcello brothers had become a government of their own.

All the brothers were married, with children, as were the Marcello sisters, Rose and Mary. Every Sunday the entire clan would have lunch at Carlos's place, where Jacqueline would produce a huge serving of spaghetti and meatballs, Carlos's favorite dish, and grandmother Louise would say grace. Although their anonymity and, to some extent, their privacy had been shattered by the Kefauver investigation, the Marcellos could count many blessings by the summer of 1953.

Yet the Kefauver investigation did not fade away for the family. As 1953 drew to a close, as a direct result of the investigation, Carlos Marcello was ordered deported as an undesirable alien. The stage was now set for a vicious battle destined to come to a climax during the first months of the presidency of John F. Kennedy.

12

Aaron Kohn:
Taking On Marcello

Not long after the federal government ordered Carlos Marcello deported, a group of concerned New Orleans citizens invited a former FBI agent to direct an investigation of the New Orleans Police Department. Once an assistant to J. Edgar Hoover, the former agent had had extensive investigative experience in Chicago. His name was Aaron Kohn, and he was destined to become the most determined opponent Marcello ever had.

Aaron Kohn had been born and raised in Philadelphia and educated in Washington, D.C., where he took his law degree. Joining the FBI in 1930, he had enjoyed a distinguished career in the bureau, much of it in Chicago, where he played key roles in the capture of such notorious gangsters of the thirties as John Dillinger, Baby Face Nelson, and Ma Barker. A slim, elegant, dark-haired man of keen intelligence, Kohn's quiet, gentlemanly bearing often fooled his adversaries, who failed to detect the tough, dogged, dedicated crime fighter he was.

When Kohn arrived in New Orleans in 1953, it did not take him long to recognize that the New Orleans Police Department and municipal administration were even more corrupt than they were reputed to be. The evidence was everywhere. Although gambling was illegal in Louisiana, Kohn found slot machines wherever he looked, bookies doing business on every street corner, and vast crowds coming and going at will from the big gambling casinos. Behind this general license, Kohn found a police department so corrupt that virtually every member of the force was either collecting or distributing graft, a practice, Kohn eventually learned, that had been going on for the past fifty years. Furthermore, he found that New Orleans Mayor DeLesseps "Chet" Morrison had come into office in 1946 thanks principally to Mafia financial support, and was paying off the debt by allowing the Mafia's illegal gambling wire service to operate freely in the downtown business district. "Finding corruption in New Orleans," observes Kohn today, "was like making a virgin gold find when the nuggets were lying on top of the ground."

Fearless in his accusations, Kohn soon called for the resignation of the New Orleans police chief and publicly denounced Mayor Morrison for working hand in hand with mobsters. At the conclusion of the investigation, several of Kohn's supporters in the business community and in civic associations formed the Metropolitan Crime Commission of New Orleans, financed entirely with private funds. They named Aaron Kohn managing director, a post he was to hold for the next twenty-four years. Soon after taking office, Kohn began to focus on what he suspected was the force behind almost all the corruption in New Orleans and surrounding parishes: the Marcello organization.

Kohn had found there was no law enforcement mechanism at work in Louisiana that threatened Carlos Marcello except the Immigration and Naturalization Service. Marcello not only had the New Orleans and Jefferson Parish Police departments and municipal administrations in his pocket but also controlled the Louisiana State Police and could usually get what he wanted from the state bureaucracy in Baton Rouge. It took an outsider like Aaron Kohn to do something about this vast, entrenched, almost institutionalized corruption. A few months after taking office, he launched a major campaign to obtain intelligence on the Marcello organization's activities. It was the first time that such an effort had been initiated in New Orleans. The Kefauver Committee investigators had done much of their work out of Washington.

One of the first things Kohn found was that all the police records of Marcello's arrests in Jefferson Parish and New Orleans had been destroyed. He made this key discovery thanks to several former police officers who had kept copies of the arrest records and had turned them over to him. Kohn then conducted a personal survey of the gambling casinos and found that not only were no law enforcement officers to be seen either in them or near them but their patrons were surprised when he told them that gambling was illegal. Once Kohn and a friend went to Marcello's New Southport Club casino, "a huge, Nevada-type operation," in Kohn's words, whose hulking floorman, known as "Concrete," recognized him as he arrived, greeted him by name, and immediately escorted him and his friend to a blackjack table. Kohn refused to play, but his friend went along and it was soon evident that he couldn't lose. With Concrete standing by, Kohn then told the dealer to cut it out and all of a sudden his friend began losing.

Turning to Concrete, Kohn asked him whom he worked for.

"Why, Mister Carlos, Sir," drawled the towering floorman, as if he had nothing to hide.

Despite opposition from Mayor Morrison, who unabashedly threatened the contributors to Kohn's crime commission, as well as Kohn's clerical personnel, Kohn stepped up his investigation of the Marcellos. Soon he himself became the victim of anonymous telephone threats, usually delivered in the middle of the night. Not taking them seriously, Kohn was, however, somewhat shaken early one Sunday morning when he went out to the driveway of his suburban home to pick up his Sunday paper. Lying inside the rolled up paper was the limp form of a white rabbit with its throat slit.

Refusing to be intimidated, Kohn continued to gather intelligence on Marcello. One of his major investigative successes was his discovery, in the mid-fifties, that Marcello had acquired, piece by piece, a huge swampland property on the West Bank. The property—some 6400 acres—was known as Churchill Farms, after its former owners, the Churchill family of New Orleans (no relation to Sir Winston). Before Kohn's investigation, people knew that the Churchills had been selling off parcels of their West Bank holdings, but no one knew to whom they had been selling. Kohn's researchers, by studying Jefferson Parish conveyances, noted that a variety of organizations—mostly land companies—had bought parcels of the property and then discovered that Carlos Marcello owned all of them. Kohn reported his findings to a local television station, causing something of a sensation in New Orleans and surrounding parishes.

During the mid-fifties Kohn learned that Carlos had remodeled an old barn on Churchill Farms, equipping it with a modern kitchen and converting part of it into a meeting room with wood-paneled walls, luxurious carpeting, and a long conference table. Kohn also found out that Carlos had built a marina on the property, known today as Pier 90, from which a boat could take off on a journey through marshes, bayous, and lakes to the Gulf of Mexico. Kohn's investigators also learned that somewhere deep in the morass of Churchill Farms Carlos had created a hunting camp, with a small rustic hut and duck blinds that Aaron Kohn believed were often used for purposes other than storing decoys, hip boots, and rain gear. In time, Kohn learned that Carlos had grandiose plans for developing Churchill Farms. Marcello had apparently contacted a noted New Orleans city planner to engineer the drainage of the property and plan the building of a large residential community with condominium apartments, shopping centers, sports facilities, and an airport. Not long after Marcello conceived these plans, Kohn's investigators learned that the state of Louisiana planned to construct, with federal funds, a bypass to Interstate 10 to run along the West Bank of the Mississippi. Kohn soon figured out that the principal beneficiary of the bypass would be Churchill Farms and reported his findings to the local media. In the end, an outraged public killed the proposed bypass.

There was no end to the sinister things Kohn succeeded in discovering about Carlos Marcello and his brothers. The nuggets, ignored for years, were scattered everywhere for the picking.

Kohn was able to attribute at least three, possibly four, murders to Marcello, including the gangland-style killing of two of Marcello's former narcotics associates, Gene Mano and Tom Siracusa. For none of these crimes was Marcello ever charged. Kohn found out that the district attorney of Jefferson Parish, Frank Landridge, was totally under Marcello's control, so much so that Landridge employed one of Marcello's most vicious enforcers, "Zip" Chimento, a man who had been convicted twice for intimidating witnesses, as chief investigator of the Jefferson Parish District Attorney's Office. He found out that although the Marcellos operated illegal slot machines and pinball machines through their Jefferson Music Company, they managed to fraudulently obtain an FCC license for Jefferson Music to operate a radio broadcast to fourteen citizen-band-wavelength receivers whose owners were involved in illegal gambling. (Kohn later forcefully brought this to the attention of the McClellan Rackets Committee.) He discovered that both Vincent and Anthony Marcello were involved in widespread illegal gambling operations, and that Pascal Marcello ran a gambling house and bar in Gretna for underage customers. Kohn also learned that Peter Marcello had spent time in a federal penitentiary, had been involved in "repeated acts of violence and brutality," and operated a string of "Venus-trap" striptease joints in the French Quarter that "enticed and defrauded unwary males." The list went on....

Meanwhile, for his efforts to expose Marcello, Kohn had to put up with the constant ridicule of his former FBI colleagues, unremitting harassment from the mayor's office, and the scorn of the New Orleans Police Department, which refused to share intelligence information with him. In time he was to learn that a Mississippi associate of Carlos's had even put out a contract on his life.

The New Orleans FBI agent assigned to keep tabs on Marcello, Regis Kennedy, "a typical Irish cop," in Kohn's words, who was nearing retirement, was convinced Kohn was barking up the wrong tree in pursuing Marcello as a Mafia boss. Apparently fooled by Marcello's "I don't know nuttin' about dat" facade, he kept insisting to his superiors in the bureau that Carlos was "just a stupid little man" who could not possibly be involved in all the criminal activities Kohn claimed he was. To Regis Kennedy and the other agents of the New Orleans FBI office, Carlos Marcello was a real estate investor and a salesman for the Pelican Tomato Company and little else.

At one point in his investigations Kohn learned from one of his informants that a Mississippi sheriff, whom he had publicly exposed as having been in Marcello's pocket, had decided to put out an independent, unilateral contract on his life. The sheriff, however, eventually got second thoughts and went to consult Carlos personally about making the hit. The two met at one of Carlos's swampland retreats. Without telling Carlos whom he planned to murder, the sheriff asked the boss what would be the best way to make his victim's body disappear. Carlos told him to come out to his car and there, in the front seat, he advised the sheriff that he should dump the body into a tub of lye, let it decompose, then pour it into the swamp. After imparting this advice, Carlos asked the sheriff whom he planned to get rid of. When the sheriff told him it was Aaron Kohn, Carlos had a quick reaction. "No, no," he said, "not dat guy," explaining that since it was well known Kohn was investigating him, his murder would bring even more heat down upon Carlos than he was getting already. Kohn smiles today over the irony that Marcello probably saved his life.

Scorned and harassed by local politicians and law enforcement officials, Aaron Kohn was eventually vindicated by two New Orleans grand juries convened in 1957 and 1958 to decide whether or not to indict several high-ranking police officials Kohn had exposed as being corrupt. To Kohn's deep satisfaction, the indictments were returned and a new era was inaugurated in New Orleans, one which, in Kohn's words, "marked a change from the time it was dangerous to be an honest cop to the period in which it became increasingly dangerous to be a dishonest cop."

Then, the following year, Kohn was further vindicated by a Senate committee to investigate corruption in labor and management chaired by Senator John L. McClellan.

Robert F. Kennedy had been appointed chief counsel of the committee. Again to Kohn's profound satisfaction, Kennedy had the committee invite him to testify on organized crime in Louisiana at the Senate hearings and asked him to come up to Washington and brief him personally on Carlos Marcello and his criminal network. At last people of consequence were taking him seriously.

And so Aaron Kohn traveled to Washington one Sunday afternoon and spent four hours in Kennedy's office telling the young shirtsleeved committee counsel all he knew about the Marcellos and the Mafia in Louisiana.

For Robert Kennedy, what Kohn told him was a unique revelation. Kennedy was familiar with the leading players in the Chicago and New York Mafia families, but knew next to nothing about organized crime in the Gulf Coast states. Kohn decided not to hold back anything. He gave Kennedy a brief history of the Louisiana Mafia since the 1880s. He traced Carlos Marcello's rise to power in the forties and fifties. He revealed what he knew about the Marcello organization: the roles Carlos's six brothers played in his criminal network, the key positions held by Joseph Poretto and Nofio Pecora, Marcello's long-standing association with his deputy in Dallas, Joseph Civello. He recited the entire litany of the Marcello brothers' crimes to Kennedy, including two of the murders he suspected Carlos had masterminded, and expatiated at length on the corrupt political climate that gave the Marcellos protection in Louisiana.

Kennedy listened attentively and took notes as Kohn talked. At the end of the long presentation Kennedy leaned across his desk and, in his youthful Cape Cod accent, said: "Well, Mr. Kohn, I thank you very much for this briefing. We are looking forward to your testimony before the committee and I can assure you that, sooner or later, we will do something about Mr. Marcello. We cannot permit this kind of corruption to exist in the United States."

13

The McClellan Committee: Round One with the Kennedys

KENNEDY: You are an associate of Mr. Frank Costello. Is that right?

MARCELLO: I decline to answer on the ground it may intend to incriminate me.

...

KENNEDY: You are an associate of Joe Civello of Dallas, Texas, who attended the meeting at Apalachin?

MARCELLO: I decline to answer on the ground it may intend to incriminate me.

...

KENNEDY: Sam Carolla, who was deported in 1947 as a narcotics trafficker?

MARCELLO: I decline to answer on the same ground.

...

KENNEDY: Do you dominate and control, Mr. Marcello, the coin machine business in southern Louisiana?

MARCELLO: I decline to answer on the same ground.

The scene was a spacious, high-ceilinged, marble-walled Senate hearing room. Chief Counsel Robert Kennedy sat upon a dais along with the committee members and assistant counsel, high above the spectators, press, and witnesses. Below him, in the forefront of the crowd, at a table strewed with papers, microphones, and wires, sat the burly Carlos Marcello, wearing a light-gray single-breasted pin-stripe suit, opaque dark glasses, and a defiant scowl that never seemed to leave his face. Next to him sat his attorney, the brilliant, fastidi-ous, Harvard-trained Jack Wasserman, and next to Wasserman sat Vincent Marcello in a conservative blue suit looking decidedly more worried and less pugnacious than his older brother. The McClellan committee to investigate labor racketeering and organized crime had been created by unanimous vote of the U.S. Senate on January 30, 1957. Robert F. Kennedy had been made chief counsel, and his brother Senator John F. Kennedy had been appointed a member of the committee. Senator John McClellan of Arkansas was chairman.

At first the committee had concentrated its attention on corrup-tion in organized labor. It was then that Chief Counsel Kennedy had unleashed his prosecutorial zeal against the leadership of the Team-sters Union, succeeding in causing the downfall of its president, Dave Beck, and the serious wounding of his immediate successor, Jimmy Hoffa.

Later, after the discovery on November 14, 1957, by the state po-lice in Apalachin, New York, of a huge secret conclave of over sixty leaders of Mafia crime families and corrupt labor unions from every major city in the country, the committee shifted its attention to the investigation of organized crime. The existence of a national syndi-cate of organized crime had been somewhat in doubt in law enforce-ment circles until the Apalachin meeting was discovered. Now its reality had been confirmed.

Although Carlos Marcello, as boss of the oldest Mafia family in the United States, had every right to a place of honor at the Apalachin meeting, he wisely declined to attend, choosing to send his most trusted brother, Joe, and his friend and associate, Dallas boss Joseph Civello, as his representatives instead. Both were stopped, identified, and briefly questioned by the state police as they tried to flee from the meeting. Like all the bosses of the nation's major crime families,

Carlos was enraged by what had happened. As it turned out, he had
every reason to be concerned. The discovery of the Apalachin crime
summit led directly to a subpoena for him to appear before the
McClellan committee.

Before witness Marcello was questioned, Aaron Kohn was called
to testify on organized crime in Louisiana and the criminal activities
of the Marcello family. During his testimony Kohn presented a short
history of the Louisiana Mafia, emphasizing the Mafia murder of Police Chief David Hennessey in 1890, and went on to relate the story
of Carlos Marcello's rise to power and the growth of his illegal enterprises, especially his vast slot machine operation.

As an illustration of how the Marcellos had corrupted the government of Jefferson Parish, he told the committee:

> "Within weeks after Sheriff Coci took office, in June 1956, his
> two deputies, his chief criminal deputy and chief civil deputy,
> were calling on bars and restaurants throughout the parish,
> ordering them to move out their present jukeboxes and slot
> machines, and advising them that the new ones would be sup-
> plied by the Marcello-controlled companies. They were given
> the alternative of doing that or being harassed by police raids."

Kohn went on to describe the range of Carlos Marcello's illegal
activities, pointing out to the committee that "every one of his brothers and one brother-in-law have been continuously active in the
growth of the Marcello mob," and going on to assert that he believed
the Marcellos would soon attain almost complete control of the political machinery and law enforcement apparatus of Louisiana.

Kohn then named all of Carlos's brothers and presented to the
committee a virtual roll call of the key players in the Marcello criminal organization, singling out Carlos's deputy in Dallas, Joseph Civello, and two of his closest lieutenants in New Orleans, Nofio Pecora
and Joseph Poretto, for special mention.

Four years and ten months later, the names Tony Marcello, Vincent Marcello, Joseph Civello, Nofio Pecora, and Joseph Poretto would
turn up on FBI reports within days of the assassination of President
Kennedy in connection with allegations made to the FBI about the
crime.

After Aaron Kohn's litany of Marcello's crimes and associates,
Robert Kennedy called one of the committee's staff investigators,
Pierre Salinger, to testify to the truth of Kohn's assertion that Jef-
ferson Parish deputy sheriffs cooperated with the Marcellos in forc-

ing bars and restaurants to take the Marcellos' slot machines. Salinger, who would one day become press secretary to President Kennedy, had conducted his own investigation of the Marcellos for the committee. That taken care of, Robert Kennedy launched into his grilling of Carlos Marcello. The cocky, defiant Marcello, alternately smirking and scowling at the youthful, inexperienced Kennedy, made the slightly disheveled 33-year-old chief counsel look somewhat like an earnest schoolboy playing cops and robbers.

KENNEDY: Mr. Marcello, did the Jefferson Parish deputy sheriffs assist you in getting locations for your coin machines?

MARCELLO: I decline to answer on the ground it may intend to incriminate me.

...

KENNEDY: Have you been able to use law enforcement officials to assist you in your businesses, Mr. Marcello?

MARCELLO: I decline to answer on the same ground.

There followed, to Kennedy's questioning, sixty-six more refusals to answer on the grounds his replies might "intend to incriminate" him. Marcello even refused to tell the committee where he was born.

The unanswered questions Kennedy put to Marcello covered a wide range of Marcello's activities. In his shrill, youthful Cape Cod—Harvard accent, the progressively irritated Kennedy asked the semi-literate 49-year-old Mafia boss about his alleged bribing of public officials in Jefferson Parish, his association with notorious gamblers Frank Costello and Dandy Phil Kastel, his relationship with Dallas Mafia chief Joseph Civello, and his ownership of New Orleans' Town & Country Motel. He asked him about the absurdly low assessed values of some of his properties on the West Bank, about his intimidation of Jefferson Parish restaurant and bar owners who would not take his slot machines and jukeboxes, about his criminal record, about his status as an illegal alien, and the government's efforts to deport him. To all questions, Marcello invoked the Fifth, scowling as he repeated his "I decline to answer" formula over and over in his slow, monotonous Sicilian-Louisianan drawl.

During the questioning some of the senators on the committee occasionally intervened to express their exasperation over Marcello's repeated invocations of his constitutional rights.

At one point, Senator Carl T. Curtis of Nebraska glared at Marcello and asked: "Do you realize that you are claiming a privilege under the Constitution of the United States, a charter of our liberty, and still you haven't ever sought to assume the responsibilities of citizenship. Isn't that correct?"

To which Marcello replied: "Senator, my attorney could answer that question."

"No, I want you to answer it. Have you ever sought citizenship?" insisted Curtis.

"I decline to answer the question," drawled Marcello.

An exasperated Senator Curtis then addressed his fellow committee members: "I think the committee should take note of the fact of how you cling to the Constitution of the United States. You have that right. It is the basic charter of human liberty. But to the other side of the ledger you have paid no attention at all."

At a later point in the hearings Senator Sam Ervin interrupted the questioning to observe: "According to the information in the possession of the committee, five years, nine months, and twenty-four days ago an order for the deportation of this—I started to say witness, but since he has given no testimony, I will say this person—this person was entered.... I would like to know how you have managed to stay in the United States for five years, nine months, and twenty-four days after you were found ordered deported as an undesirable person?...Can you give me any information on that point?"

Not receiving a reply, Senator Ervin pressed on: "I would like to know how a man who can manage to stay, a man who has been convicted of two felonies of such a serious nature as robbery and the sale of marijuana; how a man with that kind of record can stay in the United States for five years, nine months, twenty-four days after he is found to be an undesirable alien.... How have you managed to stay here?"

To which Marcello answered coolly: "Senator, not being an attorney, my attorney could answer that question."

"Well, your attorney is not a witness," observed Ervin.

"I wouldn't know," said Marcello.

"Well, I am just curious," Ervin continued. "The American people are entitled to more protection at the hands of the law than to have an undesirable alien who has committed serious felonies remain in this country for five years, nine months, twenty-four days after he is ordered deported. That certainly is an illustration of the fact that justice travels on leadened feet if it travels at all. It seems to me that the American people's patience ought to run out on this proposition, and that those who have no claim to any right to remain in America, who come here and prey like leeches upon law-abiding people of the country, ought to be removed from this country."

Senator Mundt of South Dakota then suggested that the chair "direct a letter to the attorney general inquiring as to why this deportation has not been implemented and that the attorney general's letter be made a part of the record when he replies."

After another round of fruitless attempts to get an answer out of Marcello, Senator Curtis put in his last two cents: "I notice your great fondness for American money, American protection to individual rights. But you say to tell us whether or not you have paid all your taxes would incriminate you. I think you ought to pack up your bags and voluntarily depart."

Depart Marcello then did…from the hearing. Upon being dismissed by the committee, the stocky little crime boss stood up abruptly and, joined by his brother and attorney, strode out of the Senate chamber, his chest out, his head high, having just successfully defied the United States Senate for the second time.

Committee Counsel Robert Kennedy would remember Marcello's arrogant performance on March 24, 1959, and Senator Mundt's suggestion that the attorney general be asked why the deportation order against Marcello had not been implemented, when, a little less than two years later, he and his brother came to power as President and attorney general of the United States.

PART IV

War with the Kennedys
1961–1963

"*I'd like to be remembered as the guy who broke the Mafia.*"
—*Robert F. Kennedy*

14

The Day of the Kennedys

The election of John F. Kennedy to the presidency brought into power the first chief executive and attorney general in U.S. history who had extensive knowledge of the Mafia, extensive experience in combating it, and a realistic assessment of the menace it represented to the very heart of the American system.

The American Mafia had risen swiftly to enormous wealth and influence during the forty years preceding the Kennedy administration in great part because the U.S. Department of Justice and law enforcement authorities, great and small, throughout the nation allowed the Mafia to thrive. They had even aided and abetted its growth, sometimes unknowingly, sometimes as an active partner in its advance. Politics and the Mafia fed off each other.

The accession of the Kennedys to power brought a radical change to the relationship between the federal government and the major Mafia families. Under the Kennedys there were to be no compromises with the Mafia. It was to be all-out war.

John and Robert Kennedy brought extraordinary abilities to their roles as President and attorney general. John had charisma, a talent for leadership, and a capacity to make tough decisions. Robert Kennedy brought a prosecutorial zeal to his position as chief law enforcement officer of the land seldom seen before in an attorney general. Both brothers were motivated by high ideals of statecraft and, since they enjoyed considerable independent wealth, were virtually incorruptible as far as the temptations of money were concerned. Furthermore, being young—John was only 43, and Robert, 35—the Kennedy brothers represented a rich potential. In the spring of 1963 their political future appeared limitless.

A considerable body of myth has sprung up about the character and style of the Kennedy administration. It was the historian and admirer of the Kennedys, Theodore White, who first invoked the Camelot image in an article he wrote for *Life* magazine in 1964. He quoted Jacqueline Kennedy's wistful characterization of the Kennedy White House as having resembled the mythic palace, court, and realm of King Arthur and his knights known as Camelot. This analogy gave rise in the public consciousness to the notion that under Kennedy the White House had been a seat of unparalleled splendor, sweetness, and light.

That the Kennedy White House displayed considerable splendor no one can deny. That it was a locus of sweetness and light is an untruth. Although there was much nobility in Kennedy's policies, his inner circle—the Arthurian knights—perpetrated a nasty secret war against Cuba, the violent overthrow of the Diem family in Vietnam, and an often vengeful campaign of questionable tactics aimed against the mob and their pawns in organized labor. And although John and Robert Kennedy possessed extraordinary leadership qualities and a high degree of political responsibility, there was a secretive, reckless side to both brothers' private and public lives that bore little resemblance to the chivalric spirit of the legendary Camelot.

The President had a propensity to enter into *liaisons dangeureuses* that, in retrospect, were so dangerous as to strain credulity. His most reckless extramarital adventures were with the starlet Judith Campbell, who was also a Chicago Mafia boss's girlfriend, and with the actress Marilyn Monroe. The attorney general proved equally reckless in entering into a relationship himself with Marilyn Monroe, at a time when agents of Jimmy Hoffa were keeping the actress under close electronic surveillance.

Complicating the Kennedys' plot against Cuba, their campaign against the Mafia, and the recklessness of their private lives was the strange and sinister alliance with certain Mafia bosses which the CIA had entered into, unbeknownst to the Kennedys, for the purpose of assassinating the president of Cuba.

15

The Pact with the Devil

Fidel Castro became president of Cuba on January 1, 1959, after leading a revolution against the corrupt six-year regime of the dictator Fulgencio Batista. Subsequently Castro's brother, Raul, journeyed to Moscow, where sympathetic Communist party leaders promised to help his new government, and Fidel proclaimed himself a Marxist.

Not long after he took over the government of Cuba, Castro expropriated hundreds of millions of dollars' worth of U.S. businesses on the island and closed down the gambling casinos and nightclubs owned and operated by the Mafia. Reacting to their sudden and, in some cases, disastrous loss of revenue, the Mafia leaders, led by Miami's Meyer Lansky, put out a $1 million contract on Fidel Castro.

Soon Cuban exiles in the United States began forming organizations to promote the overthrow of Castro. One of these was the Cuban Revolutionary Council (CRC), whose New Orleans chapter was to be led by the respected Cuban exiles leader Sergio Arcacha Smith and financed by his friend Carlos Marcello. Marcello had extracted a promise from Smith that, in the event Castro was overthrown and Smith took over the Cuban government, he would grant Carlos generous concessions on the island.

About a year after Castro took over Cuba the United States decided to take drastic action. On December 11, 1959, CIA Director Allen Dulles advised President Eisenhower that "thorough consideration be given to the elimination of Fidel Castro." By September 1960, CIA officers Sheffield Edwards and Richard Bissell had agreed on a plan to assassinate Castro in alliance with Mafia bosses John Roselli and Sam Giancana. They in turn would eventually bring into the conspiracy Santos Trafficante, Jr., who was a former Havana gambling casino owner and the actual boss of the Florida Mafia. Director Allen Dulles and Deputy Director General Charles P. Cabell were later briefed on the plan.

The alliance between the CIA and three of the most vicious leaders of the underworld for the purpose of plotting and carrying out the assassination of Fidel Castro created a clandestine network with the potential of a vast international Murder Incorporated. It also compromised the Kennedy administration's campaign against the Mafia. The Mafia leaders the CIA engaged were either prime targets of Attorney General Kennedy's war on organized crime or closely associated with other Mafia bosses Kennedy had targeted for prosecution.

Furthermore, the CIA-Mafia alliance made the U.S. government vulnerable to blackmail by the Mafia. All the Mafia had to do to win some concession from the government was threaten to reveal the joint plot to assassinate Castro.

Although the Kennedy brothers were behind the effort "to get rid of Castro," as Robert Kennedy once phrased the initiative in a memorandum, they did not learn of the alliance of the CIA and the Mafia until over a year after taking office. Robert Kennedy understood the seriousness of the situation immediately, displaying considerable anger at the CIA for hiring the Mafia to do its dirty work, but he failed to make sure the CIA-Mafia alliance would be discontinued.

The first CIA-sponsored attempt to assassinate Castro, utilizing its Mafia allies to carry out the execution, occurred just before the disastrous invasion of CIA-trained Cuban exiles in the Bay of Pigs in April 1961. The idea was to destroy the spirit of the Cuban armed forces before the invasion by eliminating their commander-in-chief. The plot had been hatched some weeks before in Miami's Fountainebleu Hotel where a CIA intermediary, Robert Maheu, met with Mafiosi Sam Giancana, John Roselli, and Santos Trafficante. A Cuban asset of Trafficante's was given some poison pills prepared by the CIA with which to kill the Cuban president. For reasons that remain obscure, the assassination attempt failed, as did the Bay of Pigs invasion. Further attempts by the CIA in alliance with Giancana, Roselli, Trafficante, and unnamed Cubans also came to naught. As relations between the United States and Cuba grew worse and worse, the Mafia and the frustrated Cuban exiles grew more and more hostile to both Castro and the Kennedy administration.

Did Carlos Marcello play a role in the CIA-Mafia plots to assassinate Castro? In 1979, during an FBI sting operation against Marcello and others, Marcello told government undercover agent Joseph Hauser that he did. However, in the 1975 Church Committee's Interim Report on Alleged Assassination Plots Involving Foreign Leaders, Marcello is not mentioned as having been a conspirator in the plots. If he was not involved in the plots, there is a strong likelihood that he was at least aware of them. For Marcello at the time was quite close to Santos Trafficante, Jr. The two met frequently, and both were financial backers of Cuban exiles groups. It can therefore be said, with some assurance, that if Marcello wasn't a direct participant, as he claimed he was, he must have at least been a silent, inactive, supporter of the plots. The issue is significant, for if Marcello was an active participant in the CIA's assassination plots against Castro, then he, too, along with Giancana, Roselli, and Trafficante, was in a position to blackmail the government.

Plots to assassinate Fidel Castro were far from Robert Kennedy's mind and agenda when he took control of the Justice Department in January 1961. The failed invasion of the Bay of Pigs had not yet occurred, and the first attempt to kill Fidel Castro had not yet been made.

Robert Kennedy's chief priority, as he took over as attorney general, was to mount a concerted campaign against organized crime. Whereas previous attorney generals had been content to maintain a holding action against the Mafia, Robert Kennedy sought to crush it. To his great credit he succeeded in launching a massive operation against the major crime families despite the fact that his own FBI director, J. Edgar Hoover, had insisted all his professional life that the Mafia did not exist.

To implement his policies, Kennedy bolstered the Justice Department's organized crime and racketeering section, increasing its size by 400 percent, and named Edwyn Silberling, a former prosecutor in New York District Attorney Frank Hogan's office, to head it. One of Silberling's first acts was to draw up a list of major Mafia leaders throughout the country and assign each a priority rating for increased investigation, leading, it was hoped, to eventual prosecution. Near the top of the list was Carlos Marcello.

*   *   *

In his book *The Enemy Within*, Robert Kennedy had written: "If we do not attack organized criminals with weapons and techniques as effective as their own, they will destroy us."

Kennedy had never forgotten Carlos Marcello's contemptuous defiance of him and his brother Jack at the McClellan committee hearings of March 1959. With characteristic impetuosity, he decided on a swift, audacious attack on Marcello using weapons and techniques as effective as Marcello's own. He would ambush the Louisiana Mafia boss and, in one bold stroke, throw him out of the country.

The Justice Department was aware that Marcello had acquired a forged Guatemalan birth certificate in his given name, Calogero Minacore, through the wholesale bribing of high Guatemalan officials. Kennedy's plan was to use this fake document as a basis for deporting Marcello to Guatemala.

According to Justice Department documents on the Marcello deportation case, Kennedy originally thought of deporting Marcello to Formosa, now Taiwan:

> "The General advised in extreme confidence that he had already secured authority from Formosa to deport Marcello there but he was seeking to arrange deportation to a closer country so that Marcello could be put on an Immigration and Naturalization Service plane and his deportation effected before Marcello's attorney could institute court action to delay this."

By March 15, at Robert Kennedy's insistence, the Immigration and Naturalization Service had obtained from the Guatemalan government a certified Guatemalan birth certificate for Calogero Minacore, and an entry permit for Carlos Marcello describing him as a citizen of Guatemala. With these documents in hand, Kennedy abandoned the idea of dispatching Carlos to Formosa in favor of sending him to closer Guatemala.

It was a bold plan, but an arguably illegal one, for, as Marcello's attorneys would one day declare, "a false Guatemalan birth certificate was knowingly used by the Immigration Service to fraudulently obtain a permit of entry for Carlos Marcello from the Guatemalan government."

But such legal niceties meant little to Robert Kennedy at the time. Carlos Marcello had never worried about legal niceties when he wanted to rid himself of a menace to his invisible government. He would simply make the offender disappear. Accordingly, Attorney General Kennedy wasted little time in implementing his own plans for Mr. Marcello. As soon as he was informed on March 15 that the Immigration and Naturalization Service had obtained an entry permit for Marcello from the Guatemalan government, he ordered the INS to expel him from the United States without delay.

16

The "Kidnap-Deportation"

On the morning of April 4, 1961, Carlos Marcello, accompanied by one of his lawyers, Phillip Smith, paid his required trimonthly visit, as an alien, to the offices of the Immigration and Naturalization Service in the Masonic Temple Building on St. Charles Avenue in New Orleans. While Carlos entered the building, Smith remained outside.

As soon as he reached the immigration office, Marcello sensed trouble. Usually he had to wait around before the ritual checking in. On this visit, however, he was immediately greeted by a stiff and nervous immigration agent, who told him to sit down.

Marcello remained standing before the agent's desk, wondering what was going on. Normally he would just sign in and leave.

"Will you sit down," the agent repeated.

Marcello sat down, and as he did the agent began reading from a letter written on U.S. Justice Department stationery. The letter informed Marcello that he was a citizen of Guatemala and would be immediately deported to that country. Marcello was stunned. He was about to protest when two agents suddenly appeared, handcuffed him, and escorted him to a waiting car. In Carlos's own words: "It took him about three or four minutes to read the letter. I said what for. He say well you been overdue on your visa. I couldn't understand it myself. I just, I just couldn't believe it. So by that time two immigration officers that I have never seen before, they came up and they put the handcuffs on me. Two of them, about six foot something. So I say, could I use the telephone. I say I'd like to call to talk to my attorney. They say no. I say, can I call my wife to get a toothbrush and some money. They said no, let's go."

At New Orleans International Moisant Airport a large INS passenger plane and a cordon of police were waiting on the runway for the boss of the Louisiana Mafia. Meanwhile, on the way to the airport the car bearing Carlos and his lawyer was the scene of impassioned outrage. The Mafia chieftain demanded of the agent accompanying him that he be allowed to phone his wife, and his deportation lawyer, Jack Wasserman, in Washington. Permission was denied. He demanded that he be allowed to bring along a change of clothes and some extra funds. Permission was again denied. With the three-car convoy's sirens screaming all the way to the airport, the handcuffed Marcello fumed and ranted that he was being kidnapped, that what the government was doing to him was illegal, a violation of an order issued by Supreme Court Justice Hugo Black that he be given seventy-two-hours notice before being deported. (It appears, however, that Black issued no such order.)

Once at the airport the immigration convoy was immediately surrounded by police, and Marcello was escorted by a small army of police and immigration officials to the plane, engines already running, waiting to fly him to Guatemala. Later Marcello recalled: "You would have thought it was the President coming in instead of me going out."

No sooner did Marcello board the plane than it took off. The seventy-eight-passenger aircraft was empty save for Marcello, two immigration agents, and the pilot and copilot. During the 1200-mile flight to Guatemala City the two immigration agents refused to speak to Marcello. By the time the plane arrived at its destination, Marcello was consumed with apprehension.

Meanwhile, a hysterical Phillip Smith had raced back from the plane to the terminal and phoned Carlos's brother Joe. On hearing the news, Joe immediately jumped in his car and dashed out to the airport to pick him up. Smith then called Jack Wasserman in Washington and was so incoherent Wasserman had to tell him to call back when he calmed down. "I can't understand a word you're saying," Wasserman cried.

Soon Joe Marcello arrived at the airport, picked up Smith, and the two drove to Carlos's office at the Town & Country to make another call to Jack Wasserman. If Smith was hysterical and incoherent, Joe was in a rage. As soon as they reached Carlos's office, Smith got on one phone and Joe on another. Before long the entire Marcello family was up in arms and making plans to fly down to Guatemala to be with Carlos. Jacqueline Marcello and her daughters were particularly upset. Encouraged by Carlos's brothers, they would soon be at Carlos's side.

The Marcellos had been furious at Bobby Kennedy ever since his grilling of Carlos during the McClellan hearings. Their rage was further fueled by the *States-Item* article in December quoting Kennedy as vowing to step up deportation proceedings against Carlos once he assumed office as attorney general. Now their hatred of Kennedy would know no bounds.

Smith eventually got his message across to Jack Wasserman, and on the following day, June 5, Wasserman filed suit in federal court in Washington demanding Marcello's immediate return to the United States and denouncing the government's "kidnapping" of his client as "illegal, contrary to the Constitution, and invalid."

While Wasserman was filing his suit, Attorney General Kennedy publicly announced that Marcello had been deported to Guatemala and that he was taking full responsibility for the expulsion of the New Orleans crime boss. Kennedy stated that the deportation had been carried out "in strict accordance with the law" and that he was "very happy Carlos Marcello was no longer with us." A Justice Department spokesman then explained to the press that Marcello had been deported to Guatemala after a birth certificate in Marcello's name was discovered in the Guatemalan village of San Jose Pinula.

Whether Marcello's ouster had been carried out "in strict accordance with the law" was, however, a matter of grave doubt within the Justice Department. On April 6, 1961, two days after Marcello's forced exile to Guatemala, Herbert J. Miller, Jr., then assistant attorney general, criminal division, received the following communiqué from Edwyn Silberling, then chief of the organized crime and racketeering section of the criminal division:

"In the light of the information contained in our intelligence file the United States Government may be placed in the embarrassing legal position of having made certain representations to the Guatemalan government about Marcello's birth record while it was in possession of information indicating that the birth record was a forgery."

To rid the country of the menace of Carlos Marcello, Attorney General Kennedy had been true to his intention of attacking "organized criminals with weapons and techniques as effective as their own." The action he had ordered the INS to take against Marcello was arguably illegal. It was also reckless and rash in the extreme. The abrupt, disrespectful manner in which Marcello was deported —not allowing him to get in touch with his family or his deportation attorney or to provide himself with either sufficient cash or a change of clothes—deeply offended the 51-year-old Mafia chieftain's pride. Years later Marcello told a congressional committee: "They just snatched me, and that is it, actually kidnapped me...and dumped me in Guatemala." To his intimates, Marcello would one day express a fuller measure of resentment as, in an unguarded burst of rage, he swore blood vengeance against the Kennedys.

17

Exile

Carlos Marcello spent two harrowing months of exile in Central America before surreptitiously reentering the United States. That he survived the hardships of his adventures in Guatemala, El Salvador, and Honduras was a tribute to his stamina, cunning, and self-confidence. It was also a tribute to the cohesion of the Marcello family and the power of their money.

At one of his many hearings before the Immigration and Naturalization Service, Carlos Marcello presented his version of his deportation and exile. It is one of the two accounts we have of Carlos's two-month ordeal in Central America. The other comes from Carlos's Shreveport attorney, Mike Maroun, who flew down to Guatemala to join his beleaguered client four days after his expulsion.

According to Marcello, the INS plane landed at Guatemala City's military airport in the early evening. There he was met by a Colonel Battery, who asked him: "Tell us where you want to go at, Mr. Marcellie?"

Marcello replied: "I would like to go to a hotel, anywhere."

Colonel Battery then told Marcello that there were a lot of reporters and television cameramen waiting outside the airport and at the Hotel Biltmore. Did he want to talk with them?

"No, I don't want to talk with nobody," replied Marcello, confessing that he was excited and nervous partly because he had had nothing to eat all day.

Colonel Battery then turned Marcello over to a group of officers, none of whom spoke English. After interminable unintelligible discussions, Marcello demanded to see Colonel Battery again. By now it was 11:00 P.M. Finally Battery reappeared and turned Marcello over to his secretary, a Miss Jinks, who had been born in Washington, D.C., and spoke fluent English. Battery told Marcello: "She is going to take care of you, get you an apartment for the night, and put you up because all the reporters are waiting for you at the hotel."

By Marcello's account, after Battery left, Miss Jinks asked him: "Would you like a sandwich at the Club Casablanca?"

"Yes," he said, and he and the secretary drove off in her 1956 Chevrolet to the restaurant. There Marcello had a turkey sandwich and a brandy, which made him feel "a little better."

By the time they finished eating it was 2:30 in the morning. Then the secretary suggested a solution to the problem of where Marcello would spend the night that strains credulity, but which Marcello insists did happen.

"Well I have a place for you to stay," said Miss Jinks as they left the restaurant. "My apartment."

"So she takes me to her apartment," Marcello went on, and "pointing to a king-sized bed, she said: 'You can sleep on this side and I am going to sleep on that side.' I said, 'Fine.'"

"So," Marcello continued, "she went and undressed and put the lights out. I didn't have no pajamas. I was ashamed. But she turned out the light and turned her back to me."

"I opened the wardrobe," Marcello continued, "and I seen a pair of pants and hat, lumber jacket and all, and I got to worrying about it. I said to myself, man, I said, they might kill me. Look like it's a setup. So I couldn't sleep that night."

Apparently the secretary was not in the least bit worried about sharing her bed with the deported boss of the Louisiana Mafia, for she slept soundly. He, however, stayed awake all night, ready to respond to whatever threat might come his way.

"About seven o'clock," Marcello continued, "I had put my clothes back on. I said: 'Will you call my wife and tell her where I am at?' Because she could speak Spanish, you see, and I couldn't. So she got them on the phone and my wife got on the phone. I told her I was all right, not to worry. My daughter got on the phone. They all started to crying and carrying on. They tell me my youngest brother, Sammy, is coming down with some money and clothes."

What happened next is uncertain. Somehow Marcello ended up in jail and had to promise to pay a $75,000 bribe to a high-ranking Guatemalan official to get out. The official had told Marcello that as San Jose Pinula's most famous citizen he would no doubt want to donate a new school to the village. The school would cost around $75,000.

Whatever the case, Marcello was soon out of jail and ensconced in Guatemala City's finest hotel, the Biltmore. Before long he was joined by his wife, Jacqueline, daughter Florence, son Joseph Jr., two of his brothers, Sammy and Vincent, and Vincent's wife, Sadie. It was then that his old friend and attorney Mike Maroun showed up from Shreveport. Now Carlos finally had some cash, some clothes, and some much-needed moral support.

By the time Marcello had taken up residence in the Biltmore Hotel, Guatemala City's most influential paper, *El Imparcial,* had demanded in an editorial an official explanation of Marcello's presence in Guatemala. Among other things, the editorial implied that the entry of Marcello's birth in the civil registry at San Jose Pinula was bogus.

Meanwhile, on April 10, back in New Orleans, the Internal Revenue Service had filed tax liens in excess of $835,000 against Carlos and Jacqueline Marcello. Later it was learned that this action had been instigated by Attorney General Kennedy, who, at the time, was using the IRS as a weapon in his battles with the leaders of organized crime. When Jack Wasserman phoned news of the tax liens to Marcello at his Guatemalan hotel, Marcello went into a rage. Wasserman assured him he would immediately file suit in federal court to remove the liens.

By April 12, six days after his deportation, things were not going so badly for Carlos Marcello in Guatemala City. Ensconced with his wife and daughter in a suite at the Biltmore Hotel, with two brothers and his lawyer in neighboring rooms, Carlos was meeting with various Guatemalan businessmen in the shrimp, hotel, and real estate development industries and with a representative of the agency handling Guatemala's government-endorsed slot machine operations. Marcello was not taking any chances. If Wasserman could not succeed in overturning the U.S. government's deportation order against him, he would have to seek out business opportunities in Guatemala.

For a while Carlos and his family were able to enjoy themselves in Guatemala City. The press noted their presence at the racetrack and in the city's finest shops and restaurants. But *El Imparcial* would not rest. Finally its editorials about Marcello stirred up the opposition forces to Guatemalan President Miguel Fuentes so much that about

a month after his arrival the Guatemalan government told Marcello
he could return home.

In Marcello's words:

"They said they going to give me a permit to go to the United
States, so we're all happy. We go to the airport, my wife gets
the ticket and we all, Vincent, gets a ticket. I believe I had one
of my daughters there. They got a ticket. When I went there,
they say we got orders from the State Department, you can't
get a ticket, you can't get a visa to go back. State Department
of the United States.

"So my wife she start to cry and then I say, 'Well look, why
don't you all go ahead and leave me and Mike.'

"So we went back to the hotel, and it's about eight that
night. We had the two Secret Service men staying with us. I
find it was funny they was staying there. About an hour later
three more came in there and they say: 'All right, pack your
bags. Let's go.' So they put us in a station wagon, and we go to
San Salvador, me and Mike."

Marcello was wrong about the immediate destination. It was the
neighboring state of El Salvador, but not the capital of that state. Specifically it was an army camp in the Salvadorian jungle near the
Guatemala-Salvador border, where they were left at the mercy of
Salvadorian soldiers.

The soldiers eventually took them to the capital and handed them
over to the commander of a large military barracks, where they were
confined and interrogated for several days. Marcello and Maroun had
$3000 between them, and they had to check the money in with the
barracks commander. Six days later, at 11:00 at night, an officer appeared and said: "Get ready, Mr. Marcello. We are going to deport
you to Honduras now." Marcello, stunned, pleaded, "Wait until day-
light," but the officer replied: "No, we have orders from the chief,
and you are coming now." To their relief, he returned the $3000.

The officer then assigned two guards to Marcello and Maroun
and told them to escort the two foreigners to a small airport near the
Honduras–El Salvador border, an arrangement Marcello felt was set
up for the guards to relieve him and Maroun of their cash.

Mike Maroun described what followed.

Marcello and Maroun stuffed their cash in their shoes and then were loaded by their two guards onto a decrepit bus that proceeded to climb a narrow, pitted dirt road into the mountain range forming the El Salvador–Honduras border. For six hours the bus chugged up the mountainside, with Marcello and Maroun having no idea of the fate that awaited them. Then, after the bus had penetrated about 20 miles into Honduras, the two Louisianans were unceremoniously dumped off the bus like baggage thrown in the dust, left to fend for themselves on a forested hilltop with no signs of civilization in sight.

There was nothing the two men could do now but push on down the road they had been traveling, hoping they would eventually reach a village.

There followed an ordeal that Marcello and Maroun would relate to whoever would listen for the rest of their lives.

For eight hours and 17 miles the two men made their way along the dusty, pitted road, still wearing their city clothes and their city shoes stuffed with cash. They had had little to eat or drink. Used to the virtually sea-level altitude of Louisiana, Marcello found breathing difficult along the mountaintop road. He collapsed three times in the dust, complaining that he could not go on any farther, that he was finished, and that it was that rich kid, Bobby Kennedy, who had done this to them. "If I don't make it, Mike," Carlos told Maroun at one point, as he lay exhausted in a roadside gutter, "tell my brothers when you get back, about what dat kid Bobby done to us. Tell 'em to do what dey have to do."

But Carlos always found the strength to get back up and resume his trek. Finally, as they were nearing the limits of their endurance, they arrived at a mountain village where they were able to rest and get something to eat.

When they felt strong enough to push on, they hired two Honduran Indian boys to guide them to the nearest airport. For two days and a night they struggled downhill toward the Honduran plains, exhausted but not giving up, pushing forward, marching on toward they knew not what.

As signs of civilization began to appear, Carlos and Mike noted, with increasing apprehension, that the two Indian boys had begun to whisper among themselves and point toward the two paunchy, exhausted, middle-aged men who appeared to be at the end of their strength.

Soon the downhill road became overgrown with weeds and bushes, and the Indian boys had to clear the way with their machetes. Deciding it was time to escape their potential murderers, Marcello and

Maroun deliberately fell behind, then managed to elude the boys by plunging down a pathless slope. They ended up in a burrow, bleeding from thorns, bruised by rocks, with Carlos complaining of a severe pain in his side. Later he learned he had suffered three broken ribs.

Finally, after another long downhill trek along a trail thick with underbrush, they arrived at a provincial airport. There they hired a small plane for the Honduran capital, Tegucigalpa. When they reached the city, they went straight to a hotel, where, bruised and battered and utterly worn out, they slept for two days.

Mike Maroun then returned to the United States by commercial flight to reassure Marcello's mother, brothers, sisters, wife, and children that Carlos was all right, that he was tired and bruised, but alive and able to take care of himself.

What happened next is unclear. According to Marcello's account, he stayed in the hotel in Tegucigalpa for two weeks, then decided to take the bull by the horns and reenter the United States. Somehow he was able to obtain a forged entry visa and an airline ticket to Miami. On the morning of the flight, in Marcello's words:

"I went to church. I made nine churches and I burnt a candle and I put a couple dollars in each one of the churches. [He then went to the airport, boarded his flight, and landed in Miami.] I come right into Miami. Immigration and customs searched my baggage and I just showed them the papers. I went right on through and I got in a cab and I took off.

"I got a ticket and I come back to New Orleans. I catch a cab in New Orleans and I go straight to my house. I just told the cab driver, 'Drive in the back.' I got home and my wife got all scared and all 'cause they say immigration is watching us twenty-four hours a day and all. I said don't make no difference 'cause I'm goin' give myself up anyway."

Since this account of his illegal reentry was given, Marcello's version has been authoritatively disputed by the former chief counsel of the House Select Committee on Assassinations, G. Robert Blakey, who stated in 1980 that his committee learned from a wiretap that Marcello was flown to Miami in a Dominican Republic Air Force jet.

That Marcello was able to avail himself of a Dominican Air Force jet to reenter the United States is not, on the surface, remarkable. The president of the Dominican Republic, General Rafael Trujillo, was known to be close to several U.S. Mafia bosses, including Marcello's friend Santos Trafficante. For years Trujillo's dictatorial regime was in virtual partnership with the mob in such lucrative rackets as the drug trade, casino gambling, and money laundering. And another friend of Carlos's, Washington lobbyist Irving Davidson, was the registered lobbyist for the Dominican Republic on Capitol Hill at the time.

What *was* remarkable was the timing of Marcello's return in relation to what was happening politically in the Dominican Republic in late May 1961. For it was almost precisely at the time Trujillo was assassinated by CIA-supported opposition forces that Marcello reentered the United States on a Dominican Air Force jet. (In 1975, the Senate Intelligence Committee discovered that the CIA had been plotting the assassination of Trujillo for months with the blessing of Robert Kennedy, who knew that the elimination of Trujillo was a necessary move in his war against organized crime.)

Given Trujillo's and Marcello's mutual friendships with Trafficante and Davidson, it is not difficult to conceive of Trafficante or Davidson prevailing on Trujillo to help Marcello reenter the United States, if Marcello's flight on the Dominican Air Force jet occurred before Trujillo's assassination—which it appears it did, for most sources give May 28 as the date of Marcello's return.

But there might have been still another American contact through whose intercession Marcello could have been allowed to take the Dominican jet back to the United States: his old friend Senator Russell Long, son of the late Huey Long. This possibility was suggested by a June 16, 1961, FBI report asserting that "a high-ranking U.S. government official may have intervened with the Dominican Republic on Marcello's behalf." That report went on to state that "Senator Russell Long of Louisiana, who had received financial aid from Marcello, had been very much concerned with the Marcello deportation case and was sponsoring a Louisiana official for a key INS position from which assistance to Marcello could be rendered."

Whatever the case, somebody in Carlos's invisible government had enabled him to reenter the United States without either customs or immigration officials noting his arrival. That had been a victory of sorts in what had been a deeply humiliating experience, an unprecedented affront to his pride and dignity. He had been treated with contempt and utter disrespect by the U.S. government. Who had been behind this public embarrassment? For Carlos, the INS had not been to blame. He had dealt with them many times before, and they had always tried to be fair. No, Carlos knew full well who had been responsible for this offense: Bobby Kennedy. Some day he would find a way to pay him back.

18

Marcello Returns: Kennedy Strikes Back

On June 2, 1961, Carlos Marcello's attorneys, confirming widespread rumors, announced that their client had returned to the United States and was in temporary hiding.

Upon learning this, Attorney General Kennedy, in a rage, dispatched on June 5 twenty federal agents to Shreveport, Louisiana, to conduct a search for Marcello. Since the Justice Department had learned that Michael Maroun had returned to his house in Shreveport after leaving his client in Honduras, Kennedy thought Marcello might be hiding in that city.

Later that day, Marcello voluntarily surrendered to Immigration and Naturalization Service officials in New Orleans and was ordered to be held at an alien detention center in McAllen, Texas. While he was there, a federal grand jury, acting on an urgent recommendation of Robert Kennedy, indicted Carlos for illegal reentry. On July 11, the INS ruled Marcello was an undesirable alien and once again ordered him deported, a ruling that Marcello's attorneys immediately appealed.

Meanwhile, Marcello had been released from the detention center and was back in his house in Metairie and at his nearby Town & Country office conducting business as usual.

What Carlos found upon returning to his normal routine was a family and an organization in disarray. His sudden deportation had come as a severe blow to the entire family. Carlos was their leader, their principal adviser and breadwinner, the ultimate source of whatever material well-being the Marcellos enjoyed. Without him at the helm, the Marcellos felt adrift. Jacqueline, Louise, Florence, and Jackie Jr. had been particularly upset. Their emotional and financial dependence on Carlos was absolute. Since none of Carlos's six brothers could count on the "respect" Carlos enjoyed in the Gulf states underworld, the loosely structured Marcello organization had begun to flounder in Carlos's absence. Now Carlos had to pick up the pieces and get things back on track again.

He also had to fight back at his nemesis in the Justice Department. While Carlos was in exile, Jack Wasserman had filed two lawsuits on his behalf. One was against the IRS requesting that its $835,396 tax lien against Carlos and his wife be declared null and void, and the other was against Robert F. Kennedy over the circumstances of Carlos's deportation to Guatemala. In the case of *Carlos Marcello v. Robert F. Kennedy* Marcello accused the attorney general of committing an illegal act in having him deported "kidnap style," without prior notice and on the basis of fraudulent documentation.

If Carlos Marcello had been humiliated by Robert Kennedy's mode of deporting him, Kennedy now stood to be humiliated by Marcello's counterattack. For Kennedy *had* violated a Supreme Court ruling that Marcello be given a seventy-two-hour notice before deportation could be carried out, and the documents the Justice Department had used to induce the Guatemalan government to grant Marcello an entry permit *had* been fraudulent.

While the various court actions and appeals on Marcello's deportation and reentry raged on during the fall of 1961, Robert Kennedy saw to it that Carlos would be called again to testify before the McClellan committee. The committee had been reconstituted to conduct a far-ranging investigation of illegal gambling and organized crime. Also called to testify were Carlos's brother Joe Marcello and underboss Joe Poretto.

As it turned out, Carlos did not show up for his scheduled appearance, pleading illness brought on by his recent ordeal as a helpless deportee trekking through the Salvadorian jungles. To an exasperated and somewhat incredulous committee, Jack Wasserman explained how, as a result of "the cruel and inhuman way" his client had been deported to Guatemala by the U.S. government, he was still suffering from two broken ribs caused by fainting three times on a jungle road to Honduras. Chairman McClellan told Wasserman he expected Marcello to testify when he was well.

The committee then called Joe Marcello and Joe Poretto to testify on organized crime in Louisiana. Grilling Joe on the condition of his brother Carlos's health, on which subject Joe repeatedly refused to testify, Committee Counsel Alderman threw one last impatient question at Joe: "Is he suffering from a condition called McClellanitis?" To which Joe again took the Fifth.

Joe Marcello declined to respond to all questions on his family's gambling activities, on the grounds that his answers might incriminate him. At one point Alderman asked Joe if the Marcellos were a pretty closely knit family: "You and your brothers and your older brother Carlos, all acting together in concert?" Joe declined to respond.

When it came time for Joe Marcello's partner, Joe Poretto, to testify, Poretto promptly treated the committee to a display of arrogance and contempt seldom before witnessed at a Senate hearing. Previously, as the 268-pound Poretto raised his right hand to take the oath, he had clenched his thumb and two middle fingers while extending his little finger and forefinger in the traditional Sicilian sign of *il corno*, "the horn," a gesture of defiance. Sitting down, the bulky Poretto, wearing a dark suit and opaque dark glasses, then contemptuously refused to answer any of the committee's questions on his past activities and current partnership with the Marcellos in running the Nola News racing wire services, grinning broadly at the committee as he took the Fifth over and over again. Some of the questions Poretto refused to answer alluded to his past association with members of "The Outfit" in Chicago: Moe Annenberg, the racing wire king, and Murray "The Camel" Humphreys, Sam Giancana's right hand man.

When the supposedly ailing Carlos finally did show up to testify, he refused to answer all questions put to him by the committee, including those about his health, except two: What was his name, and what was his place of birth. His nontestimony made front-page headlines in the New Orleans papers.

Although Robert Kennedy certainly had expected Carlos to take the Fifth at the hearings, he was nevertheless enraged at Carlos's arrogant repeat performance of 1959. He was particularly annoyed at Wasserman's reference to "the cruel and inhuman way" the government (read Robert Kennedy) had deported his client. It was galling to Kennedy to have to admit that so far Marcello had successfully defied every effort the government had made to investigate and prosecute him. Instead, he, the attorney general of the United States, was now on the defensive in the case of *Carlos Marcello v. Robert F. Kennedy*.

To further fan his outrage, Kennedy had to put up with an FBI director, his subordinate, who had repeatedly looked down on his efforts to ensnare Marcello. J. Edgar Hoover had little respect, and certainly no love, for the young, inexperienced attorney general. But that was not the fundamental reason why he told him, so condescendingly, that he was wasting his time pursuing the New Orleans "hoodlum," as Hoover liked to term Mafiosi. No, for J. Edgar Hoover, Carlos Marcello and his criminal network was a Pandora's box that should be left unopened. Hoover knew that the FBI simply did not have the resources and authority to go after such a powerful and elusive criminal organization. To back up his position, Hoover needed only to point out to the neophyte crime buster what a mess he had gotten the government into by his kidnap-style deportation of Carlos Marcello.

For this line of thinking, Robert Kennedy reserved his utmost contempt. Admonishing Hoover to step up the FBI's investigation of Marcello, Kennedy showed the director what he thought of his advice when, on October 30, 1961, he publicly announced the indictment of Marcello by a federal grand jury in New Orleans on charges of conspiracy in falsifying a Guatemalan birth certificate and committing perjury. Carlos's brother Joe was also charged, since it was believed that Joe was the mystery man who had gone down to Guatemala and bribed an official of the Guatemalan government to enter Carlos's name in the birth records of San Jose Pinula. Then, on December 30, 1961, with Marcello free on $10,000 bail, a five-member Board of Immigration Appeals upheld the deportation order against him, denying Jack Wasserman's appeal that it be declared invalid.

The news, coming on the eve of the new year, convulsed the Marcellos once again. The year 1961 had been difficult for the family: Carlos's deportation, the $835,396 tax assessment, the indictment for illegal reentry, the McClellan committee hearings, the indictment of both Carlos and Joe for conspiracy and perjury, and now the deportation order upheld after an unsuccessful appeal. Jacqueline and the girls would have to live in constant fear of Carlos being snatched away from them again. The brothers, all dependent on Carlos's leadership and business acumen, faced a period of uncertainty during which their livelihoods would be at stake. As for Carlos himself, the news that the deportation order had been upheld, amply reported by the press in New Orleans and Baton Rouge, could only promote an atmosphere of uncertainty in his organization with consequent damage to his business.

And who was behind all this fear and confusion and uncertainty?

People close to the Marcellos at this time have remarked that by the end of 1961, the family's hatred of Robert Kennedy knew no bounds. The mere mention of Kennedy's name at a family gathering or at a meeting of his associates at the Town & Country or Churchill Farms would trigger cries of hysteria from the Marcello women and outbursts of rage and defiance from the men.

Carlos Marcello's honor was now on the line. Bobby Kennedy was threatening to destroy everything he and his family had built up during a half century of struggles in Louisiana. With his wife and children and brothers and sisters and business associates constantly nagging him over what he was going to do about Bobby Kennedy, and his enemies and rivals in the underworld still snickering over his unceremonious deportation to Guatemala, Carlos's patience was running out. It would not be long now before his hatred of Robert Kennedy could no longer be contained.

But Carlos evidently did make at least one attempt to resolve his problem with Bobby Kennedy through diplomacy. On July 17, 1962, an FBI listening device picked up a conversation about Marcello's plight between Angelo Bruno, boss of Philadelphia's leading Mafia family, and Russell Bufalino, a Mafia capo from Pittston, Pennsylvania, that indicated Carlos had once tried to get Frank Sinatra to intercede for him with the Kennedys.

According to Bruno's taped remarks, Carlos had at some point asked Mafia bosses Santo Trafficante and Sam Giancana to persuade their friend Frank Sinatra to intervene in his behalf, through Bobby Kennedy's father, Joseph P. Kennedy, whom Bruno described as being "friendly" with Sinatra. An FBI report of October 1, 1962, on the wire-tapped Bruno-Bufalino conversation, revealed that Sinatra had apparently succeeded in getting Bobby Kennedy's ear on the Marcello case, but that, according to Bruno, Sinatra's intervention made matters worse. Instead of inducing Bobby to take it easy on the Louisiana boss, Sinatra's mission had only made Bobby more determined than ever to go after Marcello. The failure of this diplomatic effort meant that Marcello now had only one recourse in his struggle with Bobby Kennedy: war.

19

Marcello Swears Vengeance

By late summer of 1962 the web of charges Robert Kennedy had been responsible for bringing against Carlos Marcello was beginning to tighten around the Mafia boss, leaving him little room for escape. Under two major federal indictments, which would soon lead to trials and perhaps convictions and prison terms, and under a standing deportation order which could not be further appealed, Carlos was living each day under a cloud of uncertainty.

It was in this threatening atmosphere that Carlos would occasionally lose his head and, in a sudden outburst of rage, would give out hints of what he was going to do about Bobby Kennedy to people not in his closest circle but who just happened to be around him at the time.

Carlos owned a hunting and fishing camp on Grand Isle, a long bar of mud and sand in the Mississippi delta between the entrance of Barataria Bay and the Gulf of Mexico. One summer weekend when Carlos and some of his family and friends were down at the camp fishing, swimming, and basking in the sun, a black worker, one of the camp's staff of caretakers, was startled to overhear the boss launch into a tirade over Bobby Kennedy in front of a group of friends gathered at an outdoor picnic table. The worker was tidying up around the area at the time.

"Don't talk about dat sonofabitch Bobby to me!" Marcello yelled. "You know he's driving my wife fuckin' crazy. All Jackie do is cry all night thinkin' Kennedy is goin' to throw me outa the country again. She sees the stuff in the papers about the deportation and all, and she can't sleep. Bobby is drivin' my daughters crazy too. They don't want to lose their Daddy.... Well, I'll tell you boys they ain't goin' to lose their ole man. No, sir. 'Cause I gotta plan. You wait, you wait an' see if that sonofabitch Bobby Kennedy is gonna take me away from my wife an' kids."

Not long after this outburst, Carlos exploded over Bobby Kennedy again in front of other friends. This time the tirade took place in a farmhouse on Churchill Farms and went much farther than the Grand Isle eruption in explaining what he planned to do about Bobby Kennedy.

Carlos had spent part of the morning in his Town & Country office discussing various business matters with Carlo Roppolo, a close personal friend whom he had known since childhood, and Edward Becker, an acquaintance of Roppolo's from Las Vegas. Roppolo, who dabbled in the oil business, had developed an oil additive to which he had given the name Mustang and which he wanted Marcello to help him distribute in Louisiana. Becker, a former director of public relations of the Riviera Casino in Las Vegas, was now an investigator with a private detective agency based in Las Vegas. He had met Roppolo in Shreveport during an investigation of the notorious Texan swindler Billie Sol Estes, which he was conducting for one of the companies Estes had defrauded. Since Roppolo had been involved with the company Estes had swindled, his path had crossed with Becker's. When Roppolo mentioned his plan to market his new oil additive, Becker volunteered to help obtain financing for it. Soon one thing led to another and Roppolo asked Becker if he would like to meet his "uncle," Carlos Marcello, whom he wanted to interest in distributing his oil additive. Becker was well aware who Marcello was, and jumped at the chance to meet him. As it turned out, Becker and Marcello had several friends in common in Las Vegas, some of whom Marcello checked out over the phone in Becker's presence, so he quickly won Marcello's trust.

Becker, a voluble man with a quick mind and a lively wit, remembers that toward the end of the brief Town & Country session he allowed himself to laugh at Marcello's classic Mafia stare. Becker had experienced Johnny Roselli's no-nonsense stare many times in Las Vegas and was convinced that Mafia bosses practice their stare before mirrors. Carlos had thrown Becker the stare while interrupting one of his stories about Roselli. "Hey, Becker," he said, "your fuckin' mouth goin' a mile a minute. Come on, shut up an' let's get outa here. You never know who's listening around dis place."

As Becker chuckled over this, Carlos stood up, summoned an aide, and ordered his Cadillac brought to his office.

"We're goin over to Churchill Farms," he said. "I wanna show you the property. I got a lot of plans for it, an' we can talk good over dere."

This made Becker nervous. He had heard tales of people Carlos had taken a dislike to disappearing in Churchill Farms' swamps.

Before long, one of Carlos's buddies showed up with the car. He was a big hulking man named Jack Liberto, whom Carlos liked to take to the track and who was also Carlos's personal barber. Becker thought he looked big and tough enough to be a bodyguard, or something worse. With Marcello at the wheel the four men then took off for the West Bank and Carlos's 6400-acre swampland domain.

Entering the property by a narrow, bumpy dirt road, Carlos first stopped the car outside a small shrimp-packing plant by the road-side and honked the horn. Soon a black worker came out of the plant and silently handed the boss a small crate of frozen shrimp, which Carlos passed on to Liberto. "Ain't no better shrimp dan I got," said Marcello as he started up the car again.

As the Cadillac bounced along the dusty, pitted road, an occasional blue heron, or a white egret, would take flight from the bordering marshes, and from time to time one of Carlos's farmhands would slowly turn from his catfishing and tip his hat at the passing car. On either side of the road, the vast swamp with its gray, moss-hung cypresses and bright-green palmettos stretched as far as the eye could see.

As they were driving along, Carlos, at one point, turned to Becker and, gesturing toward the swamp and laughing, said: "Dere's where we get rid of de bodies."

Then he said: "Hey, Becker, you a Jew?"

Becker didn't respond.

"'Cause you know what we do with Jews, don't you, Becker?...We just roll em outa de car an into de swamp. They plenty a snakes in dere."

Becker looked down the road. Before long two rustic buildings came into view: a shed surrounded by chickens and goats, and a small farmhouse with a porch and narrow windows. Becker remembers the warm, humid September air was filled with bottle-green flies and darting swallows.

Carlos pulled up to the farmhouse and led Becker, Roppolo, and Liberto inside. Becker remembers a small bedroom with just one dresser, a sparsely furnished kitchen–dining room, and a handsomely furnished meeting room with a long table and chairs.

Carlos led his visitors into the kitchen–dining room and sat them down at a table near the refrigerator and an old gramophone. He took a platter of cheese and salami out of the refrigerator and, picking up a bottle, poured himself and his guests some scotch. Then he went over to the gramophone and put on one of his favorite Connie Francis records.

The meeting began with small talk and jokes about sexual conquests and money deals, to the accompaniment of Connie Francis's Italian songs and generous pourings of scotch.

Then, at a certain point, the voluble Becker made an offhand remark that suddenly ticked Carlos off. "Man," Becker said, "isn't it a fuckin' shame the bad deal you're gettin' from Bobby Kennedy? I've been reading about it in the papers. All that deportation stuff. What are you goin' to do about it, Carlos?"

At this, Carlos's jovial mood changed abruptly. He jumped up from the table and, reverting to Sicilian, cried out: "*Livarsi 'na pietra di la scarpa!*" (Take the stone out of my shoe!) "Don't worry about that little Bobby sonofabitch," Marcello shouted. "He's goin' to be taken care of....I got—"

"But you can't go after Bobby Kennedy," Becker interrupted. "If you do, you're going to get into a hell of a lot of trouble."

"No, I'm not talkin about 'dat," Carlos yelled, still standing. "Ya know what they say in Sicily: If you want to kill a dog, you don't cut off the tail, you cut off the head." He explained that you had to think of President Kennedy as a dog and Attorney General Kennedy as the dog's tail. "The dog will keep biting you if you only cut off its tail," Carlos went on, "but if the dog's head is cut off, the dog will die, tail and all."

Explaining further, still standing, Marcello told Becker and Roppolo that if Bobby Kennedy were killed, the President would crack down on his brother's enemies—people like himself and Hoffa—worse than before, but if the President were killed, Lyndon Johnson would do nothing. And Bobby Kennedy, whom Johnson hated, would lose all his power.

Sitting down again, Marcello then told his visitors that President Kennedy had to go, but that he would have to arrange his murder in such a way that his own men would not be identified as the assassins. No, he would have to use, or manipulate, someone not connected to his organization into a position where he would be immediately blamed by the police for the job. He had already thought of a way to set up a "nut" to take all the heat, "the way they do in Sicily."

As Carlos said this, Becker could not help noticing the fierce expression on his face. Carlos, who had downed at least two scotches, was in a sweat, his red eyes were bulging, and he was breathing heavily. Because of the intensity of his emotion, Becker quickly came to the conclusion that the Kennedy problem for Marcello had gone far beyond mere "business." Settling the score with Bobby had become, for Carlos, a deeply personal matter, a way to avenge the intolerable attack on his dignity Kennedy had inflicted on him, and reclaim honor and respect.

After Carlos's outburst over Bobby Kennedy, which had not lasted more than five or six minutes, the meeting settled down to a protracted business discussion during which Marcello did not mention the Kennedy brothers again. Wiping the sweat from his brow, Carlos told Roppolo that nobody in Louisiana could distribute his oil additive better than he could. Hadn't he gotten his own slot machines into every corner of the state? But he would have to get a decent share of the profits.

At the end of the meeting Carlos took Becker by surprise by suddenly turning to Jack Liberto saying "Hey, Jack, here's some money. Go give Becker here a good close shave. He look like he need one." And he reached into his long left trouser pocket, pulled out a wad of bills, and thrust them into Liberto's hand.

As they headed back to the Town & Country Motel, Becker began to feel a little uneasy. Maybe, he thought, Carlos was trying to set him up. In an unguarded moment, after a couple of scotches, Marcello had let the cat out of the bag and divulged his plan to kill President Kennedy to a virtual stranger. Maybe, Becker mused, ordering Liberto to give him a close shave was code for another service.

When Becker did finally find himself in Liberto's barber chair, he acquiesced at first to the shave, then had second thoughts and panicked. Liberto had placed a hot towel over Becker's face and had begun stropping his razor. Virtually blindfolded, Becker's imagination ran wild at the sound of the razor being stropped. Suddenly springing up from the chair, he took the towel away from his face and pretended to choke.

"The towel suffocated me," he told Liberto, "I couldn't breathe. Listen, let's skip the shave. But thank Carlos anyway."

Edward Becker met with Marcello and Roppolo two or three more times during his stay in Louisiana and was even invited to Carlos's huge Italianate villa in Marrero. The villa, he recalls, was surrounded by classic Italian statuary and contained an enormous aquarium and a vast store of the finest Cuban cigars. At none of these encounters did Carlos mention the Kennedy brothers again. Although Becker was familiar with Mafia braggadocio and knew it was typical of Mafia bosses to utter loud threats against their enemies, he still couldn't help from reflecting occasionally on what he had heard at Churchill Farms. What had struck him most was that Marcello seemed very serious about his intention to kill Kennedy and that he had a feeling Carlos had already discussed his plans with someone else.

That feeling was given some confirmation when, a week or so later, unknown to Becker, one of Carlos Marcello's underworld friends, Florida boss Santos Trafficante, who had recently met with Carlos in New Orleans, intimated to Cuban exile leader and financier Jose Aleman, Jr., in Miami that President Kennedy would be killed before the election of 1964.

Aleman, the son of a former Cuban cabinet minister, was active in the Cuban exiles' movement to overthrow the new revolutionary regime, and was a close friend of one of the CIA's principal Cuban conspirators in the plot to assassinate Fidel Castro. At the time Aleman met Trafficante in Miami, he was anxious to negotiate a loan to finance a large condominium development he was planning in Miami and thought that Trafficante could help raise the funds through his good friend Jimmy Hoffa. Trafficante was sympathetic to Aleman's need because he felt deeply indebted to Aleman's cousin Garcia Banyo, who had been instrumental in getting him out of Cuba unharmed after the Castro takeover.

Trafficante and Aleman met to discuss the loan in a suite in Miami's Scott Bryant Hotel, which Aleman owned. Aleman told Trafficante he needed $1.5 million and that Jimmy Hoffa had already provisionally cleared the loan which, if made, would come out of Teamsters Union pension funds. Now he needed Trafficante to put in a good word for him with Hoffa to clinch the deal.

The Teamsters chief at the time was receiving even more pressure from Robert Kennedy than his friend Carlos Marcello. Kennedy had established an entire division within the Justice Department charged with the sole task of "getting" Hoffa. And, according to Louisiana Teamster official Edward Partin, Hoffa, in the summer of 1962, was seriously thinking of thwarting that effort by killing Robert Kennedy and perhaps also his brother, the President.

When Hoffa's name came up in the conversation, Trafficante digressed a bit from discussing the loan to complain how badly the

Kennedys were treating his friend. Referring to President Kennedy, Trafficante remarked:

"Have you seen how his brother is hitting Hoffa, a man who is not a millionaire, a friend of the blue collars? He doesn't know that this kind of encounter is very delicate....It is not right what they are doing to Hoffa....Hoffa is a hardworking man and does not deserve it. Mark my word, this man Kennedy is in trouble, and he will get what is coming to him."

At this, Aleman took issue with Trafficante, telling him that he thought Kennedy was doing a good job, was well liked, and would probably be reelected.

To which Trafficante responded emphatically: "No, Jose, you don't understand me. Kennedy's not going to make it to the election. He is going to be hit."

Aleman doubled as an FBI informant. After the meeting with Trafficante, he went to the FBI field office in Miami and reported Trafficante's remarks on Hoffa and the Kennedys to the agents on duty, including Trafficante's apparent belief that John F. Kennedy would be assassinated before the next presidential election. The agents perfunctorily took down Aleman's testimony, without expressing much interest in it, and asked him to continue keeping the FBI informed of his contacts with Trafficante.

A little over two months later, on November 20, 1962, the Los Angeles FBI office called in Edward Becker to interview him about the Billie Sol Estes case. During the interview, Becker told of his meeting with Carlo Roppolo and Carlos Marcello at Churchill Farms, but did not mention Marcello's threat to have President Kennedy killed because he had not taken it that seriously at the time. Toward the end of the interview Becker agreed to provide more information to the FBI about Billie Sol Estes. The interviewing agent did not appear to be interested in Becker's meeting with Marcello, for he asked him no further questions about it.

As for Carlos's ongoing struggle with Robert Kennedy, the end of 1962 and early months of 1963 saw his position steadily deteriorate as the young attorney general, whose fight with the Louisiana Mafia chief had turned into a personal vendetta, stepped up his campaign to crush Marcello's power once and for all.

20

Marcello at Bay

It was about a month and a half after Carlos impulsively spat out his threat to have President Kennedy murdered that his frantic efforts to avoid deportation suffered a severe setback.

The Immigration and Naturalization Service deportation order was based on Carlos's status as an "undesirable alien." To be classified an undesirable alien, an individual resident in the United States, but without U.S. citizenship, must have been convicted of a federal crime. Carlos had been convicted of such a crime in 1938 for attempting to sell a large quantity of marijuana to a government undercover agent. In early October 1962, Marcello's attorneys filed a legal writ in federal court in order to have the 1938 conviction set aside, only to have a federal court rule against the substance of the writ on October 31. Now the deportation order stood upheld. In a last-ditch effort, Jack Wasserman petitioned the Supreme Court of the United States to review the deportation order against his client. If the high court refused to review the case, which it was expected to do, there would be little hope left for Marcello to remain in the United States.

The October 31 ruling against Marcello was given front-page headlines in the New Orleans *Time-Picayune* and the *States-Item,* and so the news that the INS deportation order against the Mafia chief had been upheld soon traveled throughout Louisiana. Carlos was subjected to more nagging taunts over what he was going to do about Bobby Kennedy, who everyone knew was the driving force behind the government's effort to deport him.

According to reliable sources, Carlos was continually bombarded— by his wife and children, his eight brothers and sisters and their spouses, and his closest lieutenants, men like Joe Poretto and Nofio Pecora, not to mention his lesser minions and all the public officials he had in his pocket—with questions about how he was going to handle Bobby Kennedy. Since Carlos's underworld empire, with annual revenues of $1.6 billion, was the largest single industry in the state of Louisiana, not only the Marcello family but thousands of others stood to take a beating if the man who had created and sustained this vast enterprise was thrown out of the United States.

Stories of Marcello's hatred for Bobby Kennedy, and his determination to take revenge against him for the enormous insult of the banishment to Guatemala, abound in Louisiana today, where the kidnap-deportation of the Mafia chieftain has already crossed the boundary of history into legend. One such story tells of another outburst from Carlos over Bobby Kennedy that is said to have taken place at his camp on Grand Isle around six months prior to the assassination of the President.

It was in the spring of 1963, around April or May. Carlos had invited a few of his close friends from the old Sicilian families of New Orleans to spend a weekend with him at his lodge on Grand Isle. He was having a scotch with one of them in the kitchen when the friend made a casual reference to an article he had read a while back in the *Times-Picayune* about the Supreme Court decision upholding the deportation order against him. At the mention of Bobby Kennedy's name, Carlos suddenly seemed to choke, spitting out his scotch on the floor. Recovering quickly, he formed the southern Italian symbol of *il corno*, "the horn," with his left hand, raising the little finger and the index finger while keeping the other fingers clenched. Holding the ancient symbol of hatred and revenge above his head, he shouted: "Don't worry, man, 'bout dat Bobby. We goin' to take care a dat sonofabitch!"

"Do you mean to tell me that you're gonna give it to Bobby?"

"What good dat do? You hit dat man and his brother calls out the national guard. No, you gotta hit de top man and what happen with de next top man? He don't like de brother."

"But isn't it taking a big chance to go up to Washington? You're not even allowed out of the state."

Carlos smiled and looked at his friend with condescension. Then he said: "What's a matter with you, man? When did I have to ever get to a man like dat? This is somethin' I gotta get some nut for, some crazy guy....But I tell you as sure as I stand here somethin' awful is gonna happen to dat man."

Attorney General Kennedy was, of course, delighted with the way things were going in his campaign to deport Marcello. Ever since Carlos had brazenly defied his deportation to Guatemala by secretly reentering the United States, Kennedy had vowed he would some day remove Marcello from the country forever. Kennedys played to win, and if they lost a battle, or were openly defied, they felt duty bound to seek revenge. That Bobby Kennedy's campaign against Carlos Marcellos had become a personal vendetta was well known to his closest aides in the Justice Department. This was a fight to the finish for Bobby. The Kennedy brothers might have taken a licking from Fidel Castro, but they were not going to take one from Carlos Marcello.

Yes, things were going well in the campaign to deport Marcello. But Robert Kennedy was still dissatisfied with the FBI's investigation of the Marcello criminal organization. For one thing, the FBI had recently succeeded, as never before in its history, in the electronic surveillance of major leaders of organized crime, but had not yet been able to wiretap or bug Carlos Marcello. The only other major Mafia boss who had succeeded in evading FBI electronic surveillance was Santos Trafficante.

Accordingly, in late January 1963, Robert Kennedy summoned J. Edgar Hoover to his office and told him he was dissatisfied with the bureau's investigation of Marcello. He ordered the 65-year-old bureaucrat to step up the FBI's actions against the man whom, Kennedy reminded his FBI director, two major Senate investigations had identified as the most powerful criminal in the Gulf Coast states.

Three weeks after this dressing down, Hoover directed the New Orleans FBI office—one of whose principal agents, Regis Kennedy, had consistently reported over the years that Marcello was a mere tomato salesman—to intensify its investigation of the Louisiana Mafia leader. As revealed by an FBI teletype from the director to New Orleans, Hoover ordered that a "special effort" be made to "upgrade the level of the investigation" and suggested the use of undercover informants and the necessity of initiating electronic surveillance of Marcello and his lieutenants.

It is not known what the field office in New Orleans did to carry out these orders. Many researchers and investigators knowledgeable of the situation remain distrustful of Regis Kennedy, suspecting he may have been in Marcello's pocket. Whatever Regis Kennedy's loyalties were, it now appears that little was done in New Orleans to "upgrade the level of the investigation" of Carlos Marcello, for the FBI failed to successfully perform any significant undercover surveillance of the Louisiana Mafia boss during the remainder of 1963.

In testimony before the House Select Committee on Assassinations in 1979, a former FBI agent who had been second in command of day-to-day intelligence operations concerned with organized crime in 1963 stated that the two cities in which the FBI had failed to penetrate the local Mafia organization were Dallas and New Orleans, both of which were under the control of Carlos Marcello. In regard to Marcello, the former agent testified:

> "I agree with anyone who says we never were really able to get very far with Marcello. That was our biggest gap. You just couldn't penetrate his kingdom, with the control in that state that he has. With Marcello, you've got the one big exception in our work back then. There was just no way of penetrating that area. He was too smart."

That there was "no way of penetrating that area" was proved untrue in 1979 when the FBI successfully launched a massive undercover operation against Marcello that resulted in the recording of 1400 reels of his conversations. To achieve this, FBI agents installed an electronic listening device in his Town & Country office and placed wiretap intercepts on all his phones, experiencing few difficulties in the process. In fact, it took only ten seconds for one of the agents to pick the lock on Marcello's suite of offices.

No, the reason why the FBI field office in New Orleans in 1963 was unable to "penetrate that area" had nothing to do with the intellectual powers of Carlos Marcello. It had to do with an FBI office that was so grossly deficient in its performance, not only in relation to its surveillance of Marcello but also in relation to its surveillance of another New Orleans resident at the time, one Lee Harvey Oswald, as to lead one to suspect that the office was more under the control of the Marcello organization than under that of the Justice Department in Washington. (It may be noted, in passing, that the agent who had been assigned to surveil Oswald, Warren du Brueys, replaced Aaron Kohn as director of the New Orleans Metropolitan Crime Commission in 1977. When I asked du Brueys, in 1987, whether he was still pursuing Kohn's investigation of the Marcellos, he replied: "No, we are no longer involved in that area. We have other priorities now.")

Indeed, as 1963 wore on, Marcello seemed to grow bolder and bolder in his defiance of the federal government. Some investigators have speculated that Regis Kennedy might have told Marcello about the attorney general's pressure on Hoover to step up the bureau's efforts against him, and this might have prompted Marcello to respond in kind by stepping up *his* plans to get the stone out of his shoe.

21

Intimations of Conspiracy

It had been on February 15, 1963, that J. Edgar Hoover, reacting to pressure from Attorney General Kennedy, had directed the New Orleans FBI office to make a special effort to intensify its investigations of Carlos Marcello and his criminal organization.

Approximately two months later, two individuals witnessed in New Orleans, separately and under different circumstances, what appeared to be hints of conspirational activity directed against the life of President Kennedy. Although the two witnesses were not aware of it at the time, what they saw and heard suggested foreknowledge of the assassination by a close associate of the Marcellos and a connection between the accused assassin and another Marcello associate. Their allegations were contained in FBI reports issued within a few days of the assassination.

For reasons that remain obscure, but which will receive some elaboration later on in this narrative, the two FBI reports containing the allegations either were not brought to the attention of or were overlooked by the two official investigations of the Kennedy assassination—that of the Warren Commission in 1964 and that of the House Select Committee on Assassinations in 1979—and are not to be found anywhere in the voluminous Kennedy assassination literature. One of them was given limited mention in my 1984 book

Carlos Marcello at the height of his power. Photographed at a Louisiana State Senate hearing in Baton Rouge, 1970. (*© Christopher R. Harris*)

New York's Frank Costello, called "the prime minister of the underworld" in the 1940s and 1950s, with his wife. Costello gave Carlos Marcello his big chance when he chose him to help distribute his slot machines in Louisiana. *(AP/ Wide World Photos)*

Louisiana-born Joseph Civello (right), Carlos Marcello's deputy in Dallas and a friend and business associate of Jack Ruby's, with his attorney after his arrest for having attended the organized crime summit conference at Apalachin, New York, in 1957. Civello had represented Marcello at the conclave. *(AP/Wide World Photos)*

Aaron Kohn, former FBI agent and assistant to J. Edgar Hoover and former managing director of the New Orleans Metropolitan Crime Commission. Kohn conducted the first comprehensive investigation of Carlos Marcello and briefed Chief Counsel Robert Kennedy on Marcello's criminal activities prior to Marcello's appearance before the Senate Rackets (McClellan) Committee on March 24, 1959. *(Courtesy Aaron Kohn)*

Senator John F. Kennedy questioning a witness at a Senate Rackets Committee hearing held in March 1959. His brother Robert F. Kennedy, chief counsel of the committee, and Senator John McClellan, chairman of the committee, are seated to his right. *(Hank Walker,* Life *Magazine, Time Inc.)*

Carlos Marcello (left), his brother Vincent Marcello (center), and Los Angeles racketeer Mickey Cohen (right) at the witness table. Chief Counsel Robert F. Kennedy is about to commence the questioning of both Marcello and Cohen. *(AP/Wide World Photos)*

Chairman McClellan (left) and Chief Counsel Kennedy (center) with one of Carlos Marcello's Chief slot machines. *(AP/Wide World Photos)*

Mrs. Carlos Marcello (right) with her 17-year-old daughter Florence and brother-in-law Peter Marcello, arriving at Moisant International Airport, New Orleans, from Guatemala City, after visiting her recently deported husband, April 1961. *(AP/Wide World Photos)*

Flanking their attorney, Jack Wasserman, are Carlos Marcello (left) and his brother Vincent Marcello (right) at the McClellan Committee hearing of March 24, 1959. *(AP/Wide World Photos)*

Joseph Poretto (left), one of Carlos Marcello's three most trusted associates, testifying at a Senate Rackets Committee hearing on gambling and organized crime in Washington, August 1961. With him are Carlos's most trusted brother, Joseph Marcello (right), and Marcello attorney Jack Wasserman (center). Poretto ran the Marcello organization's horse-race wire services in partnership with Joe Marcello and, for a while, managed the restaurant of the Marcello-owned Town & Country Motel. *(AP/Wide World Photos)*

Edward Becker, private investigator and Las Vegas businessman, testified to having heard Carlos Marcello threaten to kill President Kennedy. *(© Dana Anderson)*

Lee Harvey Oswald, in the summer of 1963, handing out leaflets encouraging people to join the New Orleans chapter of the Fair Play for Cuba Committee. This pro-Castro, leftist activity earned him misleading publicity. *(AP/Wide World Photos)*

View of Churchill Farms, Carlos Marcello's 6400-acre swampland property in Jefferson Parish, west of New Orleans. It was in the farmhouse at the center that, according to Edward Becker, Marcello threatened to have President Kennedy killed. *(Courtesy Life Picture Service,* Life *Magazine, 1975 Time Inc.)*

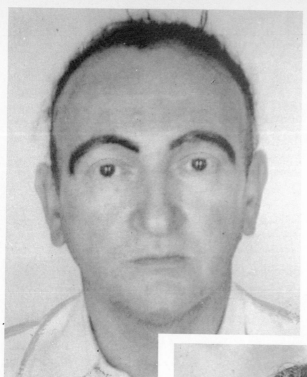

David W. Ferrie, hairles
ex-airline pilot and a
friend of Lee Harvey
Oswald's. During the
summer of 1963 Ferrie
worked as an investigato
for Carlos Marcello and
one of his attorneys.
(AP/Wide World Photos)

Guy Banister, former FBI
agent and owner and
director of a private
detective agency in New
Orleans. Carlos Marcello
was one of his clients,
David Ferrie was one of
his employees, and Lee
Harvey Oswald was seen
in his office several times
during the summer of
1963. *(Assassinations
Archives and Research
Center, Washington, D.C.)*

on the Kennedy family; the other makes its first public appearance in this book.

Eugene De Laparra was a young ex-Marine working part-time in a New Orleans bar-restaurant owned by one Bernard Tregle, an associate of the Marcellos. Tregle's establishment, the Lounnor Restaurant, known also to its customers as Tregle's Bar, was located on Airline Highway, not far from the Marcellos' Town & Country Motel. Tregle had owned other bars and restaurants, one of which, Tregle's Dreamland Barroom, had been alluded to as a Marcello-controlled establishment during the questioning of Carlos Marcello at the Kefauver hearings of 1951. According to Aaron Kohn, the Marcellos had backed Ben Tregle's bars and restaurants for years, since they were prime locations for their slot machines, pinball machines, and jukeboxes. Tregle also maintained a horse book that was connected to the Marcello gambling network, and he was the owner of several racehorses.

One day in April 1963, as De Laparra was going about his chores in Tregle's restaurant, he overheard a conversation between Ben Tregle and two friends, Norman Le Blanc, a horse trainer, and someone they referred to as the "Professor," about what seemed to be a plot to assassinate President Kennedy.

According to De Laparra, Tregle and his friends were looking at an advertisement in a detective magazine for a foreign-made rifle which sold for $12.95. Tregle stated to all present, including De Laparra: "This would be a nice rifle to buy to get the President. There is a price on the President's head, and other members of the Kennedy family. Somebody will kill Kennedy when he comes down south."

De Laparra, who also worked part-time as a groom at New Orleans' Fairgrounds racetrack, took care of one of Vincent Marcello's racehorses, and doubled as an informant for the FBI. According to a later FBI report, he had been in regular contact with three special agents in the New Orleans FBI office who testified that he had provided them with "reliable information" on illegal gambling in the New Orleans area. In his original allegation, De Laparra observed that "Vincent Marcella [sic], New Orleans racketeer," was a close friend of Tregle's and a financial backer of Tregle's business who traveled regularly to Dallas where De Laparra believed Marcello owned a nightclub.

In his eventual interview by the FBI, Eugene De Laparra did not claim to have witnessed any actual plotting against President Kennedy that April day in Tregle's restaurant, nor did his allegation suggest that Ben Tregle or Norman Le Blanc or the Professor was active in plotting the President's assassination. De Laparra simply reported that Ben Tregle appeared to have heard that there was "a price on the President's head and on other members of the Kennedy family" and that somebody would kill Kennedy when he came south.

From whom might Tregle have heard this portentous information, if indeed he did hear it from someone? It seems reasonable to suspect, given our knowledge of the Becker and Trafficante allegations, that he heard it from one of the Marcellos, either from his backer, Vincent, or from one of Vincent's brothers.

This suspicion was lent some credence by additional information De Laparra furnished to the FBI in February 1967 at the time New Orleans District Attorney Jim Garrison was launching his reinvestigation of the Kennedy assassination. In this second version of his original allegation, De Laparra told the FBI that one day, while he was working in Tregle's Bar, Tony Marcello, a brother of Carlos Marcello, came into the bar to service the pinball machine and, at a certain point, announced to Ben Tregle and three or four others at the bar: "The word is out to get the Kennedy family."

Whereupon Ben Tregle repeated Tony Marcello's remark, using slightly different language, to some people in the back room.

At about the time Eugene De Laparra heard Tony Marcello and Ben Tregle remark that there was a plot in the works to assassinate President Kennedy, a visitor to New Orleans from Darien, Georgia, was having dinner one evening at the Town & Country restaurant. There he witnessed something suspicious that, six months later, he believed might have been connected, in some way, to the assassination of President Kennedy.

According to his own testimony, made to Glynn County, Georgia, police officer Lt. Johnny Harris, the man from Darien (whom the FBI identified in most of its reports as informant SV T-1, but once referred to as Sumner) had been on a business trip to Texas and Louisiana. He had been invited one evening, along with a Texan friend, Ernest Insalmo, to have dinner in the Town & Country restaurant by two New Orleans business contacts, Salvadore Pizza, who was in the seafood business, and Benny Capeana, a wealthy construction man. Upon entering the restaurant, SV T-1 met a man he thought was the restaurant's owner, whose name he forgot, but who he later described as being of Italian ancestry, about 50 years old, 6 feet tall, around 250 pounds, with a dark complexion and gray hair combed straight back. After this encounter, SV T-1 and Insalmo were shown to the main dining room, where they noticed there were customers at only two other tables. Soon a young couple entered and sat down about two tables from where SV T-1 and his companion were sitting. The man was of medium height and slight of build and was wearing a dark suit and tie. His female friend was a blond in her early twenties and a "flashy dresser."

Before long, the man SV T-1 thought was the restaurant owner joined the couple at their table. The Georgian observed him "remove a wad of money from his pocket, which he passed under the table to the man." A few minutes later the couple left the restaurant without ordering any food or drinks.

SV T-1 thought what he had witnessed seemed somewhat suspicious, but gave little thought to it until he saw pictures of John F. Kennedy's accused assassin in the papers and on television in the days following the assassination of the President. It was then that he became convinced beyond any doubt that the man he had seen take the money from the restaurant owner seven months before had been Lee Harvey Oswald.

When, three days after the assassination, SV T-1 voiced this belief to Glynn County police officer Johnny Harris and was asked if he knew anything about the owner of the Town & Country restaurant, he replied that he knew nothing "of his background, associates, or activities."

What the informant from Georgia apparently did *not* know, then, was that the Town & Country Motel and Restaurant was owned by the Marcello family, that one of the buildings on the property was the headquarters of the boss of the Louisiana Mafia, Carlos Marcello, and that the man he met and described with near perfect accuracy was not the owner of the Town & Country but the restaurant manager, Joseph Poretto, who was also a high-ranking member of the Marcello criminal organization. In all likelihood it was probably because SV T-1 did not know anything about "the background, associates, or activities" of Joe Poretto that he had been willing to stick his neck out and declare to the police and the FBI he had seen Poretto pass a "wad of money" to the President's alleged assassin.

Eugene De Laparra and SV T-1 gave the FBI various dates in their allegations as to when they believed they had witnessed in New Orleans what they later suspected might have been conspiratorial activity connected to the assassination of President Kennedy. De Laparra believed the incident he reported had occurred in March, and SV T-1 thought his visit to the Town & Country Motel took place in either March or April.

It was also in April 1963 that the man who would one day be accused of the assassination, Lee Harvey Oswald, left Dallas, where he had been living for the past ten months, and returned to his native New Orleans.

Oswald left his job in Dallas on April 6, without telling his Russian-born wife, Marina. Six days later someone took a shot at the ultra-conservative Major General Edwin Walker, member of the right wing John Birch Society, through a window of his Dallas home; Marina Oswald later claimed that the shot had been fired by her husband, a contention that has never been conclusively proved. Then, sometime during the next twelve days, Lee decided to move to New Orleans and stay awhile with his mother's sister, Lillian Murret, and her husband, Charles, leaving his wife and daughter temporarily behind. He left Dallas by bus on the 24th and moved into his aunt and uncle's New Orleans apartment the following day. Coincidentally, it was on April 24 that the White House announced that President Kennedy would make a trip to Texas in November.

Charles Murret, known to intimates as Dutz, had served as Lee Oswald's surrogate father during his youth and adolescence, since Lee's father had died two months before he was born. At the time Oswald moved in with him in April 1963, Murret was a prosperous middle-level bookmaker in the Marcello gambling network. He worked under one of the most notorious operators in the New Orleans underworld, Sam Saia, who, Aaron Kohn testified, "had the reputation of being very close to Carlos Marcello."

22

Oswald and the Marcellos: Summer of 1963

When Lee Harvey Oswald moved into the New Orleans apartment of his Uncle Dutz and Aunt Lillian Murret on April 25, he was a desperate man. His marriage was, at best, strained; he had no job and almost no money. Whenever he had been in such straits in the past, he had turned to the Murrets; they had always lent him money when he was broke or given him a room when he had no place to spend the night. No doubt Oswald's first order of business upon reaching the Murret household that April was to discuss with Uncle Dutz how he might find a job, any job, that would enable him to rent an apartment in New Orleans for himself and his wife and daughter, who he hoped would soon be able to join him from Dallas.

Dutz Murret had no other affiliation in New Orleans as significant as the Marcello organization, and so it is reasonable to assume that it was to it that he turned to find something for his surrogate son to do.

If we are to accept FBI informant SV T-1's story, Murret was successful, for it was sometime in April that SV T-1 claimed he saw Oswald receive some money from a man SV T-1 did not know at the time was a top lieutenant of Carlos Marcello.

Oswald had practically no money when he arrived at his uncle's apartment on April 25, but by May 9 he was able to rent a $65-a-month apartment and set up a household with his wife and daughter. Where did he get the money from? Charles Murret would one day tell the Warren Commission he loaned Lee the money, but it was later learned that Murret consistently lied to the commission and never told the commission what he *really* did for a living.

It seems likely, then, that Oswald received the money from Joe Poretto in the Town & Country restaurant, as SV T-1 has suggested. But did that mean that the Marcellos were already conspiring with Oswald to assassinate John F. Kennedy, when, in Ben Tregle's words, the President came south? Not necessarily. It could have been that Poretto gave Oswald a down payment for another job, or an advance on a job the purpose of which had not yet been disclosed to him, but which later turned out to be related to the assassination.

Various investigators, including Edward Becker, have speculated on how long it took Carlos Marcello to become aware of the existence of Dutz Murret's oddball nephew after he arrived in New Orleans in the spring of 1963. Most agree that it probably did not take longer than a couple of weeks. For those who belonged to the Marcello network, New Orleans was a village within a city. If anything in the least bit out of the ordinary happened to anyone significantly connected to the network, almost everyone in it would learn what happened within days.

But it is also quite possible that the Marcellos knew about Dutz Murret's nephew before April 1963. The New Orleans papers had reported his defection to the Soviet Union in 1959, his taking a Russian wife, his decision to repatriate, and his return to the United States in June 1962. It seems reasonable to assume that the Marcello network buzzed over the strange escapades of Dutz Murret's commie nephew at these times.

Then, when that crazy nephew returned to New Orleans in April 1963, and Dutz gave out the word to the organization that the young man needed to make some money, it is safe to assume that one or more of Marcello's brothers became aware of Oswald's existence within a week or so of his arrival, especially if it was true that he had met with Joe Poretto at the Town & Country restaurant in late April. In overall charge of the Town & Country Motel complex at the time was part-owner Anthony Marcello, who, according to FBI informant Eugene De Laparra, had recently remarked in nearby Tregle's Bar, "The word is out to get the Kennedy family," and who, as we shall see later, was questioned by the FBI about his possible association with Oswald immediately after the assassination.

Oswald's arrival in New Orleans coincided with a period of setbacks that left Carlos Marcello more vulnerable to Bobby Kennedy's onslaught than ever. Sometime in April, Attorney General Kennedy received a letter from an outraged citizen claiming that a friend of his who had legitimate business dealings with Carlos Marcello had received a severe beating from two of Carlos's lieutenants. Kennedy immediately ordered the chief of his criminal division, Jack Miller, to forward the letter to J. Edgar Hoover for action. If Hoover then brought the matter to the attention of the New Orleans FBI office and an agent contacted Marcello about it, the Marcellos would have been put on notice by Kennedy that he was watching them.

But it was in May that Carlos received what seemed to be the final blow in his interminable struggle to avoid deportation. On the 27th the United States Supreme Court, in response to an appeal filed by Carlos's attorneys, declined to review the Marcello deportation action, and upheld the earlier decision of the U.S. Circuit Court of Appeals that the Immigration and Naturalization Service order to deport Marcello remain in effect. The news was prominently reported in the New Orleans papers and rapidly spread throughout Carlos's Gulf states empire.

This meant that all Carlos's appeals were exhausted. Bobby Kennedy had him cornered. Carlos had only one legitimate opportunity left to avoid deportation: he had to beat the charges of conspiracy and perjury in regard to the falsification of his Guatemalan birth certificate Kennedy had brought against him after his illegal reentry in June 1961. The case was due to be tried in November, the same month in which, Carlos had recently learned, President Kennedy was due to visit Texas.

If Carlos Marcello had been under great pressure from his family, friends, and associates to do something about Bobby Kennedy before, we can assume that after May 27 the pressure increased many times over. Now there was little time to lose. If Carlos Marcello was going to remain in the United States and maintain control of his $1.6 billion empire, he had only a few months left to thwart Kennedy's plans. During the summer and early fall of 1963 the final battle with the Kennedys would be won or lost.

Enter Dutz Murret's "crazy," hotheaded nephew and surrogate son, Lee Harvey Oswald, a young man ready for anything in the spring and summer of 1963.

For Lee Harvey Oswald, being back in the sordid milieu of his youth, after an absence of seven years, must have been painful. Although it was never revealed by the FBI and the Warren Commission in their respective investigations of the Kennedy assassination, or in any of the books on Oswald published in the sixties and seventies, Oswald had grown up in an area of New Orleans that was dominated by various illegal gambling operations controlled by the Mafia.

When Oswald was a teenager, he and his mother lived in a small apartment over a saloon at 126 Exchange Alley in New Orleans' then run-down Vieux Carré, and he attended Beauregard Junior High in the same neighborhood. Exchange Alley at the time was a squalid street lined with pool halls, bars frequented mostly by homosexuals and prostitutes, and illegal bookmaking establishments controlled by the Mafia organization then headed by Carlos Marcello's predecessor, Sam "Silver Dollar" Carolla. The nearby Beauregard School was known, according to Aaron Kohn, as "the alma mater, so to speak, of kids who frequently graduated to various criminal and underworld careers."

After Carlos Marcello took control of the Louisiana Mafia in 1947, Oswald's Uncle Dutz became connected with the new Marcello organization through one of Carlos's close associates, Sam Saia, who, according to Aaron Kohn, was "for fifteen years the biggest and most powerful operator of illegal handbooks and other forms of illegal gambling in the state."

But Lee's uncle was not the only member of the family who developed connections with associates of Carlos Marcello. His own mother, Marguerite, was well acquainted with several associates of the Louisiana Mafia boss.

For many years Marguerite Oswald had been friendly with a New Orleans underworld figure by the name of Sam Termine, who had once served as a chauffeur and bodyguard to Carlos Marcello. According to Aaron Kohn, Termine "had engaged in a number of illicit activities during his association with the Marcello organization. He had been involved in various syndicate gambling and prostitution activities as well as in the operation of a motel used for underworld activities." Once a mutual friend of Marguerite Oswald and Sam Termine was with them in a restaurant-nightclub Termine ran in Waco, Texas, when Termine spoke at length about fellow Marcello operative Dutz Murret and some of Carlos Marcello's associates in Waco. Termine emphasized that he was not the only Marcello man active in Waco at the time.

Sam Termine was not the only "Marcello man" that Marguerite Oswald knew in New Orleans either. For many years she had been friendly with a New Orleans attorney, Clem Sehrt, whom she had known since childhood, and who did a good deal of business with Carlos Marcello. In 1956 she sought him out for legal advice about her son Lee's desire to join the Marines when Lee was under the legal age for enlisting. Mrs. Oswald wanted Sehrt to find a way to alter her son's birth certificate, and Sehrt had apparently obliged.

Later Sehrt became very close to Louis Rousell, a corrupt New Orleans financier who enjoyed a close relationship to Carlos Marcello and who had a reputation as an adept money launderer. During the late fifties a police investigation revealed that two Louisiana Supreme Court justices were receiving regular payments from Louis Rousell, who was fronting for Marcello. It is believed that not long after Marguerite Oswald approached Clem Sehrt about altering her son's birth certificate, Sehrt met Carlos Marcello and began doing a considerable amount of business with him through Louis Rousell. Mrs. Oswald's relationship with Sehrt was to continue over the years.

This is not to suggest that Marguerite Oswald was herself connected to the Marcellos, which she was not, but to underscore the fact that the Marcello organization had ample opportunities to become aware of the existence of her unconventional son.

By the middle of May, barely three weeks after his arrival, Lee Oswald had succeeded in reestablishing himself in New Orleans and was beginning to lead a strange double life that hinted at connections to some clandestine organization, perhaps the CIA, perhaps the FBI, perhaps military intelligence, perhaps the Marcello network.

On May 11 Lee's wife and daughter joined him and moved into the apartment he had rented two days before. He also secured a job as a maintenance worker for a coffee company at $1.50 an hour. Although Oswald found his job with the coffee company dull, he soon found plenty of excitement in his other job, which was political agitation involving Cuba.

On May 26 Lee wrote the national director of the Fair Play for Cuba Committee asking for permission to found a New Orleans chapter. He eventually did found one, with himself as its only member.

By mid-June, before he had received a reply from the director of the Fair Play for Cuba Committee, he was distributing *HANDS OFF CUBA! Join the Fair Play for Cuba Committee* leaflets on the Dumaine Street wharf where the aircraft carrier *Wasp* was moored. Somehow he had found the money to print 1000 of these leaflets soliciting membership in a nonexistent committee.

In July a group of Cuban exiles arrived in New Orleans from Miami and joined an anti-Castro guerrilla training camp at Lacombe, north of New Orleans, near where the Marcellos maintained a hunting preserve and lodge. The training camp was located on property belonging to Mike McLaney, a former Havana casino operator with connections to Santos Trafficante and Meyer Lansky. Not long after the Miami exiles arrived, Oswald attempted to infiltrate the camp and offer his services to the exiles.

By the third week of July, Lee had lost his job with the coffee company and, as a consequence, had no visible means of support. Nevertheless, he did not bother to look for another job, but persisted in his Cuban activities, attracting a great deal of attention in the process. In early August he twice posed as a friend of the anti-Castro Cuban exiles, telling the anti-Castro militant Carlos Bringuier that he wanted to train exiles and play a role in bringing the downfall of the Castro regime. Then, a few days later, he got into a fistfight with Bringuier's group while distributing pro-Castro literature on Canal Street, a fracas that resulted in his arrest and imprisonment for disturbing the peace. Appealing to the Murrets to use their influence (with the Marcello organization?) to get him out of jail, he was finally rescued by an "old friend of the family," one Emile Bruneau, a liquor store owner, who put up his bail and paid his fine, enabling him to go free.

Years later, investigators for the House Assassinations Committee discovered that Emile Bruneau had been closely associated with two of Carlos Marcello's major associates, Nofio Pecora and Joseph Poretto. Poretto, of course was the man FBI informant SV-T-1 claimed to have observed passing money to Lee Harvey Oswald in the Town & Country restaurant.

Oswald's fight with anti-Castro elements, and his arrest and jailing, generated a lot of publicity for the young ex-defector. The Canal Street fracas was prominently reported in the New Orleans papers, and Oswald was interviewed at length about his pro-Castro sympathies on New Orleans radio. Was the Canal Street demonstration a deliberate provocation for publicity's sake? Later in the month, on August 14, Oswald again drew attention to himself by distributing pro-Castro leaflets, this time in front of the New Orleans Trade Mart. Was this Oswald's intention, or his backer's intention, to establish his credentials as a pro-Castro activist?

What was Oswald up to, displaying all this pro-Castro fervor one minute, then offering his services to an anti-Castro group the next? Was he operating on his own behalf, or at the instigation of some clandestine organization? And who was supporting him and his family and paying for the printing of the handbills and posters at the time? Was it the organization behind the man who had recently sprung him from jail?

Yes, it most likely was. For in 1979, during an FBI operation directed against Marcello and others, undercover agent Joseph Hauser got Marcello to admit he had known Oswald's uncle, Dutz Murret, and that Oswald had worked as a runner and collector for his uncle's bookmaking operation in the summer of 1963. That operation, Marcello added, was located in Sam Saia's Felix Oyster House in the French Quarter, not far from Pete Marcello's Sho-Bar on Bourbon Street.

Some corroboration of Oswald's affiliation with the Marcello gambling network was suggested by FBI informant Eugene De Laparra, who testified in 1967 that Oswald knew Ben Tregle, owner of the Marcello-backed bar and restaurant on Airline Highway not far from the Town & Country Motel. Tregle ran a horse book out of his bar that subscribed to Marcello's racing wire service, and so, in his role as a runner and collector for his bookie uncle, it is quite possible that Oswald could have had dealings with Ben Tregle. Tregle, it will be recalled, as early as March 1963, had given De Laparra the impression that he knew an assassination plot was in the works.

But was Oswald something more than a lowly runner in the Marcello bookmaking network in 1963? Did he perhaps also have a job in the Marcello anti-Castro operation?

Was Oswald being paid for his political activism in behalf of Castro's Cuba in the summer of 1963? New Orleans Attorney Dean Andrews, who performed occasional legal services for both Carlos Marcello and Lee Harvey Oswald that summer, was certain he was. Before the Warren Commission, Andrews testified that Oswald had told him he was being paid to hand out pro-Castro leaflets on the streets of New Orleans. Inexplicably, the commission declined to ask Andrews who had been paying Oswald.

Could it have been that in the summer of 1963, three months before President Kennedy was due to "come south," Oswald was already unwittingly being manipulated by the Marcello organization to play a role in a plot to assassinate the President? Had Carlos Marcello found in Oswald the "nut" he had told Becker, Roppolo, and others he was looking for to frame for the "job"?

For example, the rabidly anti-Castro Marcellos could have been paying Oswald to demonstrate on behalf of Castro so Oswald would establish a record as a pro-Castro activist. This readily accessible record would then be useful when he was framed for the assassination of the President, for it would immediately appear that pro-Castro forces were behind the crime.

Some light may be shed on this scenario by another manifestation of Oswald's double life in New Orleans during the summer of

1963: his association with a private investigator for Carlos Marcello by the name of David W. Ferrie.

Ferrie, a former Eastern Airlines pilot, had come to Marcello's attention through Marcello's New Orleans attorney G. Wray Gill, who had once represented Ferrie in a dispute with Eastern Airlines. Impressed by Ferrie's brilliance, Gill hired him in March 1962 as a legal researcher, and then assigned him in 1963 to help prepare Marcello's defense against the government's conspiracy and perjury charges. By the summer of 1963 Ferrie was meeting regularly with Gill and Marcello at Carlos's Town & Country office.

During the same period, Ferrie was also meeting regularly with a former cadet in a Louisiana civil air patrol squadron he once commanded in New Orleans, Lee Harvey Oswald. Not long after Oswald returned to New Orleans in April he ran into Ferrie, perhaps through their mutual associations with the Marcello organization. The two entered into what became a most mysterious relationship, seeing each other off and on in a variety of unusual circumstances that have perplexed scores of investigators for the past twenty-five years.

David Ferrie was a complex, bizarre individual. Brilliant, erratic, idealistic, and compulsive, he was an expert pilot, a competent research chemist, an aggressive homosexual, an amateur psychologist and practicing hypnotist, a militant anti-Castroite, a bishop of the Orthodox Old Catholic Church of North America (an offshoot of the Roman Catholic Church not recognized by the Vatican), and a victim of alopecia, a rare disease that causes the loss of all head and body hair.

Ferrie aspired to be a priest, but had been expelled from two Catholic seminaries for "erratic personal behavior." Once an airline pilot, he had been fired for having homosexual relations with young male passengers whom he would lure onto free "joy rides" aboard his scheduled flights. A dedicated cancer researcher, Ferrie kept over a hundred laboratory mice in his cluttered apartment, where microscopes and beakers were interspersed among books, papers, and personal effects. Once a soldier of fortune, Ferrie had run guns to his idol of the fifties, Fidel Castro, when the Cuban revolutionary was raiding Batista's forces from the Sierra Maestra. Then, after Castro announced he had become a Marxist, Ferrie turned against his idol and piloted bombers to Cuba on sabotage raids on behalf of various Cuban exile groups. Upon the failure of the Bay of Pigs operation, in which it is suspected Ferrie had played a role, Ferrie turned into a militant right-wing extremist. He joined the violently anti-Castro Cuban Revolutionary Front, an organization heavily financed by Carlos Marcello, and became a sworn enemy of President Kennedy, whom he accused of betraying the Cuban exiles' amphibious assault in the Bay of Pigs.

Ferrie's appearance was as outlandish as his personality and activities. Because of his total loss of hair, he was compelled to wear a wig (which some observers thought looked like monkey hair) and fake eyebrows (likened by some to tufts of carpet), both of which often went askew. Somewhere along the line he had acquired a doctorate in psychology through a correspondence course from an unaccredited school, Phoenix University in Bari, Italy, that enabled him to list himself in the New Orleans telephone directory as "Dr." David Ferrie, "psychologist." One of the reasons he had been fired as an Eastern Airlines pilot—in addition to his alleged homosexual activities—was that he had misrepresented himself as a medical doctor and psychologist in his original job application.

After the Bay of Pigs fiasco, Ferrie turned against President Kennedy with such fanaticism that once the New Orleans chapter of The Military Order of World Wars had to halt a vehemently critical address Ferrie gave on Kennedy's Cuban policy. Once he even wrote the secretary of defense a letter stating "there is nothing I would enjoy better than blowing the hell out of every damn Russian, Communist, Red, or what-have-you....Between my friends and I we can cook up a crew that can really blow them to hell....I want to train killers, however bad that sounds. It's what we need."

In addition to being employed by Carlos Marcello's attorney, Ferrie was also employed as an investigator by Guy Banister Associates, a private detective agency located at 544 Camp Street in New Orleans. When Lee Harvey Oswald was arrested in August 1963 while handing out pro-Castro leaflets on Canal Street, some of the leaflets had 544 Camp Street—an address wholly associated with *anti-Castro* groups—stamped on them. Witnesses reported seeing Oswald, Ferrie, Banister, and Sergio Arcacha Smith, leader of the Cuban Revolutionary Front, in the building together on several occasions during the summer of 1963.

Other witnesses, on a bewildering variety of occasions, also saw Lee Oswald and David Ferrie together during the summer of 1963. One witness saw them at a private party, during which the two openly discussed the desirability of a coup d'etat against the Kennedy administration. Another saw them together at Pontchartrain Beach, a New Orleans amusement park. Several witnesses on several different occasions saw Oswald and Ferrie in the Napoleon House Bar, a popular student hangout in the French Quarter. There they were overheard discussing the Kennedy administration's policies with whoever would listen. Still another witness once observed them and two "Latins" at a political meeting in Baton Rouge, openly denouncing President Kennedy's foreign and domestic policies—especially the

President's positions on Cuba and civil rights for blacks. Oswald and Ferrie evidently traveled extensively together that summer, for no fewer than six witnesses testified they saw them both in the company of an older man, perhaps New Orleans businessman Clay Shaw, perhaps Guy Banister, in Clinton, Louisiana, a small town 90 miles north of New Orleans, where the Congress of Racial Equality was conducting a voter registration drive among local blacks at the time. And still another eyewitness observed the two men in military fatigues and carrying automatic rifles, conducting what appeared to be a "military training maneuver" near Bedico Creek, a bayou 50 miles north of New Orleans.

Another individual Oswald saw during the summer of 1963 who had an association, albeit somewhat tenuous, with the Marcello organization was Guy Banister, an ex-FBI agent and, in 1963, a respected private investigator with his own detective agency. A militant supporter of the anti-Castro movement and a fervent segregationist, Banister, a friend of David Ferrie's, occasionally performed some investigative work for Carlos Marcello. For reasons that are not yet clear, Banister saw a good deal of Lee Oswald during the summer and fall of 1963. Twice, according to witnesses, Banister and Oswald visited the campus of Louisiana State University in New Orleans and held raucous discussions with the students, vehemently denouncing the civil rights policies of the Kennedy administration.

So here was Lee Harvey Oswald, the man who had gotten himself thrown in jail for fighting in the streets of New Orleans on behalf of Fidel Castro, spending a good deal of his time during the summer of 1963 with two militant anti-Castroites, David Ferrie and Guy Banister, both of whom worked for that other anti-Castroite, Carlos Marcello.

Oswald caused a big stir in New Orleans demonstrating on behalf of the Castro regime, yet no witnesses ever testified to having seen him in the company of Castro supporters during the summer of 1963, other than the anonymous individuals who helped him distribute his handbills. On the other hand, quite a few people saw him in the company of two militant members of the anti-Castro movement.

What are the logical implications of this seemingly contradictory behavior? It seems an inescapable conclusion that Oswald was not working on behalf of pro-Castro forces during the summer of 1963 but for some anti-Castro group, and that his public demonstrations in support of Castro were deceits carried out on behalf of another cause.

Since, after July 19, Oswald had no means of support other than unemployment insurance, and he could not have saved much from having worked at the coffee company for a little over two months at $1.50 an hour, it would appear that his living expenses and the cost of his pro-Castro activities must have been financed by some person, or organization, with good reason to have him identified as a fervent supporter of Fidel Castro.

When, shortly after Oswald's arrest on November 23 for the assassination of President Kennedy, it was announced that a card attesting to Oswald's membership in the Fair Play for Cuba Committee had been found in his wallet, and photographs of him handing out pro-Castro leaflets had been quickly found in the New Orleans papers, everyone directly concerned with the crime—the Dallas police, the FBI, and the nation's press—were quick to conclude that the alleged assassin of the President was some kind of a "commie nut" whose idol was Fidel Castro.

It seems Lee Harvey Oswald had carried out his assignment to perfection during the summer of 1963.

23

The Pressures Mount: September 1963

On September 25, 1963, Carlos Marcello and his fellow Mafiosi throughout the country held their breaths as they watched on national television a member of their own brotherhood publicly violating his vow of silence at a hearing before Senator John McClellan's subcommittee on organized crime.

The witness was Joseph Valachi, a former soldier in New York's Genovese family, and his appearance before the committee represented the first time in the history of organized crime in the United States that a "made" member of a Mafia family publicly testified on the inner workings of the Mafia in America. In his lengthy, often sensational testimony, delivered over a period of six days, Valachi revealed the organizational structure of the Mafia, which he referred to as Cosa Nostra ("our thing"), a new term for the American public. Valachi revealed its code, its rules and regulations, the names of the members of its national ruling body, the *commissione,* and presented a crude, somewhat disjointed, but immensely informative history of the New York Mafia families since their rise to power during prohibition. (It is worth noting, in passing, that Lee Harvey Oswald was heard using the expression Cosa Nostra in the summer of 1963, before the expression was known to anyone outside of the Cosa Nostra itself and the FBI.)

By the time Valachi was through testifying, the inner secrets of the Genovese family lay bare and the privacy of several other crime families had been seriously violated. Of the major Mafia bosses, Carlos Marcello was one of the few who emerged from the hearings personally unscathed.

What Valachi had to say about Marcello's territory underscored the independence and insularity of the Louisiana Mafia. When, during one of the hearings, Valachi was asked to tell what he knew about the Mafia in Louisiana, he replied:

"Louisiana? I don't know a thing except they don't want visitors. Once I was going to see Mardi Gras and I checked it out with Vito, which I was supposed to do if I took a trip. He said: 'Don't go.' No explanation, just 'Don't go.' They didn't want anybody there. And I was told if I ever had to go to Louisiana, Genovese would have to call ahead and get permission. Genovese himself had to get permission. It was an absolute rule."

Whether Carlos Marcello took any satisfaction from Valachi's ignorance of his operations is doubtful. Valachi's revelations still came as a blow to all the Mafia bosses, for they provided the Justice Department with a foundation of knowledge upon which it could more solidly base future assaults on organized crime.

Robert Kennedy stressed the importance of Valachi's testimony when, in a public statement after the hearings were over, he described it as "the greatest intelligence breakthrough in the history of organized crime in America" and promised to use the knowledge gained to step up his campaign against the mob. Kennedy's pronouncement on the Valachi hearings put the Mafia bosses on notice throughout the nation that the Justice Department had not slackened its pace in its war on organized crime.

Soon FBI bugs and wiretaps revealed the mob's anger over Valachi's treachery and its mounting apprehension over Robert Kennedy's crackdown. Stefano Maggadino, boss of the upstate New York Mafia, was taped on the subject of Valachi as saying: "We passed laws that this guy has got to die." Later, Maggadino's brother, Peter, was overheard exploding over President Kennedy: "He should drop dead. They should kill the whole family, the mother and the father too."

Sam Giancana could have been the spokesman for the entire mob when an FBI eavesdropping device caught him telling an underling:

"You told me...before Kennedy was appointed attorney general, but I never thought it would be this rough. You told me when they put his brother in there we were gonna see some fireworks, but I never knew it would be like this. This is murder."

Giancana was right. Kennedy's campaign against the mob *was* murder. During the almost three years he had been attorney general, his policies had resulted in a 500 percent increase in organized crime defendants indicted and a 400 percent increase in convictions. For the first time in history the Justice Department had men of the power of Giancana, Trafficante, and Marcello on the run. For the first time, also, it was bringing enormous pressure to bear on the Mafia's tools in organized labor, foremost of whom was Teamsters boss Jimmy Hoffa. At Kennedy's relentless insistence, Hoffa had been indicted twice in 1963—in May for jury tampering, and in June for fraud— and appeared certainly headed for prison.

But the war on the mob was not the only struggle Robert Kennedy was engaged in at the time. He and his brother remained active in their secret campaign "to get rid of Castro," and they were also encouraging a coup in South Vietnam that would result in the assassinations of President Diem and his brother on November 1. By September 1963, President Kennedy, through his own policies and actions and those of his brother, had probably made more powerful enemies, in less time, than any other President since Abraham Lincoln.

On September 7, one of those enemies, Fidel Castro, reacting to intelligence reports that the CIA was attempting to assassinate him, told Associated Press correspondent Daniel Harker in a widely reported interview: "We are prepared to fight them and answer in kind. United States leaders should think that if they are aiding terrorist plans to eliminate Cuban leaders, they themselves will not be safe."

The interview was published in the New Orleans *Times-Picayune* and was probably read by Lee Harvey Oswald, David Ferrie, and Carlos Marcello.

If, as is widely believed, Marcello was conspiring with Ferrie to set up Oswald to take the blame for the impending assassination of President Kennedy, Castro's remarks must have warmed Carlos's heart. Now the founder and sole member of the Fair Play for Cuba Committee of New Orleans could one day easily be linked in the public mind to Castro's September threat to retaliate against Kennedy.

Judging from the activities of Oswald, Ferrie, and Marcello in the waning days of September 1963, impulsive threats and vague intentions to assassinate President Kennedy matured into definite plans and hard decisions some time that month. These plans and decisions received some encouragement when, on September 13, the New Orleans papers confirmed that President Kennedy would make a one-day visit to Texas on either November 21 or 22.

At the time of the announcement Carlos Marcello and David Ferrie had begun planning Marcello's defense in the case of *The United States v. Carlos Marcello,* scheduled to go to trial in New Orleans in early November. In addition to conferring with Marcello at the Town & Country Motel, Ferrie was also meeting with Oswald in the French Quarter and traveling with him to various places north of town.

Several days after the confirmation of Kennedy's forthcoming trip to Texas was announced, Lee Harvey Oswald decided to make a brief visit to Mexico City, then pull up his stakes in New Orleans and return to Dallas. After spending a day with David Ferrie in Clinton, he obtained, on September 17, his Mexican tourist visa and on the 26th began his journey to the Mexican capital. There he (or quite possibly someone impersonating him, with or without his knowledge) would soon repeat his New Orleans pro-Castro charades by ostentatiously proclaiming his sympathy for Castro and his revolution wherever he went. It was also on the 26th that the press announced, for the first time, the precise day—November 22—President Kennedy would visit Dallas.

Meanwhile, in early September, Robert Kennedy, no doubt frustrated by Joe Valachi's ignorance of Marcello's fiefdom, had chewed out J. Edgar Hoover once again over the inadequacy of the FBI's coverage of Marcello and his criminal organization. The New Orleans FBI agent assigned to oversee Marcello, Regis Kennedy, was still sending reports back to Washington stating, in essence, that Marcello, as a salesman for the Pelican Tomato Company, was merely a "private businessman" who was not engaged in any discernible criminal activity. It is not known what action, if any, Hoover took after the attorney general's renewed criticism of his handling of the Marcello investigation. Judging from what we know about Carlos Marcello's activities during the next two months, it appears that either Hoover did nothing or his agents in New Orleans willfully ignored his instructions, possibly in connivance with Carlos Marcello himself.

Whatever the case, Carlos Marcello was able to operate more or less as he pleased during the months of October and November as he planned his defense against the charges brought against him by Attorney General Kennedy, and waited for his brother, the President, to venture into his territory on November 22.

24

Marcello's Dallas

Next to New Orleans, the most important city in the invisible empire of Carlos Marcello was Dallas. Dallas did not have a Mafia family of its own; its underworld was a satellite of the Marcello organization, and its leaders ultimately took their orders from Carlos Marcello.

The Marcellos had been active in Dallas and other parts of Texas for over a decade and would continue to expand their operations in the state dramatically in the years to come. For some time there had been a tacit understanding among the leaders of the major Mafia families that Texas was the Marcellos' territory, and no one else would be allowed to muscle in. As one law enforcement official put it, the Marcello network in Texas was "an independent, elaborately insulated operation."

That operation included a vast range of activities of varying degrees of legitimacy. The Marcello racing wire service was hooked up to bookies all over the state. Although there are no figures available for 1963, by 1972, according to a report by then Texas State Attorney General Crawford Martin, the Marcello gambling syndicate in Texas numbered 800 bookmakers handling gross revenues of $700 million.

In 1963 the Marcellos' slot machines could be found almost everywhere in Texas. As they had done in Louisiana, the Marcellos, throughout the fifties, had helped finance bars and restaurants that would install their machines. These were mainly in Dallas and Houston, but also in other localities. The family's Pelican Tomato Company, whose largest single customer was the U.S. Navy Department, did a huge business in Texas, importing large quantities of tomatoes from Mexico without interference from customs. In real estate, Carlos helped finance builders in Dallas and Houston, where he and his brothers also owned motels and restaurants. Carlos owned the Alamotel in Houston, and Vincent was reputed to have owned a restaurant-nightclub in Dallas. As president and co-owner with Carlos of the family slot machine and jukebox business, the Jefferson Music Company, Vincent traveled to Dallas regularly, often with his brother Sammy, to oversee the family's slot machine enterprise and other interests.

The growth of the Marcellos' power in Texas during the late forties and throughout the fifties would not have been possible without the cooperation of important Texas politicians. This cooperation had been secured by Carlos Marcello's Texan bagman, John Halfen, whose special job it had been to funnel a percentage of the Marcellos' illegal Texas profits to the political campaigns of such Texan politicos as Houston Congressman Albert Thomas, Associate Justice of the Supreme Court Tom Clark, and U.S. Senator Lyndon B. Johnson.

By the mid-fifties Carlos Marcello's racing wire serviced some 200 illegal bookmakers in Houston alone. Each bookie paid from $250 to $500 a day for the service. It was up to Jack Halfen to ensure peace between the politicians and the gambling interests. It has been estimated that of the $15.6 million a year in racetrack gambling profits realized by the Marcello-Halfen interests in Houston, Marcello took 40 percent, 25 percent went for bribes to politicians and cops, and the remaining 35 percent went to bagman Jack Halfen and his associates.

Of all the Texas politicians the Marcello-Halfen interests supported, the most powerful was Senator Lyndon B. Johnson. It has been estimated that the Marcello-Halfen group funneled at least $50,000 a year of the Marcellos' gambling profits alone to Lyndon Johnson, and in return, Johnson helped kill in committee all anti-rackets legislation that could have harmed the interests of Carlos Marcello and Jack Halfen. It was safe to say, then, that thanks partly to the influence of Vice President Lyndon Johnson, Carlos Marcello was able to operate freely in Dallas in 1963. It was no wonder that Robert Kennedy's war on organized crime got nowhere in the state in which his brother was eventually assassinated.

In the Dallas of 1963 the Marcellos were able to operate at their pleasure, unimpeded by the law, for in the best family tradition, the most important acquisition they had made in the city had been the Dallas Police force.

Running things for the Marcellos in their Dallas freedom of the early sixties was Louisiana-born Joseph Civello, ex-convict, gambler, narcotics smuggler, liquor dealer, Italian food products importer, suspected murderer, and longtime friend and associate of Carlos Marcello.

Joe Civello was one of the fifty-nine Mafia leaders arrested at the 1957 Mafia conclave in Apalachin. So close had he been to Carlos Marcello at the time that Carlos had made him his representative at the upstate New York meeting. A few days after Civello returned to Dallas from Apalachin, to an avalanche of adverse publicity in the local papers, he was observed having dinner with a Dallas Police sergeant by the name of Patrick T. Dean, who once admitted that the Dallas Police "had no trouble with the Italian families." Six years later it was Sergeant Dean who was in charge of basement security when an associate of Joe Civello's, Jack Ruby, entered the basement of Dallas Police Headquarters and murdered Lee Harvey Oswald in front of over seventy armed police officers.

Joseph Civello and Carlos Marcello were both raised in Louisiana, were both of Sicilian extraction, and were both initiated into the Mafia early in their lives. By the fall of 1963 they had known each other for many years. Civello was a partner in Marcello's racing wire service and was active in leasing Marcello's slot machines to bars, restaurants, and nightclubs in the Dallas area. FBI reports reveal frequent telephone contact between Civello and Marcello throughout the late fifties and early sixties and a shared friendship with another Dallas family of Sicilian origin, active in the city's underworld, the Campisis.

Joe and Sam Campisi owned the Egyptian Lounge restaurant, a notorious hangout of the Dallas underworld. FBI reports reveal that Civello was frequently observed furtively entering and leaving the Egyptian Lounge through a back entrance. It is believed that in the early sixties Joe Campisi was the number two mobster in the city and was considered Joe Civello's most likely successor as boss of the Marcello operation in Dallas.

Although it was never brought out at the time of the Kennedy assassination, Joe Campisi had a very close relationship with the Marcello family during the fifties and sixties. Telephone records obtained by the FBI show that there were frequent calls between Marcello's enterprises in New Orleans and Campisi's Egyptian Lounge in

Dallas. In 1978 Joe Campisi admitted he knew Carlos Marcello and four of his brothers and had visited them in Louisiana several times. Campisi told investigators he used to play golf with Vincent and Anthony Marcello and would often go to the racetrack with two or three of the brothers. Although Campisi claimed he had no business dealings with Carlos Marcello, he admitted to congressional investigators that he sent 260 pounds of Italian sausage to Carlos Marcello every Christmas, sausage he claimed, with pride, he "made special with walnuts and celery."

Occupying a position in the Dallas underworld several rungs below those occupied by Joe Civello and the Campisi brothers was a Dallas striptease nightclub owner, narcotics dealer, bookmaker, slot machines operator, and pimp who would one day murder the accused assassin of President Kennedy.

Jack Leon Ruby had been born to Jewish immigrant parents and had been raised in Chicago's West Side ghetto. There he had progressed from street gang to street gang to eventual service under the most powerful crime boss in Chicago, Al Capone. In 1946, a year before Carlos Marcello assumed power in Louisiana, the Chicago mob launched a concerted campaign to take over the rackets in the Dallas area and gain control of the Dallas Police, and in the following year Jack Ruby left Chicago for Dallas to assist in that effort. Remaining in Dallas for the rest of his life, he developed into that curious underworld hybrid, the small-time racketeer police buff.

Jack Ruby's relationship with the Dallas Police went far beyond the desire of a racketeer to ingratiate himself with those who had the power to cause him serious trouble. The Dallas Police force was, for the perennial bachelor Ruby, his chief hobby, his primary recreation. He knew by name at least seventy, perhaps a hundred, officers of the force and delighted in doing favors for them. He brought boxes full of deli sandwiches to the officers on duty at headquarters, and would often hang around headquarters for hours gassing with his policemen buddies. He would cosign loans for officers hard up for cash. He would provide them with free drinks at his nightclubs and arrange free after-hours dates for them with his sexiest strippers. So extensive and pervasive were Ruby's contacts with the police that they became legendary in Dallas. The press made use of them. Ordinary citizens made use of them. The underworld made use of them. When, on the weekend of November 23, 1963, it became necessary to silence President Kennedy's accused assassin, who was being held in custody in the Dallas Police Headquarters, those who had reason to silence him knew precisely to whom they could turn.

Although the FBI both withheld and suppressed evidence of Jack Ruby's connections to organized crime from the Warren Commission, Ruby had many acquaintances in the principal Mafia families, including at least eight associates of the Marcello organization. The most important of those Marcello associates whom Jack Ruby knew was Joseph Civello, yet evidence of the relationship between the two was deliberately suppressed by the FBI at the time of the Kennedy assassination.

That Jack Ruby knew Joseph Civello was attested to by FBI informant Bobby Gene Moore on November 27, 1963. Moore had been born and raised in Dallas and had lived and worked there until the late fifties. For a while he had been employed by Joseph Civello and his partner Frank LaMonte in their Italian import business, which Moore had strong reasons to suspect was a front for the importation of narcotics from Sicily. During the same period, from 1952 to 1956, Moore had also worked intermittently as a pianist at Jack Ruby's Vegas Club.

Bobby Gene Moore was living in Oakland, California, at the time of the Kennedy assassination. A few days after the assassination Moore saw an interview of an associate of Jack Ruby's on television, during which the associate claimed that Ruby had no connections to organized crime. Puzzled and outraged over what he conceived was a blatant falsehood, Moore went to the Oakland FBI office. There he stated that while he was a clerk in the Civello and LaMonte Italian Importing Company in Dallas, he "came to suspect that [Joseph] Civello and his partner Frank LaMonte were engaged in racket activities" because on occasion they would pointedly not allow him to open certain cartons of cheese imported from Italy, although that was his specific job. On the basis of this, he "came to believe Civello and LaMonte were importing narcotics." Moore further stated that Jack Ruby "was also a frequent visitor and associate of Civello and La Monte." As a footnote to his testimony, Moore alleged that "Judge O'Brien, a municipal judge in Dallas, was a friend of Civello and La Monte" and that he, Moore, "frequently put hams and other foodstuffs in O'Brien's car" at Civello's request.

Jack Ruby was also on very friendly terms with Civello's immediate subordinates in the Dallas Mafia hierarchy, the Campisi brothers. Ruby used to hang out for hours in the Campisis' Egyptian Lounge restaurant, and Joe Campisi would often spend some time at his table. After the assassination of President Kennedy, Ruby's roommate, George Senator, testified that Joe Campisi was "one of Ruby's three closest friends." Ruby's closeness to Campisi was also acknowledged by his sister, Eva Grant, who told investigators that her brother spent a great deal of time in the Egyptian Lounge.

In addition to Civello and Campisi, Jack Ruby associated with at least four other individuals connected to the Marcello organization, including at least two of Carlos Marcello's brothers.

Frank Caracci was a mid-level operative in the Marcello organization who owned and managed several striptease joints in New Orleans' French Quarter. Involved in extensive gambling operations in Texas and Louisiana, Caracci was friendly with Joe Civello and Joe Campisi in Dallas and was on very close terms with the Marcello brothers on his home turf. FBI reports indicate that between June and October 1963, Jack Ruby visited one of Caracci's New Orleans nightclubs, telephoned another several times, and met with Caracci personally on at least one occasion. Ruby was also in close contact with another Marcello-affiliated nightclub operator, Harold Tannenbaum, an associate of Carlos Marcello's number three man, Nofio Pecora. Tannenbaum, in fact, lived at Pecora's Tropical Tourist Court Motel in New Orleans. Between May and November 1963, Ruby made at least eighteen calls to Tannenbaum, ostensibly about the nightclub business.

The Marcellos owned, or had an interest in, several nightclubs on Bourbon Street in the heart of New Orleans' French Quarter. Bourbon Street is a village within a village. All the nightclub, restaurant, and bar owners know one another, and they usually stand near the entrances of their establishments greeting their customers. In 1963 Pete Marcello, one of Carlos's younger brothers, owned and operated the Sho-Bar, one of the gaudier strip joints and B-girl operations on Bourbon Street. Records indicate that between June and October 1963, Jack Ruby made two telephone calls to Pete Marcello's Sho-Bar and paid at least one visit to the club. After the Kennedy assassination, several Bourbon Street denizens remembered Ruby prowling the area in mid-October.

Did Jack Ruby know Carlos Marcello's brother Pete? In all likelihood, he did, and according to reliable sources he also probably knew at least two other Marcello brothers, Vincent and Sammy. If, as records show, Ruby called the Sho-Bar twice and visited it once in the summer and fall of 1963, he undoubtedly was in touch with Pete Marcello, for it was Pete who took the calls and greeted all visitors at the door. What was Ruby in touch with Pete Marcello about? In all probability the nightclub business. Ruby and Marcello often employed the same strippers. They had interests in common.

The same could be said of Ruby's relationships with Sammy and

Vincent. They also had interests in common. Vincent, as president and co-owner, with his brother Carlos, of the Jefferson Music Company, Louisiana's largest slot machine and jukebox distributor, was heavily involved in the slot machines business in Dallas. Not long after the Kennedy assassination, a man by the name of William B. Abadie, then living in Los Angeles, informed the FBI that he had worked for seven weeks in 1963 in Jack Ruby's Dallas warehouse as a slot machine and jukebox mechanic and also "wrote tickets" as a bookie in one of Ruby's gambling establishments.

Jack Ruby was therefore also involved with slot machines and bookmaking, interests that never came to light during the Warren Commission's investigation. This meant he had to have known Vincent Marcello, and probably also his assistant, Sammy, for in 1963 the Marcellos controlled a large share of the distribution of slot machines and jukeboxes in Dallas, and the family's racing wire service was hooked up to most of the city's bookies. Furthermore, Vincent was supposed to have owned a restaurant-nightclub in Dallas, as FBI informant Eugene De Laparra has suggested, and may have therefore been in competition with Ruby.

That Jack Ruby knew one or more of the Marcello brothers was never stated in the voluminous published records of the House Assassinations Committee, yet several reliable sources in New Orleans are certain he did. One of them, the present district attorney of St. Landry Parish, said he had talked to reliable people who had seen Ruby with Pete and Vincent Marcello.

But Ruby's contacts with the Marcello organization extended even beyond his acquaintance with some of Carlos's brothers. It also reached into the inner circle of Carlos's most trusted lieutenants and specifically to the number three man in the Marcello hierarchy, Nofio Pecora, whose wife, it will be recalled, was Carlos's personal secretary.

According to telephone records acquired by the FBI, on August 4, 1963, Ruby received a call from Nofio Pecora and on October 30, 1963, three weeks before the Kennedy assassination, Ruby made a call to Pecora. It is worth recalling that an associate of Nofio Pecora's, Emile Bruneau, was the Marcello associate who put up bail to get Lee Harvey Oswald out of jail in New Orleans after he had been arrested during the Canal Street scuffle.

Given Jack Ruby's friendships with the Marcellos' chief operatives in Dallas, and his relationship with at least two of Carlos Marcello's brothers and one of his top lieutenants, it appears that key people in the Marcello organization must have known a good deal about Jack Ruby by the fall of 1963.

During the months preceding the Kennedy assassination, Ruby had fallen deeply in debt and was in trouble with the IRS, to which he owed considerable sums in back taxes. Since he was such a garrulous character, Ruby's financial vulnerability must have been well known to both the Dallas Police and the Dallas underworld in the fall of 1963.

It has been observed that the Marcello organization, in its enormous embrace, was able to call upon a vast reservoir of specialized talents whenever a particular need arose. Jack Ruby's specialty was the Dallas Police force. Police headquarters was his second home. He could come and go from the premises at will. The time would come when the cultivation of this specialty would finally pay off as the debt-ridden small-time racketeer received, in November 1963, the assignment of his life.

25

Oswald and His Double

After the assassination of President Kennedy, Marina Oswald informed her interrogators that in late September 1963, her husband Lee told her he was fed up with life in the United States and wanted to return to the Soviet Union with her and their child. To accomplish this he would go to Mexico City and attempt to obtain a transit visa to visit Cuba from the Cuban Embassy, there being no Cuban consular facilities in the United States. Once in Cuba, he would try to obtain a visa from the Soviet Embassy in Havana that would enable him to return with her and the child to Russia. While in Cuba he would also spend some time fighting for Castro. "I will become a revolutionary!" he cried out to her, as he revealed his plans for their future.

Ostensibly to implement this plan, Lee extricated Marina, who was now pregnant, and his daughter from their New Orleans apartment on September 24 and sent them off to live once again with Marina's friend Ruth Paine in the Dallas suburb of Irving.

As events were to demonstrate, either Oswald deliberately lied to his wife or Marina invented the plan herself in her testimony. For, in reality, it appears certain that Oswald was going to Mexico City for a different reason, if indeed he did go to Mexico City at all. From all indications, he was going there, at the behest of his employer of the past few months, to bolster his credentials as a pro-Castro activist.

Meanwhile, that employer had begun to deploy two individuals, one who vaguely resembled Oswald and one who did not, to stage a number of incidents that could some day be used to frame the crazy ex-defector from New Orleans.

Although this scenario seems, at first glance, farfetched, the sheer weight of evidence to support it that has been accumulating over the past twenty-five years is convincing beyond reasonable doubt. For, given what we know, it appears certain that by late September the conspiracy to assassinate President Kennedy in Texas had matured into a very sophisticated operation. An important element of that operation was the deliberate framing of an individual who would emerge as a suspect immediately after the assassination. On the basis of planted evidence quickly found and compromising associations quickly discovered, he would soon be identified by law enforcement authorities as the sole killer of the President. That the conspirators hit upon the idea of deploying two Oswalds, perhaps even three, the real Lee Harvey and one or two impostors, to accomplish this aim is borne out by a long chain of once baffling, but now comprehensible, episodes commencing in Dallas in late September.

On September 25 the real Oswald was supposed to be in New Orleans about to take a bus the following day for Mexico City. Yet on that day a man representing himself as "Harvey Oswald" petitioned the office of the Selective Service in Austin, Texas, for a revocation of his dishonorable discharge from the Marines, because it hindered his chances of obtaining employment. The clerk to whom this Oswald spoke remembered him as having consciously made an effort to be obnoxious so he would not be forgotten.

On the following day, when Oswald was supposed to have been on a bus bound for Mexico City, two Cuban exiles in Dallas, Sylvia and Annie Odio, daughters of a political prisoner of Castro's, received three visitors at their Dallas apartment, two "Latins" and an American. The Latins claimed they were members of the Junta Revolucionaria, an anti-Castro group. They said they knew the Odio sisters' father's underground name and told them they were aware of the CIA's recent plots to assassinate Castro. The purpose of their visit was to enlist the Odio sisters' aid in the struggle against Castro. During the course of the conversation the American, who was introduced to the sisters as Leon Oswald, remained silent. Forty-eight hours later, one of the Latins called up Sylvia Odio and told her something about Leon Oswald. "He's a Marine, an ex-Marine, and an expert marksman," he told her. "He's kind of loco, kind of nuts. He could go either way. He could do anything—like getting underground in Cuba, like killing Castro." Then he added: "The American says we Cubans don't have any guts. He says we should have shot President Kennedy after the Bay of Pigs. He says we should do something like that."

Was Leon Oswald really Lee Harvey Oswald, or was he an impostor? Unless Miss Odio was mistaken as to the date of Leon Oswald's visit, it appears he must have been an impostor. For it is reasonably certain that the real Oswald was on a Continental Trailways bus from Laredo, Texas, to Mexico City on September 26.... Unless it was the impostor who was on the bus, and the real Oswald who was in Miss Odio's apartment.

Several passengers on board that bus later testified that someone representing himself as Lee Harvey Oswald spoke of his forthcoming business in Mexico City freely, even obtrusively, to anyone who would listen. He made a point of telling them that he was secretary of the Fair Play for Cuba Committee in New Orleans and confided to them that he hoped he would soon meet Fidel Castro in Havana.

As it turned out, Oswald, or his impostor, or both, spent six days in Mexico. He may have inadvertently given away his true allegiance by the hotel he chose there. It was the Hotel Del Comercio, a well-known meeting place of anti-Castro Cuban exiles.

Oswald's first destination the morning after his arrival was the Soviet Embassy, where, according to his wife, he went to apply for a visa to enter the Soviet Union. However, CIA headquarters and the FBI's Soviet espionage section learned through wiretaps, and highly placed informants within the embassy itself, that the man representing himself as Oswald spoke with Valery Vladimirovich Kostikov, the officer-in-charge for western hemisphere terrorist activities—including assassination—hardly an official one would consult to apply for a visa. Considerable doubt, however, has been cast on whether it was the real Lee Harvey Oswald who visited the embassy that morning because a CIA photograph of the visitor bore no resemblance whatsoever to the real Oswald.

The CIA had been routinely filming everyone who visited the Soviet Embassy. On October 10 it sent a set of stills of the man it identified as Lee Henry [sic] Oswald entering the embassy on September 27 to FBI headquarters in Washington, and the photograph turned out not to be that of Lee Harvey Oswald. Whether Oswald, or someone representing himself as Oswald, visited the Soviet Embassy that day is still a matter of controversy, for the CIA also destroyed a purported tape recording of the mysterious visitor's voice.

Later on that same day, a man representing himself as Lee Harvey Oswald went to the Cuban Embassy and told a clerk in the consular section, a young Mexican woman by the name of Sylvia Duran, that he wanted an in-transit visa to visit Cuba on the way to his ultimate destination, the Soviet Union. As he made his request, he ostentatiously displayed his Fair Play for Cuba Committee membership card and several newspaper clippings about his arrest for demonstrating for Castro in New Orleans. Feeling that the applicant's display of allegiance to Cuba was a bit overdone, and slightly suspicious, Miss Duran rejected his application, whereupon Oswald went into a fit and stormed out of the office.

After the assassination of President Kennedy, when Miss Duran saw photographs of the accused assassin in the papers, she recognized Lee Harvey Oswald's name and thought she recognized his face, but was not sure. Years later, in 1978, when a staff counsel of the House Committee on Assassinations interviewed her and showed her film footage of Oswald, she testified flatly that he was not the man who had presented himself as Oswald in 1963.

That opinion was also expressed by the head of the consular section of the Cuban Embassy at the time, Consul Eusebio Azcue, a Cuban national who interviewed the man representing himself as Lee Harvey Oswald two or three days after he had first talked to Sylvia Duran.

Apparently Oswald had returned to the Cuban Embassy to demand once more of Miss Duran that he be issued an in-transit visa to visit Cuba, and once more Miss Duran turned him down. At this second rebuff he put up such a stink that Duran had to call the head of the consular section for help. Consul Azcue then intervened and ordered the unruly man thrown out of the building. Later, when shown photographs of the man who had been arrested in Dallas for allegedly assassinating President Kennedy, Azcue denied it was the individual he had ejected from the embassy.

What are we to make of it all? Since human error in matching photographs to individuals met in fleeting, casual situations is eminently possible, and since the CIA's mistaken identification of the individual it filmed entering the Soviet Embassy could have also been due to human error, one is inclined to believe that it was at least possible that the real Oswald did visit the two embassies.

And yet there is strong evidence that suggests Lee Harvey Oswald never visited the Cuban Embassy in Mexico City that fall. For in 1978, the House Select Committee on Assassinations sent an investigator to Mexico City to look into the matter, and he returned to Washington convinced beyond all doubt that the real Oswald did not visit either the Russian Embassy or the Cuban Embassy in Mexico City and might not have even been in Mexico City when he was alleged to have been there by the FBI and the Warren Commission.

The committee's investigator was Edwin Lopez, a young attorney fluent in Spanish. After interviewing Miss Duran and Consul Azcue, he became convinced the real Oswald had never visited either one of them at their offices in the Cuban Embassy.

But it was the CIA's files of Oswald's alleged visit to Mexico City that convinced Lopez that the real Oswald had never visited the Cuban Embassy that fall. For the CIA file contained photographs of the man representing himself as Oswald visiting the Cuban Embassy on three different occasions, taken by hidden cameras from three different angles, and none of the pictures were of Lee Harvey Oswald. According to Lopez, the CIA kept the Cuban Embassy in Mexico City under around-the-clock surveillance, and so there was little chance simple human error could have accounted for mistaking the identity of the man calling himself Lee Harvey Oswald.

After completing his investigation, Edwin Lopez compiled a 300-page report, which remains classified to this day. Lopez has since declared publicly that on the basis of his investigation, he believes Lee Harvey Oswald was set up in advance to take the blame for the assassination of the President.

One thing is certain, however: that Oswald never intended to go to Cuba, fight for Fidel, and then travel to the Soviet Union, as his wife Marina claimed he had told her.

Strengthening this conclusion were the results of an investigation of Oswald's visit to Mexico City conducted by British author Anthony Summers, in 1981 and 1982, *after* the publication of his book on the Kennedy assassination, *Conspiracy,* in 1980.

Summers says that he was shown notes and memoranda upon which the 300-page Assassinations Committee's classified report on the Mexico City visit was based, including certain CIA documents. From them he learned that among the photographs the CIA's hidden cameras had taken of the person representing himself as Lee Harvey Oswald at the Cuban and Soviet Embassies in Mexico City, one was of the real Lee Harvey Oswald, and eleven were of an unknown individual. Apparently the photograph of the real Oswald had been destroyed, perhaps to protect the identity of other persons in the photograph, possible conspirators, who could have been embarrassed by their association with Oswald becoming known, and whose images could not be successfully cropped form the surveillance photograph.

Furthermore, Summers learned to his satisfaction that the CIA had recorded eight tapped telephone conversations of the man who represented himself as Lee Harvey Oswald to officials of the Soviet Embassy in Mexico City, two of which were in Spanish [which Oswald spoke] and the others in a twisted, broken Russian. Eight transcripts of these conversations were made and were sent to CIA Headquarters on October 10, 1963, or seven weeks before the assassination. The original recordings were then supposedly destroyed and the eight transcripts were never turned over to the Warren Commission, though they *were* submitted to the FBI.

Contrary to what was stated in the House Assassinations Committee's Final Report, committee staff investigators did see copies of the transcripts. They concluded that the language of the transcripts in Russian was so bad it could not have been the real Lee Harvey Oswald's; Oswald's Russian was considered nearly fluent.

From his inspection of the documents Summers could not determine what the content of the transcripts was. It appeared certain to him, however, that the Assassinations Committee *did* receive the eight transcripts and learned their contents, even though the Committee failed to reveal either the existence of the transcripts or their content in its published volumes. Summers' final opinion on the transcripts is that they were not transcriptions of the real Lee Harvey Oswald's oral remarks and that both the CIA and the FBI were aware of this soon after the assassination and did nothing to determine whose words they were, burying the whole foul-smelling matter so that the Warren Commission would never get wind of it. Yet if there ever was compelling evidence suggesting the existence of a conspiracy to assassinate President Kennedy, this was it: an Oswald impostor planting incriminating evidence against the real Oswald.

Oswald had only around $200 on him when he left New Orleans, hardly enough on which to undertake a journey that, given inevitable bureaucratic delays, could take three or four months. Furthermore, Oswald could have applied for a visa to visit the Soviet Union at any Soviet consular office in the United States.

No, Oswald, or his impostor, must have had another purpose for his visit to Mexico City. While in the Mexican capital he had vociferously advertised pro-Castro sentiments and had complained bitterly at not having been granted a visa in front of two officials of the Cuban Embassy, who he could be sure would not forget him. Once again, he had bolstered his pro-Castro credentials. When, immediately after the assassination of President Kennedy, the American ambassador to Mexico cabled Washington that he strongly suspected Castro was behind the crime, the real purpose of Oswald's visit to Mexico City was finally exposed, although no one knew it at the time.

For it now appears certain that Oswald never intended to go to Cuba or Russia. He had tried to obtain a visa to visit Cuba only to make an impression. The change of address card he made out in New Orleans just before he departed for Mexico City seems to bear this out. On the card he gave his wife's address in Irving and a post office box number in Dallas for himself.

The question of Oswald's contention, expressed to his fellow passengers on the way to Mexico City, that he had visited Mexico several times during the summer, remains perplexing. If Oswald's employer was the Marcello organization, why would he have been sent repeatedly to Mexico during the summer of 1963? It is impossible to give the answer, but it is worth noting that the Marcellos did a good deal of business in Mexico through the Pelican Tomato Company, which illegally imported huge shipments of Mexican tomatoes across the Texas-Mexico border. Immigration and Naturalization reports suggest Carlos Marcello's presence in Monterrey on several occasions in 1962 and 1963. Certainly if Oswald met with anyone of high rank in the Marcello organization in the summer of 1963, it would have been safer for them to have met in Mexico.

On October 3 the real Lee Harvey Oswald returned to Dallas, where, on September 26, the papers had confirmed that President Kennedy would visit the city on November 22. The following day he applied for a job at a concern on Industrial Boulevard, one of the three possible presidential motorcade routes, and was turned down.

After spending a few nights in the Dallas YMCA, then visiting his wife and child in Irving for a couple of days, then renting a room in a boardinghouse for a week, Oswald settled down on October 14 in an apartment at 1026 North Beckley in the Oak Cliff section of Dallas, registering in the name of O. H. Lee, without telling his wife where he was. The following day he was hired, through the efforts of his wife's friend Ruth Paine, as an order filler in the Texas School Book Depository, a building covering two of the three possible presidential motorcade routes, and on the 16th he reported for his first day of work.

Living apart from his family, under an assumed name, Oswald was assured complete privacy. Now he could attend to his business unnoticed and undisturbed. Apparently whatever business he conducted over the phone was from a public telephone in a garage near his rooming house, for a garage attendant later testified he had often made change for Oswald so he could call long-distance.

The stage was now set for the Oswald double to deliberately plant an incriminating trail of evidence against him in and around Dallas.

The real Oswald had to work at the Texas School Book Depository Monday through Friday from 8:00 to 4:45 with only a forty-minute break for lunch, which, his fellow workers testified, he always ate in the depository's cafeteria. Yet on the morning of November 1, a weekday, a man giving his name as Oswald entered Morgan's Gun Shop in Fort Worth to purchase ammunition. He drew attention to himself by acting "rude and impertinent."

On November 4, the night manager of the Dallas central Western Union office observed "Oswald" picking up several money orders. Yet the real Oswald spent that evening with his wife and child in Irving. Four days later, when the real Oswald was working at the book depository, a man named Oswald brought a rifle into the Irving Sports Shop and had three holes drilled in it for a telescopic sight. Oswald's rifle had only two holes, and they had been drilled before Oswald had purchased the weapon.

On November 8, another weekday, a man giving his name as "Harvey Oswald" went into Hutchison's grocery store in Irving to cash a check for $189. The real Oswald never cashed checks for such large amounts in stores and was not in Irving at the time.

The next day, when the real Oswald was at work, "Oswald" test drove a car in Dallas and told the salesman, Albert Bogard, he would return in a couple of weeks when he would have "a lot of money" to buy the car. The real Oswald was supposed not to have been able to drive.

On November 10, while again the real Oswald was on the job at the book depository, "Oswald" applied for a job as a parking attendant at Allright Parking Systems in Dallas. As he talked with the manager, Hubert Morrow, "Oswald" asked whether the Southland Hotel overlooking the parking lot provided a good view of downtown Dallas.

Six days later, another weekday, "Oswald" was observed by several witnesses at the Sports Drome Rifle Range in Dallas firing a 6.5-mm Italian rifle with a four-power scope with remarkable accuracy. The witnesses had seen the same rifleman at the range once before firing the same rifle. This time "Oswald" called attention to himself by shooting at another rifleman's target. An altercation ensued, with "Oswald" acting particularly obnoxious. Witnesses later testified that this Oswald returned to the rifle range again, on the 20th and 21st, the two days preceding the assassination.

What are we to make of it all? The witnesses who observed "Oswald" participating in these suspicious activities have been investigated and found to be reliable. It therefore seems an inescapable conclusion that someone impersonating Oswald was methodically planting evidence against him in and around Dallas throughout October and November 1963, and may have been doing the same thing in Mexico City a few weeks earlier. Who was this impostor? Who was behind him? Wasn't his deployment in an assassination conspiracy more consistent with the modus operandi of an intelligence agency than with the traditional ways of a Mafia organization? Did Carlos Marcello possess the necessary contacts in the intelligence community to help him conceive of, locate, and direct such a conspirator?

Yes, Carlos most certainly did have such contacts. First of all, he admitted to FBI undercover operative Joseph Hauser in 1979 that he had played a role in the 1961–1963 CIA/Mafia plots to assassinate Fidel Castro. Second, even if this was merely a boast, we know for certain that he had close connections to individuals who were directly involved with the CIA/Mafia plots, including two of the principal Mafia conspirators, Johnny Roselli and Santos Trafficante. Either one could have easily put Carlos in touch with their CIA coconspirators. Third, Carlos's close friend in Washington, lobbyist Irving Davidson, often functioned as an unofficial lobbyist for the CIA on Capitol Hill. With a mere phone call, Davidson could have put Carlos Marcello in touch with most anyone in the CIA, including the director himself.

So Carlos Marcello was not lacking in contacts with CIA people sophisticated in the art of assassination. In fact, Carlos had CIA-connected contacts capable of offering him good advice on this score at his immediate beck and call in New Orleans in the fall of 1963. One of them not only had once worked closely with the CIA but had a reputation for being an unparalleled schemer. He was, in fact, employed in scheming for Carlos precisely during the month someone calling himself Oswald was busy planting evidence in Dallas against a man who would one day be accused of murdering the President of the United States.

26

Carlos and the Master of Intrigue

After Lee Harvey Oswald left New Orleans for Mexico City, and eventually for Dallas, in late September, Oswald's eccentric friend David Ferrie began meeting with Carlos Marcello on a regular basis, ostensibly to help plan Marcello's defense against the charges the federal government had brought against him at the instigation of Attorney General Kennedy.

During October Ferrie met with Marcello several times at the Mafia boss's office in the Town & Country Motel and traveled to Guatemala on business for Marcello twice, from the 11th to the 18th and from the 30th to November 1st, presumably on missions having to do with Carlos's forged Guatemalan birth certificate and passport, one of the burning issues in Carlos's upcoming trial. Then, in November, while the case of *The United States v. Carlos Marcello* was being tried in federal court, Ferrie, by his own admission, spent the weekends of November 9, 10 and 16, 17 with Marcello at Churchill Farms.

November 1963 promised to be the most important month of Carlos Marcello's life since he had assumed leadership of the Louisiana Mafia in 1947. On November 4 he was scheduled to go on trial in federal court in New Orleans in a case that threatened to set the stage for his permanent deportation. And around the time the jury was due to decide his fate, his nemesis' brother, President John F.

Kennedy, was due to visit Dallas. That Carlos chose to spend the two weekends prior to the jury's deliberations and the President's arrival in Texas with David Ferrie was a testament to how important Ferrie had become in Marcello's life.

On the surface, Carlos Marcello and David Ferrie were about as far apart in appearance, background, personality, and interests as could be imagined. Marcello had little formal education and remained but semiliterate all his life. Ferrie was fairly well educated, having received a B.A. in philosophy from Baldwin-Wallace College, and was a very articulate and persuasive public speaker. Carlos's considerable native intelligence was almost wholly devoted to acquiring and maintaining power; he was instinctively shrewd and cunning and had a sixth sense for detecting and exploiting human frailties. Ferrie, on the other hand, was deeply interested in psychology, aeronautics, philosophy, chemistry, and medicine, and, he was proud of his correspondence-course Ph.D. Socially, Carlos had an ingratiating personality, whereas Ferrie did not. Although he was occasionally given to outbursts of rage, and was famous for his defiant scowls, Carlos could pour on the charm when it was in his interest to do so, and many men and women felt attracted to him. Ferrie was just the opposite. He usually struck people as being highly obnoxious. Dogmatic and opinionated, he invariably sought to dominate discussions and was often intolerant of all opinions that differed from his own. So far as sexual orientation was concerned, Carlos was straight whereas Ferrie was homosexual. In appearance, the short, squat, bullnecked Carlos was always neat and well-groomed, while the tall, lanky Ferrie usually looked sloppy and unkempt, and, with his wig and fake eyebrows, often gave the impression of being somewhat of a clown. In temperament Carlos was, generally speaking, steady and dependable, while Ferrie was erratic and unstable. In their respective approaches to life and work, Carlos was eminently pragmatic, while Ferrie was driven by sudden enthusiasms and, as one writer put it, "wild idealisms."

But, as different as they were in many ways, Carlos Marcello and David Ferrie also had a lot in common. Ferrie was known to his associates in the Cuban exiles anti-Castro movement as "The Master of Intrigue." He delighted in weaving elaborate plots. Once he built two miniature submarines which he planned to deploy in a complex paramilitary operation to block Havana's harbor. As an investigator for Marcello's attorney G. Wray Gill and for private detective Guy Banister, Ferrie was highly valued as an imaginative schemer. Carlos was also a lover of intrigue. As he was to admit years later, he got a tremendous kick out of getting away with some outrageous exploit, like defrauding the Teamsters' pension fund out of $1 million a month. Marcello and Ferrie also shared an adventurous, entrepreneurial spirit. They were individualists, not team players; they thrived on taking risks. Both were also highly capable organizers. Carlos had put together a huge empire of legitimate and illegal enterprises that became the largest and most prosperous industry in his state. Ferrie had organized the civil air patrol in New Orleans into a highly respected unit during World War II. Carlos's extraordinary qualities of leadership derived, in part, from what many felt was an innate hypnotic power. The same power was observed of David Ferrie: he seemed to possess an unusual ability to persuade people to do his bidding, and was known to have practiced hypnosis.

What else did Marcello and Ferrie have in common? For one, both felt persecuted by the U.S. government, especially by the IRS. We know how Carlos felt about the government. Ferrie also had his grievances. Like Marcello, he had an almost paranoid fear of the IRS, which he believed had singled him out for special punishment.

Politically, Marcello and Ferrie were both right-wing extremists, militantly segregationist and anti-Communist. Sharing an intense desire to overthrow Castro, both worked hard on behalf of the Cuban exiles.

But what the two had most in common was a detestation of the Kennedy brothers. We know from Edward Becker, and others, how Marcello felt about John and Robert Kennedy. Ferrie was no less antagonistic toward the young President. After the failure of the Bay of Pigs operation, his speech before the New Orleans chapter of the Military Order of World Wars was cut short because his critical remarks on President Kennedy were so offensive. Later, an FBI report observed that Ferrie was "publicly and privately vitriolic about President Kennedy, and had stated, on occasion, that Kennedy 'ought to be shot.'"

As we shall see, it was probably Ferrie's violently critical attitude toward Kennedy that first brought him to Carlos's attention.

It will be recalled that David Ferrie had been fired as an Eastern Airlines pilot in 1961. Among the charges Eastern filed against him was his repeated vituperative remarks against President Kennedy. Representing Ferrie in his various grievance actions against Eastern Airlines was Carlos Marcello's New Orleans attorney, G. Wray Gill.

While working for Eastern, Ferrie had joined the New Orleans branch of the Cuban Revolutionary Council, a militant Cuban exiles group with headquarters in Miami, whose delegate in New Orleans was Sergio Arcacha Smith, a man described in an FBI report as "one of the more conspiratorial Cuban exiles leaders." One of Smith's chief financial backers was Carlos Marcello. In April 1961, Ferrie took a three-week vacation from Eastern, during which it is believed he played some role, perhaps as a pilot, in the invasion at the Bay of Pigs.

It was not long after the failure of the Bay of Pigs operation that Ferrie spoke out publicly against President Kennedy, blaming him for the military fiasco, and was subsequently discharged from Eastern. Immediately after his dismissal he became a full-time partner in Arcacha Smith's counterrevolutionary activities.

The illegal reentry into the United States of Carlos Marcello after his Central American exile coincided chronologically with David Ferrie's initial association with Arcacha Smith's Cuban Revolutionary Council. By the time Ferrie joined the Cuban exiles group, Carlos Marcello had already become associated with it. According to an FBI report of April 1961, Marcello had offered Arcacha Smith a deal whereby he would make "a very substantial donation" to the CRC in return for large concessions in Cuba after Castro's eventual overthrow.

It is now believed that the initial relationship between Carlos Marcello and David Ferrie may have developed out of their mutual association with Arcacha Smith and his Cuban Revolutionary Council and their mutual use of the legal services of G. Wray Gill.

According to Carlos Quiroga, an influential Cuban exile in New Orleans who was a member of the CRC, "Ferrie lent Arcacha Smith money whenever he needed it.... He had hundred dollar bills around all the time, even after he lost his job with the airline." Where did Ferrie get the money from? It is believed he got it from Carlos Marcello.

It is also believed that Carlos Marcello and David Ferrie met for the first time in the summer of 1961, perhaps only a month or two after Carlos's return from Guatemala. It was a fateful encounter. Carlos was full of hatred and resentment of the Kennedy brothers over his recent humiliating deportation to Guatemala, and Ferrie was consumed by similar passions over President Kennedy's "betrayal" of the Cuban exiles' cause in the Bay of Pigs. Once each became aware of the other's grievances against the Kennedys, they must have indulged in an orgy of loathing, recriminations, and vows to do something about the Kennedy menace. Working for Arcacha Smith's Cuban Revolutionary Council, which, after the Bay of Pigs fiasco, turned militantly anti-Kennedy, was one way of expressing their loathing. Within a year Ferrie and Marcello would find other ways to express what became for each an all-consuming hatred of the Kennedys.

According to an FBI interview of November 27, 1963, G. Wray Gill, impressed by the brilliance Ferrie had displayed in helping to prepare his own defense against Eastern Airlines, hired David Ferrie as a researcher and investigator in March 1962, a month after Ferrie had been taken on as an investigator by private detective Guy Banister. Ferrie did not become active in the Marcello case until the summer of 1963. However, it is believed that Ferrie and Marcello saw each other occasionally in 1962 in connection with their work on behalf of anti-Castro forces in New Orleans.

It will be recalled that it was in September 1962 that Carlos Marcello told Edward Becker that he was going to have President Kennedy killed and would set up a "nut" to take the blame. And it was in April 1963 that the Marcello-backed restaurant and bar owner Ben Tregle was overheard discussing plans he had evidently learned of from Anthony Marcello to kill President Kennedy when he came south later on in the year. Among those overhearing him was an unnamed individual known to the others as the "Professor."

Since David Ferrie frequented Marcello-backed bars and restaurants at the time and had made such a point of having himself listed in the New Orleans telephone directory as "Dr. David W. Ferrie, Psychologist," and was known to lecture people in a professorial manner in bars all over New Orleans, one wonders whether the "Professor" in Tregle's bar that April day was not David Ferrie.

As we know, Ferrie saw a good deal of Lee Harvey Oswald during the summer of 1963, while he was occasionally meeting with Carlos Marcello. It was not, however, until Oswald departed for Mexico City and Dallas that Ferrie went to work full-time for Gill and Marcello on the government's conspiracy and perjury case.

That case had a complicated history. The Justice Department had brought three charges against Carlos Marcello upon his surreptitious reentry into the United States in June 1961: conspiracy to commit fraud by obtaining a forged Guatemalan birth certificate and passport, perjury in swearing he had nothing to do with obtaining the forged certificate and passport, and unlawful reentry as a deported alien. Charged also on the first two counts was Carlos's brother Joseph.

It was the government's contention that, inasmuch as it had proof that Carlos Marcello had transmitted evidence of his false Guatemalan citizenship to Italian authorities, he had conspired to obstruct the government in the exercise of its right to deport him by attempting to influence the Italian government to refuse him entry.

How Carlos Marcello became a counterfeit citizen of Guatemala is one of the more bizarre episodes in his stranger-than-fiction life.

After Marcello had been ordered deported as an undesirable alien by the Immigration and Naturalization Service in 1953, he dispatched an emissary to Rome to thwart, through the bribery of key public officials, an eventual deportation to Italy. After Carlos's representative distributed around $25,000 in cash to various high-ranking functionaries, the Italian Foreign Ministry informed the U.S. government that since Marcello was not recognized as an Italian citizen, it would be unlikely that he would be accepted by the Republic of Italy for deportation.

For a while, then, Carlos felt reasonably safe. Then, in 1956, he received word from an informant that the government had persuaded Italy to accept him for deportation. Since Carlos felt no desire to be deported to Italy, it became necessary to invent a citizenship for him in a country in which he could function if the government's deportation order against him was ever implemented. Marcello huddled with his brothers, and they decided that Guatemala would be the most· appropriate country. Guatemala City was easily accessible to New Orleans by air, telephone, and telegraph, and Louisiana shrimping fleets regularly plied Guatemalan coastal waters. If he was exiled to Guatemala, it would not be too difficult for Carlos to occasionally board a shrimp boat, sail up through the Gulf of Mexico, and slip into the waters of his 6400-acre Louisiana swamp.

Accordingly Marcello dispatched an emissary to Guatemala to find out how the government there might make him a Guatemalan citizen and how much it would cost. To carry out this mission, Carlos turned to an acquaintance of his brother Joe, Carl I. Noll. An electrical engineer and international wheeler-dealer with a criminal record and a reputation as a con artist, Noll claimed to have valuable contacts with high officials in the Guatemalan government.

Noll flew back and forth between New Orleans and Guatemala City several times and eventually struck a deal with one Antonio Valladores, a former law partner of Guatemala's prime minister, Eduardo Rodriguez-Genis. For a substantial donation, Guatemalan citizenship for Mr. Marcello could be arranged.

Subsequently, Valladores, Noll, and two functionaries of Guatemala's Department of the Interior took a trip in a government car into the hill country surrounding Guatemala City in search of a births ledger whose February 1910 records showed a space between two other names, where the record of Calogero Minacore's birth could be inserted inconspicuously. Traveling from village to village, they finally found a suitable church ledger in San Jose Pinula. In order to execute a forgery that would stand up under the strictest scrutiny,

Valladores paid a local chemist versed in making ink $100 to prepare a special ink resembling that used in 1910, and gave another $100 to an elderly citizen of the village capable of writing the birth entry in the penmanship style of the 1910 records keeper.

Returning to Guatemala City, Valladores produced an affidavit attesting to the authenticity of Marcello's birth in San Jose Pinula on February 10, 1910. On the basis of this document, the government of Guatemala issued citizenship papers for Marcello bearing the president's signature and seal, along with a forged Guatemalan passport displaying Marcello's name and photograph.

Around 1953 there followed several trips by Valladores and Noll between Guatemala City and New Orleans, during which Marcello's new citizenship papers were shown to Carlos and his brother Joe and lawyers. After all were satisfied, Carlos paid Valladores for his efforts. Noll eventually testified that the sum given Valladores and Prime Minister Rodriguez-Genis was around $100,000, a figure that has never been substantiated.

Subsequently Carlos's deportation attorney, Jack Wasserman, transmitted evidence of his client's Guatemalan citizenship to the government of Italy.

Now, ten years later, the Justice Department was claiming that Carlos Marcello had used a false Guatemalan birth certificate to influence the Italian government to refuse him entry, and therefore had conspired to obstruct the U.S. government's efforts to deport him to that country.

Having publicly stated that one of the chief aims of his administration as attorney general was to effect the deportation of Carlos Marcello, Robert Kennedy had much of his reputation riding on his conspiracy case against the Louisiana Mafia leader. If the Justice Department lost, and there was good reason to suspect that it might, Kennedy stood to lose face not only with Marcello and other Mafia bosses but also with his stubborn and intractable FBI director, who had advised him against going after Marcello in the first place.

Complicating the Justice Department's case was the indisputable fact, remarked on by one of Kennedy's chief aides at the time of Marcello's deportation, that Robert Kennedy had knowingly used a forgery—Marcello's false Guatemalan birth record—to obtain an entry permit from the Guatemalan government so Marcello could be deported to Guatemala.

To do battle against the government, the Marcello brothers had assembled a crack defense team: G. Wray Gill of New Orleans, Mike Maroun of Shreveport, and Jack Wasserman of Washington, D.C. Gill, who was also to represent Joe Marcello, had represented Carlos during the Kefauver hearings; Maroun had joined the deported Carlos in Guatemala and had endured the ordeal in El Salvador and Honduras at his side; and Wasserman, who, as the former INS counsel, knew immigration law better than anyone in the INS itself, had fought the government's efforts to deport his client since 1953.

And then there was Carlos's mysterious ace in the hole, that master of intrigue David W. Ferrie. According to his own testimony to the FBI, Ferrie played a large role on Carlos's defense team.

Ferrie at the time was operating out of G. Wray Gill's offices in New Orleans' Pere Marquette Building. From October 1st to the 11th he conferred regularly with Gill in those offices and met with Carlos Marcello several times in the Mafia boss's office at the Town & Country Motel. Then on October 11th he took a Delta Airlines flight to Guatemala, where he remained until the 18th. There followed an interval in New Orleans during which he conferred again with Marcello and his lawyers; then, on October 30, he flew via Delta to Guatemala once more, returning to New Orleans on November 1.

What did Ferrie do on behalf of Marcello during his two visits to Guatemala in October? Carlos testified in 1978 that it was Ferrie's job to investigate the background and credibility of Carl Noll. But this had been Wasserman's job and had little to do with Guatemala. It seems more reasonable to surmise that Ferrie probably contacted Antonio Valladores and Eduardo Rodriguez-Genis, whom the U.S. government had indicted as coconspirators in the case, to make sure they would vouch for the authenticity of Marcello's Guatemalan birth certificate and passport and say nothing about Carl Noll's 1956 visit to Guatemala and donation for their services. In return for this favor, Marcello would make sure their efforts on his behalf would be rewarded. During the first trip Ferrie probably met with the two Guatemalans, presented Marcello's proposal to them, and obtained their response...and their monetary demands. These would then have been given to Marcello and his lawyers upon Ferrie's return to New Orleans on the 1st. On October 30, when Ferrie flew down to Guatemala again, he was presumably bearing Marcello's final wishes and a down payment for Valladores and Rodriguez-Genis to ensure those wishes would be respected.

Evidently David Ferrie performed his missions in Guatemala well. For soon thereafter he deposited over $7000 in his bank account. When questioned about Ferrie's deposit by the House Select Committee on Assassinations in 1978, Marcello stated that he had paid Ferrie for his help in preparing his defense against the charges brought against him by the Justice Department.

27

Ruby Consults the Mob

While Carlos Marcello and David Ferrie were holding their strategy sessions at the Town & Country Motel and Churchill Farms, and Marcello's lawyers were fighting for their client's freedom in a New Orleans courtroom, 400 miles away, in Dallas, a harried, debt-ridden Jack Ruby was busy telephoning his mob contacts throughout the country, including at least two with ties to the Marcello organization.

Ruby would one day insist that these calls, which he made mostly from five home and business phones, were all to gain advice and assistance regarding a problem he was having with the American Guild of Variety Artists (AGVA). As a nightclub owner, Ruby had to deal with that union in his relations with his strippers, singers, dancers, and rival nightclub owners in Dallas. However, AGVA, at the time, was controlled by the mob and, as such, had become little more than a dues collection agency. For the most part, it ignored the nightclub owners and exploited the B girls, strippers, and dancers who worked for them. Furthermore, the range and caliber of Ruby's contacts with mob figures throughout October and November 1963 were too broad to have had much to do with his problems with AGVA. Ruby would have made a fool of himself if he had telephoned all these mobsters to discuss his petty affairs with the union, his strippers, and what he believed was unfair competition from the other Dallas strip joints, his principal business problem at the time.

Ruby had not made many calls to his Mafia contacts in September, except to those who lived in the Dallas–Fort Worth area, but his telephone records show that in October and November he suddenly felt compelled to phone Mafia pals from all over the country he hadn't been in touch with for years, others he didn't know at all. Coincidentally, the step-up in suspicious calls followed the White House's confirmation in late September that President Kennedy would be visiting Dallas on November 21 and 22.

The first suspicious out-of-state call Ruby made in October was a thirteen-minute one on the third of the month to the home of a former business associate of his, Russell D. Mathews, in Shreveport, Louisiana. Mathews, an ex-convict described by the House Assassinations Committee as "a burglar, armed robber, narcotics pusher, and murderer," was an associate of Santos Trafficante, Jr., and Joseph Campisi, both of whom were, as we know, close to Carlos Marcello. Russell Mathews was not in when Ruby called; Ruby spoke with his wife, Elizabeth, whom Ruby had never met. Since Russell and Elizabeth Mathews had recently divorced, it is assumed Ruby called Elizabeth to find out where Russell was.

A few days after the call to Mrs. Mathews, Ruby was spotted in the New Orleans French Quarter district in a striptease joint owned by Frank Caracci, another associate of Carlos Marcello, and the next day he was seen in Pete Marcello's Bourbon Street hot spot, the Sho-Bar. Not long after that, FBI agents assigned to surveil Las Vegas mobster Johnny Roselli reported that Ruby and Roselli had met in a Miami motel.

Upon his return to Dallas, Ruby made several out-of-state calls throughout October that did not appear to be suspicious. But toward the end of the month, after a mysterious trip to Las Vegas, he made five calls that were most definitely suspicious. Three of these calls, made on October 25, 26, and 31, were to California recording company executive Michael Shore, who was a friend of West Coast mobster Mickey Cohen and a close associate of the Chicago bail bondsman for the mob Irwin S. Weiner. After the call to Shore on the 26th, Ruby made a twelve-minute call to Weiner, whom he had never met, at his Chicago home.

Weiner, at the time, was one of the most powerful associates of the Chicago Mafia, known as "The Outfit". The House Assassinations Committee linked him to such criminal activities as arson, extortion, Medicare fraud, gambling, bribery, and murder, and noted he was closely associated with Chicago Mafia boss Sam Giancana, Teamsters' chief Jimmy Hoffa, and Florida boss Santos Trafficante, Jr. That Ruby called a man of Weiner's stature in the underworld to discuss his petty problems with the other Dallas strip joints strains credulity.

According to Ruby's sister, Eva Grant, after her brother called Weiner, he put in a call to a Chicago thug he had known in his youth, Lenny Patrick, a notorious member of Chicago's Outfit, suspected of having masterminded a dozen or so contract murders. Then, not long after that call, on October 30, Ruby made one of his most suspicious calls of the month, a one-minute call to Marcello Lieutenant Nofio Pecora at his Tropical Court Motel in New Orleans. But how suspicious is a one-minute call? Brief calls are standard practice in the underworld. They serve to alert the person phoned to stand by for a longer call from a public telephone or the home of a trusted friend.

Equally suspicious was a seven- to ten-minute call on November 7 that Ruby received from Barney Baker, a close aide to Jimmy Hoffa whom Robert Kennedy had described in his book *The Enemy Within* as Hoffa's "roving organizer and ambassador of violence." "Sometimes the mere threat of his presence in a room," wrote Kennedy, "was enough to silence men who would otherwise have opposed Hoffa's reign." The huge, six-foot-four, 370-pound Baker had been released from federal prison only a few weeks before he phoned Ruby. The following day Ruby made a fourteen-minute call to Baker at his Chicago apartment. Baker's boss, Jimmy Hoffa, was close to both Carlos Marcello and Santos Trafficante, and in the summer of 1962, in the presence of Louisiana Teamsters official Edward G. Partin, Hoffa had threatened to murder the Kennedy brothers.

On the same day he called Baker, Ruby placed a four-minute call to another Hoffa associate, Murray W. "Dusty" Miller, head of the southern conference of Teamsters and, according to the House Assassinations Committee, a man "associated with numerous underworld figures." Then, on November 17, Ruby received an eight-minute call from an old friend from his Chicago days, ex-convict Al Gruber. A former associate of Mickey Cohen and Jimmy Hoffa, Gruber was described by the House Assassinations Committee as a man who had a criminal record of "six arrests under three different names." Later on in the month, Gruber would visit Ruby in Dallas.

These calls made during the fifty-three days preceding the assassination of President Kennedy are the only suspicious calls made or received by Jack Ruby of which there are records. Most likely there were other calls made to the same or different mobsters from locations other than Ruby's apartment, his sister Eva's apartment, and his various places of business that were equally suspicious. The calls in question suggest that some sort of conspiracy involving Ruby and the underworld was in the making. Whether this possible conspirational activity was linked to the coming assassination of President Kennedy, or to Ruby's murder of the President's alleged assassin, or to some other as yet undetermined crime, is not known. What is clear is that a substantial number of powerful men associated with organized crime knew of Jack Ruby in the fall of 1963. They probably knew that he was broke, that he had extensive connections in the Dallas Police force, and that he was available for any assignment one of the big boys might give him.

By the third week of November it appears that Ruby had done something, or had promised to do something for the mob, and had been rewarded. For, after his trip to Las Vegas, and several meetings with Al Gruber and another old friend, Paul Roland Jones, who was known as the mob's paymaster in Dallas, Ruby went to Graham Koch, his tax attorney, on November 19 and told him he had a connection who would supply him money to settle his long-standing problems with the IRS. Four days before seeing Koch, Ruby bought a safe for the first time in his sixteen years as a Dallas nightclub operator and told an associate he was going to set it in concrete in his office. Ordinarily preferring not to keep money in the bank lest the IRS or other creditors place liens on his account, Ruby kept cash in his apartment—in bureau drawers, manila envelopes, and cookie jars. The safe, then, was an extraordinary thing. Soon he would be seen by the loan officer of his bank, William J. Cox, with $7000 in cash on his person, which he did not deposit into his account.

28

The United States v. Carlos Marcello: November 4–22

On the morning of November 1, 1963, in a federal courtroom in New Orleans, the final showdown began in Carlos Marcello's ten-year battle to avoid deportation.

The courtroom was packed. Among the many spectators, almost the entire Marcello family was on hand to hear Judge Herbert W. Christenberry charge Carlos and his brother Joe with "conspiracy to defraud the United States government by obtaining a false Guatemalan birth certificate" and "conspiracy to obstruct the United States government in the exercise of its right to deport Carlos Marcello."

The Marcello family was up in arms over the charges, which they knew had originated with Bobby Kennedy and which they believed were grossly unfair. What galled the family was their conviction that Bobby Kennedy had illegally deported Carlos in the first place. Jack Wasserman had made it clear to all of them that the Justice Department had knowingly used a false Guatemalan birth certificate to fraudulently obtain a permit of entry for Carlos from the Guatemalan government, and hence the original deportation action had been illegal. Now, they believed, a vindictive Bobby Kennedy was trying to get back at Carlos for having had the guts to defy the deportation order and reenter the country.

The Marcello forces were determined to prevail over the government in what they conceived was a duel to the finish with Attorney General Kennedy. Nothing was to stand in the way of victory. No means were to be spared in denying the government a conviction.

Meanwhile, in Washington, D.C., an anxious Robert Kennedy was taking a personal, as well as an official, interest in the Marcello trial, knowing full well how much of his own prestige was riding on its outcome. The deportation of Marcello had been a messy affair, and he had taken a good deal of criticism over it. Not the least of that criticism had come from his FBI director, who, it will be recalled, had been reluctant to move against Marcello in the first place.

Then, with his defiant reentry, Marcello had all but spat in Kennedy's face. Although it was not the attorney general's custom to phone up every U.S. attorney about to try a case for the government, Kennedy placed a call to his chief prosecutor in New Orleans, Louis C. La Cour, the day before the trial was to begin, to wish him well.

The first three days of *The United States v. Carlos Marcello* were taken up by jury selection, the reading of the charges, and Jack Wasserman's opening attack on the government's star witness, Carl I. Noll, who was then superintendent of electricians at a Minuteman base in North Dakota. Contending that Noll had a history of mental illness, Wasserman challenged his competency. He also raised the issue of Noll's criminal record: four felony convictions on charges ranging from grand larceny to the interstate transportation of stolen property.

On the fourth day, Noll, having survived Wasserman's challenges, took the stand and related the long, complex story of his mission to Guatemala on Marcello's behalf—all of which made front-page headlines in the New Orleans papers. On the fifth day, a Friday, Noll completed his initial testimony by telling the court that the Marcello brothers had promised to pay him $25,000 for his services and then never did. He also hinted that Carlos had paid a bribe of $100,000 to Antonio Valladores and Eduardo Rodriguez-Genis for the forged citizenship documents.

Among Marcello's legion of supporters attending the opening sessions of the trial was David Ferrie, who had returned from his last mission to Guatemala on November 1. Since then he had spent most of his time on the Marcello case, attending the courtroom sessions and conferring before and after those sessions with Carlos and his defense team. On the second day of the trial, November 5, he bought, by his own admission, a .38 revolver, and several days later the normally impecunious Ferrie deposited in his account in the Whitney National Bank the $7093 Marcello later admitted paying him for his paralegal services.

Ferrie and Marcello were due to spend the weekends of November 9, 10 and 16, 17 together at Churchill Farms. When, on November 25, Ferrie was questioned by the FBI about those two weekend visits, he replied that he had gone there "to map out strategy for Marcello's trial."

But what was Carlos Marcello doing planning strategy with David Ferrie when he had such brilliant legal talent available as G. Wray Gill, Mike Maroun, and the foremost deportation attorney in the country, Jack Wasserman? And why would Marcello have chosen the inaccessible Churchill Farms, whose farmhouse did not even have a phone, for his weekend "strategy" sessions with Ferrie, when his office at the Town & Country Motel was so much more convenient and so much better equipped?

Could it have been that Marcello and Ferrie were planning some other, separate, strategy together in the remote impenetrable seclusion of Churchill Farms?

Fourteen months had passed since Carlos had met in the same farmhouse with Edward Becker and Carlo Roppolo and had impulsively threatened to have President Kennedy murdered in order to neutralize his brother Bobby. Now Carlos was being tried in federal court on charges Bobby had brought against him, and the President would be down in his territory in two weeks.

Whatever the truth was behind David Ferrie's presence at Churchill Farms over the weekends of November 9, 10 and 16, 17, one fact remains indisputable: over the last two weekends before Lee Harvey Oswald allegedly murdered the President of the United States, a friend of Oswald's, David W. Ferrie, was conferring with a Mafia leader who had already threatened to have the President killed.

Judging from what we now know about the trial of Carlos and Joseph Marcello, we can piece together more or less what the trial strategy was from the weekend of November 9, 10 on, and it does not appear that David Ferrie could have played much of a role in devising it.

On the legal front, the principal strategy was to attempt to discredit the testimony of the government's star witness, Carl I. Noll, so as to cast doubt on his account of Marcello bribing Guatemalan officials to obtain a fraudulent Guatemalan birth certificate. This Jack Wasserman hoped to accomplish by calling several witnesses who had had dealings with Noll in the past. A secondary strategy was to try to show that Marcello's Guatemalan citizenship papers would not have influenced Italy's decision about accepting him as a deportee, and hence Marcello's forwarding the documents to the Italian Consulate in New Orleans was not a conspirational act designed to thwart the government's attempt to deport him. To implement this strategy, a former high-ranking Italian government official would be called to testify.

On the other front, the battleground outside the law, the Marcellos' principal strategy was to terrorize, and possibly eliminate, Carl Noll and bribe as many jurors as they could reach.

After casting around unsuccessfully for a way to fix the jury, the Marcellos finally hit upon a possible solution through the intercession of an old friend, George Alamilla, an important chicken farmer who was living and working in Belize (formerly British Honduras) at the time. Alamilla had known one of the jurors, Rudolph Heitler, for many years, and believed he could get to him on behalf of his good friend Carlos.

George Alamilla flew up to New Orleans from Belize on November 14. The Marcellos' trial had been under way for ten days, and there was little time to lose.

Carlos always dealt through intermediaries, and so he turned over the matter of fixing juror Heitler, through his old friend Alamilla, to his principal partner in the Pelican Tomato Company, Joe Matassa, without ever seeing Alamilla during his short stay in New Orleans. On November 17, while Carlos Marcello was meeting with David Ferrie at Churchill Farms, Alamilla met with Matassa at the Pelican Tomato Company's premises in New Orleans' French market. It was agreed that Matassa would furnish the money to bribe Heitler from Marcello's account at Pelican, in return for his not-guilty vote when the jury deliberated in about five days.

That same evening George Alamilla went to the home of his dear old friend, Rudolph Heitler. After some discussion, Heitler agreed to vote not guilty and to try to influence other members of the jury to do the same. For this he would expect a payment from Carlos Marcello of from $25,000 to $100,000.

When, later on, Alamilla told Joe Matassa how much Heitler wanted, Matassa balked. He told Alamilla to tell Heitler that The Little Man would pay him some decent money, but not that much, and that Heitler should be happy about the deal, whatever it was, because he would have in Carlos a "close friend for life."

As time was rapidly running out, there ensued a series of tense discussions between Alamilla, Heitler, and Matassa. Finally on November 20 Matassa gave Alamilla $600 to give to Heitler as a "good faith" payment. Heitler was to be told that the larger payment would come after he and the other jurors found "Uncle Carlos" not guilty.

As for the plan to take care of prosecution star witness Carl Noll, the Marcellos apparently resorted to out-of-state talent. According to records of Carlos's 1964–1965 trial for obstruction of justice, "in requesting the murder of Carl Noll" the Marcellos recruited an associate from Mississippi. In the end, Noll's life was spared in return for his occasional memory lapses at the trial.

Neither of these two extralegal strategies appears to have demanded the participation of David Ferrie, whose name never came up in the 1964–1965 obstruction of justice trial. Alamilla and Matassa, acting on Carlos Marcello's orders, had assumed the task of bribing juror Heitler. One of Carlos's closest lieutenants had, no doubt, been given the assignment of threatening Carl Noll and recruiting the associate in Mississippi to have Noll executed in the event he did not capitulate to the threats. As for legal strategies, it was Jack Wasserman who had obtained most of the derogatory information on Noll and who had located the witnesses who were willing to help undermine Noll's credibility. It was he and Wray Gill who had recruited the ex-Italian government official as a defense witness.

No, it appears reasonably certain that David Ferrie, who had no legal training whatsoever, could not have been much involved in mapping out strategy for Marcello's defense. Certainly the brilliant Wasserman, former chief counsel of the Immigration and Naturalization Service, would not have relied heavily on an eccentric amateur given to "wild idealisms" like Ferrie. And Carlos himself had been perfectly capable of mapping out the strategy of threatening Noll and bribing Heitler.

After Carlos's first weekend with Ferrie at Churchill Farms, the trial reopened on Tuesday, November 12, with Wasserman cross-examining Carl Noll, a grilling that lasted most of the week. Noll, who was now in fear of his life, often appeared confused on the stand. By the time Wasserman was through with him, he had succeeded in exposing several inconsistencies in Noll's account of his mission to Guatemala for the Marcellos.

Meanwhile, in Dallas, where President Kennedy was due to arrive on the 22nd, the Oswald impostor had recently made several clamorous appearances: four in Irving, one at an automobile showroom, and one at the Sports Drome Rifle Range. And Jack Ruby had recently placed calls to Nofio Pecora and Barney Baker.

As for the real Oswald, he had spent the weekend of November 9, 10 with his wife and child in Irving, returning to Dallas and his work at the Book Depository on Monday the 11th.

Three days later, on Thursday, November 14, Secret Service agent Winston Lawson decided upon the route President Kennedy's motorcade would take in Dallas on November 22. Details were communicated to the Dallas Police the following day. One of them indicated that the motorcade would pass through Dealey Plaza, via Main Street, not too far from the Book Depository where Lee Harvey Oswald worked.

Over the weekend of November 16, 17, the real Oswald disappeared entirely from view, and his whereabouts on those two days still remain unknown. Usually, if Lee did not visit his wife in Irving on the weekend, he would call her, but on Saturday the 16th he did not call. When on the 17th Marina's friend Ruth Paine called him at the number he had left with her, she was told there was no Lee Harvey Oswald living there, but there was a Mr. O. H. Lee and he was not in. This prompted Mrs. Paine to notify the FBI, which was supposed to be keeping Oswald under surveillance, that Oswald was living in Dallas under an assumed name and could not be reached by phone over the weekend of November 16, 17.

It was over that weekend that the Oswald impostor was observed at target practice at Dallas Sports Drome rifle range, and Carlos Marcello and David Ferrie held their last strategy session at Churchill Farms. Since by then the Dallas Police had been informed by the Secret Service of the route the President's motorcade would take, it is conceivable that one of Marcello's contacts in the Dallas Police Department might have passed along that information to Carlos on either the 16th or the 17th.

On Monday the 18th, the Chief of the Secret Service unit in Dallas, Forrest Sorrels, made a slight change in the motorcade route, for reasons that remain unclear, that provided for an abrupt dogleg turn to the right in Dealey Plaza from Main Street onto Houston Street and then another abrupt turn, this time to the left, onto Elm Street. This would bring the presidential motorcade right under the windows of the Book Depository where Lee Harvey Oswald worked and almost within spitting distance of the picket fence on the grassy knoll. This unprecedented route change was then communicated to both Dallas papers, the *Morning News* and the *Times-Herald*, which published the amended route on Tuesday, November 19th, three days before the assassination.

What "strategy" might Marcello and Ferrie have discussed in the farmhouse on Churchill Farms the weekend of November 16, 17?

We can imagine the scene. The incongruous pair in the small, isolated house in the midst of Marcello's sprawling 6400-acre swamp. The short, gruff 53-year-old Mafia boss and his tall, voluble 45-year-old "master of intrigue" getting down to business around the same kitchen table at which Edward Becker and Carlo Roppolo had sat with Carlos fourteen months before. For Carlos, it was down to the wire. By the end of next week he would learn the outcome of his two-and-a-half-year battle with Robert Kennedy.

Sixteen years later the House Select Committee on Assassinations would cast a very suspicious eye on Marcello's meeting with David Ferrie over the weekend preceding the assassination of President Kennedy. That the whereabouts over that same weekend of the man who would be accused of assassinating the President still remains unknown, despite the diligent efforts of scores of researchers, casts further suspicions on the meeting.

And so, on Monday, November 18, the last week of the Marcello trial began. Throughout the week crucial testimony was heard from three witnesses for the defense.

Dr. Paolo Alberto Rossi, an attorney from Rome with thirty years' experience in the Italian diplomatic service, who had been Italian consul in New Orleans from 1927 to 1931, testified that if the Italian Ministry of Foreign Affairs had given its consent to Marcello's deportation, eleventh-hour evidence in the form of a Guatemalan birth certificate would have had little effect on the deportation proceedings.

Ben Probst, a North Carolina highway contractor, testified that Carl Noll had swindled $10,000 out of him and had lied about the events of a trip to Guatemala he had made on his behalf to lease highway equipment to the Guatemalan government.

And Mrs. Yvonne Klein, a Wilmette, Illinois, building contractor, testified that Noll had swindled $50,000 out of her during trips he had made to Guatemala in connection with a $200 million construction project her company was involved in with the Guatemalan government.

Meanwhile, in the midst of this testimony, on Wednesday, November 20, Robert Kennedy celebrated his 38th birthday at a raucous party in his office at the Justice Department. Standing on top of his desk, in shirt-sleeves and loosened tie, surrounded by well-wishers, he commented with tongue in cheek on how much the stories of his war on the Mafia, his "persecution" of labor union bosses, and his use of wiretapping were going to benefit his brother's forthcoming campaign for a second term. Later on in the day, he was briefed by an aide on the progress of the Marcello trial and was assured all was going well. A favorable verdict was expected in a couple of days. For Friday the 22nd, Kennedy had scheduled a top-level meeting on organized crime to be attended by his personal staff and U.S. attorneys from all over the nation. He was looking forward to giving them the good news from New Orleans as soon as it came in.

On Thursday, November 21, the defense of Carlos and Joseph Marcello had rested its case, and President John F. Kennedy landed in Texas for a political tour. He visited San Antonio first, then Houston, before going on to Fort Worth to spend the night.

The following day, closing arguments were to be heard and a New Orleans jury would render a verdict in the case of *The United States v. Carlos Marcello*. The court proceedings would unfold during President John F. Kennedy's visit to Dallas, where he was scheduled to ride in a motorcade through the city before delivering a major address.

29

Plans and Preparations: November 20–21

On the morning of Wednesday, November 20, President John F. Kennedy had breakfast with the leaders of Congress in the White House. He touched briefly on his forthcoming trip to Texas. Despite the warnings of many that he should not go, he was flying to Houston, and then to Fort Worth/Dallas, the following day. It was to be a political trip, aimed at luring Texans to vote for him in the 1964 presidential election.

That same morning, in the center of Dallas, two police officers on routine patrol entered Dealey Plaza, through which the presidential motorcade would pass on Friday, and noticed several men standing behind a wooden fence on a grassy knoll overlooking the plaza. The men were engaged in what appeared to be mock target practice, aiming rifles over the fence in the direction of the plaza. The two police officers immediately made for the fence, but by the time they got there the riflemen had disappeared, having departed in a car that had been parked nearby. The two patrol officers did not give much thought to the incident at the time, but after the assassination of the President two days later, they reported the incident to the FBI, which issued a report of it on November 26. For reasons that have never been satisfactorily explained, the substance of the report was never mentioned in the FBI's investigation of the assassination, and the report itself disappeared until 1978, when it finally resurfaced as a result of a Freedom of Information Act request.

Late the night of Wednesday the 20th, near Eunice, Louisiana, Lt. Francis Fruge of the Louisiana State Police picked up an injured woman from the roadside and brought her to a state hospital in Jackson, Louisiana. The woman's name was Rose Cheramie, and she was a prostitute and heroin addict.

On the way to the hospital Miss Cheramie told Lieutenant Fruge that she had been making a "drug run" from Miami to Houston with two Italian male companions. They had stopped at a roadside bar and restaurant near Eunice. She had gotten a little high, and her companions had abandoned her. The owner of the restaurant then threw her out of his place. While she was trying to hitch a ride, she was grazed by a car and was slightly injured. Shortly after that, Lt. Fruge picked her up from the roadside.

As the police officer and Miss Cheramie were driving to the hospital at Jackson, Cheramie informed Lieutenant Fruge that her two male companions had told her that after a stop in Houston they were going to Dallas, where they would kill President Kennedy on the 22nd. Cheramie further elaborated to Lt. Fruge that "word was out in the underworld that Kennedy would soon be killed."

Lt. Fruge did not pay much attention that night to Cheramie's ramblings about an impending Kennedy assassination, but two days later, after he was notified of the assassination in Dallas, he went to the hospital in Jackson to order Miss Cheramie held for questioning. There he found out that on November 21 she had told two of her doctors that President Kennedy would be killed the following day. When Fruge reported Miss Cheramie's prediction to the Dallas Police, he was literally laughed out of court. They already had their man, a "commie nut" who had acted without confederates.

In the late afternoon of Thursday, November 21, that "commie nut," Lee Harvey Oswald, forsook his furnished room in Dallas for his wife's apartment in suburban Irving. He was driven there by Wesley Frazier, a coworker at the Texas School Book Depository who was a neighbor of Mrs. Oswald. According to Marina Oswald's later testimony, her husband spent a restless night in the marriage bed.

That same evening, in Dallas, around 10:00 P.M., Jack Ruby stopped by the city's principal underworld hangout, Joe Campisi's Egyptian Lounge. There he had dinner with a business associate, Ralph Paul, and had a few words with Campisi, who, it will be recalled, was a good friend of Carlos Marcello. Ruby ended up the evening at Lucas' B&B restaurant, where he was spotted by waitress Mary Lawrence with a man who, she later testified, "appeared very similar" to photographs of Lee Harvey Oswald she had seen in the papers. The real Oswald was in bed with his wife in Irving at the time. Was this the Oswald double?

Meanwhile President and Mrs. Kennedy arrived at the Hotel Texas in Fort Worth, where they would spend the night before embarking on the motorcade through Dallas the following morning.

On the morning of Friday, November 22, at around 8:20, while the President was preparing to address a group of supporters in the parking lot of the Hotel Texas, Lee Harvey Oswald left the apartment in Irving and drove with Wesley Frazier to the Texas School Book Depository. According to Frazier's later testimony, Oswald brought a long, thin package with him that he told Frazier contained some curtain rods for his room in Dallas. Frazier later suspected that the package contained the assassination weapon. However, witnesses at the Book Depository stated that Oswald was not carrying anything when he entered the depository and reported for work.

Around 11:00 A.M., a 23-year-old Dallas woman named Julia Ann Mercer was driving west on Elm Street through Dealey Plaza, past the Book Depository, when she had to stop because a green truck, parked on the curb, was blocking her lane. After a wait of a few minutes she saw a young man get out of the passenger's side of the truck, go around to the tool compartment, take out a package that looked to her like a wrapped-up rifle, then walk up the embankment to the grassy knoll with the package.

As the time for the arrival in Dealey Plaza of the presidential motorcade approached, various witnesses noticed suspicious activity both behind the grassy knoll and in the Texas School Book Depository.

As he was awaiting the motorcade, Howard Brennan, a construction worker, noticed a man in the sixth-floor southeast window of the Book Depository holding a rifle. Arnold Rowland also saw someone holding a rifle in a sixth-floor window, but it was in the southwest corner window, not the southeast. Carolyn Walther believed she saw two men in a fifth-floor window, one of whom was holding a gun. Some inmates of the Dallas County Jail overlooking Dealey Plaza thought they saw someone on the fifth floor with a gun. Two amateur photographers, Charles Bronson and Robert Hughes, took moving pictures of the depository six minutes before the motorcade arrived that revealed two men roving from window to window on the sixth floor of the depository. As the motorcade approached, Lee

Bowers, a railroad employee stationed on a control tower overlooking the train tracks behind the grassy knoll, observed two men behind the fence peering out over the plaza. Earlier he had noticed three unauthorized vehicles enter the parking lot and park by the fence.

Finally around 12:29 P.M. the motorcade appeared, slowing down to round the curve from Houston to Elm Street, and entered Dealey Plaza. One minute later shots rang out from what appeared to the many witnesses watching the motorcade to be two locations, the grassy knoll and the Book Depository. President Kennedy was struck at least two, possibly three or four, times. The fatal shot literally exploded his head. By 1:00 P.M. he was pronounced dead at Dallas's Parkland Hospital.

30

The Verdict: November 22

By 9:00 A.M. the courtroom in New Orleans was filled to overflowing, causing many would-be spectators to remain standing outside in the hallway. The New Orleans press had given the trial of Carlos and Joseph Marcello front-page headlines, thereby attracting a horde of curiosity seekers anxious to catch a glimpse of the Marcello clan.

Those who had been able to squeeze into the courtroom were not disappointed. Practically the entire family was on hand to hear the opposing attorneys present final arguments and await the jury's verdict. Forming a compact phalanx in the front rows of the courtroom were the clan's white-haired 70-year-old matriarch, Louise Marcello, surrounded by five of her sons—Vincent, Pascal, Anthony, Sammy, and Peter—and their wives and her daughters Rose and Mary and their husbands. Carlos's wife, Jacqueline, sat near them with her four children—Joseph, Florence, Louise, and Jackie Jr.—together with a dozen or so of their cousins. With defendants Carlos and Joseph completing the family tableau, the curious reveled in their once-in-a-lifetime opportunity to behold almost the entire clan, normally so reluctant to appear in public, all together in one place.

And so the closing arguments commenced. In his summation, Jack Wasserman reeled off a long list of falsehoods he contended Carl Noll had told the court, calling him a "swindler, con man, and fraud" who continually contradicted himself. In rebuttal, U.S. Attorney Louis La Cour admitted to Noll's "past bad record" and claimed that the government had never held Noll up to be anything more than what he was, telling the jury that "the choice as to Noll was not made by the government; it was made by the Marcellos" and concluding by asserting that the government had produced adequate independent substantiation of most of Noll's testimony.

While Wasserman and La Cour were presenting their arguments in New Orleans, Attorney General Kennedy was presiding over a meeting on organized crime at the Justice Department in Washington, the second session of a two-day conference, attended by his entire personal staff and U.S. attorneys from every state. Among the major items on the agenda were the investigations of Sam Giancana, Santos Trafficante, Jimmy Hoffa, and Carlos Marcello.

Aware that the trial of Marcello and his brother was ending that day, Kennedy was hoping that after a lunch break at his McLean, Virginia, estate, he would be able to report an important government victory to the conferees. The victory, he would tell them, would clear the way for Marcello's definitive, permanent deportation.

By 1:30 P.M., New Orleans time, the closing arguments of the opposing attorneys were over and Judge Herbert W. Christenberry had just delivered his fifteen-minute charge to the jury.

Just as the judge was about to officially hand the case to the jury, a bailiff suddenly strode into the courtroom and, going up to the bench, handed the judge a note. As Judge Christenberry read it, a look of shock and consternation spread over his face. Recovering quickly, he stood up and announced that President John F. Kennedy had just been shot in Dallas and was feared dead.

A wave of commotion swept over the courtroom as everyone began talking at once. Soon the courtroom was in an uproar and had to be quieted by the judge. Christenberry then handed the case to the jury and called for an hour's recess. Carlos and Joe, showing no emotion, filed out of the courtroom with their attorneys.

Meanwhile, Robert Kennedy had gone to his Virginia estate, Hickory Hill, for lunch, taking with him two of his conferees, Robert M. Morgenthau, U.S. attorney for the southern district of New York, and the chief of Morgenthau's criminal division, Silvio Mollo. They were having clam chowder and tuna fish sandwiches by the pool when, around 2:15 Washington time, the phone rang and it was J. Edgar Hoover for the attorney general. Picking up the receiver, Bobby Kennedy heard his FBI director say, in a laconic monotone: "I have news for you...the President's been shot," adding: "I think it's serious...I'll call you back when I find out more." Thirty minutes later Hoover phoned again and told Kennedy just as laconically and unemotionally as before: "The President's dead." Bobby then called off the afternoon session of his conference on organized crime; the group would never meet again.

By 3:00 P.M., New Orleans time, the court in the matter of *The United States v. Carlos Marcello* had reconvened and was awaiting the jury's verdict. Then, at 3:15, the twelve jurors reentered the court-room and Judge Christenberry asked the foreman if the jury had reached a verdict.

Carlos and Joseph Marcello, both wearing dark-blue suits and dark ties, listened impassively as the foreman read the verdict on the con-spiracy charges: not guilty; then on the perjury charges: not guilty. It was a total acquittal.

With his nemesis dead and the government's case against him de-cided in his favor, November 22, 1963, had to have been the most triumphant day of Marcello's life.

After embracing his attorneys and receiving congratulations from his family, friends, and supporters, the squat Mafia boss, with his head held high and a determined look on his face, strode out of the court-house arm in arm with his wife to a waiting car, followed by a swarm of Marcellos. According to one source, Carlos seemed "all business," and, forgoing a family celebration, left his wife and children off at the house while he went to his office in the Town & Country Motel, "looking as if he had something urgent on his mind."

Early that evening, George Alamilla and Rudolph Heitler met at New Orleans International Airport just before Alamilla was to board his return flight to Belize. At their meeting, Heitler told Alamilla that not only had he voted not guilty at the Marcellos' trial but he had also convinced several of his fellow jurors to vote not guilty. Alamilla then told his old friend he had done a great job and should go see Joe Matassa the next day to receive his reward.

What happened in the weeks and months ahead bore out the truth of the Sicilian proverb Marcello had blurted out at his September 1962 meeting with Ed Becker and Carlo Roppolo at Churchill Farms. With the head cut off, the dog would die, "tail and all." Jimmy Hoffa expressed the new order of things aptly when, after he was told of the Kennedy assassination, he snarled: "Bobby Kennedy is just an-other lawyer now."

Perhaps even less than that. After his brother's assassination,

Robert Kennedy, consumed with grief and guilt, became, in the words of one of the Justice Department's attorneys at the time, "nonfunctioning." To his slain brother's press secretary, Pierre Salinger, "he was the most shattered man" he had ever seen. Before long, Bobby's war against the mob began to wind down. Although Carlos would later be indicted for attempting to bribe juror Heitler and threatening to kill Carl Noll, for all intents and purposes the war with the Kennedys was over.

PART V

Aftermath

NOVEMBER 22, 1963— AUGUST 17, 1965

"Nothing can be honorable when there is no justice."

—*Cicero*

31

New Orleans

After receiving news of his victory over the U.S. government and Attorney General Robert Kennedy and also, almost simultaneously, word of the assassination of President Kennedy, Carlos Marcello went straight from the federal courthouse to his office in the Town & Country Motel. It was there, in his inner sanctum, that he probably learned for the first time that one of his boys, Dutz Murret's kid, had been taken into custody by the Dallas Police on suspicion of murdering a police officer and possibly also President John F. Kennedy.

If Marcello was involved in a conspiracy to assassinate the President, as a congressional subcommittee would one day guardedly suspect he had been, he was confronted with an urgent problem in the late afternoon of November 22. As soon as he learned that Oswald had been taken into custody, he would have been faced with the necessity of taking immediate action: a way would have to be found to prevent Oswald from opening his mouth, and the job would have to be done in the headquarters of the Dallas Police Department.

We have but a few hints of what Carlos Marcello did over the weekend of the Kennedy assassination. The author has located only two printed references to Marcello immediately following the conclusion of his trial and the assassination, aside from articles in the New Orleans papers about his acquittal. One comes from an FBI report on David Ferrie's postassassination activities, indicating that Ferrie telephoned Carlos Marcello's Town & Country office from a motel in Houston shortly after noon on Saturday, November 23. The other comes from the transcript of Marcello's 1964–1965 trial for jury tampering and obstruction of justice, which reveals that early in the week of November 25, Carlos's partner in the Pelican Tomato Company, Joe Matassa, told ex-juror Rudolph Heitler, in response to Heitler's repeated protests about not yet receiving the payment promised him for his not-guilty vote, that he, Matassa, was having a lot of trouble contacting "The Little Man."

From the scant information available, then, it would appear that during the weekend following the Kennedy assassination Carlos Marcello spent some time working in his Town & Country office, and that during the following week, after Jack Ruby had rubbed out the President's suspected assassin, he probably spent a good deal of time in his hideaway at Churchill Farms, where people like Joe Matassa could not bother him with complaints from uncompensated fixed jurors.

And complaints there were from ex-juror Heitler. Court records of the jury tampering trial reveal that George Alamilla pocketed the $600 Joe Matassa had given him as a down payment for juror Heitler and left for Belize the night of November 22 without giving Heitler a cent. Heitler, sensing he was being given the runaround, began phoning Joe Matassa, relentlessly demanding his money. It was then that Matassa told Heitler he was having a lot of trouble contacting Marcello.

From all indications, one individual who did not experience much difficulty in contacting Marcello after the assassination was David Ferrie, who, not long after leaving federal court with Marcello's entourage, began a series of highly suspicious activities.

Sometime between leaving the federal courthouse and early evening, Ferrie telephoned a motel Carlos Marcello owned in Houston and made a reservation for that night for himself and two young male companions, Alvin Beauboeuf and Melvin Coffey. He then placed a call to the owner and operator of the Winterland Skating Rink in Houston, inquiring about the rink's skating schedule. Three days later he would lie to the FBI about the nature of the call.

Next he picked up his two friends in his new light-blue four-door Comet station wagon and took off for Houston. They drove nonstop into the night for 350 miles, through a tremendous Texas thunderstorm, arriving at Marcello's Alamotel around 4:00 in the morning. It was from the Alamotel that, according to an FBI report, Ferrie made a collect call to Carlos Marcello's headquarters in the Town & Country Motel in the early afternoon of Saturday, November 23.

Ferrie would later tell the FBI the call was to Marcello's attorney, G. Wray Gill, but Gill was not supposed to be at the Town & Country on Saturday, and in fact was not, and so it appears more likely the call was to Carlos Marcello.

Meanwhile, as Ferrie was hurtling toward Texas, two of his associates, Guy Banister and Jack Martin, a private investigator and friend of Ferrie's who worked for Banister, got into a fight that may possibly have been related to the Kennedy assassination.

According to Martin's testimony before the House Select Committee on Assassinations in 1978, he and Banister were having drinks in a local bar when they got into a furious argument. As the argument heated up, the two went back to their offices at 544 Camp Street to continue their discussion, and after some barbed remark by Banister, Martin shouted: "What are you going to do—kill me like you all did Kennedy?" Thereupon Banister drew his magnum pistol and started beating Martin over the head with the butt, telling him to "watch himself and be careful." Finally Banister's secretary, Delphine Roberts, intervened and broke up the fight. Later Martin reported the assault to the police, but did not press any charges.

The next day, Saturday, November 23, with David Ferrie in Houston, Martin watched a television program on the Kennedy assassination during which three men discussed Lee Harvey Oswald's New Orleans friends, mentioning David Ferrie as one of them. Suddenly Martin remembered that he knew Ferrie and Oswald had been friends and that he had once overheard them talking about assassinating President Kennedy.

The following afternoon, Sunday, November 24, Jack Martin phoned a friend of New Orleans Assistant District Attorney Herman Kohlman, and told him that he suspected Lee Harvey Oswald had conspired with David Ferrie to assassinate President Kennedy. Martin then informed Kohlman's friend that Oswald and Ferrie had known each other since 1955, when they had served on the New Orleans Civil Air Patrol together. It was then, according to Martin, that Ferrie had taught Oswald how to fire a high-powered rifle with telescopic sight. Martin added that Ferrie was passionately anti-Kennedy and he, Jack Martin, had once overheard him discussing with Oswald the necessity of assassinating President Kennedy.

After releasing this bombshell, which was obviously intended for the ears of Assistant District Attorney Kohlman, Martin requested of Kohlman's friend that his identity not be revealed and hung up the phone.

The next day, Monday, November 25, practically the entire New Orleans Police force was searching for David Ferrie. Jack Martin's anonymous allegations about Ferrie's relationship with Lee Harvey Oswald had found their mark. As soon as Herman Kohlman was informed of Martin's story, he mobilized the New Orleans Police force in a massive drive to locate Lee Harvey Oswald's friend. Soon the FBI and the Secret Service joined the manhunt. But that friend was not to be found. Finally Carlos Marcello's attorney, G. Wray Gill, informed the district attorney's office that Ferrie had been in Texas over the weekend, but would soon return to New Orleans. Gill was then told to have Ferrie surrender to the district attorney upon his return, for he was wanted for questioning by the FBI and the Secret Service in regard to the assassination of President John F. Kennedy. We can imagine how Carlos Marcello must have felt when Gill gave him this news. One of his boys had been arrested in Dallas in connection with the assassination, and now another was being sought by the New Orleans district attorney for questioning. With all this going on and idiots like Jack Martin running off at the mouth, it was no wonder Joe Matassa began to have trouble contacting the Little Man.

32

Dallas

Meanwhile, in Dallas, events had moved swiftly, if clumsily, for David Ferrie's New Orleans friend Lee Harvey Oswald.

In the pandemonium following the shooting of the President, a last sighting of the Oswald impostor occurred and several arrests were made in connection with the assassination before Oswald was taken into custody as a suspect in the murder of a police officer.

The real Oswald had been encountered by Police Officer Marrion Baker and the head of the Texas Book Depository, Roy Truly, one-and-a-half minutes after the shooting, calmly sipping a Coca-Cola on the second floor of the depository. After a brief interrogation, during which Truly certified to Baker that Oswald was an employee of the depository, Oswald had been quickly released. Upon finishing his Coke, Oswald sauntered out the front door of the building, boarded a bus from a few blocks away, then got off the bus and took a cab to his rooming house. Several minutes after the shooting, a man thought to be Lee Harvey Oswald, but now believed to have been an impostor, was observed by a witness leaving the depository by the rear exit, hesitating a few minutes, then dashing down to the freeway, where he was observed convincingly by Deputy Sheriff Roger Craig climbing into a Nash rambler station wagon which promptly took off and disappeared.

Shortly thereafter, two suspects were arrested by the police in another edifice facing Dealey Plaza, the Dal-Tex Building. One of these, a young man wearing a black leather jacket and black gloves, was taken into custody and removed to the Dallas County Sheriff's Office for questioning; no record of his name, capture, or release was made. The other individual arrested in the Dal-Tex Building told the police he was a California businessman by the name of Jim Braden, and he had gone into the building after the assassination to find a public telephone. However, an employee of the Dal-Tex Building told the police the man was in the building at the time of the assassination. After a brief interrogation at the County Sheriff's Office, he was released. Miraculously a record of his arrest survived, but the sheriff's office never attempted to find out who Braden was. It was not until seven years later that a producer for CBS-TV affiliate KNXT in Los Angeles, Peter Noyes, discovered who Jim Braden really was: The name he had given to the County Sheriff's Office was one of the four aliases used by Eugene Hale Brading, a courier and liaison man for the mob with ties to Carlos Marcello, who had a rap sheet showing thirty-five arrests with convictions for burglary, bookmaking, and embezzlement. Noyes further discovered that when Braden/Brading was in New Orleans on business during the summer and fall of 1963, he used an office in the Pere Marquette Building, only a few doors down from that used by G. Wray Gill and David Ferrie. Noyes also found out that Brading had spent the night before the assassination at the same Dallas hotel, The Cabana, Jack Ruby had visited that night.

Three more arrests were made minutes after the assassination, in an open boxcar parked on the railroad tracks behind the grassy knoll. Police found three men, identified as "tramps," crouching inside the boxcar, from which they had a clear view of the picket fence guarding the knoll. Three press photographers took numerous pictures of them while they were being corralled by the police. After a brief interrogation by Deputy Sheriff Harold Elkins, they were released. No record of their arrest, their names, or their interrogation remains, only photographs taken by the photographers. Later, investigators noticed that the "tramps" seemed only dressed as tramps. In other respects they appeared quite well groomed, clean shaven and with recent haircuts. They also noted that one of them bore a strong resemblance to Lee Harvey Oswald. In 1979 a Fort Worth graphics expert hired by the House Select Committee on Assassinations identified one of the tramps as Charles V. Harrelson, a Dallas-based hoodlum with connections to Jack Ruby and Carlos Marcello.

Several other men in and around Dealey Plaza were taken into custody minutes after the assassination: another man in the Dal-Tex Building, a "Latin who could not speak English," a 31-year-old Dallas man who was kept in jail for over a week. All were released with no records of their names and testimony surviving.

What was the reason for neglecting all these potential suspects? The principal reason was that within fifteen minutes of the assassination, radio dispatchers at the Dallas Police Headquarters had radioed a description of a man wanted for questioning about the shooting of the President: "an unknown white male, approximately 30, slender build, height 5 feet 10, weight 165 pounds, reportedly armed with a .30-caliber rifle." The description closely fitted book depository employee Lee Harvey Oswald, but could have fit countless other men too. The source for the description has never been identified.

That Oswald was so quickly identified as possibly being the President's assassin, to the exclusion of all others seen behaving suspiciously at the moment of the assassination, remains especially perplexing in view of the postassassination testimony of several eyewitnesses to the crime.

Construction worker Howard Brennan had told the police about a man he had noticed in the sixth-floor southeast window of the Texas Book Depository holding a rifle minutes before the assassination; he later came to believe that man was Lee Harvey Oswald. However, as we know, Arnold Rowland also saw someone holding a rifle in a sixth-floor window but it was in the southwest corner, not the southeast, and he claimed he saw another man, unarmed, also in a sixth-floor window; Carolyn Walther's account placed two men in a fifth floor window; one man was holding a gun.

Of the 266 known witnesses to the shooting who were formally interviewed, 32 claimed the shots that struck Kennedy and Texas Governor John Connally came from the Texas School Book Depository and 51, including 2 Secret Servicemen and several police officers, testified the shots came from the area around the grassy knoll. The others thought that the shots came from both directions.

Lee Harvey Oswald had, in the meantime, gone to his room in the boarding house, changed his jacket, and picked up his pistol. While he was in his room, his landlady, Earlene Roberts, heard an automobile horn honk twice. Looking out the window to see who it was, she noticed a Dallas Police patrol car parked outside her house with two uniformed police officers in the front seats. After waiting a minute or so, the police car drove away.

What happened next is still enveloped in mystery. According to

Mrs. Roberts, the man known to her as O. H. Lee left her house shortly after the police car departed and went to a bus stop for buses heading north. It was seven minutes after one.

Eight minutes later, Dallas Police Officer J. D. Tippit, who was ordered to patrol the area Oswald was now in, was shot dead by someone, perhaps by Oswald, perhaps by someone else. About a half hour later, Oswald was seized in a neighborhood movie house, the Texas Theater, and taken into custody by the police on suspicion of having killed Officer Tippit and possibly also President Kennedy.

Before the police formally charged Oswald with anything, J. Edgar Hoover issued an internal FBI memorandum stating that the Dallas Police "very probably" had President Kennedy's killer in custody, an individual "in the category of a nut and the extremist pro-Castro crowd...an extreme radical of the left."

It was, in fact, not until five hours after his capture that the Dallas Police charged Oswald with the murder of Officer Tippit. Early the next morning, around 1:30 A.M., after hours of interrogation, no records of which have survived, Lee Harvey Oswald was charged with the murder of John F. Kennedy. During his interrogation Oswald repeated several times that he was "just a patsy," that he had nothing to do with either the murder of Officer Tippit or the assassination of the President.

33

Ferrie in Texas

What was the purpose of David Ferrie's hurried trip to Texas over the weekend of the Kennedy assassination? When asked by the FBI and the Secret Service, Ferrie replied that it was simply for recreation, that he needed to relax after the strain of preparing for Marcello's trial. On the spur of the moment he had decided to do a little goose hunting and ice skating in Texas over the weekend; that's all.

Ferrie also told his interrogators that another purpose of the trip was to explore the feasibility of opening an ice skating rink in New Orleans. He had called the owner and manager of the Winterland Skating Rink in Houston, Chuck Rolland, before leaving New Orleans, to make an appointment to see his rink the following day and discuss the problems of operating ice skating rinks in general. Ferrie told the FBI that on the afternoon of Saturday, November 23, he spent two hours at the Winterland Rink, skating and talking with Rolland about the cost of installing and operating his rink.

Later Rolland told FBI agents that Ferrie had called from New Orleans the afternoon of November 22 only to obtain the skating schedule at Winterland, and "at no time did he discuss the cost of equipping or operating an ice skating rink." Furthermore, Rolland informed the agents that Ferrie had not skated at all at his rink, but had spent his entire stay at Winterland making and receiving calls at a public telephone.

From Winterland Ferrie and his two friends went to another Houston skating rink, the Belair, where witnesses later told FBI agents the trio had not skated either.

Clearly David Ferrie lied to the FBI about his trip to Texas. He had told the interviewing agents the purpose of the trip was recreation and relaxation. But driving 350 miles nonstop through a violent thunderstorm and not getting to bed until 4:30 in the morning was certainly not a very relaxing activity. Spending three hours at skating rinks anxiously making and receiving calls at a public telephone did not appear to have been particularly relaxing either. Ferrie had told the agents he was going to do a little goose hunting and skating in Texas, yet he did neither. From what information we have, he spent most of his time in Texas on the telephone.

The trip, then, remains highly suspicious, and it should have appeared highly suspicious to the FBI and Secret Service agents who interviewed Ferrie about it. For it seems obvious now that Ferrie was sent to Texas to perform some mission, possibly one connected with the Kennedy assassination. Who sent him? What was the mission? It does not seem unreasonable to conjecture that his boss, Carlos Marcello, sent him to Texas to do something about Dutz Murret's kid, who was not supposed to be where he was, alive and in the custody of the Dallas Police. It would have been too risky to conduct the necessary telephone conversations with Marcello's Dallas deputy, Joe Civello, and Civello's liaison with the police, Jack Ruby, from New Orleans to tell them what had to be done with the President's suspected assassin. Those conversations had to be nontraceable. They had to be conducted via public phones from locations where the callers and receivers would not be recognized.

Still another factor in the equation of Ferrie's trip to Texas, though admittedly a highly conjectural one, might have had something to do with the presence of mob courier Eugene Hale Brading, alias Jim Braden, in Houston the night of November 22. It will be recalled that Brading was arrested for "acting suspiciously" in Dealey Plaza minutes after the assassination and was later discovered to have used an office in New Orleans two doors away from the offices of Carlos Marcello's lawyer, G. Wray Gill, where David Ferrie worked as an investigator.

According to Ferrie's testimony to the FBI, upon leaving the Belair Rink he and his companions checked out of the Alamotel in Houston, then drove 100 miles to Galveston, where they checked into the Drift-wood Motel around 10:00 P.M. Later, investigators noted that Ferrie had arrived in Galveston just before one of Jack Ruby's friends, Breck Wall, arrived in Galveston. At 11:44 P.M., Wall received a call from Ruby at the Galveston number of a Thomas J. McKenna. It was the last long-distance call Ruby is known to have made before shooting Lee Harvey Oswald at Dallas Police Headquarters the following morning.

On the afternoon of that day, Sunday, November 24, Ferrie placed a call to his roommate in New Orleans, Layton Martens, and, according to his FBI testimony, was shocked to learn from him that he was being accused of having been involved in the assassination of President John F. Kennedy. Ferrie immediately headed back to Louisiana. On the advice of attorney G. Wray Gill, he spent Sunday night in Hammond, at Southeastern Louisiana University, visiting a friend who was then conducting research in narcotics addiction. The next day, Monday the 25th, he left Hammond for New Orleans. Once in the city, he immédiately contacted attorney Gill, who then accompanied him to the New Orleans Parish District Attorney's Office for questioning in connection with the assassination of President Kennedy.

It was on the morning of Monday, November 25, while Ferrie was in Hammond that the FBI learned that Ferrie's library card had apparently been found on Oswald at the time of his arrest.

The information was contained in an FBI teletype of November 28 from the New Orleans field office to Director Hoover and the special agent in charge of the FBI in Dallas. Part of the teletype recounted an FBI interview with Layton Martens, conducted on November 25 in Ferrie's apartment. During the course of the interview Martens made reference to a visit to the apartment on the afternoon of November 24 by G. Wray Gill. The relevant section of the teletype read as follows:

MARTENS SAID THAT ATTORNEY G. WRAY GILL VISITED FERRIE'S RESIDENCE AND TOLD MARTENS HE WAS LOOKING FOR FERRIE WHO WAS THEN NOT AT HOME. GILL REMARKED TO MARTENS THAT WHEN LEE HARVEY OSWALD WAS ARRESTED BY THE DALLAS POLICE, OSWALD WAS CARRYING A LIBRARY CARD WITH FERRIE'S NAME ON IT. GILL INSTRUCTED MARTENS TO TELL FERRIE TO CONTACT HIM AND GILL WOULD REPRESENT FERRIE AS HIS ATTORNEY.

Who told Gill that Ferrie's library card had been found on Oswald? In the Dallas Police Department's inventory of Oswald's personal effects, no mention was made of the card. Yet it might well have been found on Oswald, not only because of what the mysterious caller told attorney Gill but also because of a question that was put to Marina Oswald by the Secret Service on Sunday, November 24.

Marina Oswald had been taken into protective custody by the Secret Service and removed to a hotel in Arlington, Texas, where she remained a virtual prisoner for three months, undergoing relentless questioning. During the course of one of her initial interrogations, on the morning of Sunday, November 24, Mrs. Oswald was asked: "Do you know a Mr. David Farry?" (sic) Marina replied she did not. Official word of Jack Martin's allegations about Ferrie and Oswald had not yet reached the New Orleans Secret Service at this point. Thus it was unlikely that the Secret Service would have known Ferrie was wanted for questioning, although it is possible that agents of the Secret Service watched the same television program Martin had seen, which had linked Oswald to Ferrie. However, it is also possible that the Secret Service learned that Ferrie's library card was found among Oswald's effects. That this was the case was apparently implied when, after Ferrie returned to New Orleans and surrendered to the authorities, an agent of the Secret Service asked him: "Did you loan your library card to Lee Harvey Oswald?" Ferrie replied that he had not. The agent never explained in his report why the question was asked.

In all probability, Ferrie first heard the rumor that his library card had been found on Oswald over the phone from his roommate Martens or from attorney Gill. That the Secret Service was also aware of this must have convulsed him. For there is evidence that soon after his Secret Service interview, Ferrie went into something of a panic and took off for Oswald's former New Orleans residence in search of information about his library card.

In 1978 Mrs. Jesse Garner, Lee Harvey Oswald's former landlady, told an investigator for the House Select Committee on Assassinations that she remembered well David Ferrie visiting her home "the night of the Kennedy assassination" inquiring whether she had come across the library card Oswald had used when he was living in one of her apartments. Mrs. Garner told the committee investigator she had declined to speak with Ferrie. Later she told author Anthony Summers that Ferrie had seemed extremely agitated that evening. It is believed Mrs. Garner was in error as to the night Ferrie visited her. It seems more probable that it was not the night of the assassination but the night of the 25th. Of course, if it had indeed been the night of the assassination, the issue of Ferrie's library card having been found on Oswald takes on an added significance.

A somewhat similar episode was related by a former neighbor of Oswald's, Mrs. Doris Eames, to investigators from New Orleans District Attorney Jim Garrison's office in 1968. According to Mrs. Eames, David Ferrie came by her house after the assassination inquiring whether she had any information regarding Oswald's library card. Ten years later she told Anthony Summers that Ferrie was so nervous that evening he appeared nearly out of his mind.

The mystery of David Ferrie's library card has never been cleared up. That someone from the Dallas Police force might have notified Carlos Marcello's attorney that the card had been found on Oswald at the time of his arrest, and then destroyed the card, suggests complicity between at least one Dallas Police officer and Carlos Marcello. For what other reason would a Dallas Police officer notify Marcello's attorney if it were not to put Marcello and Ferrie on guard? And for what other reason would that card have been subsequently destroyed were it not considered evidence of an association between Oswald and Ferrie? And, by extension, of an association between Oswald, Ferrie, and Carlos Marcello?

One would have thought that the New Orleans FBI Office would have subjected Ferrie's employer, attorney G. Wray Gill, to intensive scrutiny, but instead the interviewing agent handled him with velvet gloves and did not seem to draw any sinister conclusions from his highly suspicious testimony. Was he perhaps intimidated by the fact that Gill was Carlos Marcello's New Orleans attorney and had just won, in collaboration with Marcello's other attorney, Jack Wasserman, a sensational victory over the United States government for his client?

When questioned by the FBI about how he learned that Ferrie's library card had been found on Oswald, attorney Gill replied that he could not recall who told him the "rumor," though he supposed it might have originated with Jack Martin. Incredibly, this answer seemed to satisfy the interviewing agent.

Even more incredible was the apparent satisfaction of FBI interviewing agent Smith with attorney Gill's response to the FBI's request for records of David Ferrie's office telephone calls for the past three months. Gill cheerfully turned over only the September and October 1963 records, claiming that the November records, the crucial ones, were "unavailable." To this blatant withholding of evidence, Special Agent J. Smith offered no particular comment.

The FBI, the New Orleans Police, and the Secret Service questioned David Ferrie extensively upon his return to New Orleans on Monday, November 25, and continued their interrogation through the 26th. Transcripts of those interviews were immediately classified and buried in the National Archives. They would be neither mentioned in the FBI's summary report nor turned over to the Warren Commission. The Secret Service interview surfaced in 1967 during New Orleans District Attorney Jim Garrison's reinvestigation of the Kennedy assassination. One thirty-page FBI interview was found missing from the National Archives in 1976. Some FBI interviews of Ferrie and his associates and reports of his activities were declassified in 1977 and released as a result of Freedom of Information Act requests.

In his November 25 FBI interview with Special Agents Wall and Shearer, David Ferrie denied all the allegations that had recently been made about him. No, he did not know Lee Harvey Oswald. No, Oswald had not served under him in the Civil Air Patrol. No, he had never taught Oswald how to shoot a high-powered rifle and had never loaned him his library card.

When it came to his association with Carlos Marcello, Ferrie was quite candid with the interviewing agents. He told them he had worked hard throughout October and November helping to prepare Marcello's defense, that he had flown twice to Guatemala on behalf of Marcello in October and had met with Marcello on November 9 and 16 "at Churchill Downs[sic], which is a farm owned by Carlos Marcello, mapping strategy in connection with Marcello's trial."

The New Orleans FBI Office did not accept Ferrie's denial of knowing Oswald at face value. FBI agents interviewed a number of individuals in New Orleans about the possibility of a Ferrie-Oswald relationship, one of whom confirmed Jack Martin's allegation that the two had first met when they served with the Civil Air Patrol in 1955. He was a former schoolmate and "best friend" of Oswald's, Edward Voebel, and he told the FBI several things it apparently did not want to hear. Among others, he told the interviewing agents that Oswald was never interested in communism and that he and Oswald "had been members of the Civil Air Patrol in New Orleans with Captain Dave Ferrie" and he believed "Oswald attended a party (not sure) at the home of David Ferrie right after the members of the CAP received their stripes."

Jack Martin was interviewed by Special Agent Regis Kennedy at the New Orleans FBI Office on November 25. According to Kennedy's report of the interview, Martin stated that he had seen rifles of the type Oswald had allegedly used against the President in Ferrie's apartment, that Ferrie was a well-known amateur hypnotist who could have hypnotized Oswald, that Ferrie was "a completely disreputable person, a notorious sex deviate with a brilliant mind," and that he, Martin, "suspected him of being capable of any type of crime." Martin concluded his statement saying that he felt "Ferrie's possible association with Lee Oswald should be the subject of close examination as he personally believed that he could be implicated in the killing of President John F. Kennedy."

The Secret Service also interviewed Ferrie and prepared a summary report on him dated December 13 that virtually closed the Secret Service investigation. In the interview, Ferrie admitted he "severely criticized President John F. Kennedy both in public and in private," and stated he did not recall what he said in making these criticisms and might have used an offhand colloquial expression like "He ought to be shot." But he never made any statement that "President Kennedy should be killed" with the intention that this be done.

Ferrie again denied knowing Oswald, but freely admitted to his association with Carlos Marcello and the legal work he had recently performed for Marcello's New Orleans trial.

When the question of the library card was raised, Ferrie denied ever loaning it to Oswald, but there was no mention in the summary report of why the question was raised in the first place. To back up his claim, Ferrie produced a library card in his name that had long since expired and showed an address from which he had long since moved.

Ferrie had not yet been informed of who had made the allegations against him that had caused him so much trouble, but he guessed it was Jack Martin, a man, he told the interviewing agent, who was "well known locally for furnishing false leads to law enforcement officers, attorneys, etc." This concluding statement prompted the Secret Service to interview Jack Martin in an effort to determine his credibility.

When Martin made his original allegations about Ferrie to Herman Kohlman's friend on the afternoon of November 24, he had insisted on being given anonymity. However, Regis Kennedy's FBI interview had, so to speak, blown his cover. After November 25 it became generally known among the press and the FBI in New Orleans and Dallas that private investigator Jack Martin had been behind the allegations about Ferrie's relationship with Oswald. Martin had now lost his anonymity, and the loss filled him with dread.

Jack Martin was no fool. He knew full well about David Ferrie's relationship with Carlos Marcello. If it were to become known pub-

licly that he, Martin, was accusing Ferrie of conspiring with Oswald
to assassinate President Kennedy, suspicions of complicity in the assassination might also fall on Marcello.

Whether Martin came to this conclusion himself or was pressured
to come to it by Marcello's henchmen is not known. What is known is
that Jack Martin became a very different person when he was interviewed by the Secret Service on November 29, in his "small, run-down
apartment," as his residence was described by the reporting agent.
Apparently terrorized, Jack Martin reversed himself, telling Secret
Service Agents Rice and Gerrots that he suffered from "telephonitis
while drinking and that it was during one of his drinking sprees that
he telephoned Assistant District Attorney Kohlman and told him this
fantastic story about David William Ferrie being involved with Lee
Harvey Oswald."

Ferrie had been well known to him, Martin told the agents. He
had seen rifles in Ferrie's home, and he recalled that Ferrie had been
a Marine and had been with the Civil Air Patrol when Oswald was
enrolled in the unit. He also knew that Ferrie was anti-Kennedy and
met with Oswald over the summer. Turning all those thoughts over
in his mind, he had telephoned Herman Kohlman and told him his
story as though it was based on facts rather than on his own imagination.

That was enough for the Secret Service. After taking Martin's testimony, it shut down its investigation of David Ferrie.

The FBI's investigation, however, continued until December 18.
During its three-week duration, agents from the New Orleans field
office were able to corroborate Jack Martin's central allegation that
Ferrie knew Oswald and succeeded in discrediting Ferrie's justifica-
tion for his postassassination trip to Texas. They established that
Ferrie had lied about his activities at the Winterland Skating Rink in
Houston and had, more than likely, gone to Texas for purposes other
than rest and relaxation. Furthermore they established that Ferrie
did indeed have a relationship with Carlos Marcello, and that he had
conferred with the Mafia chieftain at Churchill Farms during the two
weekends prior to the Kennedy assassination.

What more could the FBI have wanted to know? Was it not significant that a friend of President Kennedy's alleged assassin had spent
the two weekends prior to the President's assassination conferring
with a sworn enemy of the Kennedy brothers who had been a prime
target of Attorney General Kennedy's war on organized crime?

But by December 18, what the FBI's field agents turned up in the
way of evidence bearing on the Kennedy assassination case was no

longer of any interest to the man in charge of investigating the crime. For by then, FBI Director Hoover had firmly made up his mind that Lee Harvey Oswald was the lone, unaided assassin of the President; he was fiercely determined to smother evidence to the contrary, no matter how convincing it was.

David Ferrie was now beyond suspicion and was free to reap his rewards. Not long after the FBI dropped its investigation of him, Ferrie turned up the owner of a lucrative gasoline station franchise in an affluent New Orleans suburb. His sponsor: Carlos Marcello. Years later, when questioned by a congressional committee about the gift, Marcello admitted he had made some payments to his investigator, saying they were rewards for the help Ferrie had given him in winning an acquittal on the conspiracy and perjury charges the government had brought against him. It was an explanation difficult to fault. In fighting the government's case against him, Marcello and Ferrie had a perfect alibi for their meetings, phone calls, and activities during the month of November 1963.

It is not known when, following the assassination, Carlos Marcello and David Ferrie finally met to reminisce over the events of November 22, 1963. But when they did, they must surely have spoken of the front page of the New Orleans *Times-Picayune* on November 23. There, in banner headlines it was announced: "ASSASSIN KILLS PRESIDENT WOUNDS GOVERNOR CONNALLY." And right below, another headline: "MARCELLOS NOT GUILTY, VERDICT." Then, on the next page, were the continuations of the two major front-page articles, accompanied by two illustrations. One, captioned "SCENE OF ASSASSINATION OF PRESIDENT KENNEDY," showed the Texas School Book Depository, and the other, "A MEMENTO of Lee Harvey Oswald's stay in New Orleans last summer," was a reproduction of one of Oswald's leaflets:

HANDS
OFF
CUBA!
JOIN THE FAIR PLAY FOR
CUBA COMMITTEE
Free literature, lectures
EVERYONE WELCOME!

Emphasizing the presumed assassin's pro-Castro sympathies, the article failed to mention that the only member of the Fair Play for Cuba Committee chapter in New Orleans was Oswald himself.

*   *   *

The surviving FBI and Secret Service reports on David Ferrie issued
in the wake of the Kennedy assassination fill at least 100 typewritten
pages, yet, for reasons that have never been satisfactorily explained,
both the FBI and the Secret Service saw fit to withhold their reports
on Ferrie from the official investigators of the assassination appointed
by President Johnson.

Clearly the Oswald-Ferrie-Marcello connection threatened to be
too disturbing to a government and a public that were beginning to
feel comfortable with the Oswald-the-lone-gunman solution to the assassination triumphantly proclaimed by FBI Director Hoover within
three days of the crime.

Several newsmen assigned to cover the case in Dallas seemed to
sense this when allegations about Ferrie and Oswald began circulating after November 25. Evidently Oswald's alleged link to Ferrie and
Ferrie's definite link to Marcello were much discussed by those news
reporters and television cameramen who remained on the scene during the week following the assassination. CBS producer Peter Noyes
recalls a conversation he once had with one of them, a former member of the NBC television camera team that had covered the murders of the President and Oswald. Sometime toward the middle of
the week of November 25, as interest in Ferrie was reaching a cre-
scendo in New Orleans and Dallas, the NBC man had a discussion
about Ferrie's links to Oswald and Marcello with a group of FBI
agents and newsmen that he remembered everyone found most provocative. However the FBI soon put a damper on his interest in the
subject. For, immediately after the discussion broke up, one of the
agents took him aside and told him that he should never discuss what
they had just been talking about with anyone, "for the good of the
country."

34

Ruby Silences Oswald

While David Ferrie was making his mysterious trip through Texas the weekend of the Kennedy assassination, an associate of Carlos Marcello's deputy in Dallas, Jack Ruby, was behaving just as suspiciously.

Immediately after the shooting of President Kennedy, Jack Ruby drove to Parkland Hospital, where a team of surgeons was vainly trying to save the President's life. He arrived a few minutes after Malcolm Kilduff, acting White House press secretary, announced to the world that the President was dead. While at the hospital Ruby ran into a newspaperman he knew, Seth Kantor, who had once worked for the *Dallas Times Herald* and was now a White House correspondent for the Scripps-Howard chain. They said hello and exchanged a few remarks on the killing of the President, then parted. Two days later, after murdering the President's accused assassin, Ruby denied he had been at Parkland Hospital after the assassination. Subsequently the official investigators of the President's murder accepted Ruby's denial and declined to accept Seth Kantor's testimony that he had encountered Ruby at the hospital.

After leaving the hospital Ruby went to one of his nightclubs, the Carousel, where he placed a call to Alex Gruber, the ex-convict with ties to organized crime who had visited him in Dallas earlier in the month. Gruber later told the FBI he did not remember why Ruby had called, a suspicious lapse of memory considering the fact that nearly every adult in the United States was to vividly remember what was going on in his or her life at the time of the Kennedy assassination.

Jack Ruby spent the better part of the afternoon of the 22nd making and receiving calls at the Carousel. Between 3:00 and 5:30, the period corresponding to Carlos Marcello's departure from federal court and his getting down to business in his Town & Country office, and corresponding to David Ferrie's phone calls from the Alamotel and Winterland Skating Rink in Houston, visitors noted Ruby seemed to become progressively agitated by the calls he was receiving. Finally, after taking what was to be his last call, he pocketed his revolver and went over to police headquarters. Ruby, as we know, was on such good terms with the Dallas Police force that he was able to enter police headquarters at will.

Around 7:00 P.M., Ruby, carrying a loaded, snub-nosed revolver in his right trouser pocket, was observed on the third floor of the Dallas Police Headquarters by several detectives he knew. Lee Harvey Oswald was being interrogated in room 317 by Captain Will Fritz, chief of homicide of the Dallas Police. Ruby exchanged remarks with at least three detectives in the corridor, then was observed by local radio and TV reporter Victor Robertson attempting to enter room 317 and being rebuffed by the guard outside the door. Later Ruby denied he had been at police headquarters that evening.

By 11:30 P.M. Ruby was back on the third floor of police headquarters, still carrying his revolver, when Police Chief Jesse E. Curry and District Attorney Henry M. Wade entered the corridor and announced that Oswald would be put on display in the police assembly room in the basement for all to see. The police chief wanted the world to see that Oswald had not been beaten by the police while they were attempting to extract a confession from him.

Ruby then went along with the crowd of reporters, photographers, and detectives and soon found himself in the basement assembly room staring over scores of raised-up cameras aimed at the hapless prisoner. Oswald's hands were manacled behind his back, his eyes blinded by a hundred flashbulbs going off at once, his ears deafened by all the questions simultaneously shouted at him. Soon Chief Curry had to call an abrupt halt to the "press conference" and remove the prisoner to protect him from the surging crowd.

After Oswald was led out of the room, District Attorney Wade stayed to answer reporters' questions and announce what had been learned about the identity and activities of Lee Harvey Oswald. At one point Wade told the reporters Oswald was a member of the pro-Castro Free Cuba Committee, mistaking the organization's name. Immediately Ruby corrected him, yelling out the right name, the Fair Play for Cuba Committee. How did Ruby know the correct name of the obscure committee to which Oswald belonged and which counted only one member in its New Orleans chapter, Lee Harvey Oswald? Why did Ruby pack a gun on his two visits to police headquarters on November 22? Did Ruby already know a good deal about Oswald? Was he, in reality, stalking him on someone's orders the afternoon and evening of November 22?

While Ruby was away from the Carousel the evening of November 22, the handyman at the club, Larry Crafard, took a number of phone calls from a man who refused to leave his name or a message. Later, when Crafard asked his boss about these mysterious calls, Ruby told him to mind his own business. Investigators have since wondered whether the calls might have come from public telephones along the route David Ferrie had taken from New Orleans to Houston the evening of the assassination.

On Saturday, November 23, Chief Curry decided he would transfer Lee Harvey Oswald to the custody of the county sheriff at the Dallas County Jail on Dealey Plaza around four in the afternoon. The news soon reached Jack Ruby, who was observed standing in front of the vehicular entrance of the county jail around 3:00 P.M., waiting for the delivery of Oswald. But at the last minute the transfer was postponed, because of traffic congestion in Dealey Plaza. On learning this, Ruby went over to the Dallas Police Headquarters and his listening post on the third floor. Soon Police Chief Curry decided to transfer Oswald to the county jail the next morning, a Sunday, when the traffic would be lighter. The exact time of the transfer would be decided upon in the morning.

Late that afternoon, while David Ferrie was making and receiving calls at a public phone in Houston's Winterland Skating Rink, Jack Ruby was observed by several witnesses in Dallas where there were public telephones: a parking lot, a bar, a shoe-shine parlor, the corner of Browder and Commerce Street. That evening he spent some time at the Carousel, making and receiving calls. It is not known who called him. Investigators have concluded that only one of Ruby's outgoing calls appeared suspicious, the 11:44 P.M. long-distance call he made to Dallas AGVA official Breck Wall at a Galveston number an hour and a half after David Ferrie arrived in that city.

Sometime during the early morning of Sunday, November 24, the

Dallas County Sheriff's Office and the local field office of the FBI received nearly identical warnings from an anonymous caller that Lee Harvey Oswald would be killed in the Dallas Police Headquarters basement during his transfer from headquarters to the county jail. The caller further stated that he hoped the police would hold their fire so innocent people would not get killed. The sheriff's office and the FBI duly reported the warnings to the Dallas Police.

As a result of these warnings, an elaborate transfer plan was excogitated by Chief Curry and Chief of Homicide Fritz. It was decided to use an armored van accompanied by a police car escort as a decoy during the transfer, while an unmarked car accompanied by an unmarked escort would actually transport Oswald from police headquarters to the county jail. Both the van and the unmarked car would be waiting on the ramp leading from the street to the police headquarters basement. The detectives in the basement would form a protective human corridor leading from the elevator in which Oswald would come down from the third floor to the unmarked car on the ramp. Once under way, the unmarked car carrying Oswald would break away from the convoy and take a route different from that of the van to the county jail.

But Jack Ruby had his own plan, one that, it now appears, was known to at least one member, perhaps two or three, of the Dallas Police.

Ruby's roommate, George Senator, found Jack Ruby edgy and "uptight" the morning of Sunday, November 24, as he awaited that all-important call from one of his police contacts informing him at what time Lee Harvey Oswald would be brought down to the basement for the transfer. Ruby was, therefore, very impatient with his cleaning woman, Elnora Pitts, when she phoned him around 9:00 to tell him that she would be coming around to clean, as she did every Sunday morning. Ruby surprised her by telling her to call again before coming, something he had never done before. Later Elnora Pitts told investigators that Ruby "sounded terrible strange."

Meanwhile, one of Ruby's principal police contacts, Officer W. J. "Blackie" Harrison, had gone to the Delux Diner for a coffee break. There he was notified by phone of the transfer plans and was told he would be needed to form security for Oswald at the time of the transfer. Not long after Harrison received the call, it is believed he phoned his friend Jack Ruby at Ruby's unlisted number and told him of the transfer plans.

George Senator later told investigators that after Ruby received a call at the apartment some time around 9:30, he began to pace nervously from room to room, mumbling to himself as a man laboring under an obsession.

Ruby had known all along what he had to do: silence Lee Harvey Oswald forever. Now he knew where and when he had to do it.

He knew also that he had to have a ready excuse for carrying a gun and that he had to make the killing seem like a spontaneous, unpremeditated act.

His excuse for carrying a gun was that he was taking $2000 in cash to his tax attorney to pay the federal excise tax he owed, so he had to protect himself from possible robbery. Accordingly he stuffed his pockets with nine $100 bills, thirty $10 bills, and forty $20 bills. To give the impression that his killing of Oswald was a spontaneous act, he sent a $25 Western Union money order to one of his strippers only minutes before he was due to enter the nearby police headquarters basement. What was he doing going to the police headquarters that morning? Ruby would tell his interrogators that he went to Western Union to send a money order, then thought he would go over to the police station to find out what they had done with the President's killer.

By 10:45 the police headquarters basement was crowded with over seventy police officers, around fifty reporters, and from ten to twenty press photographers and television cameramen. In charge of basement security was Sergeant Patrick T. Dean, who, it will be remembered, was so close to Dallas Mafia boss and Marcello associate Joseph Civello that he had dinner with him as soon as Civello returned to Dallas from the Mafia commission's summit meeting of 1957 at Apalachin, New York.

Ruby sent off the money order to his stripper at 11:17 and pocketed the receipt. By 11:19 he had somehow gotten into the police station basement and was maneuvering himself into position to shoot Oswald by following a television crew that was moving equipment through the basement area. Finally, he reached his friend, Officer "Blackie" Harrison, and went into a crouch directly behind him.

At 11:21, as if on cue, Lee Harvey Oswald suddenly appeared, manacled to Homicide Detective James R. Leavelle's right wrist. A barrage of flashbulbs brilliantly illuminated the target, and as the television cameras began rolling, Jack Ruby stepped out from behind Officer Harrison and fired a shot into Oswald's abdomen, wounding him fatally.

In the ensuing melee, with at least six policemen pouncing on the shooter, Ruby cried out, "Hey, you all know me! I'm Jack Ruby!"

Lee Harvey Oswald was then rushed to Parkland Hospital, where he was pronounced dead at 2:07. Jack Ruby had carried out his mission with true professionalism. It was as if his whole life as a small-time racketeer with big-time aspirations had been but a preparation, a long rehearsal, for this final assignment.

Several weeks later FBI agents interviewed Ruby's close friend Paul Roland Jones about Ruby's shooting of Oswald, and Jones told the agents he strongly doubted Ruby would have gotten emotionally upset over the assassination of the President and killed Oswald on the spur of the moment. Rather he believed Ruby would have shot him for money. Jones then went on to say that if Ruby "had been given orders by anyone to kill Oswald, Joe Civello would have known about it," informing the agents, as if they didn't know, that Civello was "the head of the syndicate in Dallas." In the FBI report of Jones's remarks, the interviewing agent neglected to add that Joseph Civello was also Carlos Marcello's deputy in Dallas.

Jack Ruby's murder of Oswald in Dallas Police headquarters before seventy-seven armed police officers was the tipoff to the milieu out of which the conspiracy to kill the President had developed. Obviously it had not been in the original assassination plan that Ruby was to kill Oswald while the suspected assassin was in the custody of the Dallas police. Something had gone awry that had necessitated this desperate, and extremely risky, operation.

Given Ruby's readily discernible connection to the underworld, it should have been apparent to the official investigators that this was the milieu from which the assassination of the President, and the murder of his suspected assassin, had come.

Clearly these crimes arose from the squalid, interconnected Dallas–New Orleans underworld of bookies, striptease joints, slot machine distributors, and drug dealers; of Pete Marcello's Sho-Bar and Jack Ruby's Carousel Club; Vincent Marcello's and Jack Ruby's slot machine warehouses; Carlos Marcello's Town & Country restaurant and Joe Campisi's Egyptian Lounge.

The members of the Warren Commission had debated what was in it for Jack Ruby to go in and rub out Oswald. The simplicity of the answer demonstrates the commission's ignorance of the code by which a man like Ruby lived.

In the Mafia if you are ordered by a superior to kill someone, and you refuse to carry out the order, you pay for your refusal with your life.

35

The Suspicions of
Edward Becker

After Edward Becker left New Orleans in late September 1962, he would occasionally think back on the scene at Churchill Farms when Carlos Marcello suddenly "went off like a bomb," as he expresses it today, and threatened to have President Kennedy killed; but by the fall of 1963 he had, more or less, put the episode out of his mind.

Becker was living in Los Angeles, working as a private investigator for ex-FBI agent Julian Blodgett, at the time Kennedy was assassinated. When he heard the news, minutes after the shooting, he did not immediately suspect Marcello might have been involved, although the thought did fleetingly cross his mind. But as he began to learn who Oswald and Ruby were, it struck him like a thunderbolt: "My god," he said to himself, "Carlos did it. I know he did. He carried out the threat. Hiring a nut to do the job, then getting one of his guys in Dallas to bump him off."

Becker was stunned by the realization and immediately began conducting his own private inquiry into what had happened in Dallas. As a professional investigator, having extensive contacts with the mob in Las Vegas and Los Angeles, including a fairly close relationship with Mafia fixer Johnny Roselli, he was in as good a position as anyone to ferret out the truth as to who, or what, might have been behind the crime.

Inquiring around, here and there, he eventually learned that Oswald's uncle and surrogate father, Dutz Murret, worked for the Marcellos in New Orleans, that he was employed in Carlos's gambling network and was also "some kind of a bar manager, or nightclub operator." He was told by his mob contacts in Las Vegas that Jack Ruby was "a tool of some mob group," that, as he told me in an interview, "he had mob connections all over the place, in Chicago, in New Orleans, Vegas, LA, Florida, you name it." He also learned through his underworld contacts that Ruby had been sent to Texas by the Chicago mob in the late forties "to get Dallas started," and "he and the other Chicago guys then blew it. So he couldn't go back to Chicago or he'd end up in the scrap. So they let him stay down there and told him to be available for whatever they might want him to do, like they do with button boys, you know, run a little dope, or some guns to Cuba, whatever.... And then he got connected with the Marcello people, who took over Dallas in the fifties, got to know a couple of the brothers, became involved with their slots and their racing wire, and there he was in the early sixties, one of their Dallas tools."

According to a distinguished Louisiana law enforcement official, "that outburst of Carlos's against the Kennedys at Grand Isle was well known. People were talking about it after the assassination.... And then the street talk in the Quarter was that Ruby knew the Marcellos and had spent a lot of time in some of their Bourbon Street dives before the assassination.... It was also common talk at the time that Ruby was being treated by one of Carlos Marcello's doctors in Jefferson Parish—for cancer of the colon—and Oswald's uncle was in thick with ole Carlos and some of his brothers in the Little Man's horse book network. In fact, everyone I knew was flabbergasted that the Warren Commission and the FBI never mentioned any of this in their reports on the assassination.... The FBI in New Orleans must have known all about Carlos's connections to Ruby and Oswald at the time...it was the talk of New Orleans; it was in the air, on the streets, everywhere, yet no mention of it ever came out of Washington, D.C."

The FBI had indeed learned about Oswald's and Ruby's mob connections over the years and during its six-week investigation of the assassination. But J. Edgar Hoover had seen to it that almost no information on these connections would be given out to the press, or transmitted to the Warren Commission. It was therefore not until the 1977–1979 House Select Committee on Assassinations' investigation of the John F. Kennedy murder that these facts were finally to see the light of day.

The Assassinations Committee eventually corroborated just about everything Becker had found out about Oswald's and Ruby's mob connections sixteen years before. It established that Dutz Murret had worked for years "in an underworld gambling syndicate affiliated with the Carlos Marcello crime family," and, through his association with Sam Saia, a major player in the Marcello gambling network, had worked "in a gambling nightclub in Royal and Iberville in the French Quarter," owned by Saia, called the Lomalinda Club, and "in other gambling clubs in New Orleans controlled by Saia." And, as we know, it established the enormous range of Jack Ruby's Mafia contacts, which included high-ranking mobsters in Los Angeles, Chicago, Las Vegas, Dallas, New Orleans, and Miami.

But what made Edward Becker believe that Carlos Marcello may have lured Dutz Murret's nephew into a plot to assassinate President Kennedy?

"Oh, come on, are you kidding?" the 60-year-old Becker remarked when I put the question to him in February 1987. "Remember Carlos had said in front of me at Churchill Farms that he was already thinking of hiring a nut to do the job, the way they do in Sicily? Well, that's the way the Mafia works in Sicily. Sometimes they entice some half-retarded illiterate kid into making a hit for them. Then they knock the kid off before he can talk."

"Look what a ready-made nut this commie ex-defector kid Oswald was. There's no question about it, with all the publicity there had been about him in the papers, Dutz Murret's nephew soon came to the attention of Carlos, or one of his brothers. Murret himself probably asked one of the Marcellos: 'Listen, what am I going to do with this nutty nephew of mine?' Murret may have even told them that his nephew was said to have once taken a potshot at General Walker. And Carlos must have thought: 'How can I use this guy? He must be good for something.' And then he gave him a couple of jobs to do to try him out. And then he, and Ferrie, or Banister, or someone, figured out what a perfect fall guy he'd make. And somehow they lured him into a plot to get Kennedy."

"As for Ruby," Becker went on, "he was the ideal guy to get Oswald. As I see it, the original game plan was to knock off Oswald soon after the assassination. When one of the conspirators blew that assignment, they had to find someone who could knock off Oswald in jail. The Marcellos knew who Jack Ruby was, don't kid yourself. They knew he had contacts in the police department, that he could get into the city jail at the right time.... As for Ruby, he probably was happy as hell to get the hit. Now he could do something big for Un-

cle Carlos. It's ridiculous to say that Ruby's job on Oswald was emotional, spur of the moment. Listen, that was a professional job if there
ever was one. Ruby just rolled in there like he had twenty years experience at it. Beautiful."

As for Marcello's possible motive in wanting to assassinate Kennedy, Becker believes it was "as much a matter of Sicilian pride as
any other....Listen, that deportation was a bitter experience for him.
To be picked up off the street and just hustled out of the country,
you know. That was the idea that Bobby had. Not only did Bobby
say, 'OK, you said you were born in Guatemala so that's where you're
going, pal,' but he also said, 'Now we'll show you in front of all your
people how weak you really are.' Carlos's pride was really shattered.
Kennedy had made a fool out of him. He had to get back his honor.
You know these Sicilians smolder a long time."

But would a Mafia boss even conceive of making such a hit, much
less actually carrying one out?

Becker was quick to reply. "Not most Mafia bosses. They tend to
be very patriotic, pride themselves on being so American. But Carlos,
yes. He was in a category all by himself. First of all, he never became
an American citizen. Remained an illegal alien all his life. And you
know that the Mafia down there in Louisiana is the oldest in the country. They have their own code, their own rules. Their boss is much
more a supreme dictator than the bosses up north. And they have
no rival bosses to contend with. Hell, for a little Napoleon like Carlos,
killing the President of the United States was nothing. He didn't even
know what the President was, what he stood for. He was just someone who was standing in his way. What the hell is a President of the
United States compared to him, the boss, Carlos Marcello? That's the
way you have to think of it. That's the kind of egotism you got down
there. Nobody's patriotic in Louisiana. Jefferson bought Louisiana
from Napoleon against the people's will. The people weren't even
consulted. They didn't want to become Americans; they wanted to
remain French. They've never been democratic in Louisiana. They've
always loved dictators down there. First they had Louis XIV. Then
they had Napoleon. Then they had the kingfish, Huey Long. Now
they got Carlos Marcello."

But would Marcello, who was normally quite prudent in his business affairs, have blurted out his intention to kill Kennedy in front
of a stranger like Becker?

"Sure. First of all, I wasn't a stranger. I was with Roppolo, who
was practically a member of the family. The Marcellos and the Rop-
polos had grown up together over there on the West Bank. Roppolo's

wife, Lillian, actually worked for Carlos. So being with Roppolo meant I was OK. Also, Carlos soon learned we knew a lot of the same people in Vegas. He even checked me out with them. And I'd already met with Carlos a couple of times before the meeting at Churchill Farms...then, as I told the House Assassinations Committee, Carlos had had a few drinks out there that day. Everybody who's dealt with Carlos knows how boastful he gets when he's had a few. You know, real Sicilian bravado. He's God Almighty with a couple of scotches under his belt. Then, there's also the short fuse. Carlos is famous for his quick temper. When he gets ticked off by something, look out. Well, I ticked him off that day at Churchill Farms when I brought up the subject of Bobby Kennedy. So, sure he would have boasted he was going to get the Kennedys in front of me. It was entirely in character."

But how could Marcello have expected to get away with it?

"Well, he *has* gotten away with it, hasn't he? He figured he owned Dallas, which he did, so he could get away with anything there. And he figured the FBI and the police would go straight for the patsy, the fall guy, straight for Oswald, which they did. Listen, killing a U.S. President was beyond any other Mafia boss's grasp, but not beyond Carlos's. He was special. He knew he could get away with anything, and he did. And look how he neutralized Bobby, just the way he told us he would. After his brother's murder you never heard a peep out of Bobby on organized crime again."

But why didn't Edward Becker go to the FBI or the Warren Commission with his suspicions regarding Marcello as soon as those suspicions were confirmed?

Becker readily admits he was too scared. If it got back to Marcello that he was ratting on him to the FBI, he would be as good as dead. Besides, Becker adds, J. Edgar Hoover did not *want* to know that Carlos Marcello was involved in the Kennedy assassination. If Becker had gone straight to Hoover with his story of the September 1962 meeting with Marcello at Churchill Farms, Hoover wouldn't have paid any attention to him, or would have tried to discredit him, and in the meantime he would have put himself in danger of a reprisal from Marcello.

It was not until May 1967 that the FBI finally learned of Edward Becker's allegation. But they did not learn it directly from Becker. Investigative journalist Ed Reid, author of *The Green Felt Jungle*, had just completed a book on organized crime titled *The Grim Reapers*. In his chapter on the New Orleans Mafia, Reid quoted an unnamed informant's account of the Churchill Farms meeting in September 1962 during which Carlos Marcello allegedly threatened to kill John F. Kennedy.

Senior officials of the FBI first learned of Ed Reid's account of the meeting at Churchill Farms over a year and a half before the book was published, because Reid was trying to strike a deal with the FBI at the time. He had gone to the Los Angeles FBI Office with a proposal to trade information he had on John Roselli for whatever information the FBI might care to give him for his current book. He then gave the interviewing agent a rough draft of his manuscript. After the agent read it, he immediately sent a memorandum to headquarters giving a full account of the Churchill Farms episode and informing the bureau that Reid's informant had been Edward Becker, a private investigator working out of Los Angeles.

When the memorandum was brought to J. Edgar Hoover's attention, the director hit the roof. Instead of ordering an investigation of Becker's allegation, he immediately ordered his subordinates to make an effort to discredit Becker as a source.

Incredibly, the individual the FBI relied on for information to discredit Becker was Sidney Korshak, a Los Angeles labor lawyer with ties to the Mafia, whom the *New York Times* characterized in 1976 as "one of the five most powerful members of the underworld" in the United States. In fact, the FBI's own files identified Korshak as an associate of reputed Chicago Mafia executioners Gus Alex and Murray "The Camel" Humphreys, and a business associate of Jimmy Hoffa, who, as we know, was on friendly terms with Carlos Marcello.

Korshak told the FBI through an intermediary that Edward Becker was "a no-good shakedown artist" who tried to shake down some of his friends for money, telling them that for a payment he could keep their names out of Ed Reid's book. The unnamed individual who had told the FBI about Korshak's opinion of Becker then got directly in touch with Reid and tried to persuade him to delete the Carlos Marcello incident from his book. Reid refused. Subsequently an FBI agent visited Reid's home in Los Angeles, in an effort to further discredit Becker's testimony and persuade Reid to delete the story. Again, Reid refused. *The Grim Reapers* was eventually published with Becker's account of the Churchill Farms meeting intact. Only the name of Edward Becker was left out.

In the end, the FBI declined to investigate Edward Becker's account of Carlos Marcello's threat against President Kennedy, dismissing it as unworthy of serious consideration. Thus the bureau did not even inform the agent in New Orleans assigned to keep track of Marcello's activities, Patrick Collins (who had replaced the lenient Regis Kennedy), of the allegation much less order him to investigate it. By then J. Edgar Hoover was so committed to defending his conclusion that Lee Harvey Oswald had acted alone in assassinating the President, and Jack Ruby had acted alone in murdering the President's alleged assassin, that he was determined to suppress all allegations of conspiracy. The attitude was in direct contradiction to a formal statement Hoover had made on May 6, 1964:

"I can assure you so far as the FBI is concerned that the case will be continued in an open classification for all time. That is, any information coming to us from any source will be thoroughly investigated, so that we will be able to either prove or disprove the allegation."

Twelve years later, after J. Edgar Hoover was long gone, the House Committee on Assassinations interviewed Edward Becker and found him to be a credible witness. The committee was able to draw out of Becker a much more detailed account of the meeting at Churchill Farms and, for the first time, an account of Becker's postassassination suspicions. The committee concluded that, in all likelihood, Carlos Marcello had threatened the life of President Kennedy at Churchill Farms on September 11, 1962.

Today Edward Becker is more convinced than ever that Carlos Marcello played a major role in the conspiracy that ultimately resulted in the assassination of President Kennedy. He does not deny that individuals from other groups, such as the Cuban exiles or "some of the CIA people Kennedy fired" or "hired guns from Trafficante," could also have had roles in the plot. But, based on all the circumstantial evidence that has come to light in the last twenty-five years, especially what the House Assassinations Committee unearthed, he is convinced Marcello was "the activist" in the plot, the prime mover.

As for the FBI's investigation of the crime of the century, which formed the basis of the Warren Commission's inquiry, Becker has only utter disdain. "Listen, I was there," he insists. "I heard Carlos say that he was going to have Kennedy killed in order to neutralize his brother Bobby, and the FBI did not even bother to investigate my allegations, which wouldn't have been very difficult to do; they only tried to discredit me, relying on the testimony of a mob lawyer who knew Hoffa and Marcello. You know what I think of Hoover's investigation of the Kennedy assassination? I think it was the biggest investigative goof-up in history—yes, in *history*—and, what is more, the FBI is still hiding that goof-up. They still haven't come clean with the American people, and with the people of the world."

36

More Intimations of Conspiracy

From what we now know about the initial responses of President Johnson, Attorney General Kennedy, and FBI Director Hoover to the assassination of President Kennedy, it seems that it would have been futile, not only for Edward Becker but for *anyone,* to have made an allegation of conspiracy in the assassination to the FBI in the wake of the crime—especially an allegation suggesting Mafia involvement— no matter how persuasive the evidence for it might have been.

In the days and weeks following the assassination, allegations of conspiracy in the slaying of the President—ranging from vague hints of possible conspiratorial activity to suggestions of the existence of complex plots—poured into FBI field offices from, it seemed, every direction. Some of them pointed an accusatory finger at Fidel Castro's Cuba, some pointed toward the Soviet Union's KGB, others toward the anti-Castro Cuban exiles, and still others toward organized crime.

The immediate reaction of Lyndon Johnson, Robert F. Kennedy, and J. Edgar Hoover to these allegations was fear. Johnson feared that if some of the allegations reported to him by the FBI were to become publicly known, they might incite war with Cuba or the Soviet Union. Kennedy feared that the allegations might reveal that his secret war against Cuba, or his overt war against organized crime, might have backfired on him and his brother. And J. Edgar Hoover was apparently terrified that if some of the allegations were found to be true, they might inflict irreparable damage to his and the FBI's reputation.

President Johnson had put FBI Director Hoover in charge of the investigation of Kennedy's murder within forty-eight hours of the shooting in Dealey Plaza. It was Hoover's responsibility to evaluate the allegations suggesting conspiracy that flooded into his office hourly from all parts of the nation and the world. As we shall see, virtually all the allegations, no matter how plausible they first appeared to be, were either ignored, quickly dismissed, or given the most superficial, cursory investigations before being summarily discredited. Although individual FBI field agents were diligent in investigating early leads suggesting the possibility of a conspiracy, when the information they had gathered reached the desk of Director J. Edgar Hoover, it died. For, as now appears certain, Hoover did not want to know of a conspiracy to kill the President, if one existed. Out of an all but paranoid sense of bureaucratic self-preservation, he was obsessed with only one aim: to convincingly pin the blame for the assassination on one man, acting alone, who could no longer defend himself because he too had been murdered. The killing of Lee Harvey Oswald had been convenient not only for the conspirators but for J. Edgar Hoover and the United States government as well.

Some of the first apparently serious allegations intimating possible conspiracy in the assassination came from Mexico City, where, as we know, Lee Harvey Oswald, or someone representing himself as Oswald, had gone in late September and had made a spectacle of himself proclaiming his pro-Castro sympathies at the Cuban and Soviet embassies.

The day after the assassination, the chief of the FBI's office in Mexico City, known as the Legat, informed FBI headquarters that the U.S. ambassador was concerned that Cubans were behind Oswald's assassination of the President. He had heard that while visiting the Cuban Embassy in early October, Oswald had offered to kill President Kennedy in retaliation for the Kennedy administration's attempts to kill Castro. Then, at noon on Monday, November 23, a man code-named "D" appeared at the U.S. Embassy in Mexico City and told embassy personnel that he was in the Cuban Consulate on September 18 and saw Cubans pay Oswald a sum of money and talk about assassinating someone. A week later it was reported that a Cubana Airlines flight to Havana had been delayed in Mexico City from 6:00 P.M. until 11:00 P.M. the day of the assassination. It was awaiting an unidentified passenger who eventually arrived by private aircraft, boarded the plane without going through customs, and took a seat in the cockpit. Observers thought the passenger looked "suspicious." As soon as the mystery man reached the cockpit, the plane took off.

There were also hints of Soviet involvement in the crime. By the evening of November 22, FBI headquarters had enough information on Oswald's recent trip to Mexico City to suggest he might also have been involved with the KGB in a plot to assassinate the President.

By then Lee Harvey Oswald's file contained a report that while in Mexico City, Oswald had gone to the Soviet Embassy and met with the consul on duty, Valery Vladimirovich Kostikov, who was also officer-in-charge for KGB western hemisphere terrorist activities, including assassination. From CIA wiretaps of the Soviet Embassy's phones it was learned that Oswald (or someone representing himself as Oswald) had confided to Kostikov that he knew of a CIA plot to assassinate Fidel Castro. Oswald's FBI file also contained an intercepted letter he had written Kostikov from Dallas on November 9, in care of the Soviet Embassy in Washington, inquiring about Soviet entrance visas for himself and his wife and two children. In reviewing this file, Hoover could not have helped suspecting Oswald might have conspired with the Soviets to assassinate the President.

There were other allegations suggesting Cuban involvement in the assassination, as well as more allegations hinting at Soviet participation in the crime, none of which were investigated by the FBI in any significant depth. Years later the Senate Intelligence Committee of 1975, 1976 and the House Assassinations Committee of 1978 conducted limited investigations and found that almost all the trails of evidence associated with the allegations had gone cold. In its final report, the House Assassinations Committee did, however, exonerate the governments of Cuba and the Soviet Union from complicity in the assassination.

But as we know, the FBI received other allegations hinting at conspiracy in the Kennedy assassination that pointed not in the direction of Cuban or Soviet involvement but toward the involvement of organized crime, more specifically toward the involvement of the Marcello organization. These received equally inadequate investigative attention.

On the afternoon of November 22, not long after the assassination, two FBI agents from the Miami office phoned Cuban exiles leader Jose Aleman at his Miami hotel. They requested an interview about Aleman's statement, in late September 1962, that Florida Mafia boss Santos Trafficante had told him Kennedy was not going to make it to the election of 1964, that he was "going to be hit."

The next morning the agents went to Aleman and, according to his later testimony, "wanted to know more and more and stayed until they had explored every possible angle." They then left, telling Aleman to keep the conversation confidential.

Aleman expected the agents to contact him again, but they never did.

When the results of the FBI's initial investigation of the assassination were announced, no mention was made of Aleman's allegation, and subsequently, the Warren Report made no reference to it in its section on "conspiracy theories."

Years later, on March 14, 1977, Jose Aleman was interviewed by a staff counsel of the House Select Committee on Assassinations, Robert Tannenbaum, about his September 1962 allegation, and Aleman confirmed that Trafficante had personally told him that President Kennedy was "going to be hit." Aleman went on to tell Tannenbaum that Santos Trafficante "had made it clear to him implicitly that he was not guessing about the impending assassination; rather he gave the impression that he knew Kennedy was going to be hit."

The day after FBI agents in Miami interviewed Jose Aleman, the New Orleans FBI was alerted by the office of the district attorney to a conspiracy allegation linking Oswald and David Ferrie in a plot to kill the President. This allegation could have been readily interpreted as also involving Carlos Marcello. It will be recalled that after submitting Ferrie to an intensive interrogation on November 25 and 26, during which Ferrie denied knowing Oswald but admitted meeting with Carlos Marcello at Churchill Farms the last two weekends prior to the assassination, the FBI had cleared him of conspiring with Oswald to kill the President, even though it found evidence that Ferrie had known Oswald and had often spoken out against President Kennedy publicly.

It will be further recalled that, curiously, the FBI pursued its investigations of Ferrie's November 22–24 trip to Texas into the middle of December 1963. And what had the agents found out during the three-week investigation they conducted *after* releasing Ferrie? Much suspicious behavior, to put it mildly: Ferrie's call from the Marcello-owned Alamotel in Houston to Marcello's headquarters in New Orleans twenty-four hours before Ruby shot Oswald, Ferrie's visit to a Houston skating rink after the assassination, where he spent several hours making and receiving calls at a public telephone. And yet, despite the suspiciousness of Ferrie's postassassination behavior, the FBI dropped its investigation of him entirely on December 18.

No sooner had the FBI disposed of one conspiracy allegation suggesting the involvement of Carlos Marcello than another arrived at the Savannah FBI office. It was immediately relayed by teletype to Director Hoover and the FBI field offices in New Orleans and Dallas. This was the allegation of informant SV T-1 that he had seen an individual who looked like Lee Harvey Oswald receive a payment of money at the Town & Country Motel from a man he believed was the restaurant owner. A Georgia police officer reported this allegation to the Savannah FBI, which transmitted it to the New Orleans office, which, in turn, had an agent interrogate Joseph Poretto, manager of the Town & Country restaurant, and Anthony Marcello, manager of the motel. Neither of them recalled having had any business dealings with someone resembling Oswald in the spring of 1963.

In an Airtel dated November 27, the New Orleans FBI notified the FBI offices in Dallas and Savannah, but not in Washington, that Joseph Poretto and Joseph Marcello had criminal records, that Joseph Marcello was a brother of Carlos Marcello, and that "all three are known hoodlums of the New Orleans Division." The Airtel concluded that Carlos Marcello was known to have had a financial interest in the Town & Country Motel and restaurant, "a known hangout for the hoodlum element." No mention of Anthony Marcello was made. Doubtless the bureau confused Anthony with Joseph.

Three days later informant SV T-1 gave an expanded version of his original allegation to Lt. Harris, which was transmitted to the FBI in Savannah, and from there was sent to Washington, New Orleans, and Dallas. In the Savannah teletype of November 29, 1963, informant SV T-1's name was unmasked inadvertently by the FBI censor and revealed to be a Mr. Sumner, who I discovered was a respected Darien businessman in the seafood industry, a brother-in-law of Lt. Harris, and later mayor of Darien. The full text of his allegation, published here for the first time, is as follows:

LT. JOHN HARRIS, GLYNN COUNTY PD, BRUNSWICK, GA., IDENTIFIED HIS [INFORMANT AS...censored] DARIEN, GA. _____ WHO DESIRES HIS IDENTITY REMAIN CONFIDENTIAL, FURNISHED THE FOLLOWING INFORMATION TO BU AGENT THIS DATE.

SOMETIME BETWEEN FEBRUARY FIFTEEN AND MARCH FIFTEEN LAST HE LEFT DARIEN AND TRAVELED TO SABENE [SIC], TEXAS, TO CONTACT BUSINESS ACQUAINTANCE, EARNEST [SIC] INSALMO. HE AND INSALMO TRAVELED TO NEW

ORLEANS, LA., WHERE THEY STAYED AT HOLIDAY INN. IN
NEW ORLEANS SUMNER CONTACTED SALVADORE PIZZA, AKA
SAL PIZZA, A BUSINESS CONTACT, OWNER PAUL PIZZA AND
SON SEAFOOD BUSINESS. PIZZA INTRODUCED _____ AND
INSALMO TO BENNY CAPEANA/PHONETIC/WEALTHY CON-
STRUCTION MAN. ONE NIGHT PIZZA AND CAPEANA TOOK
INSALMO AND _____ TO TOWN AND COUNTRY RESTAU-
RANT IN NEW ORLEANS WHERE THEY INTRODUCED INSAL-
MO TO RESTAURANT OWNER. INSALMO AND _____ STAYED
AT RESTAURANT WHILE PIZZA AND CAPEANA WENT TO WED-
DING REHERSAL [SIC]. INSALMO AND _____ WENT INTO
MAIN DINING ROOM OF RESTAURANT WHERE THERE WERE
CUSTOMERS ONLY AT TWO OTHER TABLES. _____ OB-
SERVED A YOUNG COUPLE ENTER DINING ROOM AND SIT AT
TABLE ABOUT TWO TABLES FROM WHERE HE AND INSALMO
WERE SITTING. THIS MAN GREATLY RESEMBLED PHOTO OF
LEE HARVEY OSWALD WHO _____ HAS SEEN ON TV AND IN
NEWSPAPERS. RESTAURANT OWNER JOINED COUPLE AT TABLE
AND _____ OBSERVED OWNER REMOVE WAD OF BILLS FROM
HIS POCKET WHICH HE PASSED UNDER TABLE TO MAN SIT-
TING AT THE TABLE. A FEW MINUTES LATER THE COUPLE
LEFT WITHOUT ORDERING ANY FOOD OR DRINKS. _____
CALLED INCIDENT TO INSALMO/S ATTENTION, HOWEVER, HE
DOES NOT KNOW IF INSALMO OBSERVED IT. THIS OCCURRED
ABOUT TEN PM. LATER THIS SAME NIGHT PIZZA AND CAPEANA
RETURNED TO THIS RESTAURANT AND _____, INSALMO,
PIZZA, CAPEANA, RESTAURANT [OWNER] AND INDIVIDUAL
CLAIMING TO BE WORLD/S LARGEST CHICKEN PRODUCER SAT
AROUND LARGE TABLE IN COCKTAIL LOUNGE OF RESTAU-
RANT. RESTAURANT OWNER STATED HE WAS EITHER QUOTE
WIRE MAN END QUOTE OR QUOTE TAP MAN END QUOTE FOR
QUOTE RACKETS END QUOTE IN CHICAGO, ILLINOIS. GOT IM-
PRESSION THAT INSALMO/S FATHER WAS FORMERLY A RACK-
ETEER AND WAS KNOWN TO RESTAURANT OWNER. _____
STATED THAT THIS WAS ONLY OCCASION HE MET RESTAU-
RANT OWNER AND HE KNOWS NOTHING OF HIS BACK-
GROUND, ASSOCIATES, OR RACIAL OR EXTREMIST VIEWS OR
ACTIVITIES. _____ STATES INDIVIDUAL HE BELIEVED IDEN-
TICAL WITH OSWALD WAS DRESSED IN BLUE SUIT AND DARK
TIE. HIS WOMAN COMPANION WAS WHITE FEMALE, AGE
TWENTY TWO DASH TWENTY SIX, BLONDE HAIR, FLASHY

DRESSER. HE DESCRIBED OWNER OF RESTAURANT AS WHITE
MALE, AGE FIFTY, SIX FEET TALL, TWO HUNDRED FIFTY
POUNDS, DARK COMPLEXION, GRAY HAIR, COMBED STRAIGHT
BACK.

NEW ORLEANS WIL [SIC] CONDUCT APPROPRIATE INVES-
TIGATION TO ASCERTAIN IF INDIVIDUAL DESCRIBED IN
ABOVE INCIDENT MIGHT BE OSWALD.

It will be noted that in Sumner's second version, he included some
information that he had left out of his first account: that the restaurant owner had said he had been involved in the rackets, and that
Sumner had gotten the impression that the father of his companion,
Ernest Insalmo, "was formerly a racketeer and was known to the restaurant owner."

After New Orleans FBI agent Reed Jensen interviewed Joseph
Poretto and Anthony Marcello about Sumner's allegation, the New
Orleans office requested that the Savannah FBI reinterview Sumner,
for FBI reports dated December 2, 1963, state that at Darien, Georgia:

SV T-1 was reinterviewed on 12/2/63 and a full length front
view and profile view photograph of Lee Harvey Oswald, New
Orleans, Louisiana, Police Department Number 112723, taken
on August 9, 1963, was displayed to him.

SV T-1 advised this photograph resembles the individual
he observed one night at the Town and Country Restaurant
in New Orleans between February 15, 1963, and March 15,
1963.

The restaurant owner joined the couple at their table and
SV T-1 observed the restaurant owner remove a wad of money
from his pocket which he passed under the table to the man
sitting at the table [who resembled Oswald].

SV T-1 stated this was the only occasion he met the restaurant owner and he knows nothing of his background, associates, racial or extremist views or activities.

That SV T-1 was ignorant of the Town & Country Motel's other
purpose, and was ignorant of the affiliation with Carlos Marcello of
the man who he believed was the restaurant owner, suggests that SV
T-1 did not make his allegation in order to falsely implicate the
Marcello organization in the assassination.

Having received this new and provocative information from the

FBI in Savannah, one would have thought that the FBI in New Orleans would have pursued its investigation of SV T-1's allegation further, for what could have been more suggestive of a possible relationship between Lee Harvey Oswald and the boss of the Louisiana Mafia than Oswald's receiving a payment from one of Marcello's henchmen at the boss's headquarters. But instead of delving further into the allegation, the FBI dropped the matter entirely.

It is worth examining the actual FBI reports of the interviews of Poretto and Anthony Marcello to appreciate how superficial these interviews were. On Wednesday, November 27, Special Agent Reed Jensen of the New Orleans FBI office interviewed Joseph Poretto at the Town & Country Motel and reported on the interview as follows:

JOSEPH ALBERT PORETTO, owner, Town and Country Restaurant, 1225 Airline Highway, on interview was advised of the interviewing Agent's identity, that he was not required to submit to interview, that anything he might say could be used against him in a court of law and that he could first consult an attorney. No threats, rewards, promises or other inducements were made to PORETTO in connection with this interview and he voluntarily advised as follows:

On examination of a photograph of LEE HARVEY OSWALD New Orleans Police Department number 112723, Mr. PORETTO said he had never seen this individual in person before and was positive that he had never had any business dealings or association of any kind with this person.

According to Mr. PORETTO, since the assassination of President JOHN F. KENNEDY, he had seen numerous photos and TV shots of both LEE HARVEY OSWALD and JACK LEON RUBY since that time and had never seen or known of either person prior to this time. He said he had never heard of JACK RUBY even by reputation prior to his notoriety in the newspapers.

Mr. PORETTO stated he cannot recall having had any business dealings with anyone in about March or April 1963, or at any other time, who resembled OSWALD enough for a mistaken identity.

And that was that. No further questioning. What did Special Agent Reed Jensen expect Poretto to say? That he recognized the photograph of Lee Harvey Oswald as resembling the individual to whom

he had made a payment of money in the Town & Country restaurant in April 1963?

On the same day Reed Jensen interviewed Anthony Marcello at
the Town & Country Motel:

> ANTHONY MARCELLO, Manager, Town and Country Mo-
> tel, 1225 Airline Highway, New Orleans, Louisiana, on exam-
> ining a photograph of LEE HARVEY OSWALD, New Orleans
> Police Department number 112723, advised that he had never
> seen this individual at the Town and Country Motel. He said
> that he had seen numerous photographs and TV shots of both
> LEE HARVEY OSWALD, suspected assassin of President
> JOHN F. KENNEDY and of JACK LEON RUBY, suspected
> murderer of LEE HARVEY OSWALD and he was positive that
> he had never seen either of these individuals prior to their
> notoriety through the news media. Mr. MARCELLO made
> available registration records for the Town and Country Motel.

With these perfunctory interviews, the case was closed on SV T-1's
allegation that he saw someone resembling Oswald receive a payment
from the owner of the Town & Country Motel.

There were, of course, many things the FBI could have done to
further investigate Sumner's allegation. It could have checked the registration records of the Holiday Inn in New Orleans to determine
whether Sumner and Insalmo had stayed there during the period
Sumner claimed they were in New Orleans. It could have located
Ernest Insalmo in Sabene, Texas, and interviewed him about Sumner's allegation, since Insalmo had been sitting with Sumner that
night. It could have interviewed Salvadore Pizza and Benny Capeana
to establish the date of the wedding rehearsal they attended the night
they met Sumner and Insalmo at the Town & Country restaurant.
Once that date was established, the New Orleans office could have
asked the Dallas office to find out whether Lee Harvey Oswald could
have been in New Orleans at 10:00 P.M. on that date, in the light of
his family and job commitments at the time.

But the FBI did none of these. In the end, it appears that it officially dismissed Sumner's allegation solely because Oswald had not
yet moved to New Orleans when he had allegedly been seen by
Sumner in Carlos Marcello's New Orleans headquarters, as if it would
not have been possible for Oswald to travel from Dallas to New
Orleans in order to be at the Town & Country Motel by 10:00 P.M.

Certainly he could have accomplished this after getting out of work in Dallas at 4:45 P.M. or on a weekend.

Furthermore, if the FBI had taken the trouble to investigate Oswald's living arrangements in Dallas in March 1963, it would have found that they were such as to have permitted Lee to leave his apartment without his wife noticing. For the Oswalds were then living in an apartment in Neely Street in downtown Dallas that contained a small, independent room Lee had taken for himself as a private study. The room had an interior door leading to the rest of the apartment that could be locked from the inside, and another door leading outside that enabled Lee to come and go from the apartment unobserved by his wife.

Lastly, if the FBI was really intent on testing Sumner's credibility, it could have put Joe Poretto in a lineup, since he had a criminal record, and asked Sumner to identify him.

Curiously, FBI reports on its investigation of Sumner's allegation did not question Sumner's initial description of the clothing the man he later believed was Oswald was wearing or his description of Oswald's companion. In his allegations Sumner had described Oswald as "dressed in a blue suit and a dark tie" and as having been accompanied by a "young blond woman age twenty-two to twenty-six." Lee Harvey Oswald did not often wear dark suits and ties, although there is a photograph of him dressed that way. That his blond, 22-year-old wife, Marina, would have accompanied him to the Town & Country Restaurant that night seems unlikely, though the possibility should not be ruled out.

There was, of course, also the possibility that the man Sumner saw that night in the Town & Country restaurant was the Oswald impostor. By the date on which Sumner had made his allegation, November 26, 1963, the FBI was aware of the possibility that there had been someone impersonating Oswald in Louisiana, Mexico, and Texas. The most recent example had been the phantom Oswald who visited the Cuban and Soviet embassies in Mexico City, photographs and voice recordings of whom were found not to resemble the face and voice of Oswald.

But there is testimony that either Oswald or someone closely resembling him was observed in New Orleans as early as February or March 1963, which would tend to lend credence to Sumner's alleged sighting of someone resembling Oswald in New Orleans during the same period. In 1975 a high-ranking Immigration and Naturalization Service inspector told the Senate Intelligence Committee that he was "absolutely certain" he interviewed Lee Harvey Oswald in a New

Orleans jail cell before the inspector's departure from New Orleans
on April 1.

As it turned out, the New Orleans FBI closed down its investigation of Sumner's allegation barely six days after it had been reported
to the Savannah office, without making the slightest effort to fully
resolve it.

Later, when the FBI transmitted reports of Sumner's allegation
and the FBI's interviews of Joseph Poretto and Anthony Marcello to
the commission President Johnson had established to investigate the
assassination, it did not transmit Sumner's second version of his allegation. This was the one in which he had indicated that the Town
& Country restaurant owner (i.e., Poretto) had said he was involved
"in the rackets," and in which he had gotten the impression that
Ernest Insalmo's father "was formerly a racketeer and was known to
the restaurant owner."

Nor did the FBI transmit to the Warren Commission the New
Orleans Airtel of November 27 notifying the Dallas and Savannah
FBI that Joseph Poretto and Joseph Marcello had criminal records,
that Joseph Marcello was a brother of Carlos Marcello and "all three
are known hoodlums," and that "Carlos Marcello was known to have
had an interest in the Town and Country Motel and restaurant…a
known hangout for the hoodlum element."

Thus what the Warren Commission received was an allegation apparently devoid of any sinister significance. If the commission staff
members who read the allegation had never heard of the Town &
Country Motel, Joseph Poretto, or Anthony Marcello, they would have
dismissed Sumner's report as just another crank allegation.

Was there any potential significance to Sumner's allegations? Of
course there was. We now know that in the spring and summer of
1963 Lee Harvey Oswald worked as a runner and collector for his
uncle Dutz Murret's New Orleans bookmaking operation, which meant
that he indirectly worked for Carlos Marcello.

If Sumner's observation was accurate, the Marcello-Oswald relationship antedated Oswald's return to New Orleans on April 24. Is
that possible? Of course it is. Through his uncle Dutz, Oswald could
have been contacted in Dallas by one of the Marcello brothers who
regularly visited there—either Vincent or Sammy—to take on some
as yet unknown assignment. (If we are to believe Eugene De Laparra,
Vincent Marcello used to travel back and forth between New Orleans
and Dallas in a private plane piloted by David Ferrie.)

It is believed that Oswald's July and August Fair Play for Cuba
demonstrations in New Orleans might have been planned and financed by the Marcello organization as a way of establishing Oswald's

pro-Castro credentials, an indispensable first step to setting him up to eventually take the blame for the assassination. If this was the case, the Marcello organization could also have been behind Oswald's first Fair Play for Cuba demonstration, which took place in Dallas in early April. Oswald was out of work at the time and needed money badly. In March he had bought a mail-order pistol and rifle, and in early April he began demonstrating for Castro on the streets of downtown Dallas, wearing a placard on his chest proclaiming HANDS OFF CUBA VIVA FIDEL and passing out free printed Fair Play for Cuba Committee literature. Who was putting up the money for these non-essential expenses of the unemployed Oswald?

Whatever the case, Sumner's allegation certainly demanded a much more thorough investigation than it received from the FBI.

Two days after the Savannah FBI office received Sumner's allegation, the Philadelphia FBI received still another allegation pertaining to the assassination that involved an associate of the Marcellos. It was the report of ex-Marine Eugene De Laparra, who, while working in a Marcello-backed bar and restaurant in March or April 1963, allegedly overheard the bar owner, Ben Tregle, tell two friends: "There is a price on the President's head and other members of the Kennedy family. Somebody will kill Kennedy when he comes south." De Laparra added that bar owner Tregle's principal financial backer was "Vincent Marcella [sic], New Orleans racketeer reported to travel to Dallas on many occasions."

When the New Orleans FBI investigated this allegation, it immediately ascertained that "Vincent Marcella" was Vincent Marcello, a brother of Carlos Marcello. Yet, after a brief interrogation of the bar owner and his friend, horse trainer Norman LaBlanc, who both denied knowledge of a plot to assassinate President Kennedy, the FBI investigated De Laparra's allegation no further, even though the reporting agent stated that De Laparra had provided reliable information in the past.

Once again, it is illuminating to read Special Agent Jensen's report of the interviews:

TREGLE stated that he recalls November 22, 1963, and all during that day he was around his place of business; and it is his recollection that NORMAN JOSEPH LEBLANC was either at the horse barns at Jefferson Downs Race Track or at 6115 Airline Highway that day. TREGLE said he has never known anyone frequenting TREGLE's Bar (now called the Lounnor Restaurant), called "the Professor."

According to TREGLE he believes in segregation and as a result has never agreed with President JOHN F. KENNEDY's Civil Rights Program; and in connection with this he feels that it is his prerogative to do so and express himself accordingly. He stated, however, that he can never recall at any time making any comments which could be construed as a threat on his part to kill the President of the United States or anyone else. He could not recall any incident in which he was looking at a rifle advertisement and then commenting that this rifle could be used to harm anyone; and further, he could not recall ever saying that the President of the United States would be shot if he made a visit to the Southern area of the country.

TREGLE stated that although he did not like President KENNEDY as a President he has never been associated with any organization of a political nature that had a specific purpose "fighting" the Kennedy administration's Civil Rights Program.

He stated he would never stoop to violence of any kind against anyone and he has never been associated with anyone to his knowledge who advocates violence to promote their aims and purposes. He said he considers himself a patriotic American and he is appalled at anyone who would kill an official of the United States Government, particularly the President of the country.

Needless to say, the response of Ben Tregle had little to do with Eugene De Laparra's allegation. De Laparra never accused Tregle of threatening to kill President Kennedy or of being in Dealey Plaza at the moment Kennedy was shot or of "stooping to violence." He merely stated he had overheard Tregle mentioning that there was a plan to kill President Kennedy when he came down south.

But the most pointless report of all was the apparent alibi Special Agent Regis Kennedy provided for Ben Tregle's financial backer, Vincent Marcello, who was not interviewed about De Laparra's allegation, though he was mentioned prominently in it.

On November 22, 1963, SA Regis L. Kennedy was in United States District Court, New Orleans, Louisiana, at the trial of Carlos Marcello and Joseph Marcello, who had been charged with fraud against the government. During the A.M. and P.M. sessions of the trial on this date, SA Kennedy observed Vincent

Joseph Marcello, a brother of Carlos and Joseph Marcello, at the trial.

As if to say: "No, Vincent Marcello was not hiding behind the bushes near the grassy knoll in Dealey Plaza the moment President Kennedy was shot."

As we have already indicated, De Laparra made a second allegation to the FBI about what he had overheard in Tregle's Bar in the spring of 1963. This new allegation was apparently occasioned by De Laparra's learning of the sudden death of David Ferrie during District Attorney Jim Garrison's reinvestigation of the Kennedy assassination in 1967. In his February 23, 1967, version made to the FBI office in Newark, for De Laparra was then living in New Jersey, De Laparra included some information that he had not provided on November 27, 1963, and appears to have told at least one untruth. The full text of the February 23, 1967, allegation is published here for the first time:

DELA PARRA [SIC] AROUND JUNE, SIXTY THREE WAS WORKING FOR BENNY TRAEGEL [SIC], AT TRAEGEL'S BAR, IN NEW ORLEANS, AND WHILE WORKING IN THIS BAR ON OR ABOUT SIX TWENTY TWO, SIXTY THREE, TONY MARCELLA [SIC] CAME INTO THE PREMISES TO SERVICE THE PIN BALL MACHINE. DELA PARRA ADVISED TONY MARCELLA IS THE BROTHER OF VINCENT MARCELLA, WHO OWNS MOTELS IN NEW ORLEANS.

VINCENT MARCELLA HAS ANOTHER BROTHER, WHO IS A PART TIME GAMBLER IN NEW ORLEANS.

DELA PARRA ADVISED THAT ON THIS PARTICULAR DATE, TONY MARCELLA STATED TO BEN TRAEGEL AND THREE OR FOUR OTHERS AT THE BAR THAT "THE WORD IS OUT TO GET THE KENNEDY FAMILY."

AFTER THE REMARK WAS MADE, BEN TRAEGEL CAME TO DELA PARRA IN THE BACK ROOM OF THE BAR AND REPEATED THE STATEMENT.

BEN TRAEGEL WAS LAUGHING AND ADDED THEY ARE ONLY PAYING ONE HUNDRED THOUSAND DOLLARS.

IMMEDIATELY FOLLOWING THIS INCIDENT, DELA PARRA REPORTED THE INFO TO THE NEW ORLEANS OFFICE AND IMMEDIATELY SUBSEQUENT TO THE DEATH OF PRESIDENT

KENNEDY, DELA PARRA ADVISED THAT HE FURNISHED THE
INFO AGAIN TO THE PHILADELPHIA OFFICE OF THE FBI.

DELA PARRA ADVISED THAT AFTER READING ABOUT THE
DEATH OF DAVID W. FERRIE IN NEW ORLEANS YESTERDAY,
HE WANTED TO PASS ON INFO TO THE EFFECT THAT FERRIE
WAS THE PERSONAL PILOT FOR VINCENT MARCELLA.

DELA PARRA STATED THAT HE, HIMSELF IS ALSO A HORSE
TRAINER AND USED TO TAKE CARE OF ONE OF VINCENT
MARCELLA'S HORSES.

VINCENT USED TO TAKE SEVERAL TRIPS BY PLANE TO
DALLAS.

DELA PARRA ADDED THAT BEN TRAEGEL KNEW LEE HAR-
VEY OSWALD VERY WELL.

MAIL COPY TO DALLAS.

LHM FOLLOWS.

The apparent untruth is De Laparra's claim that he reported the
incident in Tregle's Bar to the FBI in New Orleans "immediately following the incident." We know that he reported it to the FBI in
Philadelphia "immediately subsequent to the death of President Kennedy," but there is no record of his having reported it earlier. According to the FBI file on the allegation, if, in fact, De Laparra made
the allegation "immediately following the incident," the relevant report has disappeared from the file.

De Laparra's 1967 allegation is particularly illuminating in that it
explains why Ben Tregle appeared to have had foreknowledge of an
impending attempt on President Kennedy's life, as De Laparra had
contended he had in his original allegation. Who had told Ben Tregle
there was "a price on the President's head and other members of the
Kennedy family"? Now it appears one of Carlos Marcello's younger
brothers had. Would Anthony Marcello have been servicing pinball
machines in Tregle's Bar in the spring of 1963? Of course he would
have. He worked for his brothers' Jefferson Music Company at the
time, the major distributor in Louisiana of jukeboxes, slot machines,
and pinball machines. Ben Tregle's place had benefited from Marcello
financing in return for accepting Jefferson Music's coin-operated machines.

We can probably take Ben Tregle's reported remark "they are
only paying one hundred thousand dollars" with a grain of salt. De
Laparra's observation that Vincent Marcello, who ran the Jefferson
Music Company, "used to take several trips by plane to Dallas" is not

difficult to accept. Vincent's company was a major distributor of coin-operated machines in Dallas, and it probably leased machines to Jack Ruby's nightclubs. That Ben Tregle "knew Lee Harvey Oswald very well" is also possible. Since Tregle ran "a horse book" out of his bar, it is entirely conceivable that Oswald was in touch with him as a runner in the Marcello bookmaking network during the spring and summer of 1963. Tregle's Bar was also fairly close to Marcello's Town & Country restaurant, where Georgia informant Sumner claimed he saw Oswald earlier in March.

"The word is out to get the Kennedy family." It will be recalled that a similar idea had been expressed by prostitute Rose Cheramie when she told East Louisiana State Hospital physician Dr. Victor Weiss that "word was out in the underworld that Kennedy would be assassinated."

But in the end, the FBI rejected De Laparra's two allegations after conducting a virtual noninvestigation of them. Why did the FBI deny him credibility? The reason was never given at the time De Laparra made his initial allegation, but was implied later in an FBI report on him of February 27, 1967:

> De Laparra advised that during World War II he was in the U.S. Marine Corps as a result of which he suffered a nervous breakdown and from 1953 to 1954 he was in the hospital from his nervous condition. De Laparra is still receiving a 70 percent disability from the Veterans Administration due to his nervous breakdown which was prompted as the result of his military service....No further action is contemplated in this matter.

So that was the reason why the FBI disbelieved De Laparra's testimony. He was some kind of a nut.

Yet, on November 28, 1963, the FBI agent from the Philadelphia office who interviewed De Laparra when he made his original allegation stated that De Laparra had "appeared generally rational during conversation"; and on November 29, 1963, in a New Orleans FBI teletype to headquarters in Washington on the allegation, the reporting agent stated: "It is noted De Laparra has provided reliable information in the past to New Orleans [FBI agents] regarding gambling activity."

What the FBI did, then, was to officially reject De Laparra's tes-

timony on the basis of what an agent believed his psychological state
had been ten to twenty years before. According to the FBI file on De
Laparra which I received, the FBI did not test the state of De Laparra's mental health in 1963 and 1967 and made no effort to determine the precise nature of his "disability."

Could there have been anything to the De Laparra allegations?
Of course there could have been. If Tregle's Bar and "horse book"
had not been a Marcello-sponsored business, the allegations would
have been suspect. But Tregle's establishments had been characterized by law enforcement authorities as Marcello fronts as far back as
the Kefauver Committee investigation of organized crime in 1951.
What De Laparra claimed he had heard at Tregle's Bar in the spring
of 1963 was perfectly in keeping with the character and history of
the place. Tregle's was a mob hangout supported by the leading Mafia
family of Louisiana. Vincent Marcello helped finance the business,
and his younger brother Anthony helped service its jukebox and pinball and slot machines. If an allegation of foreknowledge of an intention to assassinate the President on the part of the mob would have
been made in the spring of 1963, it would have been made precisely
in such a place as Tregle's Bar.

As for the allegations themselves, that Ben Tregle had said that
there was "a price on the President's head and other members of the
Kennedy family," and that Tony Marcello had said word was out "to
get the Kennedy family," we have seen that an intention on the part
of the underworld to assassinate the President had been in the air
since the late summer of 1962, when Jimmy Hoffa had confided to
Edward Partin, Carlos Marcello had confided to Edward Becker, and
Santos Trafficante had confided to Jose Aleman that President Kennedy was "going to be hit." As one of Carlos Marcello's more trusted
brothers, Tony Marcello could well have heard of these murderous
intentions from his oldest brother and told Ben Tregle and three or
four others who hung out in his bar about them one day when he
came to the place to service the pinball machine. Given what we now
know, there was little reason why the FBI should have found De
Laparra's allegations so incredible.

What *was* incredible about the whole affair was the FBI's per-
emptory rejection of the De Laparra allegation and how the bureau
eventually prevented the Warren Commission from appreciating its
potential significance. Instead of treating this potentially significant allegation with respect, the bureau treated it as the ravings of a madman.
And when it was eventually transmitted to the President's commission to investigate the assassination of John F. Kennedy, no mention

was made that Vincent Marcello was a brother of the boss of the Louisiana Mafia, one of Attorney General Kennedy's prime targets in his war on organized crime. Unless the Warren Commission staffer who read the allegation knew of the reputation of Tregle's Bar and knew who its principal financial backer was, he was bound to dismiss De Laparra as just another crank and consign his allegations to oblivion. This was, of course, what happened to both Sumner's and De Laparra's allegations.

But what of Carlos Marcello during the days immediately following the assassination? Certainly he must have been fully aware that a good number of his associates, including one of his own brothers, had been questioned in connection with the crime. On the basis of the available evidence, what did he probably know?

By December 1, eight days after the assassination, Carlos Marcello must have known that a nephew of one of his bookmakers in downtown New Orleans had been arrested and charged with murdering President Kennedy, that an associate of his deputy in Dallas had been arrested for murdering the President's accused assassin, that his private investigator had been arrested in New Orleans for conspiring to assassinate the President, that *both* his brother Anthony and his lieutenant Joe Poretto had been questioned by the FBI as to whether they had seen the President's accused assassin in the Town & Country Motel in March, and that an associate of his brother Vincent's, Ben Tregle, had been questioned by the FBI in connection with the plan to murder President Kennedy, which Tregle had allegedly heard about in the spring.

But that was not all. Within days of the assassination, New Orleans FBI agents were also questioning some of Carlos's Bourbon Street operatives, this time not in regard to Oswald but in regard to his murderer, Jack Ruby.

Frank Caracci was a major figure in the Marcello organization and a close friend of Carlos's. A big-time gambler and Bourbon Street nightclub owner, he had gambling operations extending also to Houston and Dallas. Five days after the assassination, FBI agents went to the striptease joint he owned in partnership with the Marcellos, the 500 Club, and questioned him at length about a visit the killer of the President's suspected assassin purportedly made to the 500 Club last June. Caracci admitted that Jack Ruby had come into his club at that time looking for strippers to hire for his joint in Dallas. Caracci had instructed his night manager, Cleeve Dugas, to tell Jack Ruby to go to the nearby Sho-Bar, owned by Pete Marcello, where the hottest stripper in town, the notorious "Jada," was performing. Ruby then walked over to the Sho-Bar, watched Jada perform her outrageous act, and presumably offered her a contract to strip at his club in Dallas. In his account of Ruby's visit to the Sho-Bar, the FBI interviewing agent reported that "Bourbon Street sources recall that Mrs. Conforto danced under the name 'Jada' and was dancing at Ruby's Carousel Club in Dallas when President Kennedy was assassinated." The agent did not indicate whether Ruby had met with the man who had hired Jada, Pete Marcello, while he was at the Sho-Bar that night, but he did indicate that Ruby had met the night manager, Nick Graffagnini, a cousin of Frank Caracci's and an associate of the Marcellos'.

Given the importance of Frank Caracci and Pete Marcello to his organization, it is safe to say that Carlos Marcello received word around November 29 that the feds had been questioning his associate Caracci and either Pete or Pete's night manager, Nick Graffagnini, about Jack Ruby.

That made a total of at least eight persons associated with Carlos's underworld organization, in varying degrees of closeness, who were either arrested or questioned by the FBI in regard to the assassination of the President within a week or so of the crime.

Thus, it is safe to say that by Monday, December 1, Carlos Marcello must have been wondering whether anybody in the FBI had been putting two and two together and coming up with a suspect in the assassination named Carlos Marcello.

The person in the FBI who should have been putting two and two together was Director J. Edgar Hoover. Admittedly Hoover, at the time, was preoccupied with other conspiracy allegations, particularly those suggesting the possibility of Cuban or Soviet involvement, and was worried that the press might discover that the FBI had been lax in keeping Oswald's security file up to date. Still, by December 1, Hoover must have been aware of the same allegations we can assume Marcello was aware of by that date. (The assistant FBI director at the time, Courtney Evans, told me that "Hoover saw everything that came in.") What is more, by December 18, two weeks after the FBI had completed its initial investigation of the assassination, Hoover also knew the results of the FBI's investigation of Ferrie's post assassination trip through Texas.

And yet Hoover had his agents in New Orleans and in Texas drop their investigation of Ferrie after December 18 and make no mention of him, or of Carlos Marcello, in the FBI supplemental report of January 13, 1964, which was transmitted to the Warren Commission shortly thereafter. And he made no attempt to investigate the possibility that Ferrie and Marcello may have been involved, with

Oswald, and possibly Ruby, in a conspiracy to assassinate the President.

What are we to make of this apparently deliberate effort of Hoover's to ignore and suppress all the circumstantial evidence that his own field agents had developed, suggesting the possible complicity of Carlos Marcello in the assassination of President Kennedy and the murder of the President's accused assassin?

To answer that question, we must examine the personality, career, and motivation of the director of the FBI at the time of the assassination.

37

Hoover's Investigation

By the time of the Kennedy assassination, J. Edgar Hoover, director of the Federal Bureau of Investigation for the past thirty-nine years, had become the federal government's most powerful bureaucrat. The source of his immense power lay in his total command of the government's domestic investigative apparatus. Over the years, he and his agents had compiled dossiers on every senator, every congressman, every cabinet officer, every President since he had taken office as director during the administration of Calvin Coolidge. With his puritanical antipathy toward what he habitually referred to as "sexual goings on" and obsession with "leftist subversion," Hoover's secret files became, in the words of one member of Congress, "the greatest depository of dirt in the world." Hoover managed to get the goods on practically every man of political influence in Washington over a period of almost four decades. No one, least of all Presidents, had the courage to challenge him for fear of what the FBI director might leak out of his files to the press. In the words of his deputy director, William Sullivan, Hoover was the "greatest blackmailer of all time."

Hoover developed over the years into an authoritarian megalomaniac who eventually came to identify himself so closely with the organization he led that he and the FBI became one and the same. Presidents, one and all, had always let him get away with circumventing his titular superior, the attorney general, in favor of direct personal contact with the oval office. Until the inauguration of John F. Kennedy, Hoover had enjoyed more direct access to the President than any other Washington bureaucrat in recent history.

Along with his authoritarian megalomania, fanatic institutional loyalty, and status as the chief keeper of the nation's secrets, Hoover was obsessed with the Communist menace and was always ready to begin a new witch-hunt of "leftist sympathizers" and "subversives." Included among subversives, in addition to Communists, were also all blacks agitating for their civil rights.

Of the many blind spots in Hoover's limited field of vision, none was more opaque than his stubborn belief that organized crime did not exist in the United States. Even when the notorious national crime conclave at Apalachin, New York, attended by over sixty Mafia leaders and their pawns in organized labor, from every major city in the country, was discovered in 1957, Hoover still was not convinced that a national network of organized criminals existed. When his subordinates produced a full report on the Apalachin meeting, naming all the delegates and the Mafia families they represented, Hoover called it "baloney" and ordered all copies destroyed.

It was only natural, then, that when the 35-year-old former chief counsel of the McClellan Committee, Robert F. Kennedy, became attorney general of the United States in 1961, he was destined to clash with his subordinate, the 66-year-old director of the FBI. For Robert Kennedy had correctly identified organized crime for what it was and considered *it*, not Communist subversion, the foremost internal menace to American society.

Not long after Robert Kennedy took office as the chief law enforcement officer of the land, he did something to Hoover that no other attorney general had ever done. He took away his direct access to the President and made him report directly to him. This enraged and offended the egotistic and self-important Hoover, who would one day characterize Robert Kennedy as a "sneaky little son of a bitch."

During his brief administration as attorney general, Robert Kennedy continuously berated Hoover for dragging his feet in his investigation of organized crime. In particular, he berated him over what he believed was a wholly inadequate FBI investigation of Carlos Marcello. As we know, Kennedy had identified Marcello as one of the Justice Department's four top priority targets for prosecution in its campaign against organized crime. Although Hoover was successful in bugging and wiretapping other powerful Mafia leaders in such cities as Chicago, Philadelphia, and Buffalo, his agents in New Orleans were never able to get to Marcello. When Kennedy would ask Hoover for the latest report from New Orleans on Marcello, to his utter exasperation Hoover would send him Regis Kennedy's latest reiteration that Marcello was nothing but "a tomato salesman."

The attorney general was not the only Kennedy to be exasperated by the FBI director. The President was also exasperated by him, though for different reasons. John F. Kennedy knew that Hoover had compromising material in his secret files on him and his family going back to his father's early days as a bootlegger during prohibition. Among the dirt the director had collected on the new President were records and tapes about an affair he had during his World War II Navy days with one Inga Arvad, a married woman and former Danish beauty queen alleged to have been a Nazi sympathizer. It had been Hoover's discovery of Kennedy's first of many *liaisons dangereuses* that had been responsible for Kennedy's transfer from Naval Intelligence in Washington to PT boat school and eventually to combat service in the south Pacific.

So concerned had John F. Kennedy been about what Hoover had in his files that it is thought one of the principal reasons why, as President-elect, he appointed his admittedly inexperienced younger brother attorney general was so Bobby could keep an eye on the keeper of the files.

However, to Hoover's delight, and the Kennedy brothers' eventual embarrassment, the President and the attorney general managed to add a good deal more to Hoover's secret depository during their years in power.

The brothers were young, overconfident, and in their heyday: they had their pick of the most beautiful women in America in an era when journalists left politicians' amorous lives alone. While campaigning for the Democratic nomination, John Kennedy became embroiled with two Hollywood beauties: the starlet Judith Campbell, who was also a girlfriend of Frank Sinatra and Chicago Mafia boss Sam Giancana; and the actress, and touted "sex goddess" Marilyn Monroe. To Kennedy's acute annoyance, it was the hated Hoover who eventually forced him to stop seeing Miss Campbell, pointing out to the President over a private White House luncheon in the winter of 1962 that she was also seeing the Chicago "hoodlum" who had been involved with the CIA in plotting the assassination of Fidel Castro. However, that slap on the wrist did not deter Kennedy from continuing his relationship with Marilyn Monroe and pursuing other lovelies with reckless disregard for the possible consequences. According to recently released FBI files on John F. Kennedy's extramarital affairs, J. Edgar

Hoover's sleuths discovered Kennedy liaisons with no fewer than thirty-two women during his brief presidency.

Although Robert Kennedy was far less of a sexual libertine than his older brother, reliable evidence has accumulated over the years indicating that he too succumbed to the charms of one of his brother's paramours: the celebrated, tormented Marilyn Monroe.

As it turned out, John F. Kennedy's dalliances with Judith Campbell and Marilyn Monroe and Robert's with Miss Monroe were to make them unwitting hostages of the hated Hoover and possible targets for blackmail by organized crime.

As revealed by Anthony Summers in his 1985 book *Goddess: The Secret Lives of Marilyn Monroe*, it was Marilyn's association with Frank Sinatra that brought her into the company of some of the Kennedys' most determined enemies. One of these was the Los Angeles organized crime boss Mickey Cohen, who had links to Carlos Marcello and John Roselli and had shared one of his girlfriends, the stripper Candy Barr, with Jack Ruby. One of Cohen's rackets was sexually compromising Hollywood stars for the purpose of blackmail. It had been Cohen who engineered the torrid affair between his accomplice, Johnny Stompanato, and Lana Turner, in the hope of getting pictures of the two in bed together. (The attempt backfired when Stompanato was murdered by Lana Turner's daughter in the actress's bedroom.) Through Mickey Cohen, Marilyn met petty mob figures George Piscitelle and Sam Lo Cigno, with whom she evidently had affairs. Joseph Shimon, a former police inspector in Washington, D.C., who knew Sam Giancana and John Roselli, has testified that Marilyn Monroe also knew John Roselli, who, as we know, was also a friend of Judith Campbell's. Roselli at the time was Sam Giancana's fixer in Los Angeles, charged with subjecting the Hollywood film industry to mob control.

It now appears beyond dispute that the Kennedys' enemies in organized crime and the crime-corrupted Teamsters Union were following John Kennedy's extramarital adventures with Judith Campbell and Marilyn Monroe with the purpose of compromising him and his administration's war on organized crime.

As revealed by Anthony Summers, and also by the BBC television documentary "The Last Days of Marilyn Monroe," as early as mid-1961, private detective Fred Otash, working on behalf of Jimmy Hoffa and perhaps some members of organized crime, succeeded in wiring rooms and telephone lines in Marilyn Monroe's home and in Kennedy in-law Peter Lawford's beach house. Evidently the tapes installed picked up "sounds of lovemaking between Marilyn and John Kennedy." Years later, Chuck O'Brien, Jimmy Hoffa's stepson, testified: "Hoffa kept the tapes in his safe."

After a while, this appallingly dangerous situation was discovered by the FBI. In 1984 former FBI Assistant Director Courtney Evans, who had functioned as liaison between Kennedy and FBI Director Hoover, told British journalist Anthony Summers that he and Hoover were aware that Sam Giancana and Jimmy Hoffa were possibly attempting to blackmail the Kennedys over their relationships with Marilyn Monroe and other women.

Which brings us to Robert Kennedy's affair with Marilyn Monroe. According to the BBC's and Anthony Summers' interviews of Deborah Gould, who claims to have received her information from her former husband and former Kennedy family in-law Peter Lawford, who "confessed all" to her one day, Robert Kennedy's involvement with Marilyn started when he was sent to Miss Monroe as his brother's "messenger boy" to tell Marilyn that her relationship with the President had become too dangerous to continue. In the midst of this mission, Robert became smitten by the actress and ended up initiating a sexual affair with her himself. It was, all things considered, a reckless escapade. Robert Kennedy, married and a father of nine, was, as the attorney general of the United States, the chief law enforcement officer of the land. In 1960 he had been named "Father of the Year" by an important national magazine. Kennedy must have known he was highly vulnerable to blackmail if he did anything that would compromise his integrity as a husband, father, and high-ranking public servant. Nevertheless, with heedless abandon, he plunged into a passionate relationship with America's reigning sex goddess.

This new relationship was not ignored by the Kennedys' Mafia enemies. According to Summers and the BBC, soon Jimmy Hoffa's chief wiretapper, Bernard Spindell, and his assistant, Earl Jaycox, were eavesdropping electronically on Robert Kennedy's trysts with Miss Monroe. Hoffa and his criminal allies continued bugging and wiretapping the Lawford villa in Santa Monica and Miss Monroe's house in Brentwood.

Not only did this electronic eavesdropping pick up "sounds of lovemaking," but, according to witnesses who claimed they had listened to the tapes, it also picked up scraps of conversations between the Kennedy brothers and Miss Monroe in which such sensitive issues as Cuba, Castro, the Bay of Pigs, the question of firing FBI Director Hoover, and the investigation of Jimmy Hoffa were bandied about.

Later, firm evidence emerged that Hoffa and the mob were definitely aware of the Kennedy brothers' extramarital adventures and of how they could use what they knew as leverage against the government's efforts to prosecute them. Once, in the midst of his desperate battle to avoid prison, Hoffa told an FBI agent that he knew some "sordid details" about the Kennedy brothers' personal lives. Sam Giancana had occasion to say more or less the same thing. According to an FBI report, when Giancana and his girlfriend Phyllis McGuire were once accosted by FBI agents in Chicago's O'Hare Airport, Giancana yelled at an agent: "I know all about the Kennedys…and one of these days…I am going to tell all!"

Then in 1979, as the House Select Committee on Assassinations was concluding its investigation of President Kennedy's murder, a long-suppressed transcript of an FBI tape recording of a conversation between Florida organized crime financier Meyer Lansky and his wife surfaced that revealed that Lansky knew Robert Kennedy was "running around" with a well-known woman. To which Mrs. Lansky remarked that it probably had been Frank Sinatra who had procured the woman for Kennedy.

Finally, in 1962, things began to come to a head. In February Hoover warned President Kennedy of the danger of continuing his relationship with Judith Campbell, considering who else she was keeping company with at the time. Later, Courtney Evans, speaking on behalf of Hoover, warned Robert Kennedy about his and his brother's association with Marilyn Monroe.

Realizing they were now in potentially deep trouble, John and Robert Kennedy began to back away from the web of perilous relationships in which they had become entangled. The President severed his relationship with Frank Sinatra and had his last flings with Judith Campbell and Marilyn Monroe. By mid-June Robert had also stopped seeing Miss Monroe, and she was told never to contact John or Robert again.

But so far as Marilyn Monroe was concerned, things were far from over. In her apparent naiveté, and obvious vulnerability, she could not understand why the Kennedy brothers had abandoned her.

In early August of 1962 Robert Kennedy went to San Francisco to attend a meeting of the American Bar Association being held at the St. Francis Hotel. He and his wife, Ethel, stayed at a ranch owned by John Bates, a wealthy San Francisco lawyer and friend, located around 60 miles south of the city.

Marilyn learned that Kennedy was attending the Bar Association meeting and phoned the St. Francis from her Brentwood home several times. Kennedy did not return her calls.

Then, according to a friend of Marilyn's, Jeanne Carmen (who related her story to Anthony Summers), on the evening of August 3 Marilyn received a call from some woman, whose voice Marilyn did not recognize, who said: "Leave Bobby alone, you tramp!" The anonymous calls continued throughout the evening and into the early morning of August 4.

As the BBC and Anthony Summers reconstructed the events of August 4th, around 4:30 that afternoon, Marilyn's psychiatrist, Dr. Ralph Greenson, received a phone call from Marilyn, and he deduced from her tone of voice that she was depressed and perhaps drugged. When Dr. Greenson went over to visit the actress, he found her alternately angry and depressed. She told him that she had recently had sexual relationships with "extremely important men in government...at the highest level." And, according to Greenson, she "expressed considerable dissatisfaction with the fact that here she was the most beautiful woman in the world, and she did not have a date on Saturday night." Greenson later testified that she had expected to see a very important person that night and he had rejected her. In her last call to Dr. Greenson Marilyn asked: "Did you take away my bottle of Nembutal?" Later on that night Marilyn phoned Peter Lawford, telling him how depressed she was that Bobby Kennedy had not called her and intimating she might do something to herself. Alarmed, Lawford drove to Marilyn's house and found her desperately ill. After being rushed to the Santa Monica Hospital in an ambulance, she died. Lawford, fearing a scandal, then took the body back to Marilyn's Brentwood home and arranged things to look as if the actress had died at home in her sleep.

Years later Anthony Summers discovered that General Telephone records of the calls Marilyn had made the day and night of her death had mysteriously disappeared. An investigation into this revealed that the FBI had confiscated them within hours of Miss Monroe's death on orders from Director J. Edgar Hoover, who, in turn, had received his orders from Attorney General Kennedy.

Hoover therefore possessed information on his boss that was so potentially damaging it could, if revealed, destroy his political career. And so after August 4, 1962, Robert Kennedy, and to some extent his brother John, became, in a very real sense, a hostage of the director of the FBI. Robert Kennedy would, of course, berate Hoover from time to time for his investigative shortcomings, especially for the insufficiency of his coverage of Carlos Marcello, but he could only go so far.

Hoover was well aware of the special power he had over Robert Kennedy when, in the afternoon of November 22, 1963, he was confronted with the biggest case of his career: the assassination of President John F. Kennedy.

For one thing, Hoover knew that he could cut the attorney general and his top aides out of his investigation of the assassination entirely and get away with it, which is exactly what happened. Two of Kennedy's most trusted men in the criminal division, Jack Miller and Robert Peloquin, attempted to inject themselves into Hoover's investigation of the President's murder and were pointedly shunned by the FBI, apparently on orders from the director. Then, Hoover deliberately withheld all reports of his field agents on matters related to the assassination from both Attorney General Kennedy and Deputy Attorney General Nicholas Katzenbach. Thus Kennedy and Katzenbach never saw any of the FBI reports of allegations from informants hinting that Carlos Marcello might have been involved in the assassination.

As soon as Lee Harvey Oswald was charged with the murder of President Kennedy, Hoover began building a case against him that pointed overwhelmingly toward his guilt. So overwhelming, in fact, was the initial, undigested evidence against Oswald that, years later, Katzenbach was to tell me he thought it was a little "fishy" at the time, that the case that developed against Oswald during the three days following the assassination was, in Katzenbach's words, "too good to be true."

Take Oswald's wallet, for example. The wallet had been confiscated by the Dallas Police shortly after Oswald's arrest, and its contents were later inventoried by the FBI. The items Special Agent Manning Clements found in the wallet provided such a full portrait of their owner, including his affiliations, contacts, and recent history, as to give rise to the suspicion that someone other than Oswald knew of their existence and knew full well what sort of a portrait of the alleged assassin they would paint. Among the items listed by Clements were:

- Selective Service card in the name of Lee Harvey Oswald
- Counterfeit Selective Service card in the name of Alek James Hidell
- Certificate of Service, U.S. Marine Corps
- A counterfeit Certificate of Service, U.S. Marine Corps, in the name of Alek James Hidell
- Department of Defense identification card in the name of Lee Harvey Oswald
- United States Forces, Japan, identification card in the name of Lee Harvey Oswald

- Social security card in the name of Lee Harvey Oswald
- Card with longhand writing: Embassy USSR, 1609 Decatur NW, Washington. D.C. Consular Reznichenko
- Slip of paper bearing address of American Communist publication *The Worker*
- Fair Play for Cuba Committee membership card, with New York address, issued to Lee H. Oswald
- Fair Play for Cuba Committee membership card, New Orleans chapter, issued to L. H. Oswald and signed by A. J. Hidell
- Snapshot of Lee Harvey Oswald in U.S. Marines uniform
- Snapshot of wife Marina and child
- A Marines marksman's medal
- $13 in currency

Three items found in the wallet bearing Oswald's alias, A. J. Hidell, provided the FBI with the name of the purchaser, by mail order, of the murder weapon. Another item attested to Oswald's expertise as a marksman. Still another—the Fair Play for Cuba Committee membership card—even hinted at a plausible motive.

Would a man intent on murdering the President of the United States embark on his mission carrying such a comprehensive collection of personal documents?

It seems unlikely, unless the assassin-to-be had been given absolute assurance that he would be allowed to escape. It is much more likely that someone knowledgeable of the contents of Oswald's wallet had set him up to take the blame for the impending murder, knowing full well how delighted the police and the FBI would be to find a plausible suspect in the assassination with a background such as that revealed by the wallet.

It should be noted that Special Agent Clements did not list in his inventory a library card in the name of David W. Ferrie. If indeed Ferrie's library card was found on Oswald, it would appear that either a Dallas Police officer removed the card from Oswald's wallet prior to turning the wallet over to the FBI, or Agent Clements omitted it from his inventory for some special reason.

Deputy Attorney General Katzenbach, copropagator of the lone gunman solution to the assassination, had thought the case against Oswald was "too good to be true." It certainly was. The contents of Oswald's wallet alone enabled the first investigators of the crime to prove Oswald had purchased the murder weapon and had a plausible motive for assassinating the President.

Today, after twenty-five years of investigative research, both official and unofficial, it is generally agreed that much of the evidence used to incriminate Oswald had been planted before and after the assassination by his coconspirators, and some had been hastily fabricated by the Dallas Police and the FBI in their rush to wrap up the case. A masterful exposé of these manipulations, fabrications, and suppressions of evidence may be found in Harold Weisberg's *Whitewash* books.

This narrative is no place for a detailed analysis of the evidence against Oswald. Suffice it to say that Hoover conducted his investigation of Oswald considering him guilty from the start and was determined to show that he acted without confederates. Witnesses who were unsympathetic to the FBI's scenario were ignored. Evidence suggesting that Oswald had been framed, or that he might have had confederates, was suppressed. In this climate the investigation turned out to be nothing more than a concerted attempt to incriminate Oswald, who, contrary to American principles of jurisprudence, was assumed guilty. Since he was not afforded legal representation during his questioning and was murdered within forty-eight hours of his arrest, Oswald was never given a chance to defend himself.

But did J. Edgar Hoover in his investigation of the Kennedy assassination consciously perpetrate a cover-up? And if he did, what did he cover up?

To answer these questions, it is necessary to analyze Hoover's responses to the daily developments in the Kennedy assassination case.

J. Edgar Hoover made up his mind very early in the game that Lee Harvey Oswald was his man. The young man's apparent background coincided nicely with what had been *his* major concern as the government's principal investigator of subversive activity in the United States: communism. Oswald, for Hoover, was a leftist commie nut, apparently far removed from the chief area of concern of his detested boss, Attorney General Kennedy: organized crime.

And so, barely five hours after the assassination, before the Dallas Police had formally charged Oswald with any crime, Hoover issued an internal memorandum stating that the Dallas Police "very probably" had President Kennedy's killer in custody, "a man in the category of a nut," who was "of the pro-Castro crowd," Lee Harvey Oswald.

By late afternoon that day, FBI headquarters in Washington was in an uproar. Everybody who was anyone in the bureau was at his or her desk; telephones were squealing, messengers were running here and there, as Hoover's aides frantically scrambled to assemble all available information on the suspected assassin.

Soon William G. Sullivan, assistant director in charge of security, had a reasonably up-to-date file on Oswald on his desk. What he read must have profoundly shocked him. For there in the file was the CIA report of Oswald's recent visit to Mexico City; Oswald's meeting at the Soviet Embassy with KGB Officer Valery Kostikov; a transcript of the CIA wiretaps of Oswald's and Kostikov's conversations, in which Oswald had supposedly referred to a CIA plot to assassinate Fidel Castro; Oswald's visits to the Cuban Embassy; and his intercepted November 9 letter to Kostikov. This was in addition to all the FBI data on Oswald's recent pro-Castro agitation in New Orleans.

Yet Oswald's name had not been placed on the FBI's Internal Security Index, and the Dallas Police and Secret Service had not been notified of his recent contacts in Mexico City. How could this possibly have happened?

Sullivan went to Hoover with what he had just learned, and Hoover went straight to the White House to inform the National Security Council of the suspected assassin's recent contacts in Mexico City with the KGB's western hemisphere assassinations officer. That done, he quickly returned to headquarters to see what he could do to salvage the reputation of the negligent FBI.

When, at a Saturday morning meeting with CIA Director John McCone and National Security Adviser McGeorge Bundy, President Johnson was apprised of Oswald's recent contacts in Mexico City, Johnson is said to have exclaimed that if rumors of a possible Oswald-KGB-Castro plot spread, they could "lead us into a war that would cost 40 million lives." He then telephoned Hoover and told him to put a stop to the rumors and discourage all talk of conspiracy, especially allegations involving Cuba and the Soviet Union. The Dallas Police were then notified of the President's wishes, and Hoover ordered Dallas FBI Agent James Hosty, the agent in charge of Oswald's file, to cease interrogating Oswald and return to the Dallas office immediately. Hosty was further ordered not to divulge anything that was in the Oswald file to the Dallas Police and to cease cooperating with them and the Secret Service. It was not until after the Warren Commission had concluded its investigation of the assassination that Hosty finally learned the reason behind these orders.

Ironically, although Hosty had known about Oswald's visits to the Soviet and Cuban embassies in Mexico City, and Oswald's meeting with Valery Kostikov, his file on Oswald did not contain the information that Kostikov was the KGB officer in charge of terrorism and assassinations in the western hemisphere. For an as yet unexplained reason, headquarters had neglected to transmit this information to the Dallas office. If it had, Hosty would have probably reported it to

Felix's Oyster Bar and Restaurant in the New Orleans French Quarter, owned in 1963 by Marcello associate Sam Saia, for whom Lee Harvey Oswald's uncle and surrogate father, "Dutz" Murret, worked as a bookmaker. In the summer of 1963 Lee Harvey Oswald worked out of Felix's as a runner for the Marcello gambling network. *(Charles Nes, 1988)*

The Sho-Bar striptease joint, operated by Peter Marcello, brother of Carlos, in the French Quarter not far from Felix's. Jack Ruby visited the Sho-Bar in June 1963. *(Charles Nes, 1988)*

Jack Ruby with strippers Kathy Kay and Alice Alexander in front of his Dallas nightclub, The Carousel, shortly before the assassination of President Kennedy. *(National Archives)*

"Jada," Janet Conforto, red-haired stripper who in 1963 danced in both Marcello's Sho-Bar and Ruby's Carousel Club. She was under contract with Ruby on the day of the Kennedy assassination. *(AP/Wide World Photos)*

President and Mrs. John F. Kennedy at Love Field, Dallas, the morning of November 22, 1963, about to embark on a motorcade through the city. *(UPI/ Bettmann News Photos)*

1:30 P.M. Zapruder's Famous Film

Abraham Zapruder, a Kennedy admirer, hoisted himself atop a four-foot abutment overlooking Dealey Plaza near the end of the motorcade route. He tried out his new 8mm Bell & Howell movie camera on Marilyn Sitzman, his dress firm's 20-year-old receptionist, as she walked by. Then he asked her to climb up. "Mr. Z. had vertigo," says Sitzman (below), who returned to the scene for the first time in two decades. "He said, 'Hold onto me so I won't fall off.' " While Zapruder, who died in 1970, exposed the most intensely scrutinized 478 frames in the history of film, Sitzman witnessed the assassination. "They had just come down the hill. I heard shots, and I thought, firecrackers. All I could see was his hands going up. Then he was right in front of us," she says, gesturing toward Elm Street, 200 feet from the Texas School Book Depository. "The last shot got him in the head. Everybody was on the ground, and Mr. Z. was gone. There had been gunshots, and I was standing there all by myself." The horror of the moment struck her as she watched the movie the next morning. "The film," says Sitzman, "was more gruesome than in real life." In the artist's enlargement of a film detail, Mrs. Kennedy reacts with a quizzical look as both the President and Connally are wounded.

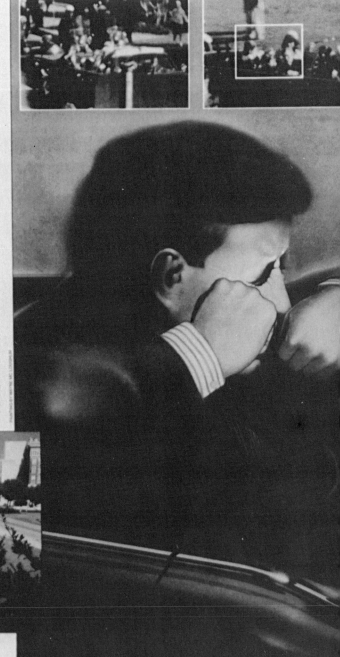

Sitzman points to fatal spot.

Hours later, President Kennedy is shot as his motorcade passes through Dealey Plaza. Governor Connally is also wounded in the attack. From a *Life* magazine artist's painting of a blowup of a frame in Abraham Zapruder's film of the assassination. (Life *Magazine* © 1983)

Lee Harvey Oswald flanked by two detectives, protests his innocence at press conference in Dallas Police headquarters, shortly after midnight, Saturday, November 23, 1963, after being accused of assassinating President Kennedy. "I'm just a patsy in this!" Oswald shouted to reporters. (© 1963 Matt Heron)

J. Edgar Hoover, director of the FBI for forty-eight years, repeatedly clashed with Attorney General Robert F. Kennedy. Hoover claimed organized crime did not exist in the United States. After the assassination of President Kennedy, Hoover tried to suppress all evidence of organized crime's complicity. (AP/Wide World Photos)

Carlos Marcello, his wife, Jacqueline, and younger brother Sammy leaving federal court in New Orleans August 18, 1965, after his acquittal on jury tampering charges arising from his November 1963 trial for conspiracy and perjury. *(AP/Wide World Photos)*

Five of the thirteen Mafiosi arrested on September 22, 1966, return with their attorneys to the site of their arrest: La Stella Restaurant in Forest Hills, New York. Clockwise: Joseph Marcello, Jr. (back to camera), attorney Jack Wasserman, Carlos Marcello, Santos Trafficante, attorney Frank Ragano, Anthony Carolla, and Frank Gagliano. *(AP/Wide World Photos)*

Carlos Marcello leaves a New Orleans courthouse after a 1968 grand jury hearing on alleged corruption in the Louisiana state government brought about by a series of articles in *Life* magazine the year before. Immediately behind Marcello is his attorney, G. Wray Gill. *(© 1968 Matt Heron)*

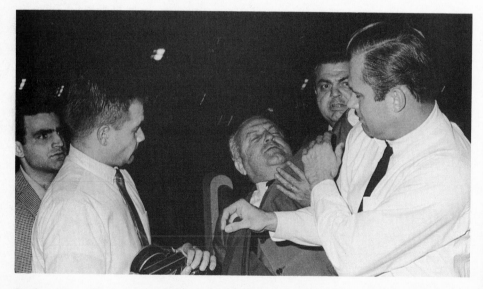

Carlos Marcello lets fly at FBI agent Patrick Collins at New Orleans airport, October 1, 1966, upon his return from the La Stella Mafia summit. Behind Carlos is his brother and family underboss, Joseph, Jr. To the left of the press photographer is Carlos's son, Joseph C. "Little Joe" Marcello. *(AP/Wide World Photos)*

the Dallas Police and the Secret Service, and the plot to kill the President might have been thwarted.

Later in the evening of November 22, after Hoover returned to headquarters, he set in motion a massive investigation of the assassination. At 9:40 P.M. he sent out a teletype to all field offices requesting they contact all informants for information bearing on the assassination. This was followed by an 11:00 P.M. teletype to all field offices requesting they make an effort to resolve all allegations pertaining to the assassination.

Around 1:35 A.M. on November 23 Oswald was finally charged with murdering the President. Later that morning, at the start of the business day, Hoover sent a memorandum to President Johnson informing him of the charges against Oswald, the evidence that had been found against him, and a few details of his pro-Castro sympathies: his membership in the Fair Play for Cuba Committee and his having demonstrated on behalf of Castro in the streets of New Orleans the previous summer.

Following that, Hoover sent a five-page top secret memorandum, with a covering letter, to the chief of the U.S. Secret Service, James J. Rowley, summarizing the results of the FBI's initial investigation of the assassination. The memorandum was pointedly not sent to President Johnson and was never turned over to the commission Johnson was to appoint to officially investigate the assassination. It was not made public until fourteen years later, when, in 1977, it was released by the FBI, along with 40,000 other Kennedy assassination documents, in response to a Freedom of Information Act lawsuit brought against the Justice Department by a private citizen. But even then, part of the document—its concluding paragraph—was entirely blanked out by the FBI censor. Subsequently, assassination researcher and author Mark Lane obtained an uncensored version of the memorandum through another Freedom of Information Act suit. The formerly blanked out paragraph read:

> The Central Intelligence Agency advised that on October 1, 1963, an extremely sensitive source had reported that an individual identified himself as Lee Oswald, who contacted the Soviet Embassy in Mexico City inquiring as to any messages. Special Agents of this Bureau, who have conversed with Oswald in Dallas, Texas, have observed photographs and have listened to a recording of his voice. These Special Agents are of the opinion that the above-referred-to individual was not Lee Harvey Oswald.

So J. Edgar Hoover had a persuasive report from his agents in Dallas that the man representing himself as Oswald who visited the Soviet Embassy and spoke with Valery Kostikov was probably an impostor.

Having to explain the existence of an Oswald impostor would have caused Hoover considerable embarrassment, for he had information on the possibility that someone had been impersonating Oswald as far back as 1960. Although he had sent two warnings to the State Department about it, he had kept the matter quiet since then and had somehow found a way to make his original memorandum disappear from Oswald's FBI file.

It was not, in fact, until 1975 that the relevant memorandum was found by a private assassination researcher among the Warren Commission documents that had been deposited in the National Archives. Members of the Warren Commission, however, testified that they had never been shown the Hoover memorandum. Furthermore, it was discovered that the two memos on the matter which Hoover had sent to the State Department were missing from the State Department's Oswald file. Apparently someone responsive to orders from Director Hoover had acted very fast after Oswald had been identified as a suspect in the Kennedy assassination.

The suppressed memorandum of June 3, 1960, from Director Hoover to the State Department had first presented the details of Lee Harvey Oswald's defection to the Soviet Union and then presented persuasive evidence that "an imposter could be using Oswald's identification data in the Soviet Union and elsewhere."

Now, on November 23, 1963, the director of the FBI, who had long suspected in silence that someone might have been impersonating Oswald, was faced, on the day after the President's assassination, with a CIA report on suspected assassin Oswald's October visit to the Soviet Embassy in Mexico City, accompanied by photographs and tapes of the man believed to have been Lee Harvey Oswald. FBI agents in Dallas had then emphatically denied that the accompanying photographs and tapes portrayed the face and voice of Lee Harvey Oswald. That an impersonator claiming to be Oswald had visited the Soviet Embassy and spoken with KGB Officer Kostikov about CIA plots to assassinate Castro clearly suggested that someone was deliberately attempting to plant evidence against Oswald in Mexico City in order to frame him for the impending assassination of the President.

Perception of this possibility, which clearly suggested the existence of a conspiracy to assassinate the President that the FBI should have detected in advance, must have made J. Edgar Hoover's blood run cold. For in addition to failing to detect a possible conspiracy, the bureau had made a monumental blunder in not placing Oswald's name on its Internal Security Index. If this had been done at the time that Oswald's, or his impersonator's, activities in Mexico City had become known to the CIA and the FBI, the Dallas FBI and Secret Service offices would have been alerted that Oswald was to be considered a security risk and therefore a threat to the President when he was due to visit Dallas in late November.

There was only one thing Hoover could do to escape what must have appeared to him to be the inevitability of public condemnation, even blame for the assassination, and that was to focus the FBI's investigation entirely on establishing Oswald as the lone assassin.

To begin implementing this decision, Hoover, on the night of Saturday, November 23, dispatched a teletype to all field offices rescinding his earlier directive of the evening of the 22nd, in which he requested his field offices to resolve all allegations pertaining to the assassination. The FBI field agents responded by conducting brief, pro forma investigations of the allegations that poured in, without attempting to resolve any of them. This strategy would protect Hoover from possible future criticism that his agents had paid no attention to the allegations that were made to the bureau in the wake of the assassination.

The next day, Sunday, November 24, at 11:21 P.M., Oswald was murdered by Jack Ruby. Consulting his files on Ruby, who had once been an FBI informant, Hoover quickly noted that Ruby had many connections to individuals associated with organized crime. Furthermore, he recognized that Ruby's silencing of the accused assassin was a typical Mafia tactic, the classic "gangland style" rubout of a potential witness.

Later on in the afternoon, after conferring with Deputy Attorney General Katzenbach, who had become acting attorney general upon the virtual collapse of Robert Kennedy, Hoover persuaded Katzenbach to go along with his plan to focus his investigation of the assassination exclusively on incriminating Lee Harvey Oswald. With Oswald no longer able to defend himself, Hoover phoned White House presidential aide Walter Jenkins and told him: "The thing I am most concerned about, and so is Mr. Katzenbach, is having something issued so we can convince the public that Oswald was the real assassin."

The next day, Monday, November 25, President Lyndon Johnson and FBI Director J. Edgar Hoover took time out to attend the monumental state funeral of John F. Kennedy, perhaps the most theatrical funeral in the nation's history. After the burial at Arlington, Johnson went to the State Department to receive the heads of government who had attended the funeral, and J. Edgar Hoover returned to his office at FBI headquarters to learn the latest developments in the assassination case.

And developments there were, in abundance. By late afternoon or early evening, Hoover was confronted with two deeply troubling conspiracy allegations.

For one, he was informed that a man, code-named "D," had shown up at the American Embassy in Mexico City and had told embassy personnel that he had been in the Cuban Consulate on September 18 and saw "Cubans pay Oswald a sum of money and talk about Oswald's assassinating someone."

As for the other allegation, he was told of a telephone call that had been received earlier in the afternoon from the New Orleans FBI office announcing the arrest of David Ferrie, an alleged friend of Oswald's on suspicion of having conspired with Oswald to assassinate President Kennedy, and his detention for questioning by the police, the Secret Service, and the FBI.

On Tuesday, November 26, official Washington went back to work. That morning President Johnson met with CIA Director McCone and told him that the FBI had primary responsibility for the investigation of Kennedy's death and directed him to make CIA resources available to the FBI. During the meeting Johnson and McCone were informed that the American ambassador to Mexico believed that the Cuban government was involved in the assassination.

By then Johnson had become extremely fearful that circumstantial evidence linking Castro to the assassination would become known to the general public. It was enough that the public already knew that the alleged assassin was apparently a Castro sympathizer. How would the public react to the allegation "D" had just made in the American Embassy in Mexico City? Johnson and his closest advisers knew they could not control the public's demand for revenge against the Cuban president in the event they strongly suspected his involvement in Kennedy's murder. And Johnson also knew that a renewed conflict with Cuba could entail a renewed conflict with the Soviet Union. He therefore gave out the word that talk of conspiracy should be discouraged by the media and law enforcement agencies, especially if it involved Cuba or the Soviet Union.

As if to underscore this wish from the standpoint of the Justice Department, Deputy Attorney General Katzenbach sent a message on the 26th to Presidential Assistant Bill Moyers as follows:

It is important that all of the facts surrounding President Kennedy's assassination be made public in such a way which will satisfy people in the United States and abroad that all the facts have been told and that a statement to this effect be made now.

1. The public must be satisfied that Oswald was the assassin; that he did not have confederates who are still at large; and that the evidence was such that he would have been convicted at trial.

2. Speculation about Oswald's motivation ought to be cut off, and we should have some basis for rebutting thought that this was a Communist conspiracy or (as the Iron Curtain press is saying) a right-wing conspiracy to blame it on the Communists. Unfortunately the facts on Oswald seem too pat—too obvious (Marxist, Cuba, Russian wife, etc.).

Later Hoover told Assistant FBI Director Alan Belmont that the FBI report he was preparing on the assassination "is to settle the dust, insofar as Oswald and his activities are concerned, both from the standpoint he is the man who assassinated the President, and relative to Oswald himself and his activities and background."

Meanwhile, allegations of conspiracy kept pouring into FBI field offices from all over the nation.

On the 26th Hoover received a long teletype from the New Orleans FBI about the interrogation of David Ferrie. The teletype told of the arrest of Ferrie, after his return from a two-day postassassination trip through Texas, and the testimony of Jack Martin, which indicated that Ferrie had taught Oswald how to fire a rifle with telescopic sight and had discussed assassinating President Kennedy with him. It went on to tell of Ferrie's association with the violently anti-Castro Cuban Revolutionary Council and of his employment by Carlos Marcello's attorney G. Wray Gill. Gill, the teletype noted, had gone to Ferrie's residence on November 24 and had told Ferrie's roommate, Layton Martens, that when Lee Harvey Oswald was arrested by the Dallas Police, Oswald was carrying a library card "with Ferrie's name on it." The teletype concluded with a sketchy account of Ferrie's recent trip to Texas, Ferrie's assertions that he did not know Oswald, and his contention that from the "end of August through November 22 he had been working on the case involving Carlos Marcello, who was charged in federal court in connection with a fraudulent birth certificate," and was with Marcello in federal court at the moment Kennedy was assassinated.

Hoover's reaction to this news was to order the FBI investigation of Ferrie continued, then to publicly stand by Katzenbach's morning message to Moyers, which he, Hoover, had drafted, and tell Alan

Belmont that the forthcoming FBI report would "settle the dust insofar as Oswald and his activities were concerned."

And yet, privately, Hoover must have been disturbed by the reports he had received from New Orleans about David Ferrie, his alleged relationship with Oswald, and his admitted relationship with Carlos Marcello.

He must have been disturbed also by the report he received later on the same afternoon from the FBI office in Savannah. It was then that Hoover first learned of the allegation of Mr. Sumner of Darien, Georgia, that in March or April he had seen someone he was sure was Lee Harvey Oswald receive a payment from the manager of Carlos Marcello's Town & Country restaurant in New Orleans. Now two allegations had come in to the bureau linking Oswald to associates of Carlos Marcello.

As if that were not enough to cause concern, the next day brought in a report of an allegation made to the FBI office in Oakland that linked Jack Ruby to an associate of Carlos Marcello's. The report of Wednesday, November 27, told of the interview with Bobby Gene Moore, in which he reported to an FBI agent that Jack Ruby had "gangster connections" in Dallas, including Joseph Civello.

J. Edgar Hoover knew full well that Joseph Civello was boss of the Mafia in Dallas, that he had attended the Mafia summit meeting in Apalachin in 1957, and that he was Carlos Marcello's agent. The idea that Ruby was close to Civello must have bothered Hoover considerably. He had already been informed that Oswald had been friendly with one of Marcello's men in New Orleans. Now Ruby too was connected to a Marcello associate.

What was Hoover's reaction to Bobby Gene Moore's allegation? Officially, he ordered the FBI in Dallas to conduct a pro forma interview of Joseph Civello, and then he ignored the sinister implications of Moore's allegation entirely. The FBI report of the interview with Civello, conducted in Dallas by Special Agents John T. McMurren and Ivan D. Lee, is as follows:

JOSEPH FRANCIS CIVELLO, 4044 Cedar Springs, advised as follows.

He has known JACK RUBY for about ten years, although he has only seen him four or five times during that period. He was never closely associated with RUBY and last saw him sometime in 1957, to the best of his knowledge. Because of this limited association, he had no knowledge of RUBY's personality, political or philosophical beliefs and could not furnish any information regarding him. He had no knowledge

of LEE HARVEY OSWALD and therefore knew of no association between RUBY and OSWALD.

End of investigation.

Then, the following day, Wednesday, November 28, still another
allegation mentioning an associate of the Marcellos arrived at headquarters. It was Eugene De Laparra's allegation that in March or April
he had overheard Vincent Marcello's friend Ben Tregle say that there
was "a price on the President's head," and that somebody would kill
Kennedy when he came south.

What was Hoover's response to these allegations? He essentially
ignored them and instead leaked news to the press on Monday,
December 2, of the FBI's investigation of the assassination, indicating Oswald was the lone, unaided assassin. Thus it was that on the
morning of December 3—five days before the FBI's initial summary
report was to be released to the public and two days before it was to
be transmitted to the President and the attorney general—a UPI story
went out to newspapers throughout the country carrying the lead:

> An exhaustive FBI report now nearly ready for the White
> House will indicate that Lee Harvey Oswald was the lone and
> unaided assassin of President Kennedy, Government sources
> say today.

Later William Sullivan wrote in his memoirs that Hoover had ordered the report leaked to the press "in an attempt to blunt the drive
for an independent investigation of the assassination."

On the afternoon of Thursday, December 5, President Lyndon
Johnson learned from an advance copy of the FBI's "exhaustive
report" that Lee Harvey Oswald was the lone and unaided assassin
of President Kennedy and that his killer, Jack Ruby, had shot him in
a fit of patriotic, public-spirited indignation, unaided and unabetted
by any accomplices.

Needless to say, no mention was made in the report of the unre-
solved allegations linking Oswald to Marcello operatives David Ferrie
and Joseph Poretto and linking Ruby to Marcello's chief of operations in Dallas, Joseph Civello. Nor was there mention of the news
that had been received from informant De Laparra hinting at foreknowledge of the assassination on the part of a Marcello associate.
Barely two weeks had passed since the assassination. The "exhaustive
report" had been based on an investigation that had focused exclusively on incriminating Oswald without even considering the possi-

ble relevance of any of the allegations that had come in suggesting he might have had accomplices.

As we shall see, Hoover's response to the assassination was subsequently foisted on the presidential commission appointed by Lyndon Johnson to "officially" investigate the crime. Since that body became wholly dependent on the FBI for raw evidentiary data, Hoover was able to subtly manipulate its investigation by withholding vital information, or by transmitting vital information to the commission smothered in enormous batches of crank allegations, with no indications that the information transmitted was potentially crucial.

Today, after twenty-five years, the spirit behind J. Edgar Hoover's response to the assassination of President Kennedy has finally come into focus. Hoover had no interest in uncovering the truth behind the assassination or in bringing the guilty to justice; he was only interested in protecting his reputation and that of the FBI. A full, open investigation of the crime, intent on uncovering a conspiracy, if there was one, was anathema to Hoover since it would threaten to expose his own and the FBI's investigatory failings. Hoover therefore conducted an investigation that ignored, or suppressed, all evidence suggesting that others, besides Oswald, might have been involved in the assassination.

What exactly was Hoover so anxious to ignore or suppress? Evidence of Cuban involvement in the assassination? No, he had ordered the Legat in Mexico City to conduct a thorough investigation of "D's" allegation, before turning it over to the CIA. (Much later it was discovered that "D" was a Nicaraguan misinformation agent trying to implicate Castro in the assassination.) The FBI was a domestic intelligence agency. The investigation of possible Cuban, or Soviet, involvement in the assassination was more properly the province of the CIA and the State Department's Office of Intelligence. Accordingly, early in his investigation, despite his awareness of the CIA-Mafia plots to assassinate Castro, Hoover made a conscious decision not to investigate possible Cuban government involvement in the assassination and instructed his agents not to conduct any interviews with the bureau's Cuban informants. As for the possibility of domestic "extremist" organizations being involved in the crime, it does not appear that Hoover went out of his way to suppress, or pointedly ignore, allegations of the involvement of segregationist, Communist, or neo-Fascist groups. No, the record that has been painstakingly pieced together over the past twenty-five years shows unmistakably that the possible conspiracy J. Edgar Hoover was most wary of, and consciously strived to cover up, was the one about which the FBI had accumulated, by December 18, the most circumstantial evidence: a plot involving the Marcello organization in New Orleans and Dallas.

There were many reasons why Hoover would have dreaded the discovery of such a plot, and they all stemmed from his overriding sense of bureaucratic self-preservation. If it was discovered that Carlos Marcello and his criminal network were behind Oswald and Ruby, Hoover would fall into disgrace and the reputation of the FBI would fall with him.

For by December 1963, a convincing paper record could have been pieced together by the office of the attorney general to show that Hoover had been repeatedly ordered by Attorney General Kennedy to upgrade his agency's investigation of Carlos Marcello, and Hoover's agents in New Orleans had repeatedly failed to take any significant steps to implement those orders. If this dereliction was revealed, Hoover would stand accused by the man he hated most in the world, Robert Kennedy, of being indirectly responsible for his brother's death by being so lax in his investigation of the man who had been behind it.

When President Johnson created the Warren Commission on November 29 to investigate the assassination, Hoover was faced with an enormous personal challenge: how to manipulate the commission so it would not come to any conclusions about the assassination that differed from his own.

As we shall see, Hoover met the challenge with consummate skill.

38

Deception and Manipulation: Hoover and the Warren Commission

When Lyndon Johnson created the Warren Commission to investigate the assassination of President Kennedy, he also created seven new threats to J. Edgar Hoover's power. Therefore, as soon as Johnson had appointed his seven commissioners, Hoover resorted to his favorite power ploy: He ordered his aides to compile secret dossiers on each member of the commission, so he would have adequate dirt in his files if a need arose.

That Hoover had perceived the Warren Commission as an adversary was first publicly revealed by the Senate Intelligence Committee in 1975. The committee had uncovered internal FBI memorandums clearly indicating that Hoover was very much concerned that the Warren Commission might possibly discover evidence in the Kennedy case that might embarrass the bureau and himself.

As it turned out, the Warren Commission became wholly dependent on the FBI's investigation of the assassination for evidence in the case. Realizing this, Hoover gave the commission only the background information and evidence he wanted it to have: that is, evidence incriminating Oswald as the lone, unaided assassin of the President, and evidence indicating that Ruby had no sinister connections with the underworld and had killed Oswald spontaneously, without confederates, out of patriotic indignation.

Hoover was fortunate to have one member of the Warren Commission anxious to convince his fellow commissioners that the assassination had been the work of one lone gunman, unaided by conspirators: former CIA Director Allen Dulles.

At the first executive session of the commission, on December 6, Dulles did a very suspicious thing. He gave each one of his fellow commissioners a copy of a book about American political assassinations which claimed that all the crimes were the work of lone, alienated madmen. This suggests that Dulles was fearful of uncovering a conspiracy in the Kennedy assassination because it might lead to the uncovering of the elaborate conspiracy he had recently been involved in to assassinate the president of Cuba.

For up until the time President Kennedy fired him as director of the CIA, after the Bay of Pigs fiasco, Allen Dulles had been involved in a CIA-sponsored conspiracy to assassinate Fidel Castro that included at least four CIA officers besides himself—Richard Bissell, J. C. King, Sheffield Edwards, and an unnamed case officer—and at least three Mafia bosses—Sam Giancana, Johnny Roselli, and Santos Trafficante—and possibly a fourth, Carlos Marcello.

Allen Dulles was well aware that if persuasive evidence were presented to the commission suggesting that Oswald or Ruby, or both, might have been used by the Mafia or the CIA, a thorough investigation might uncover the plots to assassinate the Cuban president. Accordingly, Dulles never breathed a word about the anti-Castro plots to his fellow commissioners, and did everything possible to promote the lone assassin solution to the crime.

It did not take long for that solution to be foisted on the commission, in various ways—some obvious, some subtle—by the man who conceived it.

The Warren Commission had held its first executive session on December 6. By December 9 the FBI's five-volume summary report of its investigation of the assassination had been printed and copies had been sent to the commission. On that same day Hoover made his first move toward manipulating the commission's investigation. He had Deputy Attorney General Katzenbach send a message to Commission Chairman Warren recommending that the commission immediately issue a public statement that the FBI report clearly showed Oswald was the sole assassin and that he was unaided by confederates.

That the summary report clearly indicated Oswald was the sole, unaided assassin was true. But, unknown to anyone, save Hoover, one or two of his closest aides, and a few FBI agents in New Orleans, an investigation was going on in Texas at the very moment the summary report was being distributed that threatened to produce evidence to contradict the conclusions of the report.

For, in contrast to the bureau's weak responses to other conspiracy allegations, it was going all out in December with its investigation of David Ferrie. FBI reports on this highly secret investigation, which lasted until December 18, indicate that Ferrie himself was reinterviewed by the FBI on December 5 and was further investigated by the Secret Service, which did not release its final report on him until December 13—four days *after* Hoover had issued his summary report declaring Lee Harvey Oswald's guilt as the lone, unaided assassin of the President.

What was scandalous about Hoover's premature issuance of the FBI's summary report was that the information the FBI learned about Ferrie *strengthened suspicions he might have been involved with Oswald— and perhaps with Carlos Marcello—in a conspiracy to assassinate the President.*

As all the world knows, the Warren Commission eventually came to the conclusion that Lee Harvey Oswald was the lone, unaided assassin of the President and that Jack Ruby was the lone, unaided killer of the accused assassin. It had reached this conclusion chiefly on the basis of the information J. Edgar Hoover had given it.

But what information did J. Edgar Hoover *not* transmit to the commission, or transmit without any elucidation? The list is long and deeply suspicious. Hoover did not inform the commission that Oswald's uncle and surrogate father was a member of the Marcello gambling network; that Oswald knew Marcello's private investigator, David Ferrie; that Ferrie had met with Carlos Marcello over the two weekends preceding the assassination; that Ferrie had been detained on November 25 by the New Orleans District Attorney's Office on suspicion of having been involved in a conspiracy to assassinate President Kennedy; that Ferrie had made a highly suspicious trip through Texas the weekend following the assassination and had called Carlos Marcello at his Town & Country Motel headquarters from Houston the afternoon before Ruby shot Oswald; that FBI informant Jose Aleman had reiterated to federal agents of the Miami FBI office immediately after the assassination that Florida Mafia boss Santos Trafficante had told him President Kennedy was "going to be hit"; that informants had come forth in the days immediately following the assassination with allegations hinting at Marcello involvement in the crime; that Jack Ruby had made a flurry of suspicious calls to several notorious racketeers during the two months preceding the assassination, including one to a top lieutenant of Carlos Marcello's; that Ruby was associated with two members of the Dallas underworld who were close to Carlos Marcello; that Ruby had been much more than a small-time Dallas nightclub operator, that he had also been involved in illegal gambling, the narcotics trade, and running guns to Cuba.

Not reporting to the commission the evidence of an Oswald-Ferrie-Marcello connection was one of Hoover's most flagrant sins of omission in his dealings with the Warren Commission. Most serious of all, thanks to Hoover's selective withholding of documents, the members of the commission never learned that a friend of Lee Harvey Oswald's, the openly anti-Kennedy David Ferrie, met with a sworn enemy of the Kennedys, Mafia boss Carlos Marcello, at Marcello's Louisiana estate on the two weekends immediately preceding the assassination of the President.

If the commission had been informed of these two meetings, it would have been duty bound to conduct a thorough investigation of the relationship between Oswald and Ferrie and that between Ferrie and Marcello over the months preceding the assassination. Both Ferrie and Marcello would have been called to testify before the commission.

As it turned out, the commission never called as witnesses any of the individuals referred to in the several allegations mentioning the Marcellos or their associates, which the FBI received from informants within a week of the President's murder. This included Carlos, Joseph, Vincent, and Anthony Marcello, David Ferrie, Ben Tregle, Norman Le Blanc, Eugene De Laparra, Joseph Poretto, Lt. Johnny Harris, Ernest Insalmo, informant SV T-1 (Gene Sumner), Bobby Gene Moore, Joseph Civello, and William Abadie.

And, because Hoover withheld from the commission Edward Partin's allegation about Jimmy Hoffa's threat to kill both Kennedy brothers, and Jose Aleman's testimony to the FBI that Santos Trafficante had told him President Kennedy was "going to be hit," the commission did not call Jimmy Hoffa, Edward Partin, Jose Aleman, and Santos Trafficante to testify either.

Hoover was scandalously remiss in not informing the Warren Commission that Lee Harvey Oswald's uncle and surrogate father was a bookmaker and gambler affiliated with one of Carlos Marcello's major associates. The FBI had reports in its files of Dutz Murret's involvement in the New Orleans underworld since 1944, when an

FBI crime survey of the city listed Murret as the operator of two clubs in the French Quarter that were fronts for illegal bookmaking.

Assistant counsel for the Warren Commission, Burt Griffin, told the House Assassinations Committee in 1978 that the commission had been aware of Jack Ruby's underworld connections, but since it had no evidence that Oswald had any contacts with the underworld, it discounted the possibility that organized crime could have been behind the assassination.

Equally scandalous was the fact that Hoover withheld from the commission evidence he had suggesting that someone might have been impersonating Lee Harvey Oswald since 1960 and, most recently, during Oswald's visit to Mexico City in October 1963.

The possibility of the so-called Oswald double had come up several times during the commission's deliberations and had always been discounted by the commissioners. Whenever the commission received reports of sightings of Oswald in two different locations at the same time, it always chose to believe that one of the informants was mistaken. Among other reasons for disbelieving the Oswald-double theory, the commission had noted that the FBI had never given it any reports suggesting that an Oswald impostor had been on the loose. It was not until eleven years after the conclusion of the Warren Commission's investigation that the Senate Committee on Intelligence discovered that J. Edgar Hoover had indeed been suspicious that someone had been impersonating Lee Harvey Oswald since at least June 10, 1960, and that his memorandum on the matter had never been brought to the attention of the commission. And it was not until thirteen years after the commission's demise that independent researcher and writer Mark Lane pried out of the FBI an uncensored version of Hoover's top secret memorandum of November 23, 1963, to Secret Service Chief James Rowley indicating that he had persuasive evidence that the man representing himself as Oswald who visited the Soviet Embassy in Mexico City on October 1, 1963, was probably an impostor.

Surely if the Warren Commission had Hoover's memorandums of June 10, 1960, and November 23, 1963, it would have been compelled to reinvestigate the possibility that someone representing himself as Lee Harvey Oswald had laid a trail of incriminating evidence in New Orleans, Mexico City, and Dallas during the months immediately preceding the assassination, a sure sign of a conspiracy to kill the President and frame Oswald for the murder.

*   *   *

How was Hoover able to manipulate the Warren Commission's investigation so effectively? Many examples have come to light over the years. For the purpose of this narrative, we shall examine three.

After the assassination, hundreds of allegations poured into FBI headquarters in Washington and its field offices throughout the country. At first Hoover saw no need to transmit the raw data of these allegations to the Warren Commission, as he had not seen fit to transmit raw data on other matters relating to the assassination, preferring to issue general summary reports instead.

By December 16, this practice had begun to bother certain members of the commission. On that date, the commissioners adopted a resolution designed to force Hoover to release his raw files:

RESOLVED, that the Commission request promptly from all government agencies and Departments of the government the raw materials upon which any reports given to the Commission are based....

This resolution was sent to J. Edgar Hoover, by letter, on December 17, and it made him furious. Now he was obliged to send over to the commission a good many provocative conspiracy allegations, including the reports on David Ferrie and those mentioning the Marcellos, that he would have a difficult time explaining away.

So what did Hoover do? He had his agents gather up enormous batches of miscellaneous allegations, hundreds upon hundreds of them, and send them over to the commission in lengthy "reports," accompanied by a covering letter from the director to Commission General Counsel J. Lee Rankin that read, in part, as follows:

In a number of instances the investigation in this report is incomplete in that the particular allegation has not been fully resolved. In each instance additional investigation has been instituted to fully resolve the matter.... An example of such an instance occurs wherein one Bill Baker alleged that an acquaintance of his, Joseph Noble Adams, had made various statements indicating the White Citizens Council was responsible for the assassination of President Kennedy and they were going to take care of the Attorney General. He further stated this group was composed of mistreated servicemen of which he and Oswald were also members.

Adams was subsequently located at the city jail in Austin, Texas, and upon interview, admitted he was a chronic alcoholic and that due to his alcoholic addiction it is quite possible he made the statements attributable to him, but he had very little recollection of what did occur.

The real purpose of Hoover's letter now appears transparent. In singling out the Joseph Noble Adams allegation among the hundreds submitted, he was attempting to show the commission that all these allegations were ravings of lunatics and alcoholics, not worthy of serious consideration.

It is worth noting, at this point, that whenever Hoover sent to the commission an FBI report of a conspiracy allegation involving a left-wing, or communist, individual or organization, he usually elucidated the report, describing in some detail the left-wing sympathies of the person, or organization, mentioned as alleged conspirators. But whenever he sent an FBI report to the commission of a conspiracy allegation involving organized crime, he never offered any elucidation of the report at all, and, more often than not, would not even point out that a given alleged conspirator was associated with organized crime.

What precisely happened to the allegations suggesting conspiratorial activity on the part of the Marcello organization once they reached the Warren Commission? It is hard to say. Since Hoover and his aides failed to explain their possibly sinister significance to the commission, whoever edited the twenty-six published volumes of hearings and exhibits that were eventually to accompany the Warren Commission's final report never included them in the published exhibits, and so they were never read even by any of those hardy souls who eventually took the time to plow through the twenty-six volumes. They ended up buried beneath mountains of crank allegations in the National Archives' files on the Warren Commission's investigation of the Kennedy assassination.

But why were they not subsequently picked up by the droves of journalists and independent assassination researchers who descended on the Warren Commission records after they were deposited in the archives? They were not picked up because missing from the allegations were certain key FBI documents that would have provided clues to their possible significance. These had been withheld from the commission and did not see the light of day until Freedom of Information Act lawsuits against the Justice Department began prying them loose in the late seventies and early eighties. We have already alluded to this practice as it regarded the handling of Sumner's allegation that he saw someone closely resembling Oswald receive a payment from the manager of the Town & Country restaurant in New Orleans. Without any FBI elucidations, and without any personal knowledge of the Marcello criminal organization and its headquarters in New Orleans' Town & Country Motel, there would have been no reason for a Warren Commission staffer, or later for a researcher thumbing through the crank allegations in the National Archives, to attribute any particular significance to Sumner's original allegation.

As for Bobby Gene Moore's allegation about Jack Ruby's association with Joseph Civello, we are sure it *was* read by someone on the commission staff, because there is unambiguous evidence that the original FBI report of the allegation was doctored before it was included in the commission's published exhibits.

The original FBI report, dated November 27, 1963, included Moore's allegation that Jack Ruby had been associated with Joseph Civello. But by the time it turned up in the commission's published volumes, as Exhibit 1536, the part about Ruby's association with Civello had been excised, rendering the document innocuous. Who excised it, and why? The matter remains a mystery. Apparently someone associated with the Warren Commission did not want the world to know that Jack Ruby had been in close contact with Mafia boss Carlos Marcello's deputy in Dallas. Again, Hoover sent the Bobby Gene Moore allegation to the commission sandwiched in among a huge batch of "nut stuff" without explanation.

But perhaps the most flagrant manipulation of all was Hoover's almost total suppression of Jack Martin's allegation about David Ferrie's links to Oswald, his possible involvement in an assassination conspiracy, and his mysterious trip to Texas over the weekend of the assassination. These reports were never transmitted to the Warren Commission, not even with the batches of "nut stuff."

Many other examples of how Hoover manipulated the Warren Commission's investigation have periodically come to light over the years. In 1975 the Senate Intelligence Committee discovered evidence in the FBI's files that Hoover knew about the CIA-Mafia plots of 1960–1963 to assassinate Castro, and yet never informed the Warren Commission of them. And in 1979 the House Committee on Assassinations discovered that the FBI had recorded in 1962 and 1963, through electronic listening devices, at least a half dozen conversations between various Mafia leaders and their subordinates in which either threats to kill President Kennedy or wishes to have him killed were expressed. Yet Hoover never reported these to the Secret Service, or to John and Robert Kennedy, and he deliberately withheld them from the Warren Commission.

In time, Hoover's efforts to control the Warren Commission's inquiry and promote his *idée fixe* that Oswald was the lone, unaided assassin became so obvious that it began to arouse the suspicions of several members of the commission and staff. On January 22, 1964, barely a month and a half after the commission's first executive session, Commissioners Allen Dulles and Hale Boggs, and General Counsel Rankin, held a secret executive session, the minutes of which do not appear in the final record but were discovered later among a stenotypist's notes:

DULLES: Why would it be in their [the FBI's] interest to say he [Oswald] is clearly the only guilty one?

RANKIN: They would like us to fold up and quit.

BOGGS: This closes the case, you see. Don't you see?

RANKIN: They found the man. There is nothing more to do. The commission supports their conclusions, and we can go home and that is the end of it.

BOGGS: I don't even like to see this being taken down.

DULLES: Yes. I think this record ought to be destroyed.

Another section of the same transcript reveals that General Counsel Rankin was deeply suspicious of the way the FBI had been conducting this particular investigation. As a former solicitor general, Rankin had had long experience dealing with Hoover and the FBI, and this was the first time he had found Hoover's organization coming so quickly to a firm "evaluation" of a case, without running out all leads.

RANKIN: There is this factor too that...is somewhat of an issue in this case, and I suppose you are all aware of it. That is that the FBI is very explicit that Oswald is the assassin, or was the assassin, and they are very explicit that there was no conspiracy, and they are also saying they are continuing their investigation. Now in my experience of almost nine years, in the first place it is hard to get them to say when you think you have got a case tight enough to convict somebody, that this is the person who committed the crime. In my experience with the FBI they don't do that. They claim that they don't evaluate [come to conclusions] and it is my uniform experience that they don't do that. Secondly, they have not run out all kinds of leads in Mexico or in Russia and so forth which they could probably— It is not our business, it is the very...

DULLES: What is that?

RANKIN: They haven't run out all the leads on the information and they could probably say...that isn't our business.

DULLES: Yes.

RANKIN: But they are concluding that there can't be a conspiracy without those being run out. Now that is not from my experience with the FBI.

DULLES: It is not. You are quite right. I have seen a great many reports.

As we have seen, Rankin's suspicions were well founded. There were "all kinds of leads in Mexico and Russia" and also in Cuba and the Town & Country Motel that Hoover had been supposed to "run out" and had not, while still insisting there had been no conspiracy.

A close study of what Hoover chose not to report to the Warren Commission, or chose not to elucidate for the commission, reveals inescapably that what he was trying to cover up was the possibility that members of organized crime might have been involved in the assassination, and specifically that the Marcello organization might have played a leading role in plotting and carrying out the crime. For almost all of Hoover's withholdings of information and failures to elucidate information that might have cast light on the existence of a conspiracy had to do with organized crime.

We cannot help but conclude that Hoover knew far more about the circumstances surrounding the President's murder than he ever let on. One does not deliberately withhold, or suppress, information if one considers that information innocuous.

In fairness to Hoover, the possibility must be raised that some of the Kennedy assassination allegations never reached the director's desk. Perhaps they went no farther than the desk of Assistant Director Alex Rosen, who was then chief of the bureau's general investigative division, the division Hoover had put in charge of the investigation of the assassination. When I attempted to interview Mr. Rosen on this point, he refused to cooperate. Former Assistant Director Courtney Evans, who was in overall charge of the special investigative division, told me that Hoover "saw everything," but admitted that he, Evans, did not. When I pressed him for details on this issue, asking him if he had seen all the reports on David Ferrie, he replied, "David who?" From interviews with other FBI officials knowledgeable of the routing of reports regarding the assassination, it appears more likely than not that Director Hoover did, in fact, see everything, unless Alex Rosen and his assistants deliberately withheld certain reports and allegations from him, which they could have done for not necessarily sinister reasons or reasons of bureaucratic self-preservation, but to spare the director the burden of having to read hundreds of what Rosen and his assistants might have believed were crank allegations.

It is my opinion that J. Edgar Hoover knew, or at least suspected, that Carlos Marcello and his criminal organization might have played a significant role in both the assassination of the President and the murder of the President's suspected assassin, and that he deliberately covered up evidence of this possibility out of a combination of fear and egotism. Fear that the FBI's failure to detect an assassination conspiracy involving Carlos Marcello would result in his and the FBI's disgrace. Egotism in that he was willing to cast aside his suspicions, and in so doing renounce the pursuit of truth and justice in the case, in favor of incriminating a man whose apparent credentials, as a "commie" vindicated his insistence that communism, not organized crime, was America's number one domestic enemy.

There is also another plausible explanation of J. Edgar Hoover's strangely neutral, almost passive, and seemingly even protective, attitude towards Carlos Marcello: Hoover's strange relationship with New York Mafia boss Frank Costello. For, as we know, Marcello had been Costello's protégé in the late 1930s and early 1940s and soon became Costello's right-hand man in Louisiana. In fact, it would not be an exaggeration to state that it was Frank Costello who had made Carlos Marcello's extraordinary criminal career possible.

But was there anything to the rumors that Costello and Hoover had frequent contact with one another? According to William G. Hundley, former head of the Organized Crime and Racketeering Section of the Justice Department under Attorney General Kennedy, there decidedly was. Hundley told me that he had been skeptical about the rumors he had heard about a Costello-Hoover relationship until, unexpectedly, he had a chance to learn something of the relationship from the horse's mouth.

Sometime in the fifties Hundley was in New York staying at the apartment of his friend Edward Bennett Williams. One of Williams's more celebrated clients was Frank Costello, and one morning while Hundley was there, Costello himself showed up for breakfast.

During the meal Hundley confronted Costello with the rumors he had heard about him and the FBI Director. At this, the muscular, hairy-armed Costello, in his hoarse, gravely voice, began reeling off a string of stories about his friendship with Hoover that Hundley thought at the time would have been too difficult for Costello to have invented on the spur of the moment. In the end, Hundley was convinced.

According to what Hundley says he learned from Costello over coffee that morning, when Hoover would come to New York he would meet Costello on a bench in Central Park where they would "talk things over," arriving at some sort of mutually convenient *modus vivendi*. Apparently both Costello and Hoover loved the track, and Hundley had heard that they occasionally went to the races together. When he asked Costello if this was true, Costello laughed and exclaimed: "The *horse* races! You'll never know how many races I had to fix for those lousy ten-dollar bets of Hoover's!"

The implications of such a relationship, so far as Hoover's attitude toward Carlos Marcello was concerned, are obvious. Marcello made a lot of money for Costello back in the days of Costello's gambling operations in southern Louisiana, and over the years the two had remained close friends. According to the code of the Mafia, mutual indebtedness constitutes an exceptionally strong bond. Given the apparent extent of Hoover's relationship with Costello and whatever mutual indebtedness *they* might have had, would Hoover have been inclined to move aggressively against Costello's Louisiana protégé?

The Warren Commission left behind an enormous quantity of documents. Most of them were deposited in the National Archives. Others were incorporated in twenty-six volumes accompanying the commission's final report. In 1980 two private citizens who had devoted much time, energy, and money to studying the Kennedy assassination and the investigations of it, Sylvia Meagher and Gary Owens, compiled an index to the Warren report and all the published Warren Commission hearings and exhibits. Nowhere in this ninety-four-page index can the name Carlos Marcello be found. Thanks to J. Edgar Hoover, the name never came to the attention of the Warren Commission. However, in the index Mrs. Meagher and Mr. Owens compiled for the House Select Committee on Assassinations' investigation, which was completed fifteen years after the Warren Commission published its findings, there is an entire column of entries on Carlos Marcello and members of his family. How is this possible? The answer is that by the time the House Committee on Assassinations began investigating President Kennedy's murder, J. Edgar Hoover was dead.

39

The Rubber Stamp:
The Commission's Final Report

The seven distinguished members of the Warren Commission—from Chairman Chief Justice Earl Warren to former Director of the CIA Allen Dulles to Congressmen Gerald R. Ford and Hale Boggs—represented the cream of the American establishment, a blue-ribbon panel if there ever was one. Yet a close analysis of the deliberations of the commission members and the commission's chief counsel and his assistants reveals a pronounced reluctance to get to the bottom of the crime. Their final report on the assassination of President Kennedy and the murder of his alleged assassin turned out to be little more than a rubber stamp of the hurried conclusions J. Edgar Hoover had reached within a week of the assassination.

The seven men Lyndon Johnson had chosen to serve on his commission to investigate John F. Kennedy's murder represented a spectrum of the American establishment that Johnson undoubtedly felt would not be prone to uncover any dark conspiracies capable of unsettling the collective American psyche. Each of them represented an area of the national life he might be counted on to defend against any accusations that someone or some entity associated with that area might have been involved in the assassination. Chief Justice Earl Warren, who had accepted the chair with extreme reluctance, was the highest-ranking government official on the commission and might be counted on to protect the reputation of the government he served. Former director of the CIA Allen Dulles, who had been fired by President Kennedy for his role in the Bay of Pigs disaster, could presumably be expected to look out for the interests of the organization he had served for so many years. (Years later, it was discovered that he regularly briefed CIA Chief of Counterintelligence, James J. Angleton, on the commission's secret deliberations.) Senators Richard Russell, a Georgia Democrat, and John Sherman Cooper, a Kentucky Republican, might be counted on not to look favorably on any conspiracy allegations that attempted to connect the assassination to southern white segregationists angered by the Kennedy brothers' civil rights policies. In fairness to Russell, however, the Georgia senator turned out to be the one member of the Warren Commission who refused to accept the commission's verdict of no conspiracy and the sole member, as well, who asked Chairman Warren to list him as a dissenter in the commission's final report. Warren refused.

As for former international banker and diplomat John J. McCloy, the epitome of the prudent, safe, "sound" statesman-businessman, he might be counted on to look out for the reputation of the military-industrial complex, whose overreaching power had so disturbed Kennedy's predecessor in the Oval Office. Likewise, Representative Gerald R. Ford, a close friend of J. Edgar Hoover, might be expected to make sure that any allegations linking Oswald or Ruby, or any other suspect in the assassination, to the FBI would be quickly disposed of. (Later, J. Edgar Hoover's deputy director at the time of the assassination, William Sullivan, wrote in his memoirs: "Hoover was delighted when Gerald Ford was named to the Warren Commission. The director wrote in one of his internal memos that the bureau could expect Ford to 'look after FBI interests' and he did, keeping us fully advised of what was going on behind closed doors. He was our man, our informant, on the Warren Commission.")

Finally, Representative Hale Boggs, Democrat from Louisiana, could presumably be relied on to defend the reputation of the government of Lee Harvey Oswald's home state, should the need arise. As it turned out, that need did not arise, for, as we know, J. Edgar Hoover saw to it that the name of Boggs's chief financial backer and behind-the-scenes power in the state government, Carlos Marcello, never came up during the commission's deliberations. Again, in fairness to Boggs, it should be noted that by the end of the commission's investigation he had become skeptical of the conclusions of the FBI investigation and the man who had conducted it. (Years later, a former aide to the Louisiana congressman recalled: "Hale always returned to one thing: Hoover lied his eyes out to the Commission—on Oswald, on Ruby, on their friends, the bullets, the guns, you name it...")

We know that Hoover withheld vital information from the commission, especially information about Oswald's and Ruby's links to organized crime, and deliberately failed to elucidate FBI reports that suggested that the Marcello crime family might have had something to do with the assassination. Still, the commissioners consistently overlooked what little information trickled through Hoover's strainer hinting at the possible involvement of organized crime, and they were grossly deficient in their interrogation of Jack Ruby and their evaluation of Ruby's personality and activities. Generally speaking, the commission believed the witnesses it wanted to believe and rejected the witnesses it did not want to believe, regardless of the plausibility of their testimony. Likewise, it accepted only the evidence it wanted to accept, regardless of the evidence's true worth.

One example was the treatment of journalist Seth Kantor's testimony. Kantor at the time was a White House correspondent for Scripps-Howard newspapers, a respected news reporter who had once worked for the *Dallas Times-Herald.* Jack Ruby told the Warren Commission that at no time on November 22 did he visit Parkland Hospital. However, Seth Kantor reported in his newspapers, informed the FBI, and testified before the Warren Commission that he had encountered Ruby at the hospital around 1:30 that afternoon. Kantor's account was even corroborated by another witness, Mrs. Wilma Tice, who testified that she had been next to a man she heard called "Jack" at the hospital Friday afternoon who looked exactly like the photos of Ruby she later saw in the newspapers. Yet the Warren Commission concluded that Kantor was wrong and "confused" and that Jack Ruby was truthful in asserting he did not go to the hospital after the assassination. The commission took the word of a petty mobster over a journalist noted for his accurate reporting simply because it did not want to believe that Ruby was at Parkland Hospital the moment the President died. It was too suspicious, too difficult to explain.

But the Commission did not confine its selectivity in weighing evidence to such relatively trivial issues as whether or not Jack Ruby was at Parkland Hospital when John F. Kennedy died. It also flagrantly distorted crucial evidence in the assassination case itself. The most outrageous example of this is its treatment of the wound located slightly below the President's right shoulder blade. In its Final Report the commission proclaimed that the wound was at the base of the President's neck, or six inches higher than its true location, in order to align its trajectory with the presumed exit wound in the President's throat, observed by Dallas doctors to have been situated above the shirt collar and to have had the appearance of a wound of entry—even though a transcript of the commission's deliberations indicates that both Chairman Warren and General Counsel Rankin were fully aware of the true location of the back wound. In this way the commission was able to link the back wound and the throat wound to one bullet and one gunman, thus sustaining Hoover's lone gunman solution to the assassination.

Another example of the commission's curious selectivity was its conclusion about Jack Ruby's organized crime associations. We know that Hoover deliberately failed to point out to the commission that Jack Ruby had been associated with Dallas Mafia boss and Marcello associate Joseph Civello. But the FBI did turn over to the commission records of Ruby's telephone calls during the months of October and November. Three of Ruby's most suspicious calls went to men known to be associated with organized crime: Irwin S. Weiner, front man for the Chicago mob; ex-convict Barney Baker, chief enforcer for Jimmy Hoffa; and Nofio Pecora, one of Carlos Marcello's closest associates. Incredibly, the commission saw no significance in these calls and concluded in its final report that Jack Ruby was not connected, in any significant way, with organized crime. He was just a patriotic nightclub owner and police buff who lived on the *fringe* of the underworld.

While the commission had no difficulty believing Ruby's testimony over that of Seth Kantor, when it came to believing Ruby's testimony hinting that in murdering Oswald he had been used by someone for a purpose, the commission quietly ignored him.

During Chief Justice Warren's interrogation of Ruby in the Dallas County Jail, Ruby expressed fears for his life as long as he remained in Dallas and suggested that he had been manipulated by someone when he murdered Lee Harvey Oswald.

It is well known that if the Mafia wants to kill one of its own in prison, it can easily do so. Ruby may have been reminded of this, if indeed he needed any reminding, when his friend Joe Campisi, the number two man in the Dallas Mafia, visited him in the Dallas County Jail shortly after his incarceration.

Ruby, it appears, was terrified that he might be silenced. In his testimony before Chief Justice Warren he declared: "I may not live tomorrow to give any further testimony...and the only thing I want to get out to the public, and I can't say it here, is with authenticity, with sincerity of the truth of everything, and why my act was committed, but I can't say it here." Ruby, obviously fearful that the jail room in which he was giving testimony was bugged, then pleaded over and over with Warren to let him go to Washington to give his testimony there. Warren turned Ruby's requests down eight times.

As the interrogation drew to a close, Ruby pleaded with Warren once more saying: "Unless you get me to Washington, you can't get a fair shake out of me....I have been used for a purpose." To no avail. As far as Warren was concerned, the questioning of Ruby was over.

A little over a year later, Ruby was able to make a rare public statement to reporters as he was about to enter court to be tried for the murder of Lee Harvey Oswald. His remarks were subsequently telecast over CBS-TV. After pleading to be removed to a federal jurisdiction, he called out to the newsmen: "...complete conspiracy...and the assassination too...if you knew the facts you would be amazed."

Ruby was never removed to a federal jurisdiction and did not live to tell anyone his amazing facts. In December 1966, while awaiting a retrial, he was removed from his jail cell, mortally ill with cancer, and transferred to Parkland Hospital, where he died on January 3.

Why did the Warren Commission avoid the issue of Jack Ruby's obvious ties to organized crime and his insistence that he be removed from Dallas so he could reveal the truth of why he killed Oswald?

In light of all we know more than twenty years later, it appears that the Warren Commission did not *want* to know that Ruby was part of a Mafia conspiracy to assassinate the President, if indeed he was. In fact, that was the *last* thing both the commission *and the President* wanted to know. For both President Johnson and at least three commission members stood to suffer considerable embarrassment if Giancana or Trafficante or Marcello were to go on trial for having participated in a plot to murder President John F. Kennedy.

Johnson stood to be embarrassed because, as detailed by G. R. Schreiber in *The Bobby Baker Affair*, his former protégé in the Senate, Bobby Baker, who had served him as secretary for eight years when he was majority leader, was found to have done considerable business with the Mafia in Las Vegas, Chicago, Louisiana, and the Caribbean. Johnson once referred to Baker as his surrogate son and as "one of my most trusted friends." Yet Baker's activities as a Washington fixer while working for Johnson eventually brought him a one- to three-year prison sentence on seven counts of tax evasion, theft, and fraud involving nearly $100,000 in political payoff money. And that was only the tip of the iceberg. Who knew what might come out about Johnson's surrogate son in a trial of a Mafia boss, such as Carlos Marcello, with whom that surrogate son had done considerable business? Johnson once told House Speaker John McCormack, in the presence of Washington lobbyist Robert Winterberger (who described the meeting in *The Washington Payoff*), that he believed Baker had it in his power to ruin him, perhaps even send him to prison.

But, as we know, protégé Baker's ties to organized crime were not Johnson's only concern. There also lurked the disturbing shadow of Marcello's Texas associate and political fixer Jack Halfen, who, according to investigative journalist Michael Dorman in his book *Payoff*, had, in the fifties, allegedly siphoned off a percentage of Carlos Marcello's racing wire and slot machine profits in Texas and contributed them to Lyndon Johnson's political campaigns in return for Johnson's efforts in the U.S. Senate, both on the floor and in its back rooms, to protect mob interests. According to Dorman, Johnson, because of his dependence on Halfen-Marcello money, had helped kill in committee all antiracketeering legislative proposals that could have affected Halfen's and Marcello's activities in Texas. By 1964 Jack Halfen was behind bars, but he had kept 800 feet of movie film showing himself and his wife cavorting with the Johnsons on a Texas hunting trip, and there were plenty of people in Texas willing to talk with Justice Department officials, including Attorney General Robert F. Kennedy, of the Halfen-Marcello-Johnson relationship, for a price. In fact, a former Justice Department official told me that at the time of President Kennedy's assassination, there was a thick investigative file on Robert Kennedy's desk in the Justice Department detailing the Marcello-Halfen-Johnson connection that Kennedy was debating whether to pursue. It is thought that if President Kennedy had not been killed, Attorney General Kennedy might have pursued the investigation of that connection and Bobby Baker's dealings with organized crime. This would have helped the Kennedy brothers' behind-the-scenes efforts to discredit the Vice President so they could justify leaving him off the Democratic ticket in 1964. No, the last thing Lyndon Johnson would have wanted the Warren Commission to uncover would have been a conspiracy to assassinate his predecessor, John Kennedy, masterminded by his former benefactor, Carlos Marcello.

As for commission member Allen Dulles, we have already shown why he did not want to know of a possible Mafia plot to assassinate the President. He himself had been the author of an elaborate plot, composed of CIA agents and Mafia leaders, to assassinate the president of Cuba. Suppose the existence of that plot were to become known, and suppose it could be shown to have backfired and caused the assassination of the President of the United States?

Of course, that the ongoing CIA-Mafia plot to assassinate Castro was never brought to the attention of the Warren Commission was scandalous in the extreme. What could have been more relevant? The White House Special Group was investigating the matter while the Warren Commission was still deliberating. And yet the key people knowledgeable of the plots—former CIA Director Dulles, current CIA

Director McCone, FBI Director Hoover, and Attorney General Kennedy—still withheld knowledge of the plots from the commission.

Even commission Chairman Earl Warren had reason to divert the investigation of the President's murder away from any and all indications that organized crime might have been involved. For the man who had successfully managed Warren's campaign for governor of California, his good friend Murray Chotiner, was an attorney for several notorious Mafia leaders and was particularly close to mob front man D'Alton Smith, brother of Carlos Marcello's personal secretary, Frances Pecora, and brother-in-law of Marcello's top associate, Nofio Pecora. No, Earl Warren would not care to see Frances Pecora stand up in a courtroom during the trial of her boss for conspiring to kill the President and testify to her brother's close relationship with Earl Warren's good friend and former campaign manager Murray Chotiner.

Lastly, there was commission member Hale Boggs of Louisiana, who, according to Aaron Kohn, was deeply indebted to Carlos Marcello for funding several of his political campaigns. If the commission were to consider the possibility of the involvement of organized crime in the assassination, and specifically Marcello's organization, Boggs would presumably do everything in his power to discourage it.

As for Boggs's fellow Louisianan Leon D. Hubert, one of the commission's staff of attorneys who had been specifically assigned to investigate Jack Ruby's connections to organized crime, he too had reason to shy away from considering the possibility of Marcello's involvement. Hubert had recently served as assistant district attorney in New Orleans, where, according to Aaron Kohn, he had gained the reputation of being soft on the Marcello organization.

Thus virtually all the principals concerned with the investigation of the assassination, from President Johnson to FBI Director Hoover to commission Chairman Warren to commission members Dulles and Boggs to commission counsel Hubert had good personal reasons to steer the investigation away from evidence pointing toward the possible involvement of organized crime in the assassination.

But what of the head of the Justice Department, Attorney General Robert F. Kennedy? Would not he, the notorious crime fighter, have moved heaven and earth to uncover a Mafia conspiracy to kill his brother?

As we shall see, Robert Kennedy, in the end, despite his suspicions and his grief, was just as reluctant to implicate the Mafia as President Johnson or Chief Justice Warren. For no one was more susceptible to embarrassment at the hands of the mob than he, the new leader of the Kennedy family and future candidate for the Senate and the presidency of the United States.

40

The Silence of Robert Kennedy

Robert Kennedy's two principal pursuits as attorney general had been his direction of Operation Mongoose, the administration's top secret war against Castro and his Soviet-backed regime in Cuba, and the direction of the Justice Department's war against organized crime.

We can well imagine, then, how he must have felt when he learned on November 23 that the suspect arrested for his brother's murder was found to be a member of the Fair Play for Cuba Committee who had demonstrated for Castro in New Orleans, and how he must have felt when, a day later, he learned that his brother's suspected murderer had himself been murdered "gangland style" by a Dallas nightclub operator and local racketeer who, the papers quickly reported, had once worked in his native Chicago as a messenger boy for Al Capone.

Robert Kennedy was not stupid, and he was not uninformed. He was one of the few people at the highest level of the government who knew of the CIA-Mafia plots to assassinate Castro, and he was almost alone at the level of government he represented in his awareness of the power of the Mafia.

He therefore must have quickly formed suspicions as to who, or what, might have been behind Oswald and Ruby. Given what was publicly known about the two by the afternoon of Monday, November 25, it must have seemed possible to Kennedy that pro-Castro Cubans might have been behind his brother's murder and that organized crime might have been behind the murder of the suspected assassin. To someone as knowledgeable of these two areas as Robert Kennedy, the combination of pro-Castro forces and the mob must have seemed very odd, unless Oswald had somehow been framed as a Castroite by anti-Castro forces or had intentionally misrepresented himself as a supporter of Castro.

Whatever the case, by the time of his brother's burial at Arlington, Robert Kennedy must have become painfully aware that Oswald and Ruby had been operating in the two areas he had been most concerned about as attorney general: Cuba and organized crime.

These realizations must have caused him profound anguish, adding another measure of pain to the normal burden of grief. For he could not possibly have escaped the awful suspicion that his aggressive campaigns against Castro and the mob might have backfired on his brother.

Many have testified to the degree of demoralization Robert Kennedy suffered after his brother's murder. His friend LeMoyne Billings observed that the assassination was "much harder for him than anybody," that "he didn't know where he was....Everything was just pulled out from under him." Robert Blakey, a Justice Department attorney at the time, who had been involved in the Kennedys' war on organized crime, told me that Kennedy was virtually incapacitated. William Hundley, who had headed the Justice Department's Organized Crime and Racketeering Section under Kennedy, and had overseen Carlos Marcello's prosecution in November 1963, told me in 1988 that Bobby Kennedy was so shattered that Hundley could not even get through to him about the organized crime cases he was pursuing. When Hundley finally got around to telling Kennedy about Marcello's November 22 acquittal, Kennedy just stared blankly, as if it had not registered. And Nicholas Katzenbach, who became acting attorney general immediately after the assassination, told me that Kennedy was "just out of it," that he was unable to perform the duties of his office.

So emotionally incapacitated did Bobby Kennedy become that he was unable to do any very demanding work for two months following his brother's murder. Then, when he finally felt well enough to resume his duties as attorney general in late January, he puzzled everyone by apparently taking no interest whatsoever in the ongoing investigations of his brother's assassination. Later, after the Warren Commission had concluded its investigation and issued its final report, Kennedy publicly accepted the findings of the commission, though he admitted privately he had not followed the progress of the commission's investigation and never read the report.

What explanation can we give for this seemingly contradictory behavior? The aggressive, vengeful crime fighter acquiescing, submissively, to the hated Hoover's solution to the crime, then passively accepting the conclusions of a rubber-stamp investigation he never followed and a report he never read?

Mere grief, as terrible as it must have been, does not sufficiently explain behavior so out of character. Robert Kennedy was known for his toughness and resilience, his implacability. No, Robert Kennedy must have suffered from more than grief to have been rendered virtually nonfunctioning by the assassination of his brother.

It now appears evident that during the weeks and months following the assassination, a grief-stricken and guilt-ridden Robert Kennedy, now totally ignored by Hoover and barely able to perform the functions of his office as attorney general, came to suspect that there had indeed been a conspiracy to assassinate his brother, a conspiracy in which one or both of his two principal targets in his war against organized crime—Jimmy Hoffa and Carlos Marcello—may have been involved.

That Robert Kennedy was suspicious that either Jimmy Hoffa or Carlos Marcello, or both, might have been involved in a plot to kill his brother is hinted at by certain Kennedy postassassination comments on the crime.

As we know, Robert Kennedy and William Hundley had been presiding over a conference on organized crime at the Justice Department the day of his brother's assassination and had been looking forward that morning to receiving word from New Orleans of a favorable verdict in the Justice Department's current case against Carlos and Joseph Marcello. If the verdict came in on time he wanted to announce it at the afternoon session. It would give the conference a lift. But instead of receiving word of Marcello's conviction, Kennedy received word of his brother's murder in Dallas in the midst of a lunch break at his McLean, Virginia, estate. Calling off the afternoon session at the Justice Department, Kennedy got into a discussion of the assassination with his press secretary, Edwin Guthman. According to Guthman, Kennedy said:

> "I thought they might get one of us...but Jack, after what he'd been through, never worried about it....I thought it would be me."

Who were "they"? It seems obvious that Kennedy was referring to certain leaders of organized crime, perhaps one or more of the Mafia bosses and Mafia-corrupted labor leaders he had targeted for

priority investigation and eventual prosecution. At his morning conference on organized crime, he and his section heads, Walter Sheridan
and William Hundley, had been addressing U.S. attorneys from all
over the country, on the prosecutions of Jimmy Hoffa in Nashville
and Carlos Marcello in New Orleans.

A little over two weeks later, while Kennedy was having dinner
with historian Arthur Schlesinger in Washington, the two discussed
Oswald briefly. Kennedy remarked that there seemed to be little doubt
Oswald was guilty, but there was still doubt if he had acted alone or
was part of a larger plot, "whether organized by Castro or gangsters."

And yet, despite these suspicions, Robert Kennedy knew that if
Hoffa or Marcello were involved, even though he was still attorney general, he could do nothing about investigating their possible complicity, much less initiate legal proceedings against them. This realization
must have given Kennedy such a debilitating sense of frustration and
futility that he had no choice but to swallow his suspicions and issue
a pro forma endorsement of the Warren Commission's findings, even
though he suspected they were invalid.

To understand why Robert Kennedy felt he was powerless to do
anything about investigating the possibility of Hoffa's or Marcello's
involvement in his brother's murder, we must consider the extent to
which Robert Kennedy and his family were compromised in relation
to organized crime and how, as a result, Robert Kennedy had become a virtual hostage to his enemies, including, above all, J. Edgar
Hoover.

What did Hoover and the Mafia know about the Kennedys that
would render Robert Kennedy a virtual hostage to them? The list is
long. We shall consider what Hoover knew that certain Mafia leaders
probably knew also. Hoover knew that Joseph P. Kennedy had solicited a contribution to his son's campaign for the Democratic nomination from Sam Giancana, and that when Robert Kennedy turned
the heat on Giancana, the Chicago Mafia boss let it be known that he
felt he had been double-crossed. Hoover was aware that the Kennedy
brothers knew of the CIA-Mafia plots to assassinate the president of
Cuba and did nothing to stop them. He knew of John F. Kennedy's
innumerable affairs with women of dubious reputation, both before
and during his marriage to Jacqueline Bouvier, the two most imprudent of which were with Sam Giancana's girlfriend Judith Campbell
and the actress Marilyn Monroe. Recently he had received persuasive reports from Scotland Yard that the President had been involved
with one of the call girls from the ring that had brought down Great
Britain's minister of defense, John Profumo. And he had evidence

in his files also of the attorney general's brief fling with Miss Monroe and of the tapes Jimmy Hoffa's wireman, Bernard Spindell, had secretly recorded of their encounters.

Considering what Hoover knew about Robert Kennedy and his family, could Robert have *not* accepted the FBI director's solution to the murder of his brother? Could he, as attorney general, have disputed publicly the conclusions of his subordinate J. Edgar Hoover without risking the gravest personal and political consequences?

Nicholas Katzenbach told me that when Robert Kennedy resumed his duties as attorney general in late January, he seemed to disassociate himself from the investigation of the assassination and even told Katzenbach that he preferred that there be no investigation at all. Katzenbach also told me that Hoover never sent any of the FBI teletypes and reports—the raw data on which the FBI's investigation of the assassination was based—either to him, Katzenbach, or to Robert Kennedy. This, of course, meant that Katzenbach and Kennedy never received any of the conspiracy allegations involving associates of the Marcellos. Nor did they receive transcripts of any of the taped conversations the FBI had made of various Mafia bosses threatening the lives of the Kennedy brothers in 1962 and 1963. What is more, Hoover did not send any of the raw investigatory data on Ruby to the attorney general or to his deputy. This meant that Katzenbach and Kennedy never saw the records of Ruby's telephone calls to various organized crime figures, including one to a lieutenant of Carlos Marcello's, prior to the assassination. All they received, in the end, was Hoover's massive five-volume summary report identifying Lee Harvey Oswald as the lone, unaided assassin of the President and Jack Ruby as the lone, unaided "patriotic" killer of Oswald.

Robert Kennedy was quite familiar with some of the names that showed up on certain allegations the FBI received in the weeks following the assassination. Aaron Kohn had briefed him prior to Kennedy's questioning of Carlos Marcello during the McClellan Committee hearings, and he, in turn, had questioned Marcello himself about some of them at the hearings. It is therefore safe to say that if he had received from the FBI the allegations of Jack Martin, Eugene De Laparra, Gene Sumner, and Bobby Gene Moore, and the records of Ruby's phone calls, he would have instantly recognized the Town & Country restaurant and the names Vincent Marcello, Joseph Poretto, Anthony Marcello, Joseph Civello, and Nofio Pecora, and, in horror, would have become instantly suspicious of the Marcellos.

But was there a possibility he received a copy of, or heard of, the allegations bearing those names from someone in the FBI other than

Hoover, or from someone on the staff of the Warren Commission? There certainly should have been such a possibility, for Robert Kennedy had a good friend and ally in the FBI, Courtney Evans, and supposedly had another on the Warren Commission staff, Howard Willens.

Reacting to pressure from Attorney General Kennedy to upgrade the FBI's investigation of organized crime, Hoover had created within the FBI the special division for organized crime and had put one of his most trusted agents, a veteran of twenty-five years, Courtney Evans, in charge of it. Later he selected Evans to act as liaison between the FBI and the attorney general.

Robert Kennedy had known Courtney Evans from his service on the McClellan Rackets Committee. Evans had served then as liaison between the FBI and the committee. Kennedy had liked and respected him, and their relationship had grown stronger and more intimate when Evans became liaison between him and Hoover. In time Evans became, in the words of former Assistant FBI Director William Sullivan, "a pal of Jack and Bobby," and it was widely rumored that the Kennedy brothers wanted to make him director of the FBI upon Hoover's forced retirement in 1964.

J. Edgar Hoover had been aware of these rumors, and so, immediately after the assassination, he removed Evans from his position as liaison between the FBI and Attorney General Kennedy and began shunning him. Not only that, but even though Evans had been made head of the FBI's special division for organized crime, Hoover cut him out of the investigation of the Kennedy murder entirely and made sure none of the conspiracy allegations that arrived at headquarters were routed to him. Thus, even though Evans was sitting in the midst of the frantic teletype traffic over the Kennedy assassination that was coming into headquarters from all over the nation, he never saw any of the reports mentioning the Marcellos or their associates. When, in the fall of 1987, I asked him if he had seen any of the reports on David Ferrie, he responded, "David who?" And when I asked him if Robert Kennedy saw any of the reports of conspiracy allegations, he replied: "Hoover never sent him anything."

Another friend of Robert Kennedy's who was in a position to inform Kennedy about those allegations was Howard Willens. At the time of the assassination, Willens was a 32-year-old attorney in the Justice Department's criminal division, which had been the engine room of Robert Kennedy's war on organized crime. It was around two months later (January 21) that Hoover, in response to the Warren Commission's demand for raw FBI data, began sending hundreds of FBI investigative reports to the Warren Commission. At this time, Acting Attorney General Katzenbach designated Howard Willens to serve as liaison between the Warren Commission and the Justice Department in the handling of all FBI documents sent to the commission. Soon he became an assistant to the commission's general counsel, J. Lee Rankin. Willens therefore was presumably in a position to examine all the conspiracy allegations that were made to the FBI in the wake of the assassination, including all the "nut stuff" and the allegations of Jack Martin, Eugene De Laparra, Gene Sumner, and Bobby Gene Moore. About a week after Willens assumed his liaison job with the commission, Robert Kennedy returned to the Justice Department and resumed his duties as attorney general. Robert Kennedy knew Howard Willens, and now Willens was shuttling back and forth between the Warren Commission's offices at 200 Maryland Avenue and the Justice Department, trying to handle the immense flow of FBI documents arriving at the commission. One would suppose that Robert Kennedy would have some curiosity over these documents, that he might have asked Willens to let him see some of them, but apparently he did not.

Did Howard Willens see the FBI reports of the allegations mentioning the Marcellos? If so, did he recognize their potential significance?

Since Howard Willens had been working in the division of the Justice Department that was directly concerned with Attorney General Kennedy's number one priority, his war on organized crime, it is reasonable to assume that Willens would have been familiar with the Marcello organization of Louisiana. This would mean that Willens should have immediately recognized the names David Ferrie, Carlos Marcello, Vincent Marcello, Joseph Marcello, Joseph Poretto, Joseph Civello, and the Town & Country Motel if he had managed to pluck the allegations in which these names were mentioned from the huge piles of crank allegations Hoover had sent over to satisfy the commission's request for the FBI's "raw files."

But if this were the case, why wouldn't he have brought these allegations to the attention of the Warren Commission?

We are left then, with the perplexing conclusion that either Howard Willens saw fit not to bring the allegations involving the Marcellos to the attention of members of the commission or, if he did bring them to the commission's attention, the commission chose to ignore them.

As disconcerting and unreasonable as the latter possibility is, there is some evidence to support it.

We have mentioned that the FBI report of Bobby Gene Moore's allegation arrived at the Warren Commission intact and that at some later date it was radically altered for inclusion in the commission's published exhibits.

The full, uncut FBI report of Bobby Gene Moore's allegation began with an account of who Moore was, that he had been born and raised in Dallas and had once lived in a rooming house at the rear of Hill's Liquor Store, and went on to state:

> This liquor store was a front for a bookie-type operation where bets were taken on all types of athletic events and horse races. It was operated by a man named HILL, first name unknown, and his son. This gambling place was patronized by most of the gambling element in Dallas and RUBY was a frequent visitor. Moore did not know whether or not RUBY was actually connected with the operation of the gambling place or merely a participant.

The report continued with an account of Moore's employment by Joseph Cirello [sic] and his partner Frank LaMonte at their Italian imports company, during which he came to suspect that Civello and LaMonte "were engaged in racket activities," specifically the importing of narcotics, and went on to state that "Ruby was also a frequent visitor and associate of Cirello [sic] and LaMonte."

After naming two Dallas Police officers and a judge who Moore believed were involved in illegal activities with Civello, the report went on to state:

> Ruby was also friendly with PHIL BOSCO...and Moore felt that BOSCO was also engaged in criminal activities in Dallas, although he had no specific information to substantiate this.

Then, after stating that Moore had worked as a part-time piano player for Jack Ruby at his Vegas Club in Dallas from June 1952 to 1956, the report concluded:

> Moore felt that from RUBY's association with HILL, CIRELLO [sic], and PHIL BOSCO that he was connected with the underworld in Dallas.

The report of Moore's allegation was eventually deposited in the National Archives, unexcised, as Warren Commission Document 84, but when it was published in the commission's volumes of hearings and exhibits as Commission Exhibit 1536, it appeared in a radically altered version: Only the first two paragraphs about Moore's background and his knowledge of Hill's gambling place were intact; all the rest had been cut, which, of course, meant that Ruby's association with Joseph Civello had been eliminated, along with the report of Moore's belief that Ruby "was connected with the underworld in Dallas." Found attached to the folder for the file copy of Commission Exhibit 1536 in the National Archives was an undated, unsigned note reading "Omit everything after paragraph 2."

Who was the author of that note? Was it Howard Willens? At least two serious scholars of the Kennedy assassination case believe it was.

Two questions remain. First, if Howard Willens was fully aware of the implications of the allegations suggesting the possibility of Marcello involvement, which it is reasonable to suppose he was, why didn't he forcefully bring them to the attention of the commission? And second, did he bring the allegations suggesting Marcello complicity to the attention of his friend and boss, Robert Kennedy?

In response to these questions, Willens has stated that he does not remember the specific allegations but is sure he brought "every FBI report of significance" to the attention of the Warren Commission. However, he did not feel he had the authority to bring such reports to the attention of his boss, Attorney General Robert F. Kennedy.

In 1978 the House Select Committee on Assassinations questioned Howard Willens about whether reports on organized crime figures, if there were any, were brought to the attention of the Warren Commission. Chief Counsel G. Robert Blakey pointed out to Willens that from 1959 to 1964 "the FBI, albeit illegally, had engaged in an extensive program that targeted major organized crime figures" for electronic surveillance. The bureau had "placed up to a hundred listening devices in the homes and offices of major underworld figures." Blakey then had the following exchange with Willens:

BLAKEY: Was either the existence of this program or [its] products ever brought to the attention of the Warren Commission?

WILLENS: I do not recall. I was aware that an extensive investigative program was under way with respect to organized crime. I had every reason to believe that the FBI and criminal division, which had responsibility for the overall prosecutorial effort, would bring to the attention of the Warren Commission any information developed by any source that pertained to the work of the...commission....

BLAKEY: To your knowledge, was there any effort made by the commission, by the Department of Justice, or the bureau to survey that electronic surveillance to determine whether there was any indication in it, either direct or circumstantial, that any of the major figures of organized crime might have had motive, opportunity, or the means to assassinate the President...?

WILLENS: I do not know whether any effort of that kind was made. I do not believe it was made.

Some of the conversations of members of organized crime about the Kennedys, which the FBI had picked up through wiretaps and concealed listening devices, revealed the extent of their hatred and resentment of the President and the attorney general.

On February 9, 1962, Angelo Bruno, head of the leading organized crime family of Philadelphia, was overheard talking with one of his *capiregime,* Willie Weisburg:

WEISBURG: See what Kennedy done. With Kennedy, a guy should take a knife, like one of them other guys, and stab and kill the fucker, where he is now. Somebody should kill the fucker. I mean it. This is true. Honest to God. It's about time to go. But I tell you something. I hope I get a week's notice. I'll kill. Right in the fuckin' in the White House. Somebody's got to get rid of this fucker.

Angelo Bruno agreed with Weisburg but advised him to be cautious, telling him that sometimes the man following the man who has been eliminated turns out to be worse.

On May 2, 1962, the FBI overheard Michelino Clemente, a *capiregime* in the Genovese family, express sentiments similar to Weisburg's:

CLEMENTE: Bob Kennedy won't stop today until he puts us all in jail all over the country. Until the commission meets and puts its foot down, things will be at a standstill.

When we meet, we all got to shake hands, and sit down and talk, and, if there is any trouble with a particular regime, it's got to be kept secret, and only the heads are to know about it, otherwise some broad finds out, and finally the newspapers.

At around the same time, the FBI overheard an unidentified Genovese family member saying:

"I want the President indicted, because I know he was whacking all those broads. Sinatra brought them out. I'd like to hit Kennedy. I would gladly go to the penitentiary for the rest of my life, believe me."

On October 31, 1963, the FBI picked up a conversation between two of the Maggadino brothers of Buffalo:

PETER MAGGADINO: President Kennedy he should drop dead.

STEFANO MAGGADINO: They should kill the whole family, the mother and father, too.

And yet J. Edgar Hoover had not seen fit to inform either Attorney General Kennedy or the Warren Commission of the existence of these tapes.

Howard Willens, then, was probably not to blame for those FBI reports of allegations hinting at the possibility of Marcello involvement in the assassination not reaching the Warren Commission. For now that we have obtained so many documents detailing the response of Hoover's FBI to the assassination, and Hoover's dealings with the Warren Commission, it has become apparent that the blame for this omission falls almost wholly on J. Edgar Hoover.

Seen with the advantage of twenty-five years of research into the investigations of the Kennedy assassination, it strikes us as utterly outrageous that Hoover never informed Robert Kennedy of the FBI's wiretaps of Mafia leaders threatening him and his brother, and of the several allegations that had been made to the FBI within a week of the assassination hinting at the possible involvement of the Marcello organization in the President's murder. Hoover knew full well how Robert Kennedy would have reacted if he had been shown FBI reports on allegations hinting at conspiracy in the murder of his brother that bore the names Joseph Poretto, Joseph Civello, the Town &

Country Motel, and Carlos, Joseph, Vincent, and Anthony Marcello. Kennedy would have immediately suspected that the Marcello organization might have been involved in a conspiracy to assassinate his brother.

But Robert Kennedy himself was also to blame for this outrage. He could have volunteered to appear as a witness before the Warren Commission, and as a witness, he could have alerted the commission to his suspicions in regard to Jimmy Hoffa and Carlos Marcello and asked the commission to watch for FBI reports of allegations suggesting their possible involvement in his brother's assassination. He did neither. Furthermore, he could have told the commission what he knew about the CIA-Mafia plots to kill Fidel Castro, but he did not. Instead, he went on record as accepting the results of the Warren Commission's investigation, as the following correspondence attests.

It was Howard Willens who drafted the exchange of letters between commission Chairman Earl Warren and Attorney General Robert F. Kennedy that put the seal on Robert Kennedy's capitulation to those responsible for investigating his brother's assassination.

The following memorandum from Howard Willens to commission General Counsel J. Lee Rankin tells the story:

June 4, 1964

MEMORANDUM

TO: Mr. J. Lee Rankin, General Counsel
FROM: Howard P. Willens
SUBJECT: Proposed Exchange of Letters between the
           Commission and the Attorney General.

Attached are drafts of a proposed exchange of letters between the Chairman of this Commission and the Attorney General. As I have mentioned to you, this recommended procedure is the result of my recent discussions at the Department with Deputy Attorney General Katzenbach and the Attorney General. The Attorney General would prefer to handle his obligations to the Commission in this way rather than appear as a witness.

The proposed response by the Attorney General has, of course, not been approved by him or on his behalf by the Deputy Attorney General. It represents a revision of an earlier letter which I did show to them during my conference with them today. At that time the Attorney General informed me that he had not received any reports from the Director of the Federal Bureau of Investigation regarding the investigation of the assassination, and that his principal sources of information have been the Chief Justice, the Deputy Attorney General and myself. This accounts for the specific mention of these persons in the second paragraph of his letter to the Chief Justice.

ATTACHMENTS.

The letters Willens drafted from Warren to Kennedy and from Kennedy to Warren, later signed by both parties, were as follows.

From Warren to Kennedy:

Honorable Robert F. Kennedy
Attorney General of the United States
Department of Justice
Washington, D.C. 20530

Dear General:

Throughout the course of the investigation conducted by this Commission, the Department of Justice has been most helpful in forwarding information relevant to this Commission's inquiry.

The Commission is now in the process of completing its investigation. Prior to the publication of its report, the Commission would like to be advised whether you are aware of any additional information relating to the assassination of President John F. Kennedy which has not been sent to the Commission. In view of the widely circulated allegations on this subject, the Commission would like to be informed in particular whether you have any information suggesting that the assassination of President Kennedy was caused by a domestic or foreign conspiracy. Needless to say, if you have any suggestions to make regarding the investigation of these allegations or any other phase of the Commission's work, we stand ready to act upon them.

On behalf of the Commission I wish to thank you and your representatives for the assistance you have provided to the Commission.

Sincerely,

Chairman

From Kennedy to Warren:

DRAFT
Honorable Earl Warren
Chief Justice of the United States
The Supreme Court
Washington, D.C. 20543

Dear Mr. Chief Justice:

In response to your letter of _____ I would like to assure you that all information relating in any way to the assassination of President John F. Kennedy in the possession of the Department of Justice has been referred to the President's Commission for appropriate review and investigation.

As you know, I am personally not aware of the detailed results of the extensive investigation in this matter which has been conducted by the Federal Bureau of Investigation. I have, however, received periodic reports about the work of the Commission from you, Deputy Attorney General Katzenbach and Mr. Willens of the Department of Justice, who has worked with the Commission for the past several months. Based on these reports, I am confident that every effort is being made by the President's Commission to fulfill the objectives of Executive Order No. 11130 by conducting a thorough investigation into all the facts relating to the assassination.

In response to your specific inquiry, I would like to state definitely that I know of no credible evidence to support the allegations that the assassination of President Kennedy was caused by a domestic or foreign conspiracy. I have no suggestions to make at this time regarding any additional investigation which should be undertaken by the Commission prior to the publication of its report. In the event that the members of the Commission believe that I can contribute in any way to the investigation by appearing as a witness, I will be available to do so at your convenience.

Sincerely,

Attorney General

What was the reason behind Robert Kennedy's passive response to his brother's assassination and his acquiescent acceptance of the findings of the FBI's and the Warren Commission's investigation of the crime?

Now, twenty-five years after the events of November 22, 1963, it appears that the reason was essentially political. For Robert Kennedy knew that if indeed there had been a Mafia conspiracy behind his brother's murder, especially one involving the Marcello organization, it would have been more politically embarrassing to him, and to his brother's posthumous reputation, to have the background surrounding such a plot and the incidental information that might arise out of an investigation of it revealed in a courtroom than to simply let sleeping dogs lie.

What could come out during the trial of Carlos Marcello for conspiring to assassinate the President of the United States that could possibly have been damaging to the Kennedy reputation?

The existence of the CIA-Mafia plots to assassinate the president of Cuba, for one. How would the American people have reacted to the revelation that the administration of its slain President had attempted to assassinate the president of a neighboring state?

The Kennedy brothers' respective relationships with Judith Campbell and Marilyn Monroe, for another.

We now know that the leadership of the underworld in 1963 was well aware that John Kennedy had been having affairs with Sam Giancana's girlfriend, Judith Campbell, *and* actress Marilyn Monroe and that Robert Kennedy had also carried on an affair with Miss Monroe.

Edward Becker, the private investigator who alleged he had heard Carlos Marcello threaten to kill President Kennedy in order to neutralize his brother Robert, was close to the underworld in Las Vegas and Los Angeles in the early sixties. He told me that his close friend Johnny Roselli used to comment that "everyone in the mob" knew about "Jack Kennedy's affair with Sam's girl," that it was a favorite topic of gossip in the underworld at the time. And Joseph Hauser, the convicted swindler turned government witness, whom the FBI used in a 1979 undercover operation against Carlos Marcello, corroborated Becker's observation. Hauser told me in the fall of 1987 that he had known Sam Giancana in the early sixties and that Giancana used to joke about President Kennedy's relationship with Judy Campbell all the time. Hauser said there probably wasn't a Mafia boss in the nation who did not know about the affair.

As for Mafia awareness of Robert Kennedy's relationship with Marilyn Monroe, we now know that Jimmy Hoffa's wireman, Bernard Spindell, was able to tape some of the attorney general's encounters with the actress at her Brentwood home and that Hoffa's allies in the underworld, including Carlos Marcello, were aware of the affair. That awareness was confirmed by a recently released FBI electronic surveillance transcript.

On August 20, 1962, an FBI listening device picked up a conversation between three well-known Mafia figures that made reference
to Robert Kennedy's affair with the celebrated actress. The three were
apparently concerned about possible prosecution by the government
and were thinking of exerting pressure on Robert Kennedy by threatening to break the scandal of his relationship with Marilyn Monroe.
The FBI report of the taped conversation read, in part:

> They will go for every name…unless the brother—it's big
> enough to cause a scandal against them. Would he like to see
> a headline about Marilyn Monroe come out? And him? How
> would he like it? Don't you know?…He has been in there
> plenty of times. It's been a hard affair—and this [deleted name
> of a friend of Marilyn's] said she used to be in all the time
> with him—do you think it's a secret?

But there was still another reason why it would have been potentially embarrassing for Robert Kennedy if Carlos Marcello were
brought to trial for conspiring to murder his brother: the full details
of his deportation of Marcello would come out.

We do not know precisely when Robert Kennedy was informed of
the outcome of the November 1963 trial of Carlos and Joseph Marcello—William Hundley told me it could have been the afternoon of
the assassination, but probably was not until Kennedy returned to his
desk at the Justice Department two months later, when Hundley himself gave him the unwelcome news—but during that trial, Jack Wasserman had made a convincing point that Kennedy's "kidnap style"
deportation of his client had been arguably illegal in the first place.
In any event, Kennedy was probably made aware by his advisers in
the Justice Department that the manner in which he had deported
Carlos Marcello had been ill-conceived, unfair, and arguably illegal.

In his book *The Enemy Within*, Kennedy had admonished: "If we
do not attack organized criminals with weapons and techniques as
effective as their own, they will destroy us." But had the "technique"
of grabbing a man unawares, hustling him onto a plane with only
the clothes on his back and what cash he was carrying in his wallet,
and dumping him in Guatemala with no instructions as to whom he
was supposed to report really been "effective" in the light of what we
now know?

In an eventual prosecution of Carlos Marcello for conspiring to
assassinate President Kennedy, all the embarrassing details of Attorney General Kennedy's seriously flawed deportation action would
come to light, and the press and public would inevitably conclude

that if Marcello *had* conspired to kill his brother, it would have been in retaliation for the attorney general's unfair and illegal deportation action in his regard. Therefore the assassination could be indirectly blamed on the President's brother.

Robert Kennedy's probable suspicions that the Marcellos were behind the assassination of his brother, and his realization that nothing could be done about them, do much to explain his apparent indifference to the FBI's and the Warren Commission's investigations of the assassination. In his frustration and despair, Robert Kennedy came to realize that the only sensible attitude he could take toward his brother's assassination was to remain silent. Unfortunately, his silence robbed his brother of an heroic death.

But Robert Kennedy's response to the assassination of his brother now appears to have gone beyond silence to active participation in covering up certain crucial evidence in the crime. For there are strong indications that Robert Kennedy was involved in a conspiracy to suppress key evidence that could have shown that his brother was killed as a result of gunshot wounds from more than one gunman. The evidence in question consisted of certain autopsy-related materials that the House Select Committee on Assassinations concluded in 1979 had been confiscated by Robert Kennedy in 1965 and had later been either destroyed by him, or "otherwise rendered inaccessible."

These autopsy materials consisted of black-and-white and color negatives and prints of autopsy photographs, 119 microscopic slides of sections of certain tissues, including many specimens of John F. Kennedy's wound-edge tissues; 58 slides of blood smears taken at various times during Kennedy's life, and the President's formalin-preserved brain.

Incredibly, the physical specimen evidence was never examined by the FBI or the Warren Commission during their investigations of the assassination, even though it was the key to determining the origin and trajectory of the gunshots that wounded the President and Governor Connally, and the identification of the weapons and ammunition used in the shooting. It is believed that Robert Kennedy played an important role in preventing the Warren Commission from examining these materials.

Immediately after the autopsy the photographs, x-rays, and physical specimens were transferred from the U.S. Naval Hospital at Bethesda, where the autopsy had been conducted, to the custody of the Secret Service White House detail in the Executive Office Building, adjacent to the White House. The materials were stored in a locked Secret Service file cabinet under the control of President Kennedy's former White House physician, Vice Admiral George C.

Burkley, who, in a sense, represented the rightful owner of the materials—the U.S. Navy.

And there, in that Secret Service file cabinet this crucial evidence remained, either forgotten or deliberately ignored, until over a year after the Warren Commission had issued its final report. On April 22, 1965, Senator Robert F. Kennedy instructed Dr. Burkley to transfer in person to another location what he referred to in his letter to Burkley as "the material of President Kennedy of which you have knowledge," without spelling out that what was to be transferred included the autopsy materials. The transfer of the materials was to be made from the custody of the Secret Service to the care of Mrs. Evelyn Lincoln, former personal secretary of President Kennedy, for "safekeeping" at the National Archives, where Mrs. Lincoln had been maintaining a temporary office.

What prompted Robert Kennedy to suddenly and surreptitiously order Dr. Burkley to remove the autopsy evidence from the custody of the Secret Service on April 22, 1965? It appears it must have been Kennedy's awareness, as a member of the Congress, that the Congress was then considering the enactment of a law providing for the acquisition by the United States of certain items of evidence in the assassination of President Kennedy within a year of its enactment, scheduled for the fall of 1965. This gave Kennedy little time to lose.

It is scandalous that Robert Kennedy was allowed to control these autopsy materials, since, as a family member, his interests might have conflicted with the prosecution of anyone charged with the crime. Strictly speaking, the materials were the property of the U.S. Navy, which conducted the autopsy. Mrs. Lincoln was not an employee of the National Archives at the time she received the autopsy materials. She was temporarily using an office in the Archives building to aid her in the transfer of the late President's papers to the Archives. Upon receiving various containers of autopsy materials from Dr. Burkley Mrs. Lincoln stored them in a small footlocker, in a secure closet in the office. And there they remained until approximately a month later, when Robert Kennedy telephoned her and informed her he was sending his personal secretary, Angela Novello, to remove the footlocker from her office. Mrs. Lincoln later testified that Miss Novello did, in fact, remove the footlocker and its two keys from her office in the company of Herman Kahn, Assistant Archivist for Presidential Libraries. She was not sure where Miss Novello and Mr. Kahn then stored it, but got the impression that Miss Novello took it to a courtesy storage space in the National Archives that had been made available to Robert Kennedy.

Some time later, in 1966, Attorney General Ramsey Clarke, under Lyndon Johnson, approached Senator Kennedy and asked him to comply with the law Congress had enacted on November 2, 1965, providing for the acquisition by the U.S. government of certain items of evidence pertaining to the assassination of President Kennedy, including the autopsy materials. According to Clarke's later testimony before the Assassinations Committee, Senator Kennedy proved most unsympathetic to the government's request. Heated discussions followed, and finally Kennedy agreed in the fall of 1966 to release the autopsy materials. Clarke later testified that he had discussed with Kennedy only the autopsy photographs and x-rays, that they never referred to the physical specimens.

On October 29, 1966, Kennedy family attorney Burke Marshall, on behalf of the executors of the estate of President Kennedy, which included Jacqueline Kennedy and Robert F. Kennedy, entered into a formal agreement with the U.S. government to deed the autopsy materials in the estate's possession to the National Archives. Accompanying the agreement was a complete inventory of all the materials, including the autopsy photographs and x-rays, the wound-edge tissues slides, and the President's brain.

On October 31, a number of high officials of the General Services Administration and the National Archives gathered at the National Archives to formally receive the autopsy materials from the Kennedy estate's representative and to conduct an inventory of those materials. Representing the estate were Burke Marshall and Angela Novello. Representing the government was William H. Brewster, special assistant to the General Counsel of the General Services Administration. Angela Novello gave Brewster a key and he unlocked and opened the footlocker. At this point Marshall and Novello left the room and departed from the Archives.

Accompanying the autopsy materials were a carbon copy of Robert Kennedy's letter to Dr. Burkley of April 22, 1965, and the original letter from Burkley to Evelyn Lincoln of April 26, 1965, which itemized all the materials transferred at that time, including the physical specimens. William Brewster and the other officials then removed all the materials from the footlocker and inspected them, checking each item off against the inventory, and were astonished to discover that many of the items were missing.

Most of the black-and-white and color photographs and x-rays of the autopsy listed in the inventory were present, but all the physical specimens had vanished. Photographs of the interior cavity of the President's chest were missing, as were most of those taken of the brain during a supplemental examination conducted after the official autopsy. These, of course, were the sites of Kennedy's gunshot wounds. Also missing were three plastic boxes containing microscopic slides of tissue sections, three wooden boxes containing 58 slides of blood smears, and "one stainless steel container, 7 x 8 inches in diameter, containing gross material," the gross material being the President's brain.

The government officials were appalled, well aware that the autopsy physical specimens constituted crucial evidence in the assassination case. Who had removed them from the footlocker and why?

When the House Select Committee on Assassinations investigated the highly suspicious disappearance of these autopsy materials in 1978, it concluded after an exhaustive effort, that "circumstantial evidence tends to show that Robert Kennedy either destroyed these materials or otherwise rendered them inaccessible."

It is, of course, possible that someone else destroyed the autopsy materials or otherwise rendered them inaccessible, if someone else had been able to gain access to the footlocker containing the materials, for which, it appears, only Robert Kennedy's secretary, Angela Novello, possessed the two keys. The dean of Kennedy assassination researchers, Harold Weisberg, suspects the FBI stole the materials from the footlocker simply by picking the lock. But it seems far more likely that the House Assassinations Committee's conclusions were correct.

Why would Robert Kennedy have wanted to destroy or render inaccessible this crucial evidence? The committee speculated that Kennedy might have been concerned that the tissue slides and his brother's brain might someday be put on display by the National Archives, or by some other institution. But this does not appear to be a convincing explanation since in the Kennedy executors' deed of gift to the National Archives it was specifically stipulated that "none of the materials shall be placed on public display," and that they would be made available only to persons "authorized to act for a committee of the Congress, or a Presidential committee or commission relating to the death of the late President," or to certain qualified researchers, preferably in the field of forensic pathology, whose requests to examine the materials would have to be approved by certain designated surviving members of the Kennedy family.

Besides, as has been pointed out by Henry Hurt, author of a 1985 book on the assassination, *Reasonable Doubt*, it would have been much more likely that a future hypothetical displayer, wishing to create a sensation, would want to display some of the ghastly photographs of the President's blasted face, the photographs that Chief Justice Warren admitted kept him from sleeping for three consecutive nights, than some microscopic tissue slides and preserved brain matter that would appear indistinguishable from those of any other deceased person.

In my opinion, it seems most likely that Robert Kennedy might have destroyed or rendered inaccessible the wound-edge tissue slides and bullet-riddled brain to eliminate the last remaining significant pieces of evidence that his brother had not been murdered by Lee Harvey Oswald, acting alone, but by a team of gunmen which may or may not have included Oswald.

Robert Kennedy's legal right to claim custody of the autopsy materials, not to mention his right to destroy or confiscate them, was never questioned by the officials of the National Archives and the General Services Administration who discovered to their utter astonishment, on October 31, 1966, that the physical specimens were missing. In fact, mysteriously, no documents have been located that even indicate that Robert Kennedy, or other members of the Kennedy family, were notified that some items in the Kennedy deed of gift to the National Archives were found to be missing. In other words, if indeed Robert Kennedy destroyed or hid the tissue slides, the blood smears, and the brain, the government let him get away with the destruction, or confiscation, of vital evidence pertaining to the assassination of his brother, the President.

We are left, then, with the disconcerting conclusion that Robert Kennedy's public silence in regard to his brother's assassination, and surreptitious destruction of vital evidence in the crime, suggests that he more than likely suspected all along that there had been a conspiracy to assassinate President Kennedy, possibly even had a good idea who the conspirators were, but did not want to risk having the details of the conspiracy made known because of the possible damage that knowledge might inflict on his and his slain brother's reputations.

It should be added, at this point, that not only did Robert Kennedy suppress important evidence in rendering the physical specimen autopsy materials inaccessible, but, according to the testimony of autopsy surgeon Dr. Pierre Finck, he and his sister-in-law Jacqueline had also been partly responsible for the seriously flawed presidential autopsy itself. For Robert and Jacqueline remained in close telephonic communication with certain high-ranking military officers present during the autopsy—presidential aides Admiral George Burkley and General Godfrey McHugh, in particular—from their tower suite on the 17th floor of the Naval Hospital, quietly manipulating, through them, the autopsy surgeons.

Dr. Finck testified at the 1969 New Orleans trial of Clay Shaw for conspiring to assassinate President Kennedy, that he, Finck, had been ordered by one of the high-ranking military officers attending the autopsy not to dissect the track of the bullet wound in the President's back, an order which Finck believed had originated with "the Kennedy family," meaning, of course, Jacqueline Kennedy and Robert Kennedy, who had been following the progress of the autopsy.

Why did Robert and Jacqueline not want the path of the back wound dissected? For years the Kennedy family had been hiding the fact that Jack Kennedy suffered from Addison's disease, which causes atrophy of the adrenal glands, and it is thought that the two young Kennedys prevented the autopsy surgeons from dissecting the wound in order not to expose the President's diseased adrenals. However, in preventing the dissection of the back wound the Kennedys prevented the Bethesda doctors from determining whether the bullet that entered the back did, in fact, exit from the President's throat, where the Parkland Hospital doctors in Dallas had unanimously observed a wound of entry.

Thus it was that, in their wholly understandable desire to protect the family image and the posthumous reputation of their slain brother and husband, the thirty-eight-year-old Robert Kennedy and his thirty-four-year-old sister-in-law, became unwitting accessories after the fact in the President's murder. For it was these two young people's apparent meddling in the official autopsy, beginning with their manipulation of the autopsy surgeons and ending with their disposal of the autopsy specimens, that caused the most crucial evidence in the case to be first distorted and suppressed, then irrevocably destroyed.

Silence about the Marcellos and the Kennedy assassination has not been limited to Robert Kennedy; it has also characterized the attitudes of some of his closest associates and even the attitude of the distinguished Kennedy court historian, Arthur M. Schlesinger, Jr. In his massive, "definitive" biography, *Robert Kennedy and His Times*, winner of the National Book Award in 1978, there is no mention whatsoever of Robert Kennedy's targeting of Marcello as a top priority for increased Justice Department pressure, no mention of Marcello's deportation and his defiant return, and no mention of the legal proceedings the Justice Department was bringing against him during the month of the President's assassination. Yet Robert Kennedy's pursuit of Carlos Marcello was one of the most important, and possibly fateful, undertakings of his brief career as attorney general. Incredible as it seems, considering Schlesinger's reputation as a Pulitzer Prize–winning historian, a search through the index of Schlesinger's book on Kennedy reveals that the name Marcello is not mentioned anywhere in its 1163 pages.

Robert Kennedy's demoralization in the weeks following his brother's murder was accentuated by J. Edgar Hoover's brutal and callous treatment of him starting the afternoon of the assassination. As one

Kennedy staffer expressed it, "Starting at 1:10 on November 22 they began pissing on the attorney general." Hoover removed the direct telephone to Kennedy's office from his desk, unplugged the extension, and had his secretary store the phone in a closet. When Jack Miller, the assistant attorney general for criminal affairs, flew to Dallas the afternoon of the assassination to take charge of the investigation, he was rudely ignored by Hoover's agents. When Kennedy returned to his office in the Justice Department in late January, Hoover stopped reporting to him in favor of reporting directly to the White House. Courtney Evans was removed from his liaison job and was replaced by Cartha "Deke" DeLoach, who was a good friend of Lyndon Johnson's aide Walter Jenkins. The FBI ceased sending an official car to pick up Kennedy during his travels around the country. And, as we know, Hoover pointedly excluded Robert Kennedy from the FBI's investigations of his brother's assassination. Years later Hoover boasted that he did not speak to Robert Kennedy once during his last six months as attorney general.

With his leverage with the FBI irretrievably lost, and his relationship with the new President strained and unproductive, Robert Kennedy had been effectively neutralized. Before long, his war on the Mafia would begin winding down, and he would lose interest in pursuing the Mafia bosses he had once vowed to destroy.

As might have been expected, Hoover's FBI soon began reassessing its priorities in the wake of the assassination, with consequent damage to the Kennedy campaign against organized crime. Ever alert to the government's shifting policies toward them, the mob quickly predicted what the FBI's new attitude toward them would probably be. Ten days after the assassination, an FBI listening device picked up Charles "Chuckie" English (né Inglese), one of Sam Giancana's underbosses, expressing the mob's relief to his boss:

"I will tell you something, in another two months from now, the FBI will be like it was five years ago. They won't be around no more. They say the FBI will get it [the investigation of Kennedy's murder]. They're gonna start running down Fair Play For Cuba, Fair Play for Matsu. They call that more detrimental to the country than us guys."

41

The Triumph of Carlos Marcello

By December 15, 1964, roughly three weeks after the assassination of the President, no fewer than twelve persons associated with Carlos Marcello, or with some of his closest operatives, had been either arrested or questioned in connection with the assassination.

These included Lee Harvey Oswald, the President's suspected assassin; Jack Ruby, killer of the suspected assassin; David Ferrie, a friend of Oswald's and investigator for one of Marcello's attorneys; Ben Tregle, an associate of brother Vincent Marcello's; Frank Caracci, Harold Tannenbaum, and Nick Graffagnini, acquaintances of Jack Ruby's and associates of Carlos Marcello's in the New Orleans nightclub business; Joe Campisi, a friend of Jack Ruby's and associate of the Marcellos' in Dallas; Joe Civello, a friend and business associate of Jack Ruby's and Carlos Marcello's deputy in Dallas; Joe Poretto and Nofio Pecora, two of Carlos Marcello's major associates in New Orleans; and brother Anthony Marcello.

Reports of these arrests and interrogations must have been unsettling for Carlos, but by mid-December, was Marcello worrying whether the next member of his organization to be questioned might be himself?

It is hard to say, but it seems unlikely that he was unduly concerned. For a week before, on December 9, the nation's radio, press, and television had trumpeted the results of the FBI's "exhaustive investigation" of the assassination to the nation, proclaiming that Lee Harvey Oswald was the sole, unaided assassin of the President and that Jack Ruby was the sole, unaided killer of the suspected assassin.

There remained the recently commenced investigation of the assassination by the newly appointed presidential commission headed by Chief Justice Earl Warren. What would happen to all those FBI reports on the interrogations of his brother Anthony, David Ferrie, Joe Poretto, Ben Tregle, Nofio Pecora, and Joe Civello once they were transmitted to the Warren Commission? It is reasonable to assume that Carlos might have been somewhat apprehensive over the possible destiny and use of those reports.

As we now know, Carlos had little to worry about, thanks to his unwitting protector, J. Edgar Hoover (who may not have been all that unwitting, if we consider his close relationship with Marcello's friend Frank Costello).

By late January, then, a month and a half after the last of his associates to be questioned, Joe Civello, had been interrogated by the FBI, Carlos Marcello must have felt the way he often did around noon at Churchill Farms, when the morning mists over his swamplands would have burned away and he would finally catch a glimpse of bright blue sky. It now seemed as if he and his men were in the clear. It would now take fourteen years before he himself would finally become a suspect in the Kennedy assassination.

Carlos Marcello may have been in the clear so far as becoming a suspect in the Kennedy assassination was concerned, but he was not yet entirely in the clear so far as the Justice Department was concerned.

For not long after his November 22 acquittal in the government's perjury and conspiracy case against him and his brother Joseph, the Justice Department began assembling a new case against him, one that would eventually result in his indictment for "conspiring to obstruct justice by fixing a juror and seeking the murder of a government witness." Fixed juror Rudolph Heitler had gone to the office of the U.S. attorney in New Orleans in early August 1964 and confessed that as a juror in the November 1963 conspiracy and perjury trial of the Marcello brothers, he had voted "not guilty" in return for what he had hoped would have been a substantial payment, as much as $25,000. Joe Matassa, the intermediary allegedly representing the Marcellos, had reneged and given him only two payments of $500 each. In return for a grant of immunity, Heitler told the U.S. attorney he would testify against Marcello at an eventual trial for jury tampering.

Rudolph Heitler believed he had a legitimate gripe against Marcello and his payoff man, Pelican Tomato Company President Joseph "Baby" Matassa. He had had to try repeatedly to get his money from Matassa, and Matassa had always put him off, telling him he was having trouble contacting Marcello, who, it is believed, was lying low at his Churchill Farms retreat during the postassassination period. Finally, after continuous prodding, Baby Matassa gave Heitler two cash payments of $500 each and told Heitler to be satisfied with it, that now he would have a "friend for life" in Carlos Marcello. In addition, Matassa informed Heitler that he was not the only juror who had been reached, that there had been others.

But, although he did not say anything at the time, Heitler was not satisfied and several months later renewed his attempt to get the amount he had originally requested. Finally, in June 1964, his old friend George Alamilla, pleading on behalf of Heitler, wrote Baby Matassa from Belize and tried to get a commitment out of him for a payoff to Heitler of $25,000. The attempt came to naught. On August 6, not long after Heitler saw his chances of receiving the much-coveted $25,000 payoff go down the drain, he marched off and reported the entire jury tampering episode to the office of the U.S. attorney in New Orleans.

Soon thereafter, the chief prosecution witness, Carl Noll, paid a call on the U.S. Department of Justice's offices in New Orleans and told the U.S. attorney that one of Carlos Marcello's henchmen from the Gulf Coast, Herbert Huber of Meridian, Mississippi, had approached him during the November 1963 trial and had threatened to kill him if he would not desist in his trial testimony against the Marcello brothers.

Word of these allegations reached Justice Department headquarters in Washington around the time Robert F. Kennedy resigned as attorney general and announced he would run for a seat in the United States Senate from New York. It is not known whether Kennedy learned the news. (William Hundley told me the information was probably transmitted only to Nicholas Katzenbach.) By then Kennedy had given up pursuing the Mafia and was concentrating all his attention on his forthcoming political campaign.

It was then left to Attorney General Katzenbach to announce on October 6, 1964, the indictments of Carlos Marcello and Joe Matassa on charges of conspiring to obstruct justice by "fixing a juror and seeking the murder of a government witness." Marcello now faced a maximum penalty of thirty-four years in prison and a $60,000 fine if convicted.

According to the transcript of the court record of the case, "the conspiracy meeting to fix juror Rudolph Heitler took place at the Pelican Tomato Company during a weekday four days before the assassination of the President."

The details of this conspiracy are set forth in a court record and might cast some light on another suspected conspiracy possibly involving Carlos Marcello that was unfolding at precisely the same time: the plot to assassinate President Kennedy in Dallas on November 22.

What was Carlos Marcello's modus operandi in the jury tampering conspiracy? It was to keep himself at a considerable distance from the actual commission of the crime. The man selected to actually commit the crime, i.e., offer the bribe to the juror—George Alamilla—was not even from New Orleans. He had been summoned from Belize (British Honduras) in the midst of Marcello's trial. At no time during the eight-day period was Carlos Marcello ever in direct personal contact with either Alamilla, Heitler, or Matassa. Who functioned as intermediary between Carlos and the others was never determined.

If indeed Carlos Marcello was involved in a contemporaneous conspiracy to assassinate President Kennedy, we may assume that Marcello would have employed the same modus operandi. The individuals who actually performed the assassination would have come from out of state or from outside the country and would have had no direct contact with Marcello whatsoever. They would have accomplished their mission and quickly left the country.

But where does that leave us with Lee Harvey Oswald, David Ferrie, and Jack Ruby? What roles could they have played in a Marcello-inspired assassination plot?

It would appear that if indeed there was such a plot, Ferrie's principal role would have been that of adviser to Marcello and framer of Lee Harvey Oswald. Thus it would have been Ferrie's responsibility to manipulate Oswald and his impersonator so as to make it appear immediately obvious after the assassination that Oswald had killed the President. Since Ferrie had been put in charge of Oswald, it would have been his responsibility as a member of the conspiracy to see to it that Oswald was quickly eliminated after he had been identified as the President's suspected assassin. Ferrie's last assignment, then, would have been to deliver the necessary instructions to Jack Ruby through Marcello's network in Dallas, hence the possible significance of David Ferrie's presence in Texas the day after the assassination, his collect call from Houston to the Town & Country Motel that afternoon, and his protracted use of the public telephone at the Winterland Skating Rink later on in the day.

What happened to David Ferrie after the smoke blew over following his return from Texas on November 24 and his subsequent questioning by the FBI and the Secret Service in connection with the Kennedy assassination?

The evidence shows that David Ferrie continued working for Marcello interests until at least the end of 1966. After the Kennedy assassination he left the employ of Marcello's attorney G. Wray Gill and joined the Marcello-owned United Air Taxi Corporation. Later he went to work for a well-known Marcello associate, Jacob Nastasi, in a Marcello-financed New Orleans air cargo service.

But certain recently released FBI documents suggest that Ferrie did not regard these employments as sufficient compensation for the services he had recently rendered Carlos Marcello, and, like Rudolph Heitler, he began to complain of this to people close to the boss. For, a little later, the New Orleans FBI learned from its informants that Ferrie had suddenly turned up as the owner of a lucrative service station franchise in an ideal location in suburban New Orleans. Upon investigating this, the FBI found that the franchise had been financed by Carlos Marcello.

A possible explanation of this came from a 1967 New Orleans FBI report of certain information on Carlos Marcello and David Ferrie provided by Ferrie's former roommate, Layton Martens, who had once functioned as liaison between Carlos Marcello and the Cuban Revolutionary Council delegation in New Orleans, headed by Sergio Arcacha Smith. According to the FBI report:

> MARTENS stated that DAVID FERRIE once worked for RAY [sic] GILL who is CARLOS MARCELLO'S attorney. FERRIE was an acquaintance of BANNISTER [sic] and BANNISTER did some investigatory work for MARCELLO. MARCELLO reportedly did not like Ferrie. When FERRIE left GILL'S employ he went into the gas station business which was reportedly financed by MARCELLO. MARTENS commented that he believes MARCELLO was coerced into financing this business because Ferrie had obtained incriminating information against MARCELLO.

What "incriminating information against Marcello" could David Ferrie have obtained? Was it information on Carlos Marcello's role in the Kennedy assassination? Had Marcello paid off Ferrie with the lucrative gas station franchise to keep Ferrie's mouth shut? The question was left unanswered, for by the time it was raised as a result of Martens' testimony, David Ferrie was dead. But that is another story.

The Justice Department's October 6, 1964, indictment of Carlos Marcello charged that Marcello and his lieutenants had made two secret payments to a juror "with the intent to influence his action, vote, opinion, and decision" in the case, and that in November 1963, Marcello had endeavored "to influence, obstruct, and impede" the prosecution "by requesting the murder of a principal witness for the government, Carl I. Noll."

In an uncharacteristic move, Carlos disappeared upon the announcement of the indictment, causing no fewer than ten FBI agents to fan out through the New Orleans area in search of him. After checking all his haunts—the cottage on Churchill Farms, the Town & Country Motel, the Jefferson Music Company, his brothers' restaurants—the FBI was about to give him up as a fugitive from justice. Then on October 8, Carlos suddenly emerged from hiding and surrendered at the federal courthouse, where he soon obtained his freedom by paying the required $100,000 bail.

So, once again, it was *The United States v. Carlos Marcello* in federal district court in New Orleans.

The case did not go to trial until the following year and was not decided until August 17, 1965. It was the last holdover from Robert Kennedy's campaign to destroy Carlos Marcello's power. Now Kennedy, as United States senator from New York, had turned away from his pursuit of the Mafia in favor of embracing such causes as civil rights for minorities, urban renewal, and disengagement from the Vietnamese war.

Carlos was represented at the trial by his brilliant Washington-based deportation attorney, Jack Wasserman. As the trial record shows, Wasserman succeeded in demonstrating that, although a conspiracy to bribe juror Heitler did take place, there was absolutely no proof Carlos Marcello was behind it.

Wasserman acknowledged that Rudolph Heitler, George Alamilla, and Joseph Matassa had conspired to obstruct justice at the Marcellos' trial by arranging for Heitler's not-guilty vote in return for a payment to Heitler, but he challenged the prosecution to find one instance of conspirational contact between Heitler, Alamilla, Matassa, and Marcello. As it turned out, the prosecution was unable to prove the connection. Carlos's policy of absolute insulation from his crimes had paid off again. The jury found him not guilty of "conspiring to obstruct justice by fixing a juror."

It appears that the Marcello forces took care of the charge of seek-

ing the murder of a government witness by bringing overwhelming
pressure on Carl Noll to deny his life had been threatened by one of
Marcello's henchmen and by getting the alleged henchman, Herbert
Huber, to issue a sworn statement that the government had tried to
force him to testify against Marcello at the trial. The affidavit Herbert
Huber presented at the trial read, in part:

> On Saturday, October 17, 1964, U.S. Attorney John Diuguid
> and another attorney of the Department of Justice visited me
> at my home in Meridian, Mississippi.
>   John Diuguid requested me outside of the presence of the
> other attorney to testify against Carlos Marcello and to falsely
> state that Marcello had asked me to get rid of Carl Noll.
>   At no time did Carlos Marcello ever ask me to harm or
> murder Carl Noll or anyone.

The affidavit was sworn before Marcello's attorney, Jack Wasserman, and son, Joseph C. Marcello, on October 19, 1964, and evidently
had its desired effect. The jury also returned a verdict of not guilty
on the government's charge that Carlos had endeavored to obstruct
and impede the prosecution "by requesting the murder of the principal witness for the government, Carl I. Noll."

Carlos had won over the United States government again. It was
his third consecutive major victory over the Justice Department. Now
there would be little chance of his ever being deported, and so, free
at last of the Kennedys and free of harassment from the Justice Department, he would finally be able to resume devoting his full, un-
divided energies to advancing the fortunes of his growing family and
his ever-expanding business empire. It would not be long before the
victorious Marcellos would gain effective control of the state of Louisiana and Carlos Marcello would become the wealthiest Mafia leader
in the United States.

PART VI

A Precarious Power

1965–1977

42

The Invisible Government of Carlos Marcello

"It takes time to get where I'm at. To know all these people—governors, business, the attorney general, they know me."

"[Governor] Jimmy Davis I could do business with. [Governor] Earl Long and, uh, Jimmy Davis, Earl Long."

"I had [Governor] McKeithen for eight years. That sonofabitch got $168,000 my money...."

"[Governor] Edmund [sic] [Edwin Edwards] and me all right, but I can't seen [sic] him every day...."

Carlos Marcello's boasts about his political connections, made to a young New Orleans attorney, were picked up by a small microphone that had been installed in the ceiling of his Town & Country office by the FBI in 1979.

It took that microphone, along with wiretaps on all Marcello's phones, and various recording devices on the bodies of three undercover agents, to finally inform the Justice Department of the extent of the invisible government overseen by the boss of the Louisiana Mafia.

The Justice Department had long suspected that Marcello's political influence extended to the highest levels of state and national government, but it had never been able to confirm its suspicion until it authorized the FBI, in early 1979, to mount a massive program of electronic surveillance against him.

Ironically the FBI bugs and wiretaps soon picked up suggestions of Marcello influence within the Justice Department itself, including a hint that Carlos had a connection capable of reaching all the way to the then attorney general of the United States.

The first such suggestion came as a result of the FBI's interception of a telephone conversation between Marcello and his longtime friend and occasional business associate Irving Davidson, a Washington-based lobbyist who specialized in "putting people together." Davidson was telling Marcello how he was going to get a high-ranking official of the Immigration and Naturalization Service to take care of a certain matter regarding Carlos's unending deportation case:

DAVIDSON: He [the INS official] told me the agency will go along, but there's one more place that they have to go to, uh, outside the agency. Now even if you're on [inaudible] I want you to know it's the criminal division of the Justice Department.

MARCELLO: Yeah.

DAVIDSON: And I know the name of the gentleman and I've already called, and any time I get, we're going to get an appointment.

On another occasion, the FBI bug in Carlos's Town & Country office picked up a conversation between Marcello and government undercover operative Joseph Hauser, a convicted felon, during which Carlos told Hauser he knew someone who might be able to persuade the then attorney general, Benjamin R. Civiletti, who had just taken over the job upon the resignation of Griffin Bell, to have Hauser's impending imprisonment postponed:

MARCELLO: Maybe he can make a phone call to the attorney general. Now I'm not saying I can do it. I gotta man can do it. Give me all that there and we'll make a phone call.

HAUSER (later): So how much will it cost to fix the case with Civiletti?...

(Marcello puts his fingers to his lips.)

HAUSER: Okay, I'm not gonna talk anymore. Okay, we'll talk outside.

It is not known whether Marcello actually did have a contact who could reach the attorney general of the United States. What *is* known is that he had solid connections to many other men in high places.

The leadership of the Teamsters was one. "We own de Teamsters," he once told two FBI undercover agents in a 1979 tape-recorded conversation. The "we" referred to himself, Chicago boss "Joey Doves" Aiuppa, Kansas City boss Joe Civella, and Florida boss Santos Trafficante. As we shall learn later from conversations recorded by the FBI, Carlos and his three fellow co-owners of the Teamsters were planning to own more than just the union management; they were also planning to own a big piece of the Teamsters' huge multi-billion-dollar health and welfare and pension funds.

Where else did Carlos Marcello's arm of influence reach? It had long been an open secret that it reached all the way into the United States Senate. The vehicle of that reach was one of the most powerful political families in the south, the Longs of Louisiana.

If it had not been for the Longs, the phenomenon of Carlos Marcello might never have happened. For it had been Louisiana Governor Huey Long, the legendary "Kingfish," who had been responsible for bringing Carlos's future sponsor, New York's slot machine king, Frank Costello, to Louisiana; and it had been Costello who later gave young Carlos the first big chance of his life when he entrusted him with the running of his slot machine operation on the West Bank.

Since then, as *Life* magazine pointed out in a 1970 investigative report, the Marcellos and the Longs had had a close, mutually beneficial partnership. Carlos assisted Huey Long's brother Earl in his political adventures and was a heavy contributor to the senatorial campaigns of Huey's son Russell, who became Carlos's principal contact in the U.S. Senate. Just before Robert Kennedy took office as attorney general, Carlos went to Washington to enlist Senator Long's aid in thwarting what Marcello believed would be a determined effort by Bobby Kennedy to deport him. And after the deportation and Carlos's defiant reentry, the FBI received, on June 16, 1961, a report from a reliable informant that Senator Russell Long was trying to intervene with the Justice Department on Marcello's behalf and was, in fact, "sponsoring a Louisiana official for a key INS position from which assistance to Marcello might be rendered."

But Russell Long was not the only Marcello-supported Louisiana politician in Congress. There was also Representative Hale Boggs, whose political campaigns, according to Aaron Kohn, were heavily financed by Carlos Marcello, and whom President Johnson had given an honored place on the Warren Commission.

Carlos had not failed either to add important representatives of the Louisiana halls of justice to his formidable stable of political connections.

He was, as we know, on exceptionally good terms with the New Orleans district attorney during the sixties, Jim Garrison, who, though known as a tough prosecutor, had a way of hearing no evil and seeing no evil when it came to the activities of the Marcello organization in New Orleans Parish.

Responding to public pressure, the six-foot-seven Garrison, a colorful, somewhat outlandish, but well-liked character in New Orleans, held a number of grand jury investigations of possible organized crime activity during the sixties, all of which agreed with his foregone conclusion that there was no such thing as organized crime in New Orleans Parish. However, as *Life* magazine revealed in 1970, while one of his grand juries was reaching this conclusion, a simultaneous grand jury in Houston was indicting three of Marcello's leading layoff bookmakers—Sam DiPiazza, Eugene Nolan, and Frank Timphony—for operating illegally in New Orleans and Houston. Yet even when DiPiazza and Nolan were convicted of handling millions of dollars of layoff bets right under Garrison's nose, the tall, lanky New Orleans district attorney looked the other way.

According to *Life*, during the mid to late sixties Garrison dismissed eighty-four cases brought against Marcello's men, including twenty-two cases of illegal gambling, one for attempted murder, three for kidnapping, and one for manslaughter.

Meanwhile, as reported by the House Select Committee on Assassinations in 1979, Garrison saw nothing wrong with accepting a free holiday and a $5000 gambling credit at the Sands Hotel and Casino in Las Vegas from Marcello's delegate at the Sands, Mario Marino, and allowed one of Carlos's top associates to sell him a house in the suburbs at a ridiculously low price. And Garrison proved exceptionally adept at hushing up the heart attack death of one of Marcello's leading bagmen, Vic Corona, who dropped dead one night in Garrison's Marcello-financed home during what Garrison lamely described as a "political rally."

Those who were fully aware of Garrison's cozy relationship with the Marcellos—he was also on very good terms with three of Carlos's brothers, Sammy, Vince, and Joe—were not surprised when, upon his reopening of the investigation of the Kennedy assassination in

1967, he pointedly steered his inquiry away from allegations of Mafia involvement in the assassination in what turned out, in the end, to be a long, drawn-out, fraudulent attempt to pin the blame for the President's murder on the Central Intelligence Agency.

But Jim Garrison was not the only high-ranking law enforcement officer Carlos Marcello knew. As he admitted to two wired undercover agents in 1979, he was also on very good terms with several federal judges in New Orleans:

> "If you got a federal judge, money ain't gonna do no good....I got, uh, I know half, half of 'em right here, right here, they're personal friends of mine."

An alleged connection via a third party to the chief law enforcement officer of the United States. A connection to the second highest official in the Immigration and Naturalization Service. Solid connections to the leadership of the largest and most powerful labor union in the country. Personal friendships with a distinguished U.S. senator from Louisiana and a distinguished member of the U.S. House of Representatives from Louisiana. Direct relationships with the governor of Louisiana and the district attorney of New Orleans. Friendship with several federal judges in New Orleans. To whom else in high authority did Carlos Marcello's long chain of connections reach?

To the bosses of several of the leading Mafia families in the United States, among others. Although Marcello had always denied to federal authorities that he was associated with the Mafia, in the fall of 1966 he was surprised by the police in a Queens, New York, restaurant as he was about to sit down for lunch. In the room were Carlo Gambino, boss of New York's most powerful Mafia family, Florida boss Santos Trafficante, and several high-ranking members of the Colombo, Gambino, and Genovese families. And in 1979 FBI listening devices recorded him acknowledging he was close to Chicago boss "Joey Doves" Aiuppa and Kansas City boss Joe Civella. Furthermore, he admitted to two undercover agents that he was in the Mafia, and he expressed great concern over the upcoming trial of two of his Mafia friends on the West Coast, Dominick Brooklier, boss of the Los Angeles mob, and Brooklier's underboss, Sam Sciortino. So much concern did he, in fact, have for his fellow Mafiosi in California that, according to a 1979 conversation recorded by the FBI, he was eager and willing to put up "$250,000 cash money within twenty-four hours" to fix the judge scheduled to preside over his Mafia friends' trial.

To these high-ranking connections in government, the judiciary, organized labor, and organized crime must be included Carlos's old friend, the king of Washington lobbyists, I. Irving Davidson. It was also in 1979 that the FBI learned, for the first time, that Davidson and Marcello had been in close, continuous contact with each other since the late fifties. It had been principally Davidson who had provided Marcello with most of his entrées into the agencies of the federal government, including the CIA, for which Davidson acted as a lobbyist on Capitol Hill, and into the worlds of Washington politics, international big business, and high finance. Both men had a mutual interest in the dictatorships of the Caribbean and Central America, and it is believed that Davidson, lobbyist of record for the Trujillos of the Dominican Republic, the Duvaliers of Haiti, and the Somozas of Nicaragua, more than likely provided Marcello with his entrée to those three tyrannical regimes. Lastly, it was through Davidson that Marcello had been able to extend the reach of his influence to the oil-rich Murchisons of Dallas, with whom Carlos eventually did considerable business, to certain embarrassing members of President Lyndon Johnson's camp, men such as Bobby Baker and Billie Sol Estes, and to several members of President Richard Nixon's entourage, including one political adviser, Murray Chotiner, to whom Nixon had assigned an office in the White House, and at least two of the Watergate burglars. (In 1963 Davidson was revealed to have been the go-between on a cash payoff from the Murchison oil family to Bobby Baker.)

So close had Davidson been to Marcello at the time of Carlos's deportation in 1961 that he turned out to be the only person in Washington who had Carlos's telephone number in Guatemala after Bobby Kennedy dumped him there, a fact that has given rise to the speculation that it had perhaps been Davidson who, through his good friend President Rafael Trujillo, had arranged for Marcello's illegal reentry into the United States on a Dominican Air Force jet.

Davidson's endless collection of people in high places, people who could possibly fill a key position in Carlos Marcello's invisible government, included, also, none other than FBI Director J. Edgar Hoover, who, in turn, was also a good friend of Davidson's and Marcello's friend Clint Murchison. The FBI director was a good friend of the lobbyist. The two were occasionally seen dining together in Washington restaurants, and, in later years, Davidson personally led fund-raising campaigns for the J. Edgar Hoover Foundation.

Is it possible that Carlos Marcello, through his good friend Irving Davidson, had a connection to J. Edgar Hoover, with all that might imply? The idea is not preposterous in the light of our all but certain knowledge that the FBI director used to meet privately with Marcello's first significant sponsor, Frank Costello, in New York's Central Park, among other places. If a Marcello-Hoover relationship did exist through Davidson's auspices, it would go a long way toward explaining the New Orleans FBI's strange dereliction of duty in failing to adequately oversee Marcello's activities during the months preceding the assassination of President Kennedy and Hoover's even stranger dereliction after the assassination, when he deliberately attempted to suppress all allegations suggesting the Marcellos' involvement.

But what about the lesser functionaries in Carlos Marcello's invisible government? His workaday connections? The 1979 FBI sting turned up legions of them: "Yeah, I've got em all where I want em," Marcello told an undercover agent, when asked if he had any influence with the City Council of New Orleans. "Yeah, I got de longshoremen an de building trades too," he told the government agents on another occasion.

Once Carlos implied to the same agents that he also had the Louisiana State Police where he wanted them. The three were driving at high speed from Lafayette to New Orleans in Marcello's car, with Carlos at the wheel, when one of the agents offered to drive. "You don't want to drive, man," Carlos told him. "If cops come you would go to jail, where I can get by."

Referring to a bribe Carlos was about to pay to the commissioner of administration of the state of Louisiana, Carlos told a young lawyer friend: "Man, he really jumped when I told him we could get him $129,000 cash within ninety days if he done all right."

"I used to give Police Chief Beauregard Miller $50,000 cash money every time," Carlos told his young lawyer friend one day in his Town & Country office. He went on to tell him that he made regular payoffs of from $5000 to $10,000 each to key local politicians and police officers in Jefferson Parish, St. Charles Parish, Raceland, Thibodaux, Morgan City, Franklin, Abbeville, and Lake Charles, to name a few Louisiana communities Carlos boasted he "controlled."

As we know, the FBI's 1979 sting was by no means the only investigation of the Marcello organization that had been conducted since Carlos took control of the Gulf states underworld in 1947; it was simply the most extensive and revealing. The Kefauver Committee of 1951 had done most of the pioneer spade work, uncovering, principally, the extent of Marcello's illegal gambling operations in southern Louisiana. The Metropolitan Crime Commission of New Orleans, under Aaron Kohn, had followed through with a wide-ranging investigation in the mid-fifties, and then the McClellan Senate Committee of 1959, under the zealous leadership of Chief Counsel Robert Kennedy, had built on Kohn's knowledge to further expand the Justice Department's vision of the ever-burgeoning criminal empire of the Marcellos.

And then there was *Life* magazine's courageous and thorough investigation of Marcello's grip on the political machinery and law enforcement apparatus of the state of Louisiana, published on April 10, 1970. The *Life* investigative team, under special correspondent David Chandler, found that in the late sixties Carlos could virtually do what he pleased in Louisiana, thanks to an elaborate system of alliances he had entered into with key public officials in his parish and in Baton Rouge.

Life found that Carlos had direct access to the State House in Baton Rouge through his good friend C. M. "Sammy" Downs, the second most powerful official in Governor John McKeithen's administration. It found also that Carlos controlled the head of the Louisiana State Police, Roland Coppola, and that Carlos was so close to the district attorney of Jefferson Parish, Frank Landridge, that he and Landridge shared the services of the same mob enforcer, the infamous, hulking Joseph "Zip" Chimento, who took care of strong-arm jobs for the D.A. while simultaneously working as the most feared collector for the Marcello jukebox, pinball, and slot machine business.

In addition, the *Life* investigative team discovered that Marcello controlled the Louisiana State Department of Revenue, the agency charged with collecting all state taxes. They found that Marcello's hold on this department was so complete that he was able to control the hiring and placement of tax collecting agents and was able also "to manipulate the state auditing procedures at will." This resulted in his family's virtual exemption from paying state taxes and the loss by the state of hundreds of millions of dollars in potential revenues.

But of all Carlos Marcello's dealings with the state of Louisiana, *Life* found that the most outrageous and unabashed exercise of his power over state officials was exemplified by how he was able to bully the state government into spending the taxpayers' money on improving his 6400-acre swampland property, Churchill Farms.

Marcello had purchased the huge tract on the West Bank, roughly opposite New Orleans, in 1959 for approximately $1 million. The vast, undeveloped marshland property with its small, rustic outbuildings scattered here and there among twisting bayous, spongy islands, and

ponds sprouting moss-draped cypress trunks would serve Carlos and
his men as both a refuge and a hideaway. Through its complex system of waterways, it would also provide a safe haven for small boats
laden with illicit cargoes coming up from the Gulf of Mexico. But its
ultimate purpose was as an investment.

Carlos's real estate advisers had concluded that the Churchill
Farms property, if fully diked and drained, could easily be worth $60
million as prime suburban real estate some day, especially if a state
highway could be routed through its reclaimed marshes.

Although seemingly remote, the property was easily accessible
from New Orleans and the East Bank by means of two Mississippi
bridges. But diking and draining such a large area of swampland
would cost an enormous amount of money. Not wishing to invest millions of his own personal funds, Marcello succeeded in terrorizing
the government of Jefferson Parish and the relevant Louisiana state
agencies into diking and draining the property for him at public expense.

Accordingly, Carlos got his old friend outgoing Governor Jimmie
Davis to sign a contract authorizing a regional flood control agency
to share with Jefferson Parish the cost of constructing a huge levee
to guard the eastern border of Churchill Farms from the floodwa-
ters of the Mississippi and authorizing, as well, a payment of $500,000
to Carlos Marcello as compensation for the "inconvenience" involved
in the state using his land for the building of a public improvement.

It took four years and over $1 million for the state and Jefferson
Parish to build the levee. When the job was completed in 1968, it was
time to commence the drainage. Incredibly, Carlos was able to bully
the state into installing two huge pumps in his swamp that eventually
cost the taxpayers of Louisiana around $3.5 million. Carlos then be-
gan drawing up plans for a superhighway from Baton Rouge to
Jefferson Parish to be laid down by the state, part of whose route
would run through Churchill Farms. As *Life* pointed out in its 1970
investigative report, all the effort and expense involved in diking and
draining the Churchill Farms property out of public funds was ultimately to no one's advantage but Carlos Marcello's. As predicted by
his real estate advisers in 1959, Carlos's $1 million investment in the
Churchill Farms tract had, by the early seventies, soared in value to
roughly $22 million, even though his plans for a state superhighway
to be routed through the property had not yet been approved.

As might be expected, the growth of Marcello's wealth and political
influence in Louisiana was not accomplished without violence. As *Life*

pointed out in 1970, people who attempted to cross Carlos, or his men, inevitably got killed. In 1967 one of Carlos's more prominent syndicate gamblers, Harry Bennett, was shot dead by unknown killers not long after some of Marcello's aides discovered he had met with a federal prosecutor and offered to cooperate with him in the government's investigation of the Marcello organization.

Then, roughly two years later, one of Bennett's former partners in a Marcello-controlled Gulf Coast gambling casino, Donald "Jimmie" James, was caught trying to swindle one of Carlos's close associates out of $10,000. Marcello summoned the offender to his Town & Country office and ordered him to pay up immediately, or else. James paid up the next day, and Carlos made sure word was sent throughout his organization that he *had* paid up the next day. Later, as if to drive home the lesson that simply paying back money swindled out of a family member was not sufficient redress for the initial disrespect committed, the Marcello organization took final action on the case. One afternoon, Jefferson Parish Police discovered the bullet-riddled body of Jimmie James lying on the same spot where his former partner, Harry Bennett, had been found dead two years before. Marcello never challenged these assertions and made no public denial of *Life*'s accusations.

Yes, Carlos Marcello always let it be known that people who threatened to get in his way did so at considerable personal risk. Carl Noll had allegedly been advised of this reality before he was to testify against Carlos at Marcello's 1964–1965 jury tampering trial and, as a result, suddenly lost his memory the first time he appeared on the witness stand.

As we know, it was on August 17, 1965, that Marcello was finally acquitted of the charges that had been brought against him by a federal grand jury in October 1964: "Conspiracy to obstruct justice by fixing a juror and seeking the murder of a government witness."

With this acquittal, which outraged many close observers of the case, Marcello was finally free of the series of federal charges stemming from his 1961 deportation to Guatemala and unlawful reentry into the United States, or, in other words, free of all charges stemming from his defiance of Robert Kennedy's attempt to destroy him.

Liberated, at last, from three and a half years of living under federal indictments, liberated, temporarily at least, from the threat of deportation, and liberated, finally, from the specter of Bobby Kennedy, Carlos was now free to concentrate on managing his underworld empire and assisting friends and associates who had fallen into trouble.

As the tapes of Marcello's conversations of 1979 revealed, Carlos now functioned as a sort of chief magistrate and chief executive of an invisible state. On a given day the phone would ring, and it would be a multimillionaire oil swindler from Oklahoma, currently under investigation by the FBI, who wanted Carlos to arrange for the false arrests of two prospective witnesses against him. Carlos would tell him he would see what he could do. Or the phone would ring, and it would be a New Orleans cousin of a Los Angeles mob underboss who was wondering if Carlos could do anything about fixing a federal judge. Carlos would tell him he would see what he could do. Or the phone would ring, and this time the call would be from the head of a gang of drug smugglers who had just been arrested with 800 pounds of marijuana and 200,000 Quaalude tablets on them; they needed Uncle Carlos to bail them out of jail. Carlos would tell them he would work something out.

Arrange a false arrest, fix a federal magistrate, spring a bunch of drug smugglers from jail. Judging from the confidence people had in him, Carlos's constituents seemed to feel he could get away with almost anything, which was what Carlos had always believed himself.

The truth was, of course, that Carlos Marcello had succeeded in getting away with everything all his life, from getting away with making a huge fortune in illegal gambling to getting away with defying Attorney General Kennedy—to whom his lawyers dealt the final blow by winning the jury tampering case for Carlos on August 17, 1965.

By the dawn of 1966 Carlos Marcello was well on his way to becoming the wealthiest and most influential Mafia leader in the United States, a status he would eventually attain in the early to mid-seventies. His victory over the Justice Department and the Kennedy brothers had won him enormous respect throughout the underworld. His criminal organization was now generating an estimated annual income of nearly $2 billion, making it by far the largest industry in Louisiana. As the leader of the oldest Mafia family in the United States—"the first family of the Mafia," as it was known in mob circles—Marcello enjoyed extraordinary privileges within the national syndicate. As an FBI informant learned during this period, Carlos could make "major decisions of his own without consulting the national commission." He could have, "on his own, opened the books and made new members, but because of the tact and diplomacy of Carlos Marcello, he sought commission approval in making new 'soldiers,' which the commission naturally granted."

But, as powerful and autonomous as Marcello and his invisible government had become, he was still not totally exempt from the code to which he had sworn allegiance at that tumultuous meeting at the Black Diamond Club in 1947. And so when the other bosses would summon him to help mediate a major dispute, he would not fail to honor his obligation.

Such an occasion arose in the fall of 1966 when the then most powerful Mafia leader in the country, Carlo Gambino, the so-called boss of bosses, summoned Carlos and his brother Joe to New York City. As it would turn out, this meeting of thirteen Mafiosi was to result in one of the most curious episodes in Carlos's career, a mixed blessing that would, on one hand, get him into serious trouble and, on the other, vastly increase his power in a neighboring state.

43

Summit at La Stella

On September 22, 1966, two alert New York Police officers, noting an unusual array of black limousines parked outside the La Stella Restaurant in Forest Hills, Queens, barged into the place and, in a private basement dining room, stumbled upon the largest gathering of major Mafia bosses held since the Apalachin conclave of 1957. There, seated at a long table strewed with bottles of wine, baskets of bread, and plates of antipasti, the police found thirteen men about to have lunch. Five of them turned out to be among the most powerful Mafia leaders in the nation.

Among the thirteen were four men from New Orleans: Carlos Marcello and his brother Joe; Anthony Carolla, son of former Louisiana Mafia boss Sam "Silver Dollar" Carolla; and Frank Gagliano, son of a deported mobster from the Carolla era. The others were Carlo Gambino, the lean, hawk-nosed boss of the Gambino crime family of New York, considered at the time the most powerful Mafia family in the United States; two of his *capiregime,* Joseph N. Gallo and Aniello Dellacroce; Joseph Colombo, head of the Colombo family of New York and destined to be mortally wounded in Central Park by an assassin's bullet five years later; and four members of New York's big, powerful Genovese family: acting boss Thomas "Tommy Ryan" Eboli, consiglieri Michael Miranda, and soldiers Dominick Alongi and

Anthony Carillo. The thirteenth attendee was the notorious Santos Trafficante, Jr., friend of the Marcellos, boss of the Florida Gulf Coast mob, and former conspirator with the CIA to murder Fidel Castro. Police estimated that all together the thirteen were probably responsible for over 200 contract murders.

Aided by hurriedly summoned reinforcements, the police arrested all thirteen men, charged them with "consorting with known criminals," handcuffed them, locked them up, and set bail at $1,300,000—$100,000 each. The next day the $1,300,000 was delivered, and the infamous thirteen were set free. The following afternoon Carlos Marcello, his lawyer Jack Wasserman, and brother Joe joined Anthony Carolla, Frank Gagliano, and Santos Trafficante, Jr., and his lawyer and returned to the La Stella for lunch to celebrate their freedom. It was a gesture characteristic of Marcello. All his life he had successfully defied the police and had made a spectacle of his defiance while doing so. Now he would show the New York Police they could not keep a bunch of old friends from eating lunch in an Italian restaurant in Queens.

Despite Marcello's bravado, the discovery of his attendance at what appeared to be a top-level meeting of the Mafia—a "minisummit" or a "mini-Apalachin," as some journalists called it—turned out to be personally damaging to both himself and his brother. Carlos had always insisted to law enforcement authorities that he never associated with anyone connected to organized crime and was not himself in the Mafia. Through the years, Louisiana Police officials and politicians and, as we know, even FBI agents in New Orleans had bought this contention. Now all had changed. Carlos and his brother had been discovered meeting with some of the most powerful Mafia bosses in the country. How would he explain this one? As it turned out, the excuse he gave the authorities could not have been more lame:

"I decided to see some of my old friends—so we all got together for lunch. Sure, some of these fellows had been in the rackets....But, if they're in the Mafia, I don't know a damned thing about that. This was strictly a social gathering; that's all there was to it....What's the matter with some old friends getting together for lunch?"

The disingenuous explanation fooled no one. Now Louisiana law enforcement authorities and the FBI were convinced of what they had suspected all along, that Carlos Marcello was indeed a Mafia boss and that he had contacts with some of the most powerful criminals in the national Mafia network.

What was the purpose of the La Stella summit? FBI Special Agent Harold Hughes, of the New Orleans office, conducted an investigation of the meeting and found out through reliable informants that it was a mediation effort to settle a dispute that had arisen between the Marcellos and the Carollas over Anthony Carolla's position in the New Orleans underworld. The luncheon had followed a formal meeting at another location. Apparently Anthony Carolla, as the son and heir of Carlos's predecessor, believed he had a right to a greater share of the action in the Marcello organization as well as to consideration as Carlos's possible successor. From the intelligence Hughes was able to gather, the New York dons decided in favor of Carlos and his brother: Anthony Carolla had no right to greater participation in Marcello's operations, nor was he entitled to be regarded as Carlos's successor, who, it was generally agreed, would be Joe Jr. The presence of Santos Trafficante at the meeting was necessary because of his friendship with Carlos and his vested interest in what was going on in the territory adjoining his.

Carlos and Joe had emerged triumphant from the La Stella meeting. With his sense of self-importance further inflated, Carlos felt like a conquering hero upon his return to New Orleans eight days after his arrest. Heady with triumph, he promptly lost his cool.

Carlos's participation in the La Stella summit had made headlines in the New Orleans papers, and a large crowd of newsmen, photographers, and spectators had gathered at the New Orleans International Airport to witness his triumphal return.

There are three versions of what happened next. The version Carlos stuck to has it that as Carlos was making his way through the crowd of reporters and photographers, someone he didn't know got in his way. Losing patience, Carlos took a swing at him.

However, the victim of the assault, which was photographed by a newsman and witnessed by brother Joe, was definitely not someone Carlos did not know. He was Patrick Collins, the FBI agent who had been assigned by the bureau to tail him after the retirement of Regis Kennedy. Collins had gone to the airport to let Marcello know that he was still keeping an eye on him. According to Collins's version, when he approached Carlos to welcome him back to New Orleans, Carlos shouted, "I'm the boss around here!" and hauled off and slugged him.

Which brings us to the third version. Patrick Collins had been carrying on a clandestine affair with Joe Marcello's wife, Bootsie, who had been passing on information to him about the Marcellos. As Carlos made his way through the unruly crowd, Collins, an agent known for his brashness, approached Marcello and yelled: "Hey, Carlos, guess what? I've been fucking your brother Joe's wife." For which Carlos, in an impulsive rage, let him have it.

Whichever was the correct version, Carlos was arrested by the FBI the following day and charged with assaulting an FBI agent, a federal offense. Carlos went on trial for the assault on May 20, 1968, in federal court in Laredo, Texas, his attorneys having successfully petitioned for a change of venue due to all the publicity the case had generated in New Orleans. The heavily attended trial proceedings in Laredo turned into something of a local media circus as crowds of teenage girls gathered in front of the courthouse every day to squeal over the appearance of Carlos's handsome young son, Joseph, who was treated by press and public as if he were a movie star. Amid widespread rumors of tampering, the trial ended in a hung jury, enabling Carlos to return once more to New Orleans in triumph. Subsequently the enormous publicity the trial received throughout Texas resulted in a notable expansion of Marcello's activities in that state. Suddenly, it seemed, everyone in Texas wanted to do business with him.

But the Justice Department's recently established New Orleans organized crime strike force refused to let the matter rest. Convinced that Marcello's henchmen had tampered with the Laredo jury, the U.S. attorney in New Orleans had Marcello reindicted for the assault on Collins. Carlos was then retried and convicted in Houston, Texas, on August 9, 1968. Although Carlos was sentenced to two years in federal prison, he ended up serving less than six months in the United States Medical Center for Federal Prisoners at Springfield, Missouri, where he was given extensive tests and medication and put on a strict regimen of diet and exercise.

Aaron Kohn saw Carlos both before and after his stay in the Springfield Medical Center and observes that the don never looked better than when he was released. His former bloat was gone (he had reportedly lost 40 pounds), and he no longer favored his gouty right leg. The American taxpayers had put Carlos Marcello back in shape.

The Patrick Collins affair drew an enormous amount of attention to Marcello from the Louisiana press and stirred up a great deal of sympathy for him throughout the state. During the trials in Laredo and Houston, legions of supporters flocked to his defense. According to the New Orleans Crime Commission, those who sought clemency for Marcello included "one sheriff, one former sheriff, one state legislator, two former state legislators, two former state police commanders, one president of a waterfront labor union, one bank president, two bank vice presidents, one former assistant district attorney, one chief juvenile probation officer, one former revenue agent, three insurance agency executives, five realtors, five physicians, one funeral director, and six clergymen." It was a cross section of Carlos's invisible government. Although they were unable to prevent Marcello's conviction and incarceration, it is generally agreed they played a role in getting a year and a half shaved off Carlos's sentence and in enabling him to spend the remaining six months in what amounted to a health spa for convicted felons.

But it seems there was a dark secret in the Patrick Collins affair that none of Carlos's supporters ever knew about. Before and during the trials, Carlos stuck with his story that he did not know the individual he tried to slug that day. He was merely lashing out at someone who was blocking his path. It was a weak defense, and Carlos knew it. But apparently he stuck by it to protect his family's honor. For according to reliable informants in New Orleans whom I interviewed at length on the issue, the truth was apparently that Collins *was* carrying on an affair with Bootsie Marcello and he *did* push his way through the crowd to taunt Marcello about it.

Carlos Marcello was essentially a prudent man, well aware that assaulting an FBI agent was a serious federal offense. He could never have mistaken Collins for an onlooker, for he had met with the FBI agent dozens of times. And he never would have taken a swing at Collins simply because the FBI agent got in his way. No, Carlos Marcello would have lashed out at Collins only if Collins had insulted his family's honor, which he did by boasting that he was sleeping with his brother Joe's wife. That boast had struck a nerve deep in Carlos's Sicilian guts. Was he, Carlos Marcello, going to stand by and let an enemy humiliate his brother?

Carlos Marcello would have been able to put up a reasonably sound defense against the charges brought against him if he had told the court the real reason why he assaulted Patrick Collins. There is little doubt that the jury would have sympathized with his impulsive reaction to Collins's insulting remarks. But for the sake of Joe's honor and his family's reputation, Carlos could never have permitted the world to know that an FBI agent was sleeping with his brother's wife. Rather than have this dishonor proclaimed in headlines, he decided to risk going to jail for the assault. It was a typically Sicilian decision. A family's pride and honor would not be offended by headlines about its alleged crimes or by the scorn of Senate committees, but it would be offended by headlines proclaiming the infidelity of a family member's wife, especially if that infidelity had occurred in the arms of a deadly enemy.

44

Echoes of Conspiracy: 1967

On February 13, 1967, James J. Rowley, chief of the United States Secret Service, told FBI Director J. Edgar Hoover that Chief Justice Earl Warren had recently been informed of the CIA's attempts to assassinate Fidel Castro, and that one of the underworld figures who had been involved had alleged that Castro agents in association with CIA-Mafia conspirator Santos Trafficante had retaliated by killing President Kennedy. Two days later, Hoover informed Rowley that the FBI was "not conducting any investigation" of the allegation but would "accept volunteered information."

The next day, February 16, Hoover was shown an article in the New Orleans *States-Item* disclosing that Orleans Parish District Attorney Jim Garrison was launching a reinvestigation of the John F. Kennedy assassination and that one of his chief suspects was David W. Ferrie, a former investigator for Carlos Marcello and a friend of Lee Harvey Oswald's. Reporter Rosemary James's article had been a scoop, coming out in advance of Garrison's planned press conference. FBI cable traffic during the last two weeks of February reveals that news of the Garrison investigation convulsed Hoover. Immediately he began marshaling his allies in the government and the media in a discreet, behind-the-scenes effort to discredit Garrison and undermine his investigation.

The day after the *States-Item*'s revelations, District Attorney Garrison, a tall, lanky man with a booming voice, publicly confirmed that he was reopening the investigation of the Kennedy assassination and was placing one of his chief suspects, David Ferrie, in "protective custody."

Ferrie was then put up in a New Orleans hotel by the office of the district attorney and given a bodyguard. Shortly thereafter Garrison announced to the press that he planned to indict David Ferrie soon for participating in a conspiracy to assassinate President Kennedy. Then, for reasons that remain unclear, on February 21 Ferrie was released from protective custody and allowed to return to his apartment.

The next day, early in the morning of February 22, David Ferrie was found dead in his apartment, an apparent suicide.

Word of Ferrie's sudden death traveled fast. As soon as it reached former FBI informant Eugene De Laparra, then living in New Jersey, he went straight to the FBI office in Newark on February 23 and offered the agents on duty a new, expanded version of the allegation he had made to the Philadelphia FBI office on November 27, 1963, about Ben Tregle's apparent foreknowledge of the Kennedy assassination.

This time, as we know, De Laparra revealed that it was Carlos Marcello's brother Tony who had hinted to Tregle about an impending assassination. He added that Tregle knew Lee Harvey Oswald and that Tregle's backer, Vincent Marcello, took frequent trips to Dallas in a plane piloted by David Ferrie.

But Hoover did not have much time to contemplate De Laparra's latest. Soon his attention was absorbed again by the allegation of the former CIA-Mafia conspirator. On March 4 Senator Robert Kennedy's secretary phoned Hoover and requested a copy of CIA Director of Security Sheffield Edwards' memorandum to him of May 7, 1962, briefing him on the CIA-Mafia assassination plots against Castro. Kennedy had learned of the mysterious underworld figure's allegation from Washington columnist Drew Pearson, who subsequently published a column about it on March 7.

Hoover had taken no action on the allegation, but when it came to the attention of President Lyndon Johnson, Johnson immediately ordered Hoover to conduct an investigation. Accordingly on March 20 FBI agents interviewed the as yet unnamed underworld figure's attorney and learned that the underworld figure had been hired by the CIA in 1961 to plot and carry out the murder of Fidel Castro. Later it was revealed that the mysterious plotter was Johnny Roselli. After receiving Hoover's report of the interview, President Johnson immediately ordered the CIA to brief him on the CIA's attempts to assassinate Fidel Castro. It was apparently the first Johnson had heard of the matter.

Meanwhile District Attorney Garrison's reinvestigation of the Kennedy assassination was heating up. On March 28 J. Edgar Hoover received an allegation from one of the FBI's New Orleans informants, Gordon Novel, owner of a French Quarter restaurant and an acquaintance of Jim Garrison's:

> Novel stated that Garrison plans to indict Carlos Marcello in the Kennedy assassination conspiracy because Garrison believes Marcello is tied up in some way with Jack Ruby. Novel stated that he is not certain about evidence District Attorney Garrison has on the Marcello-Ruby tie up, but it was in some way concerned with Bourbon Street nightclubs and a Bourbon Street stripper named 'Jada.'

(The reader will recall that Janet Conforto, stage name 'Jada,' had performed in 1963 in both Pete Marcello's Sho-Bar in New Orleans and Jack Ruby's Carousel Club in Dallas.)

Not long after Hoover absorbed this bit of news, Lyndon Johnson was briefed on the CIA-Mafia plots to assassinate Castro. After digesting those astonishing revelations, he had his special assistant, Marvin Watson, inform Hoover's White House liaison, Cartha DeLoach, that he was now convinced John F. Kennedy had been killed as a result of a conspiracy.

One would have thought that, after this, Hoover would have conducted a thorough investigation of Johnny Roselli's conspiracy allegation. Instead, he blithely informed the White House that the FBI planned no further investigation of Roselli's allegation. There is no record that Johnson subsequently pressed the issue.

The "affaire Roselli" had hardly blown over when J. Edgar Hoover was confronted with still another Kennedy assassination conspiracy allegation. Around May 15 the FBI learned about Edward Becker from writer Ed Reid. Hoover's knee-jerk reaction to this allegation was not to order an investigation, but to immediately order his aides to try and get Reid to expunge Becker's Churchill Farms story from his book and to find a way to discredit Becker.

No sooner was Becker disposed of than, about a month later, the Garrison investigation claimed Hoover's attention once again. On June 10, he received a report quoting a Lafayette talk-show host, Bob Hamm, on a show listed as "Garrison and the Mafia" as follows:

District Attorney Garrison believes that organized crime was responsible for the assassination. The reason being that organized crime wanted the assassination to appear as though it had been done at the instigation of Castro, and this would then, hopefully, arouse the United States to a point where Castro would be removed from power in Cuba, thereby allowing re-opening of the gambling casinos and other hoodlum interests.

It was clear, of course, to everyone in Louisiana who heard Hamm's broadcast, that "organized crime" meant Carlos Marcello.

It was indeed a curious phenomenon. Whereas during the FBI's initial investigation of the assassination and the Warren Commission's probe that followed it, organized crime and the name Marcello had been barely whispered in connection with the crime, now, two and a half years later, allegations suggesting Marcello involvement seemed to be coming in from every direction, even though District Attorney Garrison was pointedly steering *his* reinvestigation of the Kennedy murder in a completely different direction.

The Marcello-related allegations received during the spring of 1967 appear to have perturbed J. Edgar Hoover not a little, for a recently released FBI teletype of August 8, 1967, marked "URGENT," from the New Orleans FBI office to Director Hoover in apparent response to an August 7 telephone call from Hoover, reveals that the director had suddenly taken a new interest in all the allegations of November 1963 involving associates of the Marcellos' that he had so assiduously suppressed at the time. For the New Orleans teletype confirmed to the director that "Anthony Marcello, manager of the Town & Country Motel," and "Joseph Albert Poretto, owner of the Town & Country Restaurant," had been interviewed by Special Agent Jensen on November 27 in connection with SV T-1's allegation that Oswald had received a payment in the Town & Country Motel. The teletype went on to further inform him that Special Agent Jensen had also interviewed Ben Tregle and Norman Le Blanc in connection with Eugene De Laparra's allegation that Tregle had expressed apparent foreknowledge of the Kennedy assassination.

So far, 1967 had been quite a year for J. Edgar Hoover. After two years of relative quiet on the assassination front, his lone gunman solution to the crime had come under relentless fire, and he was now having to respond to one nasty conspiracy allegation after another. What was behind it all?

What was behind it was growing doubt over the conclusions of the Warren Commission, which, as we know, were almost entirely based on Hoover's investigation of the murder.

For two and a half years following the conclusion of the Warren
Commission's investigation of the assassination, the case had remained
relatively dormant. Although a good deal of skepticism had been expressed about the official explanation of the crime, and several books
had appeared that convincingly attacked the Warren Commission's
findings—the most notable of which were Mark Lane's *Rush to Judgment* and Harold Weisberg's *Whitewash*—there were no major new developments in the case until 1967.

Then, suddenly, the case seemed to crack open on half a dozen
fronts, and for the first time, significantly large segments of public
opinion became deeply skeptical of the official findings. There followed more books critical of the Warren report—Josiah Thompson's
Six Seconds in Dallas, Richard Popkin's *The Second Oswald,* and Sylvia
Meagher's *Accessories after the Fact*—the reopening of the assassination case by Jim Garrison, and a rush of new allegations suggesting
that President Kennedy had not been killed by a lone, unaided nut
but as a result of a planned conspiracy.

Concurrent with these events came a concerted effort by Jimmy
Hoffa's allies in the Teamsters, the underworld, and the federal government to prevent Hoffa from being imprisoned and then, when
the effort failed, and Hoffa went off on March 7 to the federal penitentiary at Lewisburg, to spring him from prison. In fact, Walter
Sheridan, former head of Robert Kennedy's "get Hoffa" squad, who
covered Garrison's investigation for NBC, came to believe that Garrison's investigation soon degenerated into a mob-Teamsters supported vehicle to help get Hoffa out of jail. As it turned out, Carlos
Marcello was a key figure in the "spring Hoffa" movement, assisted
by his principal fixer, D'Alton Smith, and his chief Washington contact, lobbyist Irving Davidson, who would resort to such extreme
lengths in his campaign to free Hoffa as making an attempt to use
the Garrison investigation as a means to frame the government's chief
prosecution witness for having allegedly participated in a plot to assassinate President Kennedy.

It was on March 15 that J. Edgar Hoover received word of Irving
Davidson's outrageous ploy on behalf of Hoffa in the form of a memorandum about government witness Edward Partin. The FBI report
on the memorandum read as follows:

Davidson stated he learned through affiliations with Teamsters
Headquarters in Washington, D.C. that Edward G. Partin will
be subpoenaed by a grand jury in New Orleans in the near
future in connection with his possible involvement in the as-

sassination of President Kennedy. Davidson alleged he heard there is a photograph available of Partin in the presence of Jack Ruby, but he could not furnish any additional details regarding the photograph or his source for this information.

And so, on March 15, as he was wrestling with the conspiracy allegations of Jim Garrison, Eugene De Laparra, and Johnny Roselli, J. Edgar Hoover even had to deal with one from his old friend Irving Davidson.

But it was the Roselli allegation that eventually occupied Hoover the most.

The former CIA-Mafia conspirator's allegation was first brought to the attention of the government in January 1967, when his attorney, Edward P. Morgan, got Washington columnist Drew Pearson to approach Chief Justice Warren about it. Warren then referred the allegation to the head of the Secret Service, who brought it to the attention of J. Edgar Hoover and finally to the desk of President Johnson. Roselli claimed he had been given reliable information through sources in the underworld that Kennedy had been assassinated by agents of Fidel Castro in association with former CIA-Mafia conspirator Santos Trafficante. According to Roselli's account, Oswald had been set up as a decoy at the scene of the shooting. He had been eliminated shortly after the assassination by Jack Ruby so he would not reveal the details of the plot.

Why would a Mafia don of Johnny Roselli's visibility risk certain extermination by running off at the mouth this way? Roselli was in a lot of trouble at the time he made his allegation. He was in prison for having defrauded unsuspecting businessmen and Hollywood stars out of hundreds of thousands of dollars in a card-cheating scam and was also under a deportation order from the Immigration and Naturalization Service.

Roselli had only one card left to play in his battle against the government: his past participation in the assassination plots against Castro. If he could convince the government that those plots had boomeranged into a Cuban-Mafia plot to kill President Kennedy, the government might release Roselli from prison and lift its deportation order against him in exchange for Roselli's silence. That silence might also induce the government to grant some leniency toward Roselli's friend Jimmy Hoffa.

Was there anything to Roselli's conspiracy allegation, or was it merely trumped up to blackmail the government? Quite possibly there was something to it. Roselli could very well have learned something about the assassination from his underworld sources, if the Mafia had indeed been involved in the crime. Roselli told the same story (which his lawyer told the FBI) privately to a few old friends. One of them, a midwestern newspaper publisher, told me about it spontaneously during the course of a general conversation on the Kennedy assassination. One reason for giving guarded credence to Roselli's allegation stems from the fact that some elements of Roselli's assassination scenario seem to agree with the scenario that was suggested by the House Select Committee on Assassinations twelve years later: the possibility of Trafficante sending a hit team of "Latins" up to Dallas from Miami; Marcello setting up the crazy nephew of one of his gambling associates as a decoy, or scapegoat, and then arranging for the scapegoat's elimination at the hands of his Dallas tool, Jack Ruby.

Whatever the case, we can be certain that the underworld soon became aware of the Roselli allegation, since it was eventually publicized widely by Washington columnists Drew Pearson and Jack Anderson. Although the columnists did not reveal Roselli's name, they gave his identity away to those in the know in the mob and in the CIA by revealing that the allegation had come from a former participant in the CIA-Mafia plots to murder Castro. In fact, the underworld may have known about Roselli's allegation even earlier than 1967, for Hank Greenspun of the *Las Vegas Sun* had alluded to it in an article he wrote for his paper on the CIA-Mafia plots—the first ever written on the subject—in 1966.

Therefore, it can be said with some assurance that the underworld and its political pawns and supporters knew early in 1967 that Edward Becker had pointed a finger at Carlos Marcello and Johnny Roselli had pointed a finger at Marcello's friend Santos Trafficante as possible conspirators in a plot to kill President Kennedy.

Then who comes along at about this time but New Orleans District Attorney Jim Garrison, an admitted acquaintance of Marcello's, with his explosive allegations suggesting not an organized crime conspiracy but one involving principally the CIA.

Scholars of the Kennedy assassination have since pointed out that Garrison had good reason *not* to implicate organized crime in the assassination, for he had always enjoyed a mutually beneficial relationship with Carlos Marcello. Garrison had made Marcello happy by publicly insisting that organized crime did not exist in New Orleans and by consistently ignoring Marcello's vast and blatantly open gambling network. And Marcello had contented Garrison by doing him such favors as having his Las Vegas associate Mario Marino provide him with free hotel accommodations and substantial casino credits whenever the New Orleans DA sought weekend amusement in Nevada, and arranging for him to buy an expensive home in an affluent New Orleans suburb at a cut-rate price from one of Marcello's major business associates, Frank Occhipinti.

So how was it that Garrison decided to launch an investigation of the Kennedy assassination precisely when serious allegations were being made that organized crime was involved in the murder?

There are strong indications, never confirmed by the parties concerned, that Jim Garrison was persuaded to reopen the case by two Louisiana politicians close to Carlos Marcello: Representative Hale Boggs and Senator Russell Long. According to former Justice Department official Walter Sheridan, Long induced Garrison to believe that either the CIA or the Cuban government might have had a hand in the assassination by telling Garrison of certain privileged information he claimed he had acquired as a senator from confidential intelligence sources linking Oswald to both pro-Castro Cubans and the agency. Congressman Boggs, who had been on the Warren Commission, is said to have voiced suspicions of CIA complicity to Garrison based on his conviction that the CIA had withheld vital information from the commission. Was it a mere coincidence that both Senator Long and Congressman Boggs enjoyed close personal relationships with Carlos Marcello and had benefited considerably over the years from Marcello's generous contributions to their political campaigns?

True to Boggs's and Long's suspicions, Jim Garrison directed his reinvestigation of the Kennedy assassination toward the possibility of CIA complicity by eventually indicting, to nearly everyone's bewilderment, Clay Shaw, a prominent New Orleans businessman with past connections to the CIA, for conspiring to assassinate President Kennedy, with no hard evidence to back up his charges. Garrison claimed that Shaw, the retired director of the New Orleans International Trade Mart, had known both Lee Harvey Oswald and David Ferrie and was backed by no fewer than fourteen former CIA officials, most notably a former deputy director of the CIA, General Charles P. Cabell, who had been fired by President Kennedy for his role in the Bay of Pigs fiasco.

By the time Garrison took this wild, mystifying step, his other assassination suspect, David Ferrie, had been found dead in his New Orleans apartment.

Several burning questions have been raised about Garrison's suspicions in regard to Ferrie and about Ferrie's untimely death.

Garrison knew that Ferrie had been, and continued to be, closely associated with Carlos Marcello. He knew, for example, that just be-

fore the Kennedy assassination, the then normally impecunious Ferrie
had deposited $7093.02 in his bank account, and that not long after
the murder, someone had bought him a lucrative gasoline station franchise in a New Orleans suburb. If Garrison knew this—and he stated
that he did in his book, *Heritage of Stone*—he must have known that
Ferrie's only source of income immediately preceding the assassination had been his work as an investigator for Carlos Marcello's attorney G. Wray Gill and that it had been Marcello who had bought the
gas station franchise for Ferrie after the assassination. Furthermore,
since he claimed he had conducted such a thorough investigation of
Ferrie, Garrison must also have known that not long after the assassination Marcello had secured a steady job for Ferrie with an air cargo
service firm controlled by one of his associates, Jacob Nastasi, a job
Ferrie continued to hold at least through the end of 1966. And yet
Ferrie's connections to Marcello were apparently not worth considering when it came to Garrison's suspicions about Ferrie's role in the
Kennedy assassination. For Garrison, Ferrie had been a tool of the
CIA. His connections to Marcello were irrelevant.

But what did *Marcello* think about Garrison's pointing a finger at
David Ferrie? We can only speculate that if Marcello *had* been involved with Ferrie in a plot to assassinate President Kennedy, he
would have been very disturbed over the prospect of Ferrie being
cross-examined in a courtroom.

David Ferrie was found dead in the early morning hours of
February 22 by a young male visitor who had come to see the hairless homosexual adventurer in his apartment. Upon entering the bedroom with its piles of newspapers, magazines, and books everywhere,
and its tables crowded with medicine bottles and chemical laboratory
apparatus, the visitor found Ferrie's nude body lying on the bed covered by a sheet and two brief typewritten "suicide notes," with *typed*
signatures, on a bed table. One of the notes read: "To leave this life
for me is a sweet prospect. I find nothing in it desirable, and on the
other hand, everything that is loathsome." Students of Ferrie's mysterious death have since wondered why Ferrie had not written and
signed his two suicide notes in his own hand if he had wanted them
to be believed.

Dr. Nicholas Chetta, the New Orleans Parish coroner, performed
the autopsy on Ferrie and reported that he had died of natural causes,
specifically from a cerebral hemorrhage caused by a "berry aneu-
rysm," or weak point on a blood vessel, at the base of the brain. Ferrie's cerebral hemorrhage, Dr. Chetta speculated, had probably been
brought on by stress. After all, the New Orleans district attorney had

identified him as a suspect in a conspiracy to murder the President of the United States.

Ferrie's death caused an immediate international uproar, making the front pages of the major papers of the world. Jim Garrison went on record as saying he believed the CIA had Ferrie murdered to prevent him from testifying at the upcoming trial of Clay Shaw, adding later, in a book, that "with Ferrie's death there most likely faded into oblivion the possibility of uncovering in the immediate future the full meaning of the assassination." The press, both national and international, was almost unanimously skeptical of the autopsy report. Most serious observers of the case Garrison was unfolding in New Orleans believed David Ferrie had been deliberately silenced, just as Lee Harvey Oswald had been silenced a little over three years before.

But precisely how was Ferrie silenced, and who might have been behind the silencing? Medical experts have speculated that a karate black belt could have administered a chop to the back of Ferrie's neck and caused a blood vessel to rupture at the base of the brain without leaving a mark on the skin.

Others have speculated on other ways a cerebral hemorrhage might be induced leaving no suspicious traces. In his book *Assassin*, about the corrupt regime of dictator Rafael Trujillo of the Dominican Republic, British journalist Christopher Robbins recounted how Carlos Evertze, a torturer and executioner for Trujillo, killed a suspected student activist. He knocked him out with chloroform, then drove a 4-inch extra-fine needle into his brain from underneath the right earlobe, pulled it rapidly out, and brushed away the pinpoint of blood with alcohol. "The needle method leaves no trace," wrote Robbins. "In the autopsy it seems as if the victim had a cerebral hemorrhage. The needle prick just looks like a pore."

Aaron Kohn was in New Orleans in 1967, pursuing his unending investigation of Carlos Marcello, and recalls today that he too was very skeptical of the official version of Ferrie's death. "Coroners in Louisiana are almost all corrupt," he told me, "and Ferrie's coroner, Dr. Nicholas Chetta, was no exception. Chetta had already produced several dubious autopsy reports. Whoever had reason to kill David Ferrie could easily have paid Dr. Chetta to report that Ferrie died of natural causes."

But who would have had reason to kill Ferrie on the eve of his testimony at Garrison's trial of Clay Shaw? The CIA? Not likely. Garrison's case against the CIA was known to be weak, and Ferrie had never had strong ties with the agency. At the most, he had been an occasional informant; the agency denied it had ever had anything to do with him. No, if Carlos Marcello and David Ferrie were involved in a conspiracy to assassinate President Kennedy, then Marcello would have had the most to lose from David Ferrie on the witness stand or David Ferrie plea bargaining for his freedom. Marcello would have had little difficulty finding someone in his organization willing to do the job on Ferrie, and he would have known the right man to approach Dr. Chetta about falsifying the autopsy report. It is worth noting that Dr. Chetta himself died at age 50, a little over a year after Ferrie's death, from an apparent heart attack.

Lending credibility to the belief that Ferrie might have been murdered were the fates of two of Ferrie's closest associates in the wake of Ferrie's death. The Cuban exile Eladio del Valle had once been David Ferrie's associate in the New Orleans delegation of the Cuban Revolutionary Council. The day after Ferrie's death del Valle was found executed in a Miami parking lot, his head cracked open and a bullet wound in his heart. Three months later Ferrie's closest female friend, Dr. Mary Stults Sherman, was found murdered in her New Orleans apartment. If we include Lee Harvey Oswald, she was the third close associate of Ferrie's to be murdered after the Kennedy assassination.

Jim Garrison may have been sincere in his suspicions that the CIA was behind the Kennedy assassination, and he may have been sincere in launching his own investigation to prove it. Nevertheless it remains a strong possibility that he was being unknowingly manipulated by others into conducting an investigation that would divert attention away from the possible complicity of organized crime in general, and of Carlos Marcello in particular.

This possibility is reinforced by an episode that occurred in the midst of Garrison's prosecution of his principal suspect, Clay Shaw.

As we know, an immense effort had been launched by the Teamsters and its allies in politics and organized crime to overturn Jimmy Hoffa's conviction and obtain his release from prison. Hoffa's allies knew they had to find a way to either threaten or bribe the government's chief prosecution witness, Edward G. Partin, head of Teamsters Union Local 5 in Baton Rouge, into changing his damning testimony against Hoffa. And if threats and bribes did not work, they would have to find a way to publicly discredit him.

As it turned out, the Hoffa forces' attempts at intimidation—which ranged from threats to have Partin framed for crimes he did not commit to threats of murder—came to no avail. Partin, a tough, courageous man, knew too much about Hoffa to be intimidated by threats.

Among other things, Partin knew that Hoffa had seriously contemplated killing Robert Kennedy in the summer of 1962. He knew this firsthand, because Hoffa had once expounded his murder plan directly to him at Teamsters headquarters in Washington. How would Hoffa and his allies like that to be made public? No, Edward Partin was not going to succumb to threats of violence from Hoffa, from Marcello, or from anyone else.

But perhaps Partin could be bought. The father of two young children and separated from his wife, Partin was known to be not very well off financially. Could he be bought? And if he could, what would be his price?

Walter Sheridan, former head of Robert Kennedy's "get Hoffa" squad in the Justice Department, remained close to the intrigue surrounding the effort to liberate Hoffa, and, assigned by NBC to cover the Garrison investigation in New Orleans, was also close to the action itself. According to Sheridan, the man the "spring Hoffa" forces selected to find out whether Edward Partin could be bought was one of Marcello's chief advisors and fixers, the wheeler-dealer swindler D'Alton Smith, whose sisters were married to Marcello's associates Joseph Poretto and Nofio Pecora.

In *The Fall and Rise of Jimmy Hoffa*, Sheridan wrote that, among Smith's accomplishments on behalf of the Marcellos, Smith liked to boast about getting Russell Long elected Senate whip by traveling up to Washington from New Orleans with a suitcase of Marcello cash before the Senate vote and distributing it to seven hitherto undecided senators disposed to swing their votes to Long.

We do not know if this was so, or how much it might have cost Marcello to make his friend Russell Long Senate whip, but we do know from Edward Partin's own sworn statement what Marcello offered him, through D'Alton Smith, to repudiate his trial testimony against Hoffa. The first offer of $25,000 a year for ten years was turned down as not being worth D'Alton Smith's breath. Then Smith offered Partin a flat 1 million, and Partin, who had led him on a bit, told him to go to hell.

Their threats and bribes having proved futile, Hoffa's allies hit upon a way to try and destroy Partin's reputation and credibility. As it turned out, in Jim Garrison's free-for-all investigation of the Kennedy assassination they found what they thought would be the perfect vehicle. How would Partin look if Garrison could get the public to believe Partin had been involved in a plot to assassinate President Kennedy? Accordingly, in the latter part of June 1967, Carlos Marcello's forces, led by D'Alton Smith, induced District Attorney Garrison to come up with the preposterous notion that Partin had consorted with Oswald and Ruby in New Orleans in the summer of 1963 for the purpose of planning the assassination. The sensational news was reported over station WJBO in Baton Rouge on June 23, 1967. The attempt to publicly discredit Partin had begun.

Ganging up on Partin also was Carlos Marcello's Washington lobbyist friend, Irving Davidson, who, as we have seen, attempted to brand Partin as a possible suspect in the Kennedy assassination as far back as March 15.

Fortunately for Partin, Garrison's prosecution of Clay Shaw soon became so discredited by the media and law enforcement authorities throughout the nation that Garrison himself lost all credibility and therefore found himself in no position to cast doubt upon Edward G. Partin. After the acquittal of Clay Shaw of all charges Garrison had brought against him, Garrison fell into further disrepute. It was generally agreed by almost all close observers of the case that Garrison's inquiry into the Kennedy assassination had been a monumental fraud, an outrageous abuse of the office of district attorney.

However, despite all of this, and despite the fact that Garrison made dozens of irresponsible accusations and allowed his investigation to be used by the criminal supporters of Jimmy Hoffa, he did succeed in demonstrating that the FBI had suppressed much important evidence pertaining to the assassination, and he was able to demonstrate conclusively that a significant relationship between Oswald and David Ferrie had existed. Furthermore, to his credit, he was the first assassination investigator to point out the importance of the Zapruder film of the shooting and how the autopsy of the President had been manipulated by high-ranking military officers and members of the Kennedy family and their aides.

In the end, though, Garrison's counterfeit investigation of the Kennedy assassination accomplished what its instigators probably hoped it would. It all but wrecked the movement to get to the bottom of the Kennedy assassination, and it successfully diverted attention from Carlos Marcello.

With the Garrison case in ruins and J. Edgar Hoover refusing to investigate the Becker and Roselli allegations, eleven more years would have to elapse before the Kennedy assassination case would be reopened and Carlos Marcello singled out as a prime suspect in what had by then become known as the crime of the century.

45

From Memphis to Los Angeles

MARCELLO:	The mayor's a nigger here. He's black.... He wants to do it on his own....He's a nigger, and a nigger's gonna be a nigger even if you give him some authority.
UNDERCOVER AGENT:	How come you elected a nigger mayor?
MARCELLO:	Cause these assholes went to sleep.

Carlos Marcello's remarks on New Orleans' first black mayor, Ernest Morial, recorded by an FBI undercover agent in 1979, epitomized Carlos's contempt for blacks. Blacks, to the boss of the Louisiana Mafia, were subhuman, chattel to be exploited.

Carlos, it will be remembered, had begun his business career exploiting poor young black workers at his "colored" bar in Gretna, The Black Bomber. There he sold underage blacks cheap beer and whiskey and turned the uninitiated on to marijuana by offering them free joints along with their drinks.

Later, when he became active in local and state politics, Carlos had an opportunity to exploit blacks again, this time as votes that could be bought for his candidate of the moment. In 1979 the FBI's bug in

Carlos's Town & Country office caught the boss boasting to a friend how many black votes he controlled in his home parish:

"I got a buncha niggers I gotta get together here...fifteen hundred of 'em. Fifteen hundred families, I mean....All the niggers around. The blacks over in Jefferson. Highway 90. See Highway 90 I got 1500 blacks, and in Avondale Homes, I got 4500. ...I'm tryin' to trap the whole thing...."

But Carlos Marcello's attitude toward blacks went beyond notions of them as chattel to be exploited. For, as the 1979 recordings proved and the undercover agents who taped them confirmed to me, Carlos was an avid racist and bigot who vigorously opposed the civil rights movement of the sixties and detested its leaders, especially Dr. Martin Luther King, Jr., and his white champion, Attorney General Robert F. Kennedy. A generous contributor to anti–civil rights organizations throughout the sixties, Carlos was also known to be an enthusiastic supporter of the Ku Klux Klan.

Marcello's racist attitudes and hatred of Martin Luther King, Jr., were shared by FBI Director J. Edgar Hoover, who had initiated within the bureau in the early sixties an intensive campaign to discredit the civil rights leader that often exceeded legal authority. Though Hoover's language was not quite as blunt and vulgar as Marcello's, the content of some of his remarks on Dr. King, and blacks in general, was certainly worthy of Marcello.

When Hoover was given a news release showing that *Time* magazine had nominated Dr. King "Man of the Year" in 1962, Hoover wrote in the margin: "They had to dig deep in the garbage to come up with this one." Once, at a press conference, Hoover referred to Dr. King as being "no good," "the most notorious liar," and "one of the lowest characters in the country." On another occasion, Hoover told his aides: "King is a tom cat, with obsessive degenerate sexual urges." And, according to Justice of the Supreme Court Tom Clark, Hoover once told him: "I'm not going to send the FBI in every time some nigger woman gets raped."

On the evening of April 4, 1968, Carlos Marcello and J. Edgar Hoover were gratified to receive word that Dr. Martin Luther King, Jr., had been shot dead as he stood on a second-floor balcony outside his room at the Lorraine Motel in Memphis.

Immediately after the shooting, two boarders in Bessie Brewer's rooming house, located roughly opposite Dr. King's room in the Lorraine Hotel, noticed a man fleeing down a hallway carrying a bundle that could have contained a rifle.

A few minutes later, Guy Canipe, owner of an amusement store not far from the hotel, heard someone drop a bundle in front of his store with a thump. After ascertaining that the bundle contained a rifle, Canipe summoned the police. When the police opened the bundle, they found a 30-06 rifle, two cans of Schlitz beer, the April 18 edition of the *Memphis Commercial Appeal,* a plastic bottle of after-shave lotion, some ammunition, a pair of binoculars, and a portable radio with a scratched-up identification number on it. The FBI later deciphered the partially mutilated number and found it belonged to an inmate of the Missouri State Penitentiary named James Earl Ray.

The FBI then learned that Ray was a convicted armed robber who had escaped from the Missouri State Penitentiary about a year ago. After a massive search, the FBI, assisted by the Royal Canadian Mounted Police—for Ray had initially fled to Canada—located Ray in London and had him arrested on June 7 for the assassination of Dr. King.

Four days after the assassination, a Memphis citizen, John McFerren, went to the FBI office in Memphis and told the agent on duty that on the afternoon of Dr. King's murder, while he was shopping at the Liberto, Liberto, and Latch Produce Store in Memphis, he overheard a "heavy-set white male" telling someone over the phone to go ahead and "kill the S.O.B on the balcony" and "get the job done." "You will get your $5000," the man went on. "Don't come here. Go to New Orleans and get your money. You know my brother."

McFerren, described in the FBI report as "a negroe male," was unsure who the "heavy-set white male" caller was but believed he was Frank Liberto, one of the store's owners, who had a brother in New Orleans.

On investigating the allegation, the FBI determined that Frank Liberto's New Orleans brother was Salvatore Liberto, an associate of Carlos Marcello's. This knowledge was apparently sufficient to persuade the FBI not to investigate the allegation any further.

Subsequently, a respected New Orleans–based journalist, William Sartor, who had at one time written for *Time* magazine, learned of McFerren's allegation, and how the FBI had ignored it, and decided to investigate it privately. Later he set down the results of his investigation in a manuscript he did not live to publish.

In his manuscript Sartor concluded that there was a high probability that organized crime had played a role in Dr. King's assassination, basing his conclusion primarily on a report he had received from a reliable source of a meeting James Earl Ray had in New Orleans around December 17, 1967, with a New Orleans friend, Charles Stein, and certain associates of Carlos Marcello's. The meeting, Sartor claimed, was held in either Marcello's Town & Country Motel or the Provincial Motel, another mob hangout, where motel records established that Ray had stayed from December 17 to 19.

Sartor claimed that the associates of Carlos Marcello's with whom Ray and Stein met were Salvadore "Sam" DiPiazza, Dr. Lucas A. DiLeo, and Salvadore LaCharda. Since Sartor had been informed that DiPiazza and LaCharda had direct ties to Carlos Marcello, he speculated that Ray was told at the meeting that Carlos Marcello had agreed to protect him after the assassination.

To back up his contention, William Sartor cited in his manuscript what James Earl Ray had told author William Bradford Huie in an interview for Huie's book on Ray, *He Slew the Dreamer;* Ray had left New Orleans on December 19, approximately three months before Dr. King was assassinated, with $2500 in cash, paid to him by someone whose name he would not divulge, and a promise of $12,000 more for doing "one last big job in two or three months."

Needless to say, when Sartor's manuscript was belatedly brought to the attention of J. Edgar Hoover, who had concluded within days of the assassination that James Earl Ray had murdered Dr. King, acting alone, the FBI director dismissed it out of hand and decided not to conduct an investigation of its allegations.

But in 1978 the House Select Committee on Assassinations decided that both McFerren's and Sartor's allegations deserved investigation and found that James Earl Ray had indeed stayed at the Provincial Motel in New Orleans from December 17 to 19, 1967, and that the Provincial Motel had the reputation of catering to an underworld clientele. It further established that Sam DiPiazza was a major gambler and bookmaker associated with Carlos Marcello; that Lucas DiLeo was a practicing physician in a New Orleans suburb with a police record for disturbing the peace, resisting arrest, and assault; and that Salvadore LaCharda, a former probation officer in the St. Bernard's Parish Sheriff's Office, had committed suicide three months after the King assassination. Furthermore, the committee's investigation of the McFerren allegation established that Frank Liberto's New Orleans brother, Salvatore, was indeed connected to the Marcello organization.

Both DiPiazza and DiLeo subsequently testified before the Assassinations Committee that they had never met James Earl Ray. And Carlos Marcello and Charles Stein testified before the committee, under grant of immunity, that they knew of no such meeting as that described by Sartor in his manuscript. Salvatore Liberto was not interviewed by the committee. Upon running into this stone wall of denials, the Assassinations Committee concluded that there was no support for Sartor's contention that James Earl Ray met with persons associated with organized crime in New Orleans prior to the assassination of Dr. King.

The committee did, however, discover a disconcerting FBI intelligence report of October 1961: A prominent member of the Ku Klux Klan, William Hugh Morris of New Orleans, told a Klan meeting in October 1961, in his capacity as imperial wizard and emperor of the Federated Knights of the Klan, that southern racial problems could be eliminated only by the murder of Dr. King and that he had a New Orleans underworld associate "who would kill anyone for a price." However, the committee decided not to place much importance on the report after Morris, in an appearance before the committee, denied making these statements. And that was that. The matter of Marcello involvement in the King assassination was closed.

The results of my limited investigation of the McFerren and Sartor allegations suggested that perhaps the Assassinations Committee should have probed a little deeper. For I found out that Frank Liberto's New Orleans brother, Salvatore, who, according to John McFerren's allegation, was supposed to pay the assassin of Martin Luther King, Jr., $5000, was a member of a New Orleans family of Sicilian origin, heavily involved in the city's Mafia-dominated produce markets that did a good deal of business with French market associates of Carlos Marcello's. I also concluded that the Sam DiPiazza with whom, according to Sartor, Ray met was the same Sam DiPiazza of the Marcello gambling organization who had been indicted in Texas for illegal gambling in Houston and New Orleans involving millions of dollars in layoff bets; this was at the time District Attorney Jim Garrison was claiming there was no such thing as organized crime in New Orleans Parish. A convicted felon, free on bail when he allegedly met with Ray, DiPiazza was known at the time to be a much-favored associate of Carlos Marcello's because of the large amounts of cash he generated for the boss's organization.

Given the established facts that James Earl Ray had stayed at the Provincial Motel in New Orleans from December 17 to 19, 1967, a bare three months before Dr. King was assassinated, that the Provincial Motel was a known mob hangout, that Ray was hurting for money at the time and later told William Bradford Huie that he had been paid $2500 while he was in New Orleans, with a promise of another $12,000 when, during the next two or three months, he got "one more big job done," and that Carlos Marcello had a known contempt for blacks and Martin Luther King, Jr., and sympathy for the Ku Klux Klan, it does not appear to be beyond the realm of possibility that Carlos Marcello might have ordered certain subordinates, perhaps Liberto, perhaps DiPiazza, to pay James Earl Ray a few thousand dollars to keep him going, as he stalked Dr. King from one city to another, and promised him protection and more money after he did what he had to do to the hated King.

As for J. Edgar Hoover, who must have been even more pleased over the elimination of Dr. King than Marcello had been, he took a stance on the civil rights leader's murder roughly similar to the one he had adopted in the John F. Kennedy assassination case. As he had with Lee Harvey Oswald, he proclaimed, with his customary dogmatism, that James Earl Ray was the lone, unaided assassin of Dr. King.

On the surface, Hoover had good reason to assert the lone guilt of Ray, for just as there had been a superabundance of immediately available evidence suggesting Oswald's guilt, so, in the case of James Earl Ray, there was that bundle tossed ostentatiously onto the doorstep of the Canipe Amusement Store that neatly contained everything necessary with which to identify and incriminate the suspect. How convenient it was to find, immediately after Dr. King's murder, a nice neat bundle of incriminating evidence, not far from the scene of the crime, containing the murder weapon with James Earl Ray's fingerprints all over it, a supply of ammunition fitting the weapon, various toiletries known to be habitually used by the suspected assassin, two empty beer cans bearing Ray's fingerprints, and even a portable radio with the alleged assassin's prison inmate identification number on it.

But, unlike Oswald, who had a keen mind, it appears that James Earl Ray might just have been stupid enough not to have destroyed the evidence of his crime or to have disposed of it in a less ostentatious manner than dumping it in the entrance way of a nearby store. Yet that very stupidity might have been the most convincing evidence that he had not acted alone. William Sullivan, the number three man in the FBI at the time of the King murder, expressed it this way:

"I was convinced that James Earl Ray killed Martin Luther King, but I doubt if he acted alone. Ray was so stupid I don't think he could have robbed a five- and ten-cent store. He was not only stupid, he was sloppy....Someone, I feel sure, taught Ray how to get a false Canadian passport, and how to slip out of the country. [Two areas of expertise possessed by Carlos Marcello.] And how did Ray pay for the passport and the airlines tickets?"

But that James Earl Ray might have been framed for assassinating Dr. King, or might have been helped by confederates, never seemed to have occurred to Director Hoover. Ray had killed Dr. King, acting alone, without confederates. Case closed.

Ten years later, the House Select Committee on Assassinations reversed the FBI's original finding, concluding that "on the basis of the circumstantial evidence available to it, the committee believes there is a likelihood that James Earl Ray assassinated Martin Luther King, Jr., as a result of a conspiracy." Crucial to that finding was the committee's determination that Ray, a convicted felon and fugitive from justice, would never have undertaken such a risky task as murdering the nation's most celebrated and respected civil rights leader out of his own personal racial feelings, but would have undertaken it for money. As James Earl Ray's brother told the FBI shortly after the murder: "My brother would never do anything unless he was richly paid." In view of this estimate of Ray's character, the committee was compelled to take seriously Ray's confession to William Bradford Huie that he had been paid $2500 and promised another $12,000 from someone in New Orleans while he was stalking Dr. King, from one city to another, three months before the assassination.

In its final report on its investigation of the assassination of Dr. King, the House Select Committee on Assassinations delivered a stinging criticism of Hoover's FBI. In perhaps the harshest official rebuke ever leveled at J. Edgar Hoover and the agency he directed, the committee concluded that the FBI's activities in regard to Martin Luther King, Jr., and his civil rights movement "encouraged an attack on Dr. King"; the report went on to characterize the conduct of the FBI toward the civil rights leader prior to the assassination as "morally reprehensible, illegal, felonious, and unconstitutional."

46

From Los Angeles to Watergate

Two months after Martin Luther King, Jr., was murdered in Memphis, his principal champion in the government, Senator Robert F. Kennedy, was murdered in Los Angeles.

As we know, organized crime, and its tools in organized labor, had been gunning for Robert Kennedy since the summer and fall of 1962 when Jimmy Hoffa confided his plans to murder Kennedy to his Louisiana deputy, Edward Partin; and Carlos Marcello, in the presence of Edward Becker, threatened to have President Kennedy murdered in order to neutralize his brother Robert.

Not long after President Kennedy was killed, a plot to kill Robert, also, was apparently hatched by Frank Chavez, boss of Puerto Rico's Teamsters Local 901, that eventually came to naught. It was Kennedy aide Walter Sheridan, former leader of Kennedy's "get Hoffa" squad in the Justice Department, who had gotten wind of Chavez's plans through intelligence sources within the Teamsters. Apparently Chavez was going to fly to New York from Puerto Rico during one of Robert Kennedy's senatorial campaign appearances in 1964 and do the job, but was talked out of it at the last moment. Then, in early March 1967, as Jimmy Hoffa was about to be imprisoned, federal informants learned that Chavez planned to kill Robert Kennedy, Walter Sheridan, and Edward Partin if Hoffa went to jail. As March 7, the day Hoffa was due to be imprisoned, approached, the FBI placed Chavez under twenty-four-hour surveillance and arranged for police protection of Kennedy, Sheridan, and Partin. In the end, Chavez backed off again.

But that was far from the end of the plotting against Robert Kennedy's life. When, a year later, on March 16, 1968, Robert Kennedy announced he would run for the Democratic nomination for the presidency, a shudder ran through the underworld that soon gave rise to fresh new plots against the senator's life.

In May 1968, as Robert Kennedy's campaign for the nomination shifted into high gear, an inmate informant in the prison in which Jimmy Hoffa had been incarcerated, the Federal Penitentiary at Lewisburg, told the FBI that he had overheard Jimmy Hoffa and New York Mafia boss Carmine Galante, an ally of Carlos Marcello's, discussing a "mob contract to kill Bob Kennedy."

Then, around June 1, the FBI received word from an informant that "a wealthy southern California rancher who had ties to the Minutemen and detested Robert Kennedy because of his support of agricultural workers organizer Cesar Chavez, reportedly pledged $2000 toward a $500,000 to $750,000 Mafia contract to kill the senator in the event it appeared he could receive the Democratic nomination for President."

Although there is no direct evidence that Carlos Marcello was involved in putting together a contract on Robert Kennedy's life, Marcello most certainly did have a powerful motive. For he would have been a fool indeed if he had not suspected that in the event Robert Kennedy became President he would revive the INS's stalled deportation proceedings against him. Furthermore, it was widely suspected that if Kennedy won the presidency, he would quietly reopen the investigation of his brother's murder (although he never stated publicly that he would and continued to publicly endorse the conclusions of the Warren Report). If Marcello had something to hide on that score, a Robert Kennedy presidency would pose a decided threat.

Although Robert Kennedy had, for largely political reasons, publicly endorsed the Warren Commission's findings in the investigation of his brother's murder, we know that privately he expressed skepticism of those findings.

Kennedy once expressed that skepticism to former presidential aide Arthur Schlesinger, Jr., in an October 1966 meeting with him at P. J. Clarke's saloon in New York. According to Schlesinger, Kennedy told him at that time that he believed the Warren report "was a poor job," and he was wondering how long he could continue to "avoid comment on it, which he felt he could no longer endorse."

Later, not long after Jim Garrison announced his reinvestigation of the assassination, Robert confided to Schlesinger that he thought "Garrison might be on to something." Later still, in the midst of a discussion of the Garrison probe with a member of his staff, Frank Mankiewicz, Kennedy interrupted Mankiewicz as the aide was filling him in on some of the details of the Garrison investigation saying: "Well, I don't think I want to know." What was it Kennedy didn't want to know? Mankiewicz's information on Lee Harvey Oswald's connection to David Ferrie and David Ferrie's connection to Carlos Marcello?

Marcello also had powerful underworld connections in Los Angeles at the time of Robert Kennedy's murder. He had remained on friendly terms with West Coast mobster Mickey Cohen since the days when he and Cohen had sat together at the witness table during one of the McClellan Committee hearings on organized crime in 1959. It had been on that day that both Marcello and Cohen had encountered Robert Kennedy face to face for the first time. As chief counsel for the committee, Robert Kennedy had grilled them that day, one after the other, expressing a particular contempt for them both. Two years later, Kennedy, as attorney general, had identified Cohen as a priority target for prosecution and launched a full-scale investigation of him. By 1968 Cohen had become king of the rackets in Los Angeles, particularly gambling. He controlled the Santa Anita and Del Mar racetracks, whose domination by the mob was revealed by the Kefauver Committee hearings of 1951 and the McClellan Committee hearings eight years later. Both tracks were hooked up to the Marcello wire service and bookie network. It was at the Santa Anita track that Robert Kennedy's convicted killer, Sirhan Sirhan, had worked as a groom and exercise boy while piling up debts playing the horses in his spare time. Cohen had also been a friend of Oswald's killer, Jack Ruby, with whom he had shared the favors of the notorious nightclub stripper and ex-convict Juanita Slusher Dale Phillips Sahakian, known as Candy Barr, once a performer also at Pete Marcello's Sho-Bar in New Orleans.

Ruby often boasted of his friendship with the legendary Mickey Cohen and took pride in the fact that he had had an affair with a woman who had been engaged to the Los Angeles mobster. That Robert Kennedy was shot in a city whose underworld was dominated by a friend of Carlos Marcello's and a friend of Jack Ruby's has to be regarded as potentially significant.

Furthermore, Marcello was on good terms with a young rising star in the California Mafia's San Francisco operation, Sam Sciortino, with whom he would enter into a conspiracy to bribe a federal judge in 1979. As that conspiracy unfolded, a government undercover operative recorded a heated discussion between Sciortino, Marcello, and a cousin of Sciortino's from New Orleans, Phillip Rizzuto, that contained hints, which admittedly may have been vain boasts, that the California mob may have had something to do with the killing of Robert Kennedy.

The discussion, which will be reported in greater detail later on in this book, took place in Anthony Marcello's hunting lodge in Lacombe, north of New Orleans. The undercover operative and the three mobsters were talking about fixing the California judge when, at a lull in the discussion, Rizzuto said something about Teddy Kennedy announcing he was going to make a run for the Democratic nomination. The mention of the Kennedy name then triggered a furious outburst of hostility from the three mobsters, during which Bobby Kennedy's name came up and Sciortino remarked that the "bastard thought he was gonna put us all outa business." Then Rizzuto said, "Yeah, so we put *him* outa business," and they all laughed.

It was during the FBI's 1979 electronic surveillance of Carlos Marcello that the Justice Department learned conclusively that Carlos Marcello's hostility toward Bobby Kennedy was far from dead, despite what had happened to Bobby in Los Angeles a decade before. One day, as two undercover agents were driving with Marcello from Lafayette to New Orleans, the subject of the Kennedys came up and Carlos quickly launched into a tirade against Bobby Kennedy. He proceeded with an impassioned twenty-minute account of his "kidnapping" by Kennedy and his ordeal in the jungles of El Salvador and Honduras after Bobby had dumped him "with no money, no clothes, nothin,'" in Guatemala City.

Where was Carlos Marcello at the time of Robert Kennedy's assassination? Coincidentally he was on trial, as he had been at the time of John Kennedy's assassination. This time he was being tried in Laredo, Texas, for assaulting FBI agent Patrick Collins. Coincidentally again, Justice Department reports suggest that intense jury tampering was going on behind the scenes at Laredo, as it had been going on behind the scenes in New Orleans during Carlos's deportation-related trial at the time of the assassination of President Kennedy.

According to an FBI report on the trial and Carlos's stay in Laredo, Marcello had established his temporary headquarters in a luxurious suite in Laredo's Hotel Hamilton, where, when he was not in court, he received a steady stream of "visitors from New York and San Francisco." The report did not specify who those visitors were. It was while he was with his large entourage in his Hamilton Hotel suite that Carlos learned, shortly after 1:00 A.M. the morning of June

6, 1968, that his former nemesis and possible future threat had been shot, perhaps fatally, in Los Angeles. There are no reports on what Marcello did, or said, upon receiving the news.

Who else stood to lose a lot from a Robert Kennedy presidency? Obviously Jimmy Hoffa. A Nixon presidency would almost surely spring him from prison by means of an executive pardon. A Kennedy presidency would probably keep him behind bars for his full thirteen-year sentence.

Mickey Cohen also stood to lose big if Robert Kennedy made it to the White House. Kennedy had singled out Cohen for intensive investigation and eventual prosecution back in 1961 but had to abandon his campaign against him after his brother's assassination. Kennedy had been particularly revolted by reports he had received of Cohen's practice of getting his henchmen to sexually compromise movie stars, then blackmailing them. Chances were that President Robert F. Kennedy would have his attorney general make the pursuit of Cohen a top Justice Department priority.

But there were many others who stood to lose in a big way from a Bobby Kennedy in the White House. Among them were the leaders of the major Mafia families and the mob-controlled unions, especially the Teamsters and the Longshoremen; big oil, because Kennedy wanted to repeal the oil depletion allowance; the military industrial complex, because Kennedy wanted to pull out of the Vietnamese war; and the white segregationists, who were opposed to Kennedy's support of civil rights for blacks.

And yet who turned out to be the accused assassin? A Palestinian from Israel, whose family, originally from Jordan, had been forced out of Jerusalem as a result of Israeli harassment. A Palestinian who, immediately after the assassination, appeared to have no gripes against Kennedy during his initial questioning by the police and the FBI, but who, later on, suddenly claimed he was "betrayed" by Kennedy because of Kennedy's announced intention to send fifty phantom jet fighters to Israel to protect the Jewish nation from her Arab enemies.

There seemed to be something fishy about Sirhan Sirhan assassinating Robert Kennedy out of his own free will. With the range and power of Kennedy's known enemies, it appeared curious, to say the least, to many that Kennedy would be done in because of his support of Israel. Was Sirhan Sirhan's actual role in the assassination of Robert Kennedy a diversionary one? Was it, in reality, the role of fall guy, scapegoat, a decoy to distract witnesses and the investigative authorities from the real assassin? And who was ultimately behind the crime?

The bare known facts of the Robert Kennedy assassination as of 1988, and how the assassination might have been the result of a Mafia conspiracy, are as follows.

After celebrating his victory in the California primary on the night of June 5, 1968, with a speech in the Embassy Ballroom of the Los Angeles Ambassador Hotel, Robert Kennedy was escorted from the Ballroom to the serving pantry of the hotel, which his aides had decided to use as a shortcut to the Colonial Room, where Kennedy was scheduled to hold a midnight press conference.

It was the assistant maitre d' of the hotel, Karl Uecker, who escorted the victorious candidate into the pantry, holding Kennedy by the candidate's right hand. They were preceded by around twenty people, all heading for the press conference. Once in the pantry, Kennedy was joined by a security guard, Thane Cesar, who drew up close behind him, touching Kennedy's right elbow with his left hand. Around fifty other people followed.

As the group began to proceed through the pantry, an explosion of gunshots, sounding to many like firecrackers, suddenly erupted, possibly hitting Kennedy and definitely five others. Upon being hit, Kennedy wheeled around and reached for the security guard's throat, pulling off his clip-on tie, then collapsing with it on the floor. Mortally wounded, Kennedy died in Los Angeles Good Samaritan Hospital twenty-five hours later.

Kennedy's apparent assailant had emptied his eight-shot .22-caliber pistol in the general direction of the senator. It appeared to be a random, unaimed shooting, since in addition to Kennedy, five others fell to the floor in various parts of the pantry, victims of the young Palestinian's fire.

Despite firm evidence that at least one other gun had been fired in the pantry while Sirhan's .22-caliber pistol was going off, only Sirhan, among those in the pantry possessing firearms at the time, was arrested. Later he was tried, convicted, and sentenced to death for the murder of Senator Kennedy.

Testimony that at least one other gun had been fired in the pantry came from a variety of sources.

CBS News employee Don Schulman, who was standing behind Kennedy and the security guard at the moment of the shooting, testified that he saw the security guard draw his gun and fire back at Kennedy's assailant, hitting Kennedy two or three times, apparently by mistake. And a French journalist who had been present in the pantry during the shooting reported in *France Soir* that he saw the bodyguard fire at Kennedy "from the hip, as if in a western."

The autopsy report of Los Angeles County Coroner Thomas

Noguchi and Police Examiner Wayne De Wolfer concluded that the fatal wound in the back of Kennedy's head, under his right ear, had been fired from a gun the tip of whose barrel was less than an inch from the victim's head at the moment of the shooting. Their conclusion was based on an examination of the powder burns on Kennedy's head and on other parts of his body and his jacket, for Kennedy had been hit by three other bullets fired from behind at almost point-blank range in steeply upward trajectories.

And yet, virtually all the witnesses to the shooting claimed that Sirhan Sirhan was never closer to Kennedy than 2 or 3 feet and that he fired all his shots from the front. Karl Uecker, testified in court that Sirhan never got closer to Kennedy than about 2 feet in front of him and that after his second shot, he, Uecker, pushed Sirhan over a steam table so that from the third shot on, the Palestinian was firing wildly.

Subsequently, a prominent California criminologist, William Harper, found that since the .22-caliber bullet removed from Kennedy's neck was not the same type as the .22-caliber bullet removed from one of the five other persons wounded in the shooting, it was evident that "two .22-caliber guns were involved in the assassination."

Later, in 1976, certain FBI documents on the Robert Kennedy assassination obtained by Washington attorney Bernard Fensterwald, Jr., as a result of a Freedom of Information Act request, suggested that anywhere from ten to twelve bullets had been fired at the moment of the assassination. Since Sirhan's .22-caliber pistol held only eight bullets, the other .22-caliber bullets had to have been fired from another .22-caliber gun.

Since the autopsy revealed that all the shots that hit Kennedy had been fired at virtual point-blank range from behind, in upward trajectories traveling slightly from right to left, the shots, including, of course, the fatal one, had to have come from someone who was directly behind Kennedy when Sirhan commenced firing.

Subsequent investigation revealed that Thane Cesar did, in fact, own a .22-caliber revolver at the time of the shooting, although he had told the police he had sold it before the assassination.

Cesar also told the police that the gun witness Schulman had seen him draw at the moment of the killing was his .38 service revolver. But it would have been easy for security guard Cesar to have carried a .22 in his palm, or in another holster, perhaps an ankle holster, and to have shot Kennedy with this weapon from a crouched position close to and slightly below Kennedy's right shoulder as soon as Sirhan had begun firing. From all appearances, Kennedy had instinctively reacted to his attacker in the split second of consciousness remaining to him after the first bullets struck him, for a film of the ensuing melee fleetingly shows Kennedy grabbing at his bodyguard's throat before collapsing to the floor with Cesar's clip-on tie.

Later Cesar admitted on tape in an interview by Canadian journalist Theodore Charach, the principal private investigator of the crime, that he had pulled his .38-caliber service revolver out of its holster during the shooting, but denied firing it. Following the interview Charach claimed he was approached by an unknown gunman who ordered him to hand over all his evidence, or else. Charach refused. Nothing happened. Charach continued investigating.

It was Charach who first considered the possibility of Mafia involvement in the assassination, for during his investigation of the murder, he found out that for many years the Ambassador Hotel had been owned, in part, by investors connected to organized crime, and he gradually became aware of both Sirhan's and Cesar's underworld associations. Charach also found out that not long after the Kennedy assassination, the hotel's director of security disappeared and the hotel's files for 1968 were destroyed.

Although Thane Cesar has never been officially charged with the assassination of Robert Kennedy, almost all the serious students of the crime, including forensic pathologists, criminologists, university professors, and one of Sirhan's other victims, believe that Cesar was indeed Kennedy's sole killer.

Since Sirhan's conviction for the assassination, research conducted on the past associates of both Sirhan and Cesar has revealed that in the backgrounds of both men lurked the unmistakable presence of organized crime.

While Sirhan was working as an exercise boy at the mob-controlled Santa Anita racetrack, he had been befriended by a horse trainer, Frank Donneroumas, who eventually got him a job as a groom at a horse breeding ranch in Corona belonging in part to the mob-connected entertainer and Cuban exiles leader Desi Arnaz, who counted Mickey Cohen among his circle of acquaintances. In his diary, Sirhan repeatedly referred to Donneroumas as a good friend who made him happy by paying him sums of money for various unspecified jobs.

Frank Donneroumas fled the Corona ranch sometime before the assassination. When the FBI finally caught up with him, ten months after the crime, it discovered that he was, in reality, Henry Ramistella, a minor racketeer from New Jersey (he had a rap sheet containing records of arrests for theft, violation of banking laws, narcotics possession, and perjury) who had been banished from several eastern racetracks. In addition, the FBI found that both Ramistella and Sirhan Sirhan had been good friends with Corona ranch owner Desi Arnaz, a known acquaintance of Mickey Cohen's.

Further investigation of Sirhan's background revealed that although he had professed impassioned pro-Arab statements during his trial, he had never given the impression to his friends and associates before the assassination that he was particularly pro-Arab and had, in fact, even frequently expressed a distaste for Arab food, dress, and religion. What he seemed to be interested in, investigators found, was money, easy money, the sort of money Mafia guys paid for certain jobs. At the Santa Anita and Del Mar tracks he had fallen in with a bunch of gamblers and low-level mob types, for whom he would do odd jobs for pay. At the time of the Robert Kennedy assassination, his playing the horses at the track had plunged him deeply into debt.

At the top of the southern California racetrack gambling pyramid sat the notorious Mickey Cohen. One of Cohen's preferred rackets was to set up the sexual compromising of movie actresses, the big stars of the day, by secretly filming and recording them having sex with one of his stable of Italian studs, then either selling copies of the film and tapes underground at exorbitant prices, or blackmailing the actresses in question into preventing him from selling them. It was this activity that unexpectedly resulted in the killing of Lana Turner's Cohen-planted lover, Johnny Stompanato, by Miss Turner's teenage daughter one night in the actress's bedroom. Another of Cohen's victims was Marilyn Monroe, who Mickey once set up with two of his young studs, George Piscitelle and Sam LoCigno, around the time the Kennedy brothers had become sexually involved with the star.

Racetrack mobsters like Mickey Cohen were always on the alert for hard-up gamblers, big and small, who had to cover their debts. They were useful when he had to find someone to do some nasty job. Given Cohen's near-absolute control of the Los Angeles track, and track betting, and his almost daily presence at either Santa Anita or Del Mar, it is not unreasonable to assume that one of his guys at the track might have alerted him to the existence of this Arab exercise boy who had piled up a stack of debts. As a Jew, Cohen might be more aware than most of the possibilities of exploiting the young Palestinian's smoldering hatred of Israel to further his designs.

But what of Thane Cesar? How was he connected to the mob? In his extensive investigation of the Robert Kennedy assassination, Theodore Charach discovered that Cesar had strong ties to California mobster John Alessio, a friend of Mickey Cohen's and gambling king of

San Diego, who three years after the assassination would be sentenced to federal prison for skimming millions from San Diego racetrack revenues. Charach also established that Thane Cesar had not been a regular security guard at the Ambassador but was only called in occasionally by the hotel's management for temporary assignments. In 1987 Cesar confirmed this in an interview with investigative reporter Dan Moldea during which he told Moldea he had not worked at the Ambassador for four months when he was suddenly called by the hotel management to provide additional security for Robert Kennedy on the evening of June 5.

Given Sirhan's connections to associates of Mickey Cohen's, Cesar's connection to John Alessio, Cohen's long-standing relationship with the Ambassador Hotel, his fear of a Robert Kennedy presidency, and his friendship with such determined enemies of Kennedy's as Carlos Marcello and Jimmy Hoffa, it is not difficult to envision how a Mafia conspiracy to assassinate Robert Kennedy could have developed in which Sirhan could have been recruited to act as a decoy while expert marksman Thane Cesar delivered the coup de grace.

That Sirhan might have been hired to play a role is suggested by the fact that when the normally impecunious racetrack hand was arrested by the Los Angeles Police, he was found to have four crisp new $100 bills in his pocket and no personal identification. That Thane Cesar might have been hired from the outside is suggested by his sudden, last-minute recruitment to provide security for candidate Kennedy when it had become apparent that Kennedy would win the California primary and so stood a chance of winning the Democratic nomination.

Why didn't Sirhan's defense team vigorously point out that according to the autopsy report on Kennedy, their client could not have fired the fatal shot?

As it turned out, the conduct of Sirhan's lawyers was so suspicious in this regard that it reinforced the possibility that Robert Kennedy had been killed as a result of Mafia conspiracy. Sirhan's chief defense counsel, Grant Cooper, was involved at the time in defending Las Vegas mobster Johnny Roselli and several of his codefendants in the celebrated Friar's Club card-cheating case. Cooper would soon be convicted himself of perjury in connection with his conduct in that trial. During Sirhan's trial, Cooper made no effort to use the results of the autopsy report to exonerate his client from having fired the fatal shot and even agreed to have the record show that the fatal shot had been fired from Sirhan's gun.

Sirhan's other defense counsel, Russell Parsons, performed no better for his client than Cooper. Parsons, a noted mob attorney, had once been investigated for his connections to organized crime by Robert Kennedy when Kennedy was serving as chief counsel of the McClellan Rackets Committee and had once written a letter of recommendation for none other than *Mickey Cohen*. An analysis of his defense of Sirhan reveals that he played into the hands of the prosecution to such an extent that it seemed he was deliberately trying to throw his client's case. He made no effort to show that Sirhan might have been the tool of someone else and downplayed his association with racetrack gambling. Worst of all, he willingly went along with the prosecution's contention that the fatal head wound had been inflicted by Sirhan, even though both the Los Angeles coroner and the assistant maitre d' at the Ambassador Hotel had stated under oath that Sirhan had not been in the right position to fire the fatal shot.

But if Sirhan had been part of a mob conspiracy and felt he had not fired the fatal shot (at his trial he claimed he did not remember shooting Kennedy at all), why didn't he admit to having participated in such a conspiracy? The answer is simple. Aware of Oswald's fate in the Dallas Police Headquarters, he wanted to live, and he wanted his beloved mother and his brothers and sisters to live also.

Finally, let's examine the Los Angeles Police Department. Why did it destroy such key items of evidence as the bullet-scarred ceiling tiles, door frames, and swinging door center dividers, which it took from the Ambassador pantry shortly after the assassination? Was it because, as FBI photographs were to reveal, these items contained bullet holes that would conclusively prove that more than eight shots had been fired in the pantry on the night of June 5? And why did the department seal all records of its investigation of the assassination, denying public access to them for twenty years? (They were not released until April 19, 1988, and then over 2000 key documents were found to be missing.) Was it because of the department's suspected cozy relationship with Mickey Cohen and his henchmen at the time of the assassination, a relationship alluded to during a McClellan Committee hearing in March, 1959?

To this sorry tale must be added the predictable response of J. Edgar Hoover to Robert Kennedy's murder.

In view of his well-known dislike for Robert Kennedy, and his awareness of various conspiracy theories attempting to link the director of the FBI to the assassination of President Kennedy, Hoover wanted to wrap up his end of the case as soon as possible and reassure the public that there had been no conspiracy to assassinate the aspiring presidential candidate.

Thus, despite the fact that the FBI had received reports from reliable informants that the incarcerated Jimmy Hoffa had talked with a fellow inmate about a plot to kill Bobby Kennedy and that a southern California rancher had pledged money to a $500,000 to $750,000 Mafia contract to have Kennedy murdered, Hoover announced within days of the assassination that the Palestinian immigrant Sirhan Sirhan had murdered Senator Kennedy and that there was no evidence he had been aided or influenced by confederates. Case closed.

In the ensuing months Hoover read the autopsy report indicating that Kennedy had received his fatal wound at point-blank range from behind, and he read Karl Uecker's court testimony that Sirhan never got closer to Kennedy than 2 feet in front of him. And ten months after the murder Hoover finally received the bureau's report on Sirhan's closest friend and benefactor at the Santa Anita track and at Desi Arnaz's ranch in Corona and learned that he was Frank Ramistella, a mobster from New Jersey who had been working in California under an alias because as Henry Ramistella he had been banned from most of the racetracks in the country.

Furthermore Hoover had reviewed Edward Partin's testimony of 1962 about Jimmy Hoffa's plan to murder Robert Kennedy and had even turned it over to Robert and his brother the President. And in the spring of 1967 he had been shown Ed Reid's manuscript on organized crime in which Reid had reported Edward Becker's story of Carlos Marcello's threat to murder President Kennedy in order to neutralize his brother. Still, the director stuck by his original solution to the crime: Sirhan, the lone mad gunman, acting alone.

Hoover could not have helped envision the possible conspiracy that was slowly coming into focus, and its prospect must have horrified him: a possible Hoffa-Marcello-Cohen plot to murder the man who, while serving as attorney general, had ordered J. Edgar Hoover to go after Jimmy Hoffa, Carlos Marcello, and Mickey Cohen. What a scenario! *Any* solution to the crime would be more convenient for him than that. And so the infallible director of the world's greatest investigative organization proclaimed the dogma of yet another lone mad assassin, the third such public scourge to have arisen within five years.

By now, it had become apparent to students of the three assassinations that the United States was utterly powerless to cope with a well-conceived Mafia assassination conspiracy. For the awful truth was that the Mafia had compromised too many people in high places—too many politicians, too many law enforcement authorities—and, as we have seen, through the CIA's alliance with major Mafia leaders to assassinate the president of Cuba, had even compromised the United States government itself. Uncovering a Mafia conspiracy to assassinate a major American public figure would inevitably embarrass too many important people and could conceivably also embarrass the United States.

Noted Kennedy assassination researcher Peter Dale Scott put it another way when he wrote in 1979 that the assassination appeared to have been "plotted in such a way that to unravel it would threaten major governmental interests, thus inducing a cover-up."

The elimination of Robert F. Kennedy from the 1968 presidential race, and from all future presidential races, must have come as just as great a relief to Carlos Marcello as it was to Richard Nixon. Now Carlos's favorite politician, the candidate he had supported against Kennedy in 1960 to the tune of a $500,000 cash contribution to his campaign, was sure to take over the White House in 1969.

If ever there was a candidate for the presidency whom the mob wanted elected, it was Richard Nixon. Since the earliest days of his political career in California, Nixon had seemed to walk hand in hand with the Mafia, functioning with the family bosses in an apparent symbiotic relationship that was to last right down to his resignation from the presidency in 1974, and perhaps even beyond.

Before Carlos Marcello supported Nixon in his race against John Kennedy in 1960, Nixon had received steady support from the mob since his first entry into public life. It had been Mickey Cohen who had led the mob's backing of Nixon's congressional and senatorial campaigns in California in the forties and fifties. Cohen contributed $5000 of his own money to Nixon's first congressional campaign in 1946 and raised $75,000 from Las Vegas gamblers for Nixon's run for the Senate in 1950. Among Nixon's mob backers in 1968 were Allen Dorfman, the mob-connected Teamsters financial "consultant" from Chicago, Mafia-backed Teamsters vice president Tony Provenzano, and southern California Mafia figure John Alessio, who reportedly contributed $26,000 to Nixon's 1968 presidential campaign.

With Richard Nixon's accession to the presidency on January 20, 1969, the reach of Carlos Marcello's invisible government finally extended all the way into the White House.

For one of Nixon's first acts as President was to make one of his closest advisers, California mob attorney Murray Chotiner, a special assistant with his own office in the executive mansion. Chotiner had managed Nixon's congressional and senatorial careers in California and had been responsible for persuading Eisenhower to accept Nixon as his running mate in 1952. Meanwhile, Chotiner and his brother had earned their living defending some 221 organized crime figures from government prosecution in California.

As it turned out, it was through Chotiner, a friend also of Mickey Cohen's and John Alessio's, that Carlos Marcello was able to extend his reach into the White House. For Chotiner had remained on exceptionally good terms with Marcello's chief fixer and all-purpose handyman D'Alton Smith, whose two sisters were married to two of Carlos's top henchmen, Nofio Pecora and Joseph Poretto. Chotiner had played a major role in Marcello's and D'Alton Smith's drive to thwart Jimmy Hoffa's imprisonment. Thus, although few realized it at the time, the boss of the Louisiana Mafia and three of his highest-ranking henchmen had, in Murray Chotiner, a contact at the very center of political power in the United States. Combined with Irv Davidson's many-tentacled office in downtown Washington, and Russell Long's headquarters in the Senate office building, Carlos Marcello could consider himself well represented in the nation's capital.

When Marcello's reach to Chotiner's White House office was finally attained, Carlos was facing a two-year prison term for his conviction on August 9, 1968, of assaulting a federal official, namely FBI Special Agent Patrick Collins.

Throughout Nixon's first year in office and during much of his second, Carlos and his lawyers pulled every string at their command to get Carlos's two-year sentence reduced. Finally, under Nixon's attorney general, John Mitchell—the first man since the FBI was established in 1908 to hold the office of attorney general without undergoing an FBI investigation, thanks to a special request made to J. Edgar Hoover by the new President—a federal judge reduced Carlos's prison term to six months and made arrangements for him to spend that time at the Medical Center for Federal Prisoners in Springfield, Missouri.

Marcello was released from Springfield on March 12, 1971, just in time to lend the support of his invisible government to the effort to spring Jimmy Hoffa from prison. That effort was being led by Murray Chotiner, who, according to Walter Sheridan, first had to clear Hoffa's release with the Teamsters and with the Detroit and Chicago families before President Nixon could issue an official pardon.

By December 1971, Chotiner had finally gotten everyone into line and Richard Nixon was able to commute Hoffa's thirteen-year sentence to five via an executive pardon, allowing Hoffa to go free before Christmas. Thus was Robert Kennedy's campaign to put the

Teamsters chief behind bars for at least a decade undone by his own assassination. Hoffa's and Marcello's revenge against Kennedy was now complete.

Thanks to President Nixon's sympathetic administration, Jimmy Hoffa and Carlos Marcello were now free men. While Hoffa was destined to vanish into a scrap-metal compactor at the hands of his former mob associates, Marcello went on to the most prosperous period of his life, the seventies, a decade during which he became the richest and most powerful Mafia leader in the western hemisphere.

As all the world knows, the same cannot be said for Carlos's benefactor, the President. For a year after Carlos walked out of the Springfield Medical Center, a band of Nixon mercenaries—all of whom were veterans of the 1961 Bay of Pigs operation—was caught breaking into the Democratic campaign headquarters in Washington's huge Watergate apartment complex. Though not recognized for what it was at the time, the Watergate break-in would eventually precipitate a scandal and a crisis that put an attorney general behind bars and forced a President of the United States to resign his high office in ignominy and disgrace.

47

From Watergate to the Church Committee

NIXON: How much do you need?

DEAN: I would say these people are going to cost a million dollars over the next two years.

NIXON: We could get that.

DEAN: Uh huh.

NIXON: What I mean is, you could get a million dollars. And you could get it in cash. I know where it could be gotten.

DEAN: People around here are not pros at this sort of thing. This is the sort of thing Mafia people can do: washing money, getting clean money, and things like that. We just don't know about these things because we're...not criminals and not used to dealing in that business.

The discussion of March 21, 1972, between President Richard Nixon and his young counsel John Dean was taped for posterity in the oval office during the early stage of the Watergate crisis when the leader of the break-in team was attempting to blackmail the President of the United States.

John Dean had professed innocence of how to go about doing "the sort of thing Mafia people can do: washing money, getting clean money, and things like that," because "we're not criminals and not used to dealing in that business." But his boss, the President, knew exactly what to do and where to go to get $1 million in clean cash, because he had been there before. Nixon knew that in 1960 Carlos Marcello had come up with $500,000 for his campaign against Kennedy and had personally turned the cash over to Jimmy Hoffa, in the presence of Irving Davidson, for transmission to the Nixon war chest. More than likely, Nixon also knew that Carlos Marcello had raised $500,000 in clean cash in 1967 to finance an attempt to thwart Jimmy Hoffa's imprisonment and had even had his fixer, D'Alton Smith, offer a $1 million cash bribe to government witness Edward Partin to induce him to recant his testimony against Hoffa. Yes, Richard Nixon knew from whom he could obtain large sums of clean, washed cash with which to pay off his blackmailers. And he also knew how to reach one source in a flash. All he had to do was walk over to the east wing office he had provided for his, and D'Alton Smith's, friend, Murray Chotiner, or place a call to the good friend he shared with Carlos Marcello, Irv Davidson, whose office was but a stone's throw from the White House.

That Carlos Marcello did, in fact, have the ability to raise large amounts of clean cash in a hurry was revealed by Carlos himself in a conversation recorded by an FBI undercover agent in 1979. During a discussion with the agent about Marcello's plans to bribe a federal judge, Carlos gave his word to the agent that he could raise "$250,000 cash money in twenty-four hours" to pay off the judge.

By a curious coincidence, Carlos Marcello was in Washington testifying before the House Select Committee on Crime shortly before the event occurred that precipitated the so-called Watergate crisis.

That event occurred on June 17, 1972, when five men were arrested inside the offices of the National Democratic Committee Headquarters in Washington's Watergate apartment and office complex and were charged with burglarizing the committee's files. Later it was learned that all five of the burglars had once been associated with the CIA–Cuban exiles Bay of Pigs operation of 1961 and that at least two of them, Frank Sturgis (né Frank Anthony Fiorini) and Bernard Barker, were closely associated with organized crime, and specifically with two associates of Carlos Marcello's, Meyer Lansky and Santos Trafficante, Jr.

Sometime after the Watergate burglars were arrested, it was revealed that they were, in reality, a team of mercenaries taking their orders from a cadre of White House staffers and presidential reelection committee members, known as the "plumbers," who, in turn, took their orders from President Richard M. Nixon.

At first the purposes of the Watergate break-in appeared inscrutable. But as the conspiracy began to unravel, and it became apparent that the Nixon administration had been behind the break-in, its three main purposes gradually came into focus.

One was to gather as much damaging information as possible on Senator Edward Kennedy from the files of the chairman of the Democratic National Committee, Larry O'Brien. For 1972 was a presidential election year, and despite Edward Kennedy's 1969 fall from grace at Chappaquiddick, he was still considered a prime contender for the Democratic nomination. As such, Richard Nixon, who had always been paranoid about the Kennedys, regarded Teddy as an all but mortal threat. If young Kennedy's reputation had already been battered, chiefly from self-inflicted blows, Nixon wanted to destroy it beyond repair.

A second purpose, somewhat related to the first, was to find out what skeletons in the Republican closet the Democrats had in Chairman O'Brien's files, so that Richard Nixon could already begin selecting the most appropriate weapons to contend with them if and when the skeletons were exposed.

The third purpose was the most mysterious. It was revealed by Watergate burglar Frank Sturgis in an interview with journalist Andrew St. George, published in *True* magazine in 1974. In addition to "digging up dirt on top Democrats," Sturgis told St. George that he had been ordered by Nixon's plumbers to find "a thick secret memorandum from the Castro government," "a top secret 130-page document" from the office of Fidel Castro himself, which included a detailed account of the CIA's attempts to assassinate the Castro brothers.

The 1960–61 pact with the devil had surfaced once again.

That the Watergate break-in might have had something to do with the CIA-Mafia plots to assassinate Fidel Castro was hinted at also by the mastermind of the Watergate conspiracy, E. Howard Hunt, a former CIA official who had helped coordinate the Bay of Pigs invasion.

Among the taped conversations between Richard Nixon and his aides that had helped lead to the President's forced resignation was one between Nixon and presidential aide H. R. Haldeman hinting that Hunt might have had something to do with the CIA's plots against Castro's life.

NIXON (TO JOHN DEAN):   ...this Hunt; that will uncover a lot of things. You open that scab there's a hell of a lot of things.... This involves these Cubans, Hunt, and a lot of hanky-panky....

...just say very bad to have this fellow Hunt, ah, he knows too damned much, if he was involved—you happen to know that? If it gets out that this is all involved, the Cuba thing, it would be a fiasco. It would make the CIA look bad, it's going to make Hunt look bad, and it is likely to blow the whole Bay of Pigs thing which we think would be very unfortunate—both for the CIA and for the country....

Was "the whole Bay of Pigs thing" a euphemism for the CIA-Mafia plots to murder the president of Cuba?

Some students of the enigmatic reference believe it was. But one observer who was very close to President Nixon at the time, White House aide H. R. Haldeman, thinks it went beyond the CIA-Mafia plots against Castro. In his book *The Ends of Power,* Haldeman wrote that it seemed to him "that in all of those Nixon references to the Bay of Pigs he was actually referring to the Kennedy assassination."

Apparently Haldeman had wanted Nixon to reopen the investigation of the Kennedy assassination, and Nixon had turned him down. Later Haldeman did a bit of investigating himself. He learned that Castro had known of the CIA-Mafia attempts to assassinate him all along and had even threatened to retaliate against President Kennedy and his brother Robert in a speech he gave two and a half months before the assassination in Dallas. And he learned that "after the assassination the CIA launched a fantastic cover-up. The CIA literally erased any connection between Kennedy's assassination and the CIA." The results of Haldeman's private investigation led him to conclude that the Kennedy assassination was related to the CIA-Mafia plots to assassinate Castro and that Nixon knew it was. Hence Nixon's abject fear that E. Howard Hunt might "blow the whole Bay of Pigs thing which we think would be very unfortunate—both for the CIA and for the country." Hence Nixon's desperate need to keep Hunt quiet, to get that million dollars worth of clean, washed hush money into Hunt's hands.

The CIA's secret alliance with certain Mafia leaders to murder Fidel Castro was the dirtiest government secret in the history of the United

States. Because its implications were so politically explosive, those relatively few men in the U.S. government, the Mafia, and the Cuban exiles groups who knew about it strived continuously to maintain its secrecy at all cost.

According to the 1975 Interim Report of the Senate Intelligence Committee, the original government plot to kill Castro, without the aid of the Mafia, was conceived during the last year of the Eisenhower administration by CIA Director Allen Dulles and the chief of the CIA's western hemisphere division, J. C. King. The attempt on Castro's life was to be made in conjunction with a CIA-sponsored attack on Cuba by a military force of Cuban exiles. The entire initiative had been placed under the supervision of Vice President Richard Nixon, who was made action officer for the operation. Thus it could be said that Nixon was in on the ground floor of the plotting against Castro and what became, under Kennedy, the ill-fated Bay of Pigs Cuban exiles invasion.

Meanwhile various Mafia leaders, anxious to win back their lost investments in Havana, had conceived a plot of their own to destroy the new Cuban president. Chief among these were two associates of Carlos Marcello's, Santos Trafficante and Meyer Lansky, and Marcello himself. According to FBI reports, Marcello had made a deal with Cuban exiles leader Sergio Arcacha Smith whereby in exchange for Marcello's financial support, Arcacha Smith would reward Marcello with lucrative concessions in Havana if and when Smith succeeded a defeated Castro as president of Cuba.

Later it was alleged, on good authority, that soldier of fortune and future Watergate burglar Frank Sturgis had been involved in the Mafia's initial plots to destroy Castro.

By the late summer of 1960, the CIA had gotten wind of the Mafia plots against Castro and decided to integrate them with the agency's plans to eliminate the Cuban leader. The CIA then persuaded a mob-connected aide of Howard Hughes's, Robert Maheu, to approach John Roselli on the matter. Later Roselli brought Sam Giancana into the planning, and Giancana then got his friend Santos Trafficante involved, chiefly because Santos had valuable contacts still in Cuba. The CIA-Mafia alliance to murder the president of Cuba was born. The crucial meeting between the plotters was held in Florida in October 1960. Soon after John F. Kennedy's accession to the White House in late January 1961, the conspirators began drawing up concrete plans to murder Castro. The first attempt on his life was to be made just before the Cuban exiles' planned assault on the south coast of Cuba in mid-April 1961. Either by coincidence or design, it was during this crucial phase of the plotting that President Kennedy was receiving an average of two telephone calls a week from the girlfriend of Sam Giancana, one of the Mafia conspirators.

The records of the Senate Intelligence Committee do not indicate that Carlos Marcello was in on the original CIA-Mafia plot. However, as previously noted, in 1979 Marcello told a government undercover agent that he was involved in the conspiracy. Since in 1960 and early 1961 Carlos was contributing heavily to one of the Cuban exiles leaders who would participate in the April landing in the Bay of Pigs, Arcacha Smith, it is possible that Carlos's role was limited to that support. Whatever the case, it is reasonable to assume that Carlos was fully aware of the CIA-Mafia plot to kill Castro and probably lent much to the effort in the way of advice and financial support.

Was President Kennedy aware of the plotting against Castro in the winter and spring of 1961? From the 1975 Senate Intelligence Committee's report on the plots, it appears that Kennedy was most definitely aware that an attempt on Castro's life was going to be made in connection with the Cuban exiles invasion, but there are no records indicating he knew that Mafia leaders were involved in the plotting.

That Kennedy probably knew about what has come to be known as the Bay of Pigs assassination plot is borne out by the testimony of the CIA deputy director of plans at the time, Richard Bissell, who told a Senate committee that President-Elect Kennedy was fully briefed on the planned CIA–Cuban exiles invasion of Cuba by himself and CIA Director Allen Dulles in late November 1960. Bissell further testified that he believed Dulles briefed Kennedy in "oblique terms" on the plan to assassinate Castro just before the invasion. "How 'oblique' would the terms have been?" I asked a CIA official active in the planning of the invasion at the time. "Well," he replied, "Dulles probably said something to Kennedy like: 'And don't worry about Castro, Jack, we'll be taking care of him.'"

Kennedy's knowledge of the plan to assassinate Castro as an "auxiliary operation" of the Bay of Pigs invasion, to use Bissell's expression, was also alluded to in the Senate Intelligence Committee's interim report, which stated that immediately after the failure of the invasion, Kennedy met in the White House with "the Cuban involved in the underworld assassination plot and the Bay of Pigs invasion."

This Cuban is believed to have been the "asset" Trafficante had recruited for the CIA to assassinate Castro. But did Kennedy know at the time he met with him in the White House that he had been recruited by mobster Trafficante?

Not through official channels, it appears. But he could well have learned of Trafficante's role in the conspiracy to assassinate Castro from Giancana himself if we are to believe what Judith Campbell Exner, the girlfriend Kennedy shared with Giancana, revealed in 1988. In February 1988, Mrs. Exner broke her twenty-seven-year silence on the matter and told *People* magazine, through her amanuensis, Kitty Kelley, that she had acted as a courier between Kennedy and Giancana during the period of the planning and execution of the Bay of Pigs operation, and after, and that Kennedy had also personally met with Giancana during the same period. Though Mrs. Exner's revelations confirmed what many students of the Kennedy administration had suspected, her scenario of the Kennedy-Giancana-Exner relationship has yet to be confirmed.

Whatever the case, from April 1961 on, whoever knew about the CIA-Mafia conspiracy to murder Fidel Castro was in a position to blackmail the government at will. It was the one state secret the United States would do almost anything to hide.

That Carlos Marcello knew the secret is more certain than not. As he told an FBI undercover agent in 1979, he himself was one of the CIA-Mafia conspirators, along with his friend Santos Trafficante. And, as we know, he was a close friend and supporter of Cuban exiles leader Sergio Arcacha Smith, and other Cuban exiles bent on overthrowing the Castro regime.

Who else close to Marcello knew the secret? David Ferrie, his liaison with Arcacha Smith, undoubtedly knew it. And so did his New Orleans investigator Guy Banister, and Ferrie's and Banister's friend Lee Harvey Oswald, who allegedly had spoken of the plots at the Cuban and Soviet embassies in Mexico City in October 1963. If the need arose, they too would be in a position to blackmail the government.

The mastermind of the Watergate break-in, E. Howard Hunt, also knew the dirty secret. It had been Hunt, a CIA officer at the time, who had helped coordinate the Bay of Pigs invasion and had advised Richard Bissell to "assassinate Castro before or coincident with the invasion."

And, of course, President Richard Nixon, under whose aegis as Vice President the CIA-Mafia plots to kill Castro had been born, knew the secret. And he knew that E. Howard Hunt and his team of Watergate burglars knew the secret. So it became a matter of the utmost urgency for Richard Nixon to keep Hunt and his men quiet not only about the Watergate break-in conspiracy but also about dirty secret.

Thus did the President of the United States succumb t blackmail from the man who had coordinated the Bay

sion, participated in a conspiracy to kill Fidel Castro, and master-minded the Watergate break-in. E. Howard Hunt had Richard Nixon right where he wanted him. He would keep quiet about *Nixon's* plot to murder Castro in alliance with the mob, and he would keep his Watergate mercenaries quiet about who had ultimately been behind the attempt to burglarize the Democrats' headquarters. The initial cost of this presidential capitulation would be, in the words of John Dean: "$120,000 now, and much more in the years to come." It had been Dean who brought this unwelcome news from Hunt to the President during the damning conversation of March 1973:

NIXON: You say we're going to go down the road and no more blackmail and all the rest....It's better to fight it out instead....Don't you agree you better get the Hunt thing? I mean, that's worth it, at the moment...you better damn well get that done, but fast.

DEAN: Yes, but....

NIXON: Well, for Christ's sake *get it!*

How, and from whom, John Dean eventually got the hush money is still unclear. Before Nixon personally took over the problem of the payoffs, the Watergate burglar team had been supported by Cuban exiles leader Manuel Artime, one of the conspirators in the AM/LASH plot to assassinate Castro and E. Howard Hunt's closest associate.

After Nixon assumed responsibility for distributing the hush money, he had John Dean maintain the "cover" of Artime's "Cuban Defense Fund" as the source for the money to be distributed to the blackmailers, but turned to other sources for the necessary cash. As far as is known, some of the money was left over from the Committee for the Reelection of the President, whose finance chairman had been Maurice Stans; and some came from Nixon's mob-linked Cuban friend from Key Biscayne, Bebe Rebozo, who had ties to associates of Jimmy Hoffa's, Meyer Lansky's, and John Alessio's, and possibly also to Santos Trafficante and Carlos Marcello.

Whether any of the hush money came from Carlos Marcello, whose New Orleans operation had once been characterized by the *Saturday Evening Post* as the "Wall Street of the Cosa Nostra," is not known but is suspected. For quite a few people close to Nixon voiced their suspicions that the President was strongly backed by the Mafia at the time. Special Counsel to the President Charles Colson told the *Village Voice* in 1976 that the Mafia "owned Bebe Rebozo and got their hooks into Nixon early." Attorney General Mitchell's wife, Martha, told UPI: "Nixon is involved with the Mafia. The Mafia was involved in his election." And in 1976 the *Washington Post* declared that Nixon's chief of staff, General Alexander Haig, suspecting that Nixon was controlled by the Mafia, had ordered the Army's Criminal Investigation Command to investigate the President's possible connections to organized crime.

And then there was the sensational and unprecedented presidential pardon of New Jersey Mafia boss Angelo "Gyp" DeCarlo in December 1972, not long after Nixon's reelection. DeCarlo was known to the Justice Department to have been an exceptionally brutal killer who employed torture by meat hooks and disembowelment in carrying out his contract executions. DeCarlo, in fact, had no redeeming features, and no one in the Justice Department could understand why Nixon suddenly pardoned him after the 1972 election. It is now believed that he was pardoned either because he had been able to raise additional hush money for the President's blackmailers or because he had made a substantial contribution to Nixon's reelection campaign.

After Nixon resigned from the presidency in July 1974, various scholars and investigative reporters began sifting through the immense documentation of the Watergate conspiracy and cover-up and came up with some disconcerting hints of possible links between the Watergate conspiracy and the assassination of President John F. Kennedy.

First of all, it was discovered that all the Watergate burglars and their leader, E. Howard Hunt, had been involved in the failed Bay of Pigs invasion that had so seriously undermined the prestige of the John F. Kennedy administration and had caused the Cuban exiles and various Mafia bosses, despairing over recovering their lost concessions in Havana, to cry for Kennedy's blood. During the weeks following the Kennedy assassination the FBI received reports from three Florida informants that future Watergate burglar Frank Fiorini Sturgis had had dealings with Lee Harvey Oswald in Miami over the Cuban situation and had been involved in a unilateral Mafia conspiracy to assassinate Castro. It was also discovered that Watergate burglar Bernard Barker had been very much involved with the Cuban Revolutionary Council in Miami, a Cuban exiles group that was closely linked to the Cuban Revolutionary Democratic Front in New Orleans. This Louisiana group was supported by Carlos Marcello, who funneled his financial contributions to its leader, Sergio Arcacha Smith, through his jack-of-all-trades, David Ferrie. Investigators also found credible links between Barker and Jack Ruby.

As for Bay of Pigs veteran and Watergate mastermind E. Howard Hunt, *New York Times* journalist Tad Szulc claimed he had incontrovertible evidence that the CIA official who was with the CIA station in Mexico City at the time of Oswald's visit in October 1963 was E. Howard Hunt. Szulc also claimed that Hunt probably knew something about why the CIA destroyed its tape-recordings of wiretapped calls to the Soviet Embassy of a man representing himself as Lee Harvey Oswald, but who turned out not to be Oswald, and about how it came to be that the CIA had photographed a man purported to be Oswald going to and from the embassies, who, it was later ascertained from photographs, was emphatically not Oswald.

But there were still other disconcerting links between the principals in the Watergate scandal and circumstances surrounding the Kennedy assassination. It was the Committee to Investigate Assassinations, headed by Washington attorney Bernard Fensterwald, Jr., that turned up most of these connections.

For one, the committee determined that Nixon's attorney general and fellow Watergate conspirator, John Mitchell, had ordered the Justice Department to block the release of vitally important ballistic evidence pertaining to the Kennedy assassination—evidence which had never been turned over to the Warren Commission by the FBI on the grounds of "national security." The evidence in question had, in reality, nothing to do with national security. It was simply evidence of the FBI's spectrographic analyses of the bullet and bullet fragments recovered by the FBI, and others, after the shooting. These analyses could conclusively demonstrate whether more than one gun had been fired at President Kennedy and Governor Connally. That the FBI had never turned over this evidence to the Warren Commission was, of course, deeply suspicious. But perhaps equally suspicious was Attorney General Mitchell's final position on the matter of the FBI's release of the spectrographic evidence. After a series of unsuccessful Freedom of Information lawsuits brought against the Justice Department by Kennedy assassination scholar Harold Weisberg to obtain release of the FBI's spectrographic analyses, the Justice Department shocked many assassination investigators by declaring: "In this instance the Attorney General of the United States has determined that it is not in the national interest to divulge these spectrographic analyses." Case closed.

The Watergate scandal "broke" during the second week of January

1973, as Richard Nixon was about to be inaugurated for a second term. There followed a frantic effort on the part of the President and his closest aides to cover up the conspiracy surrounding the break-in. Bernard Fensterwald's committee found, to its astonishment, that the cover-up involved no fewer than *eleven* former members and staffers of the Warren Commission. On the surface, at least, it seemed as if Richard Nixon and Company, in their effort to cover up the Watergate conspiracy, instinctively gravitated for assistance to the men who had helped Hoover, albeit perhaps unwittingly, cover up the Kennedy assassination conspiracy. What, then, did Fensterwald's committee specifically find?

It found that on the night of March 23, 1973, not long after Nixon's discussion with John Dean about obtaining hush money to pay off blackmailers E. Howard Hunt and the Watergate burglars, Nixon and one of his top aides, Charles Colson, considered appointing none other than J. Lee Rankin, former general counsel of the Warren Commission, as special prosecutor in the Watergate conspiracy case. Although Nixon ultimately decided not to appoint a special prosecutor at that time, he did ask Rankin later on if he would help prepare the presidential tapes for the Watergate investigation.

Fensterwald's committee also noted that the two other men Nixon considered for appointment as Watergate special prosecutor, one of whom was finally named to that position, were both associated with the Warren Commission. One was commission member John J. McCloy, who declined the appointment, and the other was former Warren Commission special counsel, Leon Jaworski, who had been instrumental in preventing the Warren Commission from investigating, in depth, an alleged connection between Oswald and the FBI, who accepted.

Furthermore, Fensterwald's investigators observed that Presidential Counsel John Dean hired Warren Commission Administration Aide Charles Shaffer as his defense counsel, and Presidential Assistant John D. Ehrlichmann hired Warren Commission Senior Counsel Joseph A. Ball as his defense counsel.

Finally Fensterwald's research team noted that upon the forced resignation of Vice President Spiro Agnew, after it was discovered that he had accepted kickbacks when he had been governor of Maryland, Nixon appointed former Warren Commission member Gerald Ford, a particularly strong advocate of the "lone assassin" thesis, as his new Vice President. Later, when everything began going against him and his impeachment seemed assured, Nixon asked former Warren Commission Counsel Arlen Specter, author of the "magic bullet" theory, and a man who had misrepresented crucial evidence while serving on the Warren Commission, to head his defense team and approved former Warren Commission Senior Counsel Albert Jenner as his impeachment counsel. It had been Jenner who had been in charge of investigating Lee Harvey Oswald's "background history, acquaintances, and motives" for the commission and yet had failed to discover Oswald's family connections to organized crime in New Orleans, specifically Oswald's and his uncle's association with the Marcello gambling network at the time of the Kennedy assassination.

That so many attorneys who had been associated with the Warren Commission investigation became involved in the Watergate investigation a decade later was not necessarily suspicious. The coincidence may well have had a benign explanation: that since the Warren Commission attorneys had gained unique experiences in helping to conduct Washington's foremost criminal investigation of the sixties, it was only reasonable they would be called upon to help conduct Washington's foremost criminal investigation of the 1970s. Still, it was well known by the time of the Watergate scandal that the Warren Commission had perpetrated a cover-up.

All of which leads us to Richard M. Nixon and his curiously suspicious FBI testimony after the assassination.

At the time of John F. Kennedy's murder, Richard Nixon, the narrowly defeated Republican presidential candidate, was an embittered man who was living, by his own admission, "in the shadows." Painfully aware of the questionable tactics the Kennedy forces had employed to defeat him, including their enlistment of Sam Giancana's crucial aid in delivering the vote of Cook County, Illinois, Nixon had become a vengeful man ready to do what he could to get back at the Kennedys.

Having resumed his law practice upon joining the New York law firm of Mudge, Rose, Guthrie, and Alexander, Nixon became counsel to a number of major corporations, one of which was Pepsi-Cola. On November 20, 1963, he had flown to Dallas to attend a carbonated beverage bottlers convention, remaining in the Texas city two and a half days and two nights. Then, on the morning of November 22, some three hours before President Kennedy was killed, he returned to New York on an American Airlines flight.

Approximately three months later, on February 28, 1964, the FBI interviewed the former Vice President in regard to an allegation made by Marina Oswald that her husband had told her he wanted to shoot Nixon in the spring of 1963. The bureau turned its brief report on the interview over to the Warren Commission.

Mr. Nixon advised that the only time he was in Dallas, Texas, during 1963 was two days prior to the assassination of President John F. Kennedy.

Three years later, during an interview with journalist Charles Witcover, Nixon related a slightly different version of his whereabouts on the day of his former rival's assassination, telling the journalist he had flown to Dallas the day before the assassination and had returned to New York early the following morning, when, in reality, he had flown to Dallas two days before the assassination.

What has, of course, puzzled assassination investigators is the fact that according to the FBI interview, Richard Nixon, of all people, apparently forgot where he had been on November 22, 1963, of all dates! And three years later Nixon lied again about his November 20–22 trip to Dallas, this time to a journalist. Why the two lies about the Dallas visit? Was Richard Nixon hiding something?

Upon learning of Nixon's contradictory testimony in regard to his November 20–22 stay in Dallas, Kennedy assassination researchers took note that the Marcello-financed politician was in Marcello territory during the days and hours preceding the murder of his former rival. Also, one of Nixon's fellow bottlers conventioneers, Edward Meyers, a Pepsi-Cola bottler from New York, spent part of the evening of November 21 in the company of Jack Ruby, an encounter that was, more than likely, an irrelevant coincidence, yet, nevertheless, has been one that has intrigued Kennedy assassination researchers for obvious reasons.

However, the extraordinary range and number of links connecting individuals associated with the Bay of Pigs invasion of Cuba, the CIA-Mafia plots to assassinate Castro, the alleged Mafia conspiracy to murder President John F. Kennedy, and President Nixon's Watergate conspiracy and cover-up appear to go beyond mere coincidence. What was the ultimate connective agent linking these conspiracies? Although we are not yet sure what it was, the fact that *some* connective agent linking all four conspiracies existed now appears to be a near certainty.

That feeling was further strengthened by the startling revelations of the 1975 Senate Select Committee to Study Government Operations with Respect to Intelligence Activities, known as the Church Committee, after its chairman, Senator Frank Church of Idaho. For it was the Church Committee that finally revealed to the world the dirty secret of the CIA-Mafia plots to murder Fidel Castro. The committee also established that while it believed the Kennedy brothers had not given the CIA authorization to contract with gangsters to murder Castro, the Kennedys had explicitly ordered the CIA to "get rid of Castro" and told the agency, in Robert Kennedy's words, that "no time, money, effort, or manpower should be spared toward the overthrow of Castro's regime."

Post–Church Committee research has taken the question of the Kennedy brothers' involvement in the plots to kill Castro a few steps further. According to testimony received by me from one of the CIA officials directly involved in the Castro assassination plots, it is now reasonably certain that both President Kennedy and his brother, the attorney general, gave their full stamp of approval to the so-called AM/LASH plot against the Cuban president in 1963. And according to the still unconfirmed 1988 testimony of President Kennedy's former mistress, Judith Exner, Kennedy might well have even been aware of the CIA-Mafia plots also.

It was during the Church Committee's investigation of the CIA's assassination plots, that the committee found out the CIA-Mafia plots to assassinate Castro were never reported by the FBI, the CIA, or Robert Kennedy to the Warren Commission when it was investigating the assassination of President Kennedy. Furthermore, it discovered that President Kennedy had been carrying on what appeared to be either a friendship or a secret love affair during his presidency with a girlfriend of one of the Mafia conspirators in the CIA's plots, Sam Giancana.

These discoveries, and others, led the senators to establish a subcommittee to investigate the response of the FBI and the CIA to the assassination of President Kennedy, which, in turn, led to a virtual collapse of the government's faith in the Warren Report.

Senators Richard Schweiker and Gary Hart became the driving force behind the Kennedy assassination subcommittee. What they found out, in brief, was that both the FBI and the CIA had lied to, misled, and withheld vital information from the Warren Commission to such an extent as to fatally cripple the commission's investigation and virtually prevent it from establishing the truth behind the assassination of John F. Kennedy.

Meanwhile, as the Church Committee's investigations unfolded, opening up more and more cans of worms, two of its most important witnesses were murdered, one just before he was about to testify before the committee for the first time, the other before his second scheduled appearance.

CIA-Mafia anti-Castro conspirator, and Chicago mob boss, Sam Giancana, was gunned down in the basement den of his suburban Chicago home on July 19, 1975, the day before staff members of the Church Committee were to meet him to make arrangements for his appearance before the committee in Washington five days later.

Almost a year after Giancana's murder, one of Giancana's partners in the CIA-Mafia operation against Castro, Johnny Roselli, met with Senator Schweiker and other members of the Church Committee in Washington's Carroll Arms Hotel and told them that he had good reason to believe that Cubans associated with Castro and Trafficante had been behind the Kennedy assassination and that he would testify to this effect at his next scheduled appearance before the committee. Three months later, and about ten days after a dinner in Miami with Trafficante, Roselli was murdered on board a yacht belonging to a Trafficante associate. His dismembered body was stuffed into a chain-weighted oil drum and dumped over the side. It was the first time in the history of the United States Senate that a Senate committee witness had been murdered.

Between the Giancana and Roselli murders, the committee also absorbed the jolt of Jimmy Hoffa's disappearance. Although Hoffa had not been scheduled to testify before the committee, he knew Giancana, Roselli, and Trafficante and had supported the mob's effort to destroy the Castro regime. Furthermore, many informed observers suspected he might have played a role in one or both of the Kennedy assassinations. His disappearance on July 30, 1975, meant that an important potential committee witness had been lost. Hoffa's body was never found.

Still, the Senate, to its everlasting credit, had discovered, verified, and revealed to the world the dirtiest secret ever held by the government of the United States: that its Central Intelligence Agency, originally acting on a decision taken by the executive branch of the Eisenhower administration, had entered unilaterally into a secret alliance with some of the most vicious Mafia leaders in the world to murder the president of a neighboring country.

The connective agent linking the four major conspiracies of the Bay of Pigs invasion, the CIA-Mafia operation to murder Castro, the alleged Mafia murder of President Kennedy, and the Nixon-inspired attempted burglary of the Democratic party's Watergate offices was finally beginning to come into focus. The long suspected connective was the combined forces that had generated the dirty secret: the sinister alliance between the Mafia, the CIA, and the executive branch of the United States government.

Having discovered and revealed the United States's pact with the devil, it was now up to the Congress to relate its discovery to the crime of the century. The time had come to find out what forces were behind the assassination of President John F. Kennedy.

To the surprise of many, but not to all, the trail of that effort would lead straight to Carlos Marcello.

In New Orleans on September 8, 1970, Carlos Marcello (left) testifies before a Louisiana legislative committee investigating charges of Mafia influence in the state government. One of Marcello's attorneys, Dean Andrews (behind Marcello, with dark glasses), testified in 1964 that he received an anonymous call the day after the Kennedy assassination asking him to represent Lee Harvey Oswald. *(AP/Wide World Photos)*

The funeral of Carlos Marcello's mother in Gretna, Louisiana, in September 1971. Marcello family members from left to right at top: brothers Anthony, Sammy, and Vincent; daughters Louise and Florence; and Carlos. Carlos's son, Joseph, is at the bottom left. Pallbearers at the right are Carlos's nephews. *(AP/Wide World Photos)*

New Orleans, February 1, 1975. Carlos Marcello leaves federal court with his daughter Jacqueline after being acquitted of conspiring to take over a New Orleans nightclub by force. *(AP/Wide World Photos)*

FBI Special Agent Harold Hughes (left) being congratulated by former FBI Director Clarence Kelley (1973–1978) for his successful ten-year investigation of Carlos Marcello. In 1979 Hughes coordinated the undercover operation that resulted in Marcello's conviction and imprisonment. *(FBI Photo)*

Carlos Marcello (right) and veteran Washington lobbyist Irving Davidson, defendants in the BRILAB trial, leave federal court in New Orleans after a pretrial hearing, December 9, 1980. The BRILAB undercover operation revealed that Davidson, a friend of both Lyndon Johnson and Richard Nixon, had been in close touch with Carlos Marcello since 1959. *(AP/Wide World Photos)*

Carlos Marcello after leaving federal court in New Orleans, where a judge refused to halt prosecution in the FBI's BRILAB case, December 26, 1980. *(UPI 12/26/80 Jerry Lodrgues)*

Joseph Hauser, the chief government witness against Carlos Marcello in the BRILAB trial. Hauser was the FBI's principal undercover operative. Carlos Marcello was convicted at two trials and is currently serving a cumulative seventeen-year sentence in a federal prison. *(AP/Wide World Photos)*

The principals in the 1979–1980 FBI undercover operation against Carlos Marcello meet for lunch at Impastato's Restaurant in Metairie, Louisiana. From left to right: attorney Vincent Marinello, Carlos Marcello, FBI undercover agents Larry Montague and Mike Wacks, and government informer Joseph Hauser. They are discussing the bribing of a Louisiana public official. *(Byron Humphrey)*

Carlos Marcello after hearing FBI
tapes of his conversations played in
New Orleans Federal Court, May
30, 1981. *(AP/Wide World Photos)*

New Orleans, August 3, 1981.
Carlos Marcello leaves federal
court after being found guilty
of conspiracy, bribery, and
racketeering. With him is his wife,
Jacqueline. *(AP/Wide World Photos)*

John Volz, U.S. attorney for the
eastern district of Louisiana,
victorious prosecutor of Carlos
Marcello in the New Orleans
BRILAB trial, summer of 1981.
(AP/Wide World Photos)

Irving Davidson kids around with a
New Orleans Saints sticker on his
back after being acquitted of federal
conspiracy and racketeering
charges, August 3, 1981. *(AP/Wide
World Photos)*

A dejected Carlos Marcello leaves federal court with Jacqueline after Judge Morey Sear sentenced him to ten years in prison, January 25, 1982. Marcello's attorney, Russell Schonekas, is at the right. *(AP/Wide World Photos)*

G. Robert Blakey, attorney in the Justice Department under Attorney General Robert F. Kennedy (1960–1964) and chief counsel of the House Select Committee on Assassinations (1978–1979). Blakey drafted the Racketeer-Influenced and Corrupt Organizations (RICO) Act of 1970, which has facilitated the prosecution of organized crime figures such as Carlos Marcello. *(Courtesy G. Robert Blakey)*

La Louisiane Restaurant in New Orleans' French Quarter, owned by Joseph and Sammy Marcello. Two doors away is Felix's Oyster Bar. (*John Olivier*)

Lenfants Restaurant and Nightclub on the outskirts of mid-city New Orleans, owned today by Joseph Marcello. (*John Olivier*)

Carlos Marcello's only son, Joseph, at a suburban New Orleans country club in 1987. When "Little Joe" was only in his mid-twenties, his father Carlos transferred $3 million worth of assets to him. *(A. J. Valenti)*

The home of Mr. and Mrs. Carlos Marcello, in Metairie, Jefferson Parish, as it appeared in 1988. The entire Marcello family gathers here every Sunday afternoon for lunch. *(Charles Nes © 1988)*

48

A Precarious Power

"Carlos Marcello, now 60, not only continues to dominate Louisiana, but grows richer and richer each year at public expense." So proclaimed a major article on Marcello in the April 10, 1970, issue of *Life* magazine.

"Carlos Marcello is now the second most powerful Mafia leader in the United States, ranking just after Carlo Gambino of New York," proclaimed investigative journalist Victor Riesel in his syndicated column a month later.

"We believe that Carlos Marcello has become a formidable menace to the institutions of government and the people of the United States," declared the House Select Committee on Crime in June 1972.

From the late sixties through the mid-seventies Carlos Marcello came under steadily mounting attention and attack from both the nation's press and the federal government. As a result, Carlos was compelled to conduct business under a constant state of siege.

For Carlos, each day held skirmishes of varying degrees of intensity, with enemies ranging from the Congress of the United States to the Immigration and Naturalization Service to a determined FBI agent who had sworn to get him, by the name of Harold Hughes. But despite the power and tenacity of the forces bent on his destruction, Carlos, in the end, was able to register more victories over his enemies than defeats. By the mid-seventies he had still managed to vastly increase his personal wealth and further strengthen his hold on the political machinery of his state.

However, certain forces and circumstances beyond Marcello's control were already gathering strength that would lead eventually to his abrupt and humiliating fall from power. Rich "beyond the dreams of avarice," politically influential enough to defy the government of the United States, Carlos Marcello in the mid-seventies was, unknown to him, at best in a position of precarious power.

What major challenges did Carlos Marcello survive from the late sixties on?

For one, we know he survived District Attorney Garrison's abortive probe of the Kennedy assassination, relatively unnoticed and certainly unscathed, despite the fact that three of Garrison's major suspects—Oswald, Ruby, and Ferrie—had connections to his criminal organization. For another, he survived—by what means we do not yet know—the most formidable threat to his power since the accession of John F. Kennedy to the White House: Robert F. Kennedy's quest for the presidency in 1968. And then there was the book, and all the newspaper and magazine articles. Mercifully Ed Reid's account of Edward Becker's allegation, published in *The Grim Reapers* in 1969, did not reach a very wide audience and did not generate any immediate repercussions, thanks to J. Edgar Hoover's refusal to investigate it. But the *Life* feature article on Marcello and his criminal network did momentarily paralyze his influence in the State House at Baton Rouge and temporarily cramp his style.

And then, not to be ignored among his victories of the seventies, Carlos had made a fool out of the Congress of the United States for a third time. Appearing in Washington in June 1972, shortly before the Watergate break-in, as one of the principal witnesses before the House Select Committee on Crime, which was then investigating organized crime's infiltration of professional sports, Marcello assumed his semiliterate simpleton mask that had always thrown would-be investigators off his scent in the past. The veteran of the La Stella Mafia summit told his bewildered congressional inquisitors that he was "not in no Mafia," did not know what a racketeer was, had no business interests outside of Louisiana, never contributed funds to political figures to gain influence, did not know anyone in the rackets outside of Frank Costello and Santos Trafficante, was the victim of "fake statements" by the press, and, to sum it all up, was "not in no racket and not in no organized crime."

As for Carlos's interminable battle over the Immigration and Naturalization Service's standing deportation order against him, as long as he had the cagey Jack Wasserman, the well-connected Irving Davidson, and the obliging Senator Russell Long behind him, he could consistently make fools out of the immigration people too. Since 1953 the INS had been trying to deport him, and twenty years later, after the expenditure of millions of dollars on both sides, it was still no closer to throwing him out of the country than it had been when it issued its first deportation order. Carlos Marcello was still officially an illegal alien, though he had benefited from the American system to the tune of millions upon millions of dollars.

By the mid-seventies, then, Marcello could take satisfaction in having survived all major threats to his power. Sworn enemies like Aaron Kohn remember him during this period acting just as cocky and full of himself as ever. When Kohn would occasionally run into Carlos, as was easy to do in the villagelike milieu of New Orleans, Marcello would walk briskly up to him, extend his hand, and say, in his heartiest tone of voice: "Hello, *Kohn!*"

Yet, despite Carlos's victories, despite his seemingly unquenchable bravado, forces had been gathering momentum that would crest in the late seventies and flood into Carlos's world with an insistence even his formidable defenses could not withstand.

For one, it was in the early to mid-seventies that the Federal Bureau of Investigation finally went into high gear in its investigation of Carlos Marcello and his criminal organization. In 1970, the year in which Carlos was sent off to Springfield for attempting to assault Patrick Collins, the Justice Department established a new, beefed-up organized crime strike force in New Orleans. Then, in June 1971, about two months after Marcello's release from Springfield, the FBI put a tough, brilliant young agent in charge of the New Orleans strike force's effort to nail Marcello. His name was Harold Hughes, and he immediately vowed to one day put Carlos Marcello behind bars.

Until the advent of Harold Hughes, the New Orleans FBI office had a marked tendency, as we know, to look the other way so far as the activities of Carlos Marcello were concerned. But from the summer of 1971 on, the New Orleans FBI never let the Louisiana Mafia boss out of its sight.

To let Carlos know he meant business, Hughes would drop into Marcello's Town & Country office from time to time, unannounced, to inform him that he was watching his every move and that he had better not step out of line. When Hughes would be escorted into Marcello's office by the secretary, the barrel-chested Mafia boss would greet him with a booming "Hello, *Hughes!*" and tell him to sit down. Then, leaning over his desk and meeting Hughes's eyes unflinchingly, he would remind the FBI agent he was "not goin' to fall into no trap."

The death of J. Edgar Hoover on May 2, 1972, some six weeks before the Watergate break-in, removed the last impediment to the FBI's campaign against Marcello, and Carlos began to come under increased pressure from the government. In the summer of 1972 the INS reaffirmed once more its deportation order against Carlos, a House Committee began looking into the Marcello organization's infiltration of professional sports, and in 1974 Harold Hughes's strike force began cracking down on Carlos's attempts to illegally take over several New Orleans bars and nightclubs.

Meanwhile there were also new developments on the Kennedy assassination front. In 1973 West Coast television news reporter Peter Noyes published his *Legacy of Doubt,* the first book dealing with the Kennedy assassination to convincingly advance the possibility that Carlos Marcello might have played a significant role in the crime. Ed Reid's *The Grim Reapers,* published in 1969, had only hinted at such a possibility, in one chapter of a long book covering organized crime from coast to coast. Although Noyes's book did not attract a large audience, it had considerable impact on the critics of the Warren Report, and there were legions of them, despite the Garrison debacle. Later, in 1976, an Italian documentary film, produced in Rome, titled *The Two Kennedys,* came out that emphatically blamed the murders of the Kennedy brothers on the Mafia, specifically on Carlos Marcello, at a time when suspicions of possible Marcello involvement in the assassination were restricted to relatively few people in the United States. The film's treatment of Marcello and Mickey Cohen was surprisingly well documented, containing footage that had never appeared in a television film before.

Then in 1973 the Watergate scandal broke, and in July of the following year President Nixon was forced to resign. It was during the Watergate investigation that the American people learned for the first time that the FBI and the CIA were quite capable of lying to save their skins and were both adept at covering up criminal activity.

This new public awareness of corruption in high places was reinforced by the revelations of the Church Committee in 1975 and 1976. Now Americans learned that their Central Intelligence Agency had plotted to assassinate the president of the Congo, Patrice Lumumba, had plotted with opposition forces in the Dominican Republic to assassinate the president of that country, Rafael Trujillo, and had furthermore plotted with several U.S. Mafia leaders to assassinate Fidel Castro.

Linked to these reports of sinister CIA undertakings was yet another rumor the senators wanted to get to the bottom of: that the CIA, along with the FBI, had lied to, misled, and withheld vital information from the Warren Commission during its investigation of the assassination of President John F. Kennedy.

The shocking Watergate revelations of corruption at the highest levels of government, the Senate Intelligence Committee's discovery of the CIA-Mafia plots to assassinate Castro and the deceptions practiced by the FBI and the CIA on the Warren Commission, the sudden deaths of certain key witnesses—the murders of Mafia bosses Sam Giancana and Johnny Roselli and the alleged heart attack of the CIA's William Harvey, the official in charge of the CIA-Mafia plots—all of these events so disturbed several members of the Congress that for the first time since the issuance of the Warren Report, a movement was initiated within the Congress to form a committee to reinvestigate the assassination of John F. Kennedy.

Among those most concerned with this movement were Senators Gary Hart and Richard Schweiker and Representatives Thomas Downing and Henry Gonzales. They were joined, in turn, by leaders of the congressional black caucus, who were anxious to have Congress also investigate the mysterious assassination of Martin Luther King, Jr., by another alleged "loner" who appeared to be too well financed for an escaped convict with no personal financial resources of his own.

To these must be added the voices of the most informed and persistent critics of the Warren Report: Mark Lane, Harold Weisberg, Richard Popkin, Sylvia Meagher, Josiah Thompson, Peter Noyes, Bernard Fensterwald, Jr., Peter Dale Scott, and Paul L. Hoch, all of whom, as concerned private citizens, had made significant discoveries that convincingly challenged the Warren Commission's findings.

Finally, after much wrangling, the 94th Congress in September 1976 established the House Select Committee on Assassinations to investigate the assassinations of King and Kennedy. Representative Thomas Downing was named chairman of the committee with the understanding that upon the return of the Congress to session in 1977, he would be succeeded by Representative Henry Gonzales. Chosen as chief counsel of the new assassinations committee was the brilliant Philadelphia prosecutor Richard A. Sprague, who had conducted the trial of United Mine Workers President Tony Boyle for the brutal murder of rival union leader Jake Yablonski and his wife and daughter, and had secured his conviction. Sprague immediately went to work, hiring a staff of 170 lawyers, investigators, and researchers and submitting to the House a 1977 budget for a whopping $6.5 million that included substantial funding for sophisticated new eavesdropping equipment.

There followed a period of acrimonious debate between Downing and Gonzales over Sprague's budget, the size of his staff, and how the investigations should be conducted. All of this caused such dissension among the other committee members that, for a while, the survival of the committee was seriously threatened.

In the end, Downing was forced to resign as chairman. Gonzales took his place but then was forced to resign himself over his unpopular insistence on retaining the controversial Richard Sprague as chief counsel. The House then named Representative Louis Stokes of Ohio to take Gonzales's place. Stokes, a leading member of the black caucus, promptly fired Sprague and named G. Robert Blakey, a professor of law at Cornell and a nationally recognized authority on organized crime, to take his place. Then, on March 30, 1977, the House approved the formation of a reconstituted Assassinations Committee to last until January 3, 1979, or for the duration of the 95th Congress. The new committee began its work in April operating on a substantially reduced budget of $2.5 million.

April 1977 turned out to be a fateful month for Carlos Marcello and the new Assassinations Committee. For it was then that Staff Counsel Robert Tannenbaum, who had been investigating certain conspiracy allegations that had been ignored by Hoover's FBI and the Warren Commission, recommended to the committee that it investigate possible ties between Carlos Marcello and the assassination of John F. Kennedy. It was the first time since the events of November 22, 1963, that Marcello had been mentioned by any official investigative body as a possible suspect.

PART VII

The Fall of Carlos Marcello
1978–1988

49

Congress Investigates the Crime of the Century

On January 11, 1978, Carlos Marcello appeared as a witness before the House Select Committee on Assassinations in Washington, in a secret executive session, to answer certain questions relating to the assassination of President John F. Kennedy. Marcello had been called as a witness, not as a suspect. His sworn testimony was given under a grant of immunity.

The short, heavy-set Mafia boss, now a corpulent 68, showed up in the congressional hearing room wearing his customary uniform for appearing before government investigatory committees: dark glasses and a well-tailored, if tightly fitting, double-breasted suit. The veteran committee witness, who had successfully defied Senators Estes Kefauver and John McClellan and Attorney General Robert F. Kennedy, not to mention countless special inquiry officers of the Immigration and Naturalization Service, now faced Assassinations Committee Chief Counsel G. Robert Blakey, a 42-year-old professor of law at Cornell, former Justice Department attorney under Attorney General Robert Kennedy, and author of the RICO Statute that would one day help send Carlos to jail.

Marcello was not the first Mafia boss to be questioned by the Assassinations Committee. On March 16, 1977, at a public hearing in Washington, former Chief Counsel Richard A. Sprague had interrogated Florida boss Santos Trafficante, Jr., without grant of immunity, and had received a resounding slap in the face.

Wearing his celebrated Bogartesque scowl, the tough Philadelphia prosecutor, who had sent United Mine Workers President Tony Boyle to prison for life for the Yablonski murders, asked the aging Mafia don: "Mr. Trafficante, did you ever discuss with any individuals plans to assassinate President Kennedy prior to his assassination?"

Sprague was, of course, alluding to Jose Aleman's allegation to the FBI of late September 1962 that during a conversation with Trafficante in Miami, Trafficante had told him that President Kennedy would never make it to the next election, that he was "going to be hit."

In reply, Trafficante withdrew a slip of paper from his pocket and read: "I respectfully refuse to answer that question pursuant to my constitutional rights under the First, Fourth, Fifth, and Fourteenth amendments."

To all other questions addressed to him, and there were many, the veteran of the CIA-Mafia plots to murder Fidel Castro made the same reply, invoking his constitutional rights over and over again and, in so doing, making a mockery of the House Select Committee on Assassinations, which did not possess the powers of a court of law.

When Carlos Marcello took the stand before the Assassinations Committee, roughly a year later, he turned in a vintage Marcello performance, uttering lie after lie in his inimitable, ungrammatical, Sicilian–New Orleans drawl.

Since his testimony was immunized, Carlos did not have to exasperate the committee with repeated invocations of the Fifth.

When asked if he had any involvement with organized crime, he said: "No, I don't know nuttin' about dat." (A year and a half later he would give himself away on this issue to a federal undercover agent, casually admitting to the agent he was "Maf" and expressing a deep paternal concern for some friends "in the organization" in Los Angeles who "had gotten into trouble.")

When asked if he had threatened the life of President Kennedy at a September 1962 meeting at Churchill Farms, Marcello told the committee: "Positively not, never said anythin' like dat." Then he denied that the Churchill Farms meeting between himself, Becker, and Roppolo ever took place: "The way the paper puts it and the books put it in dere, it makes it look like you had some kind of secret meetings because I have heard the book about what you are telling me."

Carlos then explained that Churchill Farms was not a place where he would conduct a business meeting, that the huge swampland property was full of duck blinds and was used only for hunting. (This lie had already been exposed by statements David Ferrie made to the FBI upon his arrest three days after the assassination, namely that he had spent the two weekends prior to the assassination with Marcello at Churchill Farms discussing legal strategy in connection with Carlos's upcoming conspiracy and perjury trial in federal court. And this lie would again be exposed by a federal undercover agent, a year and a half later, who told me that he had met with Marcello at the farmhouse at Churchill Farms to discuss important business. The agent noted while he was there that the farmhouse contained a room furnished with a conference table, with places for from six to eight people.)

When asked about his relationship with David Ferrie, Marcello admitted that Ferrie had worked for his attorney G. Wray Gill in helping him prepare his defense against the government's charges but denied that Ferrie was a friend. When asked about the $7093 that suddenly turned up in the normally impecunious Ferrie's bank account after the assassination, Marcello admitted he had paid the money to Ferrie for his paralegal services, specifying that Ferrie had been given the job of investigating the credibility of a government witness who was to testify against him at his trial. (Marcello did not explain why this required two trips to Guatemala.)

Only once during the committee's questioning did Carlos lose his cool, and that was when the name of Robert Kennedy came up.

Asked if he had heard about Robert Kennedy's intention to step up the Justice Department's investigation of the leaders of organized crime before becoming attorney general, Marcello said:

> "Yeah, but I didn't pay no attention to it at dat time."
> "When did you begin to pay attention to it?"
> "When he got to be attorney general.... He was goin' to get organized crime and all dat stuff. But the only time I really knowed about it was when they arrested me and threw me outa de country."

It was at this juncture that Carlos lost his composure. Referring to Edward Becker's allegation about Carlos's outrage over his deportation and his determination to take revenge against the Kennedys, Carlos suddenly grew red in the face and, raising his voice, all but shouted:

"I didn't need to tell no one about dat....Everybody in de
United States knowed I was kidnapped, dat what dey done was
illegal. I didn't have to discuss it with nobody. I told de whole
world it was unfair. Anybody who talked to me said it was
unfair!"

That said, there was nothing much more to say. After a few more
questions and answers, Carlos Marcello exited from the hearing, leaving the Assassinations Committee as uncertain as ever about what role,
if any, he might have played in the assassination of President John F.
Kennedy.

Although admittedly the committee's questioning of Marcello was
futile, considering that nothing he would say could ever be used as
evidence against him at a trial, still it was nevertheless somewhat incredible that Carlos was never asked whether he had a relationship
with Lee Harvey Oswald or with Oswald's uncle "Dutz" Murret, who
had worked in Carlos's gambling network for over ten years, or with
his mother, Marguerite, who had been close to several of Carlos's past
associates. A certain stonewalling on the part of the FBI might have
been responsible for this omission, for by the time of Marcello's testimony, the FBI had not yet released to the committee most of its
files on the Kennedy assassination, and the committee itself had not
yet discovered all Oswald's and Murret's connections to associates of
Carlos Marcello. Clearly the committee should have questioned Marcello much later on in its investigation when it knew much more about
him.

Upon returning home to New Orleans, Carlos and his family were
greeted the day after the hearing by a headline in the *Times-Picayune*
reading, "THE MARCELLO-JFK CONNECTION?" followed by an
article announcing, "The House Assassinations Committee is prob-
ing the possible connection between Carlos Marcello and the killing
of President John Kennedy," and going on to elaborate on the sinister implications of the Oswald-Ferrie-Marcello relationship. From
now on, the Marcello family would live under suspicion of having
been responsible for the murder of an American President.

The task the House Assassinations Committee and its chief counsel,
G. Robert Blakey, faced was monumental in scope and immense in
its possible historical significance. Since the assassination of President

Kennedy some fifteen years before, persuasive conspiracy allegations had been made suggesting the complicity of Fidel Castro or members of his government, the anti-Castro Cuban exiles, the government of the Soviet Union, the Central Intelligence Agency, the Federal Bureau of Investigation, the Secret Service, and organized crime. It was Blakey's task to investigate all these possibilities and report his findings to the American people and the world.

As it turned out, Professor Blakey was to exhibit a curiously dichotomous spirit in the way he conducted his investigation. On the one hand he evinced a seeming tendency to validate the basic findings of the Warren Commission—especially in regard to the number and provenance of the shots fired at the crime scene and the number and nature of the wounds they inflicted, but at the same time he sought to challenge the Warren Commission's central conclusion that Lee Harvey Oswald was the sole killer of the President, acting without confederates.

Of all Blakey's apparent assumptions most central was his tending not to question that Lee Harvey Oswald fired at least two shots that struck the President, in contrast to his predecessor's belief that the investigation should be conducted without presuming Oswald's guilt, that Oswald should be regarded simply as one of several suspects who may have been involved in the crime.

During the decade and a half since the assassination, a substantial body of informed opinion had developed that suggested Oswald did not kill anyone on November 22, 1963, that he had been deliberately and cunningly framed for the crime. A good deal of persuasive circumstantial evidence supported this view.

For example, by 1976, as the result of a continuing investigatory effort, it had become virtually certain to serious students of the crime that during the months preceding the assassination, someone impersonating Oswald, the so-called Oswald double (or the second Oswald, or the Oswald impostor), had deliberately laid a trail of incriminating evidence against the real Oswald that would lead the official investigations to conclude he shot the President at the behest of Fidel Castro, or the Cuban government, perhaps with the connivance of the Soviet Union.

Furthermore, compelling evidence had been developed over the years that indicated Oswald could not have possibly killed Kennedy. For example, Oswald was alleged to have fired on the President from a sixth-floor window of the Texas Book Depository at 12:30, and yet Bonnie Ray Williams, a depository worker, testified that he was eating his lunch on the sixth floor at 12:15, and saw no one else on the floor. Another witness, Carolyn Arnold, who was secretary to the vice president of the depository, testified that she spotted Oswald in the lunchroom, eating alone, at 12:15. After that sighting, the next person to spot Oswald was a motorcycle policeman, Marrion Baker, who, accompanied by the superintendent of the depository, had bumped into Oswald in the second-floor lunchroom calmly drinking a Coca-Cola only a minute and a half after the shooting broke out. Surely there was reason to doubt that Oswald (who could not have known that the President's limousine would be passing by the depository precisely at 12:30) could have gone up to the sixth floor, positioned himself to fire on the President, fired at least two deadly, perfectly aimed shots, concealed his weapon, gone back down to the lunchroom, and taken a Coca-Cola from a vending machine within fifteen minutes.

When the Warren Commission concluded that Oswald had fired on the President at 12:30, it did not have the benefit of Carolyn Arnold's precise testimony because the FBI had misrepresented it by arbitrarily changing the time of her sighting from 12:15 to 12:35. But when the House Assassinations Committee considered the problem in 1978, it had Carolyn Arnold's accurate testimony and still went along with the Warren Commission's conclusions. Many in the Kennedy assassination research community believe that the Assassinations Committee validated the Warren Commission's conclusions in regard to Oswald's role in the assassination because its chief counsel was predisposed to accept the Warren Commission's conclusions on the issue from the start.

Privately, however, Robert Blakey told me that he would not exclude the possibility that Oswald had been framed.

Also, in Blakey's defense, for a man who has been accused of wanting to make the Warren Commission's conclusions acceptable, he certainly found plenty of faults in the commission's investigation. For example, on the still controversial matter of the precise location of the President's four wounds, Blakey's Forensic Pathology Panel refuted the Warren Commission's conclusion that the President had first been shot in the right posterior base of the neck. Instead, the committee concluded the shot had entered the upper-right part of Kennedy's back, slightly below the shoulder blade, a full 6 inches below where the commission had located the wound (in order to accommodate its lone gunman explanation of the crime). Blakey also countenanced the refutation of the Warren Commission's placement of the President's head wound. The Assassinations Committee, relying on x-rays and autopsy photographs the Warren Commission had probably not seen, placed the wound no fewer than 4 inches higher

on the right posterior part of the skull than where the Warren Commission had placed it.

However, notwithstanding these successful challenges to the Warren Commission's findings on the President's wounds by the Forensic Pathology Panel, the committee itself proved unable to overcome
what soon became apparent to the Warren Commission critics and
other serious students of the assassination: a pronounced ingrained
disposition on the part of the majority of the members of the committee to protect certain long-hallowed canons of the Warren Report.
And so, even though the pathology panel moved the President's back
wound down 6 inches, and determined that the trajectory of the bullet through the President's body was virtually horizontal, even slant-
ing slightly upward, the committee nevertheless ratified the Warren
Report's controversial "magic bullet" theory that posited one bullet
fired from the southeasternmost sixth floor window of the book depository entering Kennedy's "neck" (in reality, his back), exiting from
his throat (though the path of the bullet was never dissected), then
traveling on to wound Governor Connally in three places—his up-
per back, his wrist, and his thigh—and emerging from having inflicted
all this havoc virtually unscathed. (This despite John Connally's force-
ful testimony before both the Warren Commission and the Assassinations Committee that he was absolutely certain he was struck by
the second shot and not the shot that hit Kennedy in the back.)

But by locating the wound in the back, below the shoulder blade,
a full 6 inches lower than where the Warren Commission had located
it, and by determining that its trajectory was slightly upward, the Forensic Pathology Panel had made it virtually impossible for a bullet
fired at a 45- to 60-degree angle from above to have exited from the
President's throat above the collar line, not to mention to have then
suddenly veered upward and to the right to strike Governor Connally
in the back near his right armpit. This surely could not have been
the trajectory, unless Kennedy was bending over in his seat tying his
shoelaces at the moment of the bullet's impact; bystanders' photographs of the shooting, taken seconds before and after the bullet
struck, showed he was not.

To overcome this obvious impossibility, as the committee seemed
determined to do (rather than admit the impossibility and start from
scratch in its analysis of the shot and the wound), the committee hired
a NASA engineer—an expert in trajectory analysis—to make the impossible appear possible.

The NASA scientist then fed into a computer what he believed
were the locations of Kennedy's and Connally's wounds, the align-

ment of the two men in the limousine at the moment of the shot, the slope of the roadbed, the postures of the two men at the time of the bullet's impact, and other miscellaneous information, and, abracadabra! the computer spat out a trajectory that "fit." A trajectory that validated the Warren Commission's tortuous theory that a single bullet fired from a sixth floor window of the book depository had inflicted multiple wounds on both men without losing hardly any of its mass. The committee's announcement of this validation enraged and disappointed many seasoned assassination researchers—people like Harold Weisberg, Mark Lane, and David Wrone—and caused them to lose all respect for Blakey's investigation. Subsequently the critics learned that, to come up with this validation of the Warren Commission's conclusions, the NASA engineer had to arbitrarily move the President's wound 2 or 3 inches up on the back (he believed the autopsy photographs were misleading), compute the trajectory as 20 degrees downward (in direct contradiction to the Forensic Pathology Panel's determination of a slightly upward trajectory) and assert, on the basis of a bystander's photograph, that the President was hunched over in his seat at the moment of the bullet's impact. This assertion, as we have seen, was disproved by two other bystanders' photographs taken seconds before and after the shot was fired, and was even disproved by the photo that had been singled out by the NASA engineer to sustain his trajectory analysis.

It was clear, then, to most experienced observers, that the Assassinations Committee had not set out to challenge the Warren Commission's "magic bullet" theory, but to perform acrobatics of evidence bending, if necessary, to validate it. As it turned out, the NASA trajectory analysis, by its author's own admission before the committee, allowed for margins of error that would have allowed the assassin, or assassins, to have fired from scores of other sniper locations, including the lower floors of the book depository and part of the nearby four-story Dal-Tex Building, thus rendering any firm conclusion on the provenance of the shot that inflicted the back wound on Kennedy impossible.

Likewise, the Forensic Pathology Panel proved to be emotionally incapable of going against the Warren Commission's conclusion that a bullet from Oswald's Mannlicher-Carcano rifle caused the fatal wound to the President's head. X-rays of that wound indicate that the missile exploded the President's head, disintegrating into scores of tiny bullet fragments and depositing them in the brain and surrounding tissues.

Since the type of ammunition used in a Carcano rifle is infrangible, designed to be capable of passing through several human bodies at a time without losing much of its mass, the exploding bullet that caused the fatal wound in the President's head could not have been fired from a low-velocity Carcano rifle. It could only have come from a high-velocity automatic rifle such as the M-15 carried by the Secret Service agents in the backup car immediately following the presidential limousine. In contrast to Carcano ammunition, bullets used in high-velocity automatic rifles are designed to explode on contact, which was exactly what the bullet that struck Kennedy in the back of the head did.

Since the President's fatal head wound was caused by a shot from a high-velocity automatic rifle traveling from back to front, left to right, and in a slightly upward, nearly level, trajectory, the shot must have been fired from a much lower location than the sixth floor of the book depository.

These facts notwithstanding, the Assassinations Committee concluded that the fatal head wound was caused by a shot fired from a Carcano rifle by Lee Harvey Oswald from a southwest window on the sixth floor of the Texas Book Depository.

The only differences between the Warren Commission's conclusions and those of the Assassinations Committee—in regard to the number, location, and provenance of the victims' wounds—consisted in their respective estimates of the number of shots fired at the assassination scene. The Warren Commission allowed for three shots, all from Oswald, one of which missed; and the Assassinations Committee allowed for four shots, two from Oswald that struck the President, one from Oswald that missed, and one from an unknown gunman firing from the grassy knoll that also missed.

As it turned out, only one member of the Forensic Pathology Panel dissented from these conclusions and that was the noted Chief Pathologist of Pittsburgh's Central Medical Center, Dr. Cyril Wecht, who stated both in his dissenting opinion and publicly that the members of the Forensic Pathology Panel, all of whom belonged to the conservative, establishmentarian American Society of Clinical Pathologists, were afraid to issue findings that conflicted with those of the Warren Report. In the concluding remarks of his dissenting statement, Dr. Wecht observed that so far as the committee's treatment of the forensic evidence was concerned, "the investigation of the House Select Committee on Assassinations was not an objective, fact-finding mission conducted by an impartial staff," but an attempt to make persuasive the Warren Commission's essential conclusions regarding the assassin's shots and the wounds they inflicted on the President and the governor.

But it was on the question of possible conspiracy in the assassination that Robert Blakey came to differ radically from the Warren Commission. Whereas the Warren Commission, completely in thrall to J. Edgar Hoover, bent over backward to dogmatically assert that the President had been killed by a lone, emotionally disturbed "commie" gunman, acting without confederates, Blakey became convinced fairly early in his investigation that Kennedy had been assassinated as a result of a conspiracy. Among the factors that contributed to the Assassinations Committee's ultimate finding of "probable conspiracy" were an acoustical analysis of a dictabelt recording that seemed to indicate that four shots in all were fired, one of which came from the grassy knoll;* the many ear and eye witnesses whose testimony that at least one shot came from the knoll had been ignored by the Warren Commission but now appeared both plausible and convincing to the Assassinations Committee; unimpeachable evidence that the FBI and the CIA had deceived the Warren Commission on a number of important issues and had occasionally withheld vital information from it; the committee's extensive investigation of Jack Ruby's many ties to organized crime, especially his many connections to close associates of Jimmy Hoffa's and Carlos Marcello's; and the discovery of many taped conversations between leaders of organized crime, obtained by FBI undercover agents before and immediately after the assassination, expressing their hatred of the Kennedy brothers, their rage over Robert Kennedy's campaign against them, and their desire that both brothers be killed.

On the basis of the committee's review of the FBI's pre–Warren Commission investigation of the assassination, the committee concluded that the FBI had failed to properly investigate the possibility of conspiracy to such an extent that "it would not have uncovered one had one existed." To this conclusion the committee might have added that if Hoover *had* uncovered a conspiracy he probably would have suppressed all evidence of it.

The Assassinations Committee had to confront a bewildering array of allegations suggesting conspirational activity. Most of these fell into seven areas of suspicion: the Soviet Union, Fidel Castro or the Cuban government, the anti-Castro Cuban exiles organizations, the FBI, the CIA, the Secret Service, and the "national syndicate of organized crime."

The committee was not confronted by any evidence suggesting

*The validity of the acoustical evidence has since been authoritatively disputed.

that the CIA, as an agency of the U.S. government, might have been involved in a conspiracy to assassinate President Kennedy, but it most definitely was confronted by evidence persuasively suggesting that maverick elements of the CIA, acting either on their own or in concert with members of organized crime, might have been involved. This evidence had to do with Lee Harvey Oswald's visit to Mexico City from September 27 to October 3, 1963.

It had long been known that there was extremely persuasive evidence indicating that someone representing himself as Lee Harvey Oswald, but who, in reality, was an impostor, visited the Cuban and Soviet embassies in Mexico City on several occasions during the period September 27 to October 2. This man had made a spectacle of himself so, it later seemed to investigators, his presence at the two embassies would not be soon forgotten. Particularly disturbing had been a CIA report of October 10 that a man purporting to be Lee Henry [sic] Oswald visited the Soviet Embassy in Mexico City on October 1 and spoke with Vice-Consul Valery Vladimirovich Kostikov. Kostikov, it was later learned, doubled as officer-in-charge for Western Hemisphere terrorist activities, including assassination, of the KGB. Even more disturbing was a CIA report that the individual representing himself as Oswald had actually made an offer to officials of the Cuban Embassy to kill President Kennedy. This offer was subsequently confirmed by the FBI's double agent "Solo," who was told by Fidel Castro that the man visiting the Cuban Embassy and claiming to be Oswald had indeed made the offer and it had been refused.

As if these reports were not disturbing enough in themselves, the CIA surveillance photographs of this visitor to the Cuban and Soviet embassies on at least six, possibly seven, occasions turned out not to resemble Oswald in the slightest, and the recordings of his tapped telephone conversations with officials of the Soviet Embassy turned out not to resemble Oswald's voice in the slightest or reflect his known proficiency in the Russian language. That the CIA was never able to identify the photographed individual and had destroyed the original recordings of his voice further complicated the issue.

The implications of all this were only too clear: it appeared that a conspirator had deliberately attempted to inspire terror in U.S. government officials over the national security implications of an Oswald-Kostikov meeting and an Oswald offer to Cuban officials to kill President Kennedy by laying a false trail of evidence against Oswald to induce a future official cover-up of the impending assassination.

In addition to these unsettling reports from Mexico City, there was another that had been made to a consul at the U.S. Embassy in Mexico City right after the assassination, by an individual code-named "D," who alleged that when he was at the Cuban Consulate on September 18 he saw "Cubans pay Oswald money and talk about Oswald assassinating someone." There was also a highly disturbing report by Antonio Veciana, head of Alpha 66, a Cuban exiles group determined to overthrow Castro, that in late August or early September, 1963, he saw Oswald in Dallas with a high-ranking CIA official known as Maurice Bishop.

Upon investigating these and other allegations that came to its attention, the House Assassinations Committee arrived at some pretty weak dismissals and exonerations that, in retrospect, seemed to reflect Chief Counsel Blakey's desire to pin the blame for the assassination on organized crime. An example of this seeming bias was the way the committee treated the issue of Oswald's visit to Mexico City in late September, early October, 1963.

An Assassinations Committee investigator went to Mexico City in 1978 and interviewed the two Cuban Embassy officials Oswald had supposedly met with and concluded that, not Oswald, but someone posing as Oswald, had met with them.

The same investigator read the CIA's hitherto secret file on the surveillance photographs and found that, of the twelve photographs taken, one had been of the real Lee Harvey Oswald and eleven had been of an unknown individual, and that the one of the real Oswald had been either lost or destroyed. The investigator also inspected the actual photographs of the man who was supposed to be Oswald and who was not, and discovered that they had been taken on six, perhaps seven, different occasions.

Finally, the Assassinations Committee investigator read the hitherto secret CIA file on the tape recordings of "Oswald's" tapped telephone conversations with Soviet Embassy officials and received confirmation that the original tape recordings had been destroyed. Eight transcripts of the tapes had been made, two in Spanish and the others in a Russian so "broken" its remarks could not have been uttered by Lee Harvey Oswald, who was known to have been fluent in Russian.

The investigator prepared a 300-page report on these findings, but the findings were eventually distorted in the Assassinations Committee's final report on its investigation of the Kennedy murder.

The committee reported that the CIA's photographs were the result of simple human error, *even though "Oswald" had been photographed entering the Cuban Embassy at six different times and on six different occa-*

sions. This meant that not one, but *six,* human errors had to have been made by the agency in its photographic surveillance of the Cuban and Soviet embassies during Lee Harvey Oswald's supposed visit to Mexico City in the fall of 1963. (The committee made no mention in its final report of the one photograph of the real Oswald that had been either lost or destroyed.)

In addition, the committee concluded, after interviewing a number of FBI agents who were in the Dallas field office at the time of the assassination, and who presumably had listened to the CIA's recording of Oswald's voice phoning the Soviet Embassy, that *the CIA had never sent a recording of Oswald's voice* to the Dallas FBI.

The committee's final report did not point out that previous testimony of two of the FBI agents interviewed had been impeached on another issue and said nothing about the destroyed tape recordings and the eight transcripts of the tapes, whose conversations could not have been spoken by the real Lee Harvey Oswald.

Students of the Assassinations Committee's investigation of this issue see evidence that the committee, or at least its chief counsel, did not want to believe that an impostor had operated in Mexico City because the man would almost certainly have had something to do with an intelligence agency, not organized crime, and this would weaken the committee's eventual case against the Mafia.

As veteran assassination researcher Paul L. Hoch has written:

"Such a conspirator would not be a maniac, or 'societal outcast,' but a sophisticated planner who was counting on the CIA's surveillance of the Soviet Embassy in Mexico City to detect his contact with KGB officer Kostikov....Such an individual would almost certainly have had to be associated with the global intelligence milieu, an insider privy to special knowledge of CIA procedures."

But what the committee and its chief counsel apparently did not appreciate was that the discovery of a conspirator with ties to, let us say, maverick elements of the CIA was perfectly consonant with a Mafia conspiracy to assassinate the President. Had not the CIA recently entered into a conspiracy to assassinate Fidel Castro in alliance with the Mafia? We know that Carlos Marcello told Joe Hauser he had been in on the CIA-Mafia plots to assassinate Castro. Could he not have had someone who had been associated with the CIA-Mafia plot to kill Castro aid him in a possible plot to assassinate President Kennedy?

Regrettably, the Assassinations Committee's 300-page investigative report on Oswald in Mexico City is classified and cannot be released until the year 2029. A concerted citizens effort is under way, however, to persuade Congress to declassify the report so that it may be released as soon as possible.

As for "D's" allegation, the committee received conclusive evidence that "D" was a Nicaraguan misinformation agent who was trying to implicate Cuba in the assassination. And the committee's investigation of Antonio Veciana led it to conclude that his testimony was not credible.

As for suspicions of FBI involvement in the assassination, there had been a persistent rumor that Oswald had been an FBI informant during the months preceding the assassination and might have passed on information about an assassination plot which the FBI did nothing about, by either design or neglect. The committee investigated this allegation and concluded it had no substance.

Upon completing its investigation, the Assassinations Committee came to the conclusion that neither the Soviet Union nor the government of Cuba was involved in a conspiracy to assassinate the President, despite a good deal of persuasive, but insufficiently evaluated circumstantial evidence suggesting that Castro's Cuba might have been involved. It also went on to exonerate the Cuban exiles "as a group," the FBI, the CIA, and the Secret Service from complicity. It did not, however, acquit military intelligence of possible involvement in the crime because, to its consternation, the committee learned late in its investigation that the Department of Defense had destroyed its entire file on Oswald in 1973 and had never sent the file to the Warren Commission. That a branch of military intelligence could have been involved in the assassination does not ipso facto preclude Mafia involvement either. The Assassinations Committee learned that the biggest single customer of the Marcello-controlled Pelican Tomato Company was the U.S. Navy, demonstrating that the military and Marcello did at least *some* business together. And arguably illegal business at that, for the Defense Department was committed, by executive order, to only "buy American," whereas, according to the testimony of Marcello's deportation attorney, Jack Wasserman, at an INS hearing in 1972, most of Pelican's tomatoes were imported from Mexico.

As it turned out, it was in the area of the possible involvement of organized crime in the assassination that the committee developed its strongest and deepest suspicions.

Largely because FBI electronic surveillance of members of the Mafia's national regulatory body, the *commissione,* failed to turn up so much as a hint of discussion of a plot to kill President Kennedy, the Assassinations Committee concluded that "the national syndicate of organized crime, as a group," was not involved in a conspiracy to assassinate the President.

However, the committee concluded that there were three men associated with organized crime who circumstantial evidence suggested might have participated in a unilateral plan to assassinate the President, a plan unknown to, and therefore unapproved by, the national commission. These men were Jimmy Hoffa, Santos Trafficante, Jr., and Carlos Marcello, all three of whom, the committee pointed out, were under siege from the U.S. government, and specifically from Attorney General Robert F. Kennedy, at the time of the assassination.

50

Congress Suspects Marcello

In identifying Jimmy Hoffa, Santos Trafficante, Jr., and Carlos Marcello as suspects in a possible conspiracy to assassinate President Kennedy, the House Select Committee on Assassinations based its suspicions on an impressive array of circumstantial evidence it had developed on the three men, especially Marcello.

As we shall see, much of that circumstantial evidence was intertwined. Hoffa, Trafficante, and Marcello were friends and occasionally did business with one another. Partially as a result of this, evidence against one often overlapped with evidence against another.

What evidence did the committee possess that suggested the involvement of Jimmy Hoffa in a plan to assassinate the President?

First of all, it had the testimony of government witness and Louisiana Teamsters official Edward Partin, who reported to the Justice Department that in July 1962, while he was meeting with Jimmy Hoffa in the Teamsters chief's Washington office, Hoffa had spoken at length about his plans to murder Robert Kennedy. Since Partin was on friendly terms with several powerful members of the Marcello organization, Hoffa was sure Partin could recruit someone capable of carrying out the hit. Hoffa suggested to Partin that he favored either firebombing Kennedy's car or employing "a lone gunman equipped with a rifle with a telescopic sight." When Partin informed the FBI

398

of the plot, it administered a polygraph test to Partin. The Louisiana Teamsters official passed.

According to Partin, Hoffa's assassination plans also included the murder of President Kennedy.

Edward Partin's testimony was corroborated by federal investigator Hawk Daniels, who monitored one of Partin's telephone conversations with Hoffa after the July meeting. Daniels, who became a Louisiana judge, told Anthony Summers in 1978: "I think Hoffa fully intended to carry the threats out—I really think he had the capability. It was a question of how and when, not a question of whether he had doubts as to the necessity of eliminating at least Mr. Bobby Kennedy and possibly his brother also."

A year or so after Hoffa revealed his assassination plan to Edward Partin, specifically in the late summer and early fall of 1963, Jack Ruby began telephoning a number of associates of Jimmy Hoffa's, some of whom he had never met, for no readily apparent reason. When these calls are considered in the light of Hoffa's stated plans to murder the Kennedy brothers, they arouse suspicion that Hoffa may have played some role in a conspiracy to assassinate the President or, at least, in a conspiracy to silence Lee Harvey Oswald. However, the committee admitted that, in the end, it had uncovered no direct evidence that "Hoffa was involved in a plot on the President's life." In its final report the committee noted that "as opposed to Marcello and Trafficante, Hoffa was not a major leader of organized crime. Thus his ability to guarantee that his associates would be killed if they turned government informant may have been somewhat less assured.... Indeed," the committee noted, "much of the evidence against Hoffa was supplied by a federal government informant, Edward Grady Partin," implying that since Teamsters official Partin was one of Hoffa's own men and had survived despite his collaboration with the Justice Department, Hoffa was not capable of covering up an assassination plot. "It may be strongly doubted, therefore, that Hoffa would have risked anything so dangerous as a plot against the President."

The Assassinations Committee's suspicions of Jimmy Hoffa's friend Santos Trafficante, Jr., derived principally from Trafficante's relationship with Hoffa and also, to some extent, from his relationship with Carlos Marcello.

On March 12, 1977, four days before the committee's first interview with Trafficante, the committee interviewed Jose Aleman, the wealthy Cuban exile who had alleged to the FBI in the fall of 1962 that Trafficante had told him President Kennedy "was going to be hit." During the interview, held in secret session, Aleman expanded considerably on the original allegation he had made to the FBI in the fall of 1962 and had repeated the day after the assassination. He told the Assassinations Committee that during his conversation with Trafficante, the Florida boss had said that Kennedy would "get what is coming to him" as a result of his administration's intense efforts to prosecute Hoffa. Aleman then went on to tell the committee that Trafficante had made it quite clear to him that he was not guessing, that the President was going to be killed. Rather he did, in fact, *know* that such a crime was being planned. According to the Assassinations Committee's final report, Aleman "further stated that Trafficante had given him the distinct impression that Hoffa was to be principally involved in planning the presidential murder."

A little over a year later Aleman was called to testify before the Assassinations Committee again, this time in public session. Prior to his appearance before the committee, Aleman reaffirmed his original account of his September 1962 meeting with Trafficante, but then, just before his appearance in public session, he told members of the committee staff that "he feared for his physical safety and was afraid of possible reprisal from Trafficante or his organization." Then, when he took the stand, he repeated under oath that Trafficante had said Kennedy "was going to be hit" but hedged his remark by saying that Trafficante may have only meant the President was going to be hit by "a lot of Republican votes" in the 1964 election, not that he was going to be assassinated.

When Trafficante himself appeared before the committee for the second time, on September 28, 1978, he admitted, in his immunized testimony, that he had conspired with the CIA to kill Fidel Castro but "denied any foreknowledge of, or of participation in, the President's murder."

Five years later, a penniless and despondent Jose Aleman, wholly convinced the Mafia was out to get him, committed suicide after killing his 69-year-old aunt and seriously wounding three cousins, one of whom was only 6 years old, and wounding as well four SWAT team officers of the Miami Police.

Aleman, the only son of a wealthy former minister of education in pre-Batista Cuba, had lost a fortune estimated to have once been worth around $30 million. (His investments had included the Miami Stadium, the huge Cape Florida development in Key Biscayne, and several luxury hotels in Miami.) Aleman had become convinced that his 1978 congressional testimony against Santos Trafficante had ultimately caused his financial ruin and had marked him and his family for the rest of their lives.

Tormented by these thoughts, Aleman went berserk as soon as

he woke up on the morning of August 1, 1983, and, in a wild rampage, opened fire on everyone in his house and then, after the SWAT team arrived and he had exchanged fire with them, shot himself in the temple, dying instantly.

Aleman's surviving relatives later told the press that he had been consumed with fear because of his 1978 testimony before the House Select Committee on Assassinations in which he stated that Santos Trafficante had told him in 1962 that "President John F. Kennedy would not get reelected in 1964, that he was going to get hit." "From that day on," a relative claimed, "he believed he and his family were on a Mafia hit list."

FBI wiretaps on Trafficante's phones in 1963, recording his desperation over Robert Kennedy's crackdown on his criminal empire, revealed that Trafficante had sufficient motive to rid himself of the Kennedy brothers. And he was in close touch with two other powerful men—Hoffa and Marcello—who had equally strong motives to do away with the Kennedys and had allegedly threatened to kill one or both of them. Still, as with its assessment of the possibility that Jimmy Hoffa might have been involved in a conspiracy to assassinate the Kennedy brothers, the committee concluded that it was "unlikely that Trafficante plotted to kill the President." After all, there was no evidence suggesting that Trafficante had personally plotted the President's murder, only evidence that he had foreknowledge of such a plot.

The possibility that Carlos Marcello might have played a significant role in the assassination of the President was given much more credence and attention by the Assassinations Committee. In fact, reading between the lines of the committee's guardedly worded final report, it is clear that the committee suspected Marcello's complicity above all others. For as the final report stated: "In its investigation of Marcello the Committee identified the presence of one critical evidentiary element that was lacking with the other organized crime figures examined by the Committee: credible associations relating both Lee Harvey Oswald and Jack Ruby to figures having a relationship, albeit tenuous, with Marcello's crime family or organization."

As we shall see, the Assassinations Committee's use of the word "tenuous" to describe Oswald's and Ruby's links to the Marcello crime family did not adequately express the extent and significance of those mutual associations.

Although the Warren Commission never received *any* evidence linking Oswald to organized crime, thanks to deliberate suppression of evidence by FBI Director Hoover, the Assassinations Committee discovered that Oswald's uncle and surrogate father, "Dutz" Murret, was a bookmaker in the Marcello gambling network who had functioned as a collector for top Marcello deputy Sam Saia. The committee further established that Oswald's mother cultivated friendships with two Marcello associates, Sam Termine and Clem Sehrt. It discovered as well that as a result of the Oswald-Murret family ties with Marcello associates, Oswald was bailed out of jail in the summer of 1963 by Emile Bruneau, a close associate of high-ranking Marcello aide Nofio Pecora and a friend, as well, of the head of Marcello's racing wire service, Joe Poretto, who also managed the Marcello-owned Town & Country restaurant. But most important of all, the committee established conclusively, from FBI reports that were never sent to the Warren Commission, that one of Oswald's New Orleans companions, David Ferrie, in whose company Oswald had been seen by several reliable witnesses in the months prior to the assassination, was an investigator for Carlos Marcello's New Orleans attorney, G. Wray Gill, and had admitted to the FBI that he had spent the two weekends prior to the assassination conferring with Carlos Marcello at Marcello's Churchill Farms estate.

These then were the figures Lee Harvey Oswald had contact with, who, according to the Assassinations Committee, had "tenuous" relationships with the Marcello crime family.

What the Assassinations Committee did not discover was that Oswald actually worked for the Marcello organization as a runner in its gambling network in the months prior to the assassination, and during the course of this employment had met such important associates of the Marcellos' as Joe Poretto and Ben Tregle. More likely than not, Oswald also came into contact with at least two of Carlos's brothers—Anthony and Vincent—as he made his rounds as messenger and collector for his uncle Dutz to Marcello-controlled establishments such as the Town & Country Motel and Ben Tregle's Lounnor Restaurant. Nor did the Assassinations Committee appear to be aware that Dean Andrews, the New Orleans attorney Oswald had consulted several times during the summer of 1963, who had informed the Warren Commission that Oswald told him he was being paid for demonstrating on behalf of Castro, and who claimed someone had phoned him the day after the assassination to ask him to represent Oswald as his defense attorney against the charges the Dallas Police had brought against him, was one of Carlos Marcello's attorneys.

And what did the Assassinations Committee discover about Jack Ruby's connections to the Marcello crime family?

First, the Ruby-Marcello connections in Dallas. The Assassinations

Committee established that Jack Ruby was a friend and business associate of Joseph Civello's, Carlos Marcello's deputy in Dallas and the boss of Dallas's relatively small Mafia family, a reality that J. Edgar Hoover tried to keep from the attention of the Warren Commission and which the commission itself suppressed by not mentioning it in its report or published exhibits. Furthermore, it established that Ruby was on very cordial terms with Joseph Campisi, who, the committee found out, was considered to be the number two man in the Dallas Mafia hierarchy and a man on such friendly terms with the Marcello brothers that he sent the family 260 pounds of homemade sausage every Christmas.

Campisi told the committee that he knew all of the Marcello brothers and used to go often to New Orleans to play golf and go to the track with Vincent, Anthony, and Sammy. It was Vincent who first introduced him to Carlos and Joe, and Carlos had taken to him to such an extent that he invited him several times to his fishing camp at Grand Isle, where Campisi would cook spaghetti for Carlos and all the brothers and their friends.

Joe Campisi, as we know, owned and operated a notorious mob hangout in Dallas, the Egyptian Lounge. In its interview with Campisi the Assassinations Committee obtained an admission from him that Jack Ruby had dined with him at the lounge the evening before Kennedy was assassinated. Campisi also admitted that he had visited Ruby in the Dallas County Jail eight days after the assassination.

It is one of the practices of the Mafia to visit a member of the brotherhood who has been jailed for a crime in which the brotherhood was involved soon after he first enters his cell. One of the purposes of such a visit is to remind the jailed colleague that he is to keep his mouth shut or else something unpleasant might happen to him or to a member of his family. This is usually done in subtle ways.

Joe Campisi was Ruby's first visitor after his imprisonment for murdering the President's alleged assassin. (Incredibly, the Dallas Police did not record the ten-minute conversation between Oswald's murderer and a man known to be a close associate of Carlos Marcello's deputy in Dallas.) Campisi brought his wife along with him—an unusual move, for Mafiosi almost never include their wives in meetings at which urgent matters are to be discussed, however obliquely. Former Chief Counsel Blakey speculates that Campisi brought his wife along so as not to arouse the police's suspicion. When questioned by the Assassinations Committee as to what Ruby said during their meeting, Campisi did not recall much but did remember vividly what had already become Ruby's stock answer to the question of why he killed Oswald: to spare Jacqueline Kennedy and her children the pain of an eventual trial of Lee Harvey Oswald. (Later a handwritten note of Ruby's to one of his attorneys was discovered in which Ruby admitted he was lying, that a former attorney, Tom Howard, a friend of Campisi's, told him to use the Jacqueline Kennedy story as an alibi.)

Campisi told the committee substantially what he told the FBI three weeks after the assassination: that when he and his wife arrived at Ruby's cell, they found him crying: "Here I am fighting for my life and feeling sorry for myself," Ruby was supposed to have moaned, "when I really feel sorry for Mrs. Kennedy and the kids."

Campisi's original testimony to the FBI about his meeting with Ruby in jail, which, in turn, had been transmitted to the Warren Commission, had been a masterful performance. It had conveyed the impression that Mr. and Mrs. Campisi's visit to Mr. Jack Ruby was simply a visit to an old and dear friend who had gotten into a little trouble. It reinforced Ruby's professed patriotic indignation and sympathy for Jacqueline Kennedy and her kids. But fourteen years later Campisi's story did not convince the House Select Committee on Assassinations that the purpose of his visit to prisoner Ruby was so innocent. The committee took note that Jack Ruby had dined with a Dallas-based member of the Marcello organization the evening before the assassination of the President and that the same Dallas-based member of the Marcello organization was the first person to visit Ruby after he had been jailed for the murder of the President's alleged assassin. The committee had little choice but to regard the Ruby-Campisi relationship and the Campisi-Marcello relationship as yet another set of associations strengthening the committee's growing suspicion of the Marcello crime family's involvement in a conspiracy to assassinate President Kennedy or execute the President's alleged assassin or both.

Contributing to that suspicion, the committee discovered yet another friend of Jack Ruby's with a connection to the Marcello organization. His name was James Henry Dolan, and he was the representative of the Dallas chapter of the mob-controlled American Guild of Variety Artists. The committee found out that Dolan was a close friend of Carlos Marcello's lieutenant Nofio Pecora and that Dolan had spent several days conferring with Ruby in Dallas two months before the assassination.

As for Jack Ruby's connections with the Marcello organization in New Orleans, the committee was to confirm certain connections the FBI had been aware of at the time of the assassination but had never forcefully brought to the attention of the Warren Commission. The committee was able to confirm that Ruby met with New Orleans nightclub operators and Marcello associates Harold Tannenbaum, Frank

Caracci, Cleeve Dugas, and Nick Graffagnini (one of Pete Marcello's managers at the Marcello-owned Sho-Bar on Bourbon Street) in June and October 1963 and made a telephone call on October 30 to the New Orleans office of Marcello associate Nofio Pecora, whose associate, Emile Bruneau, had bailed Lee Harvey Oswald out of jail that summer.

But there were other connections between Jack Ruby and New Orleans associates of Carlos Marcello's that the Assassinations Committee did not discover, and these were anything but "tenuous." They were the next thing to direct contact with the boss himself. For according to reliable sources in New Orleans and Dallas, it appears that Jack Ruby knew at least two of Carlos Marcello's brothers—Vincent and Tony—who ran the Marcello slot machine leasing business in Dallas, and perhaps also a third brother—Pete—who ran the family-owned nightclub in the French Quarter Ruby visited in June. At that time the Sho-Bar was featuring a notorious stripper named Jada, whom Ruby later hired to perform in his club in Dallas, and who was under contract with Ruby the day of the assassination.

In the wake of the assassination the FBI received testimony from a former part-time employee of Ruby's, William Abadie, indicating that Ruby could have come into contact with one or two of the Marcello brothers through their mutual involvement in the slot machine business. It appears virtually certain that Jack Ruby, in his dual capacity as slot machine warehouser and bookmaker, did business with Jefferson Music Company President Vincent Marcello and also perhaps with his younger brother, Tony, one of whose jobs at the time was to service the Marcello slot machines and jukeboxes leased out to various bars and restaurants.

The Assassinations Committee identified "credible associations relating both Lee Harvey Oswald and Jack Ruby to figures having a relationship, albeit tenuous, with Marcello's crime family or organization." But, as we have just seen, the associations both Oswald and Ruby had with individuals connected to the Marcello organization were more numerous and significant than the committee had realized, so much so that it is difficult to believe that the Marcello organization did not play *some* role in the assassination of the President and the murder of his alleged assassin. Given the available circumstantial evidence we now have, it is not unreasonable to suspect that this role could have been the secondary one of recruiting the scapegoat, Oswald, framing him to take the blame for the assassination, and then getting Ruby to silence him, a role that would have been a step or two removed from coordinating the team of gunmen who actually did the shooting in Dealey Plaza on November 22.

However, as suspicious as all these Oswald-Ruby-Marcello associations were, Chief Counsel Blakey rightly emphasized that they did not warrant an assumption of guilt in the assassination on the part of Carlos Marcello. "We must beware of inferring conspiracy from coincidental associations," he stated in the final report. "Only suspicion, never proof, can result from such analyses."

Where did the Assassinations Committee leave us in terms of positing a credible assassination conspiracy involving Carlos Marcello?

Before addressing that question, it is worthwhile to consider what is known about the relationship between Carlos Marcello and the committee's other prime assassination suspect, Jimmy Hoffa.

It has been established that by the time the Kennedy brothers came into power, Hoffa and Marcello knew each other and did business together at least in Louisiana, where Marcello exercised considerable influence in both the Teamsters and Longshoremen's unions. Since the two had been singled out as top priority targets in Robert Kennedy's war on organized crime, they must have sympathized with each other as they came under the young attorney general's fire.

It is pertinent, therefore, that when Jimmy Hoffa began to give serious thought to an attempt on the life of Robert Kennedy, he turned his gaze south, to Louisiana, and tried to obtain the cooperation of a Louisiana Teamsters official, Edward Partin, a man with numerous ties to associates of Carlos Marcello's.

That the relationship between Carlos Marcello and Jimmy Hoffa was particularly strong was evidenced after the assassination when it was Carlos Marcello, more than any other man, who came to Hoffa's aid as the Teamsters boss confronted imprisonment in the years 1965 to 1967. For at Hoffa's darkest hour it was to Marcello and his friend Irving Davidson that the besieged Teamsters boss and the national syndicate of organized crime turned to coordinate a national campaign to "save Hoffa" from imprisonment. FBI intelligence discovered that the mob had placed $1 million at Marcello's disposal to be used to bribe prosecution witness Partin and to make payoffs, when necessary, to judges, prosecutors, and state officials who were in a position to help thwart Hoffa's imprisonment. In taking on this large and risky responsibility, was Marcello paying back Hoffa for whatever services Hoffa had rendered to him in the Kennedy assassination?

Possibly prominent among those services could have been simply providing Marcello with useful intelligence (for instance, on the Kennedy brothers' extramarital affairs), which might have encouraged Carlos to believe he could get away with murdering John Kennedy. Knowledge of the Kennedy brothers' reckless sexual adventures could have served to convince Marcello that Attorney General Robert Kennedy would never want to conduct a thorough investigation of his brother's murder for fear Jack's sexual dalliances with the likes of Marilyn Monroe and Judy Campbell might come to light during the course of the investigation.

Carlos Marcello knew the power that getting things on people gave him. As a young convict in Angola State Prison he had won power over the warden by letting on he knew that the warden, a married man, was carrying on an affair with one of the prison's cooks. Knowing that President Kennedy had been carrying on an affair with a girlfriend of Chicago mob boss Sam Giancana, who, in turn, had been hired by the CIA to help coordinate a plan to assassinate Fidel Castro, would have helped convince Marcello that not only Robert Kennedy but also the U.S. government would not want to conduct a thorough investigation of an eventual assassination of the President.

The House Assassinations Committee's final position on the possibility of the Marcello organization's complicity in the Kennedy assassination was guarded, ambiguous, and in one or two instances clearly off base.

On the FBI's failure to effect adequate electronic surveillance of Carlos Marcello, the committee's final report stated:

> "Marcello's sophisticated security system and close-knit organizational structure may have been a factor in preventing such surveillance....A former FBI official knowledgeable about the surveillance program told the Committee 'that was our biggest gap...with Marcello you've got the one big exception in our work back then. There was just no way of penetrating that area. He was just too smart.'"

Subsequent events have proved that it was not Marcello's cleverness that prevented the FBI from bugging him; it was the laxity, the ineptitude, and possibly the venality of the agents of the FBI field office in New Orleans. For, fifteen years after the assassination, when the FBI mounted its big undercover operation against Carlos Marcello, agents assigned to bug Marcello found that Marcello was an easy mark. "We didn't have any trouble at all installing the bugs," one of the agents told me. "It was relatively easy." In fact, in 1979 the FBI was able to install a listening device in the ceiling of Carlos Marcello's inner sanctum, his office in the Town & Country Motel.

The committee was off base also on another conclusion. In assessing the possibility of Carlos Marcello's involvement in the assassination, a portion of the concluding remarks on Marcello in the committee's final report emphasized that Marcello's record of exercising prudence in the conduct of his business affairs

> "...indicated that he would be unlikely to undertake so dangerous a course of action as a Presidential assassination. Considering that record of prudence, and in the absence of direct evidence of involvement, it may be said that it is unlikely that Marcello was in fact involved in the assassination of the President."

But had Carlos Marcello been all that prudent in the conduct of his "business affairs," which must include not only his legitimate business ventures but also his criminal activities? And would he be so prudent in the future?

On the contrary, Marcello took enormous risks, time and again. Was it not highly imprudent to defy a government deportation order, and the will of so determined an enemy as Robert Kennedy, and return illegally to the United States from government-imposed exile in Central America? And was it not imprudent of Carlos, almost twenty years later, to be sucked into the wild, risky venture concocted by government undercover operatives in 1979, which eventually brought about his downfall?

But, in the end, the Assassinations Committee allowed itself to opine that perhaps Marcello *had* been involved in the Kennedy assassination. For, in its concluding statements on Carlos Marcello, the committee's final report remarked:

> "Any evaluation of Marcello's possible role in the assassination must take into consideration his unique stature within La Cosa Nostra. The FBI determined in the 1960s that because of Marcello's position as head of the New Orleans crime family (the oldest in the United States, having first entered the country in the 1880s), the Louisiana organized crime leader had been endowed with special powers and privileges not accorded to any other La Cosa Nostra members. As the leader of 'the

first family' of the Mafia in America, according to FBI information, Marcello had been the recipient of the extraordinary
privilege of conducting syndicate operations without having
to seek the approval of the national crime commission."

And then, with this as a preamble, the committee issued its final
statement on the possibility of Marcello's complicity, a statement which
qualified to a significant degree its previous conclusion that it was
"unlikely that Marcello was, in fact, involved in the assassination of
the President."

"On the other hand, the evidence that he had the motive and
the evidence of links through associates to both Oswald and
Ruby, coupled with the failure of the 1963–64 investigation to
explore adequately possible conspirational activity in the assassination, precluded a judgement by the Committee that
Marcello and his associates were not involved."

Ironically the committee came to this guarded, somewhat ambiguous, and tentative conclusion on the basis of what had turned out
to be an incomplete investigation of the possibility of Marcello's involvement in the assassination. The committee failed to consider adequately much of the available circumstantial evidence suggesting
Marcello complicity and left several promising leads unexplored.
There were two principal reasons for this failure.

First, the FBI, still up to its old tricks, withheld the huge Dallas
and New Orleans field offices' files on the assassination from the committee for so long that by the time the committee received them, it
was too late for Chief Counsel Blakey's staff to examine them in their
entirety. Thus the committee never investigated the De Laparra allegations of November 27, 1963, and February 23, 1967, and the SV
T-1 allegation of November 26, 1963.

Incredibly, then, these two potentially significant allegations, made
not by cranks but by concerned citizens within days of the assassination, one hinting at foreknowledge of the Kennedy assassination on
the part of a Marcello associate, the other suggesting a connection
between Oswald and the Marcello organization, escaped notice of both
the Warren Commission and the House Select Committee on Assassinations, thanks to the FBI's consummate ability to manipulate official investigations by simply withholding vital documents from them.

A second reason why the committee failed to adequately consider
much of the evidence of Marcello complicity had to do with time.

Congress had so limited the term of the Assassinations Committee's existence that the committee simply did not have the time to thoroughly investigate each area of possible conspiracy. This led many assassination researchers to regret the firing of former Chief Counsel Sprague, who had strenuously insisted that the investigation be an open-ended one that could be funded for at least five years.

Thus, on the question of Jack Ruby's connections with the Marcellos, the committee failed to consider the Bobby Gene Moore allegation linking Ruby to Marcello through Carlos Marcello's Dallas deputy, Joseph Civello. And somehow it missed William B. Abadie's allegation linking Ruby to two of the Marcellos' prominent activities in Dallas: their jukebox and slot machine leasing business and their racing wire service.

Furthermore, it failed to investigate Ruby's possible relationship with Carlos Marcello's brothers—Vincent, Anthony, and Peter, in particular—who escaped the attention of the Assassinations Committee almost entirely. Likewise the committee never got to the bottom of Lee Harvey Oswald's precise relationship with the Marcello organization. The committee also did not investigate Edward Becker's allegation beyond interviewing Becker and Carlos Marcello about it; it could have also interviewed the two other alleged participants at the meeting: Carlo Roppolo and "Liverde." The latter, Becker believes, was a man named Liberto who might have come from the Liberto family of New Orleans, one of whose members was suspected of having conspired with Carlos Marcello to murder Martin Luther King, Jr. In addition, although the committee cast more suspicion on Carlos Marcello as a possible conspirator than on any other single individual, it made no attempt to investigate the Marcello brothers' movements, phone calls, meetings, and activities during the months immediately preceding and following the assassination. Finally, the committee did not investigate the possibility that J. Edgar Hoover deliberately manipulated and suppressed evidence of the Marcello family's possible complicity in the murders of Kennedy and Oswald.

But the Assassinations Committee's most significant failure, which was just as much a failure of the Congress of the United States as it was a failure of the committee it created, was its unforgivable acquiescence to the original provisions of its congressional mandate: that it terminate its investigation—no matter what—in January 1979, upon the expiration of the term of the 93rd Congress.

For as time was running out in late 1978, the committee had still not reviewed the complete FBI file on the assassination, or the complete CIA file on Oswald, and was unable, because of restraints of time and money, to give adequate attention to the new leads that were constantly cropping up.

In regard to the FBI and CIA files, it appears that the committee placed far too much trust in the FBI's and the CIA's willingness to cooperate with its investigation. In the end, both investigative agencies betrayed the committee's trust and therefore, by extension, the trust of the people of the United States. As we have seen, the FBI delayed turning over to the committee some 100,000 pages of assassination documents so that when they were finally delivered, the committee staff did not have time to examine them. Likewise with the CIA. In 1981 a Freedom of Information Act lawsuit against the CIA turned up a CIA memorandum stating that the agency's file on Oswald was not completely reviewed by Assassinations Committee staff members, that some sixteen file drawers of Oswald material were never seen by the chief counsel or by any staff member of the committee.

These inexcusable omissions inevitably tend to vitiate the achievements of the committee's investigation. For alas, the investigation that was supposed to end all assassinations investigations never saw, much less reviewed, several hundred thousand pages of government documents pertaining to the crime it was mandated to investigate.

As for unpursued leads...on November 27, 1978, as the committee was nearing the end of its term, two Dallas-based investigators, Earl Golz and Gary Mack, discovered a film of the assassination scene shot by an amateur photographer six minutes before President Kennedy was fired upon. It appeared to reveal the presence of two men on the sixth floor of the Texas School Book Depository. Known as the Bronson film, after its owner, Dallas citizen Charles Bronson, the film had a curious history. Shortly after the assassination Mr. Bronson turned his film over to the FBI for examination, and according to a declassified FBI memorandum discovered in 1978, the FBI had deemed the film to be of no value to the bureau's investigation of the assassination and therefore returned it to its owner. There it remained, in Charles Bronson's custody, until Goltz and Mack found it as a result of their discovery of the 1978 FBI memo.

Several eyewitnesses had testified to the FBI after the assassination that they had seen two men moving about on the sixth floor of the book depository just before the presidential motorcade arrived in Dealey Plaza. Carolyn Walther told an FBI agent she was sure she saw two men at the sixth-floor window from which the lone gunman, Lee Harvey Oswald, was supposed to have fired on the President. Ruby Henderson also told the FBI she noticed two men at the same window as did spurned eyewitnesses Richard Carr, Arnold Rowland, and Johnny Powell. And a prisoner in the Dallas County Jail opposite the book depository told an investigative reporter that he and several of his fellow inmates saw two men standing by a sixth-floor window moments before the shooting broke out, one of whom was adjusting the scope of his rifle. The inmate had assumed they were Secret Service agents.

Furthermore, there was another film, this one taken by amateur photographer Robert Hughes, within five seconds of the first shot, that also appeared to reveal the presence of two individuals standing by windows on the sixth floor of the depository. CBS News had this film analyzed by the ITEK Corporation in 1975, and ITEK determined that indeed there were two men on the sixth floor seconds before the assassination.

The testimony of these witnesses had been ignored by the FBI after the assassination because after the murder of Oswald, followed by Hoover's swift proclamation of the Oswald-the-lone-gunman-assassin dogma, any talk of two men seen at the Texas Book Depository "sniper's perch," which Hoover had reserved exclusively for Oswald, was heresy.

The Bronson film, however, seemed to vindicate the eyewitnesses' heretical testimony. It was submitted by the Assassinations Committee to photographic expert and consultant Robert Groden for analysis, and Groden threw the committee into last-minute turmoil. He reported that the film clearly showed human forms and movements in two of the sixth-floor windows simultaneously, indicating the presence of two men on the sixth floor just before the assassination.

This was a potentially major breakthrough in the case. If the Assassinations Committee had had any fight and determination left, it would have pushed hard to persuade the new Congress to extend its term, if only for a few months, so that the evidence of the Bronson film could be adequately evaluated. Instead it only recommended to the Justice Department that the film be investigated. So far it appears that the department has not yet acted on the Assassinations Committee's recommendation.

And so, as the House Assassinations Committee was winding up its investigation and issuing its historic finding of "probable conspiracy," it found itself virtually at the beginning of a brand new investigation which it could not pursue. Hundreds of thousands of FBI and CIA documents on the assassination were still unexamined. Several tantalizing leads suggesting that the Marcello crime family might have played some role in the killing of President Kennedy and Lee Harvey Oswald could not be pursued. Extremely persuasive evidence that two gunmen were positioned on the sixth floor of the book depository minutes before the President was shot could not be fully evaluated.

And yet, with all this unfinished business on its hands, the committee made no effort to persuade the new congressional leadership to extend the term of its mandate. Granted, the committee did recommend that the Justice Department examine further the acoustical evidence suggesting the presence of two gunmen firing from two locations. Granted, it recommended that the Bronson film be further analyzed and evaluated. But apparently it never specifically recommended that the possible complicity of the Marcello crime family in the assassination be investigated.

In March 1988 the Justice Department quietly issued its long overdue response to the Assassinations Committee's recommendations for further investigation. In an undated, unsigned memorandum to House Judiciary Committee Chairman Peter Rodino, Assistant Attorney General William F. Weld stated that the Department of Justice "has concluded that no persuasive evidence can be identified to support the theory of conspiracy in the assassination of President Kennedy."

The memorandum was not made public at the time by either the Justice Department or the House. It would probably still not have seen the light of day had it not been pried loose from the Justice Department through a Freedom of Information Act request by a California doctor who went to the press with it in September 1988.

The memorandum specifically stated that the Justice Department had not seen fit to analyze the Bronson film further, and nothing was said about whether it had investigated the possible involvement of organized crime in the assassination. It appears reasonably certain, then, that Justice simply did not bother to act on the Assassinations Committee's recommendations.

And so it has been left to individual private researchers to attempt to make some headway with the case. The discussions in this book of the De Laparra and SV T-1 allegations, and the FBI's response to them, and, as we shall see, Joseph Hauser's reports of his conversations with Carlos and Joe Marcello about the assassination are three examples of this continuing effort.

Since the Justice Department's handling of the case, certainly the most important homicide case in American history, has been suspect from the start, many seasoned researchers and investigators believe that the Justice Department will never act on the case. Better to let the case die than to establish proof of conspiracy that would discredit the FBI's original investigation.

And so, given the status of the case within the Justice Department nearly eight years after the House Select Committee on Assassinations issued its finding of probable conspiracy and voiced its suspicions of the possible involvement in the crime of Jimmy Hoffa, Santos Trafficante, and Carlos Marcello, one cannot help but conclude that the United States government either does not want to know who was behind the assassination of the President or, at best, does not want the nation and the world to know who was behind the crime.

It was one thing to tell the world that an unbalanced loner killed the President and was then quickly executed for his crime by a patriotic citizen taking the law into his own hands, and quite another to admit that one of the most powerful crime families in the nation had been able to change the course of American history by violent means and get away with it.

What was Carlos Marcello's reaction to the House Select Committee on Assassinations' publicly declared suspicion that he or his "crime family or organization" might have played a role in the assassination of President Kennedy?

There is solid evidence that he was quite disturbed, for in the summer of 1979, when those findings were finally published by the government printing office, he apparently assigned the matter to his most trusted attorney, the brilliant Jack Wasserman, for investigation. Wasserman immediately set about obtaining the available FBI files on the Kennedy assassination, which included the extensive files on David Ferrie and some documents, but not all, on the allegations of Eugene De Laparra and SV T-1, as well as the Edward Becker story of Marcello's threat to kill Kennedy.

These files, amounting to well over 220,000 pages of documents, had been obtained through a lengthy and costly Freedom of Information Act lawsuit brought against the Justice Department by Harold Weisberg, noted Kennedy assassination researcher and author of several books relating to the assassination. They were the files the Assassinations Committee should have had at the beginning of its investigation but did not receive until too late. Now they were being put at the disposal of Carlos Marcello's attorney.

From correspondence between Wasserman and Weisberg that I have examined, it appears that throughout the summer and fall of 1979 Jack Wasserman foraged in Weisberg's files in an attempt to retrieve every FBI document that could relate to the possibility of his client's having been involved in the assassination.

Because of this frantic response of Marcello's principal attorney to the House Committee on Assassinations' findings, we can safely assume that those findings were a matter of deep concern to Carlos Marcello.

Did Carlos expect there would be an investigation of his possible complicity in the assassination by the Justice Department—an investigation which might have led to the convening of a grand jury and the returning of an eventual indictment for conspiracy to murder the President of the United States?

If he did, Carlos could have done no better than to put his defense in Jack Wasserman's hands. If Wasserman could successfully defend him against the Immigration and Naturalization Service for over thirty years, in what had been the longest and costliest deportation case in U.S. history, he could surely give the U.S. attorney in New Orleans, who would prosecute any assassination conspiracy case against Marcello, the battle of his life.

But Jack Wasserman never got to defend his client against the charge that he had conspired to murder President Kennedy, for shortly after Wasserman began preparing for the anticipated case, he suddenly died of a heart attack.

However, as it turned out, the Justice Department was not preparing to prosecute Carlos Marcello for conspiring to murder Kennedy when Wasserman died in 1979. Instead it was conducting an undercover "sting" operation against him that the government hoped would send the Louisiana Mafia boss to prison for the rest of his life.

The operation had begun—unknown, of course, to Wasserman—shortly after the Assassinations Committee announced its findings and closed up shop. Ironically, it was almost precisely at this time that a former convict, now in the Justice Department's witness protection program, was able to gain the Marcellos' confidence sufficiently to get Carlos and his brother Joe to talk about the Kennedy assassination. The ex-convict was Joseph Hauser, a notorious swindler and con artist whom the Justice Department had recruited to help conduct the BRILAB undercover operation against Marcello. Had the Assassinations Committee been allowed to continue its investigation for another year, it might have been able to call Joseph Hauser as a witness in secret executive session and learn the private reaction of its major suspect, and his brother, to the committee's guarded suspicion they may have conspired to assassinate the President of the United States.

51

BRILAB: The Plan to Ensnare Marcello

In June 1976 veteran Washington lobbyist Isaac Irving Davidson told his new friend Joseph Hauser, a Los Angeles–based insurance operator and convicted swindler who was anxious to extend his business operations to Louisiana, that he would introduce him to "the man who controlled things in Louisiana," "the best-connected man in America," Carlos Marcello.

Davidson went on to tell Hauser that he had known Marcello for years and knew that he controlled the Teamsters and the Longshoremen in Louisiana, along with other, minor, unions, and could get Hauser any insurance business in the state he wanted. Davidson would take care of Marcello out of the $600,000 fund Hauser had already put at Davidson's disposal to take care of the right people. Hauser, who was already involved in a promising insurance scheme with Davidson, was only too eager to do business with the legendary Mafia don, whom Davidson habitually called "the boss" to Marcello's face but would refer to in private as "Uncle Snookems."

I. Irving Davidson was a specialist in "putting people together" and counted among his close friends such apparently disparate bedfellows as Carlos Marcello, J. Edgar Hoover, Jimmy Hoffa, and Richard Nixon. He had first gotten involved with Joseph Hauser in late 1975, when he had acted as middleman between Hauser and certain

Teamsters Welfare Fund trustees in a scheme to obtain a multi-million-dollar-a-year life insurance contract for one of Hauser's companies, Farmers National Life Insurance of Miami, from the Central States, Southeast and Southwest Teamsters Health and Welfare Fund. Also involved in the scheme were Florida Mafia boss Santos Trafficante, Jr., and former attorney general under Richard Nixon, Richard G. Kleindienst, to whom, Hauser testified, he paid a $250,000 finder's fee for his help in landing the Teamsters contract.

When, in mid-June 1976, Davidson formally introduced Hauser to Carlos Marcello in Carlos's Town & Country office, Carlos told Hauser:

"I checked you out with my people and I know you is good people.... I know you make good your word."

Hauser immediately understood the code phrase "make good your word" to mean that Marcello had already received some of the money that Hauser had given to Davidson.

The following day, by placing a few calls here and there to a few key people in his invisible network, Marcello made it possible for Hauser to do business in Louisiana.

During the next thirty days Hauser and Marcello met some ten times. Marcello liked Hauser and trusted him, despite Hauser's notoriety as a con man and swindler. Among the deals they concluded was an agreement for Carlos to help Joe Hauser and Irv Davidson obtain control of the National American Life Insurance Company (NALICO) of Baton Rouge from Carlos's friends Jules and Rodger Le Blanc, and a promise from Carlos to help Hauser get all the Building Trade Union insurance business in Louisiana. Marcello also told Hauser he could deliver other union health and welfare insurance contracts as they came due, specifically the lucrative Teamsters and Longshoremen's contracts. As it turned out, Hauser was able to purchase control of NALICO for $24 million within a few days of Carlos's intervention on his behalf. For these initial services of Marcello's, which consisted mostly of phone calls to friends and associates, Davidson paid the boss $250,000.

So the meeting that Irving Davidson arranged between the Louisiana Mafia boss and the notorious insurance swindler had turned out to be, at first, most fruitful for all concerned. It was not for nothing that Davidson's business card gave his occupation as "Door Opener and Arranger."

However, unknown to all three at the time, the meeting was also destined to be a most fateful one for all concerned, especially Marcello. Several years later, it was Joe Hauser who, turning the tables on his New Orleans friend, cunningly led the hitherto invulnerable Carlos into a trap from which he would never escape, one that would eventually send him to prison for the rest of his life.

When, and how, did the Marcello-Hauser love affair go sour?

Not long after Joe Hauser bought NALICO, the Securities and Exchange Commission began investigating how Hauser had been able to gain control of the company and how he was subsequently managing it. Finding irregularities, the SEC filed a cease and desist order against NALICO and placed the company under receivership. In early 1977 Hauser lost control of the company and fell into a legal dispute with the company's former owners, the Le Blancs, who still owed him money but were pleading bankruptcy. From then on, Hauser, of course, was unable to take advantage of Marcello's union contracts.

Meanwhile, Hauser's and Davidson's scheme to obtain the Teamsters Southeast and Southwest Health and Welfare Fund life insurance contract by bribing the fund's trustees had come under investigation by the Justice Department. In 1978 Hauser was indicted, along with Davidson, on federal racketeering charges in Phoenix, Arizona. Following a lengthy trial, Hauser pleaded guilty on February 5, 1979, to criminal charges of conspiracy, bribery, and racketeering.

It was at this time that FBI Special Agent William Fleming, a specialist in undercover operations with an alert eye for convicted felons willing to turn government informer in exchange for lighter sentences, approached Joe Hauser. He proposed that the convicted swindler participate in an undercover operation against his former associate Carlos Marcello, as part of the Justice Department's nationwide sting operation, called BRILAB (after bribery and labor), "to criminally involve labor officials" suspected of being engaged in illegal activities in association with leaders of organized crime. In exchange for his participation, Hauser would receive the benefit of Justice Department attorneys' assistance at his sentencing, generous compensation payments, reimbursement of all expenses, and a place in the federal witness protection program. Hauser had been looking for a way to plea bargain for a reduced sentence, so he jumped at Fleming's proposal. Eventually Hauser's cooperation with the government allowed him to escape punishment on his ten-count Phoenix conviction for swindling $3.5 million from the Teamsters.

And so, in late February 1979, Joe Hauser joined forces with the FBI, and the undercover operation to ensnare Carlos Marcello got under way.

Curiously, it was precisely at this time that the House Select Committee on Assassinations was issuing its finding of probable conspiracy in the John F. Kennedy assassination investigation and the New Orleans *Times-Picayune* was proclaiming, in front-page headlines, the committee's suspicions of Marcello's involvement in the crime.

The government's plan to finally nail Carlos Marcello, after decades of frustrated attempts, was to set up a fictitious insurance brokerage on the West Coast, modeled after Hauser's past insurance operations. It was to be called Fidelity Financial Consultants and would be represented in Louisiana by Joe Hauser and two young associates who would actually be FBI undercover agents. Hauser, whose status now was that of a convicted felon free on bail, and his men would then induce Marcello to get key Louisiana public officials to award important union, state, and municipal insurance contracts to Fidelity in return for a share of the enormous insurance commissions on the contracts, which could conceivably amount to $100,000 a month. Carlos's conversations with Hauser, his two assistants, and the various state officials he would attempt to bribe would be recorded by electronic listening devices and wiretaps installed in his office and home by FBI technicians and by the body wires and tape recorders carried by Hauser and his men. It was hoped that Marcello would be caught red-handed offering bribes, in the form of kickbacks of the lucrative insurance commissions, to public officials who awarded contracts to Joe Hauser's Fidelity Financial Consultants.

The FBI had decided to take this route to prosecute Marcello because all normal investigative techniques—such as physical surveillance and interviews with informants—had been tried and had failed against the Louisiana boss in the past. The FBI believed this failure was due to fear of reprisal from the Marcellos on the part of confidential sources acting as FBI informants and also, in the words of one agent associated with the BRILAB operation, to "Marcello's extremely sophisticated mode of operation, designed to insulate himself from law enforcement agencies and his own criminal activities." For the FBI had learned that Marcello never dealt with people outside his trusted circle of aides. His aides, and their subordinates, acted for him. For example, Marcello's dealings with Hauser in the initial stages of their relationship always had to go through Irv Davidson.

It was therefore absolutely necessary to utilize electronic surveillance in investigating Marcello. There was no other way to penetrate to the core of his criminal enterprise. Hence also the necessity of creating a dummy business organization with which Marcello would presumably conduct much business over the phone.

And so, under the guidance of FBI coordinators William Fleming and William Weichert, the fictitious corporation was quickly established and its spanking new offices were opened in Beverly Hills. Personalized business cards and stationery were then printed by the FBI and issued to Fidelity representative Joseph Hauser and his two assistants, his "nephew" and "nephew's friend," who were, in reality, FBI undercover operatives Michael Wacks and Larry Montague. The cards and stationery proclaimed that Hauser, Wacks, and Montague represented a company associated with the Prudential Insurance Company of America, one of the largest insurance companies in the world. The prestige of the Prudential connection was emphasized on the cards and stationery by the relative size of the printing for the two company names: "Prudential Insurance Company" in boldface type at least twice as large as the type used for "Fidelity Financial Consultants."

Armed with these impressive credentials, and with body wires and attaché cases containing tape recorders hidden in false bottoms, Joe Hauser, and later Mike Wacks and Larry Montague, then prepared to leave for New Orleans to enter the lion's den.

Meanwhile, under the direction of Harold Hughes, FBI agents and technicians in New Orleans were getting ready to install a listening device in Marcello's office and to place interceptions on Marcello's phones. This was done with the authorization of the attorney general and by means of 30-day court orders signed by a federal district judge in New Orleans.

The FBI eventually established its telephone monitoring station in two apartments in a Metairie apartment complex called Chateaux Dijon. There six tape recorders were installed to tap Marcello's telephones in his Town & Country office and Metairie residence on a twenty-four-hour basis. Six FBI agents were to monitor the phone calls, in shifts, around the clock. Whenever someone would pick up the receiver of one of Marcello's phones, a horn would honk and a light would flash on the FBI's surveillance equipment. The agents would then don headphones to listen to the conversations, which were simultaneously recorded by the machines.

Before the FBI installed the hidden microphone in Marcello's office, FBI agents had rented a room in the Village Inn, a motel adjacent to Marcello's office, with a view of the office entrance. From there FBI agents monitored and videotaped the comings and goings of the Mafia boss and others. The agents also copied license plate numbers of visitors' automobiles and, in some cases, followed the departing visitors.

Installing the bug in Marcello's inner sanctum proved challenging. Still, it was a lot easier to accomplish than the New Orleans FBI office claimed it would be at the time of the Kennedy assassination, when Marcello's FBI handler insisted that Carlos was a mere tomato salesman who happened to have an impregnable security system.

The Town & Country Motel, as we know, consisted of three separate structures: the main building, containing the motel office and apartments; the restaurant, a long, low building in the shape of a typical roadside diner; and a small brick building behind the restaurant housing Carlos's suite of offices. A driveway to the right of the restaurant led back to the office building, which was somewhat removed from the other structures in the compound.

In the dead of a night chosen for its extreme darkness, a 40-foot tank truck carrying a team of armed FBI agents, some dressed in street clothes and others in typical truckers outfits, veered off Airline Highway, drove up to the motel complex, and came to a halt in front of the driveway leading to Marcello's office, blocking access to it entirely. They then got out, and the two agents dressed in work clothes put the truck's hood up and began pretending to repair the engine.

Eighteen other agents, guns at the ready, then made their way down the driveway to the little office building in back of the restaurant, prepared, in coordinator Harold Hughes's words, "to do what they had to do" if they happened to encounter any of Marcello's men.

Fortunately there were no guards around, and getting into the small, squat building posed no problems. Three of the agents then went straight to Carlos's office while the other fifteen stood guard at the entrance.

The FBI technicians wanted to install the bug behind a tile in the drop ceiling right above Carlos's desk. Working rapidly, using flashlights, they soon realized they could not obtain egress with "a hard wire," so they had to temporarily install a small FM transmitter. It took the technicians almost three hours to remove the ceiling tile, install the transmitter, put the tile back, and clean up so there would be no trace left of their presence when Marcello came to work at eight that morning.

Although Marcello's security was nonexistent, there was always the chance that the motel watchman might discover the FBI team on his rounds. But the watchman stuck to the area around the motel's apartments. At one point the night clerk on duty in the motel office went out to see what was going on with the apparently broken down truck, which a returning motel guest had brought to his attention. The agents, pretending to be working feverishly under the hood, thanked the clerk for his concern and told him they would have the engine fixed up real soon. The clerk then wished them luck and went back to his office.

Three days later the FBI team went back into the lion's den and, in a repeat performance, removed the FM transmitter from the ceiling and made the hard-wire installation. The operation had been an unqualified success.

On leaving Marcello's suite of offices the second time, one of the agents spotted on the main entrance door something he had not noticed during the first break-in: the sign, THREE CAN KEEP A SECRET IF TWO ARE DEAD.

When the team was making its getaway down Airline Highway in the tank truck, the agent told the others about it.

"Man," one of them said, "you've been seeing too many of those *Godfather*-type flicks," and as the great truck rolled down the highway, they all laughed.

The stage was now set for what was to become the most extensive, and successful, sting operation against a Mafia leader in FBI history up to that time.

52

Sting One

"They all want money....Just like all you wants money....
Everybody wants money....Anytime a politician goes in there,
he wants money...."

So observed Carlos Marcello in a taped conversation with Joe
Hauser and FBI undercover agents Mike Wacks and Larry Montague
as the FBI sting operation was getting under way.

The yearlong undercover operation coincided with the 1979 Louisiana gubernatorial campaign and election, and as it developed, the
FBI sting and Louisiana election politics became inextricably en-
twined.

The governor of Louisiana at the time was the flamboyant Democrat Edwin Edwards, a former Cajun farm boy who had clawed and
charmed his way up from local "coonass politics" to the summit of
political power in his state.

In another conversation recorded by the undercover team during
the BRILAB operation, Marcello gave his opinion of the governor:

"Edmund [sic] and me all right, but I can't seen him every
day....He's the strongest sonofabitchin' governor we ever had.
He fuck with women and he plays dice games, but he won't
drink. How you like dat?"

Edwards' lieutenant governor in 1979 was James Fitzmorris, about whom Marcello remarked in other taped conversations with the undercover agents:

"Fitzmorris? All he can do is ask a favor. He ain't worth a shit."
...
"Fitzmorris is a bullshit artist since 1948. He's been bullshitting the public, he comes close to gettin' elected with that bullshit....But he don't have enough balls to do what's right."

Edwin Edwards had decided to withdraw from the 1979 gubernatorial race, paving the way for Fitzmorris to enter the Democratic primary contest against State Public Service Commissioner Louis Lambert.

On the Republican side, the primary battle was between reform candidate David Treen and State Senator Edgar G. "Sonny" Mouton. The Louisiana statewide open primary was to be held on October 27 and the general election on December 8.

As the BRILAB operation against Marcello unfolded, the outcome of these political contests became a matter of vital concern to the principals on both sides of the operation, for it was important to the success of their scheme that the government officials Hauser wanted Marcello to bribe were associated with a candidate who stood a chance of becoming governor in 1980.

Carlos Marcello was not the only individual the Justice Department wanted Joe Hauser to pursue in the BRILAB operation. BRILAB was broad in scope. It had been conceived as capable of including the investigation of a variety of criminal activities.

Since the government believed that Hauser's friend Irv Davidson was closely associated with Carlos Marcello, it instructed Hauser also to pursue Davidson undercover, to gain his assistance in acquiring insurance business for Fidelity-Prudential and in renewing Hauser's acquaintance with Marcello. Hauser consented to the Justice Department's wish that he also record Irv Davidson's conversations. To further surveil Davidson, the FBI also secured authorization from the attorney general to tap the lobbyist's phones.

The Justice Department wanted to keep an ear on Davidson because, unlike Hauser, Davidson had kept up a continuous association with Marcello for the past twenty years. As it turned out, Davidson was involved at the time in an effort to get the Immigration Service to modify its long-standing deportation order against Marcello by offering a favor to the second highest ranking official in the INS.

Who was I. Irving Davidson, the man who, by first introducing Hauser to Marcello, indirectly and unwittingly caused his old Louisiana friend's downfall?

In his own words, he was "the grease for the machinery," a man who had spent his life "wheeling and dealing on a tightrope without a net." Davidson was the epitome of the Washington lobbyist, a schemer and promoter with a vast international network of powerful acquaintances. Comfortable with almost everybody, from sultans and sheiks to Central American tyrants and U.S. Mafia bosses, he was a man who somehow knew secrets nobody else in Washington knew. When Carlos Marcello was summarily deported to Guatemala by Bobby Kennedy and when Jimmy Hoffa disappeared off the face of the earth, the first person Washington columnist Jack Anderson phoned to get the inside stories was Irv Davidson.

Born in 1920, the son of a Pittsburgh meat market owner of eastern European Jewish stock, Davidson was a short, slight, quick little man with a perpetual grin on a face that was dominated by a huge, bulbous potato nose. Often described as "elfin," he was known for moving lightly on his feet, like, as one observer put it, "a cat on eggs." Davidson's most characteristic attitude was whispering out of the corner of his mouth a scrap of inside information in the ear of some associate. Immensely popular in Washington, he flattered a man by giving him the impression he was sharing a given secret only with him and no one else.

The interests Davidson represented in Washington were not very savory. He was a registered lobbyist for the Teamsters and had been a friend of Jimmy Hoffa. He was the registered lobbyist for the Somozas of Nicaragua, the Duvaliers of Haiti, the Trujillos of the Dominican Republic, and the wealthy Murchisons of Dallas, owners of the Dallas Cowboys, to name a few of his most powerful clients. He shared his close friendship with the Murchisons with another good friend, J. Edgar Hoover, who, it has been said, relied on Davidson for inside information no one else was able to provide. Max Kampelman, the present U.S. disarmament negotiator in Geneva, another perpetual smiler, was a fellow Washington lobbyist during Davidson's heyday, and the two were often seen together gossiping in Washington restaurants.

Irv Davidson's activities ranged the entire globe. He once sold seventy Israeli-made staghound tanks to Nicaragua. He lobbied on behalf of the CIA on Capitol Hill. He represented Fidel Castro's interests in the United States. As the registered lobbyist for Coca-Cola, he personally escorted Coca-Cola soft drink teams on missions all over the world. He did a good deal of business with the sultan of Oman and was instrumental in getting Carlos Marcello involved in business with Oman and other Persian Gulf countries. He arranged, through Jimmy Hoffa, a huge Teamsters Pension Fund loan to the Murchisons and was deeply involved in a Murchison business deal that provided funds for Lyndon Johnson's bagman, Bobby Baker. According to Edward Partin, Davidson witnessed a secret meeting between Marcello and Hoffa in late 1960 during which "a $500,000 cash payment to the Nixon campaign was made." As we have already seen, Davidson joined forces with Carlos Marcello to help keep Jimmy Hoffa from going to prison, and after Hoffa was jailed, he helped Marcello coordinate the "spring Hoffa" effort that eventually resulted in Hoffa's pardon by Richard Nixon, another close friend of Davidson's.

As the representative of all that Jack and Bobby Kennedy fought against—Trujillo, Hoffa's Teamsters, the Somozas' Nicaragua, the Texas rich, the CIA, Castro, Nixon, the mob—Davidson certainly was a representative in good standing of the interests that profited most conspicuously from the destruction of the Kennedy brothers.

It is not difficult to understand why Irv Davidson and Joe Hauser hit it off so well together. They were two men cut from the same cloth. A small, quick, dapper man, also Jewish, Hauser too was a street-smart schemer and machinery greaser with a vast collection of useful and powerful—and potentially dangerous—acquaintances eager to help him, and themselves, make money.

Although Joe Hauser was born in the village of Barnov, Poland, his complexion and facial contours were so Mediterranean—olive skin, bushy black eyebrows, black hair, mobile features—that he often struck people as more like a Latin American or southern European business magnate than the Polish refugee from the Holocaust he actually was. Hauser claimed his was the only family from Barnov that escaped the gas chambers. He himself had been interned in the Nazi concentration camp at Malthausen, condemned to die in the lethal shower rooms from one day to the next. His daring escape from the camp, a day before he was due to be gassed, allowed him to flee to America. There he arrived, as World War II was drawing to a close, with only the proverbial clothes on his back.

Before becoming a big-time insurance speculator, Hauser had knocked around trying to hustle a dollar here and there, working in New York as a butcher, in a Chicago slaughterhouse, in a jewelry factory, and in a small insurance brokerage in Los Angeles. Ambitious to make as much money as he could, as rapidly as possible, he settled on the insurance business as the ideal vehicle to make the big bucks he confesses he dreamed of day and night.

After he made his first millions as a free-wheeling, unscrupulous insurance operator, Hauser bought a $750,000 mansion in Beverly Hills, next door to Kirk Douglas's place, and began leading a wildly extravagant existence, spending and gambling his money away as if his newly won cash flow would continue forever. Among the contacts he made on the West Coast at the time were big-time Las Vegas mobster Johnny Roselli and local Mafia boss Jack Dragna.

"Look," he told a journalist in 1981, "what I did, I didn't do in a small way. Sure I gambled. Sure I wore expensive clothes. Sure I made half million dollar payoffs to people like they were nothing. Yeah, I'd blow sixty grand gambling in one afternoon. Yeah, I wore $2,000 custom-made Italian suits. What do you expect from a guy whose only realistic future at one point in his life was the gas chamber? Since my escape from the Nazis, all of my life has been a dream anyway."

Joe Hauser was able to support his extravagances by buying companies and milking them dry. His modus operandi was to purchase control of an insurance company, then, through his Mafia contacts, bribe union and government officials to award his company their organization's insurance contracts. When sufficient assets had accumulated in the company's accounts, he would then siphon them off into his and his associates' pockets, leaving the company high and dry while he quickly moved on to new pastures.

Before putting this formula into practice in Louisiana, with the blessing of Carlos Marcello, Hauser had tried it out in Florida with disastrous results. There he and Irv Davidson had gotten Tampa-based Mafia boss Santos Trafficante, Jr., to garner labor union insurance business for him by offering union officials huge kickbacks. But he wasn't so lucky this time. The feds had been watching Trafficante closely, and Trafficante, Hauser, and Davidson soon found themselves charged with dipping their fingers in the seemingly bottomless cookie jar of the Teamsters Southeast States Health and Welfare Fund. (All three were indicted, but the charges against Davidson were eventually dropped.)

Considering Hauser's notoriety as a con artist, and the fact that he had recently been convicted of attempted bribery and racketeering in Phoenix and was rumored in Phoenix to be plea bargaining with the feds, it is surprising that the wily Carlos allowed himself to be taken in. Yet, as we shall see, Marcello swallowed his friend's bait as trustingly as a Mississippi catfish sucking in a proffered worm.

That Hauser was able also to dupe his Washington pal Irv Davidson, a wary fox if ever there was one, was a further tribute to his
consummate powers of deception.

Joe Hauser's first face-to-face meeting with Carlos Marcello as a government undercover operator took place on April 2, 1979, in Hauser's
suite in New Orleans' Maison Dupuy Hotel. Hauser had his special
FBI-designed briefcase with a tape recorder in its false bottom ready
to do its job, and the FBI had installed an intercept on his hotel room
phone.

Marcello greeted Hauser cordially and then sat down on a couch
before a coffee table bearing the magic briefcase.

At first Marcello talked about the annoying problems with NAL-
ICO and the Le Blancs, whom he suspected were "stool pigeons"
because they had once sent someone to him who was wearing a recording device.

After bantering about stool pigeons and recording devices for a
few minutes, Hauser, at Marcello's insistence, placed a call to Irv
Davidson's office in Washington. Carlos instructed Hauser to tell
Davidson they were calling from the hotel telephone so they could
talk. Marcello then took the receiver and told Davidson that the three
of them were going to get involved soon in some important new business. After the call Carlos explained to Hauser that he wanted
Davidson to be aware of everything.

The FBI's intercepts of conversations between Hauser, Marcello,
and Davidson revealed to the bureau both the extent of Marcello's
and Davidson's fears of electronic surveillance and the elaborate steps
that Marcello habitually took to insulate himself from the crimes he
was planning.

During one conversation, Davidson told Hauser that Marcello believed he was "on a permanent bug." In another exchange between
the two, Davidson expressed concern that either he or Hauser was
"on a wire." During Marcello's almost daily telephone conversations
with Davidson, Marcello went to great lengths to avoid being overheard by FBI listening devices. Davidson would phone Marcello's
Town & Country office and tell Carlos's secretary he wanted to speak
with Marcello. The secretary, who knew Davidson's voice, would tell
him to phone a certain number at a certain time. Upon phoning that
number, Davidson would be told by an unknown individual to phone
another number, and he would finally make contact with the boss.

Rarely did Marcello communicate anything of substance over the phone to Hauser, with whom he was directly involved in conspiring to bribe public officials in order to obtain insurance contracts. He would almost always go through Davidson, using his special brand of cryptic language, and have Davidson inform Hauser what was going on in his own cryptic language.

At their first meeting in the Maison Dupuy Hotel, the aggressive Hauser soon got down to the business at hand. With his tape recorder rolling, he asked Carlos if he could help him get some insurance contracts soon, that his new outfit was anxious to do a lot of business in Louisiana. He then assured Marcello that Davidson would "take care of him good."

Carlos then began discussing the possibility of Hauser submitting a bid to the New Orleans City Council, which was seeking to change its health insurance coverage for 22,000 city employees from Blue Cross to another carrier. Hauser's double-bottom briefcase then picked up the following exchange:

HAUSER: So you got a lot of juice down there?

MARCELLO: Yeah, I've got 'em all where I want 'em. I got to tell 'em, "Look, put it in this company here and let 'em bid on it. Let it come out for bid." Can you bid now?

HAUSER: Yes, we could bid tomorrow.

MARCELLO: You can? All right, then you given me something to go to work on right now. What kind of deal can I make if you know what it is?

HAUSER: I have to know what benefits they want. What dollars they have to spend.

MARCELLO: All right, the City of New Orleans.

HAUSER: I have to be able to talk with someone.

MARCELLO: All right, I'll get you all the information, tell you what they paying now, what they benefit is and everything.

Carlos told Hauser he could get him all the Jefferson Parish employees health insurance contracts too. Referring to Doug Allen, president of the Jefferson Parish Council, Carlos told Hauser that both Allen and the head lawyer for the council, Harry Lee, were their "kind of people," that once the contract was obtained they would "pay who we have to pay."

Later in the discussion at the Maison Dupuy, Marcello asked Hauser if he would ever be able to get the Teamsters back. And Hauser responded: "That's up to you. I'm looking at you, my friend."

Carlos then told Hauser that Teamsters President Fitzsimmons was going to resign and that his successor would be "a guy from Kansas City or a guy from St. Louis."

Hauser asked Marcello how he was connected, and Carlos told him it would "be all right as soon as Fitzsimmons resigns."

"Are you closest to the guy from Kansas City or the guy from St. Louis?" Hauser asked.

"Don't make no difference," Marcello replied. "You just gotta go through the routine. I can handle that."

"Then you got the Teamsters under control?"

"Soon as Fitzsimmons is out."

Two days later Irv Davidson phoned Joe Hauser at the Maison Dupuy and, referring to Marcello, told him: "Our friend enjoyed meeting and talking to you again." Davidson said he had met with Marcello prior to Hauser's meeting. "He's excited about it," Davidson told Hauser. "It's all good."

There followed two months of phone calls between Marcello, Davidson, and Hauser, during which Marcello tried to keep Hauser and Davidson abreast of his progress in getting all the information he could on the City of New Orleans and Jefferson Parish employees insurance contracts. Finally, around mid-June, Carlos felt he was in a position to make concrete plans and summoned Hauser and Davidson to New Orleans for a meeting.

The meeting was held in Marcello's Town & Country office on June 22. It was the first time Hauser had met face to face with the two men he was betraying since the undercover operation began. Later he confessed to a journalist that when he put the attaché case on Carlos's desk, he could feel his "guts turning inside" and his bleeding ulcer acting up.

At one point Carlos reached across his desk, thrust his hand into the attaché case, and, while ruffling through Hauser's papers, asked: "What you got in dere? You ain't got no bug or nuttin' in dere, do ya?"

"You kiddin'?" said Hauser.

"Yeah, I'm only kidding,'" Marcello said.

Soon the three got down to business. Carlos made it clear to

Hauser that everything had to go through Davidson, that he didn't want to get too directly involved. "When you're talkin' to Irv, you're talkin' to me," Marcello emphasized.

Carlos then told Hauser and Davidson he was going to get them the New Orleans and Jefferson Parish insurance contracts and could probably also get them the Louisiana state employees' group life insurance contract and the Avondale Shipyards, which meant the Longshoremen. But they had to come up with "a lot of money to take care of everybody right." Davidson then told Carlos not to worry about that. "No problem," he told the boss. "No problem." There followed an exchange between Marcello and Hauser:

MARCELLO: I'm gonna try to get Jefferson for you first and then New Orleans. Or I might get New Orleans first.

HAUSER: Okay.

MARCELLO: In New Orleans you just gotta take care of the mayor and the council.

HAUSER: How much?

MARCELLO: I don't know yet. I still gotta feel 'em out. But the mayor he do what I say.

HAUSER: Yeah.

MARCELLO: We'll go the whole fuckin' state, if it's necessary. I'll go with you....We'll take it off the top, and whatever it is, we'll cut it three ways.

HAUSER: You're the boss, Carlos.

The meeting broke up in a mood of optimism, with Carlos assuring "the boys" everything was going "to work out okay."

Meanwhile Irv Davidson had a little undercover operation of his own going with "Uncle Snookems" that was unrelated to the government's BRILAB effort and that turned out to be a bonus for the Justice Department. For while the FBI's sting against Marcello was unfolding, Davidson was quietly attempting to induce a high-ranking official of the Immigration and Naturalization Service to modify the travel constraints and reporting requirements in force against Marcello.

Marcello in 1979 was still under the order of deportation that had been entered against him in 1956 and reaffirmed in 1961—chiefly at

the insistence of Attorney General Robert Kennedy. He had been
battling it continuously for over twenty years. Under this order,
Marcello was subject to "report for deportation when directed," "report in person to the INS quarterly," and "notify the INS of depar-
tures from Louisiana for more than forty-eight hours."

While Davidson was attempting to intervene on Carlos's behalf,
Marcello was litigating against the INS in district court in New Orleans, seeking a court injunction to remand the case to the Board of
Immigration Appeals in order to determine the legality of the original deportation order.

The Marcello deportation case had become by 1979 the longest and
costliest deportation case in U.S. history. The case had been complicated by the Kennedy-inspired "kidnap-deportation" action of 1961,
which had been arguably illegal, and the related conspiracy and perjury case against the Marcellos that followed Carlos's defiant reentry
into the country. Although the government's pressure on Marcello
had relented somewhat after the assassination of President Kennedy,
the case dragged on and on, with Marcello always succeeding in out-
witting the government, thanks to the brilliance of his deportation
attorney, Jack Wasserman. It has been estimated that the fees Marcello
had paid Wasserman for his work on the deportation case alone had
amounted to something in the neighborhood of $2 million by 1979.

The FBI's taps on Marcello's and Davidson's phones revealed that
the two men were in touch with each other practically every day, in
regard to both obtaining the insurance contracts and getting the concessions from the INS. Transcriptions of their recorded dialogues
reveal that the two spoke in a sort of code designed to confuse the
feds, who they were sure were listening in.

What the endless dialogues boiled down to was that Irv Davidson
was trying to get the INS deputy commissioner of immigration, Mario
Noto, to help lift the travel restrictions the INS had imposed on
Marcello. In return, he was offering Noto a plush job with Coca-Cola,
a company Davidson represented as a lobbyist, upon the immigration official's imminent retirement from the INS. For his labors on
Marcello's behalf, Davidson was to receive certain compensation, referred to in Carlos's taped conversations as "enough for all y'all" and
"the shrimp," and in Davidson's words as "a free cup of coffee."

One of the most revealing of the taped Davidson-Marcello dialogues concerning the INS occurred on May 14, 1979:

DAVIDSON: He [Mario Noto] told me the agency will go along,
              but then there's one more place that they have to go

> to, uh, outside the agency. Now even if you're on [in-
> audible], I want you to know it's the criminal divi-
> sion in the Justice Department.

MARCELLO: Yeah.

DAVIDSON: And I know the name of the gentleman and I've al-
> ready called and any time I get, we're going to get
> an appointment.

So there was even someone in the criminal division of the Justice
Department who might be willing to help the boss of the Louisiana
Mafia, whom the Justice Department was currently pursuing, overcome restrictions the INS, a branch of the Justice Department, had
imposed on him.

What makes the long and close relationship between Irv Davidson
and Carlos Marcello potentially so significant are the concerns and
interests of Davidson's other long and close relationships. People like
Jimmy Hoffa, Santos Trafficante, Johnny Roselli, Luis Somoza, Rafael
Trujillo, Clint Murchison, Bobby Baker, Lyndon Johnson, Richard
Nixon, and J. Edgar Hoover.

It was around the time of Irv Davidson's machinations in the Justice Department that another one of Davidson's close friends, syndicated columnist Jack Anderson, wrote an entire column on Carlos
Marcello, identifying him as "the most powerful mobster in the nation" and the House Assassinations Committee's "chief suspect in the
John F. Kennedy assassination plot."

Considering the closeness of the long-standing Davidson-Marcello
relationship, and some of the people Davidson was close to at the
time of the Kennedy assassination, one cannot help speculate on the
possible coconspirators in high places that Carlos Marcello could have
reached, through Irving Davidson, at the time of the assassination,
all of whom were arch enemies of the Kennedys: defeated presidential candidate Nixon, newly sworn-in President Johnson, and the man
Johnson had entrusted with investigating the Kennedy murder, FBI
Director J. Edgar Hoover.

Jack Anderson's column on Carlos Marcello and his suspected role
in the Kennedy assassination plot was published in the New Orleans
Times-Picayune in mid-July 1979.

FBI undercover agent Larry Montague remembers hearing about

the article but did not discuss it with Marcello at the time. "I didn't want to throw Marcello off," he told me eight years later. "I didn't want to make him suspicious by raising such an issue as the Kennedy assassination with him at that time. I considered it but came to the conclusion that I could possibly blow the whole operation if I brought it up with him.... Also, from a legal standpoint, I was supposed to confine my conversations with Carlos strictly to the operation at hand. We got the title threes only for that."

Joe Hauser was not so circumspect. The House Assassinations Committee's findings and suspicions were constantly in the New Orleans papers in the spring and summer of 1979, and Hauser occasionally mentioned them to Marcello during their innumerable conversations in the restaurants of Metairie and New Orleans.

What Hauser claims he received from Carlos was a casual admission that both Lee Harvey Oswald and his uncle Dutz Murret had worked in his downtown bookmaking network and that during the summer of 1963 Oswald worked as a "runner" for Sam Saia and Dutz Murret out of one of Saia's bookmaking establishments, the Felix Oyster House, a restaurant Saia owned on Iberville Street in the French Quarter, just around the corner from Pete Marcello's Sho-Bar.

Hauser reconstructs Marcello's remarks on his organization's relationship with Oswald, which he did not record because they were made in informal conversation, roughly as follows:

> "Oswald? I used to know his fuckin' family. His uncle he work for me. Dat kid work for me too. He worked for Sam outa his place downtown, you know, Saia's restaurant, the Felix Oyster Bar or somethin' like dat. The feds came up to de motel askin' about him, but my people didn't tell 'em nuttin'. Like we never heard of the guy, y'know."

Hauser claims he also elicited from Carlos's brother Joe a hint that the Marcellos might have been involved in the Kennedy assassination. One day Hauser brought up the subject of the Kennedys as he was reading, in Joe's presence, an account of Teddy Kennedy's 1980 campaign for the Democratic presidential nomination. Looking up from the paper, Hauser said something like: "Well, the Kennedys are at it again, Joe. Now it's Teddy. Boy, his brothers sure gave ole Carlos a rough time back when they deported him." To this Joe Marcello had remarked: "Don't worry, we took care of 'em, didn't we?"

FBI undercover agent Mike Wacks told me eight years later that he remembers Hauser telling him what Joe Marcello said.

Wacks and Montague also recall Marcello indulging in a long

monologue about his "kidnapping by Bobby Kennedy" in 1961. In the summer of 1979 they were driving from Lafayette to New Orleans in Marcello's car when Carlos saw fit to hold forth for at least a half hour on his ordeals in Guatemala, El Salvador, and Honduras.

Around the time that Jack Anderson published his column on Marcello and the Kennedy assassination, Irv Davidson received a call from Carlos informing him that he had already made the necessary arrangements for the Jefferson Parish employees insurance contract and would "straighten out New Orleans soon." But by the end of July Carlos had still not straightened out New Orleans and was thus constrained to phone Davidson in Washington and instruct him to tell Joe Hauser "to sit tight."

August is a slow month everywhere in the Deep South, but in Louisiana it is probably slower than anywhere else, so slow that business comes to a virtual standstill in the stifling midsummer heat. In downtown New Orleans the streets are almost deserted in August, as people choose to lead the air-conditioned life, venturing out into the hot, stagnant, below-sea-level air as little as possible. In this enervating atmosphere Carlos Marcello could do little with New Orleans' black mayor Ernest N. Morial—whom he habitually referred to in his conversations with Hauser as "that nigger" and whom he told both Hauser and Davidson he "controlled" (which turned out to be untrue)—and he could do even less with the New Orleans City Council. And so Carlos began casting around for another deal. Soon he came up with a scheme to make some really big money.

Carlos had set his sights on the Louisiana state employees group life insurance contract. If he could land that contract for Fidelity-Prudential, it would generate commissions of nearly $100,000 a month. Half of that he would offer as a kickback to the Louisiana state official who could get him the contract, and the other half would go to himself, Hauser, and Davidson.

Carlos learned that the Louisiana state official he might have to grease was Charles E. Roemer II, the commissioner of administration of the state of Louisiana and campaign manager for Louisiana gubernatorial candidate State Senator Edgar G. "Sonny" Mouton. As commissioner of administration, Roemer was the immediate superior of the chairman of the Board of Trustees of the Louisiana State Employees Group Benefits Program, Joe Terrell, whose trustees would render the final decision on the awarding of the state employees group life insurance contracts.

Marcello then told a friend of his in the state government, Aubrey

Young, something about his scheme and asked to be introduced to
Roemer. Young obliged, and Roemer and Marcello agreed to meet
in New Orleans toward the end of the month.

In a rare direct approach to someone outside his organization with
whom he was about to enter into a criminal conspiracy, Marcello laid
out his master plan to acquire the state insurance contract to Charles
Roemer. They met August 28 at the St. Ann in New Orleans, a modest hotel in the French Quarter that was being used as campaign headquarters for Sonny Mouton. There, in the hotel's coffee shop, Carlos
told Roemer that if Roemer awarded the state employees insurance contract to Fidelity-Prudential, the company would earn around
$86,000 a month in commissions. Of this amount, Roemer's share
would be $43,000 a month, and the remainder would go to Marcello
and his associates. Carlos added that if Roemer delivered the contract to Fidelity-Prudential within thirty to ninety days, he could give
him $129,000, or a three-month advance share of the commissions.
Meanwhile Carlos would give him an advance of $25,000 immedi-
ately after he formally agreed to help get Fidelity the contract at a
meeting Carlos planned to hold in mid-September with the other people involved: Davidson, Hauser, and Hauser's two assistants, agents
Wacks and Montague.

Later Carlos would report to a young lawyer friend, Vincent Marinello, whom he eventually brought into the conspiracy, that Roemer
"really jumped" when Carlos told him that Fidelity-Prudential could
put $129,000 in his hands within thirty to ninety days if everything
worked out all right.

According to an FBI tape, it was Aubrey Young who set up the
crucial meeting of all the conspirators at the St. Ann Hotel on September 10. He and Marcello decided that each would arrive at the
hotel at a different time. Roemer would take over a suite of rooms in
the hotel that were being used as Sonny Mouton's campaign headquarters. Marcello would be the first to arrive and would go to the
coffee shop. Davidson would then escort Hauser and the two agents
to the St. Ann for their meeting with Charlie Roemer in Mouton's
headquarters. They would first meet briefly with Marcello in the coffee shop, and then Davidson would remain with Carlos while Hauser,
Wacks, and Montague would leave to meet with Roemer. Once all of
them were together in Mouton's suite, they would reach an agreement, which one of them would communicate to Marcello and Davidson in the coffee shop to receive their approval or disapproval.

Came September 10 and right away panic broke out in the Hauser-
Wacks-Montague camp. The three were staying in the Royal Orleans

Hotel, not far from the St. Ann. But they had been led to believe the meeting was to take place in Marcello's Town & Country office, which they knew was wired. When they were informed that the crucial meeting would be held at the St. Ann, they suddenly had to worry about how to record it. Hauser, Wacks, and Montague had had a scary encounter with Irv Davidson in Washington several weeks before: Davidson suddenly took Hauser's attaché case cum recorder out of his hand and faked being dragged to the floor by its weight, saying, "You must have a recorder in here; it's so damn heavy."

The incident had made Hauser and the agents very wary of carrying an attaché case around Davidson. So just before the St. Ann meeting, they decided to dispense with their attaché cases and wire Hauser instead. But upon attaching the small recorder to the inside of Hauser's thigh, they noticed that because of Hauser's quite muscular legs, they could see the outline of the wire and the recorder beneath Hauser's trousers. They decided to dispense with the body wire too, which meant that they had to go to the meeting without any recording equipment. And this was the meeting at which they were going to get Roemer to verbally accept a bribe.

Once Roemer, Hauser, Wacks, and Montague were all together in the Mouton suite, Roemer told the three fictitious insurance men that as commissioner of administration of the state of Louisiana, he did indeed have the power to award the contracts. He then explained the process of awarding state insurance contracts and agreed to set up a meeting between his subordinate, Joe Terrell, and Hauser to discuss details. Roemer then asked to talk with one of the trio "one on one" in a men's room downstairs. It was decided that Mike Wacks should be the one, since he was technically "president" of Fidelity Financial Consultants.

Roemer and Wacks then retired to a men's room near the hotel lobby. In a corner of the bathroom, Roemer told Wacks in blunt, nononsense terms that he agreed to arrange the awarding of a state employees life insurance contract to Fidelity in exchange for half of the monthly commissions. Oh for a wire! thought Mike Wacks as he shook Roemer's hand on the deal.

The next day Roemer told his subordinate, Joe Terrell, about his plan to switch the state employees life insurance contract from CNN to Fidelity-Prudential. Then, after apparently winning Terrell's cooperation, he met with Joe Hauser in the Hilton Hotel in Baton Rouge, where he informed him that the contract could be arranged in sixty to ninety days.

Two weeks later, Marcello phoned Joe Hauser at his room in the

Royal Orleans Hotel and ordered him to pay Charles Roemer $15,000 in cash and keep $10,000 as a "saver" for "the one that's from New Orleans." Marcello's order was recorded by an FBI intercept to the delight of the operation's New Orleans coordinator, Harold Hughes, who listened to the replay not long after it was recorded. Now they had at least some of the goods on Marcello: an order to bribe a public official.

Later on that day Hauser went to the Hilton in Baton Rouge with $15,000 in cash for Commissioner Roemer and a request on the part of Carlos Marcello for five tickets to Saturday's LSU football game in Baton Rouge.

Alone with Roemer in the commissioner's hotel room, Hauser wore a wire that recorded the following exchange:

> HAUSER: Let me tell you what I got here. I got $15,000 here and the other $10,000 on Monday.
>
> But there's something I got to ask you. Carlos said he wants five tickets.
>
> ROEMER: Jesus Christ!
>
> HAUSER: Five tickets.
>
> ROEMER: Jesus Christ!

Hauser then took the $15,000 in cash out of his attaché case and handed it to Roemer, who promptly stuffed the bills into his trouser pockets and said: "Okay, thanks, but I need another $25,000."

> HAUSER: I'll see what I can do, but first I gotta get the tickets for Carlos.
>
> ROEMER: Jesus Christ. He really wants 'em, doesn't he?
>
> HAUSER: Yes.

The meeting broke up on a cordial note with a somewhat worried Roemer promising he would get the tickets to "The Quarterback" (another of Marcello's nicknames), although he didn't know where he was "going to get them from."

When Hauser told Marcello about Roemer's request for another $25,000, an FBI wiretap recorded the following exchange:

HAUSER: Would you believe that?...The balls he had!

MARCELLO: Oh, he got it. I told you he don't take no five, ten. I told you that way before.

HAUSER: That's sure.

MARCELLO: Uh look....No matter who gets in there...you know I'm a find a fuckin' way to get to 'em. I don't care who it is...even if it's Treen.

Carlos had begun to worry about the upcoming gubernatorial primaries, which were to be held on October 27. Charles Roemer would probably lose his position in the state government if Sonny Mouton lost the Republican primary to David Treen. This would, of course, jeopardize the awarding of the state contract to Fidelity.

So Carlos decided to hedge his bet on Roemer by making a tempting offer to the Republicans' probable rival for the governorship, the then Lieutenant Governor James Fitzmorris, who would soon compete in the Democratic gubernatorial primary against Louis Lambert. Carlos believed that Fitzmorris could possibly get Fidelity-Prudential certain insurance contracts that had eluded him so far: the City of New Orleans and the Avondale Shipyards, among others.

Accordingly, on September 26 Carlos summoned his young lawyer friend Vincent Marinello—"the Italian boy" he called him—to his Town & Country office. The FBI's ceiling bug above Carlos's desk recorded Carlos detailing to Marinello his whole scheme to bribe Roemer for the state insurance contract. Carlos explained how success or failure could depend on the outcome of the primaries and the election and how he therefore had to hedge his bet on Roemer by making an offer to Fitzmorris.

Carlos concluded his spiel by ordering Marinello to make an offer to Fitz, warning him not to discuss with Fitzmorris his plans to acquire state insurance business through Roemer because Fitzmorris was liable "to get crazy and go talk to the man there...uncovering everything I'm doing on the other side."

Carlos further elaborated to Marinello that if Fitzmorris agreed to help them get the City of New Orleans and Avondale Shipyards contracts, Marinello should tell Fitzmorris that $10,000 was available when the contracts were signed and they began receiving commissions from the contracts at the rate of over $100,000 a month.

Marinello, apparently somewhat awed by the figures Marcello was talking about, acknowledged to Carlos that he was talking "important money" and immediately called Fitzmorris's office to arrange for an appointment.

What followed was a three-month dance of intrigue between Carlos Marcello, Joe Hauser, Irving Davidson, Larry Montague, Michael Wacks, Charles Roemer, Vincent Marinello, James Fitzmorris, and two abstract figures representing the United States government and the people of Louisiana. The U.S. government was the choreographer and director, and the people of Louisiana, who would elect the state's next governor, symbolized Fate.

For five of the players, the imagined stakes were high. If all went well, they believed they would stand to divide anywhere from $200,000 to $500,000 a month in insurance commissions over the course of several years. For the other three, their careers in the FBI and the federal witness protection program stood to rise or fall.

Marinello made his pitch on behalf of Marcello and Fidelity-Prudential to Lieutenant Governor and gubernatorial candidate James Fitzmorris for the City of New Orleans and Avondale Shipyards contracts, offering him $10,000 now, $100,000 later, and then $50,000 a month for the life of the contracts.

Fitzmorris was guardedly receptive. He wanted to go along but observed:

> "The Edwards administration has played their cards so close to their chest, I don't know what the hell is going on...but once we get in there, talking about government programs...once we get in there we'll see what they have."

Carlos told Marinello to ask Fitzmorris if he would cooperate with Marcello if and when he became governor, warning Marinello again not to breathe a word about the Roemer deal. He also suggested he give a token to Fitzmorris now, maybe $10,000.

At his meeting with Fitzmorris, Marinello told the lieutenant governor in the presence of Michael Wacks that Wacks had "some change for you...a couple of bucks" and that "there would be more to come depending on the outcome of the election and how he performed."

The next day, September 27, Marcello called Hauser and told him to meet him and the others at Impastato's Restaurant in Metairie and to bring "the newspapers" with him. Marcello then met at the restaurant with Marinello, Hauser, Wacks, and Montague. As they were finishing their lunch, he told Hauser to give Marinello "the newspapers" for him to give to Fitzmorris later on in the day.

Carlos's order to Marinello was recorded by one of the agents:

MARCELLO: Joe's got what you need.

MARINELLO: Okay, sir.

MARCELLO: Tonight, tomorrow, whatever, when you gonna do it.

MARINELLO: I'll handle it. I'll handle it tonight, sir.

After dropping Marcello off at the Town & Country Motel, Hauser gave Marinello the $10,000 in cash and told him to take care of Fitzmorris. Marinello replied that he would do anything Mr. Marcello told him to do.

Later, after accomplishing his mission, Marinello called Hauser and told him he "delivered the newspapers" and that "everything was taken care of."

On October 8 Carlos held a meeting in his Town & Country office with Mike Wacks, whom he had come to regard affectionately "as a son." After a discussion of the current situation regarding Roemer and Fitzmorris, with Wacks's tape recorder rolling, Marcello remarked on the fact that he had to appear before the Jefferson Parish Council in connection with a dispute he was having over the disposal of parish sewage sludge on his Churchill Farms lands:

> "I gotta go give the sonofabitch right now, man. This is my business, ya understand. I got ten for somebody right now, but this is a different deal. Ain't got nothin' to do with us. See, these sonofabitchin' politicians. You know what they like."

According to Wacks, Marcello then stood up, reached into his back pockets, and pulled out two enormous wads of bills, saying: "I'm ready for 'em, ya understand? I'm ready for 'em!" And they all laughed.

Meanwhile, Charles Roemer had been making sufficient progress with Joe Terrell to induce Carlos to shake loose the remaining $10,000 he had promised him. On orders from the boss, Hauser then delivered the cash to Roemer at the Hilton Hotel in Baton Rouge on October 11. At their meeting in the Hilton, Roemer reiterated to Hauser that he had to give him another $25,000 to be used as a campaign contribution for Sonny Mouton.

The two gubernatorial primaries were indeed bearing down, and Marcello was following them closely. He was backing James Fitzmorris against Louis Lambert in the Democratic election and Mouton against

David Treen in the Republican. In the event that Fitzmorris lost, he would back Louis Lambert in the general election. Anyone but Republican David Treen. If Treen won, he would be dispensing the state patronage and more than likely he would not reappoint Charlie Roemer as commissioner of administration. "Treen is our enemy, man," an FBI listening device recorded Carlos as saying. "This motherfucker he ain't goin' to do nothin' for nobody....He and his people they is aristocrats. He not goin' for our kind of people. But them sumbitches is wheelin' an' dealin', man."

Carlos felt Fitzmorris would edge out Lambert, so he directed Marinello to "make a move on Fitzmorris," "explain what is going on," and get a firm commitment from Fitz that he would obtain the insurance contracts "for his friends" if Fitz got elected governor.

Meanwhile, in the Republican contest, Marcello had been campaigning actively for Mouton. FBI wiretaps picked up Marcello on the Mouton-Treen fight several times during the fall of 1979:

> "I'm pushin' my ass for this fellow Mouton. I gotta put some signs up. They ain't got no signs here."
> ...
> "Mouton, I think this man is goin' places, yeah."

In one tape-recorded conversation with Roemer, Marcello said he would probably be able to deliver as many as 6000 black votes in Jefferson Parish for Mouton. A few days later he told Roemer's aide Aubrey Young:

> "I got a buncha niggers I gotta get together here...fifteen hundred of 'em. Fifteen hundred families, I mean....All the niggers around. The blacks over in Jefferson. Highway 90. See Highway 90 I got 1500 blacks, and in Avondale Homes I got 4500....I'm tryin' to trap the whole thing."

As it turned out, the primaries held on October 27 resulted in Lambert's victory over Fitzmorris and Treen's victory over Mouton. For Carlos this was an alarming development.

Immediately Carlos sent Marinello to Fitzmorris to find out if there would be any chance Fitz could be appointed commissioner of administration, to succeed Roemer, if Lambert won the general election. Fitzmorris assured him that in all likelihood, Lambert would appoint him to the position.

Turning his attention to Roemer again, it now appeared virtually certain to Carlos that Treen would not reappoint Roemer commissioner of administration if he went on to win the general election. It therefore became a matter of the utmost urgency to get Fidelity-Prudential's insurance proposal over to Roemer so he could submit it to the Board of Trustees of the State Employees Group Benefits Program as soon as possible. Carlos indicated to Hauser and his assistants that Roemer still had thirty to ninety days to fulfill his end of the bargain. If they secured the contract through Roemer, they would at least have a foot in the door and could generate five or six months' commissions before the next governor reappointed a new commissioner. Hauser rushed Fidelity-Prudential's proposal over to Roemer's office. Among other things, the proposal included a letter attesting to the fact that by switching its employees benefit insurance contract to Fidelity, the state would save over $1 million a year.

As for Fitzmorris, Carlos ordered Marinello, Hauser, Wacks, and Montague to meet the lieutenant governor and get some sort of firm commitment from him. After the meeting, Marinello called Marcello and told him that Fitzmorris was going to appeal his second-place finish to Lambert and that Fitz had already made a deal with Treen to be the next commissioner of administration if Treen won the election. Fitz also added that he needed more money.

When Marinello reported this to Marcello, Carlos told Marinello that he did not want to give Fitzmorris any more money because Roemer was working hard on his deal and would probably deliver the contract in thirty days. Besides, he added, Roemer might even keep his job if Treen won.

But then something happened that shook Carlos up. Sonny Mouton, Roemer's candidate who had lost the primary election to Treen, suddenly announced he was endorsing Treen's candidacy in the general election. So Roemer's man was going with the hated Treen. This was disturbing, as Carlos told Hauser and Montague at a November 13 meeting in his Town & Country office:

MARCELLO: We got a lot of trouble, that's all I can tell you.

HAUSER: What's the matter?

MARCELLO: Shit. Ain't nothin' the matter. Just Mouton, he done gone with Treen.

HAUSER: What happened to our bet? We look like fucking fools.

MARCELLO: Well, let's see about Fitz. The boy [Marinello] is over
             at Fitz's office now. He goin' to find out who Fitz
             endorsin', Lambert or Treen.

HAUSER: Yeah, let's see....But you know Fitz is so honest.

MARCELLO: He's honest. You see, he's an honest, honest man.
             The bastard don't care for money.

HAUSER: Yeah, you're right.

MARCELLO: You wouldn't believe that, but that's the truth. He's
             a 58-year-old motherfucker been—how you say, you
             know, no money. He never did have no big money.
             That's all. If he had $20, $25,000 he had plenty
             money. Maybe—I don't think he ever had that kind
             a money in his life.

On December 9 David Treen defeated Louis Lambert in the gubernatorial election—another blow to Marcello, Marinello, and company.
    The next day Carlos told Marinello to get busy and finish the deal
with Roemer, adding that there would be an important meeting in
the state house on December 19 regarding the state insurance contract. Marinello and Marcello concurred that they would rather be
dealing with Roemer than Fitzmorris because, in Marcello's words:

"If the feds go in there, man, and shake Fitzmorris, shit, he
liable to tell everything, man. He got this. He got that.
    "No, I'm not goin' to dump no more fuckin' money on Fitz,
no way."

To Marcello's great satisfaction, the next two weeks brought nothing but good news from Roemer. The commissioner of administration had had a satisfactory meeting with the Board of Trustees of
the State Employees Group Benefits Program, and Marcello's proposal would go before the board on January 18, 1980. Carlos later
related this news to Mike Wacks, adding that it would be at this meeting "where definitely they gonna give it to us, or not, or what."
    But what had happened to Fitzmorris, who had told Marcello, via
Marinello, that he would be taking over Roemer's job in the new
Treen administration? Carlos ordered Marinello, who had become
virtually his errand boy by then, to go find out.

On January 18 Marcello was gratified to learn from Roemer that his proposal had been well received by the trustees of the Employees Benefit Program and that a final decision would be handed down on January 31.

It was at about this time that Marinello reported to Carlos that Fitzmorris was definitely not going to be the new commissioner of administration in the Treen state house, that Fitz had lied to him. Marinello said he was sorry he had given him the $10,000 but thankful he had listened to Carlos and had not "dumped all that cash on Fitz."

The news of Fitzmorris's deception brought forth a scornful exchange between Marinello and Marcello:

MARCELLO: He is chicken, more chicken than anybody I ever seen in my life.

MARINELLO: He don't have enough balls…that lyin' sonofabitch. I went to the wrong man, damn it.

MARCELLO: How old are you?

MARINELLO: Forty-three.

MARCELLO: Well you done learned somethin' now. When you as old as me, you'll know more than the fuckin' President of the United States.

Late in the afternoon of January 31, 1980, an elated Carlos Marcello summoned Vincent Marinello and the two "boys," Larry Montague and Mike Wacks, to his office in the Town & Country Motel for an important meeting. It was the first time Wacks and Montague had attended a meeting of this importance without Joe Hauser.

Arriving at the suite of offices behind the Town & Country restaurant, the three young men found the boss sitting behind his huge desk exuding even more authority, if that were possible, than he usually did. Before him on the otherwise uncluttered desk rested a neat stack of legal-sized documents.

With the two undercover agents' tape recorders spinning away, and the ceiling bug picking up his every word, Carlos triumphantly told his men he had heard from Roemer that the insurance contract was going to Fidelity-Prudential. With that, Carlos pushed the stack of papers across his desk to the two agents, telling them it was an important state bid specifications document he had received from Roemer the previous day and that they should go home and study it.

He then told Wacks and Montague they had all better start thinking about how they were going to split their $43,000-a-month share of the commissions, adding that even though Wacks and Montague had not been given a share in the original deal, he thought they should have some percentage.

"I guess you should take most of it, sir," said Larry Montague. "After all, you masterminded the deal; you did most of the work. You deserve the money."

"No," said Marcello, "it ain't the money, forget the money. I'd be just as proud as you to make the deal. I just wanna be proud dat I can do somethin' like dat."

53

Sting Two

"I'm doin' this for friends of mine in California. They Maf
like me, you know, personal friends of mine."

So proclaimed Carlos Marcello to Joe Hauser in a conversation
recorded by Hauser on October 9, 1979, at the time the Louisiana
gubernatorial primary campaigns were coming to a boil. But Carlos's
remarks had nothing to do with the Louisiana primaries. They had
to do with the upcoming trial of some of Marcello's Mafia friends on
the West Coast.

Carlos referred to these friends again in another conversation with
Hauser, this time an unrecorded one because Hauser's machine had
broken down. Hauser's notes on the conversation read:

"These people from California...they good people. They part
of the family. I don't want nuttin' to happen to 'em."

By a curious twist of fate, the imminent trial of some of Carlos's
"good people" on the West Coast, and Carlos's last-minute involvement in it, were to provide the FBI with a new opportunity to pursue Carlos undercover. They were able to launch, in a sense, a second
sting operation against him, one that, ironically, would have more

447

disastrous consequences for the aging Mafia boss than the initial operation, which, in October 1979, was approaching its most critical phase.

It also provided the government with certain information about Carlos Marcello it had been struggling to obtain for years: some admission by Marcello that he was involved in organized crime.

For years and years Marcello had publicly stated at innumerable trials and congressional hearings that he had nothing to do with the Mafia.

"I ain't in no racket. I ain't in no organized crime."

This, in its various versions, had been Carlos Marcello's eternal refrain. The last time he had uttered it to the government was at a hearing before the House Select Committee on Assassinations in 1978.

But now, in a secretly taped conversation with a federal undercover agent, he was admitting inadvertently that he was "Maf," that certain friends of his in California were "Maf," like him, and that they were "part of the family," his family, a family that extended to every major city in the United States.

And there was more to come. During this second sting operation the FBI finally learned, from listening in on Marcello's conversations, that the reputed Louisiana Mafia boss was connected to organized crime on a national scale and that the troubles of four "Maf" friends of his in California, who happened to run the Los Angeles mob, were of almost just as much concern to him as the vicissitudes of his criminal associates on his home turf.

The situation was this: Six members of the Los Angeles mob, four of whom were friends of Marcello's, had been indicted by a federal grand jury in Los Angeles on February 20, 1979, on charges of racketeering, conspiracy, extortion, obstruction of justice, and murder. They were Dominick Brooklier, boss of the Los Angeles Mafia since 1974, his underboss Sam Sciortino, capo Michael Rizzitello, and soldiers Jack Lo Cicero, Thomas Ricciardi, and Louis Tom Dragna, son of former boss Jack Dragna. Sam Sciortino had a New Orleans cousin, Phillip Rizzuto, who was a friend and associate of Carlos Marcello's and the owner of the Cafe de la Paix in the French Quarter.

The Brooklier mob indictment was a landmark in the Justice Department's war on organized crime. Reported the *Los Angeles Times:* "This is the first time in history that the entire leadership of a major Mafia family has been indicted."

* * *

It had been Phillip Rizzuto who had gotten Carlos Marcello involved in the Brooklier case.

On October 4, FBI agents monitoring Carlos Marcello's telephone overheard a conversation between Marcello and Rizzuto during which Marcello expressed unusual interest in a newspaper article he had just read about a California judge who was due to preside over the upcoming trial of his friends in Los Angeles. Referring to an earlier discussion with Rizzuto about the judge, Carlos asked what they were going to do about "this man in California."

Joseph Hauser was immediately informed by the FBI of Marcello's interest in Judge Pregerson and the trial over which he was to preside in Los Angeles. The FBI told him to be on the alert for a possible call from Marcello about it and to react to the situation as if some attempt to bribe the judge might be "in the works."

As predicted, Carlos phoned Hauser later the same day and told him about "this judge who is to preside over friends" of his next week.

The ever-alert Hauser, who had never heard of Judge Pregerson before in his life, then quickly, without a second's hesitation, told Marcello he knew the judge well and "there were things he might be able to do."

Later Carlos called his friend Rizzuto and told him that he knew someone who knew Judge Pregerson and maybe he, Rizzuto, might want to talk with him.

The stage was now set for the FBI to possibly catch Marcello in an attempt to bribe a federal judge.

Immediately after his October 4 conversation with Marcello, Hauser notified the other undercover agents in New Orleans about his conversations with Carlos. They, in turn, informed Special Agents John Barron and William Fleming of the Los Angeles FBI office, who had ultimate responsibility for supervising Hauser's undercover activities. Sensing that Marcello might make an attempt "to do something about the judge," Fleming and Barron went to work to facilitate such a possibility. They told Hauser to inform Marcello that he had a good friend who was very close to Judge Pregerson. The two agents then invented a fictitious individual they named George Ashley, who, they told Hauser, was a millionaire art dealer who happened to be an exceptionally good friend of Judge Pregerson's because Pregerson was an art connoisseur who collected valuable paintings.

Between October 4 and 11 Hauser held a number of discussions with Marcello about the judge and the trial of his Mafia friends in Los Angeles. It was during an October 9 discussion that Marcello told

Hauser all about the trial of Brooklier, Sciortino, Rizzitello, Lo Cicero, and Dragna and made the admission that the defendants were "Maf, like me" and were good friends of his.

On October 11, during a drive to Lafayette with Hauser, Wacks, and Montague, Marcello brought up the subject of Judge Pregerson and the Los Angeles trial, expressing considerable concern over it. The agents recorded the conversation:

MARCELLO: The only thing you can do, uh, I've learned that, all my life, if you got a federal judge, money ain't gonna do no good. You ain't gonna. I don't care. Unless you got your brother in there. But they ain't, you can't give 'em enough money to take it, anything like that, you understand?

MONTAGUE: I think you're right.

WACKS: Yeah. I agree.

MARCELLO: They ain't goin' to do it. I got, uh, I know half, half of 'em right here, right here, they're personal friends of mine. I better not ask for somethin' like that. They get insulted. Because they got a lifetime job.... They ain't...what you gonna give 'em? $10,000? $25,000? $50,000?...Just as soon as you give it to them, everybody knows that he got paid off. It gets around that the man is taking. Believe me, ain't no such thing as a secret. The more you add, the more people know about it.

A day or so later, over lunch with Hauser, Wacks, and Montague, Marcello reiterated his reservations about paying off a federal judge, adding a few new thoughts on the subject:

"You can't pay a little bit. Maybe two, three, or five hundred thousand dollars. That's the difference. The man makes $50,000 a year in expenses. How the fuck he gonna take $10,000?"

The next day in his Town & Country office, Marcello advised Hauser to be cautious:

"You gotta watch yourself close on this, especially with your case, and my name in there."

Then, pointing to the ceiling, as if he knew there was a bug implanted above the tiles, Carlos said:

"All right. We've talked enough. I don't want to talk no more."

For several days the FBI registered little or no movement in the matter of what action, if any, Marcello was going to take on the case of Judge Pregerson and the trial of his Mafia friends in California.

Then, on October 25, the whole thing came to a head at a meeting Carlos scheduled at his brother Anthony's hunting lodge in Lacombe, on the northeast side of Lake Pontchartrain.

This was to be Joe Hauser's most dangerous mission. Anthony Marcello's hunting lodge was located on an isolated stretch of lakefront and was removed from the main road by a long driveway. If Hauser became trapped in the place, there would be no means of escape. He would be sitting down with three mobsters—Marcello, Sciortino, and Rizzuto—who would stop at nothing if they discovered the tape recorder in his briefcase. Hauser's backup team of FBI agents would not be able to maintain visual surveillance of the meeting place and would therefore have to rely wholly on the transmitter in Hauser's briefcase to keep track of his mission.

Immediately prior to the meeting, Carlos Marcello and Joe Hauser discussed the possible bribery of Judge Pregerson over lunch at Impastato's. After reiterating once more that to make it worthwhile for a judge, who had a lifetime job to protect, it had to be very big money, Carlos told Hauser he could provide up to $250,000 in cash for the judge within twenty-four hours. Hauser, delighted he was able to record the offer, told Carlos they could discuss that possibility at the next meeting.

After lunch Marcello left Hauser off at his brother's place, then returned in twenty minutes with Sam Sciortino and Phillip Rizzuto, whom he introduced to Hauser as his "people from California." Hauser's backup then took a position near the entrance to Anthony Marcello's driveway.

On his way up the narrow, pitted driveway in Carlos's car, Hauser had noted that Anthony's hunting lodge was entirely surrounded by marshland and that there were no other buildings in sight. Clutching his special attaché case, and with his insides churning, Hauser entered the small rustic lodge with its trophies of stuffed birds. Now, as the others joined him, he felt his nerves were stretched to their limit.

It turned out to be a rough meeting. Sciortino, number two in the Los Angeles mob and a confessed murderer, faced a long prison term if he were convicted in the Brooklier trial, and he was full of anxiety and rage. Carlos felt his plight keenly, partly because Sciortino's cousin, Rizzuto, was a trusted member of Carlos's inner circle, and partly because the Brooklier indictment was such a potentially dangerous precedent for everyone in his vast extended family. Hauser was surprised to find the boss so tense.

The three mobsters and the government informer sat down by a low table, with Hauser's recorder-transmitter briefcase in full view before them.

Hauser dominated the discussion at first. He told Marcello, Sciortino, and Rizzuto that he thought he could take care of the whole thing. He had a very good friend in Los Angeles by the name of George Ashley, a millionaire art dealer who was a close friend of Judge Pregerson's. Since the judge collected paintings, Hauser thought he would be receptive to what a man of Ashley's standing in the art world might tell him. Sciortino, who had great respect for Judge Pregerson's sense of fairness, expressed his concern that Ashley's intervention might possibly cause the judge to disqualify himself. That would be detrimental to Sciortino's interest, which was to receive a guarantee of probation at the sentencing. Hauser told him not to worry about "that angle," that he was sure Pregerson would not be put off by Ashley's proposal.

There followed considerable agonizing by Sciortino and Rizzuto over what should be done. Then Sciortino suddenly exclaimed:

"Man, it would be nice if we could find some damn Mexican guy to kill Frattiano. That would solve all our problems."

Sciortino was referring to James "Jimmy the Weasel" Frattiano, the notorious Mafia hitman turned state's witness whose testimony had been instrumental in persuading the grand jury to indict Brooklier, Sciortino, et al., and whose testimony at the upcoming trial threatened to be devastating to the defendants. Sciortino went on saying that Frattiano had "tried to do the same thing with us." Sciortino then bragged that he himself had been involved in around twenty murders.

It was at this juncture that a remark by Rizzuto touched off a furious tirade against the Kennedys. At a lull in the proceedings Rizzuto informed the group that he had just read in the papers that Teddy Kennedy was going to make a try for the Democratic nomination.

"He better fuckin' not," shouted Carlos. "He better stay the fuck out of it if he knowed better."

"What a fuckin' shithead dat brother of his, Bobby, was," added

Sciortino, "bastard thought he was gonna put us all outa business, the motherfucker."

"Yeah," said Rizzuto, "so we put *him* outa business." And they all laughed.

Outside, near the entrance to Anthony's driveway, the FBI backup was listening intently to the discussions inside the house, when suddenly they lost radio contact with Hauser's briefcase. Either the transmitter had run out of power or it had been discovered and Hauser was now in trouble. The agents drove up closer to Marcello's driveway and waited.

It was getting toward the end of the meeting. Hauser's recorder-transmitter had gone dead, but Hauser was still very much alive and was still the center of attention. He had performed magnificently. Now Marcello and Sciortino turned to Hauser and told him, with a hint of desperation in their voices, that if he succeeded in bribing the judge to obtain probation for Sciortino, he would receive more insurance business than he had ever had before in his life and could then open up his own company and would no longer need Prudential. Hauser told them he would see what he could do.

After the meeting Marcello insisted on driving Hauser back to his hotel in New Orleans. Hauser's FBI backup agents were relieved to see their charge sitting in the front seat of Carlos's car as it exited from his brother's driveway. According to Hauser's trial testimony, for his recorder had remained dead, on the way into town Carlos told Hauser that taking care of Judge Pregerson was extremely important to him and to "the organization" and that money was no question. Carlos then reiterated that he could raise $250,000 in cash for the judge within twenty-four hours. It was then that he told Hauser that these "people from California" were "good people," that they were "part of the family" and that he did not want "nothin' to happen to 'em," adding that Rizzuto "was good people too," that he did a lot of "important work for the family out in Kansas City."

Just as Marcello was pulling up to Hauser's hotel, he told Hauser:

"Whatever it takes I will do. Whatever it takes.
    "If you can't get the judge, what about the guy handling the case?"

To this Hauser replied, as he said goodnight: "I'm checking to see about him, whether he's a bit player or not, to see if he's hurting for money."

*   *   *

After reviewing the tape of the October 25 meeting, Los Angeles agents Fleming and Barron instructed Joe Hauser to arrange a meeting with Sciortino in California. At that meeting Hauser would inform Sciortino that Judge Pregerson would accept an art object valued at $125,000 from Sciortino, through Ashley, in exchange for a promise not to withdraw from the case and a guarantee of probation in the event he was convicted.

On the evening of October 29, Hauser met Sciortino in the parking lot of the Holiday Inn in West Covina outside of Los Angeles and told Sciortino right away that he had "an unbelievable meeting" with Ashley. The tape-recorded conversation displayed Hauser's mastery of deceit:

HAUSER: Here's what he promised me. Judge wants to get something, okay? He doesn't trust you, but he wants to get something. If he doesn't get it, you'll go to jail.

SCIORTINO: Yeah?

HAUSER: He has guaranteed he will not pull out of the case. Guaranteed there will be no time on your probation. I said: "Now, what do I have to guarantee?" He said, "When it happens, that the man will."...Cash he never took, cash. But a painting, a nice painting. Give him a nice painting. That he would accept....I didn't want to make a commitment until I talked with you.

SCIORTINO: He says he guarantees that?

HAUSER: He guarantees that.

SCIORTINO: That's beautiful. Just me? What about the other guys?

HAUSER: I spoke to him for all three.

SCIORTINO: That's super.

Hauser went on to tell Sciortino that the plan was to give Pregerson a painting by French postimpressionist Paul Gauguin, worth $125,000, that was being offered for sale at a Los Angeles art gallery. Then he concluded his charade by telling Sciortino that this would not be the first time that Judge Pregerson took a bribe, that he once took money to fix a drug case. This, of course, was a lie.

*   *   *

On November 1 Hauser phoned Carlos Marcello from Los Angeles
to spell out the plan. FBI agents Fleming and Barron listened in:

HAUSER: I got a firm commitment from Ashley that, A. the
             judge will not disqualify himself from presiding over
             the trial, B. if Sciortino is found guilty, he'll get pro-
             bation. Now Ashley says all he wants is to give the
             judge a painting, because he's crazy with art. Sam
             [Sciortino] is committed to it. My question to you is
             this: Is Sam good for his word?

MARCELLO: Shit, yeah. Shit, yeah. He's good for his word. Yeah.
             What a paintin' cost? What you mean?

HAUSER: We're talking about a substantial amount of money.

MARCELLO: What you talkin' about?

HAUSER: Hundred ten, hundred twenty-five thousand dollars.

MARCELLO: You told Sam that?

HAUSER: Yes, I told him that.

MARCELLO: What he say?

HAUSER: He said absolutely, go right ahead and do it.

MARCELLO: Well, don't worry about it, man. I give it to you my-
             self, okay?

HAUSER: If Sam doesn't come through with the money...

MARCELLO: I'm a give it to you, okay? I'll stand good for it. 100
             percent. Okay?

HAUSER: Okay, I'll tell him.

A few weeks after pulling off this masterful deception, Joe Hauser
entered a federal penitentiary in Arizona to begin serving what turned
out to be a substantially reduced sentence for his February 1979 conviction.

In what was to be Hauser's last taped conversation with Marcello,
Carlos was unrelenting in insisting that the money for the painting
should not be paid to George Ashley until Judge Pregerson fulfilled

his commitment and gave his friend Sam Sciortino probation. At the end of the tape, Carlos was heard insisting:

"I don't want you to be holdin' no bag....And I don't want to be holdin' no damn bag either."

On November 15 the Justice Department informed Judge Pregerson of the trumped up conspiracy to bribe him, of which he had been completely unaware, and he postponed excusing himself from the Brooklier case until the FBI took down the operation.

Meanwhile, back in Louisiana the FBI had already begun to zero in on suspected corruption in the office of the commissioner of administration by delivering a subpoena to the governor of the state.

54

The Big One

"We own de Teamsters," Carlos once boasted to Hauser, Wacks, and Montague in a tape-recorded conversation, alluding to the mob's control of the nation's largest union with its billion-dollar-plus pension and health and welfare funds. "I got the only man in the United States can tell 'em [the leading Teamster officials] what the fuck to do," Carlos remarked in another recorded discussion.

The man Carlos was referring to was Joseph "Joey Doves" Aiuppa, elder statesman and current boss of Chicago's powerful Mafia organization, known as The Outfit. Carlos and Joey Doves had always gotten along fine. Joey Doves looked forward to going down to Louisiana every fall to shoot ducks and doves at Churchill Farms and at Carlos's hunting and fishing camp on Grand Isle. Together they would talk about the day when they could move in and take control of America's richest and most powerful labor union, the International Brotherhood of Teamsters.

Joe Hauser always believed it was only a matter of time before Marcello would make his move on the Teamsters. Carlos had talked about it often. It was clear that he had long coveted the $2 billion Teamsters health and welfare and pension funds, both headquartered in Chicago. But he knew he had to wait for precisely the right moment to make his big move.

457

The moment finally came in December 1979, when the government's dual sting operations against him were rapidly approaching their goal: the destruction of his power in the United States.

The government was in luck again. Just when the FBI thought it had gathered all it needed on Carlos Marcello to send him away for the rest of his life, the old Mafia boss suddenly came up with what promised to be his biggest deal of all, a complex scheme to have the two major Teamsters funds insurance contracts switched to Fidelity-Prudential. Carlos figured the deal would be worth $1 million a month in commissions. He told Wacks and Montague he would have to give a half-million-dollar-a-month kickback to the Teamsters officials who would make it possible for the union to award Fidelity the contract and split the other monthly half million between himself, Aiuppa, Fidelity-Prudential, and whichever other "families" could help him land the contract and keep hold of it. He had two others in mind: Santos Trafficante's outfit in Tampa and Joe Civella's people in Kansas City.

Mike Wacks and Larry Montague used to refer to this grandiose scheme as "The Big One" whenever Carlos would bring it up, which was often during the summer and fall of 1979. They hoped he would move on it before the FBI took their operation down. It was kind of a joke between them. As Wacks told me eight years later, he and Hauser and Montague used to discuss at off-hours how the hell they were going to get Marcello off his butt and cracking on it.

It was sometime in December, just after Joe Hauser left for federal prison to serve his sentence for his 1979 conviction, that Carlos received sufficient assurance from his intelligence sources that the time to make a move on the Teamsters funds had arrived. In a taped conversation, Carlos told Wacks and Montague that Teamsters President Frank Fitzsimmons was too unwell "to do anything about it" and Teamsters funds consultant and insurance expert Allen Dorfman, who had long exerted a dominant influence over the two big union funds, had "gotten into trouble" and was about to be removed from his position. (Dorfman would soon be shot in the head eight times by two ski-masked killers.) For all intents and purposes, then, the Teamsters had passed under the control of "the only man in the United States can tell 'em what the fuck to do," Carlos's good friend Joey Doves Aiuppa.

Carlos decided to approach Aiuppa, Trafficante, and Civella in early December to get their backing for his scheme. After making his initial overtures, he told Montague and Wacks that "all three of 'em went for it."

Carlos then told the two undercover agents that Joey Doves had agreed to come down to New Orleans and meet with him at Churchill Farms to work out the details of the scheme and do a little dove hunting, the sport that had earned Aiuppa his nickname. Since Aiuppa's word was now virtually law among the top echelon of Teamsters leadership, Carlos did not anticipate "having any problem" working out a satisfactory agreement with his good friend from Chicago.

Marcello explained to "his boys" Mike and Larry that this was "gonna be the biggest fuckin' deal ever. One million bucks a month! How do you like dat?" Wacks and Montague were overjoyed. The Big One was finally going to come down.

In anticipation of the Marcello-Aiuppa summit meeting at Churchill Farms, the FBI scrambled to get bugs installed in Carlos's swampland hideaways there and at Grand Isle. There was the farmhouse at Churchill Farms and also a shack near a duck blind on the property where Carlos used to occasionally meet with important guests. And the agents could not ignore the lodge at Carlos's hunting and fishing camp at Grand Isle.

For Wacks and Montague the prospect was almost too incredible to believe. "Can you imagine," Montague remarked to me in 1988, "the Mafia boss of Louisiana and the Mafia boss of Chicago meeting out there in a shack on Carlos's swamp to discuss a scheme of the magnitude of what Carlos was attempting to mastermind? Would the American people ever believe that future control of the nation's most powerful labor union was being worked out by two aging mobsters in a Louisiana swamp?"

But, alas, Wacks and Montague were denied the thrill of listening in on Carlos's and Joey Doves's discussions. For at the last minute, Joey Doves couldn't make it because his wife suddenly fell seriously ill.

But that was by no means the end of The Big One. The meeting was simply postponed to mid-February, the carnival season, when Trafficante and Civella could also come down to New Orleans to join the discussions. "It'll make history," Wacks told Montague, "a Mardi Gras Mafia summit, recorded for your listening pleasure by the Federal Bureau of Investigation."

According to Wacks and Montague, Carlos Marcello appeared very pleased with himself as February rolled around. It had been on January 31 that he had met with them and told them that the insurance deal with Roemer would go through. He had also believed he had solved Sam Sciortino's problem in Los Angeles by pledging from $125,000 to $250,000 toward bribing Judge Pregerson. And now he had set up a meeting between himself, Aiuppa, Trafficante, and

Civella that he was fairly sure would result in "the biggest fuckin' deal ever."

Although Mike Wacks and Larry Montague were understandably proud of the operation they and Joe Hauser had carried out "in the front lines," as Mike Wacks likes to put it, they were almost sorry that the bureau would soon have to burst Carlos's bubble. For they had come to like the feisty little man with his inimitable expressions (which Wacks collected). They liked him far more than they ever came to like the recipients of his bribes. "Roemer was a real shark," Wacks observes today, "a cold, calculating bureaucrat wholly lacking the charm of Mr. Marcello."

"Listen," says Larry Montague, "you can't place the blame wholly on Carlos for this kind of corruption. Every damn politico we approached for insurance business, as soon as we mentioned the name Marcello and hinted at kickbacks, they immediately perked up. Not one of them ever showed us the door."

And so it was with a certain regret that they phoned Carlos to tell him they were off on a much-needed vacation in Hawaii, as they left for Los Angeles a few days before the bureau took their operation down.

55

The Takedown

On February 8, 1980, federal agents appeared at Irving Davidson's Washington office and notified him that he had been under investigation, including round-the-clock electronic surveillance, for the past year in connection with a federal undercover operation involving Carlos Marcello. That said, they then proceeded to interrogate the surprised and outraged lobbyist for four hours about his relationships with the Louisiana Mafia boss and with high-ranking INS official Mario Noto.

"Listen," cried Davidson when the agents concluded their initial questioning, "if I get knocked out of the box, it's going to hurt this country. I'm involved in some sensitive stuff overseas. I'm talking to people who our own people can't talk to."

The takedown of the BRILAB investigation had begun.

Later, Davidson told the *Washington Post*: "I told those FBI people not to play superagent with me....Look at my diary here: Jan. 4, National Security Council. Do you think I planted that? I tell you that I am dealing day and night with those boys."

*   *   *

461

Carlos Marcello was first notified that something had gone wrong by Aubrey Young, the friend and former state official who had first introduced him to Commissioner Charles E. Roemer.

Marcello's insurance scheme was in a quiescent phase at the time. Joe Hauser was in prison, beginning to serve time for his Phoenix conviction. Charles Roemer was quietly pulling strings in the state house. And, as we know, agents Wacks and Montague had packed their bags and gone home, telling Carlos they were going on vacation in Hawaii.

Phoning Carlos at his Town & Country office around midday, Aubrey Young informed Marcello that Charlie Roemer had called to tell him that Governor Edwards had just been subpoenaed by the FBI to appear before a federal grand jury investigating possible corruption in state insurance matters. The February 8 conversation was recorded by the FBI:

YOUNG: Edwards just called Roemer and told him about the subpoena. He said he didn't know what to do in this. He don't know if Louis Lambert squealed or this guy, whoever he is, he might be a...

MARCELLO: It ain't my people. Don't worry about that. I'm glad you telling us, so in case they do subpoena 'em, they'll know what to do. 'Cause they in Hawaii right now. And so how you know it's for the insurance?

YOUNG: Roemer told him [Edwards].

MARCELLO: What they [the FBI] tell him?

YOUNG: Well, I don't know. He didn't tell.

MARCELLO: Well, nothin' wrong.

YOUNG: No. But here's the thing he was worried about.

MARCELLO: What's he worried about?...Tell me!

YOUNG: That maybe that guy Hauser had a plant on him, see, and he think, of course he knows Lambert dislikes him...

MARCELLO: What?

YOUNG:	Roemer thinks maybe Lambert's it and he's worried about the guy [Hauser] maybe being in prison sometime and making a deal with the FBI.
MARCELLO:	No way, man. Just like my hollering. No. No. 'Cause Ida heard it. They [agents Wacks and Montague] called me yesterday. Said "We're goin' to Hawaii." I says, "All right." I said, "Yeah," 'cause they want to come in here. "Yeah," I say. "I ain't got nothin', man, you come next week."
YOUNG:	All right. Now, the papers that Roemer gave you. He said if you got them, please destroy them.
MARCELLO:	What papers?
YOUNG:	Explaining that insurance, whatever it was. He said he gave you some papers last week. To show you how they bid. How it works.
MARCELLO:	Oh man, I done disappear with them motherfuckers. I don't need nothin' like that.
YOUNG:	He [Roemer] afraid. 'Cause you know that could get a subpoena or somethin', and he said, you know, if they ask about you, he was going to say: "Hell yeah I know you." He said, "I'm talking to him [Marcello] about oil and waste," and, you know, I said, "Well, shit, they ain't got nothing on him."
MARCELLO:	They ain't got nothin' on him. Because, fuck, there ain't nothin'.
YOUNG:	But he wanted me to come tell you. You know, they after him again. You see, they popped him.
MARCELLO:	They ain't gave.... Tell, tell Roemer we ain't gave him no money. Nobody give him nothin'. Just tell him ain't no money passed. Nothin'. No money. Okay?
YOUNG:	Y'all talkin' business. Oil and waste.
MARCELLO:	Yeah. We talkin' about our garbage deal.
YOUNG:	Oil.
MARCELLO:	If he wants to tell 'em that, tell 'im I'm, as far as me, I ain't gonna tell 'em nothin'. They can, they can

come here forty times, but I ain't, you know, I'm gonna take, tell him, look, look, tell him look, Carlos don't care if he gets subpoenaed forty times....I got subpoenaed with the, with the President, the Vice, the, the, the, the United States....

YOUNG: Told him.

MARCELLO: ...district attorney, I mean, ah, the attorney general and all. Tell him I just take the Fifth Amendment and that's it. They ain't gonna get a fuckin' thing from me.

YOUNG: I told him that. Let me tell you what. He [Roemer] don't know who it is. He knows they're after him. You see, they shooting at him again after his shit in the paper about that promotion of the fight.

MARCELLO: Yeah, I saw that. Yeah.

YOUNG: They after him, and they pay, they pay. The federal government's after Edwin too.

MARCELLO: *Man, yeah!* And then Treen done got in there trying to keep him [Roemer] from getting that job[a reference to Roemer's hopes of continuing as commissioner of administration under Treen]. He'd like to have a job and they done promised the man the job. So now he trying, you don't know what the motherfucker do.

YOUNG: You see, here's the thing. Him not knowing that, they got this white-collar crime thing going on down at the FBI. Just like they doing in Congress [a reference to the so-called Abscam investigation]. Entrapment. Entrapment. He, he don't know if that guy's. ...He's thinking now. He's reading and that. Maybe them sonofabitches are...

MARCELLO: Who that? Entrapment?

YOUNG: Entrapment, you know. Like.

MARCELLO: Oh yeah.

YOUNG: They doing those congressmen.

MARCELLO: Yeah.

YOUNG: He [Roemer] said maybe this insurance man trying to bump him off.

MARCELLO: Tell him [Roemer] the insurance man, I'd put my head on the chopping block.

YOUNG: All right.

MARCELLO: Look, the man's in jail. Forget about him, man. He ain't gonna say nothin'. And his two nephews...don't worry about it. Look, he can't give no campaign money. He ain't never. All they talk about is insurance. And they give 'em the letter to show what they can save 'em a million dollars.

YOUNG: Well, that clears him.

MARCELLO: Yeah, that's it. Gonna make him [Roemer] look good.

YOUNG: That's right.

MARCELLO: That's all. Ain't no more. Ain't no use to talk about it. Look, don't worry about it at all. Okay? And if I hear anything, I'll call you right away and say, "Look, they got subpoenaed too, and I know what."...Look, don't worry about it.

YOUNG: I ain't worried about it.

MARCELLO: 'Cause he ain't done nothing.

YOUNG: I don't know.

MARCELLO: I don't believe. He [Roemer] ain't scared, huh?

YOUNG: No, it don't bother him.

MARCELLO: He don't, he ain't scared.

YOUNG: He, he's got some balls.

MARCELLO: You wanta eat?

YOUNG: I don't know. Where you gonna eat? I got to get home. Shit man, I told my mamma, I'm so sore.

MARCELLO: I ain't ate all day. I go by Impastato's if you... [Marcello is heard calling Impastato's Restaurant in

Metairie.] Hello, Joe. What time y'all open? Oh, y'all open all day. No, no, no, no, I got, there's just three of us. We gon' come over and just, to eat, for just for an hour, and I got to leave, because I got to go to a wake. All right. We just maybe want a steak or something. Don't worry about it.

YOUNG: No, I want a salad or something.

MARCELLO: Eh? I'll be there in twenty minutes. [He hangs up the receiver.] Let's go.

YOUNG: Let me tell ya.

MARCELLO: You hungry?

YOUNG: I said, look man, I don't know that much about it, but if what you told me, you ain't got nothin' to worry. You got that letter shows that you trying to save the state money.

MARCELLO: That's right.

YOUNG: And I said, tell 'em. You been telling 'em you been …in some oil business. You tell 'em that if they ask you back here. Say, yeah, I do oil business with him [Marcello]. I do waste business with him, man. Say like me, if they ask me if I know him, I say, "Hell yeah, I know him. So what?"

MARCELLO: Yeah, it ain't nothing, man.

YOUNG: Well, that's what he's worried about, that other.

MARCELLO: No, don't, don't worry about them [the undercover agents]. Them guys is stronger than me. Okay?

YOUNG: You see, he…

MARCELLO: That's all I'ma tell you.

YOUNG: He thinks, he thinks, that Lambert's trying to hang him.

MARCELLO: Well, it could be Lambert. You don't know who it could be, you understand? You understand? Look. You got an organization. You don't know who the motherfucker is. Come on let's go eat.…

It was left to Special Agent Harold Hughes to inform Marcello who the motherfucker was. The FBI had decided to wait a few days before informing Carlos of the sting operation, so their ceiling bug in Carlos's office could pick up a few last conversations between Marcello and, it was hoped, people like Aubrey Young, Charlie Roemer, Vince Marinello, and Irving Davidson. As it turned out, Aubrey Young was the first and only one of the conspirators to call the day of the takedown, and after his call Carlos ceased making calls from his office phone except to deliver the most routine messages.

Harold Hughes showed up at Marcello's Town & Country office a few days after the takedown. After handing Carlos a subpoena to appear before a grand jury, he informed Carlos of the bitter truth. The Mafia boss sat erect behind his desk staring coldly at his long-time foe as Hughes told him what Joe Hauser and Mike Wacks and Larry Montague had been up to over the past ten months. Although he finally accepted the fact that "the insurance man" he would have put his head on the chopping block for was a turncoat and a stool pigeon, he was still reluctant to believe Wacks and Montague were FBI undercover agents. "No, them guys; they're my boys," he told Hughes. "Now you're bullshittin' me."

"No, Carlos, I'm not bullshitting you," returned Hughes. "I'm telling you the truth about them, and I'm here to tell you not to hold it against them. They're just a couple of young guys doing their job, doing what they were told to do. That's why you shouldn't try and harm them, or their families. It was nothing personal with them, and I don't want you to send your people out after them because, aside from what might happen to them, it would only make matters worse for you."

To this admonition Carlos made no reply. Telling Hughes he wasn't going to talk anymore until he spoke with his lawyer, he asked his secretary to escort the FBI agent to the door.

Not too long after Hughes left the office, Carlos received a call from Washington. It was Irving Davidson. The ceiling bug then recorded Davidson apologizing in a flood of excuses for having first introduced him to Joe Hauser. Carlos forgave him right away, telling the lobbyist that he, Davidson, "didn't know nothin' about what a motherfuckin' stool pigeon" Hauser was either, so why should he apologize? "Don't worry about it," Carlos insisted, "we still friends."

*   *   *

Needless to say, the New Orleans Mafia summit between Marcello, Aiuppa, Civella, and Trafficante, planned for Mardi Gras week, was called off, and Carlos's grandiose scheme to siphon $1 million a month in insurance commissions out of Teamsters welfare and pension funds had to be postponed indefinitely. Once again, The Big One had eluded him. Now all Carlos had to look forward to was a grand jury investigation.

Perhaps two grand jury investigations. For a week after the FBI took down the New Orleans operation, Special Agents Fleming and Barron in Los Angeles went overt with the West Coast operation and Carlos Marcello was notified he was under investigation for conspiring to bribe a federal judge.

Meanwhile, FBI agents were already busy transcribing the 1400 reels of conversation Hauser and the undercover agents had taped and the FBI listening devices and wiretaps had recorded.

The 1400 reels, consisting of over 35,000 feet of tape, constituted the largest collection of conversations of a Mafia family boss ever recorded in the history of the FBI up to that time. They were a veritable bonanza of information not only on Carlos Marcello but also on the history and state of organized crime in America.

So far as Marcello's activities were concerned, the FBI's electronic surveillance produced several intriguing by-products to the evidence it picked up relating to the BRILAB operation.

For example, during a November 1 meeting with Hauser, Marcello expressed concern that their insurance scheme might suffer after Hauser's departure for prison on November 30 and surprised Hauser by telling him he might have a contact in the office of the attorney general of the United States. Perhaps he might be able to get a postponement of Hauser's prison term:

> "Maybe he can make a phone call to the attorney general. Now I'm not saying I can do it. I gotta man can do it. Give me all that there and we'll make a phone call."

The attorney general at the time was Benjamin R. Civiletti, who had replaced former Attorney General Griffin Bell on August 16, 1979. It had been Bell who had given the final authorization for the BRILAB undercover operation against Marcello, and it had been to Bell that the findings and recommendations of the House Select Committee on Assassinations had been communicated as the FBI sting against Marcello was getting under way. However, since the House Assassinations Committee's final report with accompanying volumes of hearings and appendixes was not published until midsummer, it was newly appointed Attorney General Civiletti who received the published findings. Upon receiving the final report, with its suspicions of Marcello's possible involvement in the Kennedy assassination, Civiletti expressed his doubts whether organized crime had been involved in the assassination. Specifically he told the press that he strongly doubted whether anyone in organized crime would have used such an "unstable" individual as Jack Ruby in such an important undertaking.

Later, after Hauser provided Marcello with all the information about his conviction, Carlos volunteered that he might be able to use the influence he had on the federal parole board to get Hauser out early. Subsequently the FBI did not pick up any calls by Marcello to these supposed connections and Hauser concluded they were probably just an example of Marcello's incurable braggadocio.

One of the more significant conversations, unrelated to the BRILAB operation, that the FBI's listening device in Carlos's office picked up was a discussion between Marcello and notorious oil swindler Robert Sutton in January 1980. Sutton, a college dropout who had built a $500 million oil empire from scratch, had run afoul of the law in successfully exploiting the federal government's oil price-control program so as to realize an illegal profit of roughly $1 billion. The swindle was being called the greatest consumer fraud in American history.

Although his oil business was based in Tulsa, Sutton and some of his closest associates preferred to live in southern Louisiana. Sutton himself lived in a palatial old mansion, called Tara, in the Cajun town of Breaux Bridge. Several of his aides had taken over some of the most beautiful homes in the county.

As the FBI began closing in on him, Sutton turned to the boss of the state's invisible government for help. His major problem concerned two former associates whose imminent grand jury testimony in Tulsa could conceivably damage him. And so Robert Sutton telephoned Marcello's Town & Country office one day to find a solution. The FBI wiretap picked up Sutton telling the boss:

"Come Monday morning they [the two former associates] suppose to be at the FBI....Now I want it that they ain't gonna be able to appear....I don't want the guys beat up right now, because if something happens to 'em they could implicate me. I don't want 'em to get hurt yet, I just want 'em arrested by the police and thrown in jail."

After being assured by Sutton that he would be properly recompensed, Carlos told the 48-year-old oil swindler he would be able to perform the service Sutton needed. But later an FBI wiretap picked him up telling one of his attorneys: "I don't know. This guy looks like he's a fast talker. I don't want to get implicated."

As a result of his call to Marcello, Sutton was later indicted by a Tulsa grand jury on two charges of using gangster connections to try to prevent grand jury witnesses from testifying. This was in addition to fifteen counts of fraud and racketeering relating to his monumental oil swindle.

Another tape unrelated to the BRILAB operation that drew the FBI's attention, and still puzzles many investigators, recorded a conversation between Carlos and his brother Joe on January 23, 1980, about the murder of a federal judge, John Wood of San Antonio, on May 29, 1979.

Carlos and Joe were talking about putting up bond for nineteen people (presumably members of their organization, although that was not made clear) who had just been indicted on charges of selling 800 pounds of marijuana and 200,000 Quaalude tablets. At one point in their discussion Joe Marcello said:

> "These are the people that [were] connected with the killing of the judge in El Paso [sic]....The judge is dead. This was their three people."

Later, six men were indicted for Judge Wood's murder, including Charles V. Harrelson, a Dallas-based racketeer who, at the time of his arrest, was carrying the business card of Russell D. Mathews, another Dallas racketeer who had been a close associate of Jack Ruby's in the early sixties and who had documented connections to Santos Trafficante and Carlos Marcello.

A year after Harrelson's indictment, Gary Shaw, a Dallas news reporter and Kennedy assassination researcher, spotted a close resemblance between Harrelson and one of the three "tramps" who had been arrested in Dealey Plaza immediately after the assassination. Shaw then learned that a Fort Worth graphics expert, Jack White, who had testified on the identity of the tramps before the House Select Committee on Assassinations in 1978, had concluded, without reservation, that Harrelson was "the younger tramp." As if to confirm that possibility, rumors began circulating around Texas that Harrelson had told the officers who arrested him that he had been involved in the Kennedy assassination.

At the grand jury investigation of Judge Wood's murder, Joe Marcello was called to testify about his tape-recorded remarks of January 23 intimating he knew of three people connected to the murder. Joe categorically denied any knowledge of the subject matter of the taped conversation and said that it was not his voice on the tape. Later, sound experts and Los Angeles BRILAB prosecutor Bruce Kelton concluded that it was indeed Joe Marcello's voice on the tape, and Joe was indicted for perjury in April 1982, accused of lying before a 1980 grand jury. At his San Antonio trial Joe was ably represented by two of the most brilliant trial lawyers in the country, Roy Cohn of New York and Russell Schonekas of New Orleans, who eventually won him an acquittal on a technicality.

But the mysteries of the Marcello brothers' apparent knowledge of who Judge John Wood's killers were and Charles V. Harrelson's possible connection to the Marcellos and the Dallas tramps of November 22, 1963, remain.

Harrelson was eventually convicted of murdering Judge Wood and is currently serving a life sentence in the federal penitentiary at Texarkana. During his trial it was never determined whether he was one of the three men Joe Marcello had mentioned on the January 23, 1980, FBI tape as having been involved in Judge Wood's murder. And the presiding judge in San Antonio would not allow any testimony at the trial on Harrelson's much-publicized possible connection with the Dealey Plaza tramps and the Kennedy assassination.

Meanwhile Dallas-based researcher Gary Shaw, who is convinced Harrelson was one of the three "tramps," has been denied permission by the Federal Bureau of Prisons to interview Harrelson at Texarkana. Both the prison authorities and the prisoner himself have the power to decide who may visit a prisoner and who may not.

By May 1980, the FBI had transcribed the 1400 reels of BRILAB tapes and had turned them over to the New Orleans grand jury investigating the activities of Carlos Marcello, I. Irving Davidson, Charles E. Roemer II, Vincent Marinello, and others during the period February 1979–February 1980.

On June 17, 1980, the grand jury indicted Marcello, Davidson, Roemer, and Marinello on twelve counts of racketeering, mail and wire fraud, and "conspiracy involving an alleged scheme to obtain insurance contracts in Louisiana by bribery." The racketeering charge was a RICO violation carrying a maximum penalty of twenty years in prison. The other two charges carried maximum penalties of five years each. The case was scheduled to go to trial in New Orleans in the summer of 1981.

The federal RICO (Racketeer-Influenced and Corrupt Organizations Act) statute, drafted by G. Robert Blakey, and voted into law by Congress as part of the Organized Crime Control Act of 1970, permits federal prosecutors to go after patterns of corruption, not just individual criminal acts, and allows for long prison sentences commensurate with the damage organized crime does to individual communities and society at large. For this reason, the RICO indictment was, for Marcello, a most serious charge. Marcello's second indictment was handed down over a year later, when, on August 5, 1981, a federal grand jury in Los Angeles indicted him, Samuel Sciortino, and Phillip Rizzuto for conspiring to bribe a United States district judge. The case was due to go to trial in November 1981. If convicted, Marcello would face a minimum of ten years in prison on the charge.

Thus it was that as the summer of 1981 approached, the boss of the Louisiana Mafia faced the prospect of possibly spending the rest of his life behind bars.

But, as the New Orleans BRILAB prosecutors will affirm today, Carlos Marcello did not fear the New Orleans trial. He had been tried before in New Orleans and had always won. No, Los Angeles was one thing, but New Orleans was another. It was his home turf. Carlos firmly believed that no New Orleans jury would ever convict him of anything. He was popular in New Orleans. He had a lot of friends, influential friends, throughout the state. As the trial date approached, Carlos's Town & Country office was deluged with messages of encouragement and support from well-wishers from Shreveport to Morgan City, and friends and associates observed he was still his usual cocky, imperious self.

"They's not goin' to get me, man," he told a reporter from the *Times-Picayune* shortly before the trial began. "No way, man. Dese are my people here."

56

Trial One: New Orleans

"I can't just do things bam-bam and fuck it up....I gotta know
what I'm doin'. I gotta have confidence. If I don't have confidence, I'd rather not do business. I gotta know I'm dealin'
wit somebody dat ain't gonna do me no shit. I don't wanna
get in no damn fuckin' trouble or nuttin' like dat."

Carlos Marcello's remarks, taped by Joe Hauser in the summer
of 1979 and played before a jury in federal court in the summer of
1981, caused yet another wave of chuckles to ripple over the crowded
New Orleans courtroom. The government had made a fool out of
Marcello once again. Things were not going very well for the Louisiana Mafia boss at this trial. It was the first time tapes of Marcello's
utterances had ever been played in a courtroom. Language was not
one of Carlos's strong suits. For this reason, among others, he had
always held his tongue in public. Now, before the largest public he
had ever had—for the press was present in force—his broken, mud-
dled, obscene, arrogant language was opening him up to public ridicule time and again. Carlos Marcello was not used to people laughing
at him. Until now, people laughed at Carlos Marcello at some risk.

The tapes played on....

*   *   *

To a jury containing three black women and one black male alternate, Marcello's remarks on blacks and on New Orleans' first black mayor, Ernest Morial, taped by Joe Hauser two years before, were now boomeranging back in his face:

MARCELLO: The mayor's a nigger here. He's black. He wants to change the insurance contract to his connection. He wants to do it on his own.
                       He's a nigger, and a nigger's gonna be a nigger even if you give him some authority.

HAUSER: How come you elected a nigger mayor?

MARCELLO: Cause these assholes went to sleep.

And then there were the Mafia boss's wiretapped remarks on the black vote he boasted he controlled:

"I got a buncha niggers I gotta get together here....fifteen hundred of 'em. Fifteen hundred families I mean....All the niggers around. The blacks over in Jefferson. Highway 90. See Highway 90 I got 1500 blacks, and in Avondale Homes I got 4500....I'm tryin' to trap the whole thing...."

As these remarks by defendant Marcello reverberated in the jurors' headsets, the four black jurors were observed to be staring straight ahead with grim expressions, while some of their white colleagues seemed to be trying to stifle smiles. Never in his wildest premonitions of adversity did Carlos ever think that one day his fate would be partly in the hands of "a buncha niggers."

No, things had not been going very well for the principal defendant in the case of *The United States v. Carlos Marcello*. The FBI had mounted an extraordinarily successful undercover operation against him, one of the most brilliantly executed stings in its history. Fourteen hundred reels, thirty-five thousand feet of tape. What amounted to a continuous, yearlong divulging of secrets from the man whose motto was "Three can keep a secret if two are dead."

The trial of Carlos Marcello, Irving Davidson, Charles E. Roemer II, and Vincent Marinello began in New Orleans in late March 1981 and lasted eighteen weeks. Representing the government was trial prosecutor U.S. Attorney John Volz, assisted by former Tampa prosecutor L. Eades Hogue. Representing Marcello were Russell Schonekas, a veteran of Carlos's legal battles since the late sixties, and Henry Gonzales, former defense counsel for Florida Mafia boss Santos Trafficante. For 45-year-old John Volz, an appointee of President Jimmy Carter, this was to be the biggest case of his career so far. For Schonekas and Gonzales it was to be the showdown battle with the government in a war that had been raging intermittently since their client's 1961 abduction and deportation at the behest of Attorney General Robert F. Kennedy.

The star witness for the prosecution was to be convicted swindler, now government informant Joseph Hauser, assisted by FBI Agents Michael Wacks and Larry Montague. The New Orleans public, which had been avidly following the case since the grand jury investigation of 1980, was looking forward to the first confrontation between Hauser, Wacks, and Montague and Carlos Marcello since the BRILAB operation went overt.

As for the other defendants—Davidson, Roemer, and Marinello—only Roemer seemed to be in deep trouble. The state commissioner of administration, represented by New Orleans attorneys Michael Fawer and Matthew Greenbaum, was expected to wage an uphill fight, given the taped evidence against him. Whereas defendants Irving Davidson, represented by Washington attorney Thomas R. Dyson, Jr., and Vincent Marinello, represented by New Orleans attorney Arthur A. "Buddy" Lemann III, were given a fifty-fifty chance by the New Orleans press of being acquitted.

The defendants had been charged with conspiracy to pay bribes and kickbacks to public officials in an effort to obtain state insurance business. The counts were conspiracy, racketeering, interstate travel to engage in racketeering, and mail and wire fraud.

Jury selection for the trial had been stormy and time-consuming. The prosecution was understandably wary of prospective jurors with Italian names. The defense was understandably wary of prospective black jurors who might react adversely to Marcello's many "racial epithets" and of prospective jurors knowledgeable of Carlos Marcello's reputation as a Mafia boss.

"When I mention the name 'Marcello,' what comes to mind?" defense attorney Michael Fawer asked one prospective male juror.

"He's a powerful man. I know he owns a lot of land."

"What do you think of when you hear Charles Roemer's name?" Fawer asked the same man.

"BRILAB," the prospective juror replied.

The man was excused.

"What comes to mind when you hear the name 'Carlos Marcello'?" Fawer asked a prospective female juror.

"Honest?" the woman asked.

"Yes," Fawer responded.

"Mafia," the woman said.

The woman then added that she didn't really "know too much about Mr. Marcello and the Mafia."

She was later qualified.

One potential female juror said she heard it mentioned that "Marcello is well known in politics and has a lot of spies everywhere."

Another confessed she would be afraid to serve on the jury. She was excused.

Fawer asked one potential juror, a black male: "What if the words on the recordings have to do with your color? What if the word 'nigger' is used?"

The man said he would not be offended by such language and was qualified.

One prospective female juror said she was aware of allegations that Marcello was involved in the assassination of President John F. Kennedy, and the defense asked that she be excused because her "accusation of Mr. Marcello's involvement in the assassination of President Kennedy is potentially inflammatory."

Judge Morey Sear qualified her, however, stating that the woman apparently did not believe the allegation of Marcello's involvement in the assassination.

And so the selection process dragged on. Two days before the jury was sworn in, Irving Davidson's attorney, Thomas Dyson, forcefully requested that the entire panel be dismissed because, he argued, the prosecution had "systematically eliminated Italians from the jury."

Judge Sear dismissed the motion, saying "I suspect maybe there are other nationalities not represented on the jury."

By the time the three-week selection process was over, it was clear to all concerned that it was impossible to impanel a jury that did not know anything about Carlos Marcello. In the end, each one of the twelve jurors chosen turned out to be familiar with Marcello's reputation as an underworld figure.

After jury selection, the next battle was over whether the tapes the FBI had recorded could be played in court to the jury. The defense made a vigorous objection to allowing the jury to hear such recorded remarks as Irving Davidson's describing Marcello as the "number one guy in the mob" and likening him to "the godfather of the Philadelphia Mafia, Angelo Bruno," asserting that such remarks were "overwhelmingly prejudicial."

The defense also argued forcefully that the jury not be allowed to hear any taped conversation between Marcello and the undercover agents about the Kennedy family or the assassination of President John F. Kennedy, again on the grounds that such references would be "overwhelmingly prejudicial."

In the end Judge Sear went along with the defense on these two motions and decided that the Kennedy tapes would not be played in court but that the jury would hear all tapes pertaining specifically to the BRILAB operation. The judge also ruled that transcriptions of the tapes offered as evidence to the jury would be provided to the media.

Although this last concession was welcomed by the press, the overwhelming majority of the taped conversations would still probably remain beyond a Freedom of Information Act access.

In 1987, after stiff opposition from the Justice Department to a FOIA request for the tapes to which I *was*, by law, entitled—those admitted into evidence at the two BRILAB trials—I sued the department for release of those tapes. In the process I learned that among the tapes not admitted into evidence at the trials were three containing conversations between Carlos Marcello, the undercover agents, and others, about the John F. Kennedy assassination and the House Select Committee's investigation. According to an inventory sent by the Justice Department to my attorney, Judge Sear had put these tapes under judicial seal during the 1981 pretrial hearings, thus placing their release forever beyond the provisions of the Freedom of Information Act.

As of July 1988, the precise content of these three tapes has not been made public, and neither former Chairman Stokes nor former Chief Counsel Blakey of the Assassinations Committee has listened to them or read transcripts of their contents. Blakey told me in a July 1988 interview that he was informed of the tapes' approximate content over the phone by an FBI official after the BRILAB operation went overt in 1980. He found only one of the reported conversations—a non-conversation, as it turned out—suspicious.

As roughly described to Blakey, that conversation had been recorded by the ceiling bug in Carlos's Town & Country office. An unidentified individual had come into Carlos's office one day in the spring of 1979, when the New Orleans papers were reporting the results of the Assassinations Committee's investigation, and, after some preliminary banter, had asked Carlos how he would respond to the committee's suspicions of him. Carlos immediately told the man to shut up, that they would go outside and talk. Noises were heard of Carlos pushing his chair away from his desk and two men walking out of the room.

Curiously, while I was given a rough idea of what was on the tapes by several officials who had been associated with the BRILAB operation and trials, I was not told anything about the particular tape that had been described to Blakey.

Early in the trial proceedings the defense team presented motions to dismiss all charges against the defendants, arguing that they were victims of entrapment, selective prosecution, and prejudicial publicity. It was the government that created the conspiracy to bribe public officials with kickbacks to obtain insurance business, the defense argued. And it was the government that had singled out Carlos Marcello for "selective prosecution" out of frustration over not having succeeded in prosecuting him successfully in the past. Furthermore, Carlos Marcello's notoriety as an alleged Mafia boss and suspect in an alleged plot to assassinate President Kennedy constituted publicity so prejudicial that it would be impossible for Mr. Marcello to have a fair trial. Judge Morey Sear denied all three motions and ordered the trial to proceed.

Forced to devise a new defense strategy, what the defendants came up with was a massive onslaught on the credibility of the government's star witness, Joseph Hauser.

There was not much the defense could do about discrediting witnesses from evidence presented on tape. The defense was therefore compelled to try and discredit evidence presented that should have been on tape, but wasn't, and evidence that was on tape but gave the appearance of being deliberately fabricated in an attempt to incriminate someone.

One of the most vulnerable areas of the prosecution's case was the September 10 meeting of the conspirators at the St. Ann Hotel, for it was a crucial meeting yet, due to a variety of already mentioned unexpected circumstances, the undercover agents were unable to tape it. Thus the jury had to take Mike Wacks's word for it that Commissioner Roemer agreed, in a men's room of the hotel, to accept a kickback in return for awarding a state employees insurance contract to Fidelity Financial Consultants. In the end, the jury did accept Wacks's word, because the jurors liked and trusted Michael Wacks.

The same could not be said of Joe Hauser. As a convicted swindler and notorious con man, Hauser's credibility was extremely vulnerable and the defense put it in question repeatedly throughout the trial.

But Joe Hauser was not easily intimidated and often surprised his interrogators with his frankness and quick repartee.

"You are a con artist?" one of Marcello's attorneys, Henry Gonzales, once asked him.

"I don't think so," Hauser answered.

"Do you consider yourself a good briber?" Gonzales continued.

"Yes, sir," Hauser replied with assurance.

Hauser's credibility came under the severest attack when, after analyzing certain recordings, the defense team came to the conclusion that he had deliberately fabricated recorded conversations to incriminate important individuals, among them the attorney general of the United States and Carlos Marcello. These alleged fabrications became known to the court as "Hauser's soliloquies."

The defense contended that Hauser indulged in one of these soliloquies early in the undercover operation, on June 28, 1979, in the bathroom of Carlos Marcello's suite of offices at the Town & Country Motel. At a lull in a discussion with Marcello in the boss's office, Hauser left the office for a minute and went down the corridor to a bathroom where he recorded himself saying:

"Carlos, I'm listening. And I'm reading the papers. Okay. I'm gonna read what you're showing me. So in a sense what you're saying is that you're taking over the whole family. Oh, then we can write business throughout the country. I'm, I'm reading. Okay, I'll read it. Lemme finish reading this. You mean to tell me something like this they distribute in the mail? Oh, I see. By messenger.... I never realized numbers were such a big game."

Defense Counsel Fawer played the relevant tape, pointing out the sounds of footsteps and of doors opening and closing. Then he asked Hauser to give the court an explanation of his "toilet soliloquy." Hauser explained that he felt extremely tense and nervous in Marcello's presence and went to the bathroom for a minute to rehearse what he was going to say to Carlos next. "What will I ask him? Let's see. Maybe this.... I saw things on his desk that were dynamite."

Counsel Fawer did not bother to ask Hauser what he saw on Carlos's desk.

Instead Michael Fawer, representing the accused Charles Roemer, pushed on and asserted that Hauser had indulged in yet another taped soliloquy in Marcello's office, later on in the operation.

Referring to an offer Carlos had made to intervene on his behalf to delay his going to prison by getting in touch with a contact he had in the Justice Department, Hauser was heard saying:

"So how much will it cost to fix the case with Civiletti [then U.S. Attorney General Benjamin R. Civiletti]?...Okay, I'm not gonna talk anymore. Okay, we'll talk outside."

The defense contended that sounds on the tape of a door opening and closing just before Hauser made his remarks indicated Marcello was stepping out of the office for a minute.

"That was not a case of fabricating evidence?" Fawer asked.

"No," Hauser replied. "Marcello was present. Maybe a secretary came into the office at that moment. When I mentioned Civiletti's name, Carlos put his finger to his lips in a gesture to shut me up. I was about to go to the penitentiary and Carlos had told me he had a way to get to Attorney General Civiletti, who was Italian, like him."

While the court might have been willing to accept Hauser's explanations for his two alleged soliloquies at the Town & Country office, there was one, stemming from a meeting between Hauser and gubernatorial candidate Louis Lambert, that the court had no doubts about.

As we have seen, Marcello had been hedging his bets in the elections. When Carlos's candidate James Fitzmorris, to whom he had given a $10,000 bribe, lost the Democratic primary to Louis Lambert, Carlos felt he had to give Lambert something in case he would be elected governor over Republican candidate David Treen.

Lambert preferred his campaign donation to be in the form of cash for tickets to a fund-raising dinner. In mid-November 1979, Hauser met with Lambert in his office and offered him $10,000 in cash. Hauser had recorded the conversation:

LAMBERT: What do you want to contribute to my campaign?

HAUSER: I want to give you $10,000 in cash right now.

LAMBERT: And I'm gonna give you, let me tell you what I'm doing so you can just....Wait, right here 'til I get some tickets.

HAUSER: Oh, leave me alone, give them to L. G. Moore, leave me alone.

LAMBERT: You take the goddamn tickets and then we've done it the right way.

HAUSER: Okay.

LAMBERT: That scares you, but you just have to learn we've got a new policy.

At this point in the discussion the sounds of footsteps, presumably Lambert's, leaving the room are heard along with the sounds of a door opening and closing. Hauser, now momentarily alone in the office, takes the opportunity to say into his recorder:

HAUSER: I want it understood one thing. That's part of the business. I, I call it a kickback, you can call it anything you want.

At this point, the sounds of a door opening and closing and the sounds of footsteps are clearly audible on the tape, and Hauser completes his remarks, now no longer in soliloquy, saying:

HAUSER: ...you want to call it this...you just get this....Okay?

LAMBERT: Here take the goddamned tickets, will you.

Although Hauser denied on the stand that he was fabricating evidence—claiming there were others in the office who were coming and going—the court concluded that Hauser was, in fact, alone when he made the remark about kickbacks. However the court concluded that Hauser's conduct, while disreputable, clearly bore no relationship to the offense for which Marcello and Roemer had been convicted.

But attorney Fawer was relentless in his persecution of Joe Hauser. As part of his effort to discredit Hauser, he had a tape played to the jury of a September 23, 1979, telephone conversation between Hauser and Marcello during which Hauser tells Marcello that he was in a synagogue the day before, which was a Jewish holiday:

HAUSER: I went to the rabbi and I made a very special prayer for you.

MARCELLO: Well, thank you, Joe....We need it.

HAUSER: We all need it....The high, high rabbi made a very
             special prayer for you.

MARCELLO: Thank you.

"Was that part of the undercover operation?" Fawer asked Hauser.
"No, that was the truth," Hauser replied.

Hauser then told Fawer that his activities during the undercover operation were "not the most pleasant things I did in my life," but he
insisted that offering the prayer for Marcello was the truth.

Fawer then observed: "And a few hours later, you went to the
man for whom you made a special prayer and you carried with you
a recording device."

But as much as the defense lawyers hammered away at Joe Hauser's character and credibility, they were still unable to impugn the
credibility of the tapes on which two or more individuals were heard
talking. The tapes clearly delineated the roles of the conspirators and
illustrated their crimes. They showed that Carlos Marcello was the
ultimate boss and schemer behind the conspiracy to obtain lucrative
state insurance contracts through bribery, that he was clearly the mastermind behind the entire criminal enterprise. Also the tapes clearly
showed that it was always Marcello who gave the order to pay a given
bribe. Everyone else—Davidson, the undercover agents, Hauser, Marinello—played wholly secondary roles. They functioned only as messengers, go-betweens, sounding boards, and occasional advisers and
took no initiatives on their own.

Likewise the tapes showed beyond a shadow of a doubt that
Charles Roemer accepted a bribe from Marcello through Hauser for
the specific purpose of using his influence to award a state employees insurance contract to the company Joe Hauser represented.

Commissioner Roemer attempted to put up a defense to the accusation he accepted a bribe, but it was a lame defense that the tapes
refuted. Roemer's defense was that he accepted the money from
Marcello as a contribution to his friend Sonny Mouton's primary campaign, but that purpose is never mentioned on any of the relevant
tapes. Furthermore one of the tapes clearly showed that Commissioner Roemer was most anxious to oblige Marcello in getting the
insurance scheme off the ground.

As for Marcello's contention that he was the victim of selective
prosecution, the defense failed to show evidence that the BRILAB
operation was concocted in the criminal division of the Justice De-

partment as a means to finally "get" Marcello. Marcello's counsel Russell Schonekas was able to elicit testimony from FBI Agent Harold Hughes that Marcello had for years been the subject of an open FBI file and was considered by the FBI to be a leading figure in organized crime. Schonekas also got agents Hughes and Fleming to testify to the government's acute frustration over not being able to deport Marcello since his defiance of the deportation order of 1961 that had been instigated by Attorney General Kennedy. However Schonekas and his assistants were never able to present convincing evidence to support Marcello's contention that BRILAB was designed to "get Marcello" or that Marcello's prosecution was motivated by the government's frustration. As the prosecution was able to show, Marcello was never singled out for investigation and prosecution. Through testimony elicited from FBI Special Agent William Fleming and Joseph Hauser, the prosecution clearly demonstrated that Hauser's decision to cooperate with the government provided Fleming with a link to several individuals with whom Hauser said he had had illicit dealings in the past. Carlos Marcello just happened to be one of those individuals. The decision to go after him in an undercover operation arose, then, out of a purely fortuitous circumstance: the decision of Joseph Hauser to turn state's witness.

Those who participated in the trial as jurors or attorneys, and those who attended the proceedings as journalists or mere onlookers, all agreed that the most memorable things about it were the tape-recorded remarks of the principal defendant, Carlos Marcello.

Delivered in his unique southern drawl and Sicilian–New Orleanian Creole accent, in a broken, labored syntax and from a choice of words drawn from the code language of the Mafia and the talk of the lowest social orders, many of Marcello's expressions and pearls of wisdom were truly memorable.

Carlos Marcello, the owner of the 6400-acre Churchill Farms, on investing in land:

> "Dat's something they can't make no more—land. It's disappearing all the time. Especially around cities—New York, New Orleans, and Lafayette....They make babies every day, and every time a baby born, twenty-four years from now, they looking for a lot. They don't stay with their Mama and their Daddy."

Marcello on the snobbish West Bank community of Old Metairie, where he once maintained a home:

> "I hadda move outa there. They aristocrats and think they somebody. Their wives get drunk and got nothing for their husbands when they come home....A lotta times they puttin' on because they don't have no money."

On the Metairie Country Club:

> "You gotta die before you can get in there."

On money and New Orleans Mayor Ernest Morial:

> "Dat nigger wants money as bad as you need it, bad as everybody else wants it. Ya unnerstand? He'll take it from the right people."

On candidate for governor David Treen:

> "He an aristocrat....I don't wanna meet with him. He not goin' for all kind of people....If Treen come in there ain't goin' to be no connections."

On herons observed in the swamps from the road on the way to Lafayette with agents Wacks and Montague:

> "Herons, dat's something like a crane. You find 'em on garbage dumps. But they ain't no good to eat."

This was the speech of the man who was said to control huge labor unions, who was said to control the political machinery of an entire state, and who was suspected by a congressional committee of masterminding what had come to be called the crime of the century?

Herein lay one of the secrets of Carlos Marcello's power. As his masterful eight-month direction of the scheme to obtain Louisiana state insurance contracts through kickbacks demonstrated, Marcello was capable of successfully directing and managing a risky, complex, secret enterprise, involving the control, through bribery and fear, of public officials. And so it is not unreasonable to accept the possibility that he was able to control the political machinery of a state, or the leadership of the most powerful labor union in the country. Yet because of his lower-class grade-school language, he was always able to deceive people—especially highly educated law enforcement officials and senators sitting on committees to investigate organized crime—into believing he wasn't smart enough to plan or commit the complex crimes of which he was suspected. Carlos Marcello was surely one of the most deceptive Mafia leaders in American history. An affable, gregarious man with the business sense and entrepreneurial spirit of a founder of a major corporation, the administrative ability of a chief executive officer, and the sense of battle strategy of a four-star general, he was able to deceive people into believing he was just a plain businessman, a real estate investor, or, as his FBI case agent characterized him in the sixties, a mere "tomato salesman."

But there must have been more to the secret of Carlos Marcello's power than a combination of innate ability and deceptive manner of speech.

Mike Wacks told me that the most memorable experience he had with Marcello occurred shortly after he arrived in New Orleans to join the BRILAB undercover operation. It happened the first time he accompanied Marcello to a New Orleans restaurant:

> "As soon as we entered the dining area and sat down, the whole place fell silent. Then a half minute later the diners began whispering to one another and casting furtive glances at us. I noticed the maitre d' and the waiters hovering in conference near the entrance to the room. Then when the maitre showed up at the table with two waiters by his side, I have never seen such deference paid to someone as they showed to Mr. Marcello in my life. Soon every waiter in the place was fawning over us and I was sure every customer in the place was talking about us."

Yes, there was another component to Marcello's power: his reputation. His reputation of being a man you did not dare to cross.

Irving Davidson expressed an aspect of this other component when he gave some advice to Mike Wacks and Larry Montague in his Washington office before the two men, whom Davidson believed were Prudential insurance agents, first left for New Orleans:

> "Look, when you deal with Marcello, remember that loyalty and trustworthiness are everything to him. If you violate that, you can expect the worst to happen to you."

And, in saying that, Davidson slowly drew a finger across his neck. In the last analysis, it was the code by which Carlos Marcello lived that was the ultimate secret of his power. That ancient code, as we know, asserted that the amount of power and respect a man enjoyed was in relation to the amount of fear he could inspire. And the basis of that fear was his reputation of being a man who would not hesitate to commit murder in order to achieve his ends.

The tapes droned on....

In a series of conversations with Vince Marinello, Carlos reminisced about doing business in the good old days:

"Yeah, man, it ain't like it used to be....Yeah, man, I done got the business you don't know how many times."
...
"[Governor] Jimmy Davis I could do business with. [Governor] Earl Long and uh, Jimmy Davis, Earl Long."
...
"It ain't like before, man...all the gambling houses and all....I used to give [Police Chief] Beauregard Miller $50,000 cash money every time."
...
"I knowed everybody from fuckin' Grand Isle all the way to Raceland, man. All the way to Houma, you know....It takes me two days if I stop at each one of 'em house and to say hello, right. Yeah...it's really somethin' to see.
"I got like, uh, St. Charles Parish. I got like Raceland and Thibodaux, that's Houma. I got like Morgan City. I got two Italian buys.
"They state representatives, Guarisco and Siracusa. And all up in Franklin, them people in Abbeville and all. Lake Charles and on down....I know all these people....Go there and gotta get the right people. Say "Here $5,000, $10,000...."
...
"It takes time to get where I'm at. To know all these people—governors, business, the attorney general, they know me. They all ain't scared."

But, in recent years, Carlos told Marinello, he hadn't been able to control governors like he used to. Referring to a $168,000 bribe he claimed he gave former Governor John McKeithen in exchange for his promise to have the state build a highway through Churchill Farms, he told Marinello in a tape-recorded conversation:

> "I hate the mother fucker…take my money and don't do nothin' for me.…I had McKeithen for eight years. That sonofabitch got $168,000 my money and then that sonofabitch too scared to talk to me. How you like dat?"

Marcello then told Marinello that he offered Governor McKeithen free land on which to build the Superdome, telling the young lawyer that it would have been cheaper for the stadium to have been built in that location than on its present downtown site:

> "I was gonna give him 250 acres of ground…Churchill Farms. We set it all up for the Dome Stadium. He had everything straightened out, man. He closed up.…They losin' money where they would made money. All they needed was 20 acres for the dome. Here the train could bring the people right there. The planes could bring 'em right there. Water, everything. I got the plans."
> …
> "He [McKeithen] got so fuckin' scared, man. All of dem. So they went and paid $20, some of 'em $100 a square foot."
> …
> "It ain't no good for my reputation for somebody to take me for $125,000."

The New Orleans press, of course, had a wonderful time quoting Marcello's priceless remarks from the tapes played in court. The BRILAB trial allowed the reporters to finally have a good time with Marcello. One reporter snooping around Marcello's car noticed a book resting on the rear window shelf and found it was *The Godfather* by Mario Puzo. Following Marcello to his car after the trial session was over, the reporter asked the boss what he thought of the book. Carlos stopped a second and said:

> "Dat stuff? It's like one of them fairy tales. Like Sleepin' Beauty an de Seven Dwarfs."

In addition to talking of local politics and politicians, Carlos also liked to talk of local restaurants and food. As a consequence, the BRILAB jurors also received a good dose of culinary advice and opinion from the man whose fate they soon would be called upon to decide.

Larry Montague recalls that one of Marcello's favorite restaurants was the one his family had first established in the old Willswood Tavern on the West Bank. The place was now called Mosca's, after its first chef, Provino Mosca, who had once supervised Al Capone's kitchen. Carlos referred to it once on tape:

"I gave 'em the place there. And they made a success of the sonofabitch. You can't get no reservations there on Fridays and Saturdays."

Montague recalls that when Carlos would arrive at Mosca's, usually accompanied by five or six of "his people," the whole place would turn into "a kind of celebration." Carlos would be greeted as if he were a king. Plates of steaming hot spaghetti with clam sauce would start streaming out of the kitchen in a steady procession accompanied by bowls of salad, loaves of Italian bread, and bottles of white wine. After dinner it was Carlos's personal custom to pour Strega into everyone's double espressos. "Here, take dis," Carlos would tell one of his guests as he poured the southern Italian liqueur into what Montague recalls was the "blackest, thickest coffee" he ever saw. "Dis here will wake you up."

As all the world knows, New Orleanians love food and talk about food incessantly. In this sense the BRILAB tapes showed Marcello to be a typical New Orleanian. The tapes revealed, among many things, that Carlos preferred Italian-Creole cooking to all other cuisines. His favorite restaurants were, judging from the number of times he mentioned them on the tapes, Mosca's on the West Bank, Broussard's and La Louisiane in the French Quarter, and Impastato's in Metairie. Brother Joe at the time owned and operated La Louisiane in partnership with youngest brother, Sammy, and had an interest in Broussard's.

It is worth mentioning that Sam Saia's place, the Felix Oyster Bar, out of which Dutz Murret and his nephew Lee Harvey Oswald worked in 1963, was two doors down from La Louisiane, long a Marcello favorite and, until recently, operated by Sammy Marcello.

Yes, Carlos Marcello liked food.

In a September 1979 taped conversation that brought smiles to the BRILAB jurors' faces, Joe Hauser told Charlie Roemer in between their scheming over insurance contracts:

"Carlos been feedin' me to death. Goin' to all those restaurants. Yesterday he fed me those shrimps. He kept eating them fast as he was opening them up for me. He kept feeding them to me two and three at a time."

Hauser, a hypochondriac, perpetually worried about his health—he had a bleeding ulcer—and his weight—he was beginning to develop a paunch—would complain about Marcello's feeding him to death but would always give in to Carlos in the end if the boss insisted on his joining him for a meal.

The BRILAB jury had a chance to chuckle again over an exchange Hauser had with Carlos on November 11:

MARCELLO: Watcha wanna do this evening?

HAUSER: Don't worry about me this evening. You go home and I'll stay in the hotel.

MARCELLO: No, I got Vincent. I got myself. You wanna go eat?

HAUSER: Whatever you wanna do. I gotta eat light.

MARCELLO: Awright. But where would you like to go? You wanna go across the lake or you wanna eat light? With them other boys [Wacks and Montague] wanna eat?

HAUSER: We can go to Impastato's, is that okay?

MARCELLO: Anywhere you wanna go.

HAUSER: Impastato's...they got great fettuccine there.

MARCELLO: [Suddenly sounding full of enthusiasm] You like fettuccine, man?

HAUSER: [With an air of resignation] It's all right. Whatever you like.

The BRILAB tapes revealed that Carlos's friends and associates were forever finding special foods for him.

Aubrey Young, the former state official who first introduced Marcello to Roemer, called Carlos up once and told him: "I found out where I can get some more of that cheese."

"More of what?" asked Carlos.

"Some of that special cheese. People over in Lafayette has it."

Later Carlos phoned Hauser to tell him he'd got "some hogshead cheese. You know, Mosca. He brought me some yesterday."

Once Vince Marinello phoned Carlos to tell him he would bring him and his brother Joe a jar of *caponata,* an eggplant relish his mother made in her Greenwood Mississippi home.

"Forget about Joe," Carlos replied. "Give me mine."

The tapes droned on....From them the BRILAB jurors learned over and over again that Carlos Marcello loved spaghetti above all other dishes. In one taped conversation he told Hauser:

"I had spaghetti with my daughter....She's comin' in tomorrow with her sisters and all and she's gonna cook spaghetti ...she cook good spaghetti, man....She thought I by myself, but I got somewhere else to go tonight. You know Mosca's? [Hauser had eaten there countless times.] Didn't you eat at Mosca's last time? I'm goin' there tonight to eat with some people. Got a deal cookin'....You know, Mosca's, they make good spaghetti, man."

In November, as Hauser was getting ready to go off to prison to serve time for his Phoenix conviction, Marcello told the insurance swindler he should drink "that goat milk from Schwegmann's" for his bleeding ulcer. "I'll get you some a that milk," he told him, and then phoned Marinello about Hauser's health. The members of the BRILAB jury chuckled again over the exchange:

MARCELLO: He been bleedin'....We got him some goat milk.

MARINELLO: Oh yeah?

MARCELLO: Yeah. So now he drinkin' that goat milk. You see he want to smoke cigars. He's nervous.

MARINELLO: He must eat that pizza too.

MARCELLO: He eat everything.

But the last tape that was played to the jury was nothing to laugh about. As July drew to a close and the stifling heat of August approached, the BRILAB trial began to wind down. It was time for the prosecution and defense to present their summations.

It was the assistant prosecutor, Eades Hogue, who presented the government's summation of the case against the defendants. It was then, during his remarks, that the jurors listened to their last tape, the 160th tape played in court since the trial began. It was the recording of the February 8, 1980, telephone conversation between Aubrey Young and Carlos Marcello just after the FBI took down its yearlong undercover operation.

In the conversation, which had already been played to the jury once before, Aubrey Young told Marcello of the government's investigation, which he, Young, had learned about from Charles Roemer earlier in the day, and relayed a message from Roemer asking Marcello to destroy an insurance document Roemer had recently sent to him:

"Tell Roemer ain't no money passed," responded Marcello.

"But in fact, money did pass to Mr. Roemer," Eades Hogue told the jury. "And Mr. Marcello was aware that the money had passed for the purpose of obtaining insurance contracts.... Keep that in mind, that blatant inconsistency with the facts as you know them."

"As for Roemer," Hogue went on, "he reacted like any guilty man would react. He tells Young to tell Marcello to destroy the papers he sent him, and Marcello says: 'Oh, man, I done disappear with them motherfuckers. I don't need nothin' like that.'"

Hogue continued: "Mr. Marcello and Mr. Davidson had no qualms about corrupting Mr. Roemer, and Mr. Roemer had no qualms about being corrupted. And the majesty of a state office was sold."

"In the same telephone conversation," Hogue continued, "Marcello refuses to believe that the men he took for insurance executives could have been working for the government."

"Don't worry about them," Marcello reassures Young, "them guys is stronger than me."

"That's the confidence," Hogue observed, "that he [Marcello] had —that his conspiracy would never come to light, but, in fact, it did."

Russell Schonekas took only two hours to present his summation of Marcello's defense.

According to Schonekas, the BRILAB investigation was the federal government's last-ditch effort to snare Carlos Marcello, "a kind, old, sympathetic man who only wanted to live his life out in peace."

"He's fought 'em long enough," Schonekas told the jurors, "but now they've got him back again because they can't stand defeat." Pointing to Mike Wacks and Larry Montague, Schonekas called them "vultures waiting for the carcass."

Turning his attention to Harold Hughes, who had testified before the court that he had been pursuing an investigation of Marcello for the past ten years, Schonekas called him a "supersleuth" to whom BRILAB "offered a final opportunity to convict Marcello of a serious crime....Mr. Marcello is 71 years of age," observed Schonekas, "and if Hughes doesn't get him this time, he may never live to get him again."

Schonekas then termed the BRILAB operation "a child that was born out of mischief—mischief created by the government.

"I say there isn't any crime," Schonekas concluded, raising his voice to the jury, "but if there's any crime that Marcello is involved in, it's a crime created by those people," and he leveled a finger at the prosecution.

It was 4:00 P.M. on August 4, 1981. The New Orleans courtroom was jammed as it awaited the jury's verdict in the case of *The United States v. Carlos Marcello et al*. Present in the courtroom, all seated together in the front center of the chamber, were many members of the Marcello family. Seated near the front row were Carlos's sobbing wife, Jacqueline, and their four children: their oldest daughter, Louise Hampton, 44, a dark Italian beauty who was once a Mardi Gras Queen; son Joseph, "Little Joe," a small, intense, wiry man of 39; and daughters Florence Robards, 40, another dark beauty, and Jacqueline, "Little Jackie" Dugas, 38. Accompanying them were their spouses and several children. Immediately behind them sat Carlos's six brothers—Joe, Vincent, Anthony, Peter, Sammy, and Pascal—and his two sisters, Rose and Mary, all accompanied by their spouses, children, and grandchildren. Everyone agreed it was an impressive display of family solidarity.

Shortly after 4:00, Judge Morey Sear entered the courtroom and, taking his place on the bench, announced: "There are to be no demonstrations of any sort when these verdicts are read."

For a minute or so, all that could be heard in the courtroom was the humming and rattling of the air conditioners and the sobs of the Marcello, Roemer, and Marinello women, especially the open weeping of Jacqueline Marcello.

The twelve regular jurors then entered, trying to keep their eyes averted from the stares of the four defendants.

After the jury foreman handed Judge Sear the verdicts and received them back again, the clerk of the court asked Carlos Marcello to stand.

The short, stout, silver-haired Mafia boss rose and looked the jury foreman in the eye as he began reading the verdicts on each of the twelve counts against him.

"Count one, guilty." This was the big one: conspiracy in violation of the RICO Statute, carrying a penalty of up to twenty years in prison. Of the remaining eleven counts, Carlos was found guilty of three more: racketeering and mail and wire fraud.

Charles Roemer was asked to rise.

"Count one, guilty." The commissioner of administration looked crushed.

I. Irving Davidson, facing twelve counts, was found not guilty on all counts; Vincent Marinello's acquittal, on all three counts, came last. Each convinced the jury that he had only been a spectator to, not a participant in, the bribery scheme.

Carlos Marcello, looking as determined as always, then gathered his family together and walked briskly out of the courtroom. Taking charge of everyone, as was his custom, he went to his wife and their three daughters to see how they were holding up, then turned to his sister Rose and her old friend Cindy Marinello, Vince's mother, who was crying uncontrollably. Carlos took the arms of the two women and said: "Let's go somewhere where we can be private."

Carlos Marcello then gathered together his four attorneys, his son, and his six brothers, and the twelve men formed a barrier between the Marcello women and the press and spectators. Shouting "No comment" at the reporters who followed them, the Marcello clan made for their parked cars on Magazine Street.

Irving Davidson, who had told his family not to come to the trial, left the courthouse alone, looking downcast. "I'm upset," he told a reporter, "upset about the others," and he disappeared into the street.

Outside the courthouse a victorious John Volz told the press: "I think the trial will have a very substantial impact on the way politics is conducted in Louisiana. The jury did send a message. The message was they're not going to tolerate their public officials being corrupt anymore."

Prosecutor Volz then defended the FBI's undercover operation, saying: "This is the only way you can catch the sacred cows in this case, those who think they are above the law."

The next day, August 5, a deeply wounded Carlos Marcello was notified at his Town & Country office that he had just been indicted by a Los Angeles grand jury for conspiring to bribe a federal judge. The trial of himself, Sam Sciortino, and Phillip Rizzuto would commence in Los Angeles in late November, before he was due to be sentenced for the conviction he had just sustained in New Orleans.

Carlos Marcello and his attorneys faced an even greater challenge in Los Angeles than they had just faced unsuccessfully in New Orleans. Carlos had vainly hoped he would receive a sympathy vote from his own people, the New Orleans jurors who had just surprised him so brutally. But he could not realistically entertain much hope at all from a jury so far removed from his home turf as Los Angeles. Most observers agreed that Marcello had looked cocky and sure of himself during the New Orleans trial. But during the Los Angeles trial people found him a changed man. It seemed that it was only after that ordeal had gotten under way that he realized the enormity of the fate that awaited him.

57

Trial Two: Los Angeles

Carlos Marcello's conviction in New Orleans, followed, the next day, by his indictment in Los Angeles, left the 71-year-old Mafia boss a bewildered and deflated man. According to Harold Hughes, who continued to monitor Carlos's activities after the New Orleans trial, the number of visitors observed arriving at the Town & Country office after August 5, 1981, was sharply reduced from the normal flow, and Carlos was no longer seen in public at his usual haunts, except for an occasional stop at Mosca's.

It was not long after the double blow that Carlos was made aware, in various ways, that his influence in the state and in the mob was crumbling. According to Hughes, few people wanted to have anything to do with Carlos after his conviction. No longer would a Robert Sutton call on him to arrange a false arrest; no longer would a member of the family, a Phillip Rizzuto, call on him to help get some friends out of a jam. No, his boasts and schemes and promises, recorded by the FBI and played to the world, had gotten the Robert Suttons and Phillip Rizzutos into more trouble than they had been in before they had confided their problems to Marcello. Who could count on Carlos now? For eighteen weeks he had been held up to public scorn and ridicule in Louisiana as his schemes, and his comments on blacks, politicians, and herons, were aired in court and reported in the papers. Now all the world knew that Carlos had allowed a notorious con artist to dupe him. Who would want to enter into a deal with him now?

Who indeed? News of the FBI's sting and Marcello's conviction had sent shock waves through the entire underworld. The press had reported that 1400 reels of Marcello's conversations with federal undercover agents and others had been recorded and only 160 of these had been presented as evidence at his trial. What was on the other 1240 reels? People like "Joey Doves" Aiuppa, Joe Civella, and Santos Trafficante, who read in the papers about the tapes revealing Carlos's planned Teamsters insurance scheme, involving them, wanted to know.

They also wanted to know what kind of a deal Carlos might try to make with the government before his sentencing. Carlos knew a lot of secrets. Could the aging boss be persuaded by the feds to betray his code, so he could go home from prison, after serving a token sentence, and die, like a good Sicilian, in his own bed?

Not long after his New Orleans conviction was handed down, and it appeared likely that he would be convicted also at his upcoming trial in Los Angeles, the FBI picked up talk of a mob contract on Carlos, and agents from the New Orleans field office advised him to beef up his security.

As for some of Carlos's more grandiose projects—the development of his Churchill Farms property and pulling off The Big One with the Teamsters—Carlos could no longer even think about them. Now he could only think of two things: strategy for the upcoming Los Angeles trial and his appeal of his New Orleans conviction.

Carlos was scheduled to go on trial in Los Angeles, along with his friends Phillip Rizzuto and Sam Sciortino, on November 30, 1981. According to Harold Hughes, he was determined "to beat the rap." Getting down to work on the case, he dropped attorney Russell Schonekas, who had just lost the New Orleans BRILAB case, and hired Vince Marinello's attorney, Arthur A. "Buddy" Lemann III, who had just secured an acquittal on all counts for his client. Then, in order to have someone around in Los Angeles who talked his own language, he hired his old friend from way back, Provino Mosca, to assist Lemann.

It had been Lemann who, in his brilliant closing argument on behalf of Marinello, had claimed that the government, with its undercover operation, "had acted like a man trying to seduce a woman. He meets her, wines her, dines her, flatters her," Lemann told the jury, "and promises to marry her. And, after seducing her, he jumps up, takes off his disguise, and shouts: 'Harlot! whore! prostitute!'"

Yes, if anyone could get him off the Los Angeles charges, which could conceivably result in a ten- to twenty-year prison sentence, it would be the colorful and eloquent "Buddy" Lemann.

Carlos Marcello did not scare easily, but, according to Los Angeles prosecutor Bruce Kelton, he feared the Los Angeles trial. This was not his turf. The jury would not be composed of his people. What was more, he was extremely anxious to see his friends Sciortino and Rizzuto get acquitted, because he had been mainly responsible for the mess they were in.

Marcello had good reason to worry about the Los Angeles trial. The authors of the sting operation, FBI Agents John Barron and William Fleming, had been euphoric over its astonishing success. They and the prosecuting attorneys scheduled to conduct the trial, James D. Henderson and Bruce J. Kelton, both of the Los Angeles strike force, were determined to make a name for themselves by nailing the notorious Carlos Marcello.

John Barron liked to boast about the BRILAB operation. On February 3, 1980, a week or so before the FBI shut down the operation, Barron met with Clarence Newton, a former FBI agent, now a private investigator, and told him, with obvious pride, what he and the bureau were pulling off in New Orleans:

"Newt, I have an undercover thing that's going to make Abscam look like a kindergarten party....I got two agents who are in with Carlos Marcello....I mean so far in that he's arranged for my guys to make payoffs to a shitload of politicians who are just about to deliver to these undercover guys all the insurance business for the state of Louisiana....I'm talking so close that he thinks my guys are arranging to buy off the judge in the Brooklier case. So damned close, Newt, that I got Marcello and Sciortino asking my guys to arrange for a Mexican hit man to kill Frattiano...and its all on tape!"

So damn close. That was Carlos Marcello's problem. He had let Hauser, Wacks, and Montague get so close to him that he had held almost nothing back from them. And it was all on tape for the Los Angeles jury, and the world, to hear.

Marcello, Sciortino, and Rizzuto had been indicted on three counts: one, "conspiracy to bribe U.S. District Judge Harry Pregerson in order to obtain favorable treatment for Sciortino and others in a criminal prosecution over which Judge Pregerson was presiding"; two, "aiding and abetting each other in a corrupt endeavor to influence the judge in the discharge of his official duties"; and three, "use of interstate telephones to carry on unlawful activity."

Marcello and his attorneys had decided on a defense that portrayed Marcello as a nonculpable victim of the government's efforts to embroil him in an attempt to bribe Judge Pregerson, in which the conduct of government agents in connection with the investigation of the case was "so outrageous that it violated the defendant's rights to due process guaranteed by the Fifth Amendment."

When, on November 30, Marcello entered the federal courtroom in Los Angeles for the first time, prosecutor Bruce Kelton, who had attended much of the New Orleans trial, noticed immediately that Carlos somehow looked "diminished." "His cockiness and bravado were gone," Kelton told me seven years later. "He looked smaller, more subdued, and decidedly more worried."

And so Carlos Marcello had to endure once more the playing of tape-recorded conversations between himself, Hauser, and the undercover agents, had to endure again hearing himself, in a crowded courtroom, being conned by that sonofabitch Joe Hauser.

"I'm doin' this for friends of mine in California. They Maf like me, you know, personal friends of mine."

The first thing Buddy Lemann did, at the pretrial proceedings, was to attack the prosecution's interpretation of Carlos Marcello's remark of October 9, 1979, intimating to Hauser by the use of the abbreviated word "Maf" that he was in the Mafia. Lemann contended that on the admittedly somewhat garbled tape, Marcello had said: "They my friends, you know," not "They Maf like me, you know." After playing the tape in question several times, Lemann was able to persuade Judge Edward J. Devitt to rule that the content of the tape was so unclear, and potentially prejudicial, that it could not be admitted into evidence and therefore could not be played to the jury. Buddy Lemann had won the first round.

But, alas, for the beleaguered defendant, it was the first and last round Lemann won.

Buddy Lemann contended that the government had created the conspiracy, not the defendants, and had the court play two tapes to back up his position.

One was the October 4 conversation between Marcello and Hauser during which Marcello informed Hauser for the first time about "this judge who is about to preside over friends in California." Hauser immediately, without a second's hesitation, told Marcello the lie that he knew the judge well and "there were things he might be able to do."

"Why did Hauser tell this lie?" Lemann asked the court. "He told the lie in order to lure Marcello into a conspiracy that did not yet exist, one that was being concocted by the government."

Lemann then had the court play the October 25 tape during which Hauser told Marcello, Sciortino, and Rizzuto "the blatant fiction" about a friend of Judge Pregerson's, a wealthy art dealer, who knew that Pregerson was "corrupt" and susceptible to being influenced by an expensive gift and, in fact, had previously taken a bribe over a drug case. Hauser told the three defendants that this friend could talk to the judge about the Brooklier trial and win a guarantee of probation for Sciortino and Rizzuto in exchange for a valuable painting.

According to Lemann, there would have been no bribery plan if the FBI had not invented the fictitious art dealer who Hauser claimed was a friend of the "corrupt and susceptible" Judge Pregerson. Nor would there have been a conspiracy to bribe the judge, Lemann continued, if Hauser had not told Sciortino at their October 29 meeting "the total fiction" that the judge didn't trust Sciortino "but he wants to get something," and if he doesn't get it, Sciortino would go to jail.

In rebuttal to Lemann's argument, government attorneys Henderson and Kelton emphasized that the initial contact between defendant Marcello and the government regarding Judge Pregerson and the Brooklier case had been initiated wholly by Marcello during his October 4 telephone discussion with Hauser and that the crucial meeting of October 25, in Anthony Marcello's lodge, at which discussions regarding an approach to the judge were mentioned, had been arranged by the defendants, not the government. Finally the prosecution cited, as precedents, past cases of a similar nature in which, on appeals, it was ruled "permissible to use artifice and stratagem to ferret out criminal activity."

During these arguments, a much subdued, and sometimes inattentive, Marcello, who was now feeling his power ebbing away, day by day, was compelled to listen to the two tapes on which the hated Hauser had conned him into agreeing to offer Judge Pregerson a bribe: the one recorded at Impastato's Restaurant on October 25, in which Marcello told Hauser he could raise "$250,000 cash money within twenty-four hours" to pay off the judge, and the one of November 1, containing the brief telephone dialogue between himself and Hauser that had so elated agents Fleming and Barron who were listening in at the time:

MARCELLO: Well, don't worry about it, man. I give it to you my-
           self, okay?

HAUSER: If Sam doesn't come through with the money...

MARCELLO: I'm a give it to you, okay? I'll stand good for it. 100
           percent. Okay?

HAUSER: Okay, I'll tell him.

The verdict came forth on December 11, 1981. The jury found
Carlos Marcello guilty on all three counts, Sciortino on one count,
and Rizzuto on two counts. For his conviction Carlos stood to receive
a sentence of from ten to twenty years in a federal penitentiary.

That evening Carlos and his two attorneys returned to New Orleans, where around a month later—on January 25, 1982—they appeared in federal court for Carlos's sentencing on the New Orleans
BRILAB convictions.

The packed courtroom was tense and the hearing proved particularly trying for Carlos's wife and daughters, who wept quietly throughout the proceedings. Before the sentence was read, prosecuting
attorney Eades Hogue declared: "Marcello has participated in continuous criminal activity for fifty years...the tapes clearly indicated
that Mr. Marcello would perpetrate the same offenses, the same sort
of insurance scheme, in other states if he were not sentenced to
prison."

With Jacqueline Marcello and her three daughters sobbing audi-
bly, Judge Morey Sear then read Carlos's sentence: seven years in
prison and fines of $25,000.

Before setting bond of $300,000 for Marcello, the judge asked
the 72-year-old silver-haired Mafia boss a few questions:

SEAR: Do you claim citizenship of any country?

MARCELLO: No, sir.

SEAR: Tell me your employment over the last twelve
           months, please.

MARCELLO: I'm a real estate, uh, investor.

SEAR: Are you engaged in any business other than real es-
           tate?

MARCELLO: I'm a salesman for Pelican Tomato Company.

SEAR: How much cash you have in the bank?

MARCELLO: Hard to tell, your honor.

It was another vintage Marcello performance, playing dumb for the hundredth time. When it was over, it then took Marcello and his lawyers over an hour to post the bond. In the end, two bonding companies signed for $100,000 each and Carlos's son, "Little Joe" Marcello, wrote a personal check for $100,000.

There remained the sentencing for the Los Angeles conviction, due to take place in three months.

The sentencing of Carlos Marcello to seven years in prison on the New Orleans conviction brought the FBI's BRILAB operation to a most successful close. Finally, after over thirty years of trying, the government was able to bring one of the nation's most powerful and elusive organized crime leaders to justice. In accomplishing this the FBI had had to mount the most massive undercover operation against a single individual in its history. At one point some forty-eight special agents were working on the New Orleans operation alone. For Harold Hughes, John Barron, and William Fleming, who oversaw the operation, and for Mike Wacks and Larry Montague, who helped Joe Hauser carry it out, the BRILAB sting against Marcello was the summit of their FBI careers up to that time. But, as Bruce Kelton pointed out to me eight years after the operation began, most of the credit for its success unquestionably belonged to Joe Hauser. "The way he manipulated Marcello, known at the time as one of the cleverest and most powerful Mafia figures in the nation, if not in the world," says Kelton, "was nothing short of brilliant. I don't know of any other undercover operative who displayed more brains and guts than Joe. Time and again he put his life on the line while taping Marcello alone in his Town & Country office. And his quick thinking in the Pregerson bribery case, when he lied to Marcello about knowing the judge, was a masterstroke."

As if to confirm that opinion, Carlos Marcello was sentenced on April 13, 1982, to ten years in prison and fined $25,000 for conspiracy to bribe a federal judge. At the sentencing, Judge Edward J. Devitt, who had presided over the Los Angeles trial, told Marcello: "You've led a life of crime, the record shows that. By any evaluation, I think it's fair to say you're a very bad man."

The 72-year-old Marcello now faced a cumulative sentence of seventeen years in prison if all his appeals were denied.

The first appeal was adjudicated in New Orleans on April 15, 1983. It was then that Carlos was summoned to U.S. district court and told by Judge Morey Sear that his appeal of his New Orleans BRILAB convictions had been denied and that he had to begin serving his prison sentence immediately.

With those words, Carlos Marcello was no longer a free man. He would now be sent to the courthouse lockup to await his transfer to a federal penitentiary.

And so, as soon as Judge Sear closed the proceedings and remanded Carlos to the custody of the attorney general of the United States, two federal marshals appeared at his side to escort him to the lockup.

By chance Harold Hughes was in the courthouse elevator leading to the lockup area when the marshals brought Marcello in. As they were riding up, their eyes met and Carlos said: "Hello, Hughes." Hughes nodded. Years later Hughes told me that for the first time in his long pursuit of Marcello, Carlos looked defeated. "The gas was out of him that day," observed Hughes. "He looked like he had nothing left. He was a beaten man."

Later Carlos Marcello was taken to his old alma mater, the United States Medical Center for Federal Prisoners at Springfield, Missouri, where he was admitted on June 1 to begin serving his seven-year sentence.

Two months later Carlos was called to the warden's office and was informed that his appeal of his Los Angeles convictions had been denied. Now he faced a total of seventeen years behind bars.

It was around this time that the prison population at Springfield began talking about the new elevator man in section D: the short, bullnecked old guy with the white hair. Rumor had it he was Carlos Marcello, boss of the Louisiana Mafia, but the old guy wasn't talking.

58

Carlos in Prison

Carlos Marcello remained confined at the Springfield Medical Center for almost a year, undergoing treatments for an unspecified cancerous condition he had developed during the BRILAB operation. From all accounts, he was not in very good physical shape when he entered Springfield. In addition to cancer he suffered from the indispositions and infirmities one would expect of a man of 73 who liked to finish off a huge meal of spaghetti and meatballs with a double espresso laced with Strega and who had a propensity toward ventures so stressful and risky as to land him in prison for seventeen years. Springfield had suited him well in the past—in 1971 it had given him a new lease on life—and apparently it suited him well again. Aside from the health benefits the institution afforded, a patient-inmate at Springfield was allowed to receive more visitors and make more phone calls than he would have been permitted in a regular prison and thus was in a better position to conduct business with the outside world.

And Carlos Marcello still had much business with the world from which he had just been separated. For, according to the unwritten code of the ancient tradition to which he belonged, a Mafia boss, like the Pope, keeps his position for life. Thus, while subordinates may run the day-to-day operations of his criminal organization in his absence, the boss still makes the decisions—even though he may be making them from behind bars.

After Carlos Marcello was sent to Springfield, his most trusted brother, Joe, was supposed to have taken over as de facto boss of what was left of the Marcello organization, assisted by brothers Anthony, Vincent, and Sammy. With Carlos's political influence in ruins, and his reputation in the underworld shattered, his brothers were forced to concern themselves mostly with the family's long-established businesses: the coin machine leasing operation, the racing wire service, the bookie network, the restaurants and motels, and the management of Carlos's still-substantial real estate holdings. Foremost of the latter was the 6400-acre Churchill Farms property, whose future was now in doubt because no person, or entity, wanted to be known to do business with the infamous Marcello, and so there were no buyers now for Churchill Farms. Since Carlos was reasonably accessible at the medical center, it was not too difficult for Joe to get rulings from his older brother on the most important matters of the moment.

But in April 1984, perhaps because of an improvement in Marcello's health, Carlos was abruptly removed from the care and comfort of his Springfield spa and was transferred to the level-three Federal Correctional Institution at Texarkana, Texas, near the Texas-Arkansas state line, where he was to remain confined for almost two years.

The security of federal prisons is graded from one to six, with level one being minimum security and level six maximum. While a level-three facility such as Texarkana is three rungs removed from hell, it is still far from the paradise of level one.

Texarkana is an ominous-looking place with a reputation to match. One is struck, on approaching the prison, by its imposing 30-foot all-encompassing walls, surmounted by barbed wire and catwalks with armed guards pacing back and forth. Visitors' cars are thoroughly searched before they enter the prison compound, and visitors must pass muster at three more checkpoints before they can meet with an inmate. Even then, security is tight in the dayroom, with armed guards keeping a close watch over both inmates and visitors.

In contrast to the relatively open atmosphere of the medical center at Springfield, inmates at Texarkana are not allowed much contact with the outside world. A prisoner may make one collect long-distance call a day, no more than fifteen minutes long, and can receive a limited number of visitors (twelve in Marcello's case) on weekends from 8:30 A.M. to 3:30 P.M. All inmates are required to work or attend classes within the institution. Texarkana's warden in 1988 refused to disclose to me what Carlos Marcello's work assignment was, or who was on his visitors list. Clearly the boss of the Gulf states underworld was able to conduct far less business at Texarkana than at Springfield.

It seems that the Justice Department, which oversees the Bureau of Prisons, may have been concerned about the range and magnitude of Carlos's transactions from behind Texarkana's walls. Carlos was confined to the 900-inmate level-three main institution in the Texarkana compound rather than the level-one "satellite camp" holding 233 white-collar inmates in a small, wide-open complex outside the main institution's walls. However, since Justice Department officials were supposedly concerned about an alleged Trafficante-inspired contract on Carlos's life, considerations of security might well have been behind the decision to confine Marcello in Texarkana's formidable level-three facility.

But Marcello's confinement at Texarkana was not to last very long.

Federal prison authorities are forbidden by law to disclose why inmates are transferred from one prison to another. We can only surmise, then, that Carlos Marcello's transfer, on February 19, 1986, from the oppressive Texarkana, after serving a little less than two years there, to the relatively benign environment of the level-two correctional institution at Seagoville, Texas, had something to do with either good behavior, cancellation of the alleged contract on his life, or political pressure.

Whatever the case, Seagoville must have been a welcome respite for the aging Mafioso. The near-minimum-security correctional facility was surrounded by a mere wire fence and had the general appearance of a prep school campus. One reached the nondescript main building by walking up a tree-lined driveway and opening the unguarded front door. Most of the inmates at Seagoville were professionals—lawyers, doctors, accountants—who had doubled as embezzlers and tax cheats. Inmates were not confined to their cells all day; they were permitted to roam the grounds during certain hours and receive visitors in much more unguarded surroundings than was possible at a level-three institution such as Texarkana.

For Carlos, this was but a way station on the road to the paradise of the federal prison system—the minimum-security level-one facility. After only four months at Seagoville, Marcello was transferred again, on June 2, 1986, this time to the serene beauty of the level-one Federal Correctional Institution at Fort Worth. There he could even meet with visitors around a picnic table on a neatly trimmed lawn, well out of earshot from any damned government bug.

Why was Carlos Marcello, a notorious Mafia boss, transferred to this last heavenly rung of the federal prison system? It has been widely rumored, though never confirmed, that Carlos took advantage of his remaining political leverage to force the government's hand. Joe Hauser has speculated that Marcello was given privileged treatment because he just knew too much about too many politicians in high office, including at least one politico who was close to the President of the United States. After three years of good behavior at Springfield, Seagoville, and Texarkana, Carlos might have felt the time had come to play his trump cards.

One can only speculate as to whom Carlos might have had possibly damaging information on. Of course he had a lot on Louisiana Governor Edwin Edwards, but Edwards had almost no clout left in the Justice Department, which was investigating him for various alleged wrongdoings at the time.

Who, then, among all the high public officials Carlos might have had something on, did have enough clout within the Justice Department to influence the Bureau of Prisons?

First of all, Carlos still held the loyalty and friendship of Washington's foremost contact man, his former codefendant in the New Orleans BRILAB trial, Irving Davidson. Despite a temporary setback to his prestige, Davidson had recovered sufficiently after his BRILAB acquittal to return to business as usual. We know from the BRILAB tapes that he had had important contacts in the Justice Department in 1979. Perhaps he still had them, or had new ones, and would, this time around, be a little more discreet in exploiting them.

Then there was President Reagan's campaign manager in 1980 and 1984 and reputed "best friend," Senator Paul Laxalt of Nevada. Although Laxalt vigorously denies any improper connection with the Mafia, former FBI Las Vegas station chief Joseph Yablonsky once called him a "tool of organized crime." More than likely, Carlos knew a lot about Laxalt through their mutual association with the Teamsters. The two, along with Irving Davidson and Murray Chotiner, had helped in the effort to spring Jimmy Hoffa from prison. And as one who had told an FBI undercover agent in 1979 that he and two or three other mob bosses "owned the Teamsters," Marcello probably knew a lot about Laxalt's admitted long and close relationship with Allen Dorfman, a Teamsters pension fund "manager," mob banker, convicted extortionist, and contributor of Teamster funds to Reagan's presidential campaign. (Dorfman had been brutally murdered, "gangland style," in Chicago in 1983.) As a member of the President's inner circle, Laxalt was close to Reagan's Attorney General Edwin Meese, head of the Justice Department at the time of Marcello's 1986 transfer to Fort Worth.

However, in all fairness, there may have been a much more benign reason for Marcello's transfer to Fort Worth: the delicate state of his health. Federal prisoners at the Fort Worth Correctional Institution could avail themselves of the private health care facilities and hospitals of the Fort Worth–Dallas area, if their private financial resources allowed.

Whatever the case, the Federal Correctional Institution at Fort Worth—the epitome of the "country club" prison—must have been very much to Carlos Marcello's liking.

The level-one facility, once a private hospital, is situated on beautifully landscaped grounds on the outskirts of Fort Worth, a few miles off the Dallas–Fort Worth Freeway. Surrounded by gently sloping lawns and well-groomed shrubbery, the institutional complex is enclosed not by a wall but by a simple chain-link fence that could easily be scaled. There are tennis courts on the property and a swimming pool and softball diamond. The general atmosphere is benign, even attractive. Inmates are free to walk the grounds from 6:30 A.M. to 9:30 P.M. when they are not working at their assigned jobs. Watching a group of them strolling down a tree-shaded path, one is reminded more of the groves of academe than the grim realities of prison life.

There are approximately 900 prisoners in the facility, half of whom are women (a new phenomenon, according to the warden). All have been convicted of federal offenses, mostly so-called white-collar crimes. Each is assigned a job and works an average of forty hours a week. Some inmates work in a factory on prison grounds that manufactures traffic signs for federal highways. Others work in a data processing center for U.S. government agencies. During my tour of the institution Charles Turnbo declined to disclose what Marcello's job was or in what section of the prison he was housed. "All I can tell you is that Mr. Marcello has been a model prisoner," he said.

Opportunities for contact with the outside world are limited but are nevertheless much greater than in a level-three facility. Inmates are allowed to make collect phone calls from 6:00 A.M. to 10:00 A.M. but cannot receive calls unless they involve a family emergency. According to Warden Turnbo, some calls are monitored and some are even taped. The warden declined to elaborate on which calls were singled out to be monitored and/or taped and why.

Inmates can receive visitors between 5:00 P.M. and 8:30 P.M. three evenings during the week and Saturday and Sunday from 8:00 A.M. to 8:00 P.M., and are limited to seeing twelve different visitors a month. Visits are made in a large assembly room, seating 200 at a time, where, it appeared to me, it would be almost impossible for the prison to monitor conversations.

In fair weather, prisoners and visitors meet on the beautifully manicured lawns, where a number of picnic-style wooden tables and chairs are scattered about under shade trees which could conceivably hold bugs of one species or another. Warden Turnbo informed me that "Mr. Marcello often met with members of his family Saturday afternoons on the lawn." Carlos is said to have particularly appreciated the visits of his sturdy young grandson, Carlos Marcello II, and his three beautiful daughters, the "Mafia princesses," Jacqueline, Louise, and Florence.

It has been alleged that Carlos Marcello, then 76 and in failing health, was able to manage his businesses, both legitimate and illegitimate, from his minimum-security prison through his brothers Joe and Sammy, his most frequent visitors at Fort Worth.

FBI undercover agent Michael Wacks told me that he had heard the next most frequent visitor at Fort Worth, after Joe and Sammy, was Carlos's personal secretary. According to Wacks, Carlos had rented a house for her and her family near the prison grounds so she could easily visit the facility three afternoons a week to take dictation from the boss.

Joseph Hauser also had some ideas on Carlos's life at Fort Worth. He told me that he believed Carlos's imprisonment had diminished his power "tremendously" but added that he had also heard, on good authority, that Carlos had been able to conduct quite a lot of important business from Fort Worth. Hauser believed it was Joe Marcello who conveyed Carlos's orders to the key players in his crumbling organization.

In 1986 Carlos applied for social security benefits but was denied them. Since he is reputed to be worth millions, observers believe his application had something to do with his ongoing deportation case. Granting him social security benefits would be tantamount to recognizing him as an American citizen. Still an illegal alien and still under order of deportation by the INS, Marcello could conceivably be deported upon his scheduled release from prison on June 18, 1994.

For reasons the Bureau of Prisons has refused to disclose, Carlos's beatific stay at the level-one facility in Fort Worth was abruptly terminated on May 21, 1987, barely a year after his confinement there began. In the dead of night Marcello was taken from his cell by federal marshals and driven under heavily armed escort to the federal prison at Texarkana, where, as of this writing, he is still confined.

Why was Carlos suddenly sent back to the dungeons of level-three Texarkana after having tasted the fresh air, and sunlight, and semi-freedom of minimum-security Seagoville and Fort Worth for slightly over a year? Again the Bureau of Prisons has declined to disclose the reason. And again the reason might have had something to do with Carlos's steadily deteriorating health. For not long after Marcello was returned to Texarkana, it was reported in the Dallas *Morning News* that he had been admitted to the prison hospital for an undisclosed illness.

It was while Carlos was suffering the new indignity of his removal to Texarkana, and apparently also suffering a further decline in his health, that he made a desperate attempt to win his freedom. In October 1987, his attorney, Arthur A. "Buddy" Lemann, filed a motion in U.S. District Court in New Orleans to have his BRILAB mail and wire fraud convictions vacated, basing his case on a recent Supreme Court decision affecting previous convictions for mail and wire fraud. If Lemann was successful in pleading his case, Carlos could be released from prison in 1989.

But, alas, Judge Morey L. Sear, who had presided over the New Orleans BRILAB trial six years before, denied Marcello's petition in February 1988, thus dashing Carlos's hopes of returning to his family before his mandatory release in June 1994.

It was around the time the ailing Carlos received this deeply discouraging news that he learned that his brother Sammy had been indicted by a New Orleans grand jury for alleged participation in a multistate money-laundering operation to conceal proceeds from drug sales.

For two years IRS undercover agents had been investigating what they suspected was an extensive, interconnected drug-money-laundering operation in certain major cities of the south and southwest. Posing as brokers for important drug dealers with lots of cash for the cleaners, IRS undercover agents succeeded in penetrating the operation in Dallas, Tulsa, New Orleans, Atlanta, Baltimore, and Miami and luring various suspected money launderers into taking their dirty drug money and converting it into clean, mint-fresh bills. Among those caught red-handed—tape-recorded and videotaped— were former Nixon presidential aide Thomas Gene Crouch of Dallas and Salvadore Marcello, otherwise known as Sammy, described by the Dallas *Morning News*, which broke the story, as "the youngest brother of reputed Mafia chieftain Carlos Marcello." Ironically, one of Crouch's tasks in the Nixon administration had been to screen potential presidential appointees to the Justice Department.

The New Orleans phase of the IRS sting operation had netted Sammy Marcello and six others, including longtime Marcello attorney David Levy and his wife, Rebecca. According to Assistant U.S.

510   THE FALL OF CARLOS MARCELLO

Attorney Albert Winters, Jr., who had helped prosecute Carlos Marcello in the BRILAB trial, Levy, "a close friend of the Marcello family," was "the key figure in the [New Orleans] conspiracy." "The Internal Revenue Service," Winters stated, "was successful in placing an undercover operative in a position in New Orleans where people would launder money for him." It had been Levy who had allegedly introduced the informant to the hapless Sammy and the other New Orleans suspects.

According to the complaint filed in federal court, David Levy and Sammy Marcello met with the IRS undercover agent on November 1 and 23, 1987, to discuss the laundering of proceeds from drug sales.

At the second meeting, the Justice Department complaint stated, Sammy Marcello told the undercover informant that "he was under so much pressure from federal authorities, he felt he could not personally handle the actual laundering of the money, but would put him in touch with his 'man' in California, who could handle as much money has he [the government informant] needed to launder." Marcello was then videotaped and voice-taped putting the undercover agent in touch with Nicholas Popich of Los Angeles, who was subsequently arrested and held on $1 million bail.

Carlos was probably aware that his younger brother Sammy was in deep financial trouble at the time. Sammy's restaurant, La Louisiane, was veering toward bankruptcy. And now, at 58, Sammy, like Carlos, had succumbed to a government sting operation that would probably send him to prison for at least ten years.

Had Carlos been told in advance of the money-laundering scheme by Sammy and his old friend David Levy? More than likely he had been, since he was still head of the Marcello family and should have been kept informed of all important family business dealings. Possibly he had even given the scheme his blessing as a way to shore up Sammy's deteriorating financial condition. If such was the case, the revelation that he had allowed his brother to be sucked into the same sort of government operation that had ruined his own life must have been deeply demoralizing.

The lights were going out for Carlos Marcello. Judge Sear's denial of his appeal had dashed his last hopes for freedom. The money-laundering operation had turned out to be a bust. Now Carlos would probably have to pay for his youngest brother's legal defense. Furthermore, Sammy's indictment would have aroused suspicions in the Justice Department that Carlos had something to do with the money-laundering scheme, suspicions that might conceivably hurt his chances for early parole. What Carlos had to look forward to from 1988 on was too bleak to contemplate. He was 78 years old. Five and a half more years in the hellish isolation of Texarkana lay ahead. It would be a long, slow, lonely dying, without any of the comforts he had fought so hard all his life to attain. Was there anything he could do now to avoid this fate?

59

*The Case against
Carlos Marcello*

Yes, there was conceivably one last card Carlos could play to avoid the hell that awaited him: He could start opening his mouth. He could turn canary. The government was aware Marcello was carrying some enormous secrets within him, perhaps even the secret of secrets: had he been involved in a plot to kill President Kennedy, and what had been the details of the plot?

It was indeed an ironic situation. For, on the unlikely assumption that Carlos Marcello would give immunized testimony as to his role in a plot to assassinate President Kennedy, in return for his freedom, the Justice Department would have to release him from prison and refrain from prosecuting him for his participation in the crime of the century. How would that go down the throat of world public opinion?

But the last thing Carlos Marcello would ever do to save his skin would be to reveal secrets to the government. To turn stool pigeon would go against every grain of his being. He had made that clear to Aubrey Young in his outburst on the last BRILAB tape:

> "I'm, as far as me, I ain't gonna tell 'em nothin'. They can, they can, come here forty times, but I ain't, you know, I'm gonna take, tell him, look, tell him look, Carlos don't care if he gets subpoenaed forty times....I got subpoenaed with the,

the, the, the United States...district attorney, I mean, ah, the attorney general, and all. Tell him I just take the Fifth Amendment and that's it. They ain't gonna get a fuckin' thing from me."

Also, if Carlos had been involved in an assassination plot and revealed its details to the government, it would open up his family to retaliation from the surviving conspirators, if any, something Carlos would naturally want to avoid at all cost.

From the government's standpoint, if Carlos Marcello were induced to confess he had played a significant role in the Kennedy assassination, it could be acutely embarrassing to the Justice Department to have that confession made public. After all, the record clearly shows that the Justice Department has striven to suppress evidence of that possibility since it first discovered the Marcello-Ferrie-Oswald relationships barely three days after the murder of the President.

Would it be best, then, for both parties—the Marcellos and the government—simply to let Carlos alone, to let him take his secrets to his grave?

The question inevitably raises the issue of what the Justice Department has done, if anything, with the findings that the House Select Committee on Assassinations turned over to the attorney general for review in the summer of 1979. At that time the *New York Times* published an article stating: "Sources on the Committee said that its published report did not include a long list of investigative leads the Committee staff investigated. These leads would be made available to the Justice Department should it reopen the investigation." Has the Justice Department done anything about acting on the Assassinations Committee's recommendations? Has it done anything about "the long list of investigative leads"? No one seems to know, not even the man who conducted the committee's investigation, G. Robert Blakey, or the committee's former chairman, Representative Louis Stokes.

Given the evidence available in 1988, after twenty-five years of investigative activity, what is the case against Carlos Marcello in the assassination of President John F. Kennedy?

First, motive. The assassination of President Kennedy, and the murder of his accused assassin, gave every appearance of being desperate acts. For whoever planned and carried out the killing of the President, in November 1963, it was now or never. There was no time to lose. And, once the deed was accomplished, there was even less time to lose in silencing the suspected assassin.

In consideration of this premise, there was no more desperately threatened enemy of the Kennedys in the fall of 1963 than Carlos Marcello.

For, in the simplest of terms, in the fall of 1963, Attorney General Robert F. Kennedy, with the full backing of his brother, was bent on destroying Marcello's power once and for all. The Justice Department's conspiracy and perjury case against Carlos and his brother Joe, due to go to trial in November, was to be the first step in removing Carlos from the country forever. Carlos Marcello's possible motive, then, in killing the President, would have gone far beyond revenge, to survival. Everything he had built up over the years, as well as his very presence in the United States, was under direct attack from the Kennedys at the very moment President Kennedy was venturing into Marcello territory.

Second, evidence. The sheer volume and extent of the body of circumstantial evidence suggesting the possible involvement of the Marcello organization in the assassination that has accumulated over the past twenty-five years is now sufficiently persuasive to require evaluation and action on the part of the government. To imply, as the Justice Department has done by its inaction, that this body of evidence is meaningless requires us to brand at least eighteen witnesses and informants as either liars or lunatics, or both, and requires us, as well, to regard the extraordinarily large number of relationships shared by Lee Harvey Oswald, Jack Ruby, and David Ferrie with associates of Carlos Marcello's as mere coincidence.

It requires us to believe that government witness Edward Partin, the Louisiana Teamsters official with contacts in the Marcello organization, lied about Jimmy Hoffa's assassination plans, even though the government fully accepted his testimony against Hoffa at the trials that resulted in Hoffa's convictions. It requires us to believe that Edward Becker lied about Carlos Marcello's assassination plans, even though the House Select Committee on Assassinations accepted Becker's allegation as credible. It requires us to believe that Cuban financier Jose Aleman lied about Santos Trafficante's apparent foreknowledge of the assassination, even though the FBI had always regarded Jose Aleman as highly reliable and re-interviewed him about his 1962 allegation the day after the assassination. It requires us to believe that FBI informant Eugene De Laparra lied about Tony Marcello's and Ben Tregle's apparent foreknowledge of the assassination, even though FBI reports of De Laparra's allegations admitted that De Laparra had furnished "reliable information" to the FBI in the past. It requires us to believe that FBI informant Gene Sumner lied when he reported he had seen Joe Poretto pass money to a man he was sure was Lee Harvey Oswald in the Town & Country restaurant, even though the FBI was unable to disprove his allegation. It requires us to believe that at least ten witnesses lied about seeing Oswald and Ferrie together in the summer of 1963, even though the FBI accepted the testimony of six witnesses in Clinton, Louisiana, who claimed they saw Oswald in the company of Ferrie in their town.

It requires us to believe that Louisiana State Police Officer Francis Fruge and State Hospital physicians Dr. Bowers and Dr. Victor Weiss lied when they said Rose Cheramie had told them on November 20 and 21 that "word was out in the underworld" that President Kennedy would be killed in Dallas on November 22. And it requires us to believe that Jack Martin lied when, the day after the assassination, he told a friend of the New Orleans assistant district attorney that Ferrie and Oswald knew each other and had talked about assassinating the President—though this was independently corroborated.

Correspondingly, the Justice Department's skeptical position requires us to believe that at least five associates of Carlos Marcello, questioned by the FBI after the assassination, were telling the absolute truth when they denied allegations by FBI informants that several Marcello associates had had dealings with Oswald that summer, one or more of the Marcello brothers and one important Marcello associate had had foreknowledge of the assassination as early as that spring, and that two Marcello associates in Dallas and New Orleans had had dealings with Jack Ruby. It requires us to believe that David Ferrie was telling the truth when he told the FBI he did not know Oswald and had met with Carlos Marcello at Churchill Farms over the two weekends prior to the assassination solely for the purpose of discussing legal strategies. It requires us to believe that Joe Poretto and Tony Marcello were telling the truth when they denied seeing someone resembling Oswald in the Town & Country Motel in the spring of 1963. It requires us to believe that Ben Tregle was telling the truth when he denied he had told people in his bar that President Kennedy was going to be killed when he came south. It requires us to believe that Carlos Marcello's deputy in Dallas, Joe Civello, was telling the truth when he told the FBI immediately after the assassination that he had not heard from Jack Ruby in a year. It requires us to believe that top Marcello associate Nofio Pecora was telling the truth when he told the FBI he had not received a call from Jack Ruby on October 30, even though a call to his number was registered on Ruby's telephone records.

*   *   *

We have established that Carlos Marcello had a compelling motive to assassinate the President and that there is now an enormous body of circumstantial evidence suggesting that he and his associates were involved in the crime.

But if Carlos Marcello did indeed play a role in the assassination, how was he able to get away with it?

It is well known among serious students of organized crime that in planning and carrying out an important execution, Mafia leaders devote a good deal of time and thought to assessing what the official investigative response to the crime might be and, in turn, to calculating what their response to the investigation should be.

In weighing the possibility that Carlos Marcello was involved in a unilateral plan to assassinate President Kennedy, Marcello's ability to anticipate the investigative response and his general powers of risk assessment must be taken into account.

The BRILAB tapes revealed that whenever the question of bribing a public official was raised, Marcello always carefully assessed the degree to which he "controlled" the official before he proceeded to offer the bribe. When the problem of bribing a federal judge in Los Angeles came up, a man Carlos knew next to nothing about, he turned extremely cautious. He spent a good deal of time explaining to the undercover agents how difficult it was to get a federal judge to accept a bribe, repeating to them over and over that since federal judges have lifetime jobs, earn substantial incomes, and receive annual expense account funds of as much as $50,000, the bribe offered has to be a very large one, anywhere from $250,000 on up. And even then Carlos insisted that the judge in question should be sounded out about the proposition in advance by someone both he and the judge trusted without reservation.

In the case of a crime so enormous as the assassination of a President of the United States, it is not likely that Marcello, a family man and businessman with considerable personal and financial responsibilities, would become involved in so risky an enterprise unless he could be quite sure what the investigative response would be and whether he could survive it. To be able to get away with the assassination, Carlos would have had to anticipate the responses of the Dallas Police, the FBI, the CIA, whatever special investigative body President Johnson might choose to appoint, and a possible investigative effort, independent of the FBI, by Attorney General Robert F. Kennedy.

The Louisiana Mafia had an entente with the Dallas Police Department dating back to the 1940s when the Chicago Outfit attempted to take over Dallas using young Jack Ruby as one of its tools. Since Carlos Marcello's rise to power, his Dallas deputy, Joe Civello, did what was necessary to maintain sufficient mob influence in the department. It will be recalled that one of the Dallas Police Department's most influential officers, Sergeant Patrick Dean, had dinner with Joe Civello upon the local underworld leader's return from representing Carlos Marcello at the Mafia summit at Apalachin and had once testified that the Dallas Police "had no trouble with the Italian families." This same officer was in charge of headquarters basement security when Jack Ruby slipped in to put away President Kennedy's alleged killer. We know from FBI informants that Civello made regular payments to Dallas Police officers and that his associate Jack Ruby was on friendly terms with over fifty members of the force. Yes, Carlos knew he could count on at least some support there.

As for the FBI, it has become more and more apparent that Carlos must have exerted some control over the FBI field office in New Orleans in the early sixties. There is no other convincing explanation of why the New Orleans agents assigned to oversee Marcello failed so completely to carry out Attorney General Kennedy's order to upgrade their investigation of Carlos Marcello, including the deployment of electronic surveillance against him. Furthermore, Marcello obviously knew how acutely embarrassing it would have been for FBI Director Hoover if it were discovered that Marcello was behind a plot to kill the President. In addition, the possibility of a Hoover-Marcello entente should not be discounted. Based on the testimony of William Hundley and others, we are reasonably certain that Hoover met quite a few times with Marcello's principal sponsor, Frank Costello, when Costello was the most powerful underworld leader in the country. Given this precedent, was there any reason why Hoover should not have established an entente also with Costello's protégé? Especially since the two men shared the friendship of that self-styled master at "putting people together," Irving Davidson?

As for the CIA, we know that Marcello admitted to having participated in the CIA-Mafia plots to assassinate Fidel Castro and was close to at least one of the plotters, Santos Trafficante. Furthermore he was a supporter of the CIA-backed Cuban exiles leader Sergio Arcacha Smith, who was the New Orleans delegate of the Cuban Revolutionary Council, an associate of David Ferrie's, and one of the planners of the Bay of Pigs invasion. Since Marcello was fully knowledgeable of the CIA-Mafia conspiracies to assassinate Castro, it is safe to say that Marcello had the CIA where he wanted it. The agency would never undertake a thorough investigation of the assassination of President Kennedy if the leading suspects in the crime were knowledgeable of the CIA-Mafia plots against Castro, for fear of having its darkest secret revealed in the process.

We come to President Johnson and whatever body he might have appointed to investigate the assassination. Did Carlos have enough on Johnson so that the new President would not wish an investigation to turn up evidence of Carlos's complicity? Of course he did. Carlos Marcello's payoff man in Texas in the fifties, the notorious Jack Halfen, had been a principal financial backer of Lyndon Johnson's political campaigns in Texas from the late forties on, to the extent that it could be said that illegal profits from Marcello's slot machines in Dallas and Houston and from bookmakers' subscriptions to his racing wire service throughout all of Texas, used by Halfen to finance Johnson, were crucial to the success of Johnson's senatorial campaigns. How would it look if it came out in the press that the man accused of masterminding the assassination of President Kennedy had been an important backer of the man who had profited most from the assassination?

There remained the question of Attorney General Robert Kennedy's response to the assassination of his brother. According to Edward Becker, Marcello had stated at Churchill Farms in September 1962 that he believed the assassination of President Kennedy would destroy his younger brother's power, so that he would not be capable of galvanizing the Justice Department into launching a thorough investigation of the crime.

Events proved Marcello's alleged prediction was absolutely valid. After the assassination, both President Johnson and FBI Director Hoover turned their backs on Robert Kennedy and rendered him virtually powerless as attorney general.

But might not Robert Kennedy and his very wealthy family want to mount their own investigation of the assassination? Certainly they possessed the motivation and financial resources to do so. But Carlos Marcello knew they would not, thanks to John Kennedy's numerous extramarital indiscretions and Robert Kennedy's fling with Marilyn Monroe the year the actress died. Marcello's good friend Jimmy Hoffa had his wireman, Bernard Spindell, tape Marilyn Monroe's sexual encounters with Robert Kennedy. And we know that John F. Kennedy carried on an illicit relationship with a girlfriend of Chicago underworld boss Sam Giancana for a year and a half. That Carlos Marcello was well aware of these dangerously compromising relationships was attested to by Joseph Hauser, who told me he had discussed them with Carlos on one or two occasions during the BRILAB operation.

Yes, in assessing the likely investigative response to an assassination of the President, Carlos would have been aware he had the Dallas Police and the investigative agencies of the U.S. government precisely where he wanted them. After all, he had spent his entire life building up this indebtedness. As he told Vincent Marinello during the BRILAB operation: "It takes time to get where I'm at."

This brings us to the BRILAB operation again and its possible relevance to the question of Marcello's involvement in the Kennedy assassination. Did the tapes of Marcello's conversations, recorded during the FBI's 1979 BRILAB undercover operation, reinforce or diminish suspicions of Carlos's possible complicity in the assassination?

Unquestionably they reinforced them. First, the tapes revealed a dictatorial, manipulative, scheming Marcello, a man fully capable of masterminding three complex criminal conspiracies at the same time: a plot to obtain lucrative state insurance contracts for himself and his associates through bribing public officials, a plot to bribe a federal judge to get him to fix a case against the leadership of the Los Angeles Mafia, and a grander plot to obtain huge Teamsters pension fund insurance contracts for himself and three Mafia associates by offering large kickbacks to Teamsters pension fund trustees. Until the undercover operation surfaced, Marcello revealed himself to be in full charge of all three conspiracies, and he obviously took pride in being able to pull off a major crime involving several coconspirators and the manipulation of high-ranking state politicians. As he told undercover agent Mike Wacks when he became convinced he had successfully landed the big state insurance contracts: "I just wanna be proud I can do somethin' like dat."

Second, the tapes turned up a convincing view of the range and extent of Marcello's long suspected, but never verified, invisible government, the sort of network he could have counted on to help him cover up the assassination of a President. Carlos gave himself away on this score time and again in his boasts to the BRILAB undercover agents and his friend attorney Vincent Marinello:

"It takes time to get where I'm at. To know all these people— governors, business, the attorney general, they know me."
...

"Yeah, I got 'em all where I want 'em."
...

"I had Governor McKeithen for eight years."
...

"Maybe I can make a phone call to the attorney general. Now I'm not saying I can do it. I gotta man can do it."
...

"We own de Teamsters...."
...

"I got the only man in the United States can tell 'em [the Teamsters leadership] what the fuck to do."

. . .

"No matter who gets in there. You know I'm a find a way to get to 'em."

The BRILAB tapes also revealed that Marcello's invisible government reached to the highest levels of the federal government through his powerful contacts in Washington. The most influential of these was his friend and associate of two decades, master lobbyist Irving Davidson, who counted among his friends people of the prominence and power of J. Edgar Hoover, Lyndon Johnson, and Richard Nixon. Davidson was taped telling Marcello he would try to contact a high-ranking official in the criminal division of the Justice Department to aid him in his deportation battle.

In addition to providing us with a glimpse of the extent and workings of Marcello's invisible government, the BRILAB tapes also revealed how deeply involved in politics Carlos Marcello was. That involvement, of course, revealed itself to be wholly self-serving. Carlos had no political ideology. He played the Louisiana state elections similar to the way he played the horses, giving his support to whichever candidate he thought would do him favors were he elected.

In the 1960 presidential race between John Kennedy and Richard Nixon, Marcello knew full well who would do him favors if he were elected and who would try to do him harm. He and his brother Vincent had tasted firsthand the scorn of the Kennedy brothers during the March 1959 McClellan Committee hearings. Carlos had therefore placed a sizable bet on Richard Nixon—the now famous $500,000 cash donation to his campaign witnessed by Edward Partin, Irving Davidson, and Jimmy Hoffa. And he lost.

The assassination of President Kennedy may have been an expression of revenge and a desperate act of survival, but it was also a political act. When Nixon lost, the victors, as expected, mounted a campaign to destroy Marcello. But the results of the election could still be reversed. When Marcello played the 1979 gubernatorial election, he told Hauser: "No matter who gets in there...you know I'm a find a fuckin' way to get to 'em. I don't care who it is." So too could Carlos still find a way to get to the White House, even if by violent means. It would also have been a political act to attempt to frame a Castro supporter for the assassination. If successful, such a framing could conceivably have provoked the U. S. government into attempting to overthrow the Castro regime, thus paving the way for people like Marcello to recover their lost investments in Havana.

Marcello's unquenchable hatred of the Kennedys was confirmed also by the BRILAB tapes. On at least three occasions the undercover agents recorded Carlos's furious tirades against Robert Kennedy and the Kennedy family.

Then there were the various, incidental, unexpected revelations of the BRILAB tapes, information picked up by the FBI listening devices that was not strictly relevant to the BRILAB undercover operation but which sometimes promised some relevance to the possibility of Marcello's involvement in the Kennedy assassination.

One of the tapes, it will be recalled, hinted that Carlos and his brother Joe might have been associated with one of the killers of Judge John Wood of San Antonio. The Dallas-based racketeer Charles V. Harrelson had connections to Jack Ruby, to at least one associate of the Marcellos', and to Santos Trafficante. Harrelson had also been identified by House Select Committee on Assassinations graphics expert Jack White as possibly being one of the three "tramps" who had been arrested by the police in Dealey Plaza minutes after the assassination.

Finally, if we are to trust Joe Hauser, in view of the damage to his credibility the revelation of his alleged BRILAB "soliloquies" inflicted, Carlos and his brother Joe even went so far as to intimate to Hauser, and, on one occasion, also to Mike Wacks, that they were somehow involved in the Kennedy assassination.

The circumstances of these "veiled admissions of guilt," as they have been called, remain somewhat clouded, and the man who reported them from the sanctuary of the federal witness protection program remains somewhat inaccessible, yet they must be dealt with in any consideration of Carlos Marcello's possible complicity in the Kennedy assassination.

It will be recalled that some of these conversations came up as a result of headlines in the New Orleans *Times-Picayune* in the spring and summer of 1979 announcing the House Select Committee on Assassinations' suspicions of the involvement of Carlos Marcello in the John F. Kennedy assassination. Others came up as a result of the publication, again in the *Times-Picayune,* of Jack Anderson's syndicated column on Carlos Marcello and his suspected role in an alleged Kennedy assassination plot. Still others arose from newspaper articles on Teddy Kennedy's intention to campaign for the Democratic presidential nomination against incumbent President Jimmy Carter.

Joe Hauser used to meet with Carlos for lunch or dinner now

and then, informally, and the two would spend a couple of hours over mountains of steaming spaghetti discussing, according to Hauser, "just about everything under the sun," sometimes barely touching on the outstanding business between them. It was during one of these informal, unrecorded sessions that Hauser got Marcello talking about Lee Harvey Oswald and his family after casually mentioning an article he had recently read on the front page of the *Times-Picayune* under the banner headline: "MARCELLO–OSWALD LINK POSSIBLE."

"Hey Carlos, did you see that stuff in the paper about you and Oswald?" Hauser recalls he asked Marcello.

According to Hauser, Marcello then freely admitted to knowing Oswald and his aunt's in-laws, the Murrets, without saying anything about utilizing Oswald in a plot to assassinate the President. Carlos told Hauser that Oswald worked as a runner in his downtown New Orleans bookmaking network during the spring and summer of 1963. He also told Hauser that the FBI had come up to the Town & Country Motel a couple of times (presumably after the assassination) inquiring about Oswald and that his people had told the feds "nuttin'," "like we never heard of the guy, ya know."

This last bit of information jibes, of course, with what really did happen a few days after the assassination, unbeknownst to Hauser. FBI agents had gone to the Town & Country Motel on November 28 and 30, 1963, and asked Joe Poretto, and Anthony Marcello, whether they had seen someone resembling Lee Harvey Oswald in the motel's restaurant in March or April.

Marcello did not elaborate on his organization's relationship with Oswald any further during that discussion with Hauser, but what Carlos had said, and how he had said it, had been enough to persuade Joe Hauser that Carlos had probably been involved, in some way, with Oswald in the assassination.

But it was more what Joe Marcello had said to him in an unguarded moment, in response to one of Hauser's offhand remarks, that really convinced Hauser that the Assassinations Committee's suspicions of Marcello's complicity in the assassination might have been justified.

Joe Marcello had a much more open and expressive personality than his older brother, Carlos. He was known to be less guarded and more talkative. Yet he did not share Carlos's reputation as a liar. Law enforcement authorities had always regarded the affable, rotund Joe as a pretty straight guy who rarely got into serious trouble. At the same time it was well known that he was big enough in the Mafia to have been present at the two most important Mafia summits of recent times, the huge Apalachin conclave of 1957 and the meeting at La Stella in Queens in 1966.

Aware of all this, Joe Hauser took Joe Marcello seriously when, in the midst of an informal conversation about the Kennedy brothers, including the then candidate for the presidency, Senator Ted, the younger Marcello told Hauser not to worry about the Kennedys, boasting: "We took care of 'em, didn't we?"

Was this a vain boast, Hauser wondered at the time, or was it an honest, spontaneous reaction? In the end Hauser concluded that Joe Marcello was "implying" that the Marcellos had been involved in the assassination. In fact, Hauser explains, it seemed to him at the time that the Marcello brothers assumed that Hauser, as a bona fide member of the underworld, knew they had been involved in the elimination of President Kennedy.

Joe Hauser had received a similar impression during the tumultuous seven-hour marathon session he had with Carlos, Phillip Rizzuto, and Sam Sciortino at Anthony Marcello's lodge in connection with the Brooklier case. When the talk turned to the subject of the Kennedys, again in connection with Teddy's recently announced candidacy, Marcello, Sciortino, and Rizzuto launched into a tirade against the Kennedy brothers. Sciortino lashed out at Bobby Kennedy, accusing him of wanting to put all of them out of business, and Rizzuto said: "Yeah, so we put *him* outa business!"

Again, Joe Hauser interpreted Rizzuto's remark as assuming that everyone present, including Hauser, knew what he was talking about, that the mob had indeed put the Kennedy brothers "outa business."

Then there is the matter of the three tapes of Carlos Marcello's conversations about the Kennedy assassination and the House Select Committee's investigation that Judge Morey Sear put under judicial seal. It will be recalled that one tape revealed that Marcello purposely stepped out of his Town & Country office to discuss those matters with a visitor and that Robert Blakey considered the content of that tape "circumstantially suspicious." As of this writing, the three BRILAB "assassination tapes" remain under seal.

Finally, we are left to ponder the significance, if any, to the Kennedy assassination case, and particularly to the deaths of Lee Harvey Oswald and David Ferrie, of one last revelation arising out of the BRILAB operation, the motto Special Agent Larry Montague noticed on the door of Carlos Marcello's Town & Country office:

THREE CAN KEEP
A SECRET
IF TWO ARE DEAD

Although the BRILAB tapes did not confirm the House Assassinations Committee's suspicions of Carlos Marcello's possible involvement in the Kennedy assassination, they did strengthen them considerably. Also strengthening those suspicions has been the research that has been conducted by independent investigators and writers since the House Assassinations Committee concluded its investigation in 1979 and the BRILAB trials made their contributions to the growing body of evidence against Marcello in 1981 and 1982.

In fact, we can now affirm with reasonable certainty that upon the twenty-fifth anniversary of the assassination of President John F. Kennedy, no other conspiracy scenario seems even remotely as plausible as that suggesting the complicity of the Marcellos. Too much circumstantial evidence has accumulated over the past twenty-five years to be ignored. Thanks to what we have learned from the release of over 220,000 pages of FBI documents on the assassination, it is now clear that of the innumerable conspiracy allegations made by private citizens to the FBI in the wake of the assassination, no other alleged conspirators, and there were thousands, received as much attention from informants as the Marcellos and their associates. No fewer than four of the Marcello brothers were referred to in these allegations and the FBI reports on them: Carlos, Vincent, Joseph, and Anthony. Within five days of the President's murder, four informants, widely separated from one another and not in touch with one another, took the trouble, and the risk, to report their suspicions of the Marcellos, or their associates, to the FBI. One of them, the Georgia informant Gene Sumner, seemed unaware that the man he alleged he witnessed making a payment to someone resembling Oswald in the Town & Country Motel was associated with the Marcellos. And let it not be overlooked that the four individuals actually arrested by the police in connection with the assassination of the President and the murder of his suspected assassin—Oswald, Ferrie, Brading, and Ruby—were all connected either to Carlos Marcello or to one or more of his close associates.

How does the case against Carlos Marcello in the assassination of John F. Kennedy stand upon the twenty-fifth anniversary of the crime?

The answer is that the case is stronger than ever but is still not solid enough to be turned over to a grand jury.

The circumstantial case against Marcello has, in fact, always been strong, and it now appears reasonably certain, based on previously classified FBI and Secret Service reports, especially those on David Ferrie, that the FBI and the Secret Service realized it was strong from the very beginning. Precisely for that reason Hoover abandoned further investigation of Ferrie and shelved the allegations of Jack Martin, Eugene De Laparra, and Gene Sumner.

In confronting the possibility of the involvement of Carlos Marcello in the crime of the century, twenty-five years after FBI Director J. Edgar Hoover deliberately avoided the issue, the question inevitably arises: Did the killing of President Kennedy and his alleged assassin fit the traditional pattern of a Mafia execution? And if it did, would a powerful Mafia leader in his right mind have ever chosen such an unpromising crew to accomplish a major execution as that ragtag bunch of ne'er-do-well misfits, Lee Harvey Oswald, David Ferrie, and Jack Ruby?

Yes, the killings of the President and his suspected assassin did fit the traditional pattern of a Mafia execution, for a number of reasons.

First, the killing of the President took the form of a *public* execution, an old tradition in the Mafia, especially when the victim is regarded as a mortal enemy of the executioner. The President was brazenly gunned down before scores of witnesses, in a public square and on a public occasion for all the world to see.

Second, the rapidly identified suspected assassin, Lee Harvey Oswald, fit the time-honored Mafia mold of the scapegoat. He was an apparent loner with his own personal motive to commit the crime: in Oswald's case his apparent desire, as a devoted supporter of Fidel Castro, to take revenge against President Kennedy for his anti-Castro policies, including his administration's attempts to assassinate the Cuban leader.

Third, the quick and extraordinarily efficient *public* silencing of the suspected assassin in front of an enormous worldwide television audience before he could reveal the details of the murder plot was a Mafia practice going back to the farthest origins of the old Sicilian brotherhood. The purpose was to serve notice to other possible witnesses to the murder conspiracy as to what might happen to them if they decided to talk.

But what about the apparent unsuitability of Oswald, Ferrie, and Ruby as individuals a Mafia boss would entrust with so great and difficult a crime as the execution of a President and the framing and subsequent elimination of his suspected assassin?

It was precisely their apparent unsuitability and removal from the stereotype of the professional Mafia hitman that would have persuaded a Mafia leader to utilize Oswald, Ferrie, and Ruby in an important execution. As Carlos Marcello had "clearly indicated" to

Edward Becker, "his own lieutenants must not be identified as the assassins" so "that there would thus be a necessity to have them use or manipulate someone else to carry out the actual crime." Two young non-Italian gentiles and a paunchy middle-aged Jew. An ex-defector to the Soviet Union who passes out pro-Castro leaflets in the streets, a hairless ex–airline pilot with a history of arrests for committing "indecent acts" with young boys, and a small-time striptease joint operator—what a crew! Who would ever dream of linking these amateurs, these nonentities, to professional criminals, to the Mafia?

The selection of such an apparently unprofessional assassin as Oswald, or the framing of such a type in a murder plot, was another time-honored tradition of the Mafia.

Many Mafia executions of the past have illustrated this practice, the most celebrated one in recent years being the attempted rubout of New York Mafia boss Joseph Colombo at a public outdoor rally of the Italian-American Civil Rights League in New York in 1971. The unlikely hitman turned out to be Jerome Johnson, a young black "loner" unaffiliated with organized crime, who had probably been recruited by Colombo rival Joey Gallo, although his link with Gallo was never proved. Minutes after he shot Colombo, Johnson himself was shot dead in the ensuing melee by an unknown assailant. (Colombo lived on in a coma for seven years.)

Vincent Teresa, once number three man in the New England Mafia family headed by the late Raymond Patriarca, wrote in his book *My Life in the Mafia* that he knew it was the custom of Carlos Marcello to hire hit teams from other Mafia families, far removed from Louisiana, to perform contract murders in his realm, because one hit team was recruited by Marcello from Teresa's own crime family, the Patriarcas.

We are aware from FBI reports that during the thirty-day period preceding the assassination, Jack Ruby held telephone conversations with two of Jimmy Hoffa's most feared enforcers, both of whom were affiliated with "The Outfit" in Chicago, and also talked with a notorious mob bail bondsman affiliated with the Teamsters and the Chicago underworld.

We also have the sworn testimony of a Louisiana state trooper that on November 20, 1963, Rose Cheramie told him that she had just been driven up from Miami by two "Italians" who were heading for Dallas to shoot President Kennedy on the 22nd.

Quite possibly, then, if Carlos Marcello played a role in the Kennedy assassination, he might have recruited his professional assassination team from Chicago's Outfit or from the Trafficante organization in Florida, while having David Ferrie set up his friend Lee Harvey Oswald to take the blame. Ferrie's job would have included the deployment of an Oswald impostor, possibly someone with prior intelligence experience, to lay an incriminating trail of evidence and the necessary arrangements to have Oswald silenced immediately after the crime.

When those last arrangements failed, Ferrie had to find a way to get to Oswald in the Dallas Police Headquarters. Police buff Jack Ruby was the obvious choice. It seems that Ferrie must have reached Ruby, possibly through Civello or Campisi, during his mysterious trip to Texas following the assassination, and told him what he had to do.

The available circumstantial evidence hints at such a scenario, but we still do not have the concrete facts to confirm it. Despite the overwhelming web of circumstantial evidence suggesting the complicity of the Marcello organization in the assassination of John F. Kennedy, and despite the fact that the President's murder did bear, in thinly disguised form, the fingerprints of a traditional Mafia execution, we are still uncertain about the precise details and extent of Carlos Marcello's suspected involvement in the crime.

That said, there is at least one important element of the case about which we can be quite certain: the nature of the government's response to the assassination.

That response has been identified, unwittingly perhaps, by the government itself, through its release of innumerable official documents on the various investigations of the murder.

These documents reveal unequivocally that if indeed Carlos Marcello played a role in the assassination, then an agency of the United States government, acting "for the good of the country," let him get away with the crime.

That agency was J. Edgar Hoover's FBI. Not the FBI of the United States Department of Justice, but the FBI that was the personal fiefdom of one man.

But J. Edgar Hoover was not alone in allowing Carlos Marcello to get away with the crime of the century, if indeed Marcello was involved, for his response to the assassination was tacitly shared and supported, "for the good of the country," by Chief Justice Earl Warren, President Lyndon B. Johnson, and Attorney General Robert F. Kennedy.

As Carlos Marcello once boasted to Joe Hauser about other politicians he had the goods on: "Yeah, I got 'em all where I want 'em."

60

The Marcellos Today

The BRILAB convictions of Carlos Marcello and his subsequent imprisonment in June 1983 left the Marcello family deflated and leaderless, and the Marcello criminal network fragmented. With its former political influence virtually destroyed, and its reputation in the underworld now a laughing stock, it would not be long before the Marcello organization would find itself defenseless against the incursions of mob families from the east.

No one in the Marcello family had been able to take Carlos's place as boss or repair the damage to the family's prestige inflicted by the BRILAB operation. And Carlos's effectiveness as a leader had been severely limited by his illness and imprisonment. There was only so much business the ailing Carlos could conduct over a monitored prison phone or during weekend visiting hours with his brothers and attorneys.

Carlos's patient and long-suffering wife, Jacqueline, had been able to keep the family together with her regular Sunday afternoon luncheons of spaghetti and meatballs at the big white-columned brick house in Metairie, usually attended by a dozen or so Marcellos. But, as a woman who had always stayed out of her husband's business affairs, she was powerless to do anything about the family leadership, which was supposed to have fallen to her brother-in-law Joe.

But Joe, now supposedly the Marcello organization's de facto boss, a man heading into his mid-sixties, lacked the drive, ambition, and killer instinct of his older brother and, in the wake of BRILAB, appeared to have been gripped by a strong need to keep out of trouble, to play it safe. Staying relatively clear of the rackets that had so stimulated Carlos, Joe had turned to the business that had always served him best in the past, the restaurant business. He and Carlos had once owned the celebrated Elmwood Plantation Restaurant on the West Bank, and he was, with Sammy, part owner of La Louisiane in the French Quarter. Now Joe branched out and opened up Lenfants, a big, brassy Las Vegas–style bar-restaurant-nightclub in the new section of New Orleans, just off the big highway leading to Metairie. There, on Wednesday, Friday, and Saturday nights, he would receive the homage of the Marcellos' still large following of friends and admirers. I observed this veteran of the deportation battles, the Kennedy war, and the Apalachin and La Stella summits one evening playing host at Lenfants and was struck by how jovial and popular and happy he appeared to be. Beautiful women were greeting him with hugs and kisses. Men were embracing him and slapping him on the back. He appeared to be enjoying his role as a noted restaurateur and minor New Orleans celebrity. I had the impression he had little stomach left for the risks and battles of running what was left of his brother's criminal organization.

Nor had any of Carlos's other brothers evinced much in the way of ambition or leadership in the wake of BRILAB. The gentlemanly Vincent, also heading into his mid-sixties, busied himself almost exclusively with the family's coin machine business, the Jefferson Music Company, now sans the illegal slot machines. In this he was assisted by his brothers Sammy and Anthony, both now heading toward sixty. The one-eyed Peter, now in his early seventies, had long since sold his Bourbon Street striptease dives and was living in relative seclusion in a little house on the West Bank near Gretna; and the ever-obliging Pascal, now also in his seventies, was pretty much out of circulation, as he had been for some time.

In addition to his duties at the Jefferson Music Company, the amiable Sammy, the youngest and most charming of the brothers, also managed the French Quarter restaurant he and Joe co-owned, La Louisiane, located almost next door to Sam Saia's Felix Oyster Bar, where Lee Harvey Oswald's uncle, Dutz Murret, had once conducted his Marcello-affiliated bookmaking operations, sending his hot-headed young nephew out to the bars and horse books of New Orleans with messages and notices of moneys due.

Carlos's only son, Joseph, "Little Joe," now in his early forties, had even less drive and ambition than his uncles. Having been handed $3 million worth of assets, including a piece of the Town & Country Motel, by his father when he was only in his mid-twenties, Little Joe had never had to work for a living. A handsome, well-liked man who enjoys sports, he had never displayed the slightest inclination to follow in his father's footsteps, despite the strong filial affection he possessed for his dad, preferring a good game of golf on the links of suburban New Orleans to helping his father mastermind vast, risky criminal conspiracies. From all appearances, Little Joe's principal contribution to the Marcello enterprise has been the fathering of a son—Carlos Marcello II—whose visits to Texarkana on weekends are said to be his imprisoned grandfather's greatest joy and consolation.

Nor have the sons of Carlos's brothers shown much interest in furthering what is left of their uncle's criminal organization. Although Vincent's son, Vincent Jr., was convicted of selling cocaine at the time of the New Orleans BRILAB trial and has been a suspect in a murder, his criminal impulses have had nothing to do with his father's, or his uncles' activities. As of this writing, Vince Jr. is running a nightclub called Froggy's in a suburban New Orleans shopping mall, which has recently been attracting the more adventurous members of the city's *jeunesse dorée*.

From all appearances, the old Sicilian Mafia attitude of radical confrontation with society, or with the so-called establishment, no longer holds for Carlos's children, nephews, and nieces. These second-generation Marcellos are anxious to be accepted by New Orleans society, to become part of the establishment themselves.

But, it could be argued, for the past thirty or so years in New Orleans the barriers between society and Mafia have been breaking down. There is no longer much separation between the two social groups, as there is, say, in New York City. Members of Mafia families are not, as a rule, mentioned very often in the society columns of the major dailies in New York, whereas, in the mid-eighties, Sammy Marcello's name used to turn up now and then in the New Orleans *Times-Picayune*'s society page in connection with one event or another at La Louisiane. He gave a big dinner there in 1986 for El Salvador's director of communications and culture, an event that reportedly attracted representatives from both the crème de la crème of New Orleans society and members of the city's reigning Mafia family, including Carlos's beautiful daughter Louise, a Mardi Gras Queen in

1956 and now, as Mrs. Jefferson Hampton III, a member of a distinguished old WASP family.

And so, from 1983 on, the Marcello brothers and their offspring gradually lapsed into an easier and less risky existence than that which had been their lot while the larger-than-life Carlos had been controlling their destinies. And, as a result, by the dawn of 1988, with the 78-year-old patriarch steadily deteriorating in the gloom of Texarkana, and the family's influence in both political circles and the underworld at an all-time low, the once mighty Marcello empire had degenerated into a headless ruin assailed by one calamity after another.

The year 1988 brought many problems for the Marcellos of Louisiana. It began with the bankruptcy of La Louisiane, followed by Sammy's arrest and indictment for money laundering. These two disasters were followed by Judge Morey Sear's denial of Carlos's petition to have one of his BRILAB convictions vacated, thus condemning the Mafia boss to six more years behind bars.

Sammy's embarrassing arrest had occurred one afternoon in Lenfants Restaurant, where, since the collapse of La Louisiane, he had been helping out his brother Joe as sort of an assistant manager and fill-in host. Not long after the much-publicized arrest, Lenfants also declared bankruptcy, and it became rumored in New Orleans that Joe Marcello was now in deep financial trouble. Following that, it was learned that longtime Marcello associate and attorney David Levy, who had also been indicted for money laundering, had turned state's witness against Sammy and would testify against him, under grant of immunity, at Marcello's coming trial.

Around this time, the U.S. District Court for the Eastern District of Louisiana began releasing certain affidavits in support of applications to wiretap on the part of the FBI that clearly indicated that the Marcellos had lost almost all their power in the New Orleans underworld since Carlos's BRILAB convictions of 1981 and 1982. Those affidavits revealed conclusively that by 1986 the New Orleans French Quarter was firmly under the control of former Marcello associate Frank Caracci and his associate Nick Karno, without Caracci and Karno having to answer to any of the Marcellos.

(It will be recalled that the FBI had questioned Frank Caracci after the Kennedy assassination about his relationship with Jack Ruby.)

Furthermore, the affidavits strongly suggested that, beginning in 1986 and continuing through 1987 and into 1988, individuals asso-

ciated with the Gambino crime family of New York, headed by John
Gotti, and the Bruno-Scarfo crime family of Philadelphia, headed by
Nicodemo "Nicky" Scarfo, with the apparent blessing of Frank Caracci
and Nick Karno, had begun to move into the New Orleans rackets
that had been the exclusive province of Carlos Marcello and his criminal subordinates since the late 1940s. One of the relevant affidavits
read, in part:

> [FBI informant] CS-1 advised that in May, 1986, Frank Caracci
> and Nick Karno arranged for Erik Rasmussen and Bramer/
> Diamond to be brought into the New Orleans area from Las
> Vegas, Nevada, and New York, respectively, to establish casino-
> type gambling operations and to establish a cocaine distribution
> network. A review of FBI files indicates there are numerous
> references to Caracci and Karno as being associates of Cosa
> Nostra Boss Carlos Marcello.

In none of the 352 pages of wiretap affidavits that I acquired was
there any mention of contact between Frank Caracci and Nick Karno
and the imprisoned Carlos Marcello and his brothers in New Orleans.

The implications of the FBI wiretaps were clear. Powerful former
associates of Carlos Marcello, such as Frank Caracci and Nick Karno,
still ran things down in the French Quarter, but they were now acting on their own, not under orders from the Marcellos.

The FBI wiretap affidavits further suggested that the Gambino
and Bruno-Scarfo families, acting on the belief that gambling would
soon be legalized in New Orleans, were buying up large chunks of
valuable real estate in the French Quarter. They had also been mus-
cling in on all the illegal gambling activities associated with what remained of the Marcello organization, with Frank Caracci's apparent
blessing, and were laying the groundwork for making New Orleans
a major port of entry for cocaine and P_2P's, a chemical used in the
manufacture of illegal methamphetamines.

According to a confidential source, who acquired his information
from FBI wiretaps, what had happened was that Gambino family boss
John Gotti, sensing the void that had opened up in the Louisiana
underworld with the imprisonment of Carlos Marcello, had given the
OK to certain crews of his own family and of the Bruno-Scarfo family to respond to Frank Caracci's call for fresh new blood.

Apparently after Frank Caracci had approached Scarfo capo Jack
Diamond (alias Ronald Bramer) about coming down to New Orleans
to help set up "casino-style gambling operations and to establish a

cocaine distribution network," Diamond and another Scarfo capo, Albert "Reds" Pontani, from Trenton, had a sit-down with John Gotti in New York. There Gotti, as the head of the nation's largest and most powerful crime family, had given them permission to accept Caracci's invitation.

According to a source who heard the wiretaps, Gotti's New Orleans intelligence contacts had convinced him the Marcellos had become so weak and inconsequential that it would not even be necessary for the Scarfo people to contact Carlos or any of his brothers for permission to move in. Disdaining Joe Marcello, since they already had the blessing of Frank Caracci and Nick Karno, the Scarfos turned to aging mobster Frank Gagliano, a veteran of Sam "Silver Dollar" Carolla's gang of the pre-Marcello era, and requested a meeting. Gagliano, who, it will be recalled, had attended the La Stella summit as an ally of Silver Dollar Sam's son, Anthony Carolla, in his dispute with Carlos over the division of the spoils in New Orleans, amiably gave the Scarfo captains his formal blessing. "Sure," he is supposed to have said to Scarfo captain Reds Pontani, "go ahead. Come on in. You won't get any heat from the Marcellos. They're finished. They don't mean nothin' around here anymore."

As if to confirm that judgment, a yearlong FBI wiretap of the telephone used by Carlos Marcello at Texarkana was reported to have come up "dry."

According to a confidential source in New Orleans, knowledgeable of the FBI's continued surveillance of Carlos, one of the reasons why the protracted wiretap came up "dry" probably had something to do with the deterioration of Carlos Marcello's health in 1987 and 1988. People who visited Carlos at Texarkana in late 1987 have reported that the 78-year-old crime boss seems to have Alzheimer's disease. His memory is failing. He is often disoriented and sometimes does not remember who he is, or where he is.

In view of this disability, it can be asked whether Carlos Marcello would ever be capable of standing trial for any of his alleged past crimes in the event sufficient evidence were found for an indictment.

Not a chance, according to those who have visited Marcello at Texarkana. If, for example, a convincing case could be assembled charging Carlos with conspiracy to assassinate John F. Kennedy, and he were called to defend himself against such a charge at a trial, Marcello would be genuinely hard-pressed to remember any details of his activities in 1963.

In 1979 the Department of Justice had been put on notice by a congressional subcommittee that Carlos Marcello was a prime suspect in what the committee believed had been a probable conspiracy to assassinate President John F. Kennedy.

At that very moment, the Justice Department, through its investigative arm, the Federal Bureau of Investigation, was conducting what turned out to be a most successful undercover sting operation against the man the Assassinations Committee had identified as a prime suspect. At that time the suspected conspirator was in reasonably good health and was certainly in full possession of his mental faculties. Vulnerable as he turned out to be during the course of the BRILAB sting operation, Marcello could have conceivably been lured by the undercover agents into a discussion of his role in the alleged plot to kill President Kennedy, had he indeed been involved in such a plot. But nothing was done. The Justice Department made no effort whatsoever to utilize this ongoing sting operation against Marcello to obtain information from him about his possible role, if any, in the Kennedy assassination. In fact, the department did not even suggest to the three undercover agents that they subtly inquire of Marcello whether he had had any relationship with Lee Harvey Oswald and/ or Jack Ruby.

As it turned out, it remained for undercover operative Joe Hauser to take the initiative in this regard and attempt to get Marcello talking about the Kennedy assassination unofficially, outside the bounds and context of the government's sting operation.

If we are to believe Joe Hauser, he did succeed in getting Carlos Marcello and his brother Joe to allude "obliquely" to having played a role in a plot to assassinate President Kennedy. Hauser told the Justice Department, after the BRILAB sting was over, that Carlos and Joe Marcello had, on two separate occasions, "implied" to him that they had been involved in a conspiracy to assassinate the President. And yet the Justice Department did nothing about investigating this possibility.

Once Carlos Marcello had been convicted, sentenced, and imprisoned as a result of the BRILAB operation, the Justice Department now had the suspected Kennedy assassination conspirator under its control. It could decide, via the department's Bureau of Prisons, who Marcello could see and who he could not see. It had him effectively isolated. No one could reach him without the Justice Department's authorization. No one from the media could interview him. No one from the former House Select Committee on Assassinations could even require Judge Morey Sear to unseal the three tapes recorded during the BRILAB operation containing conversations of Carlos Marcello and the undercover agents about the Kennedy assassination.

Yes, the Justice Department now had Carlos Marcello just where it wanted him. Cut off from all inquiries into his past. Waiting for a legitimate agent of amnesia—senility or possibly Alzheimer's disease— to erase what was left of his memory so that, in the event he did possess important secrets, he could no longer remember them.

With Lee Harvey Oswald, Jack Ruby, and David Ferrie long since gone, and Carlos Marcello's memory going, there is now little chance left of getting to the bottom of the assassination of President Kennedy if Carlos Marcello or any of his associates were involved in the crime.

There can be little doubt that the Justice Department's attitude toward Carlos Marcello and the Kennedy assassination has been deeply suspect for twenty-five years.

When J. Edgar Hoover and his field agents in New Orleans became aware of the connections between Carlos Marcello, David Ferrie, and Lee Harvey Oswald, a few days after the assassination, the FBI began deliberately suppressing evidence of those connections, which, it will be recalled, were never brought to the attention of the Warren Commission. And, as we have seen, these suppressions were practiced by the FBI even as recently as the House Select Committee on Assassinations' investigation of the Kennedy assassination of 1978 and 1979, when, by delaying the turning over of its Kennedy assassination files to the committee, the FBI prevented the committee from receiving the allegations of Eugene De Laparra and Gene Sumner suggesting foreknowledge of the assassination on the part of the Marcellos and a relationship between the Marcello organization and Lee Harvey Oswald.

Meanwhile the possible key to unraveling at least some of the major mysteries of the Kennedy assassination sits in solitary confinement in a Texas prison steadily and inexorably losing his memory.

Recently Carlos Marcello's principal attorney, Arthur A. "Buddy" Lemann, appealed Judge Morey Sear's decision to deny Marcello's motion to have his BRILAB mail and wire fraud convictions vacated, thus presenting the ailing Carlos with one last chance at freedom, and assassination investigators one last chance to possibly plumb his secrets. According to a source close to the case, while there may be an outside chance Judge Sear's ruling will be successfully appealed, thus allowing Marcello the possibility of being able to die, like a good Sicilian, in his own bed, by the time the decision is handed down, Alzheimer's may have claimed the remainder of Marcello's memory and the once-all-powerful Mafia boss may not even know who he is.

Notes on Sources

CARLOS MARCELLO

Primary Sources

1. *Federal Bureau of Investigation. File on Carlos Marcello.* Most of the FBI file on Carlos Marcello that was turned over by the FBI to the House Select Committee on Assassinations in 1978 is on file at the Assassinations Archives and Research Center, 918 F Street, Washington, DC.

2. *Federal Bureau of Investigation—Freedom of Information Act Releases*

   a. The Allegation of FBI Informant SV T-1 Gene Sumner. FBI File N. 44-24016-254. Freedom of Information Act Release.

      (1) *SAVANNAH TELETYPE, 11/26/63.* To Director and SACs, New Orleans and Dallas. Page 1. The original allegation by SV T-1, Gene Sumner, to Glynn County police officer, Lt. Johnny Harris, stating he saw someone resembling Lee Harvey Oswald accepting a payment in the Town & Country Restaurant, New Orleans, from the restaurant owner (Joseph Poretto).

      (2) *NEW ORLEANS AIRTEL, 11/27/63.* From SAC, New Orleans, to SACs, Dallas and Savannah. Pages 1,2. Re Savannah teletype 11/23/63. Informing Dallas and Savannah that Town & Country Motel and Restaurant "is a known hang-out of the hoodlum element" and is owned, in part, by Carlos Marcello and managed by Joseph Poretto, who has a criminal record.

      (3) *NEW ORLEANS REPORTS OF INVESTIGATIONS OF THE SV T-1 SUMNER ALLEGATION CONTAINED IN THE SAVANNAH TELETYPE OF 11/26/63. REPORTS DATED 11/27/63.*

(a) Interview of Joseph Albert Poretto by Special Agent Reed Jensen. Dictated 11/27/63.

(b) Interview of Mrs. Ella Frabbiele by Special Agent Reed Jensen. Dictated 11/27/63.

(c) Interview of Anthony Marcello by Special Agent Reed Jensen. Dictated 11/27/63.

(4) *SAVANNAH TELETYPE, 11/29/63.* To Director and SACs, Dallas and New Orleans. Pages 1–3. Re Savannah teletype of 11/26/63. Reinterview of SV T-1 by Lt. Johnny Harris identifying informant as Gene Sumner, a businessman from Darien, Georgia. Sumner expands on original allegation and mentions names of individuals he was with at Town & Country Motel when he saw someone resembling Oswald receive a payment from the owner, who he now identifies as having been "in the rackets" in Chicago.

(5) *NEW ORLEANS TELETYPE, 11/30/63.* To Director and SACs, Dallas and Savannah. Re Savannah teletype of 11/29/63. SAC, New Orleans, observes that Oswald was not supposed to have been in New Orleans when SV T-1 allegedly observed him in the Town & Country Motel.

(6) *REPORTS OF SPECIAL AGENT JOHN P. MCGUIRE, FBI, SAVANNAH ON ALLEGATION OF SV T-1, GENE SUMNER, 12/1/63 AND 12/2/63.* Reports of McGuire's interview of SV T-1, Gene Sumner, in which Sumner reiterates his original allegation, is shown a photo of Oswald, and asserts it resembles the individual he saw accepting a payment at the Town and Country Motel.

b. The Allegation of FBI Informant Eugene De Laparra. FBI File N. 62-109060. Freedom of Information Act Release.

(1) *PHILADELPHIA TELETYPE, 11/28/63.* To Director and SACs, New Orleans and Dallas. Pages 1,2. The original allegation by De Laparra suggesting existence of a plot to assassinate President Kennedy "when he comes south." Concludes with "copy Newark."

(2) *NEW ORLEANS TELETYPE, 11/29/63.* To Director and SAC Dallas. Pages 3,4. Response to Philadelphia teletype of 11/28/63. Notes that De Laparra has provided reliable information in the past to New Orleans "regarding gambling activities." Refers to a New Orleans teletype of 11/28/63. Ben Traegel [sic] listed as "suspect" in the Kennedy assassination.

(3) *PHILADELPHIA TELETYPE, 11/29/63.* To Director. Page 1. Refers to Philadelphia teletype to Director and Dallas of 11/28/63.

(4) *NEW ORLEANS REPORTS OF INVESTIGATIONS OF THE DE LAPARRA ALLEGATION CONTAINED IN PHILADELPHIA TELETYPE OF 11/28/63. REPORTS DATED 11/30/63.*

(a) Interview of Bernard Alfred Tregle by Special Agent Reed W. Jensen. Dictated 11/29/63.

(b) Interview of Norman Joseph Le Blanc by Special Agent Reed W. Jensen. Dictated 11/29/63.

(c) Interview of Mrs. Bernard Tregle by Special Agent Ronald Hoverson. Dictated 11/29/63.

(d) Statement by Special Agent Regis L. Kennedy that he was in U.S. District Court, New Orleans, at trial of Carlos and Joseph Marcello on Nov.

22, 1963, and observed Vincent Marcello attending the trial. Dictated 11/27/63.

(5) *NEWARK TELETYPE, 2/23/67*. To Director and Dallas. Pages 1,2,3. De Laparra's second allegation suggesting existence of a plot to assassinate President Kennedy. Made the day after death of David Ferrie. Asserts that it was Tony (Anthony) Marcello who told Ben Tregle and others in Tregle's Bar that "the word is out to get the Kennedy family."

(6) *NEWARK AIRTEL, 2/27/67*. To Director. Page 1. Refers to Newark teletype of 2/23/67.

(7) *NEWARK LHM, 2/27/67*. Page 1. Summarizes Newark teletype of 2/23/67.

(8) *NEW ORLEANS TELETYPE, 8/8/67*. To Director and Dallas in response to Bucall to New Orleans of 8/7/67. Page 5 refers to Special Agent Jensen's interview of Norman Le Blanc of 11/29/63. Page 6 refers to Special Agent Jensen's interview with Bernard Alfred Tregle of 11/29/63 and requests Dallas review its files to determine report in which FD 302s of Norman Joseph Le Blanc and Alfred Tregle were reported "and furnish identity of report to bureau."

3. *U.S. Senate, Kefauver Hearings*. Special Committee to Investigate Organized Crime in Interstate Commerce. Hearings in New Orleans, Jan. 25. 26, and Feb. 7, 1951. Interrogation of Carlos Marcello, Anthony Marcello, and Joseph Poretto.

4. *U.S. Senate, Kefauver Reports*. Special Committee to Investigate Organized Crime in Interstate Commerce. Second Interim Report, Feb. 28, 1951. Third Interim Report, May 1, 1951.

5. *U.S. Senate, McClellan Committee Hearings*. Select Committee on Improper Activities in the Labor and Management Field. Hearings in Washington, Mar. 23, 24, 25, 1959, and Aug. 28, 29, 30, 31, 1961. Testimony of Aaron Kohn. Interrogations of Carlos Marcello, Vincent Marcello, Joseph Marcello, and Joseph Poretto.

6. *U.S. House of Representatives. Organized Crime Control Hearings*. May 20 to Aug. 5, 1970. Testimony of Aaron Kohn (in *Congressional Record*). Interrogation of Carlos Marcello.

7. *U.S. House of Representatives. House Select Committee on Crime*. Organized Crime in Sports (Racing). Hearings, May 9 to Jul. 27, 1972. Interrogation of Carlos Marcello.

8. *Federal Trials (excluding BRILAB)*

   a. U.S. District Court, New Orleans. *The United States v. Carlos Marcello and Joseph Marcello, Jr*. Transcript of Trial Record, Nov. 4–22, 1963.

   b. U.S. District Court, New Orleans. *The United States v. Carlos Marcello and Joseph Matasa*. Transcript of Trial Record, Oct. 4, 1964 to Aug. 17, 1965.

9. *United States Department of Justice—Immigration and Naturalization Service*. Hearings, Deportation Proceedings, Carlos Marcello, INS, New Orleans, Louisiana. Jun. 27, 1972; file N. A2–669–541. Transcript of Hearings, 453 pages. In this document Marcello related to the immigration officers the story of his 1961 "kidnap-deportation" and exile in Central America.

10. *United States House of Representatives. Select Committee on Assassinations (HSCA)*. Investigation of the Assassination of President John F. Kennedy. Final Report. 95th Congress, 2nd Session. Washington, DC: U.S. GPO, 1978–1979. Carlos Marcello is guardedly named a suspect in the assassination.

11. *United States House of Representatives. Select Committee on Assassinations (HSCA).* Investigation of the Assassination of President John F. Kennedy. Appendix to Hearings. Volume IX. Organized Crime. Staff Report on Carlos Marcello, pages 61–92.

12. *United States House of Representatives. Select Committee on Assassinations (HSCA).* Investigation of the Assassination of President John F. Kennedy. Outside Contact Report. I. Irving Davidson. Nov. 22, 1978.

13. *The BRILAB Operation and Trials. The BRILAB Tapes.*

    a. *United States District Court, Eastern District of Louisiana. United States v. Carlos Marcello, I. Irving Davidson, Charles E. Roemer, Vincent A. Marinello.* Indictment for (1) conspiracy to participate, through a pattern of racketeering activity, in the affairs of an enterprise, the activities of which affect interstate commerce; (2) a substantive violation of such participation in the affairs of that enterprise; (3) interstate travel in aid of racketeering; (4) wire fraud; and, (5) mail fraud. June 17, 1980. 25 pages. Contains a brief history of the BRILAB undercover operation, with some quotations from BRILAB tapes.

    b. *United States District Court, Eastern District of Louisiana. In the Matter of the Application of the United States of America for an Order Authorizing the Interception of Wire Communications.* Affidavits. Feb. 8, 1979 to Jan. 1, 1980. These contain a summary of Joseph Hauser's career as an insurance operator, his troubles with the law, his relationship with Davidson, his relationship with Marcello before Feb. 8, 1979, and a running history of the BRILAB undercover investigation of Marcello from Feb. 1979 to Feb. 1980. In addition, the affidavits contain many verbatim transcripts of taped conversations between Carlos Marcello, the undercover agents, Irving Davidson, Vincent Marinello, and others.

    c. *United States District Court, Eastern District of Louisiana. United States v. Carlos Marcello, I. Irving Davidson, Charles E. Roemer, Vincent A. Marinello.* Crim. A No. 80-274. Transcript of record of trial at Federal Records Center, Fort Worth, TX.

    d. *United States District Court, Central District of California. United States v. Carlos Marcello, Samuel Orlando Sciortino, and Phillip Rizzuto.* Crim. No. EJD-81-720. Transcript of record of trial at Federal Records Center, Laguna Niguel, CA.

    e. *United States v. Carlos Marcello et al.* 508 F. Supp. 586 (1981), 637 F. Supp. 1364 (1982), F31 F. Supp. 1113 (1982), 537 F. Supp. 399 (1982), 568 F. Supp. 738 (1983), 731 F. 2d 1354 (1984). These contain summaries of the New Orleans and Los Angeles BRILAB undercover operations, commentary on the trials, and many verbatim transcripts of taped conversations between Carlos Marcello, the undercover agents, and others.

    f. *The BRILAB Tapes. United States District Court For the District of Columbia. John H. Davis v. U.S. Department of Justice. Civil Action N. 88-0130 (TPJ).* Freedom of Information Act lawsuit to secure release of the approximately 160 reels of taped conversations between Carlos Marcello, the undercover agents, and others, recorded during the FBI undercover investigation of Carlos Marcello Feb. 1979 to Feb. 1980 that were admitted into evidence at the two BRILAB trials in New Orleans and Los Angeles. Approximately 1,400 reels of Marcello's conversations were recorded. Among these were three tapes of Marcello's conversations about the John F. Kennedy assassination and the House Select Committee on Assassinations investigation. These were put under judicial seal by Judge Morey Sear.

    g. *United States District Court, Eastern District of Louisiana. United States vs. Carlos Marcello et al. Criminal case N. 80-274 Section"G". Proffer. The Defendant Carlos Marcello Should Be Allowed To Demonstrate To The Instant Jury Any Prior And Present Government Bias*

Against Him Which May Have Prejudicially Influenced The Conduct of the FBI Investigation In This Case Against Marcello. (An excellent summary of the INS Deportation case against Carlos Marcello, presenting the irregularities and illegalities of the government's case.)

h. *United States District Court, Eastern District of Louisiana. United States vs. Carlos Marcello et al. Criminal Case N. 80-274 Section "G".* Motion to Vacate Conviction Pursuant To 28 USC 2255, October 7, 1987. (Marcello's appeal of his mail and wire fraud conviction. Contains a concise history of the BRILAB operation and trials).

Secondary Sources

1. *Books—General.* A selected list of books in which Carlos Marcello is prominently mentioned.

    Chandler, David Leon. *Brothers in Blood. The Rise of the Criminal Brotherhoods* (Book Four). New York: Dutton, 1975.

    Davis, John H. *The Kennedys: Dynasty and Disaster* (Parts 3, 4, 5). New York: McGraw-Hill, 1984.

    Dorman, Michael. *Payoff.* New York: Berkley, 1972. (The Marcello-Halfen connection.)

    Moldea, Dan E. *The Hoffa Wars: Teamsters, Rebels, Politicians, and the Mob.* New York: Paddington, 1978.

    Reid, Ed. *The Grim Reapers, The Anatomy of Organized Crime in America* (Chapter 9). Chicago: Henry Regnery, 1969.

    Schreiber, G.R. *The Bobby Baker Affair.* Chicago: Henry Regnery, 1964.

    Sheridan, Walter. *The Fall and Rise of Jimmy Hoffa.* New York: Saturday Review Press, 1972.

2. *Books—John F. Kennedy Assassination.* A selected list (in order of publication) in which Carlos Marcello is mentioned as a possible suspect.

    Noyes, Peter. *Legacy of Doubt.* New York: Pinnacle, 1973. The first book on the Kennedy assassination to name Carlos Marcello as a possible suspect in the crime.

    Anson, Robert Sam. *They've Killed the President—The Search for the Murderers of John F. Kennedy.* New York: Bantam, 1975.

    Fensterwald, Bernard Jr. *Coincidence or Conspiracy?* New York: Zebra, 1977.

    Kantor, Seth. *Who Was Jack Ruby?* New York: Everest House, 1978.

    Summers, Anthony. *Conspiracy. Who Killed President Kennedy?* New York: McGraw-Hill, 1980.

    Blakey, G. Robert, and Richard N. Billings. *The Plot to Kill the President.* New York: New York Times Books, 1981.

    Scheim, David E. *Contract on America. The Mafia Murder of President John F. Kennedy.* New York: Shapolsky Publishers, 1988. (Originally self-published in 1983.)

3. *Newspaper and Magazine Articles.* A selection of key articles representing major milestones in the acquisition of information on Carlos Marcello. Most of the hundreds of articles generated by the House Selected Committee on Assassinations investigation and BRILAB operations and trials are omitted.

    "Abscam (cont.). Mafiosi Call Off a Summit." *Time,* Feb. 25, 1980.

Amoss, Jim, and Dean Baquet. Articles on the BRILAB undercover operation and trials. *Times-Picayune,* New Orleans, 1980, 1981, 1982, 1983.

Amoss, Jim, and Dean Baquet. "Carlos Marcello." A three-part series in *Dixie Magazine, Times-Picayune,* New Orleans, Feb., 1982. Based on over 100 interviews. Interview with Carlos Marcello conducted through one of his attorneys, Provino Mosca.

Anderson, Jack. "Assassinations Committee Is Checking Mafia Plot." *United Feature Syndicate,* Jan. 4, 1979.

Anderson, Jack. "Carlos Marcello...Mobster." *United Feature Syndicate,* July 13, 1979.

Anderson, Jack. "House Panel Traces Mobster's Strings." *Washington Post,* Thursday, Jul. 12, 1979.

Atkinson, Jim. "Who's Behind the Mafia in Dallas?" *Dallas Magazine,* Dec. 1977.

"Carlos Marcello: Cosa Nostra Boss." *Wall Street Journal,* Oct. 14, 1970.

Chandler, David Leon. "The 'Little Man' Is Bigger Than Ever. Louisiana Still Jumps for Mobster Marcello." *Life,* Apr. 10, 1970.

Crewdson, John M. "Ex-Immigration Official Is Said to Have Assisted Crime Figure." *New York Times,* Feb. 11, 1980. (About Irving Davidson, Carlos Marcello and Mario Noto.)

Davidson, Bill. "New Orleans: Cosa Nostra's Wall Street." *The Saturday Evening Post,* Feb. 29, 1964.

Dorman, Michael. "Jack Halfen and Lyndon Johnson." *Ramparts,* 1968. (The Marcello-Halfen-Johnson connection.)

Fithian, Rep. Floyd J. "A Challenge for America. From the House Assassinations Committee Probe." *Indiana Law Enforcement Journal,* Spring 1979.

Golz, Earl. "Marcello Listens as Damaging FBI Tapes Unwind." *The Dallas Morning News.* May 30, 1981.

Lardner, George, Jr. "Investigator Detailed Mafia Leaders' Threat Against Kennedy." *Washington Post,* July 21, 1979.

Lardner, George, Jr. "U.S. vs. Marcello. Reputed Rackets Chieftain Eludes Federal Prosecutors for 30 Years." *Washington Post,* Feb. 19, 1980.

"The Marcello-JFK Connection?" *Gris Gris, New Orleans,* Jan. 15–21, 1978.

Marshall, Jonathan. "Requiem for a Mobster." *Inquiry,* Sept. 1, 1981.

"The Rise of Carlos Marcello." *Los Angeles Times,* Sept. 4, 1970.

"The Mob," Part I. *Life,* Sept. 1, 1967.

"The Mob," Part II. *Life,* Sept. 8, 1967.

Maxa, Rudy. "Confessions of a Political Dirtmonger. Ed Becker's World of Suspicions and Surmises." *Washington Post,* Apr. 17, 1980.

Oglesby, Earl and Jeff Goldberg. "Marcello-Oswald Connection Possible." *Times-Picayune,* Feb. 25, 1979.

Selcraig, Bruce. "Marcello Spins Web in Dallas." *Dallas Morning News,* Mar. 9, 1980.

"Summon Marcello, JFK Probers Urge." *Washington Post,* Apr. 1, 1977.

Taylor, Jack. "FBI Quiz Thwarts Multi-Million Dollar Mafia Plot." *Sunday Oklahoman,* Feb. 24, 1980.

Times-Picayune, New Orleans. Articles on Carlos Marcello deportation case, 1953–1988.

4. *Files of the Metropolitan Crime Commission, New Orleans.* Extensive thirty-year file on Carlos Marcello, his brothers, and associates largely compiled by Aaron Kohn when he was managing director.

5. *The New Orleans Times-Picayune Collection.* Extensive file on Carlos Marcello and his family and associates. Several thousand pages of articles and documents including the *Times-Picayune*'s 100 interviews for its three-part *Dixie Magazine* series on Carlos Marcello and an extensive interview with Carlos Marcello through his intermediary, Provino Mosca.

6. *Formal Interviews* (taped)

August La Nasa, Dec. 23, 1986. New Orleans attorney.

Aaron Kohn, Jan. 7, 11, Feb. 4, 5, Mar. 31, 1987, and Jan. 20, 1988. Former FBI special agent and assistant to J. Edgar Hoover, former director New Orleans Metropolitan Crime Commission. Investigated Carlos Marcello for over twenty years.

Harold Hughes, Jan. 18, Feb. 13, and Apr. 1, 1987. Former FBI special agent, chief of Organized Crime Strike Force, New Orleans, coordinator of the New Orleans BRILAB investigation of Carlos Marcello. Covered Carlos Marcello for thirteen years.

Richard Angelico, Feb. 9, 12, 1987, and Apr. 1, 1988. Investigative reporter, WDSU-TV New Orleans. Covered Carlos Marcello for twenty years.

Jim Amoss, Feb. 4, 1987. Metro editor, New Orleans *Times-Picayune*.

Charles Turnbo, Feb. 10, 1987. Warden, Federal Correctional Institution, Fort Worth, TX.

Alvin Beauboeuf, Feb. 11, 1987. Friend of David Ferrie's.

Edward Becker, Feb. 18, 1987. Private investigator, Las Vegas.

Courtney Evans, Jun. 10, 1987. Former assistant director, FBI. Liaison between J. Edgar Hoover and Robert F. Kennedy.

Joseph Hauser, Jul. 15, 21, and Aug. 5, 1987. U.S. government informant, BRILAB investigation of Carlos Marcello.

G. Robert Blakey, Aug. 7, 1987. Former chief counsel, House Select Committee on Assassinations.

Larry Montague, Dec. 11, 1987, and Jan. 21, 1988. FBI special agent, undercover agent, BRILAB investigation of Carlos Marcello.

Bruce Kelton, Jul. 22, 1987, and Jan. 22, 1988. Former assistant U.S. attorney, Los Angeles. Assistant prosecutor, Los Angeles BRILAB trial of Carlos Marcello.

Michael Wacks, Jan. 24, 1988. FBI special agent, undercover agent, BRILAB investigation of Carlos Marcello.

Walter Sheridan, Jun. 9, 1988. Former head of labor racketeering unit of the organized crime section, Justice Department, under Attorney General Kennedy.

William G. Hundley, Jun. 16, 1988. Chief, organized crime and racketeering section, Justice Department, under Attorney General Kennedy.

Morgan, Goudeau, Aug. 9, 1988. District Attorney, St. Landry Parish, Lafayette Louisiana.

7. *Collections*

The Papers of Paul L. Hoch, press clippings, magazine articles, FBI documents, notes on Carlos Marcello, made available to the author by Mr. Hoch.

The Papers of Anthony Summers. Press clippings, magazine articles, notes for *The Grim Reapers* by Ed Reid, miscellaneous allegations, FBI reports, Secret Service reports, on Carlos Marcello and David Ferrie, made available to the author by Mr. Summers.

8. *Informal Interviews* (not taped)

Paul L. Hoch—numerous occasions, 1987–1988. Coauthor of *The Assassinations—Dallas and Beyond.*

Bernard Fensterwald, Jr.—numerous occasions, 1987–1988. Author of *Coincidence or Conspiracy?*

Peter Noyes. Author of *Legacy of Doubt.*

9. *Written Interviews*

Joseph Hauser, Aug. 3, 1987. Mr. Hauser's answers to twenty-two questions put to him by the author.

THE ASSASSINATION OF PRESIDENT JOHN F. KENNEDY

Primary Sources

1. *Federal Bureau of Investigation. Files on the John F. Kennedy Assassination.* Approximately 221,000 pages have been released. These may be consulted at the FBI Freedom of Information Acts Reading Room, FBI Headquarters, The J. Edgar Hoover Building, Pennsylvania Ave., Washington, DC 20535, and at the libraries of several universities, such as the University of Wisconsin, Stevens Point, WI 54481, the University of California at Berkeley, and Southeastern Louisiana University at Hammond. Also available privately from: Harold Weisberg, Publisher, 7627 Old Receiver Rd., Frederick, MD 21701.

2. *National Archives and Records Services, General Services Administration.* Records of the President's Commission on the Assassination of John F. Kennedy (the Warren Commission). Record Group 272. National Archives, Washington, DC. The Warren Commission Documents—known as CDs, including many FBI reports that were not published in the Warren Commission's twenty-six volumes of Hearings and Exhibits: see 4 below.

3. *The State of Louisiana v. Clay L. Shaw, Criminal District Court, New Orleans* (the Garrison Investigation). Forty volumes. The Linus A. Sims Memorial Library, Southeastern Louisiana University, Hammond.

4. *President's Commission on the Assassination of President John F. Kennedy* (the Warren Commission). Hearings and Exhibits. Twenty-six volumes, Washington, DC: U.S. GPO, 1964.

5. *President's Commission on the Assassination of President John F. Kennedy. Report* (the Warren Report). Washington, DC: U.S. GPO, 1964.

6. *United States House of Representatives. Select Committee on Assassinations (HSCA).* Assassination of President John F. Kennedy. Final Report. 95th Congress, 2nd Session. Washington, DC: U.S. GPO, 1979.

7. *United States House of Representatives. Select Committee on Assassinations (HSCA).* Investigation of the Assassination of President John F. Kennedy. Hearings and Appendixes

to Hearings, twelve volumes. 95th Congress, 2nd Session. Washington, DC: U.S. GPO, 1978–79.

8. *United States Senate. Select Committee to Study Governmental Operations with Respect to Intelligence Activities (the Church Committee)*. Book V. The Investigation of the Assassination of President John F. Kennedy: The Performance of the Intelligence Agencies (the Schweiker-Hart Report). 94th Congress, 2nd Session. Washington, DC: U.S. GPO, 1976.

9. *Central Intelligence Agency. Papers on the Assassination of President John F. Kennedy*. Fifteen volumes, 3847 pages. Linus A. Sims Memorial Library, Southeastern Louisiana University, Hammond.

Secondary Sources

1. *Books.* A selection of the seminal books (in order of publication) on the assassination, excluding those identifying Carlos Marcello as a prime suspect. For these see the preceding section.

Joesten, Joachim. *Oswald: Assassin or Fall Guy?* New York: Marzani & Munsell, 1964.

Lane, Mark. *Rush to Judgment: A Critique of the Warren Commission's Inquiry into the Murders of John F. Kennedy, Officer J.D. Tippit, and Lee Harvey Oswald.* New York: Holt, Rinehart and Winston, 1966.

Popkin, Richard H. *The Second Oswald.* New York: Avon-New York Review of Books, 1966.

Epstein, Edward Jay. *Inquest: The Warren Commission and the Establishment of Truth.* New York: Viking, Bantam, 1966.

Weisberg, Harold. *Whitewash, The Report on the Warren Report.* Hyattstown, MD: H. Weisberg, 1966. (Followed by *Whitewash*, Vols. II, III, IV, 1967–1974.)

Meagher, Sylvia. *Accessories after the Fact: The Warren Commission, the Authorities and the Report.* Indianapolis: Bobbs-Merrill, 1967.

Thompson, Josiah. *Six Seconds in Dallas. A Micro-Study of the Kennedy Assassination.* New York: Bernard Geis, 1967.

Garrison, Jim. *A Heritage of Stone.* New York: Putnam, 1970.

Weisberg, Harold. *Post-Mortem. JFK Assassination Cover-Up Smashed.* Frederick, MD: H. Weisberg, Publisher, 1975.

Hoch, Paul L., Peter Dale Scott and Russell Stetler. *The Assassinations. Dallas and Beyond. A Guide to Cover-Ups and Investigations.* New York: Random House (Vintage Books), 1976.

Scott, Peter Dale. *Crime and Cover-Up: The CIA, the Mafia and the Dallas-Watergate Connection.* Berkeley: Westworks, 1977.

Evica, George Michael. *And We Are All Mortal: New Evidence and Analysis in the Assassination of John F. Kennedy.* West Hartford, CT.: University of Hartford Press, 1978.

Lifton, David. *Best Evidence: Disguise and Deception in the Assassination of John F. Kennedy.* New York: Macmillan, 1980.

Kurtz, Michael. *Crime of the Century. The Kennedy Assassination from a Historian's Perspective.* Knoxville: University of Tennessee Press, 1982.

Hurt, Henry. *Reasonable Doubt. An Investigation into the Assassination of John F. Kennedy.* New York: Holt, Rinehart and Winston, 1985.

2. *Unpublished Manuscripts*

Hoch, Paul L. *The Oswald Papers: The FBI versus the Warren Commission.* Draft, 1974. Copyright Paul L. Hoch.

Hoch, Paul L., Peter Dale Scott, Russell Stetler, and Josiah Thompson. *Beyond Conspiracy.* Unedited and uncorrected galleys, 1980. Copyright Hoch, Scott, Stetler, Thompson.

3. *Newspaper and Magazine Articles, a Selected List*

Alavarez, Luis W. "A Physicist Examines the Kennedy Assassination Film." *American Journal of Physics, 44, 1976, pp. 813-827.*

Branch, Taylor, and George Crile III. "The Kennedy Vendetta." *Harper's,* 251, Aug. 1975, pp. 49–63.

Donahue, Howard. "Evaluation of the Pathology of the Wounding of John F. Kennedy." *Biological Aspects of Forensic Science,* Apr. 26, 1982.

Gallery Magazine. "Special Gallery Report. The JFK Assassination." Jul. 1979.

Kurtz, Michael. Lee Harvey Oswald in New Orleans: A Reappraisal." *Louisiana History,* 21, 1980, pp. 7–20.

Lowenstein, Allard K. "The Kennedy Killings." *Argosy,* February 1976, pp. 28–33, 86.

Malone, William Scott, and Jerry Policoff. "Fear and Loathing on the Assassination Trail." Unpublished article. (On The House Select Committee on Assassinations' investigation of the JFK assassination).

Malone, William Scott, and Jerry. "A Great Show, A Lousy Investigation." Special Report. *New Times.* Sept. 4, 1978. (On the House Select Committee on Assassinations' investigation of the JFK assassination).

Reppert, Ralph. "Kennedy Assassination: A Different View." *Baltimore Sun Sunday Magazine,* May 1 and 8, 1977.

Silva, Helga. "Fear of Mafia and Future Led Aleman to Fatal Finale." *Miami Herald,* Aug. 2, 1983.

Wecht, Cyril H. "Pathologist's View of JFK Autopsy: An Unsolved Case." *Modern Medicine,* Nov. 27, 1972, pp. 28-32.

Wecht, Cyril H., and Robert P. Smith. "The Medical Evidence in the Assassination of President Kennedy." *Forensic Science,* 3, 1974, pp. 105–128.

York, Marva. "Exile Tormented Before Fatal Spree." *Miami News,* Aug. 1, 1983.

4. *Reviews and Newsletters on the Assassination of John F. Kennedy and Related Matters*

   a. *The Third Decade: A Journal of Research on the John F. Kennedy Assassination.* Published bimonthly at State University College, Fredonia, NY 14063. Editor and Publisher: Professor Jerry D. Rose.

   b. *Echoes of Conspiracy.* A newsletter on research, investigations, and writings pertaining to the assassinations of John F. Kennedy, Martin Luther King, Jr., and Robert F. Kennedy, and related subjects. Editor and Publisher: Paul L. Hoch, 1525 Acton Street, Berkeley CA 79407.

5. *Bibliographies and Indexes*

    a. Guth, DeLloyd J., and David R. Wrone. *The Assassination of John F. Kennedy—A Comprehensive Historical and Legal Bibliography, 1963–1979.* 398 pages, Westport, CN, and London, England: Greenwood Press, 1980.

    b. Meagher, Sylvia, in collaboration with Gary Owens. *Master Index to the J.F.K. Assassinations Investigations: The Reports and Supporting Volumes of the House Select Committee on Assassinations and the Warren Commission.* 435 pages, Metuchen, NJ, and London, England: Scarecrow Press, 1980.

    Note: See bibliographies on the John F. Kennedy assassination in Kurtz, *Crime of the Century*, 1982; Blakey and Billings, *The Plot to Kill the President*, 1981; Davis, *The Kennedys: Dynasty and Disaster*, 1984; Hurt, *Reasonable Doubt*, 1985; and Scheim, *Contract on America*, 1988. These bibliographies take up where Guth and Wrone left off.

6. *Interviews*

    G. Robert Blakey, former chief counsel, House Select Committee on Assassinations, Sept. 8, 13, 19, 1983, and Jan. 3, 1984.

    Nicholas Katzenbach, former attorney general of the United States, Sept. 23, 1983.

    Edward Becker, Feb. 18, 1987.

    Anthony Summers, Jun. 15, 1988.

7. *Collections*

    The Papers of Paul L. Hoch. Extensive collection of papers and official documents of the John F. Kennedy assassination, and the FBI, Warren Commission, and House Select Committee on Assassinations investigations, made available to the author by Mr. Hoch.

    The Papers of Anthony Summers. Research notes for Mr. Summers' book, CONSPIRACY, *Who Killed President Kennedy?* and subsequent post-publication research notes on Lee Harvey Oswald's visit to Mexico City, Sept. 27-Oct. 3, 1963, including notes on the working papers of the House Select Committee on Assassinations 300-page classified report on Oswald in Mexico City which Mr. Summers obtained from a Committee investigator.

PLOTS TO ASSASSINATE
PRESIDENT FIDEL CASTRO

Primary Sources

1. *United States Senate. Select Committee to Study Governmental Operations with Respect to Intelligence Activities* (the Church Committee). Interim Report: Alleged Assassination Plots Involving Foreign Leaders. Nov. 20, 1975. 94th Congress, 1st Session, Washington, DC: U.S. GPO, 1975.

2. *United States Senate. Select Committee to Study Governmental Operations with Respect to Intelligence Activities* (the Church Committee). Final Report, Book V: The Investigation of the Assassination of John F. Kennedy: Performance of the Intelligence Agencies. 1976. 94th Congress, 2nd Session. Washington, DC: U.S. GPO, 1976. (See pp. 68–80 on AM/LASH plot.)

3. *United States House of Representatives. Select Committee on Assassinations (HSCA).* Investigation of the Assassination of President John F. Kennedy. Appendix to Hearings. Volume X: The Evolution and Implications of the CIA-Sponsored Assassination Conspiracies against Fidel Castro. Staff Report, pp. 147–195.

Secondary Sources

1. *Books and Articles*

Ashman, Charles. *The CIA-Mafia Link.* New York, Manor Books, 1975.

Exner, Judith Campbell (with Ovid Demaris). *My Story.* New York: Grove Press, 1977.

Frattiano, Jimmy (with Ovid Demaris). *The Last Mafioso.* New York: Bantam, 1981.

Giancana, Antoinette. *Mafia Princess.* New York: William Morrow, 1984.

Hinckle, Warren, and William Turner. *The Fish Is Red: The Story of The Secret War against Castro.* New York: Harper & Row, 1981.

Hunt, E. Howard. *Give Us This Day.* New York: Arlington House, 1973.

Kostman, Jim. *What Johnny Knew: L'Affaire Roselli and the Cover-Up of the JFK Assassination.* Unpublished monograph, 1976.

Marchetti, Victor, and John D. Marks. *The CIA and the Cult of Intelligence.* New York: Alfred A. Knopf, 1974.

Morrow, Robert D. *Betrayal: A Reconstruction of Certain Clandestine Events from the Bay of Pigs to the Assassination of John F. Kennedy.* Chicago: Henry Regnery, 1976.

Phillips, David A. *The Night Watch.* New York: Atheneum, 1977.

Powers, Thomas. *The Man Who Kept the Secrets. Richard Helms and the CIA.* New York: Knopf, 1979.

Prouty, Leroy Fletcher. *The Secret Team: CIA and Its Allies in Control of the United States and the World.* Englewood Cliffs, NJ: Prentice-Hall, 1973.

Scott, Peter Dale. *Crime and Cover-Up: The CIA, the Mafia, and the Dallas-Watergate Connection.* Berkeley: Westworks, 1977.

Smith, Joseph B. *Portrait of a Cold Warrior.* New York: G. P. Putnam's Sons, 1976.

Wyden, Peter. *Bay of Pigs—The Untold Story.* New York: Simon & Schuster, 1979.

2. *Interviews*

Richard Helms, former director of the Central Intelligence Agency, Sept. 23, 1983.

Samuel Halpern, former executive assistant to the Task Force on Cuba and one of the four men directly involved in the AM/LASH operation against Castro, Mar. 28, 1984.

Thomas Hughes, former director of the State Department's Bureau of Intelligence and Research, Mar. 30, 1984.

John McCone, former director of the Central Intelligence Agency, Jan. 12, 1984.

THE ASSASSINATION OF
MARTIN LUTHER KING, JR.

Primary Sources

1. *United States House of Representatives. Select Committee on Assassinations (HSCA).* Investigation of the Assassination of Martin Luther King, Jr. Final Report. Conspiracy allegations: William Hugh Morris, pp. 382, 383; John McFerren, pp. 385–387; William Sartor, pp. 387–389.

2. *United States House of Representatives. Select Committee on Assassinations (HSCA).* Investigation of the Assassination of Martin Luther King, Jr. Appendix to hearings, Vol. XII. Staff Report: An analysis of James Earl Ray's Trip to New Orleans, Dec. 15–Dec. 21, 1967, pp. 267–282.

3. FBI Report on McFerren Allegation, File N. 157-10673, 4/22/68.

Secondary Sources

1. *Books*

   Huie, William Bradford. *He Slew the Dreamer.* New York: Delacorte Press, 1970.

   Sartor, William. Unfinished manuscript on the assassination of Martin Luther King, Jr. (HSCA MLK document N. 110334).

THE ASSASSINATION OF
ROBERT F. KENNEDY

Primary Sources

1. Los Angeles Police Department. Files on the Investigation of the Assassination of Senator Robert F. Kennedy. California State Archives, 1020 O Street, Room 130, Sacramento, CA 95814. (50,000 square feet of written material, 2500 photographs, 150 pieces of physical evidence, 200 reel-to-reel tape recordings. Films, videotapes, audiotapes. Released Apr. 19, 1988.)

2. Federal Bureau of Investigations. Files on Assassination of Senator Robert F. Kennedy. Assassination Archives and Research Center, 918 F Street, N.W., Suite 510 (AARC), Washington, DC 20004. (Approximately 5000 pages of FBI documents dating from 1968 to 1972. Freedom of Information Act releases from 1976 to 1979.)

3. Federal Bureau of Investigation. Files on the Assassination of Senator Robert F. Kennedy. The Robert F. Kennedy Assassination Archives, Southeastern Massachusetts University, North Dartmouth, MA 02747. (Approximately 35,000 pages of FBI documents obtained through Freedom of Information Act requests.)

Secondary Sources

1. *Books and Articles*

   Charach, Theodore. "Why Sirhan Could Not Have Killed Robert F. Kennedy." *Knave Magazine*, Part I (March 1977) and Part II (April 1977).

Harp, S. Duncan. *The Tangled Web. An Inquiry into the Assassination of Senator Robert F. Kennedy.* Unpublished book-length manuscript. Copyright 1977 by S. Duncan Harp.

Houghton, Robert A., with Theodore Taylor. *Special Unit Senator: The Investigation of the Assassination of Senator Robert F. Kennedy.* New York: Random House, 1970.

Kaiser, Robert Blair. *"RFK Must Die!" A History of the Robert Kennedy Assassination and Its Aftermath.* New York: Dutton, 1970.

Lowenstein, Allard K. "The Murder of Robert Kennedy." *Saturday Review,* Feb. 19, 1977.

Moldea, Dan. "Who Really Killed Bobby Kennedy?" *Regardie's Magazine,* June 1977.

Noguchi, Thomas I., and Joseph DiMona. *Coroner.* New York: Simon & Schuster, 1963.

Scheim, David E. *Contract on America: The Mafia Murder of President John F. Kennedy.* New York: Shapolsky Publishers, 1988. (See Chapter 21, pp. 277–297.)

Stone, Gregory. *Robert F. Kennedy Assassination.* Current Status of the Evidence. Unpublished Monographs, 1984–1987.

Turner, William W., and John G. Christian. *The Assassination of Robert F. Kennedy: A Searching Look at the Conspiracy and Cover-Up, 1968–1978.* New York: Random House, 1978.

2. *Special Collections*

The Robert F. Kennedy Assassination Papers. The Robert F. Kennedy Assassination Archives, Southeastern Massachusetts University, North Dartmouth, MA. (Twenty cubic feet of articles, official documents, taped interviews, recorded hearings, trial exhibits, diagrams, photographs, and charts. Includes the Castellano-Nelson collection; the papers of Robert B. Kaiser, author of *RFK Must Die!*; the Lowenstein-Stone collection; and the papers of Dr. Philip Melanson.)

3. *Films*

The Second Gun. American Films Ltd. Theodore Charach and Gerard Alcan, 1973, 2 hours. Available in VHS at the Assassination Archives and Research Center (AARC).

Interviews. RFK Assassination Investigation. Conducted by Theodore Charach. Available in VHS at AARC.

The Two Kennedys. Rome, 1976. Italian documentary on the Kennedy assassinations. Producer: Alfredo. Bini. Director and writer: Gianni Bisachi. VHS edition, Ben Barry Associates Productions, 1976.

GENERAL BIBLIOGRAPHY

Note: Limited to books and articles used as sources of information for this book.

Books

Asbury, Herbert. *The French Quarter—An Informal History of the New Orleans Underworld.* New York: Pocket Books. (Photocopy without date of publication.)

Bernstein, Carl, and Bob Woodward. *All the President's Men.* New York: Simon & Schuster, 1974.

Cohen, Mickey, with John Peer Nugent. *In My Own Words*. Englewood Cliffs, NJ: Prentice-Hall, 1975.

Davison, Jean. *Oswald's Game*. New York: W.W. Norton, 1983.

Demaris, Ovid. *The Last Mafioso*. New York: Times Books, 1981.

Flammonde, Paris. *The Kennedy Conspiracy: An Uncommissioned Report on the Jim Garrison Investigation*. New York: Meredith, 1969.

Haldeman, H.R., with Joseph DiMona. *The Ends of Power*. New York: Times Books, 1978.

Kane, Harnett T. *Louisiana Hayride*. New York: Bonanza Books, 1941.

Kelley, Clarence M., and James Kirkpatrick Davis. *Kelley. The Story of an FBI Director*. Kansas City–New York: Andrew, McMeel & Parker, A Universal Press Syndicate Affiliate, 1987.

Kendall, John Smith. *History of New Orleans*. Chicago: Regnery, 1922.

Kennedy, Robert F. *The Enemy Within*. New York: Harper & Brothers, 1960.

Lowenstein, Allard K. Edited by Gregory Stone and Douglas Lowenstein. *Lowenstein: Acts of Courage and Belief*. New York: Harcourt, Brace, Jovanovich, 1983.

Lukas, J. Anthony. *Nightmare. The Underside of the Nixon Years*. New York: Viking Press, 1973.

Maas, Peter. *The Valachi Papers*. New York: Putnam, 1968.

Marchetti, Victor, and John D. Marks. The CIA and the Cult of Intelligence. New York: Knopf, 1974.

Morgan, John. *No Gangster More Bold. Murray Humphreys: The Welsh Political Genius Who Corrupted America*. London: Hodder and Stoughton, 1985.

Navasky, Victor. *Kennedy Justice*. New York: Atheneum, 1977.

Schlesinger, Arthur M., Jr. *Robert Kennedy and His Times*. Boston: Houghton Mifflin, 1978.

Schorr, Daniel. *Clearing the Air*. Boston: Houghton Mifflin, 1977.

Shaw, J. Gary, with Larry R. Harris. *Cover-Up: The Governmental Conspiracy to Conceal the Facts About the Public Execution of John Kennedy*. Cleburne, TX: Shaw, 1976.

Sullivan, William, with Bill Brown. *The Bureau. My Thirty Years in Hoover's FBI*. New York: W.W. Norton, 1979.

Summers, Anthony. *GODDESS. The Secret Lives of Marilyn Monroe*. New York: Macmillan, 1985.

Teresa, Vincent, with Thomas C. Renner. *My Life in the Mafia*. Garden City, NY: Doubleday, 1973.

Williams, T. Harry. *Huey Long*. New York: Bantam, 1969.

Articles

Cannizaro, Steve. "Marcello Brother, 6 Others Arrested." *Times-Picayune*, New Orleans, Feb. 3, 1988. (About arrest of Sammy Marcello.)

Coxe, John E. "The New Orleans Mafia Incident." *The Louisiana Historical Quarterly*, Oct. 1937, pp. 1067–1109.

Kendall, John Smith. "Who Killa De Chief? The Murder of Police Chief David Hennessey." *The Louisiana Historical Quarterly*, Apr., 1939, pp. 492–530.

MISCELLANEOUS U.S. GOVERNMENT DOCUMENTS

Federal Bureau of Investigation

1. David William Ferrie. New Orleans Field Office file 89-69A-100 to 3299.

2. Joseph Albert Poretto. New Orleans Field Office file 62-9-33-411.

3. Internal Memorandum. From Assistant Attorney General, Criminal Division to Director, FBI, Jun. 7, 1978. RE: House Select Committee on Assassinations. (Justice Department's recommendation that Assassinations Committee's request for FBI's Dallas and New Orleans Field Office files on the John F. Kennedy assassination be denied.)

United States District Court, Eastern District of Louisiana

1. Affidavits in Support of Applications of The United States of America For an Order Authorizing The Interception of Wire Communications. Misc. N. 2142, 1986, 1987.

   a. 352 pages of Affidavits of FBI Special Agents executed throughout 1986 and 1987 revealing extent of the infiltration of crews of the Bruno/Scarfo and Gambino crime families in various rackets in New Orleans once controlled by the Marcello organization.

2. United States v. Carlos Marcello *et al.* Criminal Docket N. 80-274, Section "G," *Government's Memorandum of Law Concerning the Sufficiency of Evidence to Convict Defendant Vincent A. Marinello on Counts 1, 2, 11, and 12 of the indictment.* (15-page memorandum giving concise history of the BRILAB bribery scheme.)

3. United States v. I. Irving Davidson *et al.* Criminal Action N. 80-274, Section "C," *Defendant Davidson's Proffer Regarding Challenges for Cause to the Prospective Jurors, Severance, and Change of Venue.*

United States Secret Service

1. Investigation of David W. Ferrie, November 24–29, 1963 by Special Agent In Charge, John W. Rice and Special Agent Anthony E. Gerrots. Report dated 12/13/63. File N. C0-2-34, 030.

Federal Bureau of Investigation

1. File on Joseph Francis Civello. N. 92-2824. Assassination Archives and Research Center, Washington, D.C.

Federal Bureau of Investigation

1. File on Jack Leon Ruby. Assassination Archives and Research Center, Washington, D.C.

   a. The Allegation of William Abadie, 12/7/63, Los Angeles, CA. Los Angeles file 44-895. In which Abadie asserted Jack Ruby was involved in gambling in Dallas and maintained a slot machine and juke box "warehouse shop" and a bookmaking establishment often frequented by the Dallas Police. Ruby described by Abadie as "a quite, intense racketeer, gambler, and hustler."

   b. The Allegation of Bobby Gene Moore, 11/27/1963, Oakland, CA. File SF 44-494, DL 44-1639. In which Moore asserted Jack Ruby was associated with Dallas Mafia boss Joseph Civello and was "connected with the underworld in Dallas."

Acknowledgments

Books about the Mafia, the Kennedy assassination, and the FBI are difficult to research because very few people are willing to talk with you. The vow of *omertà* is not exclusive to the Mafia. Equally robust walls of silence also surround the Kennedy past and the records of the Federal Bureau of Investigation. For this reason, among others, I am especially grateful to everyone who persevered in providing me with information for this book.

Books such as this are also expensive to research, for often, as was the case with *Mafia Kingfish,* one must take chances and invest in promising, though risky, prospects that often turn out to be dry holes; and so you have to begin searching and drilling all over again. For this reason, I am also especially grateful to those individuals and institutions, aside from the publisher, who helped finance this book.

Foremost among these was the Harry Frank Guggenheim Foundation, whose Board of Directors awarded me a research grant without which I doubt this book, as it came to stand, could have been written. I wish to thank both the foundation's Board of Directors, chaired by Peter Lawson-Johnston, and its program officer, Karen Colvard, for their belief in my project, their willingness to support it, and the encouragement that their faith and support gave me to go forward. I hope this book will do justice to the vision of the late Harry

Frank Guggenheim, who created his foundation to aid research in the field of human violence, aggression, and domination.

Since, as I have already noted, walls of silence surround the three main protagonists of this book, I have had to rely heavily on documentary sources. I therefore owe a large debt of gratitude to the custodians of four major collections of documents who, promptly and generously, responded to my always urgent requests, often above and beyond the call of duty. These were Bernard Fensterwald, Jr., and James H. Lesar, respectively president and vice president of the Assassination Archives and Research Center in Washington, D.C.; Paul L. Hoch, noted John F. Kennedy assassination investigator and author, and custodian of an exceptionally comprehensive file of Kennedy assassination materials; Harold Weisberg, author of several important books on the assassination of President Kennedy and its investigations, and custodian of over 200,000 pages of FBI documents on the assassination which he obtained in 1977 and 1978 as a result of a protracted lawsuit against the Justice Department under the provisions of the Freedom of Information Act; and Jim Amoss, metro editor of the New Orleans *Times-Picayune*, who placed his own personal files and his newspaper's considerable files of documents and papers on Carlos Marcello at my disposal.

In addition to making their collections of documents available, the above individuals were of great assistance to me in many other ways.

Mr. Fensterwald was a constant source of expert advice and moral support throughout the research and writing of the book. A recommendation from him helped obtain for me the research grant I received from the Harry Frank Guggenheim Foundation.

Mr. Lesar, a veteran of Harold Weisberg's Freedom of Information Act battles, conducted a long and expertly waged lawsuit against the Justice Department on my behalf to obtain the tape-recorded conversations of Carlos Marcello, and others, that resulted from the FBI's 1979–1980 undercover investigation. Known as BRILAB, this sting operation ultimately led to convictions of Mr. Marcello at two trials and his eventual imprisonment.

Paul Hoch provided me with essential advice throughout the research and writing of the book with unfailing generosity and perspicacity. Since there are certainly few people in the country, if any, who know as much about the John F. Kennedy assassination and its various investigations as Mr. Hoch, his counsel constituted a vital contribution to my book.

Next I wish to thank all my excellent researchers, both those willing to be identified and those who preferred not to be named on these pages. These were Frank Olivier, Yvonne Olivier, Barbara Tsao, Amy Stevens, Robert Ranftel, and four citizens of New Orleans who have chosen to remain anonymous. Yvonne Olivier served as picture editor for the book, and I am grateful to her for her perseverance in chasing down certain illustrations often in the face of considerable obstacles and frustrations.

Others who performed valuable research for the book or who supplied me with important documents and information on an informal, nonremunerative basis were Paul L. Hoch, James H. Lesar, Bernard Fensterwald, Jr., Dan E. Moldea, Mary Ferrell, Harold Donahue, Jerry Rose, Jim Amoss, Scott van Wynsberghe, Richard Angelico, Aaron Kohn, David E. Scheim, Greg Stone, Anthony Summers, Harold Weisberg, Harold Hughes, and Larry Montague.

A special debt of gratitude goes to all those who agreed to be formally interviewed by me, some of whom I importuned several times. These included Aaron Kohn (six times), Harold Hughes (three times), Edward Becker (twice), August La Nasa, Charles Turnbo, Richard Angelico (three times), Paul L. Hoch, Bernard Fensterwald, Jr., G. Robert Blakey, Jim Amoss, Joseph Hauser, Michael Wacks, Larry Montague, Anthony Summers, Bruce Kelton, Nicholas Katzenbach, Richard Helms, Samuel Hepburn, Harold Weisberg, Alvin Beauboeuf, Tony Sherman, Walter Sheridan, William G. Hundley, Peter Noyes, Courtney Evans, Morgan Goudeau, and about a dozen individuals who have chosen to remain anonymous. Details of these interviews are given in the Notes on Sources.

I am greatly indebted also to the authors of certain staff reports included in the thirteen volumes of hearings and appendixes accompanying the final report of The House Select Committee on Assassinations' investigation of the assassination of John F. Kennedy. Foremost among these are Gaeton J. Fonzi, Edwin Lopez, Michael Ewing, Patricia Orr, Ralph Salerno, Gary T. Cornwell, G. Robert Blakey, and T. Mark Flanagan, Jr.

Correspondingly I owe thanks to the authors of major magazine and newspaper articles on Carlos Marcello and to the authors of chapters on him in certain books. These authors and their works can be found in the Notes on Sources. Likewise, I am indebted to the authors of various articles and books on the John F. Kennedy assassination and the assassinations of Robert F. Kennedy and Martin Luther King, Jr., listed in the Notes on Sources.

I believe all of us owe a significant debt of gratitude to the various informants who had the sense of civic responsibility, the fearlessness, and the sense of justice to come forth in the wake of the John F. Kennedy assassination and make allegations to the FBI suggesting the possible involvement of organized crime in the assassination, even though the government paid little or no attention to them at the time. These courageous citizens are also mentioned in the Notes on Sources.

Finally, I owe a primary debt of gratitude to the vice president and publisher of McGraw-Hill's General Books Division, Gladys Justin Carr, for her belief in the worth of the book proposal I submitted to her in the spring of 1986, and for her faith in my ability to do justice to it, that resulted in this book.

Likewise, I owe a great deal of thanks to my editor, Lisa Frost, for her encouragement and support throughout the researching and the writing, for her expert grasp of the complex subject matter of the book, and for her judicious suggestions as to how the original manuscript could be improved. My thanks also go to the book's copy editor, Leslie Anne Weber, whose meticulous reading of the manuscript substantially improved both its grammatical and factual accuracy, and to proofreader Susan Jacobs for her superb ability to detect discrepancies.

On a personal level I wish to thank certain friends and relatives who helped me, and put up with me, during what turned out to be a most demanding ordeal. My friend and agent, Marianne Strong, was compelled by me to respond to numerous emergencies throughout the writing, some of them financial, and I thank her for helping me cope with them. Craig Fuller of Chemical Bank also helped respond to some of these emergencies, and I thank him for his personal attention to my often urgent banking needs.

My thanks go to those who helped type the manuscript: Nancy Davis; Carol Deacon-Cumings and Maureen Simmons of Soho Typing; and Sahodra Nathu. And my thanks also go to my efficient photo copiers, William S. Marbit, Henry Trattner, and Andy Green of Readers, Inc.

Among those who gave me the benefit of their love and support, I am deeply grateful to Nancy W. Davis and Maude B. Davis. And finally to Sahodra Nathu, who put up with me during the writing and helped me with the book in countless, unanticipated ways, a process that often entailed much personal sacrifice on her part, I owe more thanks than I am able to express. Her presence in my life since I began working on the book has been an indispensable source of encouragement, help, companionship, and love.

John H. Davis

Index

Bronson, Charles, Bronson film, 177, 411–413
Brooklier, Dominick, 311, 448, 449, 450, 452, 456, 497, 499, 523
Brooks, Harry, 59
Brown Bomber, the, 28, 29, 32, 38, 337
Bruneau, Emile, 128, 144, 402, 405
Bruno, Angelo, 105, 284, 477
Bruno-Scarfo family, 531–533
Bufalino, Russell, 105
Bundy, McGeorge, 246
Bureau of Prisons, 471, 505, 508, 509, 534
Burkley, George C., 291–292, 293, 295

Cabell, Charles P., 86, 331
California Mafia, 346–348, 352–353, 356–357, 519
    federal indictment and trial, 447–456, 468
Camelot, 84
Campbell, Judith, 84, 238, 239, 241, 278, 289, 364–365, 407, 518
    (*See also* Exner, Judith)
Campisi, Joe, 140–141, 142–143, 164, 176–177, 208, 271, 298, 403–405, 527
Campisi, Sam, 140, 141, 142
Canipe, Guy, 339, 342
Capeana, Benny, 120, 221, 224
Capone, Al, 30, 54, 59, 63, 141, 275, 488
Capro, Joseph, 45
Caracci, Frank, 143, 164, 233–234, 298, 405, 531–533
Carillo, Anthony, 320
Carlos Marcello v. Robert F. Kennedy, 102, 103
Carmen, Jeanne, 241–242
Carolla, Anthony, 45, 47, 59, 319, 320, 321, 533
Carolla, Sam "Silver Dollar," 19–20, 28–29, 30, 32, 33–34, 35, 36–37, 39, 41, 43, 44–46, 47–48, 49, 74, 319, 533

Carousel Club, 203, 204, 205, 208, 234, 326
Carr, Richard, 412
Carter, Jimmy, 475, 521
Castro, Fidel, 85–87, 115, 129, 130–133, 136–137, 146–151, 192, 205, 216, 217, 227, 240, 246–247, 250, 251, 254, 275–276, 278, 327, 329, 386, 387, 392, 393, 426, 520
    and Cuban exiles, 85, 86–87, 111, 127–128, 130–131, 147, 148, 156, 157–159, 216, 240, 269, 276, 331, 360, 363, 365, 366, 386, 394
    plot to kill, 84–87, 111, 136, 147, 154, 218, 238, 246, 248, 254, 257, 263, 273, 275, 278, 286, 289, 320, 324–327, 329, 330, 355–356, 361–366, 367, 371–374, 379, 384, 395, 400, 407, 517, 525
    threatens retaliation against Kennedy, 136, 362
    throws out Mafia, 85, 363
Castro, Raul, 85
CBS, 202, 271, 349, 412
Central Intelligence Agency (*see* CIA)
Cesar, Thane, 349, 350–351, 352–353
Chandler, David, 314
Charach, Theodore, 351, 352–353
Chateaux Dijon, 420
Chavez, Cesar, 345
Chavez, Frank, 344–345
Cheramie, Rose, 176, 231, 515, 526
Chetta, Nicholas, 332–334
Chicago Mafia, 164–165, 210, 214, 238, 271, 275, 278, 309, 311, 370, 373, 457, 516, 518, 526
    and Teamsters pension funds, 457–460
Chimento, Joseph "Zip," 71, 314
Chotiner, Murray, 273–274, 312, 356–358, 360, 506
Christenberry, Herbert W., 167, 180, 181